AF361554

An Evangelical Adrift

An Evangelical Adrift
The Making of John Henry Newman's Theology

Geertjan Zuijdwegt

The Catholic University of America Press
Washington, D.C.

Cataloging-in-Publication Data available from the Library of Congress
Names: Zuijdwegt, Geertjan, author.
Title: An evangelical adrift : the making of John Henry Newman's theology /
    Geertjan Zuijdwegt.
Description: Washington, D.C. : The Catholic University of America Press,
    [2022] | Includes bibliographical references and index.
Identifiers: LCCN 2022038647 (print) | LCCN 2022038648 (ebook) | ISBN
    9780813235585 (cloth) | ISBN 9780813235592 (ebook)
Subjects: LCSH: Newman, John Henry, Saint, 1801–1890. |
    Cardinals—England—Biography.
Classification: LCC BX4705.N5 Z85 2022 (print) | LCC BX4705.N5 (ebook) |
    DDC 282.092 [B]—dc23/eng/20221014
LC record available at https://lccn.loc.gov/2022038647
LC ebook record available at https://lccn.loc.gov/2022038648

To Elizabeth

Contents

Acknowledgments

This book was nearly ten years in the making. It grew out of an almost unrelated research project. I intended to study Victorian critics of the Catholic John Henry Newman, but instead, I wrote a biography of the Anglican Newman. It was the book on Newman I had always wanted to read but could never find. In some ways, the book originates from my first encounter with Newman as an undergrad, when I randomly picked up a copy of the *Apologia* from a box of library doubles. It was an old Fontana paperback of the 1864 edition, which included the whole exchange with Charles Kingsley. I recall relishing Kingsley's feisty charges, Newman's brilliant parries, and the majestic sense one got of two men clashing in earnest about what they believed. But although I liked the *Apologia* and was fascinated by Newman's thought, I could never quite find out where it came from. From 1833 onward, everything seemed pretty clear, but before that, Newman's development seemed rather confusing. There was some flirting with scepticism, a teenage conversion, a decade of evangelicalism, and a drift toward liberalism. And the upshot of it all was a man who kickstarted the Tractarian Movement to make the Church of England more Catholic. It made no sense to me, and the literature was of little help. Time and again, whatever current research project I was engaged in, I found myself returning to the puzzle of Newman's early development. At last, I decided I would try to solve it. Such an idiosyncratic trajectory makes for many debts of gratitude.

Research for this book has been funded by generous grants from the Research Foundation—Flanders (FWO) and the KU Leuven Faculty of Theology and Religious Studies. The patience of the latter, especially, I will never forget. Librarians and archivists abroad (especially at Oxford, London, and Cambridge) have been of great assistance. The people at the KU Leuven interlibrary loan service were invaluable, and so was Daniel Joyce, the Birmingham Oratory archivist. Many thanks to Mark Chapman for facilitating a year of intensive research at Oxford and to Peter Nockles for his conversation and introductions there. A productive and enjoyable research stay at the National Institute for Newman Studies in Pittsburgh gave me the opportunity to explore the relationship between Newman and Whately. I am grateful to Mike Shea for introducing me to the Culler microfilm there and for being a friend ever after. Two books deserve special mention. I owe my introduction to Newman's evangelical theology to Thomas Sheridan's *Newman on Justification*, and Frank Turner's *John Henry Newman* taught me how to get context and history right. Without them, this book would not have been written. I have benefited from those who commented on earlier drafts of this work, or parts of it. Thanks to Terrence Merrigan, Mark Chapman, Jacques Haers,

SJ, Peter Nockles, Andrew Meszaros, and two anonymous reviewers for the Catholic University of America Press this has become a better book. Needless to say, the responsibility for remaining flaws is mine. No one has engaged with the ideas in this work like Bradford Manderfield. He has been the best of friends. I thank my children, Kees and Anna, for suffering my absence as well as abiding my presence. All my love goes to my wife Elizabeth, who supported me throughout and to whom I dedicate this book.

Abbreviations

Add.	*Addresses to Cardinal Newman with His Replies etc., 1879–1881.* Edited by W. P. Neville. London: Longmans, Green, and Co., 1905.
Apo.	*Apologia pro vita sua: Being a Reply to a Pamphlet Entitled "What, then, Does Dr. Newman Mean?"* London: Longman, Green, Longman, Roberts, and Green, 1864.
Ari.	*The Arians of the Fourth Century, their Doctrine, Temper, and Conduct, Chiefly as Exhibited in the Councils of the Church, between* A.D. *325, and* A.D. *381.* London: J. G. & F. Rivington, 1833.
AW	*Autobiographical Writings.* Edited by Henry Tristram. London: Sheed and Ward, 1956.
Diff.	*Lectures on Certain Difficulties Felt by Anglicans in Submitting to the Catholic Church.* London: Burns & Lambert, 1850.
Ess.	*Essays: Critical and Historical.* 2 vols. London: Basil Montagu Pickering, 1871.
GA	*An Essay in Aid of a Grammar of Assent.* London: Burns, Oates, & Co., 1870.
Hist.	*History of My Religious Opinions.* London: Longman, Green, Longman, Roberts, and Green, 1865.
LD	*The Letters and Diaries of John Henry Newman.* 32 vols. Vols. 1–8, 23–31: edited by Charles Stephen Dessain, Thomas Gornall et al. Oxford: Clarendon Press, 1973–1999; Vols. 9–10, 32: edited by Francis J. McGrath and Gerard Tracey. Oxford: Oxford University Press, 2006–2008; Vols. 11–22: edited by Charles Stephen Dessain et al. London: Thomas Nelson, 1961–1971.
Mir.	*Two Essays on Scripture Miracles and on Ecclesiastical.* London: Basil Montagu Pickering, 1870.
OUS	*Sermons, Chiefly on the Theory of Religious Belief, Preached before the University of Oxford.* 1st ed. London: J. G. F. & J. Rivington, 1843.
PaS	*Parochial Sermons.* 6 vols. London: J. G. & F. Rivington, 1834–1836; J. G. F. & J. Rivington, 1839–1842.
PlS	*Plain Sermons, by Contributors to the "Tracts for the Times."* London: J. G. F. & J. Rivington, 1843.
Serm.	*Sermons, 1824–1843.* 5 vols. Edited by Placid Murray, Vincent Ferrer Blehl, and Francis J. McGrath. Oxford: Clarendon Press, 1991–2012.
VV	*Verses on Various Occasions.* London: Burns, Oates & Co., 1868.

BL   Bodleian Library

BOA   Birmingham Oratory Archive

CRN   Charles Robert Newman

JHN   John Henry Newman

OCL   Oriel College Letterbook

ODNB   *Oxford Dictionary of National Biography* (online edition)

Parker   Kenneth L. Parker, ed. *Newman's Oriel College Senior Library Record.*
            Pittsburgh: National Institute for Newman Studies. https://digital-
            collections.newmanstudies.org/library-records.

Introduction

There seems to be no end of making books on Newman, and anyone adding
yet another stone to the cairn must at least go through the ritual of making
excuses for doing so.[1]

Newman studies, like every other field, has its *enfants terribles*. Fifty years ago,
a certain P. J. FitzPatrick dared take the side of Charles Kingsley against Newman
and was forgotten as a reward for his effort. The same could have happened to
Frank Turner in our own day. His revisionist studies met with determined resistance in the Newman community, and only recently did the tide change. The challenge of Turner's work is one of the excuses for this book. Perhaps an apology
is in order for every book inflicted on what must be the most saturated publishing
market in history, so a new book on Newman certainly requires some justification.
FitzPatrick already saw that in the 1960s, and since then, publications on Newman
have multiplied beyond number. Newman's recent canonization ensures there is
no end in sight.

But then again, there is much to write about. John Henry Newman (1801–
1890) had a long, busy, and eventful life. He started out as an Anglican, began a
crusade to revitalize the Church of England, converted to Roman Catholicism,
brought the Oratory of St Philip Neri to England, founded a university in Ireland,
and was created cardinal. Meanwhile, he published a vast opus of varied and often
exquisite prose—history, philosophy, theology, criticism, autobiography, two
novels—and some impressive poetry to boot. Of the manuscripts he left, many
papers and most sermons were published in the century after his death, as well
as thirty-two volumes of correspondence. It is no wonder that such a vast amount
of material from one of the towering intellects of the Victorian era has attracted
scholars from many disciplines, whose output has become immense and unwieldy.
So why would I want to add "another stone to the cairn?"

The simple answer is because a keystone is missing. This book is a theological
biography spanning the period between Newman's teenage conversion to evangelicalism and the beginning of the Tractarian Movement. By almost any measure,
these years were the most formative of his life. By the early 1830s, he explicitly
rejected much of the theology he had espoused in the early 1820s and had developed a highly original, deeply personal, and quite radical alternative, whose fundamental notions continued to shape his thought for the rest of his life. Whether
we look at the extent of the change (covering almost every facet of his theology)

---

1. G. Egner [P. J. FitzPatrick], *Apologia pro Charles Kingsley* (London: Sheed and Ward, 1969), xi.

or at its depth (redefining most of his fundamental theological notions), every later change pales in comparison, even his conversion to Roman Catholicism in 1845. And yet, we have no accurate account of this change: the period in which it occurred is comparatively neglected, the significance of the change is usually overlooked, its nature and content are misrepresented, and its scope is narrowed. This is reason enough for a new study. But it is all the timelier because it clarifies a set of issues that have arisen in Newman research in the past two decades, which threaten to create lasting but perhaps avoidable scholarly division.

Clearing the Field

Although Newman always was and continues to be a contentious figure, it seems fair to say that he devoted his life to the cause of religion. Divisions arise about why he did so, and what his religion was. Did his religion really change as much as it seems, or was it the same throughout his life? And why did he profess what he did: because he genuinely believed it, or for some other reason? Although many commentators conclude that Newman deeply believed what he taught, a small but significant minority has averred that his religious profession was not quite so honest, arguing, usually, that he fled from his own sceptical intellect into superstition. In the nineteenth century, this was a common line of argument. It began with some of Newman's erstwhile friends and colleagues at Oriel College in the late 1830s and became near-canonical in the controversy over *An Essay on the Development of Christian Doctrine*, the book that defended his conversion to Roman Catholicism in 1845. The *Apologia pro vita sua*, Newman's 1864 attempt to vindicate the integrity of his religious journey satisfied some, but by no means all, so similar critiques continued to be voiced throughout the Victorian era, even by some of its most prominent intellectuals.[2] In the first decades after his death, when Newman studies became a predominantly Catholic affair, this tradition of criticism fell into oblivion. It flared up briefly among Newman's modernist interpreters (like Henri Brémond and George Tyrrell), but in the concerted effort to suppress modernism and salvage Newman from its taint, their readings, too, were forgotten.

---

2. Geertjan Zuijdwegt, "Scepticism and Credulity: Victorian Critiques of John Henry Newman's Religious Apologetic," *Journal for the History of Modern Theology* 20, no. 1 (2013): 1–24; "Richard Whately's Influence on John Henry Newman's Oxford University Sermons on Faith and Reason," *Newman Studies Journal* 10, no. 1 (2013): 82–95; "Newman's Disputed Honesty: A Case Study in Victorian Religious Controversy," *Louvain Studies* 34 (2010): 361–84; Erik Sidenvall, *After Anti-Catholicism? John Henry Newman and Protestant Britain, 1845–c.1890* (London: T&T Clark, 2005); Lawrence Poston, *The Antagonist Principle: John Henry Newman and the Paradox of Personality* (Charlottesville: University of Virginia Press, 2014); J. M. I. Klaver, "The Apologia," in *The Oxford Handbook of John Henry Newman*, ed. Frederick D. Aquino and Benjamin J. King (Oxford: Oxford University Press, 2018), 454–74, esp. 459–65.

It is owing to his antimodernist defenders in the early twentieth century that Newman was saved for Catholic theology, even though his place there has never been entirely beyond dispute. But having a field of study dominated by partisans comes at a price. Not only was Newman's theology canonized, but also his accounts of how it came to be and what it was all about. Perhaps quite intentionally, the *Apologia* became the model and the measure of future biographies.[3] To take an instance that concerns us immediately, the *Apologia* devoted thirty pages to the years up to 1833, and 270 to the remaining twelve. Given that Newman defended himself against Charles Kingsley's attack on his integrity as an Anglican, this made perfect sense. He was on trial for his Tractarian opinions, and what came before was needed only to set the stage. Later biographers replicated the procedure without its excuse. Wilfrid Ward could still appeal to Newman's express wishes, but even Charles Dessain spends less than one-tenth of his biography on what he rather vacuously titles, "The First Thirty Years."[4] Although quite a few scholars are more elaborate, Dessain is far from alone.[5] But there is a more pressing issue than space. The *Apologia's* narrative is one of basic continuity of views. Again, Newman was well within his rights to select those aspects from his history that made for a harmonious story. He was under no obligation to anyone. But more critical acumen might have been expected from later biographers, especially because the *Apologia* itself hints that there was more to Newman's early development than he cared to tell.

For one, we learn that Newman was once an evangelical, or at least that his views after his adolescent conversion were shaped by evangelical authors of the moderately Calvinistic variety. We also learn that his views were no longer evangelical by the time he began the Tractarian Movement, but how he stopped being an evangelical he does not explain. Similarly, Newman tells us that his Tractarian "battle was with liberalism."[6] But we also learn that he was tending to liberalism himself in the mid-1820s, a tendency that was checked when he got ill and lost a loved one.[7] None of this is very enlightening, nor did it need to be. But these

---

3. See Maisie Ward, *Young Mr. Newman* (London: Sheed & Ward, 1948), vii–viii.

4. Wilfrid Ward, *The Life of John Henry Cardinal Newman*, vol. 1 (London: Longmans, Green, and Co., 1912), 3. Ward's two-volume biography devotes only fifty-one pages (out of more than 1,100) to the first half of Newman's life. See also Charles Stephen Dessain, *John Henry Newman* (London: Thomas Nelson, 1966), 1–14 (out of 169).

5. The ratio is similar in Ian Ker, *John Henry Newman: A Biography* (Oxford: Clarendon Press, 1988), 1–53 (out of 745). Meriol Trevor's two-volume work, *Newman: The Pillar of the Cloud* and *Newman: Light in Winter* (London: Macmillan, 1962) devotes 109 pages (out of 1,283) to the first third of Newman's life.

6. *Apologia pro vita sua: Being a Reply to a Pamphlet Entitled "What, then, Does Dr. Newman Mean?"* (London: Longman, Green, Longman, Roberts, and Green, 1864), 120, hereafter *Apo.*; see also 94–95, 108–9, 111, 130–32.

7. *Apo.*, 72.

enigmas might have troubled commentators more than they have. To learn, without much explanation, that someone is evangelical, and then is not, and tends to be a liberal, only to resist liberalism a few years later, should evoke curiosity aplenty. Why did Newman stop being an evangelical, and what, then, did he become? What was this tendency to liberalism, and how did it relate to his evangelicalism (or did it)? Why did it become undone, and why did he hate liberalism so much afterwards? And what do these epithets mean in the first place? These are questions to be answered, not avoided.

To some extent, Newman realized that his account in the *Apologia* raised as many questions as it answered. He explained liberalism as he understood it in a long note appended to the 1865 edition, though never how it applied to himself. He did not address the issue of evangelicalism in later editions of the *Apologia*, but he did compose another autobiography in 1874 in which he examined his youthful evangelical convictions.[8] In some ways, these explications helped, but they also created problems of their own. As he got older, Newman maintained that he had never been a real evangelical at all (at least, most scholars have concluded that's what he said). With a few notable exceptions, his partisans ignored his evangelical theology accordingly, for how could it be significant if it was never real? Newman's liberal tendencies, too, were easy enough to ignore, given that he did little to specify them. And thus, the basic continuities of the *Apologia* were replicated in later scholarship. The image is that of an adolescent religious prodigy whose conversion provided him with elements of thought and belief—sometimes embryonic, but often quite mature—which grew harmoniously, first into Tractarianism and then into Roman Catholicism. This description of mainline Newman scholarship might be oversimplified, but that it captures a deeply cherished understanding of Newman's development is shown by the largely negative Catholic response to the late Frank Turner's massive 2002 biography, *John Henry Newman: The Challenge to Evangelical Religion.*

Consciously revisionist, Turner challenged the reliability of the *Apologia* and the uncritical use scholars make of it to interpret Newman's life up to 1845.[9] Turner's central contention was that Newman's professed opposition to liberalism in the *Apologia* was meant to conceal "his antipathy as the Newman of Oriel and St. Mary's to evangelical Protestantism, a dislike bordering on hatred that had

---

8. *History of My Religious Opinions* (London: Longman, Green, Longman, Roberts, and Green, 1865), 285–97, hereafter *Hist.*; "Autobiographical Memoir," *Autobiographical Writings*, ed. Henry Tristram (London: Scheed and Ward, 1956), 19–108, hereafter *AW*. With many excisions, Anne Mozley integrated the memoir into her *Letters and Correspondence of John Henry Newman, During his Life in the English Church*, vol. 1 (London: Longmans, Green, and Co., 1891).

9. Frank M. Turner, *John Henry Newman: The Challenge to Evangelical Religion* (New Haven, Conn.: Yale University Press, 2002), 5–7. See Simon Skinner, "History *versus* Hagiography: The Reception of Turner's *Newman*," *Journal of Ecclesiastical History* 61, no. 4 (2010): 764–65.

been the single most energizing force in his thought and theology during the 1830s and early 1840s"—a claim Turner reiterated in the introduction to his 2008 critical edition of the *Apologia*.[10] For Turner, the *Apologia* was Newman's conscious effort to make his story and person relevant to the religious debates—Protestant as well as Catholic—of the 1860s.[11] Newman simply recast his early antievangelicalism as a more fashionable antiliberalism:

> The rhetoric he used to attack what he termed liberalism in the 1860s and 1870s he had first devised in the 1830s to characterize and denounce contemporary evangelical Protestant religion. He later simply transferred that language to his critique of mid- and late-Victorian religious and cultural targets.[12]

The *Apologia's* "battle with liberalism" was little more than a ruse: a clever attempt, on Newman's part, to make his legacy more enduring, and a successful one at that given its reception history.

There was much more to ruffle Catholic feathers in Turner's biography, from suggestions about Newman's (latent) homosexuality to imputations of nastiness in engaging controversy, and most reviews from that quarter were severe.[13] More worrisome is the fact that Turner's study was "quietly embargoed" in mainline Newman studies.[14] That, at least, was Oxford historian Simon Skinner's indignant argument in the *Journal of Ecclesiastical History*. He scathingly portrayed Catholic Newman studies as a "coterie of like-minded celebrants" whose confessional commitments prevent them from valuing a monument of historical research like Turner's *Newman*. The issue, to cite Skinner's title, was one of "history versus hagiography." If nothing else, Skinner's battle cry awoke some students of Newman from their dogmatic slumbers, including myself. But its effect was not just to spur better historiography. In some quarters, the legitimate call for meticulous historical inquiry became one of being for or against Turner. The issue shifted, one is tempted to say, from taking "Newman's utterances at face value" to taking Turner's word for it.[15] Obviously, both are questionable procedures. What Newman says about his own history deserves serious attention, if only because it comes from someone with unique—though far from infallible—access to the subject under consideration: himself. Still, its primary function is heuristic;

---

10. Turner, *John Henry Newman*, 9; Frank M. Turner, "Editor's Introduction: The Newman of the *Apologia* and the Newman of History," in John Henry Newman, *Apologia Pro Vita Sua and Six Sermons*, ed. Frank M. Turner (New Haven, Conn.: Yale University Press, 2008): 1–115; Skinner, "History *versus* Hagiography," 765.

11. Turner, *John Henry Newman*, 9–10; Turner, "Editor's Introduction," 55.

12. Turner, "Editor's Introduction," 59; see also 68–69.

13. See Skinner, "History *versus* Hagiography," 767–81.

14. Skinner, "History *versus* Hagiography," 779.

15. Skinner, "History *versus* Hagiography," 769.

his interpretations are pointers in the quest for historical explanation, to be tested against the best evidence, if and where available.

Turner's claims are easier to evaluate. His account is open to a more straightforward form of empirical falsification since it presumes no special access to its subject matter but rests—if not wholly, at least ultimately—on a body of historical evidence. Accordingly, the advice to those troubled by Turner's revisionist claims is simple: if you do not agree, stop complaining and do the research. And if you do agree, make sure you do not just take Turner's word for it. The question, after all, is, or should be, one of "history versus history."

Ironically, it is precisely as history that Turner's monumental effort falls short. Even more ironic, it does so for the same reason as many traditional accounts: because it leaves the puzzles of Newman's early development unsolved. Although not the first to do so, Turner has rightly highlighted Newman's turn against evangelical religion in 1830, its consequent emergence as one of his main polemical targets, and its all but complete absence from the *Apologia*, which focuses on liberalism instead. This is a puzzle, to be sure, but Turner's solution—that antiliberalism was a ruse for antievangelicalism—is mistaken. To understand the mistake, consider another puzzle. Newman, as Turner affirms, was once an evangelical. From 1830 onward, we find this same Newman espousing a very different theology and attacking evangelicalism from the pulpit. How did he get from *a* to *b*? One obvious way to go about answering this question is to detail theological shifts in the intervening period, but this is what Turner does not do. Instead, he replicates some of the standard account, with a focus not on the content of Newman's change in views but on the psychological forces that supposedly drove it.[16] The result is meagre. "Energized by anger, disappointment, and frustration" over a series of conflicts with his radical evangelical brother Francis, Newman "lifted the private battles located in his family to a universal plane of criticism."[17] Put simply, John began to preach the importance of religious obedience at St Mary's because Frank would not listen to him at home.

The main problem with this explanation is not its crude psychologism, although this, too, is a problem, but the fact that Turner overlooked (or ignored) all the sources that do account for the shift. Excepting correspondence and journal entries, his massive biography ignores nearly all of Newman's writing prior to 1830. Turner cites none of Newman's published articles or many manuscript papers, and uses only two out of more than 200 sermons.[18] Surely, it borders on historiographical recklessness to claim that "contingency after contingency determined the emergence of Newman's religious character and thought" when one

---

16. Turner, *John Henry Newman*, 110–35.
17. Turner, *John Henry Newman*, 134.
18. Turner, *John Henry Newman*, 128, 130–31.

has not consulted the bulk of relevant sources.[19] Admittedly, most of these sources were hard to come by at the time Turner wrote his biography, but others had succeeded in accessing them before, and they are all on Dwight Culler's microfilm of the Birmingham Oratory Archive, which Turner used extensively. Whether willful or not, the omission means that Turner could only take up Newman's theology in medias res, when it already had a history of over a decade. Accordingly, there was nothing left for him but to explain Newman's rejection of evangelical religion in psychological terms.

This is one historiographical flaw the present study is intended to remedy. To do so, I carefully trace Newman's gradual departure from evangelical thought. Contrary to most mainline studies, I argue that this entailed a fundamental transformation affecting almost every aspect of Newman's theology. Against Turner, I argue that this change had a coherent rationale. It was the product of careful and consistent reasoning and reflection shaped, but not determined, by contingent factors: people met, events experienced, conflicts fought, books read, assignments taken.

Besides helping to solve the puzzle of Newman's relationship to evangelicalism, this study also helps to solve the puzzle of Newman's relationship to liberalism. Here, my argument is slightly more complex. I argue that Newman's idea of liberalism emerged in response to the sea change in English social, political, and religious culture that occurred between the late 1820s and early 1830s. Both Newman's understanding of liberalism and his response to it were part of a developmental process largely distinct from his coincident qualms about evangelicalism. After 1833, the Tractarian Newman began to discern a tendency toward liberalism in much of the Protestant theology of the day, especially in evangelical religion and in the thought of his erstwhile friends and colleagues at Oriel. I argue that Newman was bound to make this discovery because his own evangelical theology in the mid-1820s had embodied the liberal tendencies he now derided. His own drift toward liberalism was not (as the conventional reading has it) a tertium quid, intervening between his evangelical and Tractarian periods, but a modification of his evangelical theology, which was congenial to it, or which—so he later believed—even invited it. Accordingly, the *Apologia's* emphasis on liberalism is not a ruse but a simplification. The Tractarian Newman began to attack evangelicalism wholesale not only but primarily because he believed that, like most Protestant theology, it tended toward liberalism. When created cardinal in 1879, Newman stated: "For thirty, forty, fifty years I have resisted to the best of my powers the spirit of liberalism in religion."[20] Measured by the tools of the historian,

---

19. Turner, *John Henry Newman*, 110.

20. John Henry Newman (hereafter JHN), "Biglietto Speech," *Addresses to Cardinal Newman with His Replies etc., 1879–1881*, ed. W. P. Neville (London: Longmans, Green, and Co., 1905), 64, hereafter *Add.*

this contentious claim must be judged as true. It might not have been the only thing he resisted, but it was the crucial thing.

Object, Design, Method

To describe this study as a theological biography simply means that it is an intellectual biography with a focus on theology. Such an approach seemed right for one who, as all hands agree, spent half or more of his waking hours focused on religion, either directly (praying, celebrating, catechizing, preaching), or indirectly (reading, thinking, writing, teaching, or talking about it). The fact that theological perspectives have long been too dominant in Newman studies—now gradually recognized and remedied—does not render them invalid.[21] The emphasis of this study is on themes, ideas, and arguments. I focus on what Newman believed and taught more than on who he was, or what he did. I do not discuss the elements of his personal history that did not influence his theological development.[22] No attempt is made to offer a comprehensive interpretation of his personality, nor do I appeal to psychological drives, complexes, or mechanisms to explain his adoption of certain views. There are many such analyses, at times quite captivating ones, but their evidential base is often too slim to render them much better than speculation. They are usually quite reductive, too, taking the development of Newman's thought as the product of (un)conscious affects, be they religious (deep spiritual instincts or desires) or naturalistic (a sense of paternal failure or sibling rivalry). Although I acknowledge the importance of such affects, I believe that thought is relatively autonomous and that a (developing) set of convictions can have its own integrity and rationale.

It is safe to say that Newman was the thinking type. Much of his intellectual development was driven by what could be called a process of reflective intensification. He discovered an idea—say church, conscience, moral character, or mystery—and then gradually and consistently proceeded to deepen his understanding of it and think through and accept what it implied until it became a foundational concept in his theology. But none of this happened in a vacuum. Newman was a social thinker, that is, one who thought in encounter with others: his family (his

---

21. See Colin Barr and Simon Skinner, "Political and Social Thought," in *The Oxford Handbook of John Henry Newman*, ed. Frederick D. Aquino and Benjamin J. King (Oxford: Oxford University Press, 2018), 395–97.

22. Besides the major biographies by Ward, Trevor, Ker, and Turner, those interested in the details of Newman's personal and family life can consult M. Ward, *Young Mr. Newman*; Sean O'Faolain, *Newman's Way* (London: Longmans, Green, and Co., 1952); David Newsome, *The Parting of Friends: The Wilberforces and Henry Manning* (Grand Rapids, Mich.: William B. Eerdmans, 1993); and Edward Short, *Newman and His Family* (London: Bloomsbury, 2013). For Newman's intellectual formation at Oxford and his vision of education, see Dwight Culler's unsurpassed *The Imperial Intellect: A Study of Newman's Educational Ideal* (New Haven, Conn.: Yale University Press, 1955), 1–79.

parents and sisters, his brothers Charles and Frank, his aunt Elizabeth), his mentors, guides, friends, and pupils (Mayers, Whately, Hawkins, Pusey, Keble, Froude, the Wilberforces), and his authors (Scott, Sumner, Erskine, Butler, Clement, Origen). Much of my story concerns the ways these dead or living people influenced the development of Newman's thought. He was a social thinker in a second sense as well. An avaricious reader and a keen observer, he knew what was happening around him, in culture, society, and politics. He also knew his way around the world. For all the otherworldliness that came with his semicloistered existence as an Oriel fellow, he was savvy about money and power and a masterly tactician in various campaigns, once styling himself "the rhetorician" of the Tractarian Movement.[23] Although this aspect of Newman's personality is beyond the scope of the present study, his informed critique of culture is key to my argument.

As befits a biography, the basic organizing principle of this study is chronology. I trace the transformations of Newman's theology roughly in the order of their occurrence. The first chapter analyses Newman's 1816 conversion to evangelical religion, along with the theology he adopted and began to systematize in the early 1820s. Chapter 2 expands on fundamental theological ideas of faith, reason, and revelation that Newman acquired as an adolescent by charting their development under the influence of English Enlightenment apologetics and in controversy with his apostate brother Charles. Chapters 3, 4, and 5 describe three distinct transformations that befell Newman's theology in the mid-1820s. Chapter 3 details what Newman later styled his drift toward liberalism by analysing his understanding of the nature, object, and value of doctrine, in particular, the atonement and the Trinity. Chapter 4 treats Newman's shift toward High Church theology, which has garnered so much comment both from himself and from later scholars. Chapter 5 traces the development of Newman's idea of conscience and its relation to natural religion. The terminus for each panel of this triptych is 1827, a time at which Newman was no longer evangelical but not yet anything else: an evangelical adrift.

Chapter 6 analyses the period between late 1827 and early 1829, when dramatic events in Newman's personal life—illness and death—along with a new set of friends estranged him further from evangelical thought, while solidifying the insights he had gained since 1825. Between 1829 and 1832, Newman's new vision took definite shape. Chapters 7, 8, and 9 narrate the conclusion to this comprehensive

---

23. JHN to Richard Hurrell Froude, February 2, 1836, in *The Letters and Diaries of John Henry Newman,* vol. 5, ed. Charles Steven Dessain, Thomas Gornall et al. (Oxford: Clarendon Press, 1973–1999), 225, hereafter *LD* 5. The citation for the entire work is: *The Letters and Diaries of John Henry Newman,* 32 vols. Vols. 1–8, 23–31, ed. Charles Stephen Dessain, Thomas Gornall et al. (Oxford: Clarendon Press, 1973–1999); vols. 9–10, 32, ed. Francis J. McGrath and Gerard Tracey (Oxford: Oxford University Press, 2006–2008); vols. 11–22, ed. Charles Stephen Dessain et al. (London: Thomas Nelson, 1961–1971).

theological transformation from two distinct angels. Chapter 7 examines Newman's definite rejection of evangelical theology and his alternative vision of both the religious subject and the object of religious belief. Chapter 8 shifts the focus from evangelicalism to liberalism. It describes the emergence of the idea in Newman's thought along with his denunciation of its driving principle: reliance on the intellect in religious inquiry. Chapter 9 analyses Newman's attack on an amorphous but pervasive liberal worldview whose theological resemblance to Socinianism (or Unitarianism) he deplored, and which he countered by emphasizing the mysteriousness of religious truth and the doctrinal authority of the early church. The final chapter makes a foray into the first years of the Tractarian Movement, when Newman began to discern and attack liberal tendencies in the systems that had shaped his early thought: evangelicalism and Oriel theology.

Although this study details the comprehensive transformation of Newman's early theology, it is not exhaustive. I have written on a parsimonious principle. Only those views qualify as products of change for which sufficient evidence exists that he either did not hold them earlier or with a widely different sense or import. Some changes are overdetermined. Many more sources contribute to a shift than are required to account for it. In most cases, I select only the most important ones, those that are sufficient for explanation. Some theological developments are treated only tangentially, such as his thought on the relation between the Jewish and Christian dispensations, the liturgy, or the Roman Catholic Church. Others are not touched upon at all, such as his interest in and exposition of prophecy or his views on education. Nor is each strand of influence discussed (think of Romantic novelists and poets, like Walter Scott and Robert Southey). The reasons for these omissions are various. Some themes were not at the center of his theological development (for example, his take on prophecy). Others are important mostly in hindsight (thus, Roman Catholicism only really became an issue in 1833). In the case of the Romantic authors, which he read in his teenage years, the evidence to establish their influence on specific developments is slight or diffuse, even though Romanticism colored his religious outlook as a whole.[24]

There are many historiographical pitfalls when dealing with an author like Newman, who not only reinterpreted his own development throughout his life but continued to revise his writings for later editions or republications; a fact commonly known but methodologically neglected. I consistently use the first version of Newman's texts where available. Sometimes, this means using the manuscript over the published version, as in the case of the *Oxford University Sermons*, which Newman preached between 1826 and 1843 (the year he published them with many revisions). In most cases, it means using the first published version:

---

24. See David Goslee's uneven but still insightful *Romanticism and the Anglican Newman* (Athens, Ohio: Ohio University Press, 1996).

the original journal article or encyclopedia entry, the first edition of the *Arians* and of the *Parochial* and *Plain Sermons*. The latter pose an additional problem. Most of Newman's pre-1829 sermons have survived only in manuscript form. Until they appeared in the recent five-volume edition of his Anglican sermons, only six out of 184 had been available. By contrast, many of the sermons written between 1829 and 1833, including most of the significant ones, were published in the following years.[25] Because the manuscripts of these sermons were destroyed, later revisions, whether for subsequent preachings or for publication, can no longer be traced.

It is hard to determine the historiographical import of this constraint. On the one hand, the manuscripts of Newman's unpublished sermons sometimes show significant revisions for later preachings. On the other hand, the substance of his university sermons—the only published sermons preserved in manuscript—was not altered upon publication in 1843. Moreover, the sermons originally composed in 1830 and 1831 are largely consistent both with one another, whether published in 1834 or 1843, and with manuscript sermons of the same period. This suggests that Newman published the sermons in substance as they were preached, although (occasionally significant) revisions occurred. While many manuscripts from the Newman archives have been published, many have not. The present study draws on much of this unpublished material. In presenting it in print, I have been more concerned with readability than with exact graphic reproduction. Some specifics are preserved, such as underlining for emphasis, but abbreviations have been silently expanded (e.g., Christ for Xt, religion for rel[n], should for sh[d], or which for w[h]). I ask forgiveness of readers who would have preferred greater precision.

Theology and Egotism

This book is a theological biography, not a study in theology. Its aim is neither to forward a theological theory nor to present *the* position of Newman and to evaluate its merits, coherence, or relevance within a specified theological framework. There are many studies of the latter variety and excellent ones at that, even though they often tend to overlook the developing character of Newman's thought. And yet I hope that my approach, which is to integrate analyses of Newman's developing theological views with the story of his personal quest for religious truth, will be a (modest) contribution to the study of theology. I could

---

25. They were incorporated in the first three volumes (1834, 1835, 1836) of his *Parochial Sermons*, 6 vols. (London: J. G. & F. Rivington, 1834–1836; J. G. F. & J. Rivington, 1839–1842), hereafter *PaS*, and in the fifth volume of *Plain Sermons, by Contributors to the "Tracts for the Times"* (London: J. G. F. & J. Rivington, 1843), hereafter *PlS*.

envisage it along the following lines. Toward the end of *The Varieties of Religious Experience*, William James contrasts science and religion in terms of their respective attitudes to what he calls "the personal point of view"—repudiated by science, extolled by religion.[26] "The pivot round which the religious life . . . revolves," James argues, "is the interest of the individual in his private personal destiny. Religion, in short, is a monumental chapter in the history of human egotism."[27]

This judgment concludes James's detailed investigation of individuals' religious attitudes, convictions, and expressions, and its immediate context is his discussion of the survival theory of religion, the idea that religion is an anthropomorphic remnant from primitive stages of human development. Such a theory assumes that science can adequately represent reality only if it abstracts as much as possible from personal language and experience and frames its theories in "universal and impersonal terms."[28] James thinks this assumption is mistaken. He boldly counters: "so long as we deal with the cosmic and the general, we deal only with the symbols of reality, but *as soon as we deal with private and personal phenomena as such, we deal with realities in the completest sense of the term.*"[29]

James's conviction was rooted in his radical empiricism, but that philosophical position need not detain us. What matters is his basic point: that abstract ideas or theories, however magnificent, are thought by a subject, who has certain attitudes toward them and possesses self-awareness. It is only "such a concrete bit of personal experience" that James regards as "a *full* fact."

> That unsharable feeling which each one of us has of the pinch of his individual destiny as he privately feels it rolling out on fortune's wheel may be disparaged for its egotism, may be sneered at as unscientific, but it is the one thing that fills up the measure of our concrete actuality, and any would-be existent that should lack such a feeling, or its analogue, would be a piece of reality only half made up.[30]

We relate to the world in deeply personal ways, which are constitutive of its (and our) reality. A science that would ignore these "egotistic elements of experience" and replace them with abstractions would miss what is real. This applies to theology as much as to any other science. After all, the "axis of reality runs solely through the egotistic places—they are strung upon it like so many beads."[31]

---

26. William James, *The Varieties of Religious Experience: A Study in Human Nature* (London: Longmans, Green, and Co., 1928), 491.

27. James, *The Varieties of Religious Experience*, 491.

28. James, *The Varieties of Religious Experience*, 491.

29. James, *The Varieties of Religious Experience*, 498.

30. James, *The Varieties of Religious Experience*, 499.

31. James, *The Varieties of Religious Experience*, 499–500.

Many, by now, will have been reminded of Newman's famous dictum that in thinking and writing about religion (or metaphysics or ethics), "egotism is true modesty."[32] "In religious inquiry," he explains, "each of us can speak only for himself, and for himself he has a right to speak."[33] This comment prefaces the discussion of the evidences of Christianity in *An Essay in Aid of a Grammar of Assent* (1870). When these are concerned, Newman argues, a person's "true sobriety and modesty consists, not in claiming for his conclusions an acceptance or a scientific approval which is not to be found any where, but in stating what are personally his own grounds for his belief in Natural and Revealed Religion."[34] Here, as in the longer citation from James, the idea of the personal is strikingly overdetermined. Newman's "personally his own" and James's "individual destiny privately felt" are equally pleonastic ways to emphasize that the acquisition of truth has a deeply personal dimension, that personal meanings are involved that a purported scientific objectivity cannot capture. Newman was no radical empiricist, and he would have rejected James's pragmatist take on doctrine as an instance of rationalism, but he shared the conviction that when it comes to the how, the what, and the why of people's religious beliefs, there is no way around the personal.

If James and Newman are right, the most adequate picture of a person's theology emerges when viewed within the framework of their personal quest for religious truth. It is such a picture that I aim to draw. For James, being religious means leaving the purportedly scientific observer standpoint and genuinely confronting ourselves with "questions connected with our individual destinies."[35] The present study does not leave the observer standpoint, but it does portray the theological development of one who hardly ever—if at all—occupied that standpoint, that is, one who was always deeply concerned about his individual destiny and that of those for whom he felt responsible. Its goal is not to convince anyone that the development of Newman's theology was right but rather to establish what this development was and understand the way it was shaped by his search for appropriate ways of relating to God. The resulting portrait shows that, for Newman, even seemingly arid or arcane theological questions were never detached from questions of individual destiny. His theological questions were religious questions, questions whose answer made a difference. Perhaps such an awareness, that theological views and arguments—even foreign or long forgotten ones—can be profoundly meaningful for those who held (or still hold) them, can render service to the discipline of theology, which sometimes forgets that its subject matter is entwined with people's sense of individual destiny.

32. JHN, *An Essay in Aid of a Grammar of Assent* (London: Burns, Oates, & Co., 1870), 379, hereafter *GA*.

33. *GA*, 379–80.

34. *GA*, 380–81.

35. James, *The Varieties of Religious Experience*, 500.

CHAPTER 1

A Young Evangelical

From the age of fifteen to his early twenties, John Henry Newman was an evangelical in the Church of England. All the major biographers recount, however briefly, the evangelical first decade of Newman's actively religious life, and all agree that the event with which it began—his adolescent conversion—was a landmark experience that, some way or another, continued to shape his future self. Still, there is something remarkable about the way in which Newman's early evangelicalism is treated. With the notable exception of Paul Vaiss, all the biographers describe Newman's evangelical period from the viewpoint of his personal religiosity rather than his theology.[1] They abound in portrayals of his religious discipline at the time, which was strict and introspective and has drawn some harsh comments, but they hardly ever touch on the evangelical theology he embraced.

This is all the more remarkable because few scholars hesitate to interpret Newman's life by his theology when other periods are concerned, such as his time in the Oxford Movement or his conversion to Rome. One explanation could be that, unlike his early religiosity, his early theology is difficult to integrate into the seamless sort of narrative that most biographers prefer. This would presume at least an awareness of the sources, however, for which there is barely any evidence. Admittedly, these sources have been hard to come by. Except for two articles in the evangelical *Christian Observer*, Newman's theological papers prior to 1824 remain unpublished, while the sermons he preached as curate of St Clement's (1824–1826) have been comprehensively available only since 2012. Still, there seems to be more to it, since the few scholars who did wish to address the subject, such as, John Linnan, Thomas Sheridan, and Paul Vaiss, managed to access the sources with little trouble.[2] Only a general lack of interest can account for the neglect of such important material.

Ironically, it might be Newman himself who is to blame for much of the disinterest in his early thought. As an old man, he questioned the genuineness of his

---

1. Paul Vaiss, *Newman. Sa vie, sa pensée et sa spiritualité* (Paris: L'Harmattan, 1991).

2. John E. Linnan, "The Evangelical Background of John Henry Newman, 1816–1826," 2 vols. (PhD diss., Université Catholique de Louvain, 1965); Thomas Sheridan, *Newman on Justification* (Staten Island, N.Y.: Alba House, 1967). Even so, the obscurity of both the sources and the (scanty) literature continues. Gareth Atkins, a prominent historian of Anglican evangelicalism, gives no evidence of even knowing about their existence in his recent chapter on Newman's evangelicalism. See his "Evangelical Writers," in *The Oxford Handbook of John Henry Newman*, ed. Frederick D. Aquino and Benjamin J. King (Oxford: Oxford University Press, 2018), 173–95.

early evangelicalism and insisted that his conversion had never been properly evangelical at all. It had lacked the special, sudden, and forceful religious emotions prescribed by the evangelical literature—a fact he recognized as early as 1821.[3] Many scholars have extrapolated from these observations to downplay the significance of Newman's evangelical period as a whole, usually in service of a more "Catholic" reading of his "first conversion" and its outcome. Although this line of interpretation clearly militates against Newman's usual descriptions of his adolescent religion, both at the time and in later life, it had only a few challengers.[4] Critics like Linnan and Vaiss have rightly insisted on the import of Newman's early evangelicalism. His adolescent conversion, they argue, not only *made* him an evangelical but *was* "an Evangelical conversion"—*pace* Newman.[5] Perhaps the latter dispute is only a quibble about words, given how much depends on definitions here. But we need not assess the elderly Newman's claims about his adolescent religion just yet, not before we have traced the many cues to his early theological development in the patchy and self-censored, but still ample, source material.

Newman's Adolescent Conversion

On May 15, 1812, the Court of King's Bench sentenced London publisher Daniel Isaac Eaton to eighteen months' imprisonment in Newgate gaol for a blasphemous libel.[6] It consisted of Eaton's having published and sold a small book by his friend, the famous American revolutionary and notorious Deist Thomas Paine (1737–1809). The book was titled *The Age of Reason. Part the Third. Being an Examination of the Passages in the New Testament, Quoted from the Old and Called Prophecies concerning Jesus Christ.*[7] The pamphlet, Paine's last, was never intended to be the final installment of *The Age of Reason*, his scurrilous two-part attack on Christianity published in 1794–1795, but it was right in line with his earlier work. Rife with ridicule, it was a case-by-case demolition of the Gospel writers' application of Old Testament prophecies to Jesus. Never one to mince words, Paine gloried throughout in mocking "the collection of lies, and contradictions called the Holy Bible . . . the rubbish called revealed religion."[8] Eaton knew that rebranding the book as the long-anticipated third part of *The Age of Reason* would work wonders

---

3. JHN, "Autobiographical Memoir," *AW*, 80; "June or July 1821," *AW*, 166; "July 26, 1826," *AW*, 172.

4. See Linnan, *The Evangelical Background,* 293–346; Vaiss, *Newman,* 43–58.

5. Linnan, *The Evangelical Background,* 346; Vaiss, *Newman,* 57.

6. Thomas Jones Howell, ed., *A Complete Collection of State Trials and Proceedings for High Treason and other Crimes and Misdemeanors,* vol. 31 (London: 1823), 927–58.

7. Thomas Paine, *The Age of Reason. Part the Third. Being an Examination of the Passages in the New Testament, Quoted from the Old and Called Prophecies concerning Jesus Christ* (London: Daniel Isaac Eaton, 1811).

8. Paine, *The Age of Reason. Part the Third,* 5.

for its success, and he sold it under the new title in his shop at Ave Maria Lane, right behind St Paul's Cathedral.

One day in 1811, a certain London banker entered Eaton's shop—it was right on the way from his firm in Lombard Street to his house in Southampton Street—and bought Paine's pamphlet. That banker was John Newman Sr. Whatever he thought when he bought Paine's text, he certainly did not foresee that the semi-clandestine booklet passing over Eaton's counter would end up in the archive of a Roman Catholic congregation in Birmingham, founded by his eldest son, a man who went on to become cardinal and is now canonized.[9] Had he known, John Newman would not have liked it. If his youngest son Francis is to be believed, John Sr. had no pretentions to being especially religious. He styled himself "a man of the world," and admired Benjamin Franklin and Thomas Jefferson, those other great American revolutionaries.[10] He seems to have made no show of his views on religion, but he also did little to hide them. Although he was barely involved in the religious education of his children, Frank still concluded, at 17, that his "father was an entire freethinker."[11] John Jr. seems to have suspected as much at an even younger age. When he was 14, he stumbled upon his father's copy of Paine's pamphlet. In the *Apologia*, he recollects reading "Paine's Tracts against the Old Testament" at that impressionable age and finding "pleasure in thinking of the objections which were contained in them."[12] He also remembered telling his father that he had read David Hume's attack on miracles in the *Enquiry*, "but perhaps," he adds, "it was a brag."[13] This is a revealing remark, not because he might have read Hume but because it was something he could brag about. Apparently, there was little shame attached to reading overt critiques of Christianity among the Newmans.

None of this is to say that religion had no place in the Newman household. They went to church on Sundays, had "a short prayer or hymn night and morning," and the women of the family—their mother Jemima, but especially their grandmother and aunt on the Newman side (both named Elizabeth)—had the children read out the Psalms of the day.[14] But when Thomas Mozley later

---

9. Birmingham Oratory Archive A.8.5, hereafter BOA.

10. Francis William Newman (hereafter FWN), *Contributions Chiefly to the Early History of the Late Cardinal Newman* (London: Kegan Paul, Trench, Trübner & Co., 1891), 7.

11. FWN to Moncure Daniel Conway, in Moncure Daniel Conway, *Autobiography: Memories and Experiences*, vol. 1 (London: Cassell and Company, 1904), 396. Thomas Mozley, who had never known his father-in-law, even claimed he was a Freemason, presumably on his wife Harriett's authority. See *Reminiscences: Chiefly of Oriel College and the Oxford Movement*, vol. 1 (London: Longmans, Green, and Co., 1882), 12.

12. *Apo.*, 58.

13. *Apo.*, 58. See David Hume, *An Enquiry concerning Human Understanding*, ed. Peter Millican (Oxford: Oxford University Press, 2007), 79–95 (109–31).

14. FWN to Moncure Daniel Conway, in Conway, *Autobiography*, vol. 1, 396.

depicted his mother-in-law Jemima, who was of Huguenot descent, as a Calvinistic evangelical, John and Frank strenuously objected. "She would be called an Arminian and Remonstrant," John wrote to him, "The only Sermons she seemed to know were [John] 'Tillotson's'"—a latitudinarian divine of the seventeenth century.[15] In hindsight, Frank thought his religious education had been minimal. "I remember how I used to puzzle what Christ's *blood* had to do with us," he later recalled.[16] John felt he had been "brought up from a child to take great delight in reading the Bible," but he, too, had to admit: "I had no formed religious convictions till I was fifteen."[17] Among the Newmans, in short, religion was present, but not prominent. There was little instruction, little overt piety, a goodly amount of latitudinarian moderation, and, in the person of John Sr., more than a hint of Enlightenment rationalism and political radicalism. It was not to spurn his father's authority that John read Paine in puberty but to seek his esteem. Having too much religion, not too little, is what estranged him from his father's values.

During his last months at Ealing School, in the autumn and winter of 1816, Newman experienced a religious conversion. He later called it a "great change of thought" and "the beginning of a new life."[18] It happened at a time of personal and family crisis. The London bank in which his father was a partner had gone under in the financial crisis that followed the end of the Napoleonic wars and closed in the spring of 1816.[19] Because of the trouble, Newman had to remain an additional term at Ealing while his father was set up by his former partners as a brewer at Alton (Hampshire), a painful family episode that Newman as late as 1874 wished to have omitted from future memoirs of his life.[20] On top of this, Newman suffered a "keen, terrible" physical illness over the summer at Ealing, which he later claimed had made him "a Christian."[21] During those troubled months, Newman came under the influence of Walter Mayers, an evangelical clergyman and classics master at Ealing, whose conversation and sermons, along

15. JHN to Thomas Mozley, June 9, 1882, *LD* 30, 94; see also 99n3.

16. FWN to Moncure Daniel Conway, in Conway, *Autobiography*, vol. 1, 396.

17. *Apo.*, 55.

18. *Apo.*, 58; "Autobiographical Memoir," *AW*, 29. In 1822, Newman dated the period of his conversion from August 1 to December 21, 1816 (*AW*, 181). For two psychological approaches, see, for a Jungian angle, Terrence Merrigan, "*Numquam minus solus, quam cum solus*—Newman's First Conversion: Its Significance for his Life and Thought," *Downside Review* 103 (April 1985): 99–116; for an Eriksonian interpretation, see Walter E. Conn, *Conscience & Conversion in Newman: A Developmental Study of Self in John Henry Newman* (Milwaukee, Wisc.: Marquette University Press, 2010), 13–25, esp. 18–25. On Newman at Ealing, see Culler, *The Imperial Intellect*, 1–5.

19. *LD* 1, 18–19; *AW*, 150; JHN to Thomas Mozley, June 9, 1882, *LD* 30, 94.

20. *LD* 1, 26–28; "Autobiographical Memoir," *AW*, 29; Stephen Dessain, "Newman's First Conversion," *Newman Studien* 3 (1957): 40.

21. JHN, "June 25, 1869," *AW*, 268.

with the Calvinistic books he recommended, occasioned Newman's decisive turn toward religion.[22]

Newman assessed his conversion differently at different times, but he always considered it a radical change. "Thy wonderful grace turned me right round . . . at the age of fifteen," he could still confess in 1859, "Thou didst change my heart, and in part my whole mental complexion at that time."[23] What he changed from is not so easy to establish as what he changed to. His childhood religiosity was imaginative and romantic, but little more about it is known.[24] As a teenager, he took an intellectual and moral turn, probably in (unconscious) imitation of his father's stance. He read Paine, and perhaps Hume and Voltaire, and started to toy with doubt. Morality, moreover, began to seem preferable over devotion. "I should like to be virtuous but not religious," he used to think, a sentiment that also neatly summed up his father's outlook.[25] By the summer of 1816, all of this was changing. John was now a boy in need of deliverance. He was embarrassed and confused by his father's professional failure, scared for the family's future, and physically ill. He feared the heavy hand of God. In such a crisis, the sedate rationalism of his father's religious outlook could offer neither support nor conviction. Before the evangelical tale of sin and redemption, the attraction of moral excellence and worldly happiness dwindled, and intellectual qualms gave way. His conversion cut "at the root of doubt, providing a chain between God and the soul (i.e. with every link complete)." [26] Newman was certain now. "I know I am right. How do you know it? I know I know. How? I know I know I know &c &c."[27]

More than a change in behavior, conversion is a change of perspective. Drastic turns away from sin are usually preceded by a new perception of the extent or depth of one's sins. Newman's case was no exception. To John Keble, he later related how, "as a boy of fifteen," he was "living a life of sin, with a very dark conscience and a very profane spirit."[28] He had casually entertained religious doubt and derived pleasure from Paine's vulgarities. And his morals had been compromised, as well. One of the few remaining fragments from the immediate postconversion period (an extempore Latin prayer) suggests what darkened his

---

22. *Apo.*, 58–59 (the name Walter Mayers is included from the 1865 edition onward; see *Hist.*, 4); "JHN to Richard Greaves," February 27, 1828, *LD* 2, 57. For biographical information on Mayers and a collection of his sermons, see *Sermons, of the late Rev. Walter Mayers* (London: James Nisbet, 1831). Newman and his mother were subscribers to the volume.

23. JHN, "December 15, 1859," *AW*, 250.

24. See *Apo.*, 55–56; *AW*, 149–50. In 1820 and 1821, Newman wrote a memoir detailing his religious notions as a child. Only a few fragments survive. The rest he burned as an old man (*AW*, 145, 149; *LD* 28, 92n2).

25. JHN, "January 19, 1823," *AW*, 169.

26. *AW*, 150.

27. *AW*, 150.

28. JHN to John Keble, June 8, 1844, *LD* 10, 260.

conscience. He asks to be safeguarded from the temptation to worldly recreations like dancing, from gluttony, and from the enticements of the flesh. This last petition is accompanied by a fervid "O wretched me! I have sinned," which suggests that at least some of it had to do with his incipient sexuality as a teenager.[29] "I was more like a devil than a wicked boy," he concluded in 1859.[30] From the vantage point of Western culture today, it is tempting to dismiss a comment like this—reminiscent of Augustine's reflections on stealing pears—as pious hyperbole. But we cannot plumb the depths of another person's conscience. At the least, it shows that Newman continued to regard his adolescent conversion as a turning away from sin.

Conversions, however, are not just about turning away: they are also a turning toward. Newman was converted to God. As he famously put it in the *Apologia*, he rested "in the thought of two and two only supreme and luminously self-evident beings, myself and my Creator"—the world and everybody else faded from view.[31] Many commentators have, with good reason, dwelled on this key aspect of Newman's conversion as instituting a relationship with God that was "face to face, *'solus cum solo'*" (alone with the Alone).[32] But his conversion was also, and perhaps more so, an experience of deliverance, so that the figure of the Redeemer eclipsed that of the Creator. In a versified extempore prayer written at the end of 1816, Newman expresses his religiosity in terms of complete devotion to God, out of gratitude for his personal salvation from sin through Christ's atoning sacrifice:

> Let me always, my God & king
>   In Thy dear Name rejoice
> And daily to Thy praises sing
>   With ever grateful voice
> I am a worm, and Thou art good
>   To save a wretch like me,
> Who always has Thy grace withstood,
>   And turned his back on Thee.
> O grant that I may persevere
>   And finally obtain
> A glorious crown, purchased for dear,
>   That ever may remain

29. "Serva me carnis a [*sic*] illecebris. Heu miser ego! peccavi." *AW*, 151. See Ward, *Young Mr. Newman*, 59.

30. JHN, "December 15, 1859," *AW*, 250.

31. *Apo.*, 59. From the 1865 edition onward, "absolute" is substituted for "supreme," probably for reasons of theological and philosophical accuracy (*Hist.*, 4).

32. *Apo.*, 318. See Dessain, "Newman's First Conversion," 47–48; Merrigan, "*Numquam minus solus*," esp. 112.

> Purchased for dear, for by the Blood
> Of Jesus it is given
> Who suffered death, the Just & Good,
> That we may live in heaven.
> O may I scorn each mundane joy,
> And meditate on Thee.
> May heaven all my thoughts employ,
> Then happy shall I be.[33]

Both in style and content, the verse echoes the *Olney Hymns* of John Newton and William Cowper. Its sixth line, "To save a wretch a like me," is straight out of *Amazing Grace*, and self-identifying as a "worm" (fifth line) is ubiquitous in Newton's hymns, which are also paralleled in the narrative structure of Newman's poem, with its evangelical sequence of sin, redemption, sanctification, and glorification.[34] The final stanza displays the ascetical bent of Newman's early religiosity, a reaction, no doubt, to the looming loss of family prosperity and easy living. In response, he took a decisive turn away from the pleasures of the world to interior communion with God.

The Principle of Dogma

Newman's mental turn inward—the *solus cum solo*—simultaneously effected a mental turn outward, to God as the exterior object of faith. He discovered that there was a truth about God, something definite to be known. This is why he could describe himself as without "formed religious convictions" prior to his conversion, while falling, upon his conversion, "under the influences of a definite Creed" and receiving "impressions of dogma" into his intellect.[35] As a child, he certainly had a religious sensibility and a lively religious imagination. The few remaining fragments testify to that. But his conversion gave his faith an intelligible object: a God who had made himself known. This could be called the intellectual character of Newman's conversion, provided that we understand "intellectual" not as pertaining to a subjective faculty—the intellect—distinct from emotions, desires, and intuitions, but objectively, as expressive of the fact that the reception of definite intelligible content became part and parcel of his religiosity.[36] Newman

33. *AW*, 151. Even at the time, Newman regarded the verse as "doggerel" (*AW*, 150).

34. [John Newton and William Cowper], *Olney Hymns* (London: W. Oliver, 1779), esp. 53–54; see also 143.

35. *Apo.*, 55, 58; Dessain, "Newman's First Conversion," 45.

36. Stephen Dessain ("Newman's First Conversion," 48–50) has made much of Newman's conversion being intellectual in the former sense—which it no doubt was, *too*—almost to the exclusion of its moral and affective dimensions. Conn, by contrast, holds that Newman's conversion was "a basic moral conversion rooted in Christian values" rather than an affective or cognitive one

worded it quite precisely in the *Apologia*: "From the age of fifteen, dogma has been the fundamental principle of my religion."[37] The insistence here is not on "the great dogmas of the faith" (in the plural) he mentions a few lines later but on "dogma" (singular) understood as a "fundamental principle," that is, a constitutive category that determines the structure of religious belief as a whole.

Put simply, the principle of dogma means believing definite things about God because God has revealed them. Newman acquired this principle, or at least its rudiments, from the evangelical clergyman Thomas Scott (1747–1821), "the writer," he later wrote, "who made a deeper impression on my mind than any other, and to whom (humanly speaking) I almost owe my soul."[38]

Newman was particularly impressed with *The Force of Truth* (1779), a spiritual autobiography that narrates Scott's theological progression, as an Anglican clergyman, from Socinianism (or Unitarianism) to orthodox evangelicalism. English Socinians were committed to God's absolute unity. They rejected the Trinity, the divinity of Christ, and the incarnation, as well as the atonement (in any of its traditional renderings), usually because they found these doctrines logically incoherent.[39] Scott gradually became convinced that the Socinian appeal to reason was misguided. He explains how he ultimately accepted the doctrine of "a Trinity of coequal persons in the Unity of the Godhead" on the plain authority of the Bible.[40] He diligently collected all scripture texts pertaining to the issue and found that they taught both the unity of God and the divinity of Christ and the Holy Spirit. Before, he had rejected the doctrine of the Trinity on the grounds of its logical impossibility. On his former view, "the Son and Holy Spirit . . . must either be *mere creatures*, or . . . there must be three Gods."[41] Now, he felt constrained to accept the doctrine of a Trinity-in-unity on the plain authority of scripture, however incomprehensible it might be. "I was driven from my reasonings," Scott recollects, "and constrained to submit my understanding to divine revelation."[42] Submission to God cuts right through the Gordian knot that the intellect ties for

---

(*Conscience & Conversion*, 24). This, too, is an overstatement; the (scanty) source material does not justify a conclusion either way. All three aspects—affective, moral, and intellectual—were at play. Assigning definite priority to the one or the other says more about the interpreter than about Newman's conversion.

37. *Apo.*, 120.

38. *Apo.*, 50.

39. Michael R. Watts, *The Dissenters: From the Reformation to the French Revolution* (Oxford: Clarendon Press, 1978), 371–82; Michael Ledger-Lomas, "Unitarians and Presbyterians," in *The Oxford History of Protestant Dissenting Traditions*, vol. 3, *The Nineteenth Century*, ed. Timothy Larsen and Michael Ledger-Lomas (Oxford: Oxford University Press, 2017), 108.

40. Thomas Scott, *The Force of Truth: An Authentick Narrative*, 8th ed. (London: L. B. Seeley, 1808), 53.

41. Scott, *The Force of Truth*, 32. Scott derived the phrasing of the dilemma from Samuel Clarke's *The Scripture-Doctrine of the Trinity* (London: James Knapton, 1712).

42. Scott, *The Force of Truth*, 55.

itself when it tries to reason out religious doctrine. It was a simple and robust solution that would have appealed to a boy of Newman's cast of mind, which wedded a love of the romantic to a penchant for logic.

Newman's earliest papers show that he was indeed taken by Scott's story. In late 1816 and early 1817, he followed Scott's lead and compiled lengthy collections of scripture texts in proof of "the Divinity of Jesus Christ [and] the Holy Ghost" and in support of the Athanasian Creed, along with drafting the outline of an essay on the importance and biblical grounds of belief in the Trinity and the atonement.[43] Like Scott, Newman identified the lack of a proper concept of faith as the central problem of Socinian theology. In a note of October 1819, he wondered "what the Socinians understand by *faith*." "As I understand the Bible," he argued, "faith is *a* (perhaps *the*) most difficult Christian grace." It is "the believing of something which is beyond our powers of reason and contradictory to the imaginations of our sinful nature."[44] Newman's point was emphatically not to relish incomprehensibility. The memory of his own doubting days was still too fresh. He merely wanted to get religion's epistemic ordering right. The key question when confronted with doctrinal claims like those of the Athanasian Creed is not whether we can make sense of them but whether they can be proven from scripture. Newman was convinced that many common objections to Christianity were premised on a disregard for this principle. His former dabbling in rationalist critique now only increased his eagerness to get to the bottom of the argument for unbelief. This concern never left him. It was the subject of his famous last article, *The Development of Religious Error* (1885), but he began his writing career on the same note, with a piece that could have borne the same title.[45]

In May 1821, Newman published a two-page letter in the evangelical *Christian Observer* to show that many common critiques of revelation were unreasonable.[46] He did so by means of an extended analogy between scientific and religious inquiry. Contrary to popular prejudice, Newman argued, the pursuit of scientific knowledge, especially in mathematics and physics, inculcates attitudes conducive to Christian belief. It teaches us "how little we know, how little we can comprehend, and how erroneous oftentimes are the conclusions to which à priori

---

43. *Apo.*, 60–61. Newman's archive contains five early theological papers on this issue: (i) two very similar sets of compilations of scripture texts in proof of the divinity of Christ and the Holy Spirit, dated 1816/1817 by Newman (BOA A.9.1.a), (ii) two equally similar sets of scripture references in support of the Athanasian Creed, one dated 1816 by an archivist, the other dated 1817 by Newman, and containing some additional remarks (BOA A.9.1.b), and (iii) the outlines of the essay, undated, but conjecturally put at 1817 by an archivist (BOA A.9.1.b).

44. JHN, "October 10, 1819," *AW*, 161.

45. JHN, "The Development of Religious Error," *Contemporary Review* 48 (October 1885): 457–69.

46. [JHN], "On the Study of the Mathematics," *Christian Observer* 20, no. 5 (May 1821): 293–95; *LD* 1, 102–5.

speculations would lead us."[47] Such epistemic humility is easily forgotten when it comes to evaluating Christianity. For instance, some people object to the means God has chosen to reveal himself: "Why did not God, instead of separating the Jews as a peculiar people to preserve the true religion, reveal His will at once to the whole world? . . . 'If the Gospel were written on the sun,' said Paine, 'it would be believed by all.'"[48] Newman had been bothered by this argument ever since he read Paine as a teenager. In response, he now observed that analogous objections would be considered presumptuous when raised against the order of nature, which also seems to be organized on a less than ideal plan. The earth, for instance, is "in shape a *spheroid*", not perfectly round, it "describes an *ellipse* round the sun," not a circle, and it does so "with an *irregular* motion," not a regular one.[49] But to find fault with the Creator on such grounds would be rash and arrogant. We lack the knowledge to form a judgment on the best way to organize the universe, just as we lack the knowledge to judge of God's chosen mode of revelation.

The analogy with science not only supplies the proper response to "objections arising from the *difficulties* of revelation"—the "why"-type of questions— but also to objections arising from "those mysteries which have been said to involve *contradictions* and *impossibilities*."[50] Such mysteries give rise to "how" questions. "How can the Divine Being exist in three Persons? How can God and man be one Christ?"[51] Such questions might be hard to answer, but science, too, has its seeming contradictions. Take the mathematical proposition that "two lines, the assymptotes [*sic*] of curves for instance, may be always drawing nearer to each other, yet never meet."[52] Although this is no easier to conceive than the doctrine of the Trinity, no one objects to asymptotes because they are rather unlikely. The point here is not, as earlier, to recommend an attitude but rather to inculcate a method. To assess the truth of a particular set of claims, be they scientific or religious, we ought to evaluate the proofs by which they are substantiated, not their contents. We believe Newton's conclusions "because the arguments which prove their truth are sound. The nature of those conclusions makes no difference to our belief . . . be they difficult, mysterious, incomprehensible, seemingly contradictory, it matters not: they are *proved*."[53]

In science, this methodological principle is easy enough to abide by, but in religion it is regularly flouted. No scientifically minded person would argue against Newton's theory by "asserting the falsity of the conclusion from some à priori con-

---

47. [JHN], "On the Study of the Mathematics," 293; *LD* 1, 102.

48. [JHN], "On the Study of the Mathematics," 294; *LD* 1, 103.

49. [JHN], "On the Study of the Mathematics," 294; *LD* 1, 103.

50. [JHN], "On the Study of the Mathematics," 294; *LD* 1, 103.

51. [JHN], "On the Study of the Mathematics," 294; *LD* 1, 104.

52. [JHN], "On the Study of the Mathematics," 295; *LD* 1, 104.

53. [JHN], "On the Study of the Mathematics," 295; *LD* 1, 104.

ception of his own fancy," and yet, "this very thing is done daily with the Bible."[54] Instead of assessing Christian doctrine by an impartial evaluation of the evidence that it is revealed, unbelievers reject it because they cannot fathom its contents.

> Men begin at the wrong end of the scale of reasoning; and having refuted, as they conceive, a doctrine by arguments resting on the basis of pre-conceived ideas, they proceed up the ladder, and arrive at once at the portentous determination, that all the proofs which have been advanced in support of that doctrine, and the book which contains an avowal of that doctrine, must be erroneous.[55]

People assume without warrant that "'a true religion can have no mysteries'; and then infer either that Christianity is not a true religion because it contains mysteries"—the position of Deists like Paine—"or that it contains no mysteries, because it is a true religion"—the Socinian position. Although it involves flawed reasoning, Newman believed that this topsy-turvy mode of arguing was motivated by emotional and moral, rather than intellectual, concerns. Deists and Socinians "fear lest the Gospel should be true; they hate the light, their heart is not inclined to spiritual duties and therefore they approach the examination of the Scriptures with prejudice."[56] Only when these prejudices are dispelled can a rational assessment of the truth of revelation take place.

Although Newman defended the mysterious, he did not glory in it, unlike William Beveridge, another of his formative authors. Beveridge was so alive to God's essential unknowability that he considered "those apprehensions of GOD to be the truest, whereby we apprehend him to be the most incomprehensible."[57] The Trinity was "a Mystery which I cannot possibly conceive, yet 'tis a Truth which I can easily believe."[58] The harder it is to understand, the easier it is to believe, Beveridge almost seems to say.

Newman did not share this attitude. For him, the difficulty of certain doctrines was a drawback, not a boon, and a source of distress more than joy. Even though he argued that difficulties in the content of revelation are no objection to its truth, he also claimed that "Christianity does not require us to believe any thing absurd or contradictory: its most incomprehensible doctrines are not opposed to reason."[59] Perhaps, this was meant to quiet himself as much as his readers. Shortly after submitting his article, he records having dreamt of a "spirit" that came to

54. [JHN], "On the Study of the Mathematics," 295; *LD* 1, 104.
55. [JHN], "On the Study of the Mathematics," 295; *LD* 1, 104.
56. [JHN], "On the Study of the Mathematics," 295; *LD* 1, 104.
57. William Beveridge, *Private Thoughts upon Religion* (London: K. Smith, 1709), 52.
58. Beveridge, *Private Thoughts upon Religion*, 35.
59. [JHN], "On the Study of the Mathematics," 295; *LD* 1, 104.

talk to him. This "mysterious visitant" explained "that it was absolutely impossible for the reason of man to understand the mystery . . . of the Holy Trinity, and in vain to argue about it; but that every thing in another world was so *very, very plain*, that there was not the slightest difficulty about it."[60] Even without adopting a Freudian theory of dreams as wish fulfilment, the deep gratitude Newman felt on waking "for so kind a message" shows that the difficulty of the doctrine had been causing him some anxiety.[61] This ongoing struggle explains why the idea of faith as the acceptance of revelation on the basis of divine authority—the principle of dogma—was so important to Newman. He felt that if we do not accept doctrines simply because God has revealed them, the door is wide open to Deist or Socinian critiques of their content, and the whole Christian edifice will come tumbling down.

An Evangelical Theology

Newman's conversion did not just make him a Christian. It made him an evangelical Christian. He had come to realize that human beings are not as they are supposed to be. Some way or another, they must change in order to be with God. It was a foundational insight that continued to drive much of his theology, even after all that was distinctively evangelical about it had disappeared. But for the time being, this thought took on all the hues of the moderately Calvinistic evangelicalism under whose influence he had been converted. Let us briefly review the main characteristics of that variety of Christianity, as it had emerged out of successive evangelical revivals in England since the 1730s.[62]

Evangelicals agreed with other orthodox Protestants on many points of doctrine, but they had a distinct set of theological emphases or priorities. David Bebbington has encapsulated these central tenets in his by now famous quadrilateral, as: "*conversionism*, the belief that lives need to be changed; *activism*, the expression of the gospel in effort; *biblicism*, a particular regard for the Bible; and what may be called *crucicentrism*, a stress on the sacrifice of Christ on the cross."[63] As Bebbington implicitly acknowledges, a fifth characteristic, at least for eighteenth- and

60. JHN, "June 1, 1821," *AW*, 166.

61. JHN, "June 1, 1821," *AW*, 167.

62. Boyd Hilton, *A Mad, Bad, and Dangerous People? England 1783–1846* (Oxford: Oxford University Press, 2006), 174–84.

63. David W. Bebbington, *Evangelicalism in Modern Britain: A History from the 1730s to the 1980s* (London: Routledge, 1989), 2–3. Although not without its criticisms, Bebbington's quadrilateral has become the standard working definition for modern historians of evangelicalism. See Timothy Larsen, "The Reception Given *Evangelicalism in Modern Britain* Since its Publication in 1989," in *The Emergence of Evangelicalism: Exploring Historical Continuities*, ed. Michael A. G. Haykin and Kenneth J. Stewart (Nottingham: Inter-Varsity Press, 2008), 21–36; and the literature at Haykin, "Evangelicalism and the Enlightenment: a Reassessment," in the same volume (37–60, 49n61).

early nineteenth-century evangelicalism, would be an emphasis on human corruption.[64] These four or five characteristics are closely connected. Together, they constitute a distinct form of organizing Christian theology. Because of complete human sinfulness (*corruption*), human lives must be changed (*conversionism*). This change is brought about by faith in Christ's atoning sacrifice (*crucicentrism*) as authoritatively proclaimed in scripture (*biblicism*). Gratitude for the salvation received by faith in Christ leads the believer to a lively spirituality and good works, the marks of true conversion (*activism*). This narrative ordering of evangelical characteristics already shows that besides its concern with certain objects of belief, evangelicalism also has a specific understanding of the believing subject.

Sheridan Gilley notes, perceptively, that the particular strength of evangelicalism "lay in the integration of its dogmas with common religious experience."[65] Like all substantive varieties of Christianity, evangelicalism is not just about an object, a system of beliefs, but also about the subject, how a believer has to feel, think, and act. This is especially evident in the evangelical emphasis on conversion, which is precisely a particular way of affectively, cognitively, and practically appropriating Christianity's content. Affect is the motive force here, as shown in the substantial body of conversion literature that developed out of the eighteenth-century evangelical revivals in England and the United States, which narrated conversions according to well-established patterns of misery, redemption, and gratitude.[66] One could sum up, albeit too simplistically, the relation between evangelical doctrine and subjectivity as the application to each believer's personal experience of this threefold organizing principle of Reformed theology—misery, deliverance, gratitude—with varying emphases depending on the strand of evangelicalism concerned.[67] Evangelicalism, then, as a specific form of Protestantism, provides a distinct and highly integrated account of doctrine and experience (or, in more classical terms, of *fides quae* and *fides qua*).[68] Newman's early theological manuscripts offer a textbook account of this evangelical system.

Immediately after his final term at Ealing, Newman was entered at Trinity College and went up to Oxford. Toward the end of his undergraduate years, the relig-

---

64. Bebbington, *Evangelicalism in Modern Britain*, 3. See Patricia Meldrum, *Conscience and Compromise: Forgotten Evangelicals of Nineteenth-century Scotland* (Carlisle: Paternoster, 2006), 117ff.

65. Sheridan Gilley, *Newman and His Age* (London: Darton, Longman and Todd, 1990), 16.

66. Bebbington, *Evangelicalism in Modern Britain*, 5–10.

67. D. Bruce Hindmarsh, *The Evangelical Conversion Narrative: Spiritual Autobiography in Early Modern England* (Oxford: Oxford University Press, 2005), 323–24; Mark R. Stevenson, *The Doctrines of Grace in an Unexpected Place: Calvinistic Soteriology in Nineteenth-Century Brethren Thought* (Eugene, Ore.: Pickwick Publications, 2017), 205–7. The Heidelberg Catechism (1563) is the *locus classicus* for this organizing principle.

68. This distinction is often traced to Augustine's observation that, "those things that are believed (*ea quae creduntur*) are one thing, and the faith by which they are believed (*fides qua creduntur*) is another thing" (*De Trinitate* XIII,5).

ious fervor with which he had begun university had waned somewhat. In 1821, he noted how, "in 1819 and the beginning of 1820, I hoped great things for myself, not liking to go into the Church, but to the Law," the latter, incidentally, being his father's wish.[69] His relative failure in his B.A. examination in November 1820, which he merely passed rather than gain any honors, apparently checked these "dreams of a secular ambition."[70] And in 1821, we find the young Newman "more devoted to the evangelical creed" than ever before.[71] His renewed religious vigor made him return to composing theological pieces, just as he had done in the year following his conversion. The most important of these, for gauging the nature of his theology, is the cumbrously titled *A collection of Scripture passages setting forth in due order of succession the doctrines of Christianity*. It is his "evangelical synthesis," as Sheridan calls it.[72] As its title suggests, the text consists mainly of long strings of quotations from scripture, but they are interspersed with Newman's summaries of their doctrinal gist. The *Collection* falls naturally into two parts, which mirror the distinction between *fides quae* and *fides qua*. The first part deals with the doctrinal content of Christianity (*fides quae*) from a salvation historical perspective (fall—redemption by Christ—gift of the Holy Spirit). The second and largest part deals with the subjective appropriation of this doctrinal content (*fides qua*), that is, with "[t]he truth and effects of the above doctrines in the experience of the elect."[73] It is divided into four sections that mirror the presentation in the first part, and they are titled, "On the unconverted man," "On conversion," "On good works the necessary fruits of faith," and "On indwelling sin."[74] All in all, the text represents Newman's strenuous effort over the course of at least six months to systematize his evangelical views.[75]

As a true evangelical, Newman placed the atonement at the center of Christian theology. "The doctrine of the atonement," he had noted in October 1819, is "the key stone of Christianity."[76] In the first part of the *Collection*, he argued that because of Adam's fall, humankind became totally depraved and could no longer fulfil the demands of God's moral law: "Man does <u>only</u> evil <u>continually</u>, he drinketh iniquity like water, he is altogether filthy, his heart is desperately wicked, he has no good thing in him."[77] From the vantage point of God's justice, mankind was "condemned to eternal misery." But, in his mercy, God "provided

---

69. *AW*, 150.

70. JHN, "Autobiographical Memoir," *AW*, 45; Culler, *The Imperial Intellect*, 12–22.

71. JHN, "Autobiographical Memoir," *AW*, 80.

72. Sheridan, *Newman on Justification*, 50.

73. JHN, *A collection of Scripture passages setting forth in due order of succession the doctrines of Christianity*, June 1821, BOA A.9.1, 25.

74. JHN, *Collection*, BOA A.9.1.c; Sheridan, *Newman on Justification*, 52–58; Vaiss, *Newman*, 89–93.

75. Newman dated the document June 1821, but he had begun it before, and continued to work on it until January 1822 (see *LD* 1, 119n4).

76. JHN, "October 10, 1819," *AW*, 161.

77. JHN, *Collection*, BOA A.9.1, 11.

a stupendous scheme by which He was enabled consistently with His holiness to extend salvation to mankind." In the incarnation, the Son became man, and, "as the substitute of mankind, He fulfilled the Holy law of God, He died the death of a sinner."[78] What we have here is a penal substitutionary theory of the atonement: Christ satisfied the requirements of the divine law by undergoing the punishment meted out for us, so that God could mercifully accept his sinful creatures "without disparagement to His justice."[79] In this way, Christ reconciled God and humankind. His righteousness can now be "imputed" to those who believe in His atoning sacrifice, so that they are justified.[80] This justification is understood forensically and extrinsically. It consists of, in the words of one of Newman's later papers, "a change of state — i.e. from God's wrath to his favor," not in a change of nature.[81] For this latter, and subsequent, change, Newman reserved the term regeneration. Regeneration is the work of the Holy Spirit, who "proceeds from the throne of the reconciled Father, to infuse into the souls of the elect that life which was lost at the fall."[82] Simply put, justification sets God right with us, while regeneration sets us right with God. All of this was classic evangelical doctrine. It agreed perfectly, for instance, with Scott's essays on justification and regeneration, in which Newman was well-versed.[83]

In the second part of the *Collection*, Newman treated the convergence between "the structure of the Gospel Covenant" and "the feelings & experience of the Christian."[84] Conversion is the point where doctrine and experience meet. By being converted, a person appropriates the doctrinal content of Christianity in a life-changing manner. This idea was the fulcrum of Newman's early theology. In the *Collection*, he described the process of conversion in starkly emotional terms—"feeling" is the dominant operative factor. The "first stage" of the individual's conversion is the "gloomy season" in which "he is 'convinced of sin.'"[85] He resolves to do better, but fails, tries again, fails again; "gloom & horror weigh upon his soul."[86] At this point of moral crisis, he is confronted with "the offer of pardon." "He reads in Scripture the good tidings of salvation — he is invited, yea intreated, to draw near & accept the gift of eternal life."[87] For a time, he can

---

78. JHN, *Collection*, BOA A.9.1, 11.

79. JHN, *Collection*, BOA A.9.1, 23.

80. JHN, *Collection*, BOA A.9.1, 23.

81. JHN, *The Nature of Holiness*, BOA A.9.1.g, 4. The manuscript is untitled—the title given is conventional. Its cover has "1822 or 1823?" in Newman's hand.

82. JHN, *Collection*, BOA A.9.1, 24.

83. Thomas Scott, *Essays on the Most Important Subjects in Religion*, 7th ed. (London: L. B. Seeley, 1814), 179–214; JHN to Lord Lifford, September 12, 1837, *LD* 6, 129.

84. JHN, *Collection*, BOA A.9.1.c, 15.

85. JHN, *Collection*, BOA A.9.1.c.4, 11.

86. JHN, *Collection*, BOA A.9.1.c.4, 12.

87. JHN, *Collection*, BOA A.9.1.c.4, 12.

hardly believe his luck, but then, "Lo, he hath laid hold on the appointed mean of justification . . . he believeth!"[88] Now his new life begins, the life of faith in Christ. "He knows and feels that in the sight of God, he is perfectly pure & righteous. . . . How great then is his gratitude! — he feels more than he can express the excessive lovingkindness of that Redeemer who hath purchased him with His own blood." "Gratitude to God" will now be his "grand motive . . . to good works."[89] In this process of sanctification, the fledgling believer must learn to grapple with the remains of his natural inclination to sin.[90] But if he once more adopts a sinful course, God will recall him, often by means of "temporal calamities," and the sinner will return to God through suffering.[91] The struggle with "indwelling sin" teaches the believer "more entirely his own nothingness & the all-sufficiency of his Saviour," which is how God brings "good out of evil" for the elect.[92] The entire depiction of conversion, then, neatly mirrors the scheme of salvation outlined in the first part of Newman's text: from depravity, via redemption, to grateful, holy living.

Conversion and Calvinism

No other early text of Newman is as rife with pathos and archaic affectation as the *Collection*. He never wrote anything like it again. But he continued to hold and express its evangelical conception of conversion for some years to come, albeit in less high-flown prose. Three aspects of this notion of conversion need further explication: (i) its radical nature, (ii) the mode of its occurrence, and (iii) God's sovereignty in effecting it. Taken together, they help us to configure the type of evangelical Newman was.

As to the first, Newman noted in an 1820 journal entry: "it is *absolutely necessary* for *every* one to undergo a *total change* in his heart and affections, *before* he can enter into the kingdom of heaven."[93] As in the *Collection*, this change is located at the level of emotions and desires. In a fictitious dialogue between Spenser (Newman) and Merton (an objector to evangelicalism), Newman underscored the totality of the change. To Merton's objection that it "is not in man's nature" to have the feelings required by the gospel, Spenser retorts, "since we cannot have feelings which are not in our nature . . . the feelings of our nature must be changed," which is precisely what scripture teaches.[94] Newman stressed the same idea in a paper on

<hr>

88. JHN, *Collection*, BOA A.9.1.c.4, 13.
89. JHN, *Collection*, BOA A.9.1.c.4, 7.
90. See p. 122.
91. JHN, *Collection*, BOA A.9.1.c.6, 13.
92. JHN, *Collection*, BOA A.9.1.c.6, 11.
93. JHN, "September 29, 1820," *AW*, 165.
94. JHN, *Dialogue—Merton—Spenser,* January 1822, BOA A.9.1.e, 4, 6.

the nature and attainment of holiness. We need "a mighty revolution, a radical change of heart & sentiment" if we "would be saved."[95] Again, the change takes place on the affective level. Holiness, he argued, "consists in a certain state of the heart & affections — including, indeed, good works & religious observances, but only as the external signs & evidences of an inward principle."[96] This principle is "the love of God," which, being "altogether foreign to our natures," must be newly "implanted" there.[97]

The second aspect of conversion is that although it is a radical change, it need not be a sudden one. Newman thought that conversions usually take some time, as his own had. He owed this view to Walter Mayers, who also emphasized the necessity of "a change from our natural state" but insisted that "conversion . . . is very rarely *sudden* or *instantaneous* but generally s*low* and *gradual*."[98] Newman concurred. His essay on holiness describes the sinner's "<u>revolution</u> of sentiment" as a matter of time, "attended by reflection, meditation & reading of the Scriptures under the influence of the Holy Spirit."[99] Although the tone of this later paper is more reserved than that of the *Collection*, Newman retains in it the same basic structure of conversion. It follows the same pattern in every case: "[i] sense of God's holiness & our own vileness, [ii] sorrow for sin, [iii] belief in Christ as the savior of the world, [iv] justification;—& adoption or the being made the children of God in Christ Jesus, [v] peace with God & faith working by love, [vi] good works."[100] When someone has arrived at the last stage—living a "godly life"—she can be sure that conversion has taken place.[101] Conversion is complete when one has passed through the stages of misery and redemption to that of holy living. From then on, the believer is regenerate: no longer engaged in conversion but in progressive sanctification.

The idea of conversion as a circumscribed process of radical change leads to a black-and-white understanding of people as either converted or not. This is due to the third noteworthy aspect of Newman's take on conversion: its emphasis on God's sovereignty. Unlike Wesleyan Methodists but like most evangelicals in the Church of England, Newman was a Calvinist. The resultant emphasis on God's sovereignty had implications on both doctrine and of the experience of the believer. Regarding doctrine, Newman maintained that God has freely elected some people (and not others) to salvation. "Before the foundation of the world," he wrote in the *Collection*, "He predestinated certain individuals — according to

<hr>

95. JHN, *Nature of Holiness*, BOA A.9.1.g, 2.
96. JHN, *Nature of Holiness*, BOA A.9.1.g, 1.
97. JHN, *Nature of Holiness*, BOA A.9.1.g, 2.
98. Walter Mayers to JHN, April 14, 1817, *LD* 1, 32.
99. JHN, *Nature of Holiness*, BOA A.9.1.g, 3.
100. JHN, *Nature of Holiness*, BOA A.9.1.g,5.
101. JHN, *Nature of Holiness*, BOA A.9.1.g, 4.

the good pleasure of his will, not from anything good in them — to be saved."[102] Election was based in the divine will, not, as with the Arminians, in God's foreknowledge. Unlike high or hyper-Calvinists—a rarer breed both within and without the Established Church—Newman never held the obverse doctrine, of predestination to damnation.[103] Along with this commitment to unconditional election went an understanding of grace as efficacious or irresistible.

In June 1817, just after he moved to Oxford, he went to the University Church of St Mary the Virgin to hear a sermon by William Crowe, poet and Public Orator at the university.[104] He came away disillusioned. Crowe's claim that "the grace of God is always everywhere present" so provoked Newman that he wrote a rebuttal in his journal.[105] The grace Crowe talked of, Newman argued, is either efficacious or not. If efficacious, everyone would be converted, which is observably not the case. If not, it is not really grace, since grace, by definition, "implies an efficacious aid from God." Crowe could reply that people's hearts are "not always disposed to it," but that does not solve the problem: only God can rightly dispose the heart, but we see that not everyone is properly disposed, so God does not give grace to all.[106]

This position raises a theological difficulty. Evangelical preachers often urgently invited people to accept the gospel message, but this seems a perverse practice if those people cannot genuinely respond to it. Some high Calvinists, for this reason, "were unwilling to offer the gospel freely to all people" and did not indiscriminately preach the atonement.[107] Newman did not go to such lengths. He considered this difficulty in the *Collection* and concluded that although we can respond to gospel preaching only through "the entire & immediate influence" of the Holy Spirit, the Spirit chooses to employ human exhortations as "<u>signs</u> or <u>instruments</u> of rousing & stimulating us."[108] God still does all the work, but he uses instruments, and preaching is the preferred tool.

Newman applied a similar logic in another 1821 paper, a comment on St Paul's injunction to work out our own salvation—a challenging command for those who believe that God sovereignly effects conversion. Newman argued that St Paul's injunction only applies to the process of sanctification, not to regeneration. St Paul means that we should labor "to become more & more released from the bondage

<hr>

102. JHN, *Collection*, BOA A.9.1, 11.

103. *Apo.*, 59. See Mark Stevenson's recent historical survey of Calvinistic soteriology in England from 1660, through the Evangelical Revival, and up to the early nineteenth century (*The Doctrines of Grace*, 16–66); see also Ian J. Shaw, *High Calvinists in Action: Calvinism and the City—Manchester and London, c. 1810–1860* (Oxford: Oxford University Press, 2003), 10–25.

104. W. P. Courtney, "Crowe, William," rev. Rebecca Mills, *ODNB*.

105. JHN, "June 29, 1817," *AW*, 162.

106. JHN, "June 29, 1817," *AW*, 162.

107. Stevenson, *The Doctrines of Grace*, 38, 42.

108. JHN, *Collection*, BOA A.9.1.c.3, 15, 16.

of sin" *after* we have believed in Christ, have been justified, and have received a new nature from the Spirit.[109] This is clear from St Paul's presupposing that we *want* to be free from sin, which we do not want by nature. Such a "longing after holiness" is the free gift of God. He "imparts <u>a will</u>," and this grace "<u>cannot</u> be resisted."[110] This is but another way of phrasing the radical change God sovereignly brings about in conversion. About this, we can do nothing, but once this change has occurred, there are things we can do. We can partake of the means of grace: prayer, the reading of scripture, self-examination, the Lord's Supper. This is not work exactly, but it does involve effort. Effort, however, does not necessarily mean merit: "there is nothing good in the <u>very using the means</u>; the good is in <u>the will</u> which is the <u>cause</u>, in <u>the power</u> which is the effect of using them," and these are given by God.[111] Like the exhortations of preaching, religious practices are mere instruments in the hands of God whose efficacy depends on God's prior intervention and posterior blessing. It is a testimony to Newman's intellectual honesty that he could conclude a few months later that St Paul's injunction is a mere figure of speech, like saying "the sun rises"; correct from a human point of view but not from that of "strict doctrinal exactness."[112]

When it comes to religious experience, the emphasis on efficacious grace grounded one of evangelicalism's most appealing traits: a personal assurance of salvation. Unlike their gloomier Puritan forebears, for whom assurance was rare and tortuous to acquire, many evangelicals cheerily held that assurance was a normal condition for the believer, usually acquired upon conversion.[113] For evangelicals of a more robustly Calvinistic description—like Newman—the doctrine of assurance also entailed the idea of final perseverance, that is, a knowledge not only of one's present but also of one's ultimate state of salvation. Given God's irresistible grace, God's election to salvation cannot be conceived to miscarry. Once we know we are saved, we are saved once and for all. In the *Apologia*, Newman tells us that he discovered the doctrine in one of the Calvinist books Mayers gave him: a work by William Romaine (1714–1795), whose title and

---

109. JHN, *Comment on Phil 2,12&13*, June 1821, BOA A.9.1.e, 2. See Sheridan, *Newman on Justification*, 44–48. The text was "composed at the request of [Frederick Edward] Pegus," who matriculated at Oxford in 1817.

110. JHN, *Comment*, BOA A.9.1.e, 2.

111. JHN, *Comment*, BOA A.9.1.e, 3. See also "February 2, 1823," *AW*, 170.

112. JHN, "October 15, 1821," *AW*, 168.

113. Bebbington, *Evangelicalism in Modern Britain*, 42–50. In the Westminster Confession (1648), a reformed confession influenced by Puritan theology, assurance is considered as not belonging "to the essence of faith, but that a true believer may wait long, and conflict with many difficulties, before he be partaker of it" (Art. 18). As several scholars have pointed out, many later evangelicals retained something of the Puritan approach to assurance, so that Bebbington's assessment is overly optimistic (see many of the contributions in Haykin and Stewart, *The Emergence of Evangelicalism*, and Stevenson, *The Doctrines of Grace*, 209–10).

further contents he had forgotten. It probably was the *Discourses upon Solomon's Song*, which contained Romaine's most emphatic defense of a personal assurance of final salvation as well as a notion of grace identical to Newman's.[114] As soon as he read about "the doctrine of final perseverance," Newman recalls in the *Apologia*, "I received it at once, and believed that the inward conversion of which I was conscious . . . would last into the next life, and that I was elected to eternal glory."[115] Or as he had put it in August 1821, "I have . . . a 'full assurance of hope,' concerning my final perseverance, and have had it from the time of my conversion."[116] His experience of deliverance, it seems, was so overpowering that only the Calvinist idea of final perseverance could adequately capture its scope.

Living Religion

In the *Apologia*, Newman immediately felt the need to add that his belief in final perseverance did not have "any tendency whatever to lead me to be careless about pleasing God."[117] This is a revealing comment. Within the Church of England, the most common charge against Calvinistic evangelicals, and against Romaine in particular, was that their doctrine of assurance entailed antinomianism, "the view that the believer is not bound by the moral law."[118] With regard to some high Calvinists, this criticism was not completely off target, but it was misguided in the case of evangelicals at large. It certainly did not apply to the young Newman, who was painstakingly strict in his religious discipline, especially from 1821 onward, when he engaged in extensive critical self-examinations, no longer read newspapers on Sunday, and completely avoided the theatre.[119] Although no one could claim he had too little zeal, his parents thought he had too much. He liked to quote scripture freely and partook of the Lord's Supper more often than was usual, so that his mother feared he "began to be righteous overmuch, and was verging upon enthusiasm"—that other bugbear of English religious common sense.[120] She also blamed him for carrying along Frank, who too had been converted at Ealing. Tensions ran even higher with his father. An incident in the Long Vacation of 1821 is illustrative. "After dinner today," John records in his diary on September 30, "I was suddenly called downstairs to give my opinion whether I

---

114. See William Romaine, *Discourses upon* Solomon's Song, *preached at St Dunstan's Church* (London: T. Chapman, 1789), esp. 45–73 and 231–45.

115. *Apo.*, 59.

116. JHN, "August 4, 1821," *AW*, 174.

117. *Apo.*, 59.

118. Bebbington, *Evangelicalism in Modern Britain*, 63.

119. JHN, "January 23, 1821," *AW*, 181; "August 18, 1821," *AW*, 175; "September 1, 1821," *AW*, 175; "October 23, 1821," *AW*, 177; "January 12, 1822," *AW*, 180; "February 21, 1822," *AW*, 183; "June 2, 1822," *AW*, 186; "April 13, 1823," *AW*, 171, etc.

120. JHN, "August 13, 1821," *AW*, 175.

thought it a sin to write a letter on a Sunday."[121] Frank, it appeared, "had refused to copy one," and "a scene ensued more painful than any I have experienced."[122] Clearly, John refused to budge. Although their father was reconciled to them the next day, he continued to struggle with their evangelical fervor. And he already had trouble enough as it was.

The brewery business had never suited John Newman Sr., and on November 3, 1821, he was declared bankrupt. Suddenly, the family's prospects looked bleak.[123] He wrote to John on Saturday, October 27, to tell him he would go to church the next day and would take comfort from the thought of the entire family, both in London and at Oxford, praying as one for divine assistance, "however negligent we might have been of our duties to God and ungratefully insensible of our advantages"—an avowal of past laxity primarily to be applied to himself.[124] John Jr. responded to the family crisis with the same religious fervor as five years before. He wrote to his Aunt Betsy of the "privilege of what is called misfortune." "I exult and triumph, and my heart beats high," he exclaimed, "at the thought that God is cutting away all ties which might bind me to the world."[125] Much of this was overstrained emotion. He knew well enough that he would soon be responsible for his own finances and for those of Frank, who had just come to Oxford.[126] It was, at least in part, to meet this challenge that he conceived the idea of standing for a fellowship at Oriel, the top college of the day. And thus, a mere week after he had confidently deprecated "wealth, or fame, or great influence" to his aunt, the thought of Oriel made him feel almost suffocated with "vain glory" and ambition for "the honours of the world."[127]

Despite turning to religion himself after going bankrupt, John Sr. could not handle his eldest son's feverish response to his latest professional failure. Things came to a head over the Christmas holidays, when they clashed right after church on January 6. They had been to Kentish Town Chapel in Highgate Road, where Johnson Grant, the minister, preached a sermon on the turning of the year. John Jr. found it "a very good discourse," especially Grant's observation that "affliction is an awful thing, for calamity either leaves us better or worse."[128] John Sr. seems not to have liked it much. Grant asked his parishioners whether they had been "purified" by the "furnace" of affliction. "Has an avidity for worldly pursuits and

---

121. JHN, "September 30, 1821," *AW*, 176.

122. JHN, "September 30, 1821," *AW*, 176.

123. See *LD* 1, 113; JHN, "January 23, 1822," *AW*, 181.

124. Mr Newman to JHN, October 27, 1821, *LD* 1, 114.

125. JHN to Elizabeth Newman, November 7, 1821, *LD* 1, 115, 116.

126. JHN to Mr Newman, November 14, 1821, *LD* 1, 116.

127. JHN to Mr Newman, November 14, 1821, *LD* 1, 115; "November 15, 1821," *AW*, 177; Ernest Nicholson, "Eveleigh and Copleston: The Pre-Eminence of Oriel," in *Oriel College: A History*, ed. Jeremy Catto (Oxford: Oxford University Press, 2013), 247–90.

128. JHN, "January 6, 1822," *AW*, 179.

for worldly pleasures been reduced in our minds within the sober and solemn bounds prescribed by the Gospel?" he wondered.[129] This would be a lot to stomach for anyone recently bankrupt, let alone for one as little inclined to devotion as John Newman Sr. After church, he took it all out on his son. He accused him of "encouraging a nervousness and morbid sensibility," calling his evangelical religiosity "a disease of mind."[130] He confidently predicted that John would change his opinions within a few years (John, of course, was sure this would never happen) and told him to do "nothing ultra" in the meantime.[131] He criticized John's letter in the *Christian Observer*, which was "more like the composition of an old man, than of a youth just entering life with energy and aspirations," and he was no less sparing of the journal itself. "My opinion of the *Christian Observer* is this, that it is a humbug."[132] In short, he was done with the pious talk. He wanted action.

Within the week, John Sr. told his son that it was time to carve out a future for himself. Unsurprisingly, John Jr. "determined on the Church," rather than the law. The choice suited his religious inclinations as well as his previous decision to try for an Oriel fellowship, but it was not what his father wanted.[133] Although the odds were stacked against him, he was strangely confident until a week or two before the Oriel examinations, which began on April 6 and lasted for five days. But on April 12, he could jubilantly note in his journal: "I have this morning been elected Fellow of Oriel. Thank God, thank God."[134] It took another two years before he realized his other, even more consequential determination. On June 13, 1824, he was ordained a deacon at Christ Church Cathedral, and a year later, on May 29, 1825, he was ordained to the priesthood. Although he never stopped being "ultra," his opinions did begin to change almost right away, just as his father, who did not live to see it, had predicted. And yet, even though his evangelicalism came undone at least partly because he became a minister in the Church of England, he had not been taking his Anglicanism lightly.

An Anglican Evangelical

It is possible to define and describe evangelicalism with little regard to confessional boundaries, as I have done so far, but such boundaries were, of course, in place. Newman was a Church of England evangelical, not a dissenting evangelical (like Baptists or Methodists), and this fact was as important to him as it had been to Thomas Scott. He never trivialized his ecclesial membership. Immedi-

---

129. Johnson Grant, *Course of Sermons for the Year*, vol. 1 (London: Rivington et al., 1833), 4.
130. JHN, "January 6, 1822," *AW*, 179.
131. JHN, "January 6, 1822," *AW*, 179. See also "January 12, 1822," *AW*, 180.
132. JHN, "January 6, 1822," *AW*, 179.
133. JHN, "January 11, 1822," *AW*, 180.
134. JHN, "April 12, 1822," *AW*, 186; Culler, *The Imperial Intellect*, 26–35.

ately after his conversion, he tried to square his rudimentary evangelical theology with the doctrinal teachings of the Church of England, as expressed, primarily, in the Thirty-Nine Articles.[135] This was the real point of the compilations of scriptural texts in support of Trinitarian doctrine he composed during and after his conversion. Like Scott's, they quite literally sought to make good what the eighth article promised: that the Apostles', the Nicene, and the Athanasian Creed, "may be proved by most certain warrants of Holy Scripture."[136] His defense of the Athanasian Creed, especially, which was binding on Anglicans but not on dissenters, shows that he wanted to be faithful member of the Established Church.

Like Scott, Newman had little difficulty, at first, integrating evangelicalism and Church of England theology. But wider society was not so hospitable to the attempt. At the time, evangelicals were "a small minority within the church, held in contempt or hated by most churchmen."[137] They were charged with enthusiasm because of their emphasis on the experience of conversion, with antinomianism because of their understanding of assurance, and popularly brushed aside as Methodists. For that reason, evangelicals at large felt the urgent need to show that they, and not their detractors, were the "true churchmen," faithful to the reformers, as well as to the articles, the *Homilies*, and the prayer book.[138]

Newman was no exception. At Oxford, he experienced the popular sentiment against evangelicalism first-hand. In his dialogue between Spenser and Merton, Merton applies various disparaging labels to Spenser, ranging from "field-preacher," over "Calvinist," to "one of the newbirth gentry."[139] In response, Newman drew on Church of England sources. Spenser ends his case for a radical new birth with citations from a handful of bishops and the first *Book of Homilies*, while the manuscript concludes with a lengthy appendix citing influential divines in support of the same point.[140] As late as 1825, Newman used the Anglican reformers to support

135. These "Articles of Religion" emerged out of the Reformation struggles in the English church and were accepted in their current form in 1571.

136. Unless otherwise indicated, citations of Church of England formularies, liturgical services, etc., are taken from the 1662 edition of *The Book of Common Prayer* (Cambridge: John Baskerville, 1762).

137. Kenneth Hylson-Smith, *Evangelicals in the Church of England, 1734–1984* (Edinburgh: T. & T. Clark, 1989), 67.

138. Garreth Atkins, "'True churchmen'? Anglican Evangelicals and History, c. 1770–1850," *Theology* 115, no. 5 (2012): 339–49.

139. JHN, *Dialogue—Merton—Spenser*, BOA A.9.1.e, 3, 5.

140. JHN, *Dialogue—Merton—Spenser*, BOA A.9.1.e, 7–9, 10–18. The first, or "former," *Book of Homilies* is a collection of sermons mainly written by Thomas Cranmer (1489–1556) and enjoined by Article XXXV as containing "a godly and wholesome doctrine." The divines Newman cited as in favor of an evangelical understanding of regeneration are (in the text): Joseph Hall (1574–1656), Edward Reynolds (1599–1676), Jeremy Taylor (1613–1667), John Wilkins (1614–1672), and (in the appendix): Hugh Latimer (1487–1555), John Lightfoot (1602–1675), Thomas Jackson (1579–1640), and Joseph Mede (1586–1639).

evangelical doctrine. His sermon on "justification through faith only" reads like a vindication of Scott's road to evangelical Anglicanism, with Newman using the same quotations from Richard Hooker that Scott presents in the *Force of Truth* as having led to his evangelical understanding of justification by faith.[141]

For Newman, evangelicalism was not just a possible interpretation of Church of England theology but the only right one. Evangelical and Anglican theology stood or fell together. He argued as much in a somewhat confused, but interesting paper written in May 1821: *On the necessity of a thorough reception of the doctrines contained in the 9th article & first part of the 10th, to a belief in the rest.* It claimed that the commonly felt disdain for the Thirty-Nine Articles resulted from a failure to accept the "complete degeneracy of our nature" taught in article IX and X—a doctrinal emphasis typical for evangelicals.[142] Newman began the piece with an observation. In polite society, he noted, "nothing is of more common occurrence than to hear frequent objections to the articles of our Church."[143] Newman identified a kind of epistemic hubris, fueled by the increase and dissemination of (scientific) knowledge among an ever-larger segment of the population, as the main cultural threat to traditional formulations of religious truth. "Indeed," he argued, "it were impossible in so intelligent & liberal an age as the present, when every one feels himself able to form & free to declare his own opinions, that the <u>pure</u> & <u>unbending</u> <u>doctrines</u> of our Church should be otherwise than hostilely received."[144] Usually, such hostility did not result in open rejection. Many depended for their livelihood, career, or reputation on keeping their peace with "the Establishment." Such people tended to "<u>pervert</u>" rather than reject the "unpalatable doctrines & rigid morality of the Gospel & the Church of England." Only those in a "more independent situation" would "deny the Scriptures & articles" altogether.[145] These latter critics, ironically enough, had a better grasp of the theology of the articles than their shiftier counterparts. Overt objectors "readily detect the 'Evangelical,' or, as they choose to call it, the 'Antinomian' flavour of the articles," Newman argued, and they "pity the <u>liberal</u> clergy who have to come with such a millstone round their neck to the contest."[146] While the liberal Anglican must gloss over parts of the articles, the open critic can candidly

141. Scott, *The Force of Truth*, 34–42; JHN, No. 61, "Justification through faith only," March 6, 1825, in *Sermons, 1824–1843*, 5 vols., ed. Placid Murray, Vincent Ferrer Blehl, and Francis J. McGrath (Oxford: Clarendon Press, 1991–2012), vol. 5, 179–91, esp. 184–87, hereafter *Serm.* Richard Hooker (1554–1600) was one of the most important and influential sixteenth-century Church of England theologians.

142. JHN, *On the necessity of a thorough reception of the doctrines contained in the 9th article & first part of the 10th, to a belief in the rest,* May 1821, BOA A.9.1.e, 1, 3.

143. JHN, *On the necessity,* BOA A.9.1.e, 1.

144. JHN, *On the necessity,* BOA A.9.1.e, 1–2.

145. JHN, *On the necessity,* BOA A.9.1.e, 2.

146. JHN, *On the necessity,* BOA A.9.1.e, 2.

admit their real bearing, witnessing, unwittingly, to "the truth of what is commonly called the 'Evangelical' interpretation of Christianity."[147]

Although the overt impugner might understand the articles better than the scholiast who explains them away, Newman still considered direct critiques more dangerous, especially for the young. Impressionable, and with few prior ideas about the articles, young people enter society and encounter,

> I will not say <u>objections</u> advanced against our reformers, but a certain contemptuous tone of language adopted concerning them as if they were very well-meaning men, who advanced far into the light which the Papacy had so discreetly shaded from the eyes of her Sons, but whose minds were necessarily contracted, & ideas bigotted [*sic*] by the mist & confusion in which they had so long been shrouded.[148]

Among the (upper) middle class of Regency England, it seems, the articles were not so much considered untrue as outdated and irrelevant. "It was all very well in those days," the fashionable critic would argue, "but in an age such as this when knowledge is so widely diffused, it is most preposterous to insist on dogmas which cannot stand their ground." "I approve of articles," he would add, "it imparts a dignity to an established church; it hinders an impolitic latitude of opinion in its ministers, but really for a man to wish us to assent to such an assortment of abstract & barren propositions cannot be tolerated by any enlightened mind."[149] Such sentiments, expressed as matters of course, would easily mislead a credulous youth. He might take to the articles and find that the one enjoining "the thorough reception of the Athanasian Creed," with its damnatory clauses, "opposes the <u>liberality</u> of his à priori conjectures," while "the Calvinism which seems to lie on the surface of the 17th"—the article on election—"actually dismays him."[150] In time, such reflections might lead a young person to conclude that doctrinal truth is indeed an indifferent matter. One wonders how much of Newman's own experience is reflected in this sketch.

It is tempting to read Newman's analysis as a classically conservative response to the influence of (Lockean) liberalism, with its emphasis on individual liberty and societal progress, on public perceptions of religion, but social criticism was not his main goal. His principal object was theological: to show that the reason so many people take offence at the articles was rooted in their "rejection of the doctrine of human corruption."[151] Newman held that no one could assent "to the mysterious doctrines of Christianity without a full conviction of the naturally

147. JHN, *On the necessity*, BOA A.9.1.e, 2.
148. JHN, *On the necessity*, BOA A.9.1.e, 3.
149. JHN, *On the necessity*, BOA A.9.1.e, 3.
150. JHN, *On the necessity*, BOA A.9.1.e, 3–4.
151. JHN, *On the necessity*, BOA A.9.1.e, 4.

depraved condition of mankind." "This conviction," he argued, "is the keystone of the arch; take it away & the other doctrines are loosened & fall."[152] Although the ensuing argument lacks clarity, its gist is clear. Christian doctrine is a solution to a specific problem: sin. Take the problem away, and there is no more need for the solution. If sin is only "venial," there is no eternal punishment, and thus no need for the "sufferings of a Divine Being" to redeem sinners, which justifies the Socinian conclusion that "Jesus is a mere Man."[153] Similarly, if people are "naturally upright," good works can be performed without faith and suffice for salvation, which undoes the articles' teaching that works are "the necessary fruits of faith" and that God sovereignly elects the saved.[154] To "a man who does not <u>feel</u> the complete degeneracy of our nature," in short, "the machinery of the Gospel covenant will appear needlessly intricate & the materials preposterously costly."[155]

Moving from the doctrinal to the fundamental theological level (a distinction he did not draw) Newman argued that if our reasoning capacities are unimpaired by sin, revelation as such becomes superfluous. What is at stake here is the principle of dogma itself, not individual dogmas. If reason can determine religious truth, "there is no use in the Sacred Scripture <u>as a revelation,</u>" for then, "its authority is not decisive," and people are "allowed to choose <u>what</u> they will acknowledge & <u>what</u> reject."[156] Once the principle of dogma falls, all dogmas fall with it. Such a position,

> carrying us far beyond the bounds of any particular article, overthrows them all . . . and hurrying through the ocean of controversy takes without opposition the different vessels of Romanism, Socinianism, Mysticism & all in fact that cruise under the colours of Christianity, till it lands us in safety on the philosophic shore of Deism.[157]

It is one thing, though, to show that Christian doctrine is premised on the idea of human corruption, but quite another to hold that people actually reject the one because they have first rejected the other—Newman's original contention. Toward the end of his text, Newman quite suddenly realized the disjunction, and he ended on a note of disappointment "for having spent so much time *operosè nihil agendo*."[158] For a biographer, of course, the essay is much more than nothing.

---

152. JHN, *On the necessity*, BOA A.9.1.e, 4.
153. JHN, *On the necessity*, BOA A.9.1.e, 5.
154. JHN, *On the necessity*, BOA A.9.1.e, 6.
155. JHN, *On the necessity*, BOA A.9.1.e, 4.
156. JHN, *On the necessity*, BOA A.9.1.e, 6.
157. JHN, *On the necessity*, BOA A.9.1.e, 6.
158. JHN, *On the necessity*, BOA A.9.1.e, 7. The Latin is from an exclamation widely attributed at the time to a dying Hugo Grotius: "*Heu! Vitam perdidi operosè nihil agendo*"—"Alas! I have wasted my life laboriously doing nothing."

It witnesses to Newman's acumen for (conservative) social criticism, his penchant for logical and systematic thought in theology, his fundamental commitment to the principle of dogma, and, perhaps most importantly, his conviction that only an evangelical take on the Gospel could ensure assent to the articles of the Established Church.

The latter claim was especially contentious. Newman wrote his early papers at a time when evangelical allegiance to the Church of England was hot in the public debate. Herbert Marsh, the Bishop of Peterborough, had just instituted an examination for candidates for ordination in his diocese, intended to weed out evangelicals from their ranks.[159] In response, successive issues of the 1821 *Christian Observer*, to which Newman subscribed, attacked Marsh's eighty-seven questions and defended evangelical theology by means of authoritative Anglican texts, like the *Homilies*.[160] Evidently, the dialogue between Spenser and Merton was Newman's attempt to contribute to the debate on the evangelical side. It is quite likely that his paper on 'working out one's own salvation' was also elicited by Marsh, who used St Paul's text to argue that a person *does* have an active "share in the work of his salvation."[161] Marsh had troubled evangelical waters before with his strictures on the British and Foreign Bible Society in 1812.[162] The Bible Society was one of multiple panevangelical organizations set up at the turn of the century with the aim of uniting Anglican and dissenting evangelicals in a common purpose, in this case, the free distribution of Bibles.[163] In the spring of 1823, Newman began to consider membership in earnest, and he subscribed a year later.[164]

In the meantime, he had consulted Marsh's critical pamphlet and composed a reply.[165] Like many churchmen, Marsh objected to the close association of Anglicans and dissenters in the Bible Society because he thought the downplaying of denominational differences it implied could easily lead Anglicans to dissent. Distributing the Bible, moreover, held no guarantee that its readers would come to the Church of England. The Bible alone, Marsh contended, might lead the reader into any of the many forms of Protestantism, be they heterodox or orthodox,

---

159. Robert K. Forrest, "Marsh, Herbert," *ODNB*.

160. For Marsh's questions, see "Reviews of Pamphlets, &c., on the Peterborough Question," *Christian Observer* 20, no. 3 (March 1821): 160–90, 161–64. See also the continuation and conclusion of this review in the following two numbers of the *Christian Observer* (20, no. 4 [April 1821]: 235–58, and 20, no. 5 [May 1821]: 295–316).

161. "Reviews of Pamphlets," *Christian Observer* 20, no. 3 (March 1821): 161.

162. Herbert Marsh, *An Inquiry into the Consequences of Neglecting to Give the Prayer Book with the Bible*, 4th ed. (London: Rivingtons, 1812); Atkins, "True Churchmen?" 343.

163. Hylson-Smith, *Evangelicals in the Church of England*, 96–99; Roger H. Martin, *Evangelicals United: Ecumenical Stirrings in Pre-Victorian Britain, 1795–1830*, Studies in Evangelicalism 4 (London: The Scarecrow Press, 1983), esp. 80–146.

164. JHN, "June 8, 1823," *AW*, 192; "May 16, 1824," *AW*, 199.

165. JHN, *Remarks on Herbert Marsh's Pamphlet on the Bible Society*, April 1823, BOA A.9.1.e.

for the Bible does not carry true doctrine on its face.[166] Accordingly, Anglicans could not rest satisfied with handing out Bibles alone but should distribute the prayer book along with it, to safeguard its proper interpretation.

Newman's response expressed the ecumenical spirit typical for evangelicals of the age. "Does not this objection," he inquired, "in some degree arise from not considering religion as a work of the heart — All truly pious individuals agree in substance, however they may differ in forms."[167] On Newman's view, true religion was the product of conversion of heart, and where such conversion has truly occurred, people will inevitably hold substantially the same Christian truths. Reading the Bible is sufficient to achieve this end: "those who come humbly to it will understand enough for salvation."[168] He granted that clergymen should do all they could to instruct their parishioners in Anglican doctrine, and even "circulate prayer-books," but he did not see the impropriety of a distinct society also distributing "the pure and unencumbered Bible."[169] In fact, he considered the Bible Society's ecumenical character a benefit rather than a drawback, citing the fact that it "promotes charity among members of different sects" as a reason for joining it.[170] Once again, his evangelical convictions had been challenged from within the Church of England, and, again, he managed to find a tensile equilibrium between his evangelical theology and his denominational identity.

But neither anti-Calvinism nor the Bible Society was the most pressing problems for Anglican evangelicals. The central issue was that of the relationship between baptism and conversion. Evangelicals insisted that an experience of conversion is necessary to be regenerate (that is, to receive the new life required by scripture). It was, perhaps, their most defining characteristic. But they were confronted with a set of liturgical statements (contained in the *Book of Common Prayer*) that seemed to deny that regeneration depended on such a change. The various baptismal services declared that baptism makes a child regenerate, while the catechism stated that baptism conveys a "new birth."[171] The former especially troubled evangelical Anglicans. They must, at times, have felt the sting of William Pitt the Elder's quip about the Church of England's "Calvinistic creed" and

---

166. Marsh, *An Inquiry*, 7–11.

167. JHN, *Marsh's Pamphlet*, BOA A.9.1.e, 2.

168. JHN, *Marsh's Pamphlet*, BOA A.9.1.e, 3.

169. JHN, *Marsh's Pamphlet*, BOA A.9.1.e, 3.

170. JHN, *Marsh's Pamphlet*, BOA A.9.1.e, 8.

171. See Bebbington, *Evangelicalism in Modern Britain*, 9. In the service for public baptisms, the minister prays for "*this infant*, that *he* coming to thy holy Baptism, may receive remission of *his* sins by spiritual regeneration." After the act of baptism, the minister declares "that *this Child is* regenerate," and shortly after gives God thanks "that it hath pleased thee to regenerate *this Infant* with thy Holy Spirit." The service for private baptisms, in addition, described baptism as "the laver of Regeneration." In the catechism, the response to the question: "What is the spiritual and inward grace [of baptism]" is "A death unto sin, and a new birth unto righteousness."

"Popish liturgy."[172] Newman certainly felt the tension. At the time of his conversion, he tried to adjudicate between the respective views on baptism of Scott and Richard Mant, whose 1812 *Bampton Lectures* fervently advocated baptismal regeneration as the true doctrine of the Church of England and antagonized Anglican evangelicals accordingly.[173] Shortly afterwards, he read William Beveridge's *Private Thoughts upon Religion*—a gift from Walter Mayers—and found that he, too, regarded "Baptism as the mean whereby we receive the Holy Spirit, although not the only mean."[174] Puzzled, he queried Mayers, who acknowledged the "strong expressions in our baptismal service" but argued that they should not be interpreted in Mant's strict sense.[175] Mant's idea of baptism as "the only vehicle of regeneration," Mayers contended, is irreconcilable with actual experience:

> [Mant's] statements are contradicted by thousands around us, who though they have been admitted by Baptism into the *visible* church of Christ, are evidently not living as members of the *invisible* church, or as those whom the scriptures would denominate "renewed in the spirit of their minds."[176]

Since the lives of so many baptized people do not conform to what the Bible teaches about the new life of the Spirit, they cannot be regenerate yet. They still need the conversion that will make them so.

Newman fully adopted Mayer's argument, and it grounded his rejection of baptismal regeneration for almost a decade. In the *Collection*, he drove the issue to the point of irony. Can human means change an unconverted heart? How about "the waters of baptism," he wondered almost cynically:

> easy receipt, & of inestimable virtue! sovereign specific for the sanctification of a country, simple remedy for the radical disease of our nature! We have brought our children to the font — how rapturous will it be to observe, as reason begins to act, the daily unfolding & discovery of a regenerated nature, of an holy will & godly affections!

Only to conclude: "Alas, experience teaches a different lesson, & we are constrained to admit that neither the hand of the baptizer . . . nor anything human is a sure and certain method powerful to <u>force</u> the <u>gift</u> of God."[177] The appeal to

---

172. The remark is said by Edmund Burke to have occurred in Pitt's parliamentary speech of May 19, 1772. See P. J. Marshall and Donald Bryant, eds., *The Writings and Speeches of Edmund Burke*, vol. 4 (Oxford: Oxford University Press, 2015), 308.

173. Richard Mant, *An Appeal to the Gospel* (Oxford: J. Parker, 1812); JHN, *Scott vs. Mant on Baptism*, BOA A.9.1.b. The manuscript is a brief collection of references from scripture and various theologians, dated 1816 by Newman, and titled by an archivist.

174. JHN to Walter Mayers, January 1817, *LD* 1, 30.

175. Walter Mayers to JHN, April 14, 1817, *LD* 1, 32.

176. Walter Mayers to JHN, April 14, 1817, *LD* 1, 32.

177. JHN, *Collection*, BOA A.9.1.c, 16.

experience that grounded Newman's rejection of baptismal regeneration was not based only on his observations of the outside world, it derived just as much from his own process of conversion. In an 1820 journal entry, he wondered whether children "receive this change [regeneration] in baptism?" and replied: "For myself I can answer that I did not; and that, when God afterwards in His mercy created me anew, no one can say it was only *reforming*."[178] His conversion made Newman not just a different being but a new being.

Six years on, Newman's view had changed completely. With regard to his own conversion, he now noted in his journal: "my feelings were not *violent*, but a returning to, a renewing of, principles, under the power of the Holy Spirit, which I had *already* felt, and in a measure acted on, when young."[179] It was much more like a reforming than a new creation after all. But this change in assessment had a context. Newman had just come to accept the doctrine of baptismal regeneration, which made the evangelical notion of conversion as a radical postbaptismal change theologically obsolete. By 1826, the tension between the evangelical understanding of regeneration and its counterpart in the liturgy of the Church of England had been resolved in favor of the latter, but this is matter for a later chapter. Here, it is important because it brings us back to the opening question of this chapter: the evangelical nature of Newman's conversion and of his early theology.

Conclusion

In his *Autobiographical Memoir*, Newman framed his conversion within a narrative shaped by his later conviction of "the indefectibility of genuine certitude" developed in the *Grammar of Assent*.[180] Since he had given up some of his evangelical beliefs, he concluded that he could never have been certain about them. As a young man, he had assented to evangelicalism as a whole, and this included mistaking mere belief—in final perseverance, for instance—for certitude. Newman did not just reinterpret his doctrinal adherence to evangelicalism. He also dismissed its erstwhile experiential appeal, claiming that it "had from the first failed to find a response in his own religious experience."[181] Its "emotional and feverish devotion and its tumultuous experiences were foreign to his nature."[182] This interpretation—of Newman, by Newman—has given rise to obverse conclusions. Linnan dismisses it as a *post hoc* rationalization and argues that Newman both was an evangelical *and* experienced an evangelical conversion.

178. JHN, "September 29, 1820," *AW*, 165.
179. JHN, "July 26, 1826," *AW*, 172.
180. JHN, "Autobiographical Memoir," *AW*, 80.
181. JHN, "Autobiographical Memoir," *AW*, 79.
182. JHN, "Autobiographical Memoir," *AW*, 82.

Stephen Dessain, by contrast, concludes that "Newman was never a real evangelical" at all.[183]

The obvious response to the latter claim is that if Newman was no evangelical, there never was a person who looked as much like one without being one. If we adopt Dessain's logic (that Newman never was a real evangelical because he stopped being one after a decade or so) we might as well argue that he was never a real Anglican. Some people, Anglican as well as Roman Catholic, might welcome this conclusion, and they are welcome to it. But we should note that it is the elusive adjective "real" that does all the work in this argument. There can, in principle, be good reasons—and for Newman there were—to discount his early evangelicalism, qua evangelicalism, as a confused whim, despite all the appearances to the contrary. Hence, it is not surprising that scholars eagerly following Newman's lead have paid scant attention to his evangelical theology. But even if one regards Newman's evangelicalism as of little importance in the final (theological) analysis, or in view of his religious development as a whole—both questionable positions—this does not mean that it was of little importance to Newman at the time. This is what Linnan suggests (although he does not say it) and what is at stake for any historically sensitive biographer: Newman's sense of self at the time. From this viewpoint, there can be no doubt that the young Newman should be called what he called himself: evangelical.

This leaves us the question of Newman's conversion itself. Here the sources are more fragmentary and less univocal. On the one hand, Dessain's claim that Newman "had never been through the conventional experiences of conviction of sin, terror, despair, followed by full assurance of salvation" is unpersuasive.[184] The evidence reviewed above suggests that this was, in fact, quite like what Newman experienced at the time of his conversion, and he never denied it. He maintained only that his "own feelings were *not* violent" in the manner usually described in evangelical literature; then again, neither were Scott's.[185] On the other hand, Newman had already noted in 1821 that his conversion had been "so different" from all the descriptions he ever encountered in the evangelical literature, that in his *Collection* he was "obliged to adopt the language of books" for fear of going "by what *may* be an individual case."[186] There seems to have been something odd about Newman's conversion, something that did not quite cohere with the usual evangelical narrative, but whether this is enough to discount Newman's conversion as evangelical still seems little more than a quibble about words.

<hr>

183. Dessain, "Newman's First Conversion," 50.
184. Dessain, "Newman's First Conversion," 50.
185. JHN, "July 26, 1826," *AW*, 172; "Autobiographical Memoir," *AW*, 80.
186. JHN, "June or July 1821," *AW*, 166.

The fact is that we are confronted with an aged Newman's claims about the innermost dynamic of his personal convictions: to have lacked certitudes, which at the time he thought he had, and to have been averse to emotions he tried to embrace. These claims remain, on principle, opaque to the biographer. Even if Newman's perception was slanted by theory, he had access to his own history in a way that others have not. And even the theoretical slanting cannot be dismissed out of hand. Newman's mature view of the nature and structure of the human mind, might, for all we know, be true. But its truth or falsity cannot be assessed here and will probably never be settled conclusively either way. We should, therefore, take Newman as we find him in the first decade of his actively religious life: a teenage boy who experienced a conversion that turned him away from sin and to God, who embraced evangelicalism in consequence, and who soon put pen to paper to systematize his views and carve out for himself a legitimate place in the Church of England.

The struggle for confessional identity is a key corollary to the fact that Newman's theological development began with a conversion. For Newman (unlike for, say, Keble), what it meant to be a Christian in the Church of England was never self-evident. He did not so much grow into his confessional identity as awaken to it quite suddenly, when his conversion had made him an evangelical. As a result, his theology was under construction right from the start. He needed to harmonize evangelical theology (which, at that point, functioned as the proper and natural interpretation of his conversion experience) with the doctrinal and liturgical tradition of his church, just as he would years later with Patristic theology. One could say that his long quest to establish the true nature of the Church of England began here, when he was an evangelical seeking to claim Anglicanism as his own. In both cases, evangelical and Tractarian, he had to contend with the clamors of many of his coreligionists, and both attempts were ultimately unsuccessful, at least as far as Newman himself was concerned. In the latter case, it was Anglicanism that could not bear the strain of Patristic theology. In the former case, it was evangelicalism that had to give way to Church of England theology. This process took time, however, and it was not as straightforward as he later made it out to be.

CHAPTER 2

A Brother's Apostasy

John Newman Sr. was not the only doubter in the Newman family. John and Frank had found Jesus at Ealing, but there was a now forgotten middle brother, Charles, who was not as inclined to spiritual religion.[1] Although he was probably as talented as his brothers, Charles never became a great Victorian. He was psychologically unstable and had his family worried about his sanity and sustenance for most of his life. In the early 1820s, John and Frank tried to engage him in their intense religious routines, but Charles did not take to evangelicalism.[2] In fact, he did not take to religion at all. In the summer of 1823, Charles began to raise doubts about Christianity to John—similar ones, perhaps, as their father's, but with more existential urgency. He wavered for a while, but soon after John Sr. died in the summer of 1824, his doubts hardened into resolute unbelief. Unlike his father, who might not have been the best of Christians but made no show of his opinions, Charles was an outspoken apostate, eager to discuss his views. Dealing with Charles was a challenge for the whole Newman family, but John Jr. bore the brunt of it. He was not only best equipped to deal with the situation—eldest male, recently ordained, first-rate education—but also Charles's chosen interlocutor. In 1825, the two brothers engaged in a prodigious exchange of letters—often convoluted but always interesting—which lasted for six months and counts among the most intense exchanges of Newman's life.[3]

Newman came to the discussion with a lot of background. Ever since his pubescent approaches to scepticism, he had been interested in the grounds of belief. From Scott, he had learned the traditional conception of Christian faith as belief in some intelligible content because God has revealed it, the principle

---

1. Biographical material on Charles Robert (1802–1884) includes John's memorandum of May 1874, *LD* 1, 182–83; *LD* 2, 38; *LD* 3, 86; *LD* 4, 131–35; Thomas Purnell, "Charles Robert Newman," *Athenaeum*, March 29, 1884, 408; Charles Robert Newman [hereafter CRN], *Essays in Rationalism*, ed. George Jacob Holyoake and J. M. Wheeler (London: Progressive Publishing Company, 1891); Sean O'Faolain, *Newman's Way*; and Martin J. Svaglic, "Charles Newman and his Brothers," *PMLA* 71, no. 3 (1956): 370–85. Edward Short offers the only sustained attempt at a biographical study in *Newman and His Family*, 115–39.

2. See *AW*, 174–75.

3. The correspondence was copied out into eight notebooks (BOA A.4.2), "partly by Newman himself, partly by other members of the family" (*LD* 1, 212). It comprises John's and Charles's letters and five papers, three by Charles (titled *No 1*, *No 2*, and *No 3*), and two by John (*Paper A* and *Paper B*). Only John's letters are included in *LD*. For a brief account of John's side of the correspondence, see G. R. Evans, "Newman's Letters to Charles," *Downside Review* 100 (1982): 92–100.

of dogma. But he continued to delve into questions concerning the reasonableness of Christianity. He studied John Locke during the Long Vacation of 1818, and in 1819, he acquired a copy of William Paley's definitive summary of eighteenth-century apologetics, the two-volume *A View of the Evidences of Christianity* (1794), whose margins he filled with numerous comments and summaries of Paley's arguments.[4] Newman's own first-ever publication, the 1821 letter to the *Christian Observer*, was an attempt to contribute to the debate. At Oriel, Newman began to associate with some of the apologetic luminaries of the day: Richard Whately, who had made a splash parodying Hume's objections against miracles in his *Historic Doubts Relative to Napoleon Buonaparte* (1819), and John Davison, who developed the apologetic argument from prophecy in his Warburtonian lectures.[5] From 1823 to the middle of 1825, moreover, Newman regularly attended the divinity lectures of Charles Lloyd, who, as he later recalled, primarily "employed his mind on the grounds of Christian faith."[6]

From this milieu of living and dead thinkers, Newman acquired an approach to apologetics that had been developed in the early Enlightenment by a group of avant-garde Anglican thinkers—scientists, philosophers, and theologians—and had become paradigmatic by the early nineteenth century. The apologetic model of the English Enlightenment had become a self-evident frame of reference for most educated people at the time, almost like evolutionary theory today. Naturally, Newman used this model as the prism for interpreting and countering his brother's apostasy, who, as naturally, refused to be fit into a mould that was made to his disadvantage. Yet, Newman's debt to this model has scarcely been noticed. In part, this is because it has become foreign to our intellectual world. Excepting a handful of evangelical apologists, who, perhaps unwittingly, perpetuate parts of this tradition, its reasoning has become unfamiliar and unappealing to educated

4. JHN to Hans Henry Hamilton, [May? 1821], *LD* 1, 105; *AW*, 40. Newman's copy of Paley's *Evidences*, 15th ed. (London: John Murray, 1814) is kept in the Birmingham Oratory library. It is inscribed "John Henry Newman 1819."

5. Richard Whately, *Historic Doubts relative to Napoleon Buonaparte* (London: J. Hatchard, 1819); John Davison, *Discourses on Prophecy* (London: John Murray, 1824); and Richard Brent, *Liberal Anglican Politics: Whiggery, Religion, and Reform, 1830–1841* (Oxford: Clarendon Press, 1987), 150–53.

6. JHN, "Autobiographical Memoir," *AW*, 71. Apologetics was, indeed, the main focus of Lloyd's lectures, which dealt with atheism, Deism, Unitarianism, and—extensively—the evidences of Christianity, drawing on Paley and Nathaniel Lardner (1684–1768). See E. S. Ffoulkes, *A History of the Church of S. Mary the Virgin, Oxford* (London: Longmans, Green, and Co., 1892), 401–3; William J. Baker, *Beyond Port and Prejudice: Charles Lloyd of Oxford, 1784–1829* (Orono: University of Maine at Orono Press, 1981), 97–106. All of this shows that an emphasis on the evidences of Christianity in the tradition of Locke and Paley, usually associated with Cambridge, was equally characteristic of the Oxford of the 1820s. Newman's appreciation of Johann David Michaelis (see below), translated and edited by the Cambridge exegete Herbert Marsh, also bespeaks an interest generally associated with Cambridge. Lloyd, who had a "liking for exegetical criticism," might have influenced Newman in this regard (JHN, "Autobiographical Memoir," *AW*, 71). See David M. Thompson, *Cambridge Theology in the Nineteenth Century: Enquiry, Controversy and Truth* (Aldershot: Ashgate, 2008), 13–47.

Christians today. Newman's early adoption of this tradition has also been obscured by his later qualms about its take on faith and reason. If his letters to Charles are read at all, they are made to fit this later, more critical stance.[7] Finally, even though these letters are part of a dispute, no one mentions the letters to which they respond, which obscures the issues at stake.[8] The present chapter provides a contextualized and comprehensive account of Newman's earliest apologetic, but before detailing the dispute between John and Charles, we need to familiarize ourselves with its intellectual backdrop.

English Enlightenment Apologetics

It would take most people today significant intellectual and imaginative effort to comprehend the inner logic and wide appeal of the apologetic tradition that developed during the English Enlightenment (from c. 1660 to 1800). What many now consider one of the aspects of Christian belief most challenging to reason—the miracles of scripture—was then regarded as *the* evidence by which Christian belief was rationally justified.[9] In our age, in which hardly anyone is immune to demythologizing interpretations of the Gospels, it seems easier to affirm the incarnation or the Trinity than to believe that Jesus of Nazareth walked on water or multiplied a few loaves of bread and some fish into a meal for five thousand people. But for early modern Anglican divines, such miracles were precisely what made it reasonable to believe in Christian doctrine. And not only theologians thought so. Leading scientists and philosophers of the day developed the theory underlying this appeal to miracles with nuance and precision.[10] Its appeal, moreover, proved surprisingly lasting. At the time of the outrage over *Essays and Reviews* in the early 1860s, it was still the dominant model among mid-Victorian Protestants.[11]

---

7. Edward J. Enright, "The Letters to Charles Newman as Background to the *Grammar*," in *Personality and Belief: Interdisciplinary Essays on John Henry Newman*, ed. Gerard Magill (Lanham, Md.: University Press of America, 1994), 161–72; Evans, "Newman's Letters," 99; and Gilley, *Newman and His Age*, 56–57.

8. Only Francis McGrath cites fragments of Charles's first letter in *John Henry Newman: Universal Revelation* (Macon, Ga.: Mercer University Press, 1997), 28–30. Short (*Newman and His Family*) has not consulted Charles's letters and accordingly misrepresents both the content and the import of the controversy. In a long letter to Charles of August 19, 1830, John himself summarized the course of the controversy (JHN to CRN, August 19, 1830, *LD* 2, 266–81).

9. Lorraine Daston, "Marvelous Facts and Miraculous Evidence in Early Modern Europe," *Critical Inquiry* 18, no. 1 (1991): 93–124; Peter Harrison, "Miracles, Early Modern Science, and Rational Religion," *Church History* 75, no. 3 (2006): 493–510.

10. Robert M. Burns, *The Great Debate on Miracles: From Joseph Glanvill to David Hume* (Lewisburg, Pa.: Bucknell University Press, 1981).

11. Josef L. Altholz, "The Mind of Victorian Orthodoxy: Anglican Responses to *Essays and Reviews*, 1860–1864," *Church History* 51, no. 2 (1982): 186–97.

To map this tradition, I draw on its three most influential progenitors: the Anglican theologians Edward Stillingfleet (1635–1699) and John Tillotson (1630–1694) and the philosopher John Locke (1632–1704). Although they quarrelled at times, they shared a common religious outlook, usually termed latitudinarianism, and were in basic agreement about the principles that shaped Enlightenment apologetics.[12]

To believe in revelation, one must first believe in God. As John Tillotson put it in one of his sermons: "Before I can be persuaded that any Revelation is from God, I must be persuaded there is a God."[13] Most English Enlightenment thinkers held that substantial religious knowledge could be attained by natural means, that is, reason and the experience of the external world. Such so-called natural religion included beliefs—in God's existence, unity and attributes (infinite goodness, wisdom, and power), the immortality of the human soul and an ultimate judgment of human conduct (a "future state")—as well as behavioral prescripts (worship, prayer, and virtuous living).[14] Pious and upright pagans from classical antiquity were instanced as evidence that such beliefs and prescripts were not just demonstrable by reason but also attainable in practice, although its prevalence was a topic of debate.[15] Next, Enlightenment apologists argued that the God known through the "light of nature" had further revealed himself in history. Their argument was premised on the conviction that whatever God reveals is true. Given God's "infallible and unerring Knowledge, together with his Goodness and Authority," Tillotson noted, God "neither can be deceived himself, nor will deceive us in any thing that he reveals to us."[16] Accordingly, to believe that a particular "Religion is true," we only need to "be satisfy'd, that it is from God; for being once satisfy'd of that, there can remain no doubt of the truth of anything that comes from him."[17]

---

12. John Spurr, "'Latitudinarianism' and the Restoration Church," *The Historical Journal* 31, no. 1 (1988): 61–82; Richard Kroll, Richard Ashcraft, and Perez Zagorin, eds., *Philosophy, Science, and Religion in England, 1640–1700* (Cambridge: Cambridge University Press, 1992); Martin I. J. Griffin, *Latitudinarianism in the Seventeenth-Century Church of England*, ed. Richard H. Popkin and Lila Freedman (Leiden: E. J. Brill, 1992); and Brian Young, *Religion and Enlightenment in Eighteenth-Century England* (Oxford: Oxford University Press, 1998).

13. John Tillotson, *The Works of the Most Reverend Dr. John Tillotson*, vol. 2 (London: 1722), 433. See also Robert Boyle, *The Christian Virtuoso* (London: 1690), 13–14; John Locke, "A Discourse of Miracles," in *Posthumous Works of Mr. John Locke* (London: A. and J. Churchill, 1706 [written: 1701–2]), 220; and Griffin, *Latitudinarianism*, 50–52, 73–76.

14. M. A. Stewart, "Arguments for the Existence of God: The British Debate," in *The Cambridge History of Eighteenth-Century Philosophy*, ed. Knud Haakonssen (Cambridge: Cambridge University Press, 2006), 712; Tillotson, *Works*, 432–35.

15. Stewart, "Arguments for the Existence of God," 711. Tillotson (*Works*, 434) put forth Socrates as the paragon of a heathen who embraced the truths of natural religion.

16. Tillotson, *Works*, 438.

17. Tillotson, *Works*, 526.

In so far as it understood faith as belief in the necessarily veracious "Testimony or Authority of God," Enlightenment apologetics remained wedded to traditional theological categories.[18] Logically, it construed concrete acts of faith as follows. For every x, if x is revealed, x is true; this x is revealed, therefore this x is true. On this model, the truthmaker for x is not its content but its provenance. When revelation is concerned, Edward Stillingfleet argued, "the truth of a doctrine depends not on the evidence of the things themselves"—the plausibility or full intelligibility of the content of the doctrine—"but on the authority of him that reveals it."[19] Still, there are limits to what God can reveal. All apologists agreed that revealed doctrine could not contradict certain knowledge about God or nature. "God never persuades a Man of any thing that contradicts the Natural and Essential Notions of his Mind and Understanding," Tillotson argued. Thus, God cannot persuade anyone that "there is no God; and that he is not Wise and Just, and Good."[20] Hence also the error of transubstantiation, which is incompatible with our certain knowledge of the "*essential* and *inseparable properties* of *bodies*," as Stillingfleet put it.[21] In the philosophy of John Locke, this idea received the rigorous epistemological formulation that shaped the eighteenth-century debate.[22]

In his *Essay on Human Understanding* (1689), Locke radically distinguished knowledge from all other forms of human conviction. Although knowledge is certain, its scope is limited, including a set of mathematical, metaphysical, and moral propositions, but excluding, for instance, the conclusions of the natural sciences.[23] Still, human beings are not left in the dark. "The faculty which God has given man to supply the want of clear and certain knowledge, in cases where that cannot be had, is *judgment*."[24] Such judgment concerns probable propositions and "is called *belief, assent,* or *opinion,* which is the admitting or receiving any proposition for true, upon arguments or proofs that are found to persuade us to receive it as true, without certain knowledge that it is so."[25] Religious faith is a species of such judgment. It is distinct from reason by the grounds on which it holds propositions to be true. Whereas reason is "the discovery of the certainty

18. Tillotson, *Works*, 437.

19. Edward Stillingfleet, *Origines Sacrae, or a Rational Account of the Grounds of Christian Faith* (London: Henry Mortlock, 1675), 228.

20. Tillotson, *Works*, 442.

21. Stillingfleet, *Origines Sacrae*, 239.

22. M. A. Stewart, "Revealed Religion: The British Debate," in *The Cambridge History of Eighteenth-Century Philosophy*, ed. Knud Haakonssen (Cambridge: Cambridge University Press, 2006), 685.

23. John Locke, *An Essay concerning Human Understanding*, vol. 2, ed. John W. Yolton (London: J. M. Dent, 1961), 145–66; 247 (bk. 4, chap. 3; chap. 14.1); Nicholas Jolley, "Locke on Faith and Reason," in *The Cambridge Companion to Locke's "Essay concerning Human Understanding,"* ed. Lex Newman (Cambridge: Cambridge University Press, 2007), 439; and E. J. Lowe, *Locke on Human Understanding* (London: Routledge, 1995), 181–82.

24. Locke, *Essay*, 247, 248 (bk. 4, chap. 14.1, 3).

25. Locke, *Essay*, 250 (bk. 4, chap. 15.3).

or probability of such propositions or truths, which the mind arrives at by deduction made from such *ideas* which it has got by the use of its natural faculties, viz. by sensation and reflection," faith "is the assent to any proposition, not thus made out by the deductions of reason, but upon the credit of the proposer as coming from GOD, in some extraordinary way of communication."[26] This mode of communicating is called revelation, and we assent to it because we judge that the "proposer"—prophet, messiah, or apostle—speaks the words of God, who "can neither deceive nor be deceived."[27]

Since judgments are always about probabilities, nothing can be admitted as revelation that conflicts with certain knowledge. Our conviction that God has revealed something can never be as sure as "the knowledge we have from the clear and distinct perception of our own *ideas.*"[28] In the realm of probability, however, revelation reigns supreme.

> GOD, in giving us the light of *reason*, has not thereby tied up his own hands from affording us, when he thinks fit, the light of *revelation* in any of those matters wherein our natural faculties are able to give a probable determination: *revelation*, where God has been pleased to give it, *must carry it against the probable conjectures of reason.*[29]

The idea here is that the one God speaks to us in two complementary ways. One is by reason, or "natural *revelation*," as Locke once called it, which provides us with a limited portion of certain knowledge of God and the world.[30] The other is faith, or revelation proper, which operates in the vast domain of probability and where it occupies a special place.

For Locke, judgments of probability are based on two complementary grounds, the "testimony of others" and the "conformity of anything with our own knowledge, observation, and experience."[31] We believe that Julius Caesar crossed the Rubicon in 49 BC because we read of his invasion of Italy in several ancient historians, and because it is quite likely that he did so given the socio-political circumstances of the time, his character, and his rivalry with Pompey.[32] It is important to note the inevitably subjective character of probability judgments. Probability is always probability *for someone*. To take Locke's own example, it is easy for *him* to believe a report that someone walked on ice in wintry England, whereas it was literally beyond belief for the King of Siam, when he heard, from

---

26. Locke, *Essay*, 281 (bk. 4, chap. 18.2).
27. Locke, *Essay*, 292 (bk. 4, chap. 19.11).
28. Locke, *Essay*, 282 (bk. 4, chap. 18.4).
29. Locke, *Essay*, 285 (bk. 4, chap. 18.8).
30. Locke, *Essay*, 289 (bk. 4, chap. 19.4).
31. Locke, *Essay*, 250 (bk. 4, chap. 15.4).
32. Locke, *Essay*, 257 (bk. 4, chap. 16.8–9).

a Dutch ambassador, "that the water in his country would sometimes, in cold weather, be so hard that men walked upon it and that it would bear an elephant."[33] This instance shows that the two grounds of judgment are inversely proportionate: the more incredible an event appears, the more "probability relies on testimony."[34] In the case of belief in revelation, this logic is pushed to the extreme. The propositions of revelation "challenge the highest degree of our assent, whether the thing proposed agree or disagree with common experience and the ordinary course of things or no . . . [because] the testimony is of such an one as cannot deceive nor be deceived, and that is of God himself."[35] Since God's testimony is infinitely reliable, it warrants belief in very unlikely events or propositions. We can be as dumbstruck as the King of Siam with regard to the content of revelation, and still believe it, because it is grounded on God's own testimony, instead of the mere word of a Dutchman.

In terms of content, revealed propositions are "above *reason*": they pertain to matters in which reason can form either no judgment at all, or only a probable judgment.[36] Propositions of the first class, such as "that part of the angels rebelled against GOD" or "that the dead shall rise and live again," are simply "beyond the discovery of *reason*, and purely matters of *faith*, with which *reason* has, directly, nothing to do."[37] With regard to propositions of the second class,

> concerning which [the mind] has but an uncertain evidence and so is persuaded of their truth only upon probable grounds, which still admit a possibility of the contrary to be true without doing violence to the certain evidence of its own knowledge and overturning the principles of all reason, in such probable propositions, I say, an evident *revelation* ought to determine our assent, even against probability.[38]

The improbability of a doctrine's content, then, constitutes no objection to its truth, because its truth is determined by *"revelation*, as another principle of truth and ground of assent."[39] If geological research, for instance, indicates that a universal flood never occurred, revelation, as "another principle of truth," still obliges us to believe the biblical story about Noah because geology is only based on probable reasoning. The key question, in short, is not what revelation says,

---

33. Locke, *Essay*, 251 (bk. 4, chap. 15.5).

34. Locke, *Essay*, 251 (bk. 4, chap. 15.5).

35. Locke, *Essay*, 261 (bk. 4, chap. 16.14).

36. Locke, *Essay*, 285 (bk. 4, chap. 18.7).

37. Locke, *Essay*, 285 (bk. 4, chap. 18.7).

38. Locke, *Essay*, 286 (bk. 4, chap. 18.9).

39. Locke, *Essay*, 286 (bk. 4, chap.18.10). See John Locke, "Mr. Locke's Reply to the Bishop of Worcester's Answer to his Second Letter," in *The Works of John Locke*, vol. 3 (London, 1794), 480–82; Nicholas Wolterstorff, *John Locke and the Ethics of Belief* (Cambridge: Cambridge University Press, 1996), 128.

but who says it. As Locke put it, "whether the proposition supposed to be revealed be in itself evidently true or visibly probable or, by the natural ways of knowledge, uncertain, the proposition that must be well grounded and manifested to be true is this, that GOD is the revealer of it."[40]

In practice, this meant proving that the Bible (and the Bible alone) contained God's revelation to mankind. The particular linkage of scripture and revelation in Enlightenment apologetics was the product of post-Reformation controversies between Anglicans and Roman Catholics about the locus of religious authority. In *The Religion of Protestants* (1638), William Chillingworth contrasted Roman Catholic reliance on the infallible authority of the church with Protestant reliance on scripture, as containing "all the material objects of Faith," and thus forming a "complete and total" rule of faith, famously declaring: "The BIBLE only is the Religion of Protestants!"[41] This hyperbole should not be understood in a modern fundamentalist sense. Scripture, for Chillingworth, was not coextensive with revelation: "the books of Scripture are not so much the objects of our faith, as the instruments of conveying it to our understanding."[42] Given this take on scripture as the vehicle for transmitting the revealed message, the apologist must prove two distinct propositions: that the vehicle is reliable and that the message transmitted is indeed revealed.

Enlightenment apologists had few doubts about the historical reliability of the Bible. They uniformly accepted both the biblical canon and most, if not all, traditional ascriptions of authorship. Tillotson, for instance, felt assured by "credible and uncontroul'd Report"—i.e., by reliable historical testimony—that "St. *Matthew* wrote the Gospel which goes under his Name," and summarily dismissed further objections:

> It bears his Name, hath always been received for his; and if this will not satisfy, I cannot prove it farther, it is too late now to prove it by any other Argument. St. *Matthew* is dead, and those who saw him write it, and those who received it from them, so that we cannot go to enquire of them in order to our Satisfaction.[43]

Once securely identified, the biblical authors were presented as competent witnesses who had either received direct revelations themselves (like John in the Apocalypse), were personally involved in the events they related (like John in his Gospel), relied on trustworthy eyewitness reports (such as Mark and Luke), or all

---

40. Locke, *Essay*, 292 (bk. 4, chap. 19.10).

41. William Chillingworth, *The Religion of Protestants a Safe Way to Salvation* (Oxford: Leonard Lichfield, 1638), 55, 375. For the sake of readability, Chillingworth's spelling has been silently modernized.

42. Chillingworth, *The Religion of Protestants*, 116.

43. Tillotson, *Works*, 448; see also 471–72.

of these (Moses). Stillingfleet develops the prototypical argument. Moses was a reliable historian because he had no "*ambitious design* of *advancing himself* and *his posterity*," candidly portrayed the many "*lesser failings* and *grosser enormities*" of the Patriarchs, the people of Israel, and even of himself, and stood out by the "*simplicity* and *plainness*" of his style.[44] The same goes for the Apostles. They were eyewitnesses with no ulterior motives, wrote impartially and in great circumstantial detail, and endured "*reproaches, persecutions, all manner of hardships*, nay, . . . *death itself*" for the propagation of their message.[45]

Enlightenment apologists were well-aware that it is one thing to argue that Moses is as reliable a historian as Tacitus or Thucydides, but quite another to claim that his books contain a message from God. We can only prove the latter, Locke argued, by "outward signs" of divine activity unmistakable to reason.[46] The one category of "signs" that met this requirement was the miraculous—broadly understood so as to include prophecies and their fulfilment. "Miracles," wrote Tillotson, "are the principal external Proof and Confirmation of the Divinity of a Doctrine."[47] Locke made the same point more vigorously in *A Discourse of Miracles*. "Supernatural signs [are] the only means God is conceived to have to satisfie Men as rational Creatures of the Certainty of any thing he would reveal," he argued. They are the "Foundation on which the Believers of any divine Revelation must ultimately bottom their Faith." [48] Such signs must exhibit a clear teleology aligning them with God's revelatory purposes.[49] In the medieval church, and among Roman Catholics generally, miracles often presumed rather than proved faith, or evidenced things other than doctrine, such as personal sanctity. This was unthinkable for English Enlightenment apologists.[50] Only the establishment of a true religion—Christianity—was a rational end for such a rough remedy as God's overruling his own laws of nature. In that case, however, the ordinary logic of probability judgments is turned on its head: the more extraordinary the miracle, the better suited to its goal. As Locke had it in the *Essay*:

Where . . . supernatural events are suitable to ends aimed at by Him who has the power to change the course of nature, there, under such circum-

---

44. M. A. Stewart, "Revealed Religion," 684; Stillingfleet, *Origines Sacrae*, 135–38.

45. Stillingfleet, *Origines Sacrae*, 276; see also 273–300.

46. Locke, *Essay*, (bk. 4, chap. 19.15).

47. Tillotson, *Works*, 498; see also 535.

48. Locke, "A Discourse of Miracles," 227–28, 230.

49. Scripture provided ample warrant for this idea. In the Bible, the process of revelation rarely consists in a direct and public divine communication (such as the heavenly voice in the synoptic account of Jesus' baptism by John) but rather is usually mediated by concrete figures who often rest their claim to divine authority on the miracles they perform (see, for e.g., Moses: Ex 4:1–8; Jesus: Mt 11:3–4, Jn 3:2, 15:24; the Apostles: Acts 14:3, Heb 2:4).

50. Harrison, "Miracles, Early Modern Science, and Rational Religion," 502.

stances, they may be the fitter to procure belief, by how much more they are beyond or contrary to ordinary observation. This is the proper case of *miracles*, which, well attested, do not only find credit themselves, but give it also to other truths, which need such confirmation.[51]

In the case of miracles, the inverse proportion between an event's likelihood and the testimony needed to substantiate it is reversed. Since miracles are God's only way to convince us of a message he wants to get across, their intrinsic improbability tells for, not against them.[52]

Perhaps surprisingly, this appeal to miracles tallied with the new natural philosophy developed by the Royal Society scientists, who both enlarged the natural realm and drew clearer borders between the natural and the supernatural. Medieval cosmology, whose elaborate hierarchy of being included multiple unchanging heavens and celestial bodies moved by separate intelligences which influenced material things on earth, was abandoned for an understanding of all of nature, including the heavens, as governed by uniform laws.[53] Lorraine Daston has shown how the category of the "preternatural"—including, for instance, portents like comets and monstrous births—was gradually "naturalized" and lost much of its religious signification.[54] Both the gradual disappearance of the "third ontological domain"[55] of the preternatural and the cosmological simplification involved in a law-based understanding of nature contributed to a more dichotomous conception of the natural and the supernatural. In such an ontology, a miracle could be defined, quite simply, as "a supernatural Effect," which "exceeds any natural Power that we know of to produce it."[56] Soon, miracles became the only sure tokens of God's revelatory activity.

By resting faith primarily on external proofs, external, that is, to the content of revelation, Enlightenment apologists walled off that content from criticism. But such fortifications did not impress all. Deist critics of Christianity conspired to scale these walls. The unity of purpose and ideas implied in the conventional denominator is relative. If anything, Deism denotes a family resemblance rather than strict theological and philosophical unity. Deists were united by a set of traits—none, perhaps, shared by all, but most shared by many—including a strong emphasis on reason and natural religion, an explicit rejection of at least substantial segments of the biblical revelation, and a marked suspicion of miracles, priest-

---

51. Locke, *Essay*, 261 (bk. 4, chap. 16.13).
52. Locke, "A Discourse of Miracles," 219–21. See Burns, *The Great Debate on Miracles*, 50–57.
53. Edward Grant, *Planets, Stars, and Orbs: The Medieval Cosmos, 1200–1687* (Cambridge: Cambridge University Press, 1994), 488–617.
54. Daston, "Marvelous Facts and Miraculous Evidence," 107–13.
55. Daston, "Marvelous Facts and Miraculous Evidence," 99.
56. Tillotson, *Works*, 495.

hood, and other forms of religious authority.[57] They resolutely rejected the idea of faith as belief on authority, as well as truths "above reason." The "only Criterion of true Religion," Thomas Morgan argued, is "the Nature, Reason, and Fitness of Things, as appearing to the Understanding."[58] The idea of a divine message received on grounds that disregard its content was unintelligible to a Deist like Morgan. As a result, the concomitant distinction on the level of scripture—between revelation (the divine message) and its credentials (the miracles)—also disappeared. Deists treated all biblical material as one, aiming their critiques of scripture equally at its doctrinal content and its miracle stories.

Deists saw little need for the God known by nature to reveal himself any further, and, given their more confident estimate of the capacities and range of natural reason, judged the Bible more severely. If the God of nature had wanted to reveal himself, they argued, he could reasonably be expected to have done so in a more conspicuous and less objectionable manner. Thus, the profusion of miracle stories in other religious traditions seriously challenged the evidential import of the biblical miracles—if miracles are claimed in every religion, why do they only buttress Christian revelation? Some of the biblical miracles, moreover, were morally dubious (think of the story about Jesus' sending a host of demons into a drove of pigs that consequently jumped off a cliff, which must have cost the owner an arm and a leg) or perceived as out of keeping with Jesus' general character, such as his turning large amounts of water into wine, or cursing a fig tree.[59] They complemented such *a posteriori* critiques—to use Robert Burns's term—with *a priori* objections to the concept of miracle, some of which predated, and probably inspired Hume's argument in the *Enquiry*. They argued that God could not, or would not, alter the orderly course of nature he had established, or that, even though *God* was at liberty to do so, *we* could never be sure that he had done so, since the constant experience of the natural phenomena that lead us to believe in an orderly universe always outweighs the strength of any testimony that can be adduced for the occurrence of miracles—Hume's objection.[60]

<hr>

57. Robert E. Sullivan, *John Toland and the Deist Controversy: A Study in Adaptations* (Cambridge, Mass.: Harvard University Press, 1982), 205–34; James A. Herrick, *The Radical Rhetoric of the English Deists: The Discourse of Scepticism, 1680–1750* (Columbia: University of South Carolina Press, 1997), 26–39; and Burns, *The Great Debate on Miracles*, 70–130.

58. Philalethes [Thomas Morgan], "A Letter to Eusebius," in *The Moral Philosopher*, vol. 2 (London: 1739), 29.

59. Both Thomas Woolston and Peter Annet relentlessly criticized Jesus' miracles in this fashion (Burns, *The Great Debate on Miracles*, 77–79; Herrick, *The Radical Rhetoric of the English Deists*, 82–87, 140–1).

60. Diego Lucci and Jeffrey R. Wigelsworth, "'God does not act arbitrarily, or interpose unnecessarily:' Providential Deism and the Denial of Miracles in Wollaston, Tindal, Chubb, and Morgan," *Intellectual History Review* 25, no. 2 (2015): 170–72.

In response to the Deist attacks on revelation, most eighteenth-century apologists, whose ranks, by now, comprised dissenters as well as Anglicans, stuck to their guns. William Law's answer to Matthew Tindal is typical: "A course of plain undeniable miracles, attesting the truth of a revelation, is the *highest* and *utmost* evidence of its coming from God, and not to be tried by our judgments about the *reasonableness* or *necessity* of its doctrines."[61]

Gradually, however, the weight of the argument shifted from proving that miracles evidence a revelation—now simply assumed—to proving that miracles actually happened. Charles Leslie's popular *A Short and Easie Method with the Deists* instances this shift "from the evidence *of* miracles to the evidence *for* miracles," as Daston calls it.[62] "The *Truth of the Doctrine of* CHRIST," Leslie argued, "will be sufficiently evinced if the *Matters of Fact*, which are recorded of him in the Gospels be *True*; for his *Miracles*, if *True*, do vouch the *Truth* of what he delivered."[63] And thus, English apologists developed increasingly elaborate arguments for the historical reliability of scripture. Take the Presbyterian minister Nathaniel Lardner. In addition to writing a twelve-volume *Credibility of the Gospel History* (1727–1755), he published collections of early patristic and ancient Jewish and pagan testimonies to Christianity, all to demonstrate the credibility of the Apostles as witnesses and the historical reliability of their writings.[64] When Newman was confronted with his brother's proclamation of unbelief, it was this long tradition of thought and argument that shaped his response.

Charles Newman's Crisis of Faith

On February 23, 1825, Charles Newman informed his brother John that he had made up his mind on the question of religion. "I . . . have come to a judgment which no doubt will surprise you: for it is entirely against Christianity."[65] But John was hardly surprised. He had been aware of Charles's fits of religious doubt for at least a year and a half. In August 1823, he reports a long conversation with Charles on the subject of Christianity. Charles's objections centered on the doctrine of hell. "The antecedent improbability of eternal punishment is so great that it is absurd to believe it," he argued.[66] John could only deplore this line of argument. It did precisely what his 1821 piece for the *Christian Observer* had sought to forbid: evaluate a

---

61. William Law, "The Case of Reason, or Natural Religion, Fairly and Fully Stated," in *Works of the Reverend William Law*, vol. 2 (London: J. Richardson, 1762), 110. The book was first published in 1731. I owe the reference to Herrick (*The Radical Rhetoric of the English Deists*, 153) who garbles the citation.

62. Daston, "Marvellous Facts and Miraculous Evidence," 114. See Herrick, *The Radical Rhetoric of the English Deists*, 163–79.

63. Charles Leslie, *A Short and Easie Method with the Deists* (London: C. Brome, 1699), 6.

64. Alexander Gordon, "Lardner, Nathaniel (1684–1768)," rev. Alan P. F. Sell, *ODNB*.

65. CRN to JHN, February 23, 1825, BOA A.4.2.1, 1. Cited in *LD* 1, 212.

66. JHN, "August 9, 1823," *AW*, 192.

doctrine on the basis of its contents rather than its proofs.[67] Accordingly, John aimed to remedy what to his mind could be nothing else than deep-seated prejudice on Charles's part. He argued that by nature we are "bad judges of our guilt" and thus not fit to assess the doctrine of eternal punishment.[68] We can only grasp its meaning if we engage in religious praxis, that is, read the Bible, pray "for grace to understand it," and strive to live an upright life.[69] Charles did not think much of such preparation. "Man is not so bad," he retorted, "your way of asking for grace is very roundabout; so much machinery; why not read the Bible, and employ reason at once?"[70] John reiterated his earlier advice in a letter of December 1823, stressing the importance of sound religious convictions and of seeking truth in a serious and sincere way.[71] In this incipient stage of Charles's crisis of faith, John still treated his brother—for all his doubts—as a believer, who needed, and appeared receptive to, religious exhortation more than argument. Rather than put forth the evidences, John aimed to quell the real source of Charles' trouble: his emotional and moral qualms about the doctrinal content of Christianity.

At first, this approach seemed to work. Frank wrote in his dotage that Charles "disowned us all, on my father's death, as 'too religious' for him."[72] But if any disowning occurred, it certainly did not happen right away. Around the time their father died, in August 1824, John spent quite some time with Charles, who even recommended a popular religious work to him, with which John was "much pleased."[73] Charles's religious doubts seemed to be on the wane. As John pointedly reminded him in March 1825, "a few months ago, your judgment was *on the whole* in favor of Christianity."[74] But the lull in Charles's crisis of faith was temporary. By Christmas, his doubts had been rekindled. The Newman family spent the holidays in Strand-on-the-Green (London), where they read together—among works of a more religious description—"Owen's (of Lanark) Essays."[75] The reference is to the Deist Robert Owen's *A New View of Society* (1813), which, as John later explained, was read at Charles's behest.[76] Owen's book was pivotal in the development of Charles's

---

67. See pp. 23–25.

68. JHN, "August 9, 1823," *AW*, 193.

69. JHN, "August 9, 1823," *AW*, 193.

70. JHN, "August 9, 1823," *AW*, 193.

71. JHN to CRN, December 12, 1823, *LD* 1, 169–70.

72. FWN, *Contributions*, viii.

73. JHN to Mrs Newman, October 18, 1824, *LD* 1, 195. See also *LD* 1, 193, 194. The book was the early eighteenth-century Calvinist Samuel Clarke's *A Collection of the Promises of Scripture under their Proper Heads* (Philadelphia: J. H. Cunningham, 1820). It is still among the books in Newman's study at the Birmingham Oratory.

74. JHN to CRN, March 3, 1825, *LD* 1, 213.

75. *LD* 1, 206.

76. *LD* 1, 206; Robert Owen, *A New View of Society: or, Essays on the Formation of the Human Character, Preparatory to the Development of a Plan for gradually ameliorating the Condition of Mankind*, 3rd ed. (London: 1817).

unbelief. Charles probably became familiar with Owenism in late 1824, and when he read *A New View*, it struck him like a revelation. By the time he informed John of his definitive rejection of Christianity, he was a devoted Owenite. "Mr. Owen & the Cooperators are approximating to truth," he wrote in February, "all the rest of the world are acting & thinking on false principles."[77]

Although *A New View* propagated extensive societal and educational reforms—partly enacted in Owen's own cotton mills at New Lanark—it seemed restrained in its criticism of religion. But, as Robert Davis has pointed out, the book's central thesis was "profoundly irreconcilable with orthodox Christianity."[78] The basis for Owen's reformism was the idea that human character is completely determined by circumstances. Accordingly, changing those circumstances for the better of necessity results in societal improvement: "By far the greater part of the misery with which man is encircled *may* be easily dissipated and removed; and . . . with mathematical precision he *may be* surrounded with those circumstances which must gradually increase his happiness."[79] Owen, in short, rejected human free will in favor of circumstantial determinism. This determinist anthropology provided Charles with the theoretical groundwork to justify his initial qualms about the doctrine of eternal punishment. When human beings are not responsible for their actions, divine punishment becomes, as Charles put it, "quite ridiculous."[80] On the same reasoning, he somewhat reluctantly relinquished the positive corollary to the doctrine of hell. "I was rather surprised," he wrote to John, "when I found I must give up the idea of glory everlasting . . . but it cannot be helped."[81] Owen had argued that it was because of the ideas of eternal punishment and reward, present "in all systems which have hitherto been taught to the mass of mankind, that the misery of the human race has to so great an extent proceeded."[82] Charles followed suit: "I do not deny the beauty of Christ's precepts; but to make a <u>system</u> of them I consider very injurious: in fact it is religion immediately or obliquely that brings evil most abundantly into the world."[83] Charles realized that Christianity supplied people with a reason to act virtuously, but "Mr. Owen's principles & system"—in full operation at New Lanark—provided a more than adequate substitute: "Mr. Owen for practical motives to action . . . beats St. Paul hollow."[84]

<hr>

77. CRN to JHN, February 23, 1825, BOA A.4.2.1, 2. See also p. 5: "My opinion is that the whole world except Mr. Owen & the Cooperators are mad: the latter are approximating to truth."

78. Robert A. Davis, "Robert Owen and Religion," in *Robert Owen and His Legacy*, ed. Chris Williams and Noel Thompson (Cardiff: University of Wales Press, 2011), 95.

79. Owen, *A New View of Society*, 28; Davis, "Robert Owen and Religion," 95–98.

80. CRN to JHN, February 23, 1825, BOA A.4.2.1, 3. See O'Faolain, *Newman's Way*, 75.

81. CRN to JHN, February 23, 1825, BOA A.4.2.1, 5.

82. Owen, *A New View of Society*, 107.

83. CRN to JHN, February 23, 1825, BOA A.4.2.1, 2.

84. CRN to JHN, February 23, 1825, BOA A.4.2.1, 5, 1.

John was saddened by Charles's letter, but unimpressed by its argument. Charles had written rashly and ramblingly, declaring "the whole world . . . mad" and dismissing all previous authors for and against Christianity as "a pack of fools," always excepting Owen, of course.[85]

In fact, Charles admitted himself he was "fidgetty [*sic*]" and had "a mental itch," which prevented him from fully developing his arguments.[86] This was certainly not the way to persuade a cautious and intelligent brother of having formed a careful judgment on Christianity. John's response of March 3, 1825, mingled sorrow and sympathy for his brother's "unquiet state of mind" with occasional flares of indignation at Charles's reckless reasoning.[87] Charles, however, remained undeterred, and John felt obliged to enter "into a defence of Christianity" against his brother—"a most painful, and most heart-rending event."[88] The ensuing correspondence lasted for six months, from March through August, with an interruption in May and June. Throughout, the brothers were at cross-purposes. John naturally interpreted Charles's apostasy within the framework of English Enlightenment apologetics. Accordingly, he persistently attempted to convince Charles of his unreasonableness in rejecting a revelation on the basis of its contents, while trying, at the same time, to engage him on the proper ground of debate, the evidences for Christianity. Charles, by contrast, was elated at his discovery of Owenite determinism, and used it—without defending it—as the key to explaining Christianity in purely naturalistic terms. He simply would (or could) not see the pertinence of John's distinction between contents and evidences. As a result, little constructive engagement took place in the first stage of the dispute. Battle lines were drawn, and positions taken, but no headway was made. It was only when correspondence was renewed in July, when Charles began to comprehend and counter the argumentative framework John had set up in the first stage of the dispute, that a more meaningful exchange commenced.

Drawing Battle Lines

Right from the start, John identified the distinction between the contents and the evidences of revelation as the fulcrum of the debate. Faced with Charles's Owenite objections to eternal punishment and reward, John commented: "how monstrous is it to attempt overturning a system by *a-priori* objections to its doctrines; while the great body of external evidence on which it is founded remains untouched!"[89] As in his 1821 article, he drew an analogy with the sciences. Charles's

---

85. CRN to JHN, February 23, 1825, BOA A.4.2.1, 5, 4.
86. CRN to JHN, February 23, 1825, BOA A.4.2.1, 1, 5.
87. JHN to CRN, March 3, 1825, *LD* 1, 213.
88. JHN to CRN, March 24, 1825, *LD* 1, 220.
89. JHN to CRN, March 3, 1825, *LD* 1, 214.

mode of proceeding was like endeavouring "to refute Newton, not by showing some flaw in his reasoning, but by expatiating on the antecedent absurdity, the ridiculousness of supposing the earth to go round the sun."[90] Charles had accused Christians of being too prejudiced to see their religion in a dispassionate light. John reversed the accusation and stressed the objective historiographical methodology used to evaluate the evidences for revelation, based as it was "upon the obvious and general canons by which we judge of the truth or falsehood of *every thing* we hear; not on rules peculiar to religion, or modelled by it." Given that "purely logical principles" were at stake in assessing the reliability of historical testimony to miracles, Charles should aim his objections at the evidences, rather than the content of Christianity.[91]

Passionate about his newfound Owenism, Charles was impervious to what must have struck him as just another of John's theological niceties. In his response of March 11, he claimed with renewed vigor: "we have no divine revelation & Christianity is from beginning to end a human invention."[92] Charles's approach in this letter epitomizes his attitude in the first half of the dispute. Instead of demolishing the eighteenth-century case for the truth of Christianity, he sidestepped the tradition of Enlightenment apologetics and doggedly pushed his own agenda: using Owen's circumstantial determinism to argue that all of biblical history could be "most extremely easily accounted for on natural principles."[93] "Human nature," Charles maintained, "is so extraordinary that no reliance whatever is to be placed on the record of the Evangelists."[94] Given the atmosphere of religious excitement in which Jesus lived and worked, his miraculous cures could easily be attributed to "the power of imagination" (i.e., suggestion) operating both in him and in the diseased.[95] "I have such an opinion of human nature under the circumstances," Charles wrote, "that I can even believe that [St Matthew] persuaded himself he saw miracles performed which he did not see."[96]

All of this was more assertion than argument, and John began to get annoyed. In his response of March 24, he tried to acquire a clearer picture of Charles's understanding of the evidences for Christianity, but first he explained his own conception of the scope and limits of evidential apologetics. Echoing, once again, his 1821 article, John pointed out that he considered "the rejection of Christianity to arise from a fault of the *heart*, not of the *intellect*."[97] For John, unbelief could only be founded on prejudice of a morally reprehensible nature. It "arises, not from

---

90. JHN to CRN, March 3, 1825, *LD* 1, 214.
91. JHN to CRN, March 3, 1825, *LD* 1, 214.
92. CRN to JHN, March 11, 1825, BOA A.4.2.1, 13.
93. CRN to JHN, March 11, 1825, BOA A.4.2.1, 16.
94. CRN to JHN, March 11, 1825, BOA A.4.2.1, 14.
95. CRN to JHN, March 11, 1825, BOA A.4.2.1, 14.
96. CRN to JHN, March 11, 1825, BOA A.4.2.1, 15.
97. JHN to CRN, March 24, 1825, *LD* 1, 219.

mere error of reasoning, but from pride or sensuality." Unbelievers reject Christianity simply because they are uncomfortable with its moral and spiritual claims. Thus, "a dislike of the *contents* of Scripture is at the bottom of unbelief." Attacking the evidences is "quite *an afterthought*." Rather than considering the evidences for Christianity in an unbiased manner, hostile unbelievers attacked them in a *post hoc* effort to justify their prior repudiation of the content of Christianity. Accordingly, people like Charles "reverse the legitimate process of reasoning, and act in a manner which would be scouted as unfair were they examining Newton's Principia or Lavoisier's Chemistry"—again the analogy with science.[98]

One implication of John's argument was that a mere process of reasoning could never undo unbelief, since it had distinct moral and affective origins. "The most powerful arguments for Christianity do not *convince*, only *silence*," John wrote, "for there is at the bottom that secret antipathy for the doctrines of Christianity, which is quite out of the reach of argument."[99] John's point here is *de facto* rather than *de jure*. He does not mean that the evidences are not convincing in theory: they are. He means only that they fail to be so in practice because unbelievers are viciously obstinate. It is key to rightly understand John's argument here. In ideal circumstances, that is, in the case of an unbiased inquirer, the evidences for revelation *do* establish the truth of Christianity. In this sense, considering the evidences is the proper starting point for religious inquiry. As he put in his 1821 *Collection*, it is only when "we have travelled through the evidences for the truth of Christianity, and arrived at a settled conviction of the entire inspiration of the whole Bible" that we begin to "inquire what we are to do to inherit eternal life."[100] Yet, evidence has little impact on the person who has rejected Christianity because of its content, because such a rejection stems from a separate stratum of one's being: the moral and affective. As a result, such a person will not, in practice, be convinced of the truth of Christianity by means of the evidences, even though she should be. Even if her intellect is satisfied, moral and emotional qualms remain. John's purpose, therefore, in arguing with Charles was "not so much to show Christianity *true*, as to prove it *rational*; nor to prove infidelity *false*, so much as *irrational*."[101] John's rhetoric, of course, was less than flattering to Charles, who stood convicted of knavery either way. The only thing he stood to gain, as far as John was concerned, was to be a reasonable knave, rather than a foolish one.

Despite his reservations about what evidential apologetics could achieve in practice, John wholeheartedly threw himself into a defense of the reasonableness of Christianity. To do so effectively, he wanted to ascertain Charles's exact position.

98. JHN to CRN, March 24, 1825, *LD* 1, 219.
99. JHN to CRN, March 24, 1825, *LD* 1, 219.
100. JHN, *Collection*, BOA A.9.1, 10.
101. JHN to CRN, March 24, 1825, *LD* 1, 219.

He roundly admitted: "I feel myself unable to commence the attack till I know in
what quarter the foe is; and whether I am spending my blows on imaginary assail-
ants, or advancing to the actual seat of the war."[102] Accordingly, he drew up a series
of queries—overwhelming in both number and scope—to gain a more complete
picture of Charles's opinions. By means of thirty-five pointed questions, summar-
izing the major themes in Enlightenment apologetics, John urged Charles to discuss
(i) the reliability of the Gospel testimony (including its antiquity and the credibility
of its authors), (ii) the character and motivation of Jesus and the Apostles (whether
they were impostors or enthusiasts), (iii) miracles (their occurrence, explanation,
and reception), (iv) the rise of Christianity (its rapidity and its causes), and finally,
(v) the idea of revelation (and its establishment by miracles).[103] John, in short, stipulated that if Charles wanted to proceed rationally, he ought to refute a century-and-
a-half of Enlightenment apologetics before attacking the contents of revelation.

Charles immediately answered John's letter, on March 26, but, as he admitted
himself, in a manner "destitute of all method & design."[104] Instead of answering
John's queries, which he promised to do soon, he reiterated his Owenite objections to the doctrine of hell, asserting that, "the idea of men's being condemned
to hell in the next life arises from a total mistake of his nature."[105] Yet, he concluded with a question that was germane to the discussion. "Do you conceive,"
he asked of John, "that, if some of the books of the Bible can be proved to have
all the signs of being written by unassisted men, while at the same time they profess to be written by the inspiration of the Deity; — that the credit of the whole
Bible is shaking?"[106] Slowly, Charles began to see the direction in which John
wished to steer the discussion.

In his response of April 14, John answered Charles's question by explaining
the Lockean epistemological underpinnings of the distinction between the contents and evidences of revelation. Like Locke, John admitted that scripture could
not be divinely revealed if it would teach logical impossibilities, such as "that two
and two made five," or "flagrant immoralities" at odds with our natural knowledge
of God's attributes.[107] Likewise, clear marks of "forgery" in the "structure and

---

102. JHN to CRN, March 24, 1825, *LD* 1, 219.

103. JHN to CRN, March 24, 1825, *LD* 1, 219–20; Evans, "Newman's Letters," 96–97.

104. CRN to JHN, March 26, 1825, BOA A.4.2.1, 26.

105. CRN to JHN, March 26, 1825, BOA A.4.2.1, 25.

106. CRN to JHN, March 26, 1825, BOA A.4.2.1, 26.

107. JHN to CRN, April 14, 1825, *LD* 1, 226. In his first university sermon, John insisted
more generally: "we cannot imagine that He [God] would by His inspired servants set forth as articles
of faith, doctrines which contradict previous truths which He has written on the face of nature"
(No. 151, "The temper of mind injoined by Christianity, that which is indispensable in conducting
scientific inquiries," July 2, 1826, BOA A.9.4, 4–5; published as "The Philosophical Temper, First
Enjoined by the Gospel," *Sermons, Chiefly on the Theory of Religious Belief, Preached before the University of
Oxford* [London: J. G. F. & J. Rivington, 1843], 5, hereafter *OUS*).

contents" of scripture would tell against its divine inspiration.[108] So far, John answered Charles's question in the affirmative. Yet, John also followed Locke in arguing that when probable propositions are concerned, revelation overrules reason. "A revelation," John argued, "implies the disclosure of something before unknown . . . something otherwise indiscoverable," which "*may* prove agreeable to our own experience, but *as* certainly it may turn out to be beyond its reach."[109] Although revelation can neither be patently absurd nor obviously immoral, it might well contain doctrines that appear highly improbable. To drive home his point, John constructed an analogy on the basis of recent astronomical theorizing on the phenomenon of shooting stars. Until the end of the eighteenth century, shooting stars were generally regarded as atmospheric phenomena, like lightning, what John called "meteors." In the early nineteenth century, however, they came to be viewed as "real bodies," or stars.[110] Now suppose, John argued, that "a revelation had been made in the last age to inform us they *were* really stars, this report would be contrary to all our previous philosophy."[111] Yet, someone who rejected such a revelation on the basis of its content, would act unreasonably,

> *not* because *prior* to the revelation (using all the light he had) he had come to the *probable* conclusion that they were meteors; but that *now*, when a professed revelation was offered him, he *assumed* that his opinion relative to falling stars was so demonstratively true, that instead of examining the claims of the revelation, he might try it by its *contents*.[112]

John's point here is the same as Locke's. As long as revelation does not contradict our certain knowledge, it is to be evaluated on the basis of its proofs rather than its contents.

The conclusions John drew from Locke's theory had an immediate bearing on the dispute at hand. For John, the epistemic modesty implied in the Lockean understanding of revelation was of a distinctly moral nature. Humility was required to keep one's pretentions to knowledge in check by duly distinguishing certain knowledge from probable opinion, so as to be open to the newness of revelation. Charles, by contrast, had exhibited pride in "rejecting the *credentials* of Christianity *because* you dislike the *contents*," that is, letting his personal qualms about the doctrine of hell override the rational claims of the evidences for Christianity on his belief.[113] John insisted, therefore, that, "The *credentials* . . . of a

---

108. JHN to CRN, April 14, 1825, *LD* 1, 226.

109. JHN to CRN, April 14, 1825, *LD* 1, 225.

110. JHN to CRN, April 14, 1825, *LD* 1, 225; John North, *Cosmos: An Illustrated History of Astronomy and Cosmology* (Chicago: University of Chicago Press, 2008), 527–28.

111. JHN to CRN, April 14, 1825, *LD* 1, 225.

112. JHN to CRN, April 14, 1825, *LD* 1, 225.

113. JHN to CRN, April 14, 1825, *LD* 1, 225., 228, 227.

revelation are for the most part distinct from its contents — and by the former is it primarily to be tried." Only a discussion of the evidences would provide a way forward in the discussion. "Let us stand on ground where both can stand," he argued, "where there are some common principles and some certainty of soundness in the premises [*sic*]."[114] Until Charles had properly taken the implications of the distinction between contents and evidences into account, John argued, he had "no right to pen another line about Mr Owen's system: a system, which it would not be difficult but irrelevant to answer."[115]

After John's letter of April 14, the controversy between the two brothers came to a standstill. On May 11, Charles informed John that he wanted to drop the controversy for the present, because he felt mentally healthier and was looking for employment.[116] Nevertheless, Charles included a six-thousand word paper, titled *No 1*, dated May 9, in which, he alleged, "I have answered most of the queries which you put to me."[117] John was supposed to receive both the letter and the paper from his mother, but she only forwarded the letter, because she was concerned about the toll the dispute was taking on John's health. She wrote John, probably to his relief, that because he had "so much other urgent business on his mind," Charles's lengthy paper would follow in the Long Vacation.[118] Meanwhile, Charles would join his mother and sisters in Strand-on-the-Green at the end of May and stay for the summer. Here, the matter rested for two months.

Engaging Revelation

When correspondence recommenced in July, the two eldest Newman brothers were once more at cross-purposes, so that the second stage of the dispute was as convoluted as the first. Amidst the profusion of letters and papers flying back and forth, even the protagonists had a hard time keeping track of each other's meaning, let alone the present-day reader. John strenuously attempted to retain some order in the exchange and used all of his analytical acumen to extract the few pertinent arguments from Charles's rambling compositions. Charles, by contrast, cared little for structured argument and was unwilling or unable to focus on one or two key points. His texts, in fact, become increasingly manic, displaying a remarkable sort of elation at being able to level attack after attack at Christianity. By the end of the dispute, neither John nor Charles had moved an inch. Nevertheless, the second stage of the controversy was more meaningful than the first. In the first stage, John and Charles had done little more

114. JHN to CRN, April 14, 1825, *LD* 1, 226.
115. JHN to CRN, April 14, 1825, *LD* 1, 226.
116. CRN to JHN, May 11, 1825, BOA A.4.2.2, 39.
117. CRN to JHN, May 11, 1825, BOA A.4.2.2, 39.
118. Mrs Newman to JHN, May 12, 1825, *LD* 1, 231.

than entrench their respective positions; now some forays were made into enemy territory, and actual engagement took place. Discussion centered on two distinct but related focal points: (i) scripture and the evidences for revealed religion, and (ii) the relation between natural and revealed religion.

Engaging Scripture: John, Charles, and the Evidences of Christianity

Initially, some of the misunderstandings that marked the first stage of the dispute seemed to have been cleared up during the two-month lapse in correspondence. John spent the week from June 25 to July 2 with his family in Strand-on-the-Green, where Charles broached the topic of religion. John attempted once more to explain "the unreasonableness of judging of a revelation by its *contents*."[119] He thought he had been successful, for Charles had pleaded guilty. "You indeed yourself acknowledged the other day," John wrote on July 7, "that an aversion to the contents of Scripture is the *grand objection* in your mind to revelation."[120] Debating the evidences, therefore, was beside the point:

> It will then be but child's play to be arguing about external evidences, while all the time you have this hidden and insuperable obstacle in your mind; which, 'hushed' at present 'in grim repose,' will afterwards rise up to overthrow whatever structure I may raise against you.[121]

For John, Charles's admission of what John had consistently alleged changed the nature of the controversy. Rather than focus on the evidences, John now required Charles to *prove* the principle on which he had acted, namely, *"that we have a right to judge of the contents of a revelation by our own preconceived notions."*[122] But Charles prevaricated. He had sunk his teeth into John's queries on the evidences and was unwilling to defend his earlier objections to the contents of revelation. "My principal dependence," he wrote on July 20, "is <u>not</u> as you suppose on the argument which may be brought against the contents of Scripture."[123] To prove as much, he directed John to his paper *No 1*, which John had finally received, and soon added papers *No 2* and *No 3*.

As far as the evidences are concerned, Charles's papers did little more than continue his earlier attempt to account for the biblical narrative on naturalistic principles. Paper *No 1*, which dealt primarily with the Old Testament, presented

---

119. JHN to CRN, July 7, 1825, *LD* 1, 240; see also *LD* 1, 239.
120. JHN to CRN, July 7, 1825, *LD* 1, 240.
121. JHN to CRN, July 7, 1825, *LD* 1, 240.
122. JHN to CRN, July 7, 1825, *LD* 1, 240. The quote is from Thomas Gray's *The Bard* (1757).
123. CRN to JHN, July 20, 1825, BOA A.4.2.2, 36. In his paper *No 2*, Charles seemed to retract his argument from the contents of Christianity as well (CRN, *No 2*, July 20, 1825, BOA A.4.2.3, 1).

an elaborate naturalized history of the main events recounted in scripture, without distinguishing between the divine message—what John regarded as the content of revelation—and prophecies or miracle stories—the evidences of revelation. Echoing a characteristic Deist trope, Charles referred Old Testament miracle stories to superstition and manipulation by the Israelite priesthood.[124] Prophecies, he explained by an *ex eventu* strategy supplied by Thomas Paine, whose pamphlet he, too, had read.[125] Paine maintained that the Old Testament prophecies applied to Jesus by the four Evangelists were "not prophecies of the person called Jesus Christ," but described events or persons contemporaneous with the prophet.[126] Charles generally followed Paine's lead but had more historical-critical acumen in particulars. In discussing whether the suffering servant of Isaiah 53 was predictive of Jesus—one of the classic evidences from prophecy—Paine had rejected Hugo Grotius's suggestion that this prophecy applied to Jeremiah, rather than Jesus, on the basis of Isaiah's living prior to Jeremiah. Charles, however, was aware of the multiple authorship of Isaiah and noted in the margin of his father's copy of Paine's treatise: "Payne [*sic*] ought to have considered that the book of Isaiah [was] written by different persons."[127] Accordingly, he could interpret Isaiah's prophecy as a mere description of Jeremiah, and so explain it in strictly natural terms.[128] Most of Charles's paper was concerned with an alternative genealogy of the Christian religion. It described how the central ideas of Christianity—sin, sacrifice, redemption, and a messiah—had gradually and naturally developed from the time of the Patriarchs, so that in first-century Judaism, all that was "wanting to complete the Christian scheme, was the Christ himself."[129] In this charged religious climate, Jesus, a highly sensitive religious individual, began to believe he was the Messiah, started to teach and expound scripture, and consciously tried to fulfill the Old Testament prophecies. After his tragic death, his disciples began "to experience the amazing power of faith" and continued his mission.[130]

John was not impressed by what he regarded as mere conjectures, and he was exasperated at Charles's refusal to engage his central contention that "it is unfair to judge of the genuineness of a revelation by the things revealed."[131]

<hr>

124. CRN, *No 1*, May 9, 1825, BOA A.4.2.2, 43, 50, 53, 56; Herrick, *The Radical Rhetoric of the English Deists*, 32–34.

125. On John's prior request, Charles included Paine's treatise, which he had probably inherited from his father, with his letter of July 20, challenging John to refute it.

126. Paine, *The Age of Reason. Part the Third*, 11. See pp. 16–17 in this book.

127. BOA A.8.5; Paine, *The Age of Reason. Part the Third*, 33.

128. CRN, *No 1*, May 9, 1825, BOA A.4.2.2, 57–59.

129. CRN, *No 1*, May 9, 1825, BOA A.4.2.2, 61.

130. CRN, *No 1*, May 9, 1825, BOA A.4.2.2, 63.

131. JHN to CRN, July 26[?], 1825, *LD* 1, 246–48, 247. There is no reason to suppose, with Ken Parker, that Newman's argument in this letter against judging of a revelation by its contents was influenced by William Van Mildert's Boyle Lectures, which Newman had read on July 22 and 23

Believing that mutual understanding was beyond reach, he gave up the point for the present. "I am not allowed to *convince* you, I must now attempt to *confute* you," he wrote on July 26.[132] Accordingly, he returned to discussing the evidences and pointed out that "the greater part" of his queries, which Charles so boisterously claimed to have answered in *No 1*, were left "without answer at all."[133] Meanwhile, Charles had written paper *No 2* and began *No 3* on receiving John's letter of the 26th.[134] Although both papers dealt explicitly with John's queries, they added little to Charles's argument. *No 2* and *No 3* continued the conjectural account of the origins of Christianity "on principles, which allow nothing supernatural to have taken place."[135] Jesus, Charles reiterated, had imbibed the religious fervor of his age and regarded himself as the promised messiah. He tailored his ministry to fit prophetic expectations, healed people by natural means, and imparted his enthusiasm to his followers, who, in turn, gave a miraculous account of his life in the Gospels. All of this was done in good faith. Jesus and his disciples "were perfectly sincere & no Impostors"; they were merely deluded enthusiasts.[136]

If Charles's attribution of most of the scriptural narrative to human imagination rather than divine intervention was classically Deist, John responded along the equally classic lines of Enlightenment apologetics. His *Paper A*, written between August 23 and August 28, dealt with the authenticity of the Gospels.[137] It contained little original work. On transcribing it at a later date, John noted: "principally from Michälis [*sic*] and Less."[138] John had indeed consulted the influential Lutheran theologians Johann David Michaelis (1717–1791) and Gottfried Less (1736–1797) with a view to answering Charles, but his principal source was Thomas Hartwell

---

(*LD* 1, 245), as this had been Newman's line of argument from the start of the controversy. Van Mildert's argument is simply more evidence of how widespread the distinction between contents and credentials was among Protestant apologists. See Kenneth Parker and C. Michael Shea, "Johann Adam Möhler's Influence on John Henry Newman's Theory of Doctrinal Development: The Case for a Reappraisal," *Ephemerides Theologicae Lovanienses* 89.1 (2013): 89; William Van Mildert, *An Historical View of the Rise and Progress of Infidelity*, vol. 2, 4th ed. [1st ed. 1806] (London: Rivington, 1831), 1–33.

132. JHN to CRN, July 26[?], 1825, *LD* 1, 246.

133. JHN to CRN, July 26[?], 1825, *LD* 1, 247.

134. BOA A.4.2.3, 1, 9. Both papers were sent, with an accompanying letter, on August 1.

135. CRN, *No 2*, July 20[?], 1825, BOA A.4.2.3, 1.

136. CRN, *No 3*, August 1, 1825, BOA A.4.2.3, 14. Here Charles was more moderate than Paine, who even questioned the historical existence of Jesus (see *The Age of Reason. Part the Third*, 69). Charles commented in the margin: "the man named Jesus Christ did no doubt exist" (BOA A.8.5).

137. See *LD* 1, 253, 255.

138. JHN, *Paper A*, August 28, 1825, BOA A.4.2.4, 7. John consulted Lardner as well. On August 22, he noted in his diary "busied in collecting material for answer of Charles" (*LD* 1, 253). On the same day, he borrowed from the Oriel College Library Lardner's *A Large Collection of Ancient Jewish and Heathen Testimonies*, in *Works*, vols. 7–9, ed. Andrew Kippis (London: J. Johnson, 1788) (Parker).

Horne.[139] *Paper A* was an abbreviated but largely verbatim rendition of the section "On the Genuineness and Authenticity of the New Testament" in Horne's *An Introduction to the Critical Study and Knowledge of the Holy Scriptures* (1818).[140] Like his eighteenth-century sources, John held that the truth of Christianity hinged on the genuineness of the Gospels. On the Enlightenment model, as we have seen, the gospel message was proven true once the gospel testimony to miracles was proven reliable, or, as Horne—paraphrasing Michaelis—put it: "the arguments that prove the authenticity of the New Testament also prove the truth of the Christian religion."[141] In *No 2* and *No 3*, Charles had claimed that the "Gospels & Acts are <u>compilations</u>," collected from various sources and acquiring their final form only in the beginning of the second century.[142] They were the products, moreover, of religious enthusiasm. John retorted that there was no historical reason to doubt the integrity or early date of the Gospels, and every reason to believe them genuine.[143] In proof of this assertion, *Paper A* cited both internal and external evidence for the authenticity of the Gospels, appealing to their style and contents, on the one hand, and to testimonies of early Christians, heretics, and pagans, on the other, to demonstrate that the Gospel writers were reliable contemporary witnesses to the events they described.[144]

Charles did not understand the importance John attached to the authenticity of the Gospels. In a letter to his mother, he observed that John's *Paper A* "had been beating the air," because he did not deny that the original Gospels were preserved in the present Gospels. He specified, moreover, that he regarded "the miraculous accounts as the principal parts afterwards added."[145] John responded at length on September 26, arguing that Charles position still implied that he held

139. See JHN, August 18, 1825, *LD* 1, 252; Johann David Michaelis, *Introduction to the New Testament*, vol. 1, ed. Herbert Marsh (Cambridge: J. Archdeacon, 1793); Gottfried Less, *The Authenticity, Uncorrupted Preservation, and Credibility of the New Testament*, ed. Roger Kingdon (London: F. C. and J. Rivington, 1804). Lloyd recommended Less in his lectures (Ffoulkes, *A History of the Church of S. Mary the Virgin, Oxford*, 402).

140. Thomas Hartwell Horne, *An Introduction to the Critical Study and Knowledge of the Holy Scriptures*, vol. 2 (London: T. Cadell and W. Davies, 1818), 339–67. Newman borrowed the first and second volume of the work from the Oriel College Library on July 24, 1825 in the context of researching his article on miracles for the *Encyclopaedia Metropolitana* (Parker). Horne was far from original himself, relying—again, often verbatim—on Michaelis, Less, Lardner, and James Thomson's article "Scripture" in the third edition of the *Encyclopaedia Britannica* (vol. 17 [Edinburgh: A. Bell and C. Macfarquhar, 1797], 106–74). Thomson also drew explicitly on Michaelis and Lardner. This network of influence, incidentally, shows the paradigmatic status of Enlightenment apologetics around the turn of the century.

141. Horne, *An Introduction to the Critical Study and Knowledge of the Holy Scriptures*, 340; Michaelis, *Introduction to the New Testament*, 4–12, esp. 12.

142. CRN, *No 3*, August 1, 1825, BOA A.4.2.3, 9.

143. JHN to CRN, August 25, 1825, *LD* 1, 255.

144. JHN, *Paper A*, August 28, 1825, BOA A.4.2.4, 7–22; Horne, *An Introduction to the Critical Study and Knowledge of the Holy Scriptures*, 342–52, 357–63.

145. John's summary, in BOA A.4.2.6, 14; *LD* 1, 258.

part of the Gospels to be spurious, and that little of them remained when the miracle stories were taken out.[146] John's emphasis on the genuineness of the Gospels should not be interpreted as an argument for the verbal inspiration of the Bible. For all his commitment to the authenticity of the Gospels, John did not hold that the truth of Christianity depended on minute accuracy in the scriptural narrative. In fact, John allowed for a surprisingly wide margin of error in both the Old and the New Testaments. His response to one of Charles's direct charges against the argument from prophecy bears this out.

Believing he had answered John's questions exhaustively in his papers *No 2* and *No 3*, Charles felt at liberty to level his first "direct attack on the Bible" in the accompanying letter of August 1.[147] His argument was straightforward: Ezekiel had prophesied that the kingdom of Egypt would cease to be a powerful nation; this prophecy was not fulfilled because Egypt had flourished in subsequent periods, for instance, under the Ptolemies and the Fatimide Caliphate.[148] John's response was twofold. On the one hand, he devoted his *Paper B* to denying the factual correctness of Charles's assertions. Drawing on Edward Gibbon, John argued that from soon after Ezekiel's prophecy, the Egyptian people had been ruled by foreign dynasties, so that the native Egyptians, the Copts, had had no share in the power Egypt possessed in later years. Ezekiel's prediction, in consequence, had come true.[149] More interestingly, however, John denied the pertinence of Charles's objection. In a letter accompanying *Paper A* and *B*, which was composed on August 25 but sent only on September 3, John remarked: "I can never allow the principle that any thing in a book of the *Old Testament*, can overthrow *Christianity*. . . . There is every difference between thinking the *books not inspired* or corrupted and interpolated, and the *religion false*."[150] He applied the same line to the New Testament. Michaelis and Less, John argued, "*reject the Apocalypse*," others "think part of St Matthew and St Luke spurious," while Edward Evanson "supposes all the gospels spurious except Luke, and even that interpolated" but still "strenuously advocates the truth of Christianity."[151] John's argument was partly rhetorical; he did not share these views but wanted to demonstrate a principle: "the New Testament is not *Christianity*, but the *record* of Christianity."[152] This was John's real point. *Paper B* was merely meant to

146. JHN to CRN, September 26, 1825, *LD* 1, 258–60.
147. CRN to JHN, August 1, 1825, BOA A.4.2.3, 21.
148. CRN to JHN, August 1, 1825, BOA A.4.2.3, 22–23; Ezekiel 29:15, 30:13.
149. JHN, *Paper B*, August 28, 1825, BOA A.4.2.5.
150. JHN to CRN, August 25, 1825, *LD* 1, 254.
151. JHN to CRN, August 25, 1825, *LD* 1, 254. The latter reference is to Edward Evanson's *The Dissonance of the Four Generally Received Evangelists, and the Evidence of their Respective Authenticity* (Ipswich: B. Law, 1792).
152. JHN to CRN, August 25, 1825, *LD* 1, 254. Compare Chillingworth's distinction between the books of scripture and the truths they contain.

demonstrate that Charles's objection *could* be met, even though it was, strictly speaking, "irrelevant."[153]

John and Charles's wrangle over scripture—and the resulting confusion—clearly shows the continuing import of the distinction between the contents and the evidences of revelation for the discussion. John regarded this distinction as axiomatic, and even when he stopped defending it explicitly, it was implied in his argument. He conceived of Christianity first and foremost as a message delivered in history by Jesus and his earliest followers. Human knowledge of this divine communication was obtained through its historical records, in particular the New Testament, which contained both the divinely revealed message itself and the proofs that showed this message to be divine. Occasional mistakes or interpolations in the records neither disproved the historical reality of the revelation nor invalidated the substantial truth of its message. The historicity of the New Testament miracles, moreover, was sufficiently attested to demonstrate the supernatural origin of the New Testament teachings.[154]

John's notion that the Bible was the record of a historical revelation, rather than that revelation itself, simply made no sense to Charles. Like many Deists before him, he identified revelation with the Bible as a whole and held, accordingly, that it should not contain any mistakes.[155] Charles, moreover, believed that the evidences were not as neutral a territory as John supposed. The proof from miracles and prophecies was based, as John had argued, on common rules for evaluating testimony. These rules, however, depended on a particular view of human psychology, stipulating the likelihood—given certain texts—of their authors having been either deluded or deceptive. Thus, eighteenth-century apologists like George Lyttelton and Charles Leslie had devised criteria to demonstrate, respectively, the trustworthiness of Luke's testimony to Paul's miraculous conversion and of Moses's and the Apostles' testimony to miracles.[156] Charles pointed out, however, that Lyttelton and Leslie had not properly considered the possibility that "Paul was deceived by his own mind" (*pace* Lyttelton) and that a "belief of miracles which never took place might be imposed on the mind of the Israelites" (*pace* Leslie).[157] For Charles, the "external evidences" promised a spurious objectivity, since we are "profoundly ignorant of that science which they do essentially

---

153. JHN to CRN, August 25, 1825, *LD* 1, 254.

154. JHN to CRN, August 25, 1825, *LD* 1, 254.

155. JHN to CRN, August 19, 1830, *LD* 2, 278.

156. George Lyttelton, *Observations on the Conversion and Apostleship of St. Paul* (London: R. Dodsley, 1747); Leslie, *A Short and Easie Method*.

157. CRN to JHN, July 20, 1825, BOA A.4.2.2, 37–38. John Davison (*Discourses on Prophecy*, 43) adduced these same two works as conclusive arguments for Christianity. It seems likely that John, who had read Davison in April 1825, had recommended them to Charles in conversation on July 1, and that Charles felt compelled to respond (see *LD* 1, 228, 239).

involve, human nature."[158] We are simply "in the dark as to how human agency is motioned and influenced, . . . [and] our knowledge of the circumstances which impelled it in the case before us is extremely narrow & imperfect."[159] The evidences, therefore, cannot serve as a neutral starting point for religious inquiry.

John never engaged this line of argument, nor could he have felt much need to do so. Given the widely accepted and, to him, perfectly satisfactory criteria for evaluating testimony developed in the eighteenth century, Charles's argument, based as it was on a mere declaration of ignorance, seemed a flimsy basis on which to jeopardize the Enlightenment apologetic tradition. Yet, it was premised on a fundamental principle that did need to be addressed: the intrinsic improbability of supernatural events. This principle, prevalent in both Hume and the Deists, stipulated that supernatural events are so inherently improbable that the amount of evidence required for proving them is all but insurmountable. It undergirded Charles's argument that if the biblical stories can be explained in naturalistic terms, however contrived, there is no reason to suppose they are supernatural in origin. As long as a more or less plausible naturalistic account of the phenomena is at hand, such as Owen's determinism, one should never resort to supernatural explanations. This was the crux of the discussion between John and Charles, and it resolved itself into their respective perspectives on how the God of nature was likely to reveal himself.

God and the Gods: John, Charles, and Natural Religion

Recall that the Enlightenment defense of Christian revelation was premised on the possibility of natural knowledge of God. Given God's known goodness and benevolence toward his creation, on the one hand, and the sorry state of humankind, on the other, apologists like Paley thought it highly probable that God would reveal himself to enable ignorant and sinful human beings to return to their Maker. Such a revelation could only be miraculous. As Paley noted, "in the same degree as it is probable . . . that a revelation should be communicated to mankind at all, in the same degree is it probable . . . that miracles should be wrought."[160] For Enlightenment apologetics, then, the identity of the God of nature and the God of revelation was guaranteed by miracles, which, as genuine interruptions of the course of nature, could only be performed by its Creator. John had raised this point in his questions to Charles on March 24: "If there is a moral Governor of the world, is there any great antecedent improbability in his

<hr>

158. CRN, *No 1*, May 9, 1825, BOA A.4.2.2, 41.

159. CRN, *No 1*, May 9, 1825, BOA A.4.2.2, 41–42.

160. William Paley, *A View of the Evidences of Christianity*, 2nd ed., vol. 1 (London: R. Faulder, 1794), 3. See Stewart, "Revealed Religion," 703.

revealing his will to man? . . . and if not, is there any conceivable way of attesting it, besides that of miracles? . . . is there any great antecedent improbability in miracles being wrought?"[161] Charles responded to these questions in *No 3*, arguing that the Christian revelation was not what could have been expected from the God of nature.

Somewhat hesitantly, Charles granted that divine providence was likely to reveal itself, but, he added, "this (you must allow) He has not done," because only "a very small portion of the Race" has ever heard of the Christian revelation.[162] This was due to the ineffective means God was supposed to have used to establish Christianity. "There are a thousand other conceivable ways," Charles argued,

> infinitely better than [miracles] by means of a number of men 2000 Years ago, & then employing educated persons to convince us in those latter ages by an elaborate, & what no man can by any means be certain is not after all, a fallacious process of argumentation that there is sufficient evidence that such Miracles really took place.[163]

For Charles, as for the Deists, the idea of revelation entailed universal accessibility. It seemed unworthy for the God of nature—knowable by everyone—to communicate further aspects of his will only to a privileged few.[164] Instead of requiring a convoluted, evidential apologetic, Charles argued, the content of revelation "might force an infallible conviction on the human mind, that it was divine. Or God might write his law on the Sun."[165] Again, Charles was taking his lead from Paine, who, we will recall, had argued that the "news of salvation by Jesus Christ [ought to have] been inscribed on the face of the Sun and the Moon" in order to be a revelation worthy of the God of nature.[166]

John had instanced Paine's objection in his 1821 article as an example of a difficulty of revelation analogous to difficulties in the scientific study of nature.[167] It exemplified the error of judging revelation on the basis of what we think it ought to be, rather than on the basis of evidence. Charles, in fact, had already raised a variant of Paine's objection in conversation on July 1, arguing that it seemed "unlikely Providence should rest such important doctrines as those of Scripture upon *one kind of proof*."[168] In reply, John returned to a theme from his earlier letters.

---

161. JHN to CRN, March 24, 1825, *LD* 1, 220; Evans, "Newman's Letters to Charles," 97–98.

162. CRN, *No 3*, August 1, 1825, BOA A.4.2.3, 15.

163. CRN, *No 3*, August 1, 1825, BOA A.4.2.3, 15.

164. Herrick, *The Radical Rhetoric of the English Deists*, 28–32.

165. CRN, *No 3*, August 1, 1825, BOA A.4.2.3, 15.

166. Paine, *The Age of Reason. Part the Third*, 88.

167. [JHN], "On the Study of the Mathematics," 294; *LD* 1, 103. See p. 24 in this book.

168. JHN to CRN, July 7, 1825, *LD* 1, 240.

It was *"impracticable"* for God to rest revelation on anything other than external evidence, because unassisted human reason is too ill-equipped to judge of the contents of revelation.[169] John had already said as much on April 14, when he warned Charles that "the mind cannot arrive at religious truth . . . without God's dispersing its prejudices."[170] Accordingly, he had urged Charles "to have recourse to the Author of Nature himself for direction."[171] Charles had not responded to this admonition, so John repeated it on July 26, maintaining that his recommendation to pray "for divine assistance" was not based on Christian revelation but "on the natural feelings of every one who acknowledges a Providence."[172]

John's advice was premised on his belief in the identity of the God of nature with the God of revelation. To John, it was self-evident that turning to the God knowable by natural reason would lead one to the Christian God. This identity, however, was far from obvious to a Deist like Paine, who rejected Christianity precisely on the basis of its incompatibility with belief in the God of nature. "HE THAT BELIEVES IN THE STORY OF CHRIST IS AN INFIDEL TO GOD," was the fierce conclusion to his pamphlet.[173] Charles shared Paine's sentiment and even appeared to question whether any relation to the God of nature was possible. "To what God ought I then to pray?" he asked John on August 1, "To your's [*sic*]? That would truly be giving up the argument. To Jupiter? To Jaggernaut? To Allah?"[174] With a touch of irony, he observed that the past and present plurality of religious belief and practice showed that following one's natural religious inclinations led to "an idolatry that Jehovah hates" rather than to the worship of the Christian God.[175] John believed that Charles's response jeopardized belief in God's existence, and he refused to engage its sceptical implications: "I fairly warn you that in all my arguments, I shall consider myself at liberty to assume, if necessary, that point."[176] Charles, moreover, had misunderstood John's idea of natural religion. Human beings naturally and rightly feel dependent "on a superior being," although they are often "wrong in their conceptions of the *object* of that dependence."[177]

For Charles, however, the fact of religious plurality provided a new way of tackling John's distinction between the evidences and the contents of revelation. "If ever a Hindoo or a Mahometan entertains doubts of the truth of his religion (doubts which you will allow in his case are right & just) he must necessarily have

169. JHN to CRN, July 7, 1825, *LD* 1, 240.
170. JHN to CRN, April 14, 1825, *LD* 1, 228.
171. JHN to CRN, April 14, 1825, *LD* 1, 228.
172. JHN to CRN, July 26, 1825, *LD* 1, 247.
173. Paine, *The Age of Reason. Part the Third*, 89.
174. CRN to JHN, August 1, 1825, BOA A.4.2.3, 20–21.
175. CRN to JHN, August 1, 1825, BOA A.4.2.3, 21.
176. JHN to CRN, August 25, 1825, *LD* 1, 253.
177. JHN to CRN, August 25, 1825, *LD* 1, 253.

begun with . . . a dislike of the <u>doctrines</u> & contents of his superstition," Charles argued on August 1.[178] The same was true of the ancients. Charles rhetorically asked: "Ought Horace & Cicero & Ovid to have suspended their judgment till they had examined carefully . . . whether there was sufficient evidence that a divine personage called Ceres did really some centuries before work many miracles & establish the awful Eleusinian Mysteries?"[179] Charles's point was simple: if adherents of a non-Christian religion had a right to judge their revelation by its contents, so had he. John's unproblematic identification of the God of nature with one particular God of revelation—the Christian one—was unwarranted. In this light, the distinction between the contents and the evidences of revelation appeared less rigid than John supposed. If the contents of an alleged revelation could serve to disqualify one religion, they could serve to disqualify all. Charles, therefore, challenged John's Lockean argument that the "credentials" of a revelation "are no more contained in the message itself which it purports to bring from heaven than an ambassador's instructions from his sovereign are his credentials."[180] "A person might appear at a foreign Court," Charles objected, "with the passport and pretensions of an ambassador, yet the instructions he brought might be of such a description as to act as <u>moral anticredentials</u>, totally to make void his claims."[181] Charles argued, in short, that any given religion, Christianity included, could legitimately be assessed by a balancing of contents and evidence. Since the credentials of revelation were established by probabilistic arguments, they should be weighed against the probability, or lack thereof, of the contents of revelation. "Can you assert," Charles asked John, "that there is such infallible certainty in [Christianity's] technical credentials, that is, its external evidence, as to make any improbabilities or apparent inconsistencies in its moral credentials, that is, the contents of the revelation of no weight or avail against it?"[182]

John did not address this epistemological segment of Charles's argument. He simply denied that Christianity, unlike non-Christian religions, contained such "moral anticredentials" and reiterated the Lockean dictum that revelation could not contain "mathematical contradictions or flagrant immoralities."[183] This rule, he argued, provided an adequate criterion to adjudicate between contending religions. Since Hinduism, Islam, and the religions of ancient Greece and Rome were immoral or self-contradictory, Charles's appeal to religious plurality was pointless.[184]

---

178. CRN to JHN, August 1, 1825, BOA A.4.2.3, 18.

179. CRN to JHN, August 1, 1825, BOA A.4.2.3, 19. This was once again a common Deist line of reasoning (see Burns, *The Great Debate on Miracles*, 72).

180. JHN to CRN, July 26, 1825, *LD* 1, 246–47.

181. CRN to JHN, August 1, 1825, BOA A.4.2.3, 19.

182. CRN to JHN, August 1, 1825, BOA A.4.2.3, 19–20.

183. JHN to CRN, August 25, 1825, *LD* 1, 253.

184. JHN to CRN, August 25, 1825, *LD* 1, 253.

Charles, in the meantime, was elated by his discovery that the proofs of Christianity were merely probabilistic and wrote again on August 25 without awaiting John's reply. He was so convinced of his argument that he construed John's slack response as a sign of incipient doubt on John's part.[185] If the proofs of Christianity had "borne the stamp of undoubted certainty," Charles admitted, arguments from the contents of Christianity would indeed be futile.[186] But since the evidences are "but presumptive, the fair proceeding undoubtedly must be to match & balance them against those adverse improbabilities" drawn from revelation's contents.[187] Charles believed John's earlier emphasis on the distinction between the proofs and the contents of revelation was based "on the assumption that there was <u>certain</u> evidence for the truth of Christianity."[188] He now felt that he had driven John to admit that there was no such certain evidence, and thence surmised John's religious doubts. John received Charles's letter of the 25th on the 29th, after he had finished his *Paper A* and *B*. Naturally, he took offence at Charles's insinuations. In a postscript to *Paper B*, he dismissed them as "a fresh and very painful proof of your present distempered state of mind."[189] He ignored Charles's epistemological argument and simply requested Charles to answer his *Paper A* and *B*. But Charles was so convinced by now that he had "overwhelmingly proved that the Christian religion is not a divine revelation" that he considered the discussion closed.[190]

Conclusion

On May 6, 1883, the old Cardinal Newman noted at the head of *Paper B*: "I am not sure that this Paper on Egypt is worth any thing — but I believe no other part of the controversy <u>is</u>."[191] This was a harsh judgment, shaped by six decades of apologetic experience on John's side, and of solidified atheism on Charles's side. Although the 1825 controversy had brought the two eldest Newman brothers no closer to accepting each other's position, it forced John to develop a more coherent defense of the Christian revelation and to reflect on the nature of unbelief. His response reflected the standard contemporary approach to

185. CRN to JHN, August 25, 1825, BOA A.4.2.6, 2, 10, 13.
186. CRN to JHN, August 25, 1825, BOA A.4.2.6, 3.
187. CRN to JHN, August 25, 1825, BOA A.4.2.6, 4.
188. CRN to JHN, August 25, 1825, BOA A.4.2.6, 4.
189. JHN to CRN, Postscript to *Paper B*, August 29, 1825, BOA A.4.2.6, 1. See *LD* 1, 255.
190. CRN to JHN, August 25, 1825, BOA A.4.2.6, 10. According to John's letter of August 19, 1830 (*LD* 2, 276–77), two letters followed. Charles wrote a Latin letter on October 20 in which he told John he wanted to respond at a later date. John replied with a letter that does not appear to have been preserved, but which Charles found "unjustifiable" (CRN to JHN, May 28, 1830, BOA A.4.2.6, 24).
191. JHN, *Paper B*, BOA A.4.2.5, 1; *LD* 1, 255.

apologetics, rooted in over a century of Enlightenment religious conflict. Yet, at the end of the discussion, Charles began to identify potentially significant problems with this tradition. His resolute termination of the controversy left John unable to address these problems in correspondence, but he continued to think them through. Soon, he began to redefine his position and take a line that was more decidedly his own. We will come back to these developments below (in chapter 6). But first, we return from apologetics to theology.

CHAPTER 3

Liberal Tendencies

On June 13, 1824, Newman was ordained a deacon at Christ Church Cathedral.[1] A few weeks later, he took the curacy of the parish of St Clement's, a post which he only resigned in February 1826, to become tutor of Oriel. "During these years of parochial duty," he noted in his *Autobiographical Memoir*, "Mr Newman underwent a great change in his religious opinions."[2] The demise of his evangelicalism set in. With the retrospective calm that characterized his old age, Newman described the gradual shedding of his evangelical convictions as a rather tranquil process, shaped by the general "atmosphere of Oriel Common Room," the particular influence of two Oriel fellows (Edward Bouverie Pusey and Edward Hawkins), and his parochial experience.[3] But in reality, the process that turned him from evangelical into High Church Anglican was neither serene nor straightforward. His journal entries for 1824 and 1825 witness to a sense of perplexity and uncertainty about the outcome of his religious quest.[4] For a time, as Walter Conn observes, Newman "lost his firm cognitive bearings."[5] His gradual extrication from intellectual confusion is traced in detail in the next chapter. This chapter shows that his progression from evangelical to High Church theology was not only less serene than he later made it out to be but also not nearly as linear.

Newman admitted as much in the *Apologia*. Without much explanation, he indicates that between the committed evangelical of the early 1820s and the proto-Tractarian of the early 1830s hovered the spectre of the liberal. For a time in the mid-1820s, he noted, "I was drifting in the direction of liberalism."[6] This remark has proved something of an enigma for scholars. Although noticed by most, it is explained by few, and by none satisfactorily. Even Frank Turner, who otherwise has much to say on Newman and liberalism, merely comments that Newman does not "significantly delineate" "the details" of this "personal drift towards lib-

---

1. He was ordained to the priesthood a year later, on May 29, 1825.
2. JHN, "Autobiographical Memoir," *AW*, 73.
3. JHN, "Autobiographical Memoir," *AW*, 73–80.
4. See JHN, "July 21, 1824," *AW*, 201; "August 15, 1824," *AW*, 201; "August 24, 1824," *AW*, 202; "September 3, 1824," *AW*, 202; "January 13, 1825," *AW*, 203; "February 21, 1825," *AW*, 205; "October 30, 1825," *AW*, 207.
5. Conn, *Conscience & Conversion in Newman*, 38.
6. *Apo.*, 72. From the 1865 edition onward, "liberalism" is replaced with "the liberalism of the day" (*Hist.*, 14).

eralism," and safely ignores the remark for the remainder of his text.[7] Now, it is true that Newman provides preciously few particulars. Besides, liberalism is a complex concept in his thought. Yet, a lot is at stake in getting the meaning of his remark right, because it offers a key to understanding the development of his theology in general, and of his religious polemics in particular.

Liberalism in the *Apologia*

Since Newman's claim to have drifted toward liberalism as a young man appears in the *Apologia*, we must look at the *Apologia* to find out what he meant by the term. Our initial sense of the concept will, therefore, be limited and pro-visional—there is at least thirty years of material prior to the *Apologia* that bears on the issue—but it is sufficient for our purposes in this chapter. In the 1864 edition of the work, Newman did not define liberalism in any detail, beyond noting that he spoke of "liberalism in *religion*," not in politics, and that he meant by it: "the anti-dogmatic principle and its developments."[8] This is not much, but it is something. The definition, cryptic though it be, identifies liberalism as the exact opposite of the "principle of dogma," which occurs in the same passage and has been discussed above.[9] Liberalism, like its counterpart, is a fundamental principle that structures an entire worldview, which consists not in the affirmation but in the denial or undermining of the idea that there is a definite truth in religion.[10] Its outcome is religion "as a mere sentiment," that is, a religion that is solely con-cerned with the emotional states of the believing subject, because it is no longer directed toward a definite external object.[11] For Newman, such religion was "a dream and a mockery": a dream because the emotional states it engenders no longer correspond to external reality, and a mockery because it mimics real religion without actually holding it to be true. "As well can there be filial love without the fact of a father," he scathingly concluded, "as devotion without the fact of a Supreme Being."[12] This is the most that can be extracted from what is but a half-page of the *Apologia*, and Newman realized it was not enough.

The 1865 edition of the *Apologia*, which now went by its subtitle alone: *History of My Religious Opinion*s, elaborated on liberalism in a lengthy "Note A," because,

---

7. Turner, "Editor's Introduction," 87. In his earlier biography, Turner does not notice the remark at all.

8. *Apo.*, 105, 120. The first quotation is omitted from the 1865 edition, presumably because of the added note on liberalism that would have made Newman's religious take on liberalism clear enough.

9. See pp. 21–22.

10. As Newman put it in his *Biglietto speech* fifteen years later, "Liberalism in religion is the doc-trine that there is no positive truth in religion, but that one creed is as good as another" (*Add.*, 64).

11. *Apo.*, 120.

12. *Apo.*, 120.

as Newman admitted, "merely to call it the Anti-dogmatic Principle is to tell very little about it."[13] The note consists of two parts. First, Newman traced the growth of liberalism at Oxford in the first decades of the nineteenth century, but without specifying who those Oxford liberals were, or what they held. Second, Newman listed eighteen theses capturing some of the "developments" of the antidogmatic principle that, as a Tractarian, he "earnestly denounced and abjured."[14] He also provided a concise definition of liberalism as

> the mistake of subjecting to human judgment those revealed doctrines which are in their nature beyond and independent of it, and of claiming to determine on intrinsic grounds the truth and value of propositions which rest for their reception simply on the external authority of the Divine Word.[15]

Liberalism, in short, makes the truth or importance of a doctrine depend on human judgment. We accept or value doctrine only as long and insofar as it makes sense to us. In effect—and this is Newman's point—this approach undermines the idea that dogma represents an external object, which might, but need not, conform to our human conceptions.

As far as the truth of revelation is concerned, this definition captures quite precisely the understanding of revelation we have been discussing so far. Liberalism involves the judging of a revelation on the basis of what it says rather than on the basis of who says it, whereas we ought to believe in a revelation because it comes from God, not because it makes sense or appeals to us. Newman never wavered in his opposition to this first aspect of liberalism. As early as 1821, he associated such a reliance on human judgment and the concomitant hostility to revealed doctrine with the liberality of the age. In his op-ed for the *Christian Observer*, he challenged reason's capacity to determine the how and why of revelation. Just as we believe scientific theories because they are derived from sound evidence, we believe Christian doctrine because we can prove that it originates with God. He staunchly defended this principle in his correspondence with Charles, who had violated it by rejecting Christianity on the basis of its content (the doctrine of eternal punishment). This is by now familiar territory. The second aspect of the *Apologia's* definition of liberalism, concerning the relative value of revealed propositions, breaks new ground. What is at stake here is theology—the structuring of Christianity's content—rather than apologetics—the grounding of Christianity's truth claim. Here, too, the liberal approach is to "subject to human judgment" what is beyond it, that is, to assign relative value to doctrines by considering their respective appeal.

13. *Hist.*, 285.
14. *Hist.*, 294–96.
15. *Hist.*, 288.

The theses at the end of Note A explain what Newman had in mind here, but the character of these theses is the subject of debate.

As Newman had expected, Note A came in for extensive criticism. Although he stood by his definition of liberalism, Newman admitted to Richard Holt Hutton that its purpose was historical, like most of the note, offering "the best analysis of my meaning in time past." Similarly, the theses were not meant as "strictly logical" deductions from the definition but rather propositions related to it—"developments"—which, historically, "the Tracts etc opposed."[16] To disarm further criticism, a few lines to this effect were included at the end of Note A from 1869 onward.[17] Frank Turner meets Newman's claim about the historical thrust of Note A with utter scepticism. Newman, he argues, intentionally modelled his eighteen theses on the condemnations in Pius XI's *Syllabus Errorum* and his encyclical *Quanta Cura*—both published the year before—so as at once to ingratiate himself with English ultramontanists (by aligning himself with the papal agenda) and to pacify liberal English Catholics (by downplaying the extremeness of the papal documents).[18] The historical value of the theses, therefore, is next to nothing. They witness only to Newman's concerns in 1865, not to his convictions in the 1830s. I cannot engage all the particulars of Turner's argument here, but observe that this reading of Note A fits his overall hermeneutic for the *Apologia* as Newman's creative rewriting of history for present-day purposes. It never seems to occur to Turner that Newman might have discerned, in the 1830s, the same cultural and religious tenets that Pius XI addressed in the 1860s. On the face of it, however, there is nothing unlikely in this latter scenario, and it gains plausibility when, by and by, we will return to Newman's theses. For now, it is enough to examine the first, which bears directly on the issue at hand: the young Newman's drift toward liberalism.

"No religious tenet is important," proposition 1 reads, "unless reason shows it to be so."[19] By itself, this is only a partial restatement of the general definition of liberalism, reiterating the idea that reason, or human judgment, can determine the value or importance of a doctrine, but Newman makes it more specific by means of a revealing illustration: "Therefore, e.g., the doctrine of the Athanasian Creed is not to be insisted on, unless it tends to convert the soul; and the doctrine of the Atonement is to be insisted on, if it does convert the soul."[20] This is so

---

16. JHN to Richard Holt Hutton, June 3, 1865, *LD* 21, 482.

17. See Turner, "Editor's Introduction," 75. Those lines read: "I need hardly say that the above Note is mainly historical. How far the Liberal party of 1830–40 really held the above eighteen Theses, which I attributed to them, and how far and in what sense I should oppose those Theses now, could scarcely be explained without a separate Dissertation" (*Apo.* [1875] 297).

18. Turner, "Editor's Introduction," 71–75.

19. *Hist.*, 294.

20. *Hist.*, 294.

curious a way to instance liberalism that it could not but have puzzled the *Apologia's* first readers. Those who regarded liberalism in a historical vein would have associated its manifestations in the 1830s with utilitarianism, or the Whig reforms of church and state, while those with a more contemporary focus would have thought of John Stuart Mill's *On Liberty* (1859) or the biblical criticism of *Essays and Reviews* (1860). Hardly anyone would have regarded an undue emphasis on conversion as a particularly liberal trait. And it makes no sense at all from Turner's vantage point. Whatever Pius IX condemned—and he condemned a lot—he was not concerned with those who valued doctrine for its power to convert. The reason this instance is so puzzling is that its conception of liberalism was neither contemporary, nor even properly historical. It was personal.

The idea of conversion—Newman's focus in this illustration—was as foreign to liberal discourse then as it is now. Instead, it puts us squarely within the evangelical frame of reference. If anything, it was evangelicalism that approached doctrine in general, and the atonement in particular, as geared toward conversion. Such an approach instances liberalism because, by valuing doctrine only insofar as it is conducive to conversion, it imposes a human rationale on what is beyond it: revealed truth. At no other time in the *Apologia* does Newman use an evangelical tenet to instance a liberal principle. The reason he does so here is personal. For a time, this liberal tendency had characterized his own evangelical theology, and writing Note A made him think of that time. If the illustration is confusing, therefore, it is not because he was writing for an audience, as Turner has it, but because he entirely forgot about his audience. And he forgot about it, because he was thinking of himself. Proposition 1 is the only theological tenet of liberalism he admits having given into, albeit "partly," and "before I began to publish."[21] Together with the illustration, this admission neatly delineates the content as well as the timeframe of Newman's liberal tendencies.

Before analysing these tendencies in detail, three preliminary remarks are in order. First, Newman's "drift toward liberalism" was precisely that: a drift. It was tending toward a position, not firmly taking one. Second, it was unintentional. Newman never aspired to be a liberal, nor did he know, at the time, that he was tending toward liberalism. Finally, it was one tendency among several. In apologetics, Newman adhered to the principle of dogma, while in theology, his drift toward liberalism was counteracted by the pull of High Church principles and doctrines. As a result, his religious thinking between 1824 and 1828, when his liberal inclinations were abruptly cut short,[22] was in a state of flux, marked by

21. *Hist.*, 296. He also admits to having given into the idea that, "The civil power has no positive duty, in a normal state of things, to maintain religious truth" (no. 12) and, "perhaps," the idea that "There is no such thing as a national or state conscience" (no. 11).

22. *Apo.*, 72.

stronger inner contradictions than at any time before or after. We see this tension in the sermons he preached at St Clement's, by far the most important source for gleaning his theological development in the mid-1820s. On the one hand, these sermons (especially the earlier ones) witness to his increasing systematization of the connection between doctrine and conversion, what he would later regard as a liberal tendency. On the other hand, these sermons (especially the later ones) witness to a loss of confidence in many aspects of evangelical theology, occasioned by his gradual acceptance of the doctrine of baptismal regeneration, what he would later regard as a High Church tendency. These lines of development were inversely proportionate. As his High Church inclinations waxed, his evangelicalism waned, along with its liberal propensities. But this is matter for the next chapter. First, we must consider the liberal modulations of Newman's early evangelical theology.

The Nature and Goal of Revelation

When Newman began to take duty at St Clement's in July 1824, he brought his evangelical theology to the pulpit. Recall that he regarded the atonement as the centerpiece of Christian theology and conversion as the defining aspect of Christian life. These two dimensions, the doctrinal and the experiential, were inseparable, since to be converted is, essentially, to believe in Christ's atoning sacrifice on the cross. Conversion is usually brought about by "the word of God and instruction," as Newman had it, that is, by preaching.[23] And given that "the sacrifice of Christ is uniformly held up in Scripture as the means of converting man from sin to holiness," his preaching, like that of most evangelicals, centered on the atonement.[24] Upon sending his first sermons to his mother, he explained: "I am aware they contain truths, which are unpalatable to the generality of mankind — but the doctrine of Christ crucified is the only spring of real virtue and piety, and the only foundation of peace and comfort."[25] The intrinsic relationship between conversion and the atonement was not just one theological conviction among others. It was the organizing principle for much of Newman's preaching at St Clement's.

From September 1824 to September 1825, Newman preached a tripartite course of sermons "treating of the scheme of Christian doctrine," of which

23. JHN, *Nature of Holiness*, BOA A.9.1.g., 2.

24. JHN, No. 29, "The effects on the mind of the doctrine of the Cross," October 31, 1824, *Serm.* 1, 269. "This hen is the grand and characteristic doctrine of our holy faith, an atonement for sin," he had argued a week before (No. 27, "The atonement of Christ," October 24, 1824, *Serm.* 1, 320). See Roderick Strange, *Newman and the Gospel of Christ* (Oxford: Oxford University Press, 1981), 96–97.

25. JHN to Mrs Newman, July 28, 1824, *LD* 1, 181.

about half is preserved.[26] Its structure paralleled, in all essentials, that of the *Collection*.[27] Its first part dealt with "the grand and peculiar doctrines of the gospel," which, as in 1821, were three: "our natural corruption," "the doctrine of the atonement of sin through Christ," and "the doctrine of sanctification through the Holy Spirit."[28] The second part dealt with faith, "by which those doctrines are received into the heart."[29] It delineated the nature of faith, and its various roles, as "the means of justification," "the root and principle of sanctification," and as "producing comfort, peace, joy, and assurance."[30] The third and final part of the course dealt with "the particular effects of faith on the heart and life," that is, its power to "purify us from sin, [and] excite us to good works."[31] After the *Collection*, this sermon course was Newman's second (and final) attempt to systematize his evangelical theology. Regarding both the doctrinal content of Christianity (fall, redemption, sanctification) and its application to the life of the believer (faith, gratitude, good works) it kept to the pattern of the *Collection*. But where the *Collection* conceptualized the relationship between the realms of doctrine and experience loosely and associatively, the sermon course offered a systematic account of the intrinsic connection between revelation and conversion.

This account was grounded in two convictions about the nature of revelation. First, Newman considered revelation as a *scheme*. He already spoke of the "Scheme of Salvation" in the *Collection*, but in his sermons at St Clement's, it became his preferred way of referring to revelation as a whole.[32] The term expresses the fact that revelation is a system whose parts all work together to achieve a certain end. It was precisely for this reason—to elucidate the "*scheme* of Christian doctrine"—that Newman preached his sermons as a series, so that his hearers might clearly "see the *connexion* existing between the parts of the system [of religion]."[33] Knowledge of this system is the particular privilege of Christian faith. Whereas the ancient

26. JHN, No. 103, "Holiness the end of the Gospel," September 4, 1825, *Serm.* 5, 292. Francis McGrath has titled the three parts as follows (*Serm.* 5, 447–48): 1. The Trinity and Man's Salvation (September–November 1824, nine sermons, four preserved); 2. On Faith (February–March 1825, six sermons, three preserved); 3. On Sins (June–September 1825, eleven sermons, eight preserved).

27. See pp. 28–30.

28. JHN, No. 103, "Holiness," *Serm.* 5, 292.

29. JHN, No. 103, "Holiness," *Serm.* 5, 292.

30. JHN, No. 103, "Holiness," *Serm.* 5, 292, 293.

31. JHN, No. 103, "Holiness," *Serm.* 5, 293, 292.

32. JHN, *Collection*, BOA A.9.1, 5. The expression, or one of its cognates, occurs in the following sermons at St Clement's: No. 14, *Serm.* 5, 61, 62, 66; No. 12, *Serm.* 2, 267; No. 17, *Serm.* 5, 93; No. 23; *Serm.* 5, 106; No 27, *Serm.* 1, 319; No. 29, *Serm.* 1, 269; No. 40, *Serm.* 2, 9; No. 46, *Serm.* 1, 327; No. 51, *Serm.* 1, 280; No. 57, *Serm.* 5, 174; No. 67, *Serm.* 5, 198; No. 90, *Serm.* 5, 253; No. 99, *Serm.* 5, 287; No. 103, *Serm.* 5, 292–95, 297; No. 104, *Serm.* 2, 343; No. 108, *Serm.* 5, 314; No. 110, *Serm.* 5, 332; No. 111, *Serm.* 5, 335, 336, 339; No. 123, *Serm.* 2, 384, 387. It occurs in Newman's preaching until at least 1829, but with decreasing regularity.

33. JHN, No. 17, "Character of God and His holy law," September 12, 1824, *Serm.* 5, 93.

Israelites only had a "dim and distant view of the scheme of restoration," Christian faith "invests the scheme of providence with the Sun's universal light — we now see it as a whole — and discover the bearings and tendencies of many parts before unknown."[34] The content of revelation, then, should be viewed as a system, not as a set of individual propositions, and knowledge of this system is faith. Now this system has a *goal*: it is a "scheme of salvation," of "redemption," of "restoration," and this is the second fundamental aspect of Newman's idea of revelation.[35]

For the evangelical Newman, revelation had a specific teleology, which was explicated in the final sermon of his course, *Holiness the end of the Gospel*. Revelation, as the title indicates, is a means to an end, from which the entirety of revelation derives its meaning. This *"end* of the gospel," Newman maintained, "is to make us *holy*." God's "distinguishing attribute" is holiness, "and as He is holy, so are we to be holy."[36] Because God is holy, he wants to make us holy. Since we are not, he has done certain things so that we may be. Thus, "the Christian scheme of salvation is a *remedy*. . . . It presupposes a falling away, and is intended to effect a *recovery*."[37] Conversion, in short, is the goal of revelation; it is what the revealed system was intended to effect. Recall that the evangelical Newman regarded the "heart and affections" as the locus of conversion. If conversion is a change, what changes, first and foremost, is people's desires and emotions. This change is necessary because, of ourselves, we simply do not want to be religious. For the "natural man," religion "is in itself distasteful and bitter," Newman argued in the first sermon he ever wrote.[38] God, therefore, intervenes in people's lives to overturn "the natural enmity of their hearts towards godliness, and the downward and earthly tendency of their affections."[39]

The means by which God does so, is the gospel message. The *Collection* already portrayed the doctrine of the atonement as the means *par excellence* to redirect people's emotions and desires:

> His [Christ's] purity inspires terror at our transgressions, His love fills us with shame at them — self-abasement & gratitude follow — and the soul released from the spirit of fear & the penalties of the law begins to pant after a resemblance of its Redeemer's Holiness.[40]

---

34. JHN, No. 108, "On the *principles* common to all revelation," September 25, 1825, *Serm.* 5, 314; No. 57, "Nature and object of faith," February 20, 1825, *Serm.* 5, 174. See No. 99, "The Christian promise not temporal," August 14, 1825, *Serm.* 5, 287.

35. JHN, No. 14, "Illumination," August 22, 1824, *Serm.* 5, 61; No. 108, "On the *principles*," *Serm.* 5, 314

36. JHN, No. 103, "Holiness," *Serm.* 5, 293. See also, for example, No. 29, "The effects," *Serm.* 5, 269; No. 33, "Office of the Holy Spirit in renewing our nature," November 14, 1824, *Serm.* 5, 133; No. 123, "On the internal evidence of the evangelical doctrine," December 11, 1825, *Serm.* 2, 385.

37. JHN, No. 103, "Holiness," *Serm.* 5, 294.

38. JHN, No. 1, "The work of man," June 27, 1824, *Serm.* 5, 20.

39. JHN, No. 1, "The work of man," *Serm.* 5, 21.

40. JHN, *Collection*, BOA A.9.1.c.3, 13, 14.

It argued, moreover, that "the covenant of grace was <u>calculated</u> to effect" these feelings and longings.[41] God intended revelation to change people's emotions and desires, and that is why he chose to reveal himself the way he did. This fundamental principle, that revelation is a means to an end, is only hinted at in Newman's earlier papers, but it becomes the ground of his systematic exposition of the relation between doctrine and experience in his sermons at St Clement's. The propositional expression of revelation (doctrine) is related to the concrete life of the believer (experience) *because* revelation is a means to an end: it is given *so that* people's lives might be changed. On such a model, it is the burden of theology to explicate the relationship between revelation and experience, that is, explain *how* doctrine brings about conversion. And this is precisely what Newman did in his sermon course.

Faith, Conversion, and the Atonement

In *Holiness the end of the Gospel*, Newman recapitulated the account of the relationship between doctrine and conversion he had offered in the previous sermons:

> *Man* is in a peculiar state — a peculiar provision has been made for our sanctification, which would not have been necessary were we not radically unclean in heart and affections — This provision is the death of Christ, which, while it atones for our sins, and obtains for us the gift of the Spirit has also a natural tendency to create corresponding feelings in our minds, and under the grace of the same Spirit actually does make an impression on us. — The doctrines concerning the Son and Spirit of God being received by faith, have a sanctifying power — The Gospel displays the glorious excellences of God — faith conveys this display to the soul and creates in it an intimation of those excellencies. — The holiness and love of God as seen in Christ create in us holiness and love towards God.[42]

The basic elements of the evangelical scheme of salvation described here (corruption, redemption, faith, sanctification) are by now familiar. What matters is how Newman construes their relations. Besides its objective component (settling the claims of God's justice upon us), the atonement has a communicative purpose. It is a "display" of God's attributes—"holiness and love"—which creates a particular "impression" as well as certain "feelings" in the subject. It does so through faith, which grasps the "display" that God provides of himself in revelation, and "creates" a desire in the subject to emulate what she sees. Faith, then, is the point at which the objective reality of doctrine and the subjective reality of conversion

---

41. JHN, *Collection*, BOA A.9.1.c.3, 14.
42. JHN, No. 103, "Holiness," *Serm.* 5, 294.

intersect. Newman summed up the idea in an earlier sermon of the course: "The *object* of faith is the *holiness* and *mercy* of God — faith is the *channel*, through which this object operates upon the heart."[43]

Newman's understanding of faith and revelation was heavily indebted to the work of the Church of Scotland theologian Thomas Erskine of Linlathen (1788–1870), an evangelical of growing renown in the early 1820s.[44] "I knew, when young, Mr. Erskine's first publications well," Newman recollected late in life, "I thought them able and persuasive."[45] Judging by his sermons, he found them persuasive, indeed. Erskine's earliest books, *Remarks on the Internal Evidence for the Truth of Revealed Religion* (1820) and *An Essay on Faith* (1822) presented a theory of revelation and conversion that provided, in outline, the systematic framework for Newman's own theory.[46] Like Newman, Erskine attributed a distinct teleology to revelation: "the intention of the Gospel . . . is to renew the character of man after the likeness of God. It is to give happiness and holiness to the human heart."[47] "And this intention is accomplished," he continued, "by the revelation of the character of God in the work of redemption."[48] For Newman and Erskine, revelation achieves this end "because the objects which are revealed to us for our belief, have a natural tendency to produce a most important and blessed change on our happiness and our characters"—this is why they are revealed in the first place.[49] Erskine's key metaphors to describe the mode of revelation—"manifestation," "impression," "exhibition"—are, like Newman's, drawn from the realm of visual communication, and their object is God's character, as displayed primarily in the atonement. There, Christ "exhibited, in suffering and in death, that combination of holiness and mercy, which, if believed, must excite love, and if

43. JHN, No. 59, "Nature and object of faith," February 27, 1825, *Serm.* 5, 177. Only the abstract of this sermon survives.

44. Nicholas R. Needham, *Thomas Erskine of Linlathen: His Life and Theology* (Edinburgh: Rutherford House Books, 1990); Trevor A. Hart, *The Teaching Father: An Introduction to the Theology of Thomas Erskine of Linlathen* (Edinburgh: Saint Andrew Press, 1993); and Don Horrocks, *Laws of the Spiritual Order: Innovation and Reconstruction in the Soteriology of Thomas Erskine of Linlathen* (Carlisle: Paternoster Press, 2004).

45. JHN to George T. Edwards, January 2, 1883, *LD* 30, 168–69. See Strange, *Newman and the Gospel of Christ*, 98–99. Several of Newman's sermons at St Clement's contain explicit references to Erskine: No. 29, *Serm.* 1, 268ff; No. 123, *Serm.* 2, 381ff; No. 57, *Serm.* 5, 165ff; *Serm.* 1, 268n1; *Serm.* 2, 381n1. In the autumn of 1825, he recommended Erskine to his best friend John William Bowden ("October 30, 1825," *AW*, 207).

46. The Birmingham Oratory Library contains both works bound into a single volume, annotated by Newman: *Remarks on the Internal Evidence for the Truth of Revealed Religion*, 5th ed. (Edinburgh: Waugh & Innes, 1821) and *An Essay on Faith*, 2nd ed. (Edinburgh: Waugh & Innes, 1822). Newman delved into these works in "1823 or 1824" (JHN to George T. Edwards, January 2, 1883, *LD* 30, 169).

47. Erskine, *An Essay on Faith*, 43.

48. Erskine, *An Essay on Faith*, 43.

49. Erskine, *An Essay on Faith*, 89; see also 101: "The moral effects of it [the Gospel] on the character constitute the great reason of its being urged on our belief."

loved, must produce resemblance."[50] For Erskine, too, faith is where object (God) and subject (the believer) intersect. Accordingly, we need an analysis of the mechanics of faith—for lack of a better term—to understand how doctrine effects conversion.

The Structure of Faith

In a February 1825 sermon on the "nature and object of faith," Newman stressed the pivotal role of faith in Christianity's conceptual framework: "if we obtain clear and accurate notions on this point, we shall find the other parts of the Christian system fall, as it were, into their natural places."[51] In a first section of the sermon, Newman defined faith as reliance on testimony. Faith is *"knowing through a medium — knowing through another —* To have faith concerning a thing, is to feel convinced of it from reliance on something else which gives the information."[52] This formal definition of faith as a species of cognition applies to everyday forms of belief as well as to religious belief. The only difference is its object, which, in the latter case, transcends the realm of sense. Newman, therefore, defined religious faith as "being impressed with the reality of unseen things from confidence in the person who tells us of them."[53] This definition sounds classical, but its phraseology betrays Erskine's influence. Although Erskine subscribed to the Enlightenment understanding of faith as "assent to the truth of Divine testimony," he argued that this was to say very little about it. What determines the nature of faith in the individual is what it is about. "An assent cannot be given to anything without receiving an impression corresponding to it in all respects," Erskine maintained, "for the meaning of belief is just the impression made on the mind by the object presented to it."[54] Erskine means that every belief has some intelligible content— it is *about* something—and this content gives faith its import in concrete cases. In a theological (and not in an apologetic) context, this was Newman's line, too. When belief in the truth of revelation is at stake—in apologetics, that is—he regarded faith simply as an assent to testimony, based on evidence for its reliability, not on its content. But in the realm of theology, faith is determined by its content, because apprehending the right kind of content creates the right kind of believer.

Newman maintained that genuine faith has three dimensions: the cognitive (or apprehensive), the affective, and the practical. These three dimensions are causally connected: faith is practical *because* it is affective, and it is affective *because* it is apprehensive. First, faith is necessarily *"practical,"* that is, it results in practice

---

50. Erskine, *Remarks on the Internal Evidence*, 62.
51. JHN, No. 57, "Nature and object," *Serm.* 5, 165.
52. JHN, No. 57, "Nature and object," *Serm.* 5, 166.
53. JHN, No. 57, "Nature and object," *Serm.* 5, 169.
54. Erskine, *An Essay on Faith*, 128–29, see also 44.

"wherever the object admits of practice."[55] This is one condition of a person having faith—that she act on it—and it implies a second, as its ground. If faith is "evidenced by action," Newman argued, "it must be necessarily connected with the heart."[56] Since every action is performed for some kind of motive, and "every motive has reference to some passion," faith always involves emotion and desire.[57] The active dimension of faith, in other words, is premised on its affective dimension: "faith only leads to practice *by* affecting the heart."[58] To use Newman's own example: if someone tells you your house is on fire, the "alarm and terror" you feel will make you drop whatever you are doing to check up on the situation.[59]

It is clear from this instance that affect, in turn, depends on apprehension: to feel and act in this way, you must know what it *means* for a house to be on fire. Faith produces its desired emotional and practical effects only if its content is understood. To use another of Newman's examples: if I am told that I can attain a spiritual benefit, like "holy joy," I will not merely for that reason desire it, because "I do not know what a holy joy *means* — worldly joy I understand too well, but the other I do not understand and therefore cannot be said to believe in it." As a result, "I make no effort to attain it, not because I do not like it, but more properly because I do not even understand it."[60]

Once again, Newman echoes Erskine, whose early work focused on the causal relationship between understanding, on the one hand, and emotions and practice, on the other. Erskine stressed the primacy of understanding within the causal structure of faith. "I may understand many things which I do not believe," Erskine argued, "but I cannot believe any thing which I do not understand."[61]

> A man may with great propriety say, I understand the Cartesian system of vortices, though I don't believe in it. But it is absolutely impossible for him to believe in that system without knowing what it is. . . . Now there is a meaning in the Gospel, and there is declared in it the system of God's dealings with men. This meaning, and this system, must be understood, before we can believe the Gospel.[62]

Once the Gospel is understood, it can be believed, and then "the effect on the character necessarily follows."[63] Conversely, if faith has no effects on the "heart

---

55. JHN, No. 57, "Nature and object," *Serm.* 5, 167.
56. JHN, No. 57, "Nature and object," *Serm.* 5, 167.
57. JHN, No. 57, "Nature and object," *Serm.* 5, 168, 167.
58. JHN, No. 57, "Nature and object," *Serm.* 5, 171–72.
59. JHN, No. 57, "Nature and object," *Serm.* 5, 167.
60. JHN, No. 57, "Nature and object," *Serm.* 5, 168.
61. Erskine, *An Essay on Faith*, 28.
62. Erskine, *An Essay on Faith*, 28–29.
63. Erskine, *Remarks on the Internal Evidence*, 57–58.

and conduct," this must result from misapprehending its content.[64] Like Erskine, Newman argued that once "the main object of religious faith"—God's holiness—is believed and apprehended, it "necessarily produces very important effects upon the mind."[65] No one can "really believe in, i.e. feel and be imprest [*sic*] by, the holiness of God and His law, without being filled with pain and (as it were) disgust at the continual defilement of his thoughts words and actions." Conversely, "the man who feels no such distress at himself at all, does not at all believe or feel that first article of revealed religion, the existence of a holy and spiritual God."[66] Feeling, in turn, gives rise to action: "in the very same proportion in which he feels that God is a God of holiness, so will he strive and labour . . . to purify himself as God is pure."[67]

Although Newman's presentation of the causal relationship between understanding, emotion, and practice mirrors that of Erskine, he is less emphatic about the primacy of understanding. His jumbling of terms that are technically distinct in Erskine—to "believe in" God's holiness is to "feel" it and to be "impressed by" it—seems to make belief, feeling, and understanding coterminous in practice, albeit distinct in theory. But his treatment of defective modes of faith shows that apprehension is still paramount. First, Newman pinpoints people whose faith constitutes neither an "impression upon the heart" nor an "influence on the conduct"—it is neither "*warm*" nor "*practical*."[68] Such faith is mere profession, because God's "character really understood and believed in, must affect at once the heart and conduct."[69] The absence of the affective and practical dimension of faith, in other words, is due to a lack of understanding. Second, there are "those who seem to evidence their faith by *practice*, without having their heart affected by it."[70] This, too, is a sham form of faith, because "unless their heart is right with God, they *cannot* in reality be leading a Christian and holy life."[71] Again, this follows from Newman's theoretical framework. If faith leads to practice only *through* the affections, there can be no genuine Christian practice without corresponding affections. But if someone does not have such affections, she cannot have "faith in the right object," that is, she must have misunderstood what faith is about.[72] Finally, there are "those who *seem* to have their hearts affected without their conduct being influenced."[73] This case is the obverse of the former. Since the right

64. Erskine, *An Essay on Faith*, 81.
65. JHN, No. 57, "Nature and object," *Serm.* 5, 169.
66. JHN, No. 57, "Nature and object," *Serm.* 5, 169.
67. JHN, No. 57, "Nature and object," *Serm.* 5, 170.
68. JHN, No. 57, "Nature and object," *Serm.* 5, 170.
69. JHN, No. 57, "Nature and object," *Serm.* 5, 171.
70. JHN, No. 57, "Nature and object," *Serm.* 5, 171.
71. JHN, No. 57, "Nature and object," *Serm.* 5, 172.
72. JHN, No. 57, "Nature and object," *Serm.* 5, 172.
73. JHN, No. 57, "Nature and object," *Serm.* 5, 173.

kind of affections issue in the right kind of action, the only conclusion can be that their affections are misguided. Proper affections depend on a proper apprehension of the object of faith, and thus the mistake at play here is that "such people understand little of the *holiness* of God and have little acquaintance with the corruption of their own hearts."[74] In all three cases, in short, defective faith is caused by a lack of understanding.

Newman had already emphasized the primacy of understanding in the first sermon he ever preached (at Over Worton, the parish of his former teacher Walter Mayers). It described three gifts by which the Holy Spirit renews the mind: "*illumination, sanctification,* [and] *comfort,*" and argued that the latter gifts depend upon the former.[75] "We cannot be holy or at peace," Newman insisted, "unless our minds are first enlightened with heavenly knowledge."[76] Thus, "sanctification and peace of mind both depend on knowledge."[77] He still retained this idea a year and half later. It is only by the "knowledge" of Christ, he argued in a sermon of December 1825, that "the heart is raised to love Him and renewed in holiness." Such knowledge "is the ground of joy peace and comfort, and the very principle and root of holiness in heart and life."[78] Faith, then, as a comprehensive disposition embodying cognition, emotion, and practice, is ultimately determined by what it understands of its object. This object produces a certain intelligible content in the mind—an "impression," as Newman and Erskine called it—that elicits an affective response, which, in turn, leads to practice.[79] That much is clear now. What remains to be seen is what this "impression" is, and how it functions concretely.

The Object of Faith

For the evangelical Newman, the object of faith was twofold, comprising God's holiness and mercy. Revelation presents us with that object by being, as Erskine put it, a "manifestation" of God's character.[80] This concept of manifestation, and the cognate ideas of "display," "exhibition," and the like, denote a perspicuity, on the part of revelation, that corresponds to the understanding required for real faith. If faith is based on understanding, revelation must be perspicuous. If not, revelation's inner teleology—"God operating on the characters of men through a manifestation of his own character"—would miscarry.[81] The atonement

---

74. JHN, No. 57, "Nature and object," *Serm.* 5, 173.
75. JHN, No. 2, "Waiting on God," June 23, 1824, *Serm.* 5, 6.
76. JHN, No. 2, "Waiting on God," *Serm.* 5, 10.
77. JHN, No. 2, "Waiting on God," *Serm.* 5, 10.
78. JHN, No. 123, "On the internal evidence," *Serm.* 2, 386.
79. Erskine, *An Essay on Faith,* 44.
80. Erskine, *An Essay on Faith,* 55–56.
81. Erskine, *Remarks on the Internal Evidence,* 12. See also *An Essay on Faith,* 48.

is the ultimate manifestation of God's character: the "blood of the atonement,"
Erskine noted, is "a channel which displays all the perfections of God."[82]
Newman likewise asserted: "Redemption is . . . the great manifestation of the
divine character."[83] Or as he put it in a sermon of December 1825: "the sacrifice
of Christ for us is . . . a declaration, a manifestation of the glorious character of
God — to make known unto us the divine excellence and impress upon us an
admiration and affection towards it."[84] Newman developed this theme in several
sermons, but most elaborately so in *The effects on the mind of the doctrine of the Cross*,
the seventh of his course. Like Erskine, he argued that it was for these "effects"
that Christ's sacrifice was made known to us, since we could still have been "saved
by His merits," even "without our being informed of the fact."[85] If God had
merely wanted to "pardon us," he commented in a later sermon, "there would
have been no need of revealing to us the sacrifice of Christ."[86] But "the great
excellence of the doctrine of Christ crucified" is that, "while it reconciles our
offended creator to us, it has a powerful tendency to draw us to God."[87]

In the atonement, the two central aspects of the divine character—"love and
holiness"—are "manifested" and harmonized in a unique way.[88] Half-paraphras-
ing and half-citing Erskine, Newman explained the idea as follows:

> The sacrifice of Christ has connected sin with the blood of a benefactor,
> and obedience with the last request of a friend expiring in tortures for us.
> — Thus God is justified, as a lawgiver, in dispensing mercy to the guilty —
> a pledge is given us of the sincerity and reality of that mercy, and the divine
> character is made at once the object of our esteem and of our gratitude. We
> are taught by the cross of Christ that it forms no part of the Almighty's
> scheme of forgiveness to break the eternal connexion which must exist
> between sin and misery — yet on the other hand we learn His infinite love
> which extends its invitations and entreaties of reconciliation as wide as the
> ravages of sin.[89]

The atonement, then, shows that God remains pure and holy. He wants to have
nothing to do with sin, which continues to merit only death. But the atonement

<hr>

82. Erskine, *An Essay on Faith*, 88.

83. JHN, No. 12, "Illumination," August 22, 1824, *Serm.* 5, 61.

84. JHN, No. 123, "On the internal evidence," *Serm.* 2, 384; see also 383; No. 29, "The effects,"
Serm. 5, 272: "The sacrifice of His Son is in itself a most stupendous and affecting display of the
excellencies of the divine character."

85. JHN, No. 29, "The effects," *Serm.* 5, 269.

86. JHN, No. 123, "On the internal evidence," *Serm.* 2, 385–86.

87. JHN, No. 29, "The effects," *Serm.* 5, 273.

88. JHN, No. 29, "The effects," *Serm.* 5, 272.

89. JHN, No. 29, "The effects," *Serm.* 5, 273; Erskine, *Remarks on the Internal Evidence*, 73–75.
See also JHN, No. 123, "On the internal evidence," *Serm.* 2, 384–85.

also demonstrates God's love, because he takes that death upon himself. This manifestation of God's character, in turn, produces the affections required of the true believer; it causes "a mighty revolution and change of feeling."[90] While it convinces us of "our extreme guiltiness"—since our sin required God's "only Son to suffer and die for us"—it also imparts "the assurance of reconciliation," because our claim to God's mercy is securely grounded on Christ's sacrifice.[91] Accordingly, "we are excited and touched by His love, while we are awed and humbled and spiritualized by His holiness."[92] The first affect, gratitude for the atonement, is what leads people to engage in good works. "It is this wonderful display of love," Newman argued in another sermon, "which incites the believer . . . to activity in well doing."[93] The second affect, awareness of sin, makes us realize our dependence on Christ whatever good we do. "Gratitude," in sum "makes us active, consciousness of sin keeps us humble — and both gratitude and sense of sin lead us to stake all upon the merits of Jesus Christ."[94]

Newman's systematic account of the relation between the atonement and conversion can be summed up as follows: God intends revelation to change people's lives; revelation does so by means of the doctrine of the atonement, which, if understood and believed, radically alters people's affections, and thereby leads to good works. In outline, though not in detail and emphasis, this account is the same as Erskine's. Its causal sequence hinges on the presence of faith, in its restricted sense of assent to something understood. If faith is there, the mechanism works: God's intention is realized, and people's lives are changed. If faith is not there, the mechanism fails. Where the doctrine of the atonement is not received, there can be no conversion. Note that Newman's systematization of his evangelical theology is precisely that, a systematization. His convictions are the same as in his earlier texts, but they are conceptually and causally related in an orderly manner, so that they now form parts of a system. It should be clear, by now, that this account does exactly what the *Apologia* sought to forbid, namely, "insist on the doctrine of the atonement because it converts the soul." This is not yet to evaluate it, nor to brand it liberal. For now, it is a mere observance of fact, because we need to consider a second aspect of Note A's illustration of liberalism before we can assess the tendency of Newman's evangelical understanding of doctrine.

The obvious negative corollary to the positive insistence on some doctrines because they effect conversion is the disregard for other doctrines that have no

90. JHN, No. 57, "Nature and object," *Serm.* 5, 171.
91. JHN, No. 19, "The corruption of human nature," September 19, 1824, *Serm.* 2, 314; No. 29, "The effects," *Serm.* 5, 270. See also No. 4, "The wounded spirit," July 25, 1824, *Serm.* 5, 39–40; No. 27, "the atonement of Christ," October 24, 1824, *Serm.* 2, 320.
92. JHN, No. 29, "The effects," *Serm.* 5, 273.
93. JHN, No. 20, "Parable of the Good Samaritan," September 12, 1824, *Serm.* 5, 103.
94. JHN, No. 29, "The effects," *Serm.* 5, 274.

such tendency. The instance Newman offered in the *Apologia* was the doctrine of the Athanasian Creed. This is a significant example, because compared to the other creeds sanctioned by the Thirty-Nine Articles (the Nicene and the Apostles' Creed), the Athanasian Creed stands out for its extensive delineation of the immanent Trinity and the relation between Christ's divine and human natures. It is easy to see how its doctrines would seem arid and speculative to an evangelical concerned with converting people. Compared to the drama of Christ's sacrifice, there is little to stir our emotions in the assertion that we should not be "confounding the Persons, nor dividing the Substance" or that the Spirit is "neither made, nor created, nor begotten, but proceeding." Accordingly, it cannot come as a surprise that this negative part of Newman's illustration in the *Apologia* was as biographically laden as its positive corollary, the insistence on the atonement.

Trinitarian Doctrine

We saw in the first chapter that Newman's teenage conversion issued in a vivid perception of the importance of dogma. Proving the several clauses of the Athanasian Creed from scripture was one shape this conviction took. There can be no question that Newman affirmed the content of the Athanasian Creed. But despite his belief in its truth, reflections on the immanent Trinity (the Godhead as it is in itself) did not suit his scriptural mode of theologizing. As an evangelical, he always treated the Trinity from an economic perspective (the Godhead as seen to operate in salvation history). Already as a teenager, he understood the distinctions in the Godhead within the framework of the "scheme of redemption."[95] In the *Collection*, his account of the Trinity became even more emphatically economic. Instead of treating it as a substantive doctrine in its own right, in the manner of the Athanasian Creed, he derived both the content and the function of Trinitarian doctrine from the exigencies of the scheme of salvation. Within the drama of redemption,

> He [Christ] revealed the three Persons of the Divine Essence . . . in a relative situation and aspect. The Father was the God against whom man sinned, the Son was the God who was to satisfy the justice of the Father & fulfil the obedience of the elect, the Spirit was the God who was to call, regenerate & sanctify these vessels of mercy prepared afore unto glory. Thus in a <u>relative</u> and <u>covenanted</u> sense, the Father was to <u>send</u> the Son, and the Father & Son the Spirit, and the Son & the Spirit to be <u>sent</u>.[96]

95. JHN, *Trinitas or Humanitas*, BOA A.9.1.b. The conjectural date of 1817, suggested by one of the Birmingham Oratory's former archivists, is confirmed by comparison with a manuscript titled *Athanasian Creed* and dated 1817 by Newman himself (BOA A.9.1.b), which was preparatory to this text.

96. JHN, *Collection*, BOA A.9.1, 12.

Two things are of note in this passage. First, it portrays the distinctions between the persons in the Godhead as relative, that is, relative to us and relative to the scheme of salvation. Revelation does not unveil the distinction of persons in the Godhead in an absolute sense but within revelation's redemptive teleology, that is, as it relates to us. Secondly, its distinction between the persons in the Godhead is functional; it is based on their respective roles in the scheme of salvation. The Father takes on the role of offended justice, the Son of satisfying its claims, the Spirit of applying to individuals the ensuing benefits. Newman soon abandoned this rather crude mode of ascribing contrasting attributes to Father and Son, which almost suggests a conflict of interest within the Godhead, but his understanding of the distinctions in the Trinity as relative and functional continued to characterize his theology.[97]

This tendency was only reinforced by his reading of Erskine two or three years later. In the *Remarks*, Erskine had challenged the value of abstract presentations of Trinitarian doctrine from the vantage point of the teleology of revelation. In the creeds, Erskine argued, the doctrine of the Trinity "is stated by itself, divested of all its Scriptural accompaniments; and is made to bear simply on the nature of the Divine essence, and the mysterious fact of the existence of Three in One."[98] Such an abstract presentation is misguided, because the simple fact of a Trinity, "taken by itself, cannot in the smallest degree tend to develop the Divine character, and therefore cannot make any moral impression on our minds," which is the goal of revelation. Scripture, by contrast, makes Trinitarian doctrine "subservient to the manifestation of the moral character of God," that is, to his "combined justice and mercy in the redemption of sinners."[99] Conceived in this salvation-historical way, the doctrine does "produce a moral effect upon our characters," which "the abstract fact that there is a plurality in the unity of the Godhead" never could.[100] Newman, too, subordinated Trinitarian doctrine to the conversionist teleology of revelation, and for the same reason.

In his Trinity Sunday sermon for 1825, he criticized those who consider "the mystery of the Trinity a bare abstract naked uninteresting dogma, which is to be believed indeed, but has no connexion with purity of life and comfort of heart."[101] Their mistake results from a misapprehension of the nature of doctrine:

97. In his first ever sermon on the Trinity, of which only the abstract is preserved, Newman subsumed the entire work of salvation under the love of the one God, thus skirting oppositional descriptions of Father and Son. Trinitarian doctrine, however, continued to be derived from the "scheme of salvation": "The two grand doctrines of justification and sanctification reveal the second and third Persons of the Trinity" (JHN, No. 23, "The Trinity displayed in the gospel scheme of salvation," October 10, 1824, *Serm.* 5, 106).

98. Erskine, *Remarks on the Internal Evidence*, 95.

99. Erskine, *Remarks on the Internal Evidence*, 95.

100. Erskine, *Remarks on the Internal Evidence*, 97, 96.

101. JHN, No. 81, "On the Trinity," May 29, 1825, *Serm.* 3, 283.

> It is almost a fundamental truth in religion, that all doctrines are *practical*, all
> have a reference to our moral state. The end of the gospel, is *holiness* — and
> the doctrines are to be received by faith, *in order to* make us humble, grateful,
> obedient, submissive, heavenly minded, pure in heart. — Indeed could an
> article of faith be proved to have *no* tendency directly or indirectly to sanctify
> the soul, I confess it would be a more plausible objection to the truth of
> that doctrine than almost any other.[102]

This is probably Newman's most emphatic assertion of the principle that the
exclusive aim of revelation is conversion.[103] The affective and practical import of
a doctrine is no longer just a measure of its value but a criterion of its truth. This
idea jars with many of his other convictions, and we will return to it at the end
of the chapter. For now, it is enough to note the practical bent of his approach
to the Trinity. It is not just that Trinitarian distinctions derive their meaning from
the scheme of salvation (as in the *Collection*), they also need to serve a practical
purpose. This practical take on the Trinity was not derived just from Erskine but
also drew on the theology of his mentor at Oriel, Richard Whately (1787–1863).

Whately on Revelation

When Newman became a fellow of Oriel in April 1822, he found it hard to
adapt to his new social circle. He was extremely shy and frightfully self-conscious
about his social deportment. His evangelical convictions isolated him even further,
because none of the other fellows shared them.[104] His senior colleagues, however,
were determined to make something of a youth whose remarkable potential they
had discerned during his fellowship examinations, and they put it to Whately to
draw Newman out. Genial, boisterous, and loquacious, Whately liked to hammer
out his ideas in spirited argument with his protégées, and Newman was a willing,
able, and welcome anvil.[105] The period of their initial acquaintance was brief—
Whately accepted a living in Halesworth in August 1822—but productive. Whately
asked Newman to turn his manuscript dialogues *On Reasoning* into a regular treatise,
which appeared shortly afterwards as the entry *Logic* in the *Encyclopaedia Metropolitana*.[106] At Halesworth, Whately remembered Newman and arranged for him to

---

102. JHN, No. 81, "On the Trinity," *Serm.* 3, 283.

103. Erskine, *Remarks on the Internal Evidence*, 59; *An Essay on Faith*, 105.

104. JHN, "Autobiographical Memoir," *AW*, 65–66. This section incorporates material from
my "Richard Whately" in *The Oxford Handbook of John Henry Newman*, ed. Frederick D. Aquino and
Benjamin J. King (Oxford: Oxford University Press, 2018), 196–216, reproduced with permission.
DOI: 10.1093/oxfordhb/9780198718284.013.10.

105. JHN, "Autobiographical Memoir," *AW*, 66–67.

106. JHN, "Autobiographical Memoir," *AW*, 67; Richard Whately, *On Reasoning*, BOA A.6.21;
Gillian R. Evans, "'An organon more delicate, versatile, and elastic': John Henry Newman and
Whately's *Logic*," *Downside Review* 97 (1979): 177–86; Culler, *The Imperial Intellect*, 38–42.

contribute a piece on Cicero to the *Metropolitana*. Because the editor, Edward Smedley, liked it, he invited Newman to write an entry on Apollonius of Tyana and the question of miracles.[107] When Whately returned to Oxford as principal of St Alban Hall, in 1825, he made Newman his vice-principal. For a year, Newman was Whately's jack of all trades, acting as "Tutor, Chaplain, Bursar, and Dean" in a hall that had sunk into disarray under previous heads.[108] When Newman relinquished the position in February 1826, upon becoming tutor of Oriel, both regretted the parting. From 1822 to 1826, then, Newman was under Whately's theological influence, for whose exercise there was ample opportunity given Whately's habit of talking incessantly.[109] When Whately later maintained that they had "consulted together . . . about almost all the principal points in my publications," this meant little more than that he had spoken while Newman listened.[110] It did ensure, however, that Newman acquired a solid grasp of Whately's thought.

It is, perhaps, surprising that the views of an Oxford don like Whately and an Edinburgh evangelical like Erskine should converge, and in many respects, they did not. But in the one respect that they did, they shaped young Newman's thought. Like Erskine, Whately was strongly convinced of the practical purpose of revelation. Revelation is given, Whately argued in his 1822 Bampton Lectures, "not for the increase of our speculative knowledge, but . . . in order to our serving God, and conforming our lives to his commands."[111] In an 1825 essay devoted entirely to this conviction, he maintained that revelation is of an "exclusively *practical* character"; it reveals what "concerns us practically to know, with a view to the regulation of the heart and conduct," and nothing more.[112] For both Whately and Erskine, this practical take on revelation served as a test for the proper interpretation of doctrine. "The most *practical* interpretation of each doctrine that can fairly be adopted is ever likely to be the truest," Whately argued. Accordingly, he laid it down as "an important general rule," that

> if the other reasons be equal, or nearly equal, in favour of two different interpretations of any doctrine, one of which represents it as a mere speculative point of faith, and the other as having some tendency to influence the heart or conduct, this latter is to be adopted, as the more conformable to the general plan of revelation.[113]

---

107. See pp. 171–77.

108. JHN, "Autobiographical Memoir," *AW*, 69. See Culler, *The Imperial Intellect*, 47–48.

109. JHN, "Autobiographical Memoir," *AW*, 69.

110. Richard Whately to JHN, November 3, 1834, *LD* 4, 356.

111. Richard Whately, *The Use and Abuse of Party-Feeling in Matters of Religion* (Oxford: J. Parker, 1822), 182.

112. Richard Whately, *Essays on Some of the Peculiarities of the Christian Religion* (Oxford/London: John Murray, 1825), 184, 195; see also, for example, 196, 199, 206.

113. Whately, *Peculiarities of the Christian Religion*, 218–19.

Erskine proposed a similar "test" by which to evaluate doctrines: "Are they good and profitable in their influence on the heart and conduct?" If not, "we may be assured that we have mistaken the doctrine."[114] Newman, as we have seen, formulated the same rule even more strictly in his sermon on the Trinity. Of course, Whately's concrete conception of the practical goal of revelation differed from that of Erskine and Newman. Whately was no evangelical and would have frowned upon their understanding of conversion and its relation to the atonement. Besides, Whately's understanding of the teleology of revelation was grounded on a philosophical as well as a theological rationale.

In addition to specifying the goal of revelation, Whately developed a theory about the nature of revelation. If there is one unifying thread in his early work, it is this. Time and again, he insisted that God is not "revealed to us as He is in Himself, but as He is relatively to ourselves."[115] This conviction dovetailed with the idea that the goal of revelation is practical. All we need to know, for practical purposes, is how God relates to us, not what his own mode of being is. Despite its apparent simplicity, this idea of the relative nature of revelation was rooted in a philosophical theory that was, for its time, quite subtle. Its groundwork had been laid by Whately's mentor, Edward Copleston (1776–1849), the provost of Oriel College, who gleaned it, in turn, from a near-forgotten work of the theologian William King (1650–1729). The theory earned Oriel an accolade from the *Edinburgh Review* (which was otherwise not so friendly to Oxford) as being "at present the school of Speculative Philosophy in England"—a commendation eagerly cited by Newman when he informed his father that he was elected fellow.[116] Although speculation was, ironically enough, what Copleston and Whately sought to avoid, the epithet was not ill-chosen. Quite some speculative philosophy was involved in their rejection of the speculative dimension of revelation.

In 1821, Copleston published his *Enquiry into the Doctrines of Necessity and Predestination*, part of which attacked Calvinist theories of divine foreknowledge and predestination by means of a distinct theory of analogical predication. Copleston argued, uncontroversially, that since we have no direct means of perceiving God, our knowledge of him can only be derived from his operations as displayed in nature and in scripture. On this basis, we ascribe properties to God, such as wisdom or power.[117] What Copleston wanted to determine was the character of such ascriptions, and this part of his theory was more controversial. For Copleston, ascribing something like wisdom to God does not mean that God has

---

114. Erskine, *An Essay on Faith*, 105.

115. Whately, *The Use and Abuse of Party-Feeling*, 187–88.

116. James Mackintosh, "Stewart's *Introduction to the Encyclopaedia*," *Edinburgh Review* 36 (October 1821): 254n; JHN to Mr. Newman, April 16, 1822, *LD* 1, 135.

117. Edward Copleston, *An Enquiry into the Doctrines of Necessity and Predestination* (London: John Murray, 1821), 117.

intellectual attributes *resembling* those of human beings; for all we know, their nature might be utterly different. What we really say, when we predicate wisdom of God, is not that God has an attribute "wisdom" that resembles our wisdom but that God performs certain actions, which, if *we* were to perform them, would involve what *we* call wisdom:

> We ascribe *wisdom* and *foresight* to him, because he does what cannot be performed by us without the help of those faculties. That these faculties in him are of a nature different from our own we must be very sensible—but because of the similarity of their effects we give them the same name.[118]

We perceive, in short, a resemblance between the way we relate to our actions, and the way God does, and it is the similarity of these relations we describe when we predicate wisdom of God.

This mode of predication Copleston calls analogy. It does not denote a resemblance of two natures, but a resemblance of two relations.[119] Whether God has any attribute that resembles human wisdom we cannot know, because "things most *unlike* and discordant in their nature may be strictly *analogous* to one another," Copleston argued. For instance,

> A certain *proposition* may be called the *basis* of a system. The proposition is to the system what the basis is to a building. It serves a similar office and purpose: and this last relation being well known is of use to illustrate the other which was less known. E.g. The system *rests* upon it: it is *useless to proceed* with the argument till this is well established: if this were *removed*, the system must fall.[120]

By nature, a proposition is as unlike bricks and mortar as anything, but in relation to a theory, a proposition can fulfil the same role as a foundation in relation to a house. Copleston applied this theory only to the immediate subject of his treatise, God's intellectual attributes, but Whately included God's moral attributes as well. Even when "we call God just or merciful," he argued, "we can mean nothing *more* than his being and acting in *relation* to certain objects, in the same manner as a just and merciful man would."[121] Thus, when we read in scripture that God pardons people who have offended him, we call him merciful, because that is what

118. Copleston, *An Enquiry*, 117.

119. Copleston, *An Enquiry*, 122–23.

120. Copleston, *An Enquiry*, 123. This take on analogy—commonly referred to as analogy of proportionality—was more or less what was understood by the term in classical antiquity.

121. Richard Whately, *The Right Method of Interpreting Scripture, in What Relates to the Nature of the Deity, and His Dealings with Mankind, illustrated in a Discourse on Predestination by Dr. King* (London: John Murray, 1821), iv–v.

we would call a man who would pardon someone who has offended him. Compared to medieval discussions of analogical predication—with which Copleston and Whately would hardly have been familiar—this theological use of analogy is crude, but in the first half of the nineteenth century, it must have seemed groundbreaking. Whately, at least, thought so. It was his panacea for all theological problems, providing a solution "to every . . . mysterious doctrine revealed in Scripture" and forming "the proper basis of all sound theology."[122] The doctrine of the Trinity was a case in point.

Whately and Newman on the Trinity

In an appendix to his *Logic*, dealing with "ambiguous terms," Whately commented on the misleading connotations of the word "person" in Trinitarian theology. Originally, he argued, it had been introduced into theology "in its classical sense," as indicating an (assumed) "character."[123] Nowadays, however, the modern sense of the term, signifying a "distinct Substance," was regularly imported into theology. On this understanding, "three divine Persons" would be "precisely equivalent to 'three Gods.'"[124] Whately's anxiety about tritheism was no figment of the imagination. The High Churchman William Lyall once told him, as Whately recalled to Edward Hawkins, that "there were just as much, & in the same sense, three persons in the Deity, as there were then 3 persons in my room; but that there was a mysterious unity of design & cooperation of agency."[125] Lyall's position clearly fell short of the unity attributed to God in scripture, but the modern usage of the term "person" invited his mistake. For that reason, Whately modelled his own view on the Church of England Catechism, which sets "before us the relations in which the Most High stands towards us, of Maker, Redeemer, and Sanctifier."[126] This wiser and more scriptural approach respects the purpose and nature of revelation, which is "to reveal to us, with a view to our practical benefit, not what God is in Himself, but what He is relatively to us."[127] Belief in the Trinity means that "we believe God to stand in three relations *to us*," whatever he might be in himself.[128] And only this purely economic conception of the Trinity safeguards its practical import. Scripture "reveals to us the Father, that we may

122. Whately, *The Right Method of Interpreting Scripture*, ix.
123. Richard Whately, *Elements of Logic* (London: J. Mawman, 1826), 291. He based this conclusion on the original use of the Latin *persona* as denoting "a *Mask* which actors wore on the stage," just as the Greek *prosopon* (291). See *The Use and Abuse of Party-Feeling*, 198.
124. Whately, *Elements of Logic*, 291, 292.
125. Richard Whately to Edward Hawkins, December 25, 1826, OCL 2.176, 5.
126. Whately, *Elements of Logic*, 292; see also *Peculiarities of the Christian Religion*, 205–6, 208.
127. Whately, *Elements of Logic*, 293.
128. Whately, *Peculiarities of the Christian Religion*, 208; see also *Elements of Logic*, 293.

worship, and thank Him . . . the Son, that we may humbly rely on his atonement
. . . and the Holy Spirit, that we may implore His inward aid."[129]

Newman's 1825 sermon on the Trinity closely echoed Whately's understanding of the doctrine. "The incomprehensible persons of the Trinity," he argued,
"are revealed not as they are *in themselves* but as they are *to us*, not as to their *nature*
but as to their *working*."[130] Scripture does not tell us "any thing about the nature
itself of the three Persons in the Godhead." Instead, it directs "our attention to
their *doings* and *providences*."[131] In consequence, our response should be practical,
rather than speculative: no "mere acknowledgement of [God] as three in one"
but "a practical reliance in Him as Creator, Redeemer, and Sanctifier."[132] In this
way, Newman could retain a functional approach to Trinitarian distinctions without the polarity implied in the *Collection*. In a marginal note, he referred to
"Whately's Bosworth Lectures" as substantiating his overall position.[133] This lec-
ture series is not preserved, but it evidently contained the core of Whately's teaching on the Trinity.[134] Newman, then, shared Whately's emphasis on the economic
Trinity—what God *does*, rather than what he *is*—as well as his practical focus.

This does not mean that Newman ever denied a threefold distinction in the
immanent Godhead—he never did—only that he regarded the nature of this distinction as unknowable:

> though the Father, Son, and Holy Spirit are one and the same God, yet there
> is some *distinction between* them — what we do not know — and this distinc-
> tion we attempt to express by the word 'person' . . . a word which does not
> mean the same as when we apply it to men, but which intimates that the
> Father is not the Son, the Son not the Holy Ghost, and the Holy Ghost not
> the Father.[135]

For Newman, the distinction between the persons of the Trinity was not just
economical: God is as really three as he is one. But there our knowledge ends.
Revelation only tells us *that* there is a distinction in the immanent Godhead, not

---

129. Whately, *The Use and Abuse of Party-Feeling*, 193; see also *Peculiarities of the Christian
Religion*, 208.

130. JHN, No. 81, "On the Trinity," *Serm.* 3, 284; see also 285.

131. JHN, No. 81, "On the Trinity," *Serm.* 3, 284.

132. JHN, No. 81, "On the Trinity," *Serm.* 3, 285.

133. JHN, No. 81, "On the Trinity," *Serm.* 3, 284n7. The editors' suggestion that this refers to
Whately's Bampton Lectures is mistaken. The Bosworth Lectures took their name from the founder
of the lectureship, John Bosworth (rector of Tortworth, 1768–1786) and consisted of eleven lectures
on theological subjects for Oriel undergraduates. See *Remains of the Late Edward Copleston, D.D., Bishop
of Llandaff*, ed. Richard Whately (London: John W. Parker, 1854), 293; Neil Ker and Michael Perkin,
A Directory of the Parochial Libraries of the Church of England and the Church in Wales (London: Bibliographical Society, 2004), 337.

134. See p. 312n40.

135. JHN, No. 81, "On the Trinity," *Serm.* 3, 280.

what it is. This aspect of his position is important to note, because it suggests that he was not in agreement, or perhaps not even familiar, with the theory of analogical predication that grounded Whately's conception of the Trinity. On Whately's theory of analogy, it is hard to accommodate Newman's conclusion that the distinction between the divine persons revealed in the economy of salvation also entails a distinction in the immanent Godhead, even if an unknowable one. Since analogy does not mean resemblance between entities, but resemblance between relations, no analogical predicate entails a claim about the immanent Godhead, but only about God as he relates to something else. Accordingly, asserting that God acts in creation as Father, Son, and Spirit, does not entail that a corresponding threefold distinction is present in the immanent Godhead. It might be, for all we know, but all we can say for certain is that the one God acts as three, so that *relative to us* he is three-in-one. Whately's theory of analogy, in short, threatens to burn all bridges between the economic and the immanent Trinity.

It might seem trifling to make so much of the divergence between Newman's position and that of Whately. Both believed that the *nature* of the distinctions in the Godhead is unknowable, but while Whately held that even the *fact* of these distinctions is unknowable, Newman believed that there *is* a threefold distinction in the Godhead, represented by the names Father, Son, and Spirit. This difference, slight as it might seem at this early stage, was the germ from which a serious theological conflict would develop. The first hint of divergence was a minor dispute that followed the Easter sermon Newman preached at Oriel College Chapel in 1827. Copleston liked the text when he read it, and recommended it to Whately and Hawkins, whose marginal comments on the manuscript survive.[136] The sermon, *On the Mediatorial Kingdom of Christ*, developed the idea stemming from the early Reformation tradition that there are two divine kingdoms, or realms of jurisdiction, to which human beings can belong. By nature, they belong to the universal kingdom of God's providence. By grace, they belong to the kingdom created by Christ's redemptive work, "His *mediatorial* Kingdom."[137] The bone of contention in Newman's sermon was not this distinction but the inferences he

136. JHN, "February 21, 1828," *AW*, 211; No. 160, "On the Mediatorial Kingdom of Christ," April 15, 1827, *Serm.* 1, 329–42.

137. JHN, No. 160, "Mediatorial Kingdom," *Serm.* 1, 329–42. For Newman's earlier treatments of the subject, see No. 46, "Christ's divine and mediatorial kingdoms," December 26, 1824, *Serm.* 1, 322–28; No. 51, "Nature and history of the Mediatorial kingdom," January 2, 1825, *Serm.* 1, 277–85; No. 158, "On the Mediatorial Kingdom of Christ," December 25, 1826, *Serm.* 1, 293–301; for a later treatment, see No. 175, "On the mediatorial Kingdom of Christ (generally)," September 7, 1828, *Serm.* 1, 258–67. The distinction between God's universal and Christ's mediatorial kingdom provided the theological rationale for the early Calvinist version of the two kingdoms theory as applied to the relation between state (providence) and church (redemption). For its development in Calvin and Reformed orthodoxy, which parallels Newman's account, see David Vandrunen, "The Two Kingdoms Doctrine and the Relationship of Church and State in the Early Reformed Tradition," *Journal of Church and State* 49, no. 4 (2007): 743–63.

drew from it about the person of the Son as head of the mediatorial kingdom. Given that the Son's mediatorial kingdom is both limited in extent and provisional (it does not include everyone and only lasts till the last judgment), Newman concluded that "the Son of God, as Mediator, is *inferior to the Father*," as well as to his own "eternal dominion as God."[138] From the perspective of the economy of salvation, then, the Son must be regarded as inferior to the Father, and that is how he is usually represented in the "scheme of redemption:" "in a subordinate character, in the form of a servant."[139]

Newman's representation stemmed from a concern to safeguard the personal unity of Christ as God and man. For some years, he had been struggling with the New Testament passages that describe the Son as subordinate to the Father. One of his solutions, reflected in earlier sermons on the theme, was "to understand 'the Son' always of our Lord's human nature."[140] Thus, he would distinguish between "the *absolute* Kingdom of Christ as *God*, and His *mediatorial* Kingdom as *man*," or observe, in another sermon, that "the Son of God as the Head of this Kingdom *as man* is *inferior to the* Father."[141] The problem with this interpretation is that it drives a wedge between the Son's divine and assumed human nature. It is hard to see how Christ's personal unity is preserved when his divine and human natures are so neatly distinct that terms and functions can be predicated of the one to the exclusion of the other. In the 1827 sermon, therefore, Newman adopted a different framework to understand the subordination of the Son. Instead of attributing inferiority to his human, in contrast to his divine nature, he portrayed the Son's subordination to the Father as a constituent aspect of the economic Trinity, in contrast to the Son's equality with the Father in the immanent Trinity. In this way, Christ's divine and human natures need not be severed, and his personal unity is safeguarded.

Both Whately and Hawkins balked at Newman's sermon; Hawkins mildly so, but Whately thought Newman verged on heresy. "Arianism," he maintained, "is a conclusion which on your views is inevitable."[142] Although his charge has often been taken as obvious, Whately's reasoning was not as straightforward as most scholars suppose.[143] It might seem that he simply meant that Newman's idea of the Son as inferior to the Father entailed that the Son is less divine than the Father, but more was at stake.

---

138. JHN, No. 160, "Mediatorial Kingdom," *Serm.* 1, 334, 337.

139. JHN, No. 160, "Mediatorial Kingdom," *Serm.* 1, 335.

140. JHN, "Memorandum," May 13, 1827, *LD* 2, 16.

141. JHN, No. 46, "Christ's divine and mediatorial kingdoms," December 26, 1824, *Serm.* 1, 323; No. 158, "On the Mediatorial Kingdom of Christ," December 25, 1826, *Serm.* 1, 297, first emphasis added.

142. JHN, No. 160, "Mediatorial Kingdom," *Serm.* 1, 337; see *Apo.*, 71.

143. Gilley, *Newman and His Age*, 63; Stephen Thomas, *Newman and Heresy: The Anglican Years* (Cambridge: Cambridge University Press, 1991), 15–16.

Newman, for one, was puzzled by Whately's criticisms. In a memorandum of May 13, 1827, he admitted that he had presented only "*a partial view* of the doctrine" and might have emphasized the unity of Father and Son more but found no other flaw in his exposition.[144] He had reason to be confused. He had stressed his economic viewpoint throughout the sermon, and explicitly designated the Son as "God," "the eternal, self-existing Lord of all things."[145] This outright denial that there ever was a "before" when the Son "was not,'" precluded a directly Arian interpretation of his sermon. Whately did not overlook these statements. What he found disturbing about Newman's sermon was not so much its depiction of the Son as inferior to the Father as the idea undergirding this depiction: that the names Father, Son, and Spirit correspond to real relational distinctions in the Godhead. The accusation of Arianism was only a corollary to this deeper criticism.

Although Whately's comments were slightly confused, their gist is clear. To Newman's assertion that "the Son of God . . . Himself God . . . *took human form*," Whately replied: "Where is it said that He (the Mediator and Redeemer) *took* human form?" and cited 1 Timothy 2:5 in proof: "There is one God and one Mediator between God and [man], the man Christ Jesus."[146] When Newman used this verse himself later on in the sermon, Whately reiterated: "Is not this (as well as numberless other texts) against the notion of any divine character in the Son distinct from the Father who is the One God?"[147] Whately's problem was with the distinction between Father and Son in the immanent Godhead and, as a corollary, with the idea that the Son, in distinction from the Father, had become incarnate. Whately believed that Christ was God, but he would not affirm that Christ's divine nature was that of one person in the immanent Trinity, in contradistinction to the other two.[148] When Newman once again mentioned the Son's "incomprehensible condescension in humbling Himself for us," Whately noted: "This is too deep for human minds and language; and the *impression which it leaves on the feelings* of those who dwell on it . . . will inevitably be either Tritheism, or such a *conscious danger* of it as will turn men's thoughts from the whole subject."[149]

For Whately, the idea that one of the divine persons had assumed human nature, unavoidably created the impression that this person was a separate entity, and thus another God. He agreed that some of the texts Newman adduced were

---

144. JHN, "Memorandum," May 13, 1827, *LD* 2, 15–16.

145. JHN, No. 160, "Mediatorial Kingdom," *Serm.* 1, 335.

146. JHN, No. 160, "Mediatorial Kingdom," *Serm.* 1, 331.

147. *Serm.* 1, 333. Hawkins added a cautionary comment here, addressed to Whately: "Doubtless there are hosts of Texts on the great doctrine of the Unity — but there is some mysterious distinction too."

148. Although the evidence is too scant to draw firm conclusions, Whately's comments suggest that he wanted to "*confine* true and proper divinity to the Father" and conceived of the person of Christ as a human nature "united with the Father" (*Serm.* 1, 337, 336).

149. *Serm.* 1, 335.

"*difficult* to be explained of the human nature of Christ"—his own preferred solution—but insisted that to "speak of the divine nature of the Son as something distinct from the Father so as to avoid both Tritheism, and the hurtful consequences of a dread of it, seems to me . . . impossible."[150] This comment is terminologically confused—Newman never as much as hinted that the *nature* of the Son was distinct from that of the Father—but it illustrates, once again, Whately's own leanings. For him, a distinction between divine persons in the immanent Godhead could only mean a distinction between divine natures, which would lead either to tritheism, or, by way of reaction, to the Socinian denial of the Trinity. Whately's talk of Arianism was only an afterthought. If we hold (as Newman did) that one person in the immanent Godhead became incarnate, Whately reasoned, that person must be a distinct being. If this distinct being, in turn, is considered inferior to the Father, it must be a being of lesser divinity, and thus we arrive at an Arian conception of Christ. But his latter step in the argument depends on the former. At bottom, Whately rejected Newman's position because he could not conceive of a meaningful way to distinguish persons in the immanent Godhead that did not entail belief in more than one God.

Although Whately never affirmed such distinctions in the immanent Godhead, he also never denied that they existed. He just did not think we can speak intelligibly about them. "The doctrine of these distinctions may be *true*," he admitted in one of his comments, "but if it could be miraculously made clear to our minds, I doubt whether our language could express it."[151] Accordingly, when a reader of the *Logic* asked Hawkins whether Whately was a Sabellian, Whately could indignantly deny the charge. "You might have told your young querist," he wrote to Hawkins, "that if by Sabellianism he meant the doctrines <u>imputed</u> to Sabellius, viz: that the Father suffered on the cross, & that Father, Son & Holy Ghost are only <u>names</u>, all of the same signification, these I reject & have never advocated."[152] The key to this response is that Whately could deny forms of modalism like that of Sabellius because he refused to give *any* metaphysical signification to the names Father, Son, and Spirit. He could not regard them as signifying "persons" in any intelligible sense, but he also did not assert that they were *mere* "names," signifying only three modes or aspects of the one God's activity. Whately refused to draw either conclusion; he simply remained agnostic as far as the immanent Trinity was concerned, and recommended Newman to do the same. It is "surely better to waive the discussion," he commented, "and dwell on the *practical* doctrine of the Trinity, viz: the relations of God to us."[153]

150. *Serm.* 1, 336.
151. *Serm.* 1, 336.
152. Richard Whately to Edward Hawkins, December 3, 1826, OCL 4.349, 2.
153. *Serm.* 1, 336.

In later life, Newman called his sermon "one of my first *declared* departures from Whately's teaching."[154] That it was a departure, we have seen, but there was nothing "declared" about it. He certainly had not been trying to take a stand against Whately, whose criticisms not only surprised him but also cowed him into submission. In his memorandum on the sermon, he noted:

> I . . . cordially dislike all discussions concerning the *nature* of God, and speculations about the *mode* of His Existence as Three and One. . . . I do not even like the words Trinity, Person, Procession etc etc — indeed any systematic exposition but what is *relative to us* and *practical*.[155]

A month later, he repreached his 1825 sermon on the Trinity unaltered, retaining its Whatelyan emphases.[156] Nevertheless, the seeds of future divergence were sown. *On the Mediatorial Kingdom of Christ* was by no means "the high point of Newman's liberalism," as Sheridan Gilley has it.[157] It was, instead, one of Newman's first, albeit unwitting, steps away from the liberalism he would later attribute to Whately. It must have been some time after this episode that he realized, when he and Whately "were talking freely together, that *perhaps* his [Whately's] view concerning the Persons of the Blessed Trinity was, that, all that they were said to be in revelation, was only *relatively to us*; as if there were not really and absolutely any Trinity in the Godhead."[158] But what this realization led to is matter for later chapters. Now, it is time to draw together the different strands of argument of the present.

Conclusion

Recall that Newman defined liberalism in the *Apologia* as determining the truth and/or relative value of a doctrine on intrinsic grounds, by means of human reason, rather than on the authority of God, who revealed it. He concretized the second aspect of this definition as a preference for one set of doctrines over another because it produces a certain effect. To illustrate this approach, he pointed to an insistence on the atonement, because it effects conversions, along with downplaying the Athanasian Creed, because it does not. To the casual observer, it was noted, this example is less than enlightening, not because it has no concrete

---

154. *LD* 2, 185n4.

155. JHN, "May 13, 1827," *LD* 2, 16.

156. *Serm.* 1, 279.

157. Gilley, *Newman and His Age*, 63. Despite recognizing the (potential) Sabellianism of Whately's theology, Stephen Thomas misrepresents both Newman's position and the theological issue at stake (*Newman and Heresy*, 15–19).

158. JHN to William Monsell, October 10, 1852, *LD* 15, 177.

historical referent but because its referent is so utterly particular that it easily escapes notice. What Newman was referring to was the drift of his own early theology along with the influences that shaped it. Following Erskine, he averred that the goal of revelation is to effect conversion. All doctrine is geared toward this end. The "Scripture doctrines lose their force and meaning unless regarded with reference to our new creation unto holiness," he argued in one of his sermons.[159] The doctrine of the atonement is particularly suited to bring about conversion. It is the ultimate manifestation of God's character as at once holy and merciful; holy, so that we would realize our sin, merciful, so that we would turn to our Savior for forgiveness. Within this teleology of revelation, the doctrine of the Trinity derives its meaning from being a manifestation of God's relations to us as Creator, Redeemer, and Sanctifier. The distinctions in the immanent Godhead—expressed in the Athanasian Creed in the exact terms that Newman so disliked: "Person" and "Procession"—do not serve any practical purpose and are therefore better left alone.

Although these views correspond to the liberal position denounced in the *Apologia*, they only witness to Newman's theology, not to his intentions as a theologian. This is an important distinction and a necessary one given the ambiguity of the *Apologia's* definition of liberalism. In the *Apologia*, Newman adduces convictions he used to hold, that is, that conversion is the one goal of revelation, that the atonement is its primary means, and that the Trinity is only meaningful in relation to it, to instance a mistaken reliance on "reason'" or "human judgment." For the Newman of the *Apologia*, valuing one set of doctrines over another because it produces conversions objectively entails a reliance on reason instead of divine authority. But it is far from clear that the evangelical Newman—subjectively—adopted these ideas because he relied on reason. He might well have believed that his understanding of the relation between doctrine and conversion was itself part and parcel of revelation. His firm conviction that it was scripture and not reason that presented the doctrine of the atonement as *the* means of conversion suggests as much.[160] Before ten years were over, he came to believe that this conviction was gravely mistaken. Revelation countenanced no such idea. Whatever his intentions had been, he now saw that from an objective point of view, his theology had not been premised on a simple acceptance of revelation as the word of God but rather on a systematization of the scheme of revelation that was of human, not divine, origin. Accordingly, when he began to denounce the theological approach of Whately and his Oriel coterie as well as that of Erskine, he did so from a personal, not just a theoretical, awareness of its dangerous implications. By attacking the ideas of Whately and Erskine as "liberal"

---

159. JHN, No. 103, "Holiness," *Serm.* 5, 294.
160. See p. 84.

and "rationalistic" in the mid-1830s, he also pronounced judgment on his own theological leanings of a decade before. And yet, he was right to specify in the *Apologia* that he only partly gave into this form of liberalism. He had never fully embraced the positions of Erskine and Whately.

Erskine's conviction that "I cannot believe any thing which I do not understand" entailed the full perspicuity of revelation. The *Apologia* instanced this view as another tenet of liberalism. The second of Note A's eighteen propositions was a nearly verbatim rendering of Erskine: "No one can believe what he does not understand. Therefore, e.g., there are no mysteries in true religion."[161] Newman had never gone to such lengths. He consistently argued instead that revelation includes mysterious truths, which we believe not because of what they say but because of who says them. In theology, however, this formal aspect of faith as assent to testimony was eclipsed by a focus on faith's intelligible content. Mysteries were still true, but relatively insignificant, because they contributed little to the goal of revelation: conversion. Thus, Newman continued to affirm a threefold distinction in the immanent Godhead but did not make much of it. Instead, he tried to make Trinitarian doctrine meaningful and relevant to his parishioners by adopting Whately's purely economical and practical account of the Trinity. But just as in Erskine's case, he adopted Whately's logic while balking at his conclusions. This is why he was "drifting toward" rather than espousing liberalism in the mid-1820s. He was drawn to, and in large measure adopted, what he would later regard as liberal tenets, but he stopped short of their logical issue, be it the complete perspicuity of revelation or agnosticism about Trinitarian distinctions.

These reflections help to explain Newman's surprising assertion, in the 1825 sermon on the Trinity, that a lack of practical import is an objection to the truth of a doctrine. At first sight, this is an instance of judging a revelation by its content, a practice he had always opposed. As he put in his 1826 *Essay on Miracles*, "our *speculations* concerning the divine attributes and designs, professing as they do to decide on the truth of Revealed doctrines, in fact go to supersede the necessity of a Revelation altogether."[162] But two reasons militate against such a reading. For one, Newman, as noted, probably believed that his conviction of the practical goal of revelation was not derived from speculation but from scripture. More importantly, however, Christian doctrines are not *wholly* mysterious. The distinction of persons in the immanent Trinity is incomprehensible, but the economic roles of Creator, Redeemer, and Sanctifier have meaning and practical import. Accordingly, Newman paid little heed to the mysterious bits and focused

---

161. *Hist.*, 294.

162. JHN, "Apollonius Tyanaeus—Miracles," *Encyclopaedia Metropolitana*, vol. 10, *History and Biography*, vol. 2, 635; *Two Essays on Scripture Miracles and on Ecclesiastical* (London: Basil Montagu Pickering, 1870), 52, hereafter *Mir.*

on what we do understand, because only that has a sanctifying tendency. He had no qualms about valuing doctrines for their perspicuity and practical import, but he still considered the mysterious bits to be true. Even in his sermon on the Trinity, he argued that since the distinction of persons in the immanent Trinity concerns "the nature of God," about which we "cannot possibly know anything . . . except as far as He Himself tells us of it," we accept it simply because of Christ's "*credibility* as a witness," as being "the Messenger of the Gospel."[163] Doctrinal statements like the Athanasian Creed functioned negatively, as boundaries not to be crossed. They did not positively shape the young Newman's theology. But this, too, was to change.

163. JHN, No. 81, "On the Trinity," *Serm.* 3, 281–82.

CHAPTER 4

High Church Transformations

Between the early 1820s and the early 1830s, Newman's theology was deeply transformed. Much of what he had firmly held at the beginning of that decade he abjured just as resolutely at its end. This change is commonly described as a turn from evangelical to High Church, or even proto-Catholic theology. As far it goes, that is a true statement, but it needs to be unpacked carefully to do Newman justice. To begin with, it was one development among several.

Initially, it was counteracted by the liberal modulations of his evangelicalism discussed in the previous chapter, and it coincided with the fundamental shift in his conception of conscience and natural religion discussed in the next. Second, using party-epithets obscures the idiosyncratic character of Newman's developing theology. It is true that in the early 1820s, he held many things that evangelicals hold, while in the early 1830s, he held many things High Churchmen, or even Catholics hold. But he did not abandon one established system or group for another. Third, the standard account usually opts for only one level of theological analysis: that of explicit doctrinal commitments.[1] It tends to describe Newman's development as the substitution of a set of High Church doctrines (such as baptismal regeneration) for a set of evangelical ones. Change is analysed as exchange: trading one thing for another.

Although indispensable, such a doctrinal model is overly static; useful, perhaps, to chart someone's orthodoxy but not to gauge intellectual development. At best, it can establish perimeters of development, but not its rationale. For one, individual doctrines are part of a system. Accordingly, theological development not only concerns individual doctrines but also the logical relations and relative emphases amongst a set of doctrines. Newman's acceptance of baptismal regeneration, for instance, made him rethink the nature of election and the role of the visible church in mediating grace and truth. This systematic dimension is recognized in the better specimens of the doctrinal approach, such as Thomas Sheridan's exceptionally thorough *Newman on Justification*, but their scope and depth remain limited.[2] More fundamental levels of transformation are even more rarely identified. Doctrines and doctrinal systems are grafted onto a wider set of

---

1. Perhaps unintentionally, Newman himself set the pattern for this approach in the *Apologia* and the *Autobiographical Memoir.*

2. Many of the sources discussed in the present chapter are treated, often at more length, in Sheridan's valuable work, with whose conclusions I am in broad agreement.

convictions and (methodological) principles that govern an individual's theological outlook or vision. Such convictions—say, about the nature of doctrine (what it means for something to *be* a doctrine)—cannot itself be expressed in terms of doctrines or doctrinal systems (think of Newman's take on the nature and teleology of revelation). But shifts in these kinds of convictions, concerning theological enquiry, the nature of doctrine, the religious subject, and human agency, are part and parcel of Newman's theological transformation.

Finding the right level of analysis is not the only challenge for providing an adequate account of Newman's theological development in the eight years or so prior to the Tractarian Movement. In the last two decades, serious questions have been raised about its coherence and theological rationale. Frank Turner's psychologizing reading of Newman's rejection of evangelicalism is an instance already discussed. Another is that of Paul Vaiss, who portrays Newman's development as theologically driven but fickle and incoherent in character. Newman oscillated between evangelical and High Church convictions from the mid-1820s right up to the eve of the Tractarian Movement, going through "a most definitely Evangelical phase" as late as 1832.[3] While Turner ignored much primary material, Vaiss uses Newman's published and unpublished writings to the full, but his reading of some of his main sources—the sermons Newman preached in 1832—is selective and often misleading.[4] Besides, his argument proves too much. It is true, as Vaiss observes, that Newman reused several earlier, (purportedly) evangelical sermons in 1832. But what Vaiss does not mention is that Newman still preached most of those sermons unaltered as late as 1841—a date which neither Vaiss nor anyone else wishes to include in Newman's "evangelical phase."[5] In contrast to Vaiss and Turner, I argue that the transformation of Newman's evangelical thought was both coherent and radical, that is, it came about by means of an intelligible series of theological steps but produced a theological outlook that was

3. Paul Vaiss, "Newman's State of Mind on the Eve of His Italian Tour," in *From Oxford to the People: Reconsidering Newman & the Oxford Movement*, ed. Paul Vaiss (Leominster: Gracewing, 1996), 203. See also Vaiss, *Newman*, chaps. 18, 19.

4. Thus, a citation intended to demonstrate Newman's 1832 commitment to "the total corruption of human nature" (Vaiss, "Newman's State of Mind," 207) is taken from a sermon which denies that doctrine explicitly (JHN, No. 192, "The flesh," March 19, 1829, *Serm.* 2, 209; see pp. 204–5 in this book.

5. Of the ten sermons Vaiss cites, seven were preached virtually unaltered as late as 1838, 1840, or 1841. See Vaiss, "Newman's State of Mind," 221–22, n. 7–19; JHN, No. 339, "On the Holy Spirit—His Nature and Office," June 10, 1832–June 3, 1838, *Serm.* 4, 184; No. 332, "On our national sins—for the Fast Day," March 21, 1832–January 30, 1838, *Serm.* 3, 202; No. 192, "The flesh," March 19, 1829–January 1, 1841, *Serm.* 2, 207; No. 255, "St Bartholomew a pattern of guilelessness," August 24, 1830–April 13, 1841, *Serm.* 3, 60; No. 188, "On Justification by faith only," January 18, 1829–August 22, 1841, *Serm.* 2, 166; No. 337, "Revelation of God in the New Testament," May 1, 1832–May 1, 1841, *Serm.* 3, 333; No. 323, "On the Ministerial Order, as an existing divine institution. Ordination Sermon," December 18, 1831–August 24, 1840, *Serm.* 4, 78.

fundamentally different from his former evangelical perspective.[6] The present chapter traces the first step in this development: the changes in Newman's systematic theology between 1825 and 1827, the period in which he abandoned much of the evangelicalism described in chapter 1 for a doctrinal position that was, in a qualified sense, High Church.

The Problem of Baptismal Regeneration

Perhaps so many scholars have limited their analysis of Newman's theological development to the level of doctrine because his change of thought began with a clearly identifiable doctrinal issue: that of baptismal regeneration, one of evangelicals' most pressing concerns with Church of England theology. In the first chapter, I argued that Newman's religious identity in the early 1820s consisted of a fusion of evangelical convictions with Church of England commitments. Although his papers of the time show that he did not regard their identification as obvious, he initially experienced little tension between them. In his 1821 *Collection*, he concurred with Walter Mayers's view that regeneration cannot take place in baptism, because so many baptized people live deeply sinful lives. In his paper on holiness (written in 1822 or 1823), he still expressly dismissed the doctrine of baptismal regeneration but in a more careful manner. In one of his 1817 letters, Walter Mayers had appealed to Ezekiel Hopkins (1634–1690), a Puritan divine, to argue that baptism has some salvific efficacy, but only "after an external manner"; it does not issue in regeneration or conversion: the inward change of heart or nature necessary for salvation.[7] Newman adopted a similar solution. "Baptism," he argued, "<u>as such</u>, in no case conveys to the convert change of heart."[8] Instead, it issues in "a <u>change of state</u>," which gives us "certain privileges, viz. adoption, justification, the right of asking for God's Spirit & the hope of heaven."[9] Baptism, then, sets God right with us: God no longer regards us as in a guilty *state*, but, in Christ, as in a justified *state*. Christ's righteousness, in other words, is imputed to us. This baptismal change is external: it does not change who we are but how God perceives us. With the internal change of *nature*, which sets us right with God (by our acquiring holiness through the operation of the Holy Spirit), baptism has nothing to do. This is a separate change, which results from a consciously experienced process of conversion.

---

6. Lawrence Poston's claim that Newman's "core Evangelicalism never left him" is, therefore, misleading at best (*The Antagonist Principle*, 39).

7. Walter Mayers to JHN, April 14, 1817, *LD* 1, 33; Ezekiel Hopkins, "The Nature and Necessity of Regeneration; or, the New-Birth," in *The Works of the Right Reverent Father in God, Ezekiel Hopkins*, vol. 2, ed. Josiah Pratt (London: L. B. Seeley, 1809), 468.

8. JHN, *Nature of Holiness*, BOA A.9.1.g, 7.

9. JHN, *Nature of Holiness*, BOA A.9.1.g, 7.

In early 1824, the theological confidence exuded by Newman's earlier papers was on the wane. "It is painful to think how unsettled my principles are," he wrote in his annual birthday reflection on February 21.[10] At Oriel, he had forged new friendships, which made him rethink some of his evangelical assumptions. In the spring of 1823, he became intimate with Edward Pusey, who had just been elected to an Oriel fellowship. Pusey was no evangelical. Newman confessed in his diary that he even suspected him of being "prejudiced against Thy children."[11] Nonetheless, Pusey was the first person at Oriel with whom Newman felt sufficiently at ease to speak freely about religion.[12] In Pusey, he befriended, perhaps for the first time, a nonevangelical whose deep and sincere religiosity was beyond question.

Newman had similar feelings about another Oriel fellow, Edward Hawkins, who, unlike Pusey, was Newman's senior by more than ten years and thus more of a mentor than a peer. "I have just come from hearing Hawkins preach a most beautiful sermon," Newman noted in a diary entry of December 1822, "I trust, and hardly can doubt, God is leading him."[13] Still, Hawkins did much to increase Newman's theological confusion. "Hawkins," he wrote in his 1824 birthday reflection, "has been declaring his opinions on some points, as appears to me, very erroneously."[14] But he no longer felt as sure of his own position as he had before: "feeling I am as a poor child without sense or strength, I trust God will enlighten me, and tell me what is the truth."[15]

Although these new friendships had an unsettling effect, Newman's renewed concern with the doctrine of baptismal regeneration had less to do with the influence of Pusey and Hawkins than with a specific event: his approaching ordination as a deacon on June 13, 1824. As in everything religious, he was uncommonly earnest about this step. "I have the responsibility of souls on me to the day of my death," he would comment the day after.[16] He realized that being a minister of the Church of England was different from being a mere private member; it entailed graver responsibilities and a stronger institutional commitment. As a minister, the baptismal service's references to regeneration were no longer mere food for theoretical argument but concerned him personally. Of each child he would baptize, he would now have to declare: "*this Child* is regenerate"— an uncomfortable prospect for a conscientious young man who did not think this

10. JHN, "February 21, 1824," *AW*, 196.

11. JHN, "May 17, 1823," *AW*, 191.

12. JHN, "April 13, 1823," *AW*, 190; "May 2, 1823," *AW*, 190; "May 17, 1823," *AW*, 191; "October 24, 1823," *AW*, 194; "February 1, 1824," *AW*, 195–96; "March 15, 1824," *AW*, 197–98; "December 16, 1824," *AW*, 203; "Autobiographical Memoir," *AW*, 74–76.

13. JHN, "December 1, 1822," *AW*, 188.

14. JHN, "February 21, 1824," *AW*, 196–97.

15. JHN, "February 21, 1824," *AW*, 197.

16. JHN, "June 14, 1824," *AW*, 201.

was true. In the months preceding his ordination, therefore, he searched anew the authoritative texts of the Anglican theological tradition with regard to "the question of Regeneration."[17] In addition to scripture, the Apocrypha, and the *Homilies*, he studied Richard Mant's annotated version of the *Book of Common Prayer*, which adduced a variety of Anglican authorities to defend the idea that regeneration takes place in baptism and not at some separate time of conversion.[18] But he was slow to make up his mind and remained sorely troubled even after his ordination.

To begin with, Hawkins did not leave him alone. Only a month into his ministry, Newman records a conversation in which Hawkins criticized his rigid distinction between "real and nominal Christianity."[19] In the first sermon he ever wrote, Newman had strongly contrasted the converted and the unconverted, "those in the path that leadeth to life" and those "in that of endless misery."[20] He elaborated on the absolute incapacity to become holy of any human being, who has "in himself neither the *power*, nor the *will*, nor even the *knowledge* of his radical *unholiness*."[21] Hawkins objected, perhaps not so much to Newman's theology as to his mode of presenting it. "The majority, he said, of my congregation would not be touched by my preaching; for they would be conscious to themselves of not doing *enough*, not of doing *nothing*."[22] The binary take on conversion that characterized Newman's evangelicalism would not do for the pulpit.[23] Evidently, the conversation had an impact, for three weeks later, he noted that the "question of regeneration perplexes me very much."[24] Perhaps he brought up his qualms to Hawkins, but whether he did or not, four days later, on August 19, Hawkins gave him a book that was to be a major catalyst of change in his theology: John Bird Sumner's *Apostolical Preaching* (1815).[25]

As its title indicates, the subject of Sumner's book was the one Hawkins had problematized: preaching. Sumner's core argument was that the Christian minister should model his preaching on that of the Apostles, especially on the epistles of St Paul.[26] Although Sumner was an evangelical, he applied his argument directly against Calvinism: not so much against its characteristic doctrines as such, but

17. JHN, "March 13, 1824," *AW*, 197.

18. See, for example, Richard Mant, ed., *The Book of Common Prayer* (Oxford: J. Parker, 1820), 388–89, 391, 402–4.

19. JHN, "July 21, 1824," *AW*, 201.

20. JHN, No. 1, "The work of man," June 27, 1824, *Serm.* 5, 21.

21. JHN, No. 1, "The work of man," *Serm.* 5.

22. JHN, "July 21, 1824," *AW*, 201.

23. JHN, "Autobiographical Memoir," *AW*, 77.

24. JHN, "August 15, 1824," *AW*, 201.

25. *LD* 1, 19.

26. John Bird Sumner, *Apostolical Preaching Considered, in an Examination of St. Paul's Epistles*, 6th ed. (London: J. Hatchard and Son, 1826), 19–36.

against the expedience of preaching them. This, at least, Sumner professed. In reality, he more than implied that those doctrines were false.[27] In quick succession, Sumner argued that (double) predestination (or active reprobation), individual election, efficacious (or irresistible) grace, final perseverance, and the necessity of a postbaptismal conversion are not taught explicitly by St Paul, and sometimes directly contradicted, so that they should not be preached, and perhaps not even be held. We will look at some of Sumner's arguments in detail below, when we consider their influence on Newman's theological development. For now, it is enough to observe that reading the work drove Newman to a point of crisis. On August 24, he noted in his diary: "Sumner's book threatens to drive me either into Calvinism, or baptismal regeneration, and I wish to steer clear of both, at least in preaching."[28] Sheridan expresses puzzlement at this comment. Because he believes that the doctrines of predestination and individual election "never really had any appeal" for Newman, he thinks Newman should have heartily welcomed Sumner's arguments.[29] But as we have seen in chapter 1, Newman's evangelicalism was more Calvinistic than Sheridan allows. Except for the idea of active reprobation, he held all the Calvinistic tenets Sumner condemns. Hence, his comment is not as puzzling as Sheridan suggests. Sumner forced a painful dilemma on Newman: either to be a consistent (high or hyper-) Calvinist, or to adopt the doctrine of baptismal regeneration; there was no middle way.

It is important to observe that the terms Newman used to express the dilemma he faced—"Calvinism" and "baptismal regeneration"—are not on a par: one designates a theological system, the other a theological doctrine. This conceptual disparity is instructive because it indicates how Newman experienced the problem of baptismal regeneration. By all that this doctrine implied—to which he could not yet assign the name of a system—it undermined the theological system he had held so far. This claim requires some unpacking. On the evangelical "scheme of salvation," which Newman had embraced and defended in his papers of the early 1820s, grace operates in a strikingly straightforward manner. Sumner spoke of the "tremendous *simplicity* of the Calvinistic scheme."[30] God has elected certain individuals to be saved; they will therefore experience a conversion, which will carry them on to eternal salvation. The guiding principle throughout is God's sovereignty, which is expressed in the doctrine of efficacious, or irresistible grace: whomever God wishes to save, he saves. Along with the idea of conversion as a radical change, this model issues in a stark binary between converted and unconverted. Everyone who experiences conversion and shows its fruits (good works),

<hr>

27. Sheridan, *Newman on Justification*, 83.
28. JHN, "August 24, 1824," *AW*, 202.
29. Sheridan, *Newman on Justification*, 83.
30. Sumner, *Apostolical Preaching*, 42.

knows that she is among the elect and will be saved. Conversely, everyone who has not experienced conversion and does not lead a holy life is, so far, on the road to perdition. Conversion does not come in degrees: one has either experienced a radical change and is on the path to holiness, or one has not.

It is this doctrine of efficacious grace, with all its consequences, that, Sumner argued, "absolutely nullifies the sacrament of baptism."[31] If baptism is not understood as being "accompanied with such an effusion of the Holy Spirit towards the inward renewing of the heart, that the person baptized. . . . By this amendment or regeneration of his nature is enabled to bring forth fruit," then it is only "an empty rite, an external mark of admission into the visible church, attended with no real grace, and therefore conveying no real benefit, nor advancing a person one step towards salvation."[32] Sumner puts the dilemma about as forcefully as can be: either you adopt the Calvinistic idea of efficacious grace and stop baptizing infants altogether, or you give up that idea and all it implies and accept that baptism brings about all the regeneration we need. These were the stakes, and Newman felt them keenly. "Last night," he wrote in the diary entry of August 24, "I was so distressed and low about it, that a slight roughness from someone nearly brought me to tears, and the thought even struck me I must leave the Church."[33] Such a state of limbo could not last, and he soon began to make up his mind.

The Search for a Solution

At the end of 1824, Newman had a series of conversations with Pusey on the doctrine that had made him so anxious—"I inclining to separate regeneration from baptism, he doubting its separation."[34] This was the last burst of evangelical conviction on the subject. By January 1825, Newman hesitantly concluded that he "must give up the doctrine . . . of regeneration as apart from baptism."[35] The "great stand is to be made," he argued, "*not* against those who connect a spiritual change with baptism, but those who deny a spiritual change altogether."[36] What matters is that one is changed from being sinful to being holy. As long as people admit this, it matters little whether they consider this regenerative process to be initiated by baptism, or by an experience of conversion. All who hold that such a change is necessary "should unite against those who make it (regeneration) a mere opening of new prospects, when the old score of offences is wiped away,

---

31. Sumner, *Apostolical Preaching*, 181.
32. Sumner, *Apostolical Preaching*, 181–82.
33. JHN, "August 24, 1824," *AW*, 202.
34. JHN, "December 16, 1824," *AW*, 203
35. JHN, "January 13, 1825," *AW*, 203.
36. JHN, "January 13, 1825," *AW*, 203.

and a person is for the second time put, as it were, on his good behaviour."[37] Such a view reduces regeneration to justification, which brings the forgiveness of sins but contributes nothing to inward change. Of course, underscoring the commonality of all who believe in regeneration (be it through baptism or conversion) does not help to decide which account of regeneration is right, but Newman also had positive reasons to accept baptismal regeneration.

A key one was his growing experience as a pastor, which quickly taught him how right Hawkins had been to criticize his binary view of conversion. When he set about his ministry at St Clement's in June 1824, he did so with all his customary earnestness. He introduced himself to all the families of his parish, avidly visited the sick and dying, started a Sunday school, and began to collect money to build a new church to hold the parish's expanding population.[38] Parish work introduced him to a completely new sphere of action and experience. Instead of the learned, upper-crust society of an Oxford College, he was now dealing with working-class people—"labourers, mechanics, small shopkeepers, and servants attached to different Colleges"—who often lacked the intellectual and religious consistency of his colleagues at Oriel, but were still not all bad.[39] Before long, Newman was forced to admit that "the good thoughts which careless men often have" indicate that grace is at work in their lives.[40] Since such people lack the evidence of a conversion in an evangelical sense— a consistently holy life—he could only attribute the presence of such grace to baptism. Soon after, he ascribed his "change of sentiment as to Regeneration" in large measure to "the fact that in my parochial duties I found many, who in most important points were inconsistent, but whom yet I could not say were altogether without grace."[41] What struck him in doing parish work, in short, was the obverse of what had struck him (and Mayers) before. He was no longer so appalled at the badness of the baptized that he denied their regeneration, but so surprised by what goodness they displayed, that he could only account for it through baptismal grace.

A second reason why baptismal regeneration appealed to him was the practice of infant baptism. In an echo of Sumner, Newman wondered, "unless God is likely to vouchsafe grace in baptism, why ordain it for infants?"[42] The only plausible reason to baptize infants is that it does them good. And scripture does, in fact, intimate that infants can receive grace: "What did our Lord mean by bid-

---

37. JHN, "January 13, 1825," *AW*, 203.
38. Newman's fundraiser resulted in the building of the current St Clement's Church on the Marston Road.
39. JHN, "Rebuilding of St Clement's," December 1, 1824, *LD* 1, 201.
40. JHN, "January 13, 1825," *AW*, 204.
41. JHN, "July 17, 1825," *AW*, 206.
42. JHN, "January 13, 1825," *AW*, 204.

ding children to come to Him, if not for spiritual blessings?"[43] Still, Newman was hesitant. "I do not like to apply the term 'regeneration' to the privileges of baptism," he noted in January, "though I do not use it on the other side."[44] A sermon fragment of April shows that he was overcoming this reluctance. "Baptism," he argued, "is a sign and pledge both of justification and regeneration."[45] Although he now explicitly linked baptism to regeneration, he still held that regeneration depends on faith. Infants, therefore, can only receive "the blessings of baptism, because though they have not actually faith and repentance, yet they promise them both by their sureties."[46] As soon as they "come to years of understanding," children must "show *themselves* that lively faith which at baptism was promised for them," because otherwise they at once "cease to be members of Christ."[47] The regenerative effects of baptism, then, are not intrinsic to the sacrament but are conditional both upon the faith of the sponsors and upon the later faith of the baptized. Gradually, though, Newman construed the tie between the act of baptism and the reception of the Holy Spirit more closely.

When he was ordained to the priesthood, on May 29, 1825, Newman quite naturally compared his feelings and views to those of a year before, when he had been ordained deacon:

> I hope I was not exactly uncharitable, then; still I certainly thought that there might be some among them who were coming to the Bishop out of their own heads, and without the Spirit of God. But when I looked round today, I could hope and trust that none were altogether destitute of divine influence. . . . Then, I thought there were many in the visible Church of Christ, who have never been visited by the Holy Ghost; now, I think there are none but probably, nay almost certainly, have been visited by Him.[48]

Newman, in a word, conceived the Holy Spirit to operate more liberally than he had thought before. He also held that these operations were conditional on baptism, but he did not think that baptism, in and of itself, conveyed the Spirit to the baptized. "I do not even now actually maintain that the Spirit always or generally accompanies the very act of baptism, only that the sacrament brings them into the kingdom of grace, where the Spirit will constantly meet them with His influences."[49] People do not receive the Spirit in baptism but come within range of his continual operation. They change locales, so to speak, rather than being

43. JHN, "January 13, 1825," *AW*, 204.
44. JHN, "January 13, 1825," *AW*, 204.
45. JHN, No. 70, "Personal interest in Christ," April 10, 1825, *Serm.* 5, 225.
46. JHN, No. 70, "Personal interest in Christ," *Serm.* 5, 225
47. JHN, No. 70, "Personal interest in Christ," *Serm.* 5, 225.
48. JHN, "May 29, 1825," *AW*, 206.
49. JHN, "May 29, 1825," *AW*, 206.

changed themselves. The Spirit, therefore, remains external to the baptized person: she is in an optimal position to receive the Spirit, but the Spirit is not actually present within her. To move from this view to one that sees the Spirit as inwardly changing the believer in baptism is at once a small step and an enormous leap. It is a small step, because the Spirit is already so close to the believer that he practically inheres in her. He is there for the asking and will be there when asked for. It is a giant leap, because to cross this boundary between external and internal is to make grace an inhering principle in the believer, prior to and independent of any exertion on her part. The Spirit is there; not just there for the asking.

Although it took a while before Newman took this step (or leap), he did conceive of the relation between the Holy Spirit and the baptized in ever-closer ways. In a sermon November 20, 1825, *Our admittance into the church our title to the Holy Spirit*, he asserted categorically that "the Holy Spirit is given *generally* to all the visible church," that is, to "all who are by baptism admitted into the Christian body"—a claim which he had not yet been willing to make in May.[50] He did not view this general gift as changing the individual inwardly, however, even though he occasionally verged on such a notion (when, for instance, he exhorted his congregation to "stir up the gift of God that is in you").[51] The main thrust of the sermon, however, is, as its title indicates, that baptism *entitles* us to the Holy Spirit. The baptized have "the direct promising of the Holy Spirit to sanctify them whenever they ask for it"; they have "a title . . . to claim at once the aid of the Holy Ghost in order to give them a new heart and spirit."[52] At first sight, this might not appear so different from his position in the early 1820s, when he maintained that baptism gives us the "right of asking for God's Spirit."[53] But there is every difference between the right *to ask* for something (which implies the possibility of refusal) and *entitlement*, which is the right *to receive* something. On his earlier view, the baptized person had a right to ask for the Holy Spirit, but she still required a distinct experience of conversion before she could be said to have received it. Newman now relinquished this condition.

In a March 1826 sermon, he formulated an even bolder view. He stated that "holy baptism" is "attended by the giving of the Holy Ghost" and drew on St Peter's First Epistle to argue that it "doth . . . *save us*."[54] More precisely, it puts us into a "state of salvation."[55] The term "state" no longer denotes the earlier contrast between justification—a *state* of acceptance—and regeneration—a *change*

---

50. JHN, No. 118, "Our admittance into the church our title to the Holy Spirit," November 20, 1825, *Serm.* 5, 361; see also 362.

51. JHN, No. 118, "Our admittance into the church," *Serm.* 5, 364.

52. JHN, No. 118, "Our admittance into the church," *Serm.* 5, 361–62.

53. JHN, *Nature of Holiness*, BOA A.9.1.g, 7.

54. JHN, No. 144, "On infant baptism," March 12, 1826, *Serm.* 1, 173, 174; 1 Pt 3:21.

55. JHN, No. 144, "On infant baptism," *Serm.* 1, 175.

of nature. The sermon, in fact, studiously avoids those terms. Instead, it subsumes their respective contents under the overarching idea of salvation. "Acceptance with God" and "the renewing of the Holy Ghost" are two aspects of the one "state of salvation" which "baptism conveys."[56] Baptism, Newman argued, admits us "to the fellowship of the Holy Ghost, who is thenceforth pledged and sealed to us whenever we come to God for that precious gift in Christ's name."[57] The notion of fellowship is more intimate than that of entitlement. It is not just that the Spirit is bound to come to us when we ask for him, but that, when we ask for him, we ask for someone whom we have already befriended, someone who is actually already with us. In fact, the Spirit does not wait to be asked. That is why we baptize *infants*. In baptism,

> we provide for them a present guide, Sanctifier and Comforter, directly they begin to think — a Holy One who will suggest good thoughts and desires into their minds as soon as natural evil begins to work within them — who will enlighten and lead them to the truth and give them eyes to see their sin and misery, and fix their faith upon the cross of Christ, and fill them with a desire for a spiritual heaven.[58]

Right away, the Holy Spirit begins to change the child's nature, even though to "continue in a state of salvation," the child must display faith once it is capable of it. Such baptismal regeneration is no longer conditional upon the faith of the sponsors. If "it is said that children promise repentance and faith by their sponsors in baptism," Newman now argued, "it is only meant that their sponsors promise they will do all in their power to lead them to God," not that their faith makes baptism efficacious.[59]

Regeneration and Sanctification

Newman's change of mind on baptismal regeneration coincided with gradual alterations in his understanding of sanctification. From the time of his conversion, he had believed that the goal of a Christian life is to become holy, because holiness fits us for heaven. In 1817, Walter Mayers explained to his young pupil that "in describing a meetness for heaven the scriptures . . . depict a state of holiness as absolutely necessary."[60] Newman's first sermons echoed this conviction. Holiness, he insisted, is "absolutely *necessary*, if we would see happiness in another world,"

<hr>

56. JHN, No. 144, "On infant baptism," *Serm.* 1, 175.
57. JHN, No. 144, "On infant baptism," *Serm.* 1, 176.
58. JHN, No. 144, "On infant baptism," *Serm.* 1, 176–77.
59. JHN, No. 144, "On infant baptism," *Serm.* 1, 177.
60. Walter Mayers to JHN, April 14, 1817, *LD* 1, 32.

because "none can enjoy the spiritual pleasures of heaven except he first acquire a taste for them on earth."[61] Holiness binds our earthly and heavenly states together. It establishes a continuity between what we are now and wat we will be. As he put it in the abstract of another sermon: "heaven is the perfection of holiness."[62]

Accordingly, the most important question for any Christian is how she can become holy. Newman's initial answer conceptualized sanctification as a two-step process. Becoming holy begins with conversion (or regeneration): the conscious experience of a radical redirection of one's affections and desires from sin to God. This is step one. But even after conversion, "the believer's nature is still corrupt & carnal," as the 1821 *Collection* had it.[63] This "remaining corruption of the regenerate" necessitates a continuous struggle to overcome "indwelling sin."[64] This is step two. Regeneration is only "the first stage of sanctification."[65] Although it constitutes a radical change of the affections and desires, it must still be enacted in practice. Becoming holy, therefore, takes time and effort, but effort should be understood aright here.

Recall Newman's early conviction that "good works & religious observances" do not constitute holiness, which is "something higher . . . than mere morality or mere churchgoing." Good works are only "external signs & evidences of an inward principle," which is sovereignly bestowed by the Holy Spirit upon conversion.[66] Still, this principle can be nurtured, not by trying to do good but by using the means of grace. The regenerate Christian, Newman argued in a June 1821 note,

> wants to do good works & profess the Christian virtues, such as humility, patience, self-denial, sincerity, charity, resignation, content, meekness, benevolence. How is he to attain to that which he cannot do without power from above? Why, by doing that which he <u>can do</u> without power from above — viz, use those rites & outward observances which God has appointed as the means of receiving <obtaining> power to act religiously.[67]

These means, we will recollect, are "reading the word of God, praying, self-examination" and "partaking the Lord's supper."[68] They are channels of grace, which, when used by the regenerate, further their sanctification and issue in the desired "good works" and "Christian virtues."

When Newman started to preach at St Clement's in the summer of 1824, he was insecure about his earlier theology and did not want to commit to any definite

---

61. JHN, No. 1, "The work of man," *Serm.* 5, 23.
62. JHN, No. 7, "The peculiar bliss of heaven," July 25, 1824, *Serm.* 5, 43.
63. JHN, *Collection*, BOA A.9.1.c.6, 11.
64. JHN, *Collection*, BOA A.9.1.c.6, 11.
65. JHN, *Comment*, BOA A.9.1.e, 2.
66. JHN, *Nature of Holiness*, BOA A.9.1.g., 1.
67. JHN, *Comment*, BOA A.9.1.e, 2–3.
68. JHN, *Comment*, BOA A.9.1.e, 1. See pp. 32–33 in this book.

views of regeneration. He chose, therefore, to avoid the term altogether and talk of sanctification instead. As before, he distinguished between "salvation from the *guilt and punishment* of sin" and "salvation from its *tyrannizing influence*," and argued that God provides both:

> Christ has atoned for our sins and thus rescues us from the *punishment*, and the Holy Spirit cleanses our hearts from evil and purifies them unto every good work. Christ in short, has by his death reconciled *God* to *us* . . . and the Holy Spirit, by his sanctifying grace, reconciles *us* to God.[69]

Because of his doubts about regeneration, Newman did not identify a clear starting point for the process of sanctification, but he still rigidly distinguished those who are engaged in it from those who are not, as Hawkins was quick to point out. The latter group Newman portrayed as still in need of "the Holy Spirit who enlightens us, who worketh in us, to will and to do."[70] The former group he adjured to persevere in the means of grace. The Christian who is enlightened by the Holy Spirit "has to beat down his pride — to mortify his sinful affections — to purify his passions. He wishes, he strives to do it — but the remains of . . . natural corruption . . . thwart and impede him at every step."[71] The only way to solve this impasse is to "be constant in the means of grace"—the chief of which is prayer.[72]

As before, Newman was wary of suggesting that a holy life can be acquired by aiming at it directly, so to speak, that is, by trying to do good. Instead of attempting to sanctify herself by good works, the Christian must pray to be sanctified by the Spirit: "it is not enough that we *originally* received grace from God, we must be receiving fresh supplies daily by incessant communion with our divine Savior."[73] Newman emphasized prayer (and the means of grace more generally) as the only route to sanctification because he feared that a direct focus on good works would obscure the centrality of faith as "the principle by which (under God) we [are] enabled to die unto sin and live unto holiness."[74] He held that good works acquire their value solely from faith. However much good people do, if they "do not walk in the Spirit," they are lost; "in the eyes of a pure and holy God, they are odious, because their doings spring not from *faith*."[75] As he pithily

---

69. JHN, No. 4, "The wounded spirit," July 25, 1824, *Serm.* 5, 40–41.

70. JHN, No. 1, "The work of man," *Serm.* 5, 22. See also No. 4, "The wounded spirit," *Serm.* 5, 38–39; No. 5, "Prayer," July 25, 1824, *Serm.* 5, 47–48; No. 13, "Parable of the vineyard," August 22, 1824, *Serm.* 5, 74.

71. JHN, No. 2, "Waiting on God," June 23, 1824, *Serm.* 5, 11.

72. JHN, No. 2, "Waiting on God," *Serm.* 5, 12. See also JHN, No. 5, "Prayer," *Serm.* 5, 44–52; No. 12, "Religion alone sufficient for man," *Serm.* 2, 271; No. 14, "Illumination," August 22, 1824, *Serm.* 5, 64–65.

73. JHN, No. 5, "Prayer," *Serm.* 5, 44.

74. JHN, No. 73, "On faith, hope, and charity," May 8, 1825, *Serm.* 5, 230.

75. JHN, No. 5, "Prayer," *Serm.* 5, 47.

put in another early sermon, "a *good* man, in Scripture, means a true believer in Christ Jesus."[76] Much of his early preaching was premised on this contrast between faith and works. Works are suspect not only because they entail notions of merit and reward antagonistic to the "free salvation of the gospel" but also because a focus on the exteriority of conduct obscures the interiority of sanctification.[77] The typical Pharisee, after all, is "one who rests principally in forms and external good works, and thinks little of the purification of the heart."[78]

In his sermon course on "the scheme of Christian doctrine," Newman drew on Erskine to systematize an understanding of good works as springing from the affective change that results from apprehending the doctrine of the atonement.[79] While doing so—between September 1824 and September 1825—he gradually adopted the doctrine of baptismal regeneration. On his new view, sanctification began with baptism, rather than a distinct experience of conversion. As a result, he no longer believed in a radical affective change prior to growth in holiness, even though he continued to hold that good works issue from an affective change rooted in faith. This shift is reflected in his sermon course. In its earlier parts, when he was still unsure about baptismal regeneration, he described sanctification without explicating its temporal dimensions. It remains unclear whether faith changes the affections instantaneously (as soon as the doctrine of the atonement is apprehended) or whether this takes time. But by the end of the course, in a sermon of July 1825, he explicitly guarded against the former interpretation. He began by recapitulating the gist of his course, which had discussed "the characteristic doctrines of the gospel," and their "reception into the heart *by faith*" in order to "purify and renew the inward man."[80] Still reluctant to treat good works directly, he had approached these sanctifying "effects of faith" by means of their "contrary vices" from the conviction that "to dissuade from unholiness is to urge to holiness."[81] Following the same method, he would now criticize "worldliness" so as to promote "spirituality of mind."[82] Before entering upon the subject, however, he wanted to emphasize the gradual nature of affective change.

Many people, Newman argued, think that faith, "being the transference of our affections *from* the creature *to* the Creator, must at once dislodge worldliness."[83] Now "this would be quite true, *if* our faith were perfect." But it is not. Instead, faith is a "living and growing" reality, which varies indefinitely in individuals:

---

76. JHN, No. 6, "Self-righteousness," July 18, 1824, *Serm.* 5, 29.

77. JHN, No. 15, "Parable of the Pharisee and the publican," August 29, 1824, *Serm.* 5, 82.

78. JHN, No. 15, "Parable of the Pharisee and the publican," *Serm.* 5, 80.

79. JHN, No. 103, "Holiness the end of the Gospel," September 4, 1825, *Serm.* 5, 292. See pp. 84–95 in this book.

80. JHN, No. 89, "against worldliness," July 10, 1825, *Serm.* 5, 243.

81. JHN, No. 89, "against worldliness," *Serm.* 5, 244.

82. JHN, No. 89, "against worldliness," *Serm.* 5, 244.

83. JHN, No. 89, "against worldliness," *Serm.* 5, 244.

The more faith we have the more we overcome the world — as faith grows and spreads within us, worldliness is subdued, and brought under — but faith may be true faith as far as it goes though it is but partial and slight — there is no inconsistency then in supposing a person <man> a true believer and yet in some degree worldly.[84]

At bottom, this was a critique of the evangelical account of regeneration, and Newman drew out the implication himself. "It is indeed a very serious error," he argued, "to suppose faith perfect, and the regenerate character <a man who has once turned to God> at once purged <cleansed> from all his former sins, and changed in heart and principle."[85] In part, this was a critique of his own earlier position, perhaps his first. Although he had never denied the tenacity of indwelling sin, he had held for years that regeneration is precisely the kind of radical change of "heart and principle" he now criticized. He now feared this view would slacken people's efforts to become holy: "I say it is a *serious* error, because it will lead us to account faith as a sort of charm, which will necessarily produce good works without our caring more about it."[86] It is difficult, though not impossible, to reconcile this critique with other parts of the sermon course, which represent the logic that leads from faith, via the affections, to praxis as almost inexorable. Even though it is still faith that changes the affections, Newman was beginning to allow that a direct focus on doing good—"caring more about it"—is part and parcel of becoming holy.

In this process of rethinking sanctification, Newman settled on the category of habit to denote what changes in the subject when she becomes holy. In a sermon on January 2, 1825, entitled *Preparation for death*, he reiterated his usual take on sanctification as a preparation for the afterlife: "according as the mind has been exercised in habits of holiness or worldliness, so is it fitted or not fitted to enjoy the pure delights of heaven."[87] But what is new here is the mention of "habit." In previous sermons, he had used the term only to denote negative religious states. He had spoken of "inveterate habits of sin," "habits of worldliness," and "habits of irreligion," but he had not used it positively, in the sense of holy habits.[88] This makes sense. To one schooled in Aristotle, as Newman was, habit denotes a stable disposition, acquired by practice. Sin could easily be understood that way, since it depends wholly on human agency, but Newman had rejected the idea that sanctification depends on human efforts to do good. Good works

<hr>

84. JHN, No. 89, "against worldliness," *Serm.* 5, 244.

85. JHN, No. 89, "against worldliness," *Serm.* 5, 244.

86. JHN, No. 89, "against worldliness," *Serm.* 5, 245.

87. JHN, No. 50, "Preparation for death," January 2, 1825, *Serm.* 5, 157.

88. JHN, No. 1, "The work of man," *Serm.* 5, 21; No. 28, "Parable of the barren fig tree," October 17, 1824, *Serm.* 5, 119; No. 36, "God's word a refuge in trouble," November 21, 1824, *Serm.* 5, 136.

are the outcome, not the means, of sanctification. He retained this idea in the new sermon, where 'habit' only denotes a stable disposition, not its acquisition by practice. Thus, he attributed our failure to break "confirmed habits of religious sloth" not to lack of trying but to trying in the wrong way. We fail, "because we seek to do that only 'with *our* might' which demands no less than a divine arm to effect." Instead of *doing*, therefore, we should be *asking*: "thus only shall we be able to 'do our work with *our might*,' when we first ask for the might of Christ."[89] Sanctification, then, as before, depends on prayer as the means to receive the continual infusion of divine grace that we need to become holy. Still, the introduction of the category of habit bodes a change.

In the summer of 1825, Newman returned to the issue of sanctification. In a sermon of August 7, he set out, once again, to clarify the relation between sanctification and eternal life. He considered it evident that "our present virtue" does not "entitle us on the score of merit to the reward of heaven."[90] Still, there must be a "*connexion* between holiness here and happiness hereafter," otherwise St Paul—in the text for Newman's sermon—would not have made eternal life conditional on holiness: "If ye through the Spirit do mortify the deeds of the body, ye shall live."[91] In explanation, Newman once more portrayed holiness as the bond between this life and the next. Holiness, he explained, "is a *condition* of salvation, not because there is any merit in it, but because we could not enjoy salvation without it . . . sanctification and the bliss of heaven are *in kind* the very same."[92] And thus, "this life is a *preparation* for another . . . here we are to acquire certain habits of mind without which we cannot enjoy heaven."[93] Although formulated more strongly than before, this idea was not new. What changed was his presentation of the means to acquire such habits:

> Self discipline then, self denial, mortification, prayer, self examination, the ordinances of grace, and endeavours and struggles after holiness are the means, which under the grace of God, are to bring our hearts into that state of feeling which is meet and right for heaven.[94]

This inventory includes the means he had emphasized before—prayer, self-examination, ordinances of grace—but added an agentic dimension aimed directly at good works. He explained such efforts to acquire holiness in terms of habit formation:

89. JHN, No. 50, "Preparation for death," *Serm.* 5, 158.
90. JHN, No. 97, "Future reward not merited by us," August 7, 1825, *Serm.* 5, 279.
91. JHN, No. 97, "Future reward not merited by us," *Serm.* 5, 281, 279. See Romans 8:13.
92. JHN, No. 97, "Future reward not merited by us," *Serm.* 5, 282.
93. JHN, No. 97, "Future reward not merited by us," *Serm.* 5, 281.
94. JHN, No. 97, "Future reward not merited by us," *Serm.* 5, 282.

The more we exercise ourselves in any art or pursuit, the more skilful we become. In like manner the more we exert ourselves in acts of humility, the more humble we become — in acts of faith, the more believing — of charity, the more loving — of meekness, the more meek and long suffering.[95]

This is a crucial shift. For the first time, Newman applied the secular paradigm of habit formation to the spiritual life. In 1821, he had denied outright that we can acquire "the Christian virtues" by performing virtuous acts, and this conviction still dominated his early preaching at St Clement's. Now, he not only stated that holiness consists of relatively stable dispositions but also that it is acquired by practice.

This shift in Newman's account of sanctification owed much to Joseph Butler's *Analogy of Religion* (1736), a quintessential Oriel read. Studying it was "an era" in Newman's theological development and shaped his thought in diverse, lasting, and profound ways.[96] Newman variously dated his first reading to 1823 and 1825, but there are few, if any, traces of its influence until he began to study it in earnest in June 1825.[97] In the *Analogy*, Butler elaborated an anthropology that emphasized the human capacity for improvement. Human beings are so constituted that "they are capable of naturally becoming qualified for states of life, for which they were once wholly unqualified."[98] And not only can people improve, they can do so lastingly. "We are capable, not only of acting, and of having different momentary impressions made upon us, but of getting a new facility in any kind of action, and of settled alterations in our temper or character."[99] This is what Butler called "the power of habits," which "are to be formed by exercise," that is, by "repeated acts."[100] If these habits concern virtue (rather than mere bodily or technical skill), Butler added, such acts must not only be recurrent but also be based on "inward practical purposes." Only acts that are meant to be virtuous, can be virtuous: "it is only these inward principles exerted, which are strictly acts of obedience, of veracity, of justice, and of charity."[101] Obviously, if we do

---

95. JHN, No. 97, "Future reward not merited by us," *Serm.* 5, 282.

96. *Apo.*, 67; Jane Garnett, "Joseph Butler," in *The Oxford Handbook of John Henry Newman*, ed. Frederick D. Aquino and Benjamin J. King (Oxford: Oxford University Press, 2018), 135–53.

97. *AW*, 192; *Apo.*, 67; *LD* 1, 238, 262. Only one instance merits discussion. When making up his mind on regeneration in January 1825, he noted in his diary: "I confess it seems more agreeable to the analogy of God's works, that there should be no harsh line, but degrees of holiness indefinitely small" (JHN, "January 13, 1825," *AW*, 204). The idea of an analogy between the workings of providence and the operation of grace is pure Butler, but the context and the phrasing of the remark suggest that it was rather the admission of a Butlerian objection (leveled by Pusey or, more likely, Hawkins) than the product of direct engagement with the *Analogy*.

98. Joseph Butler, *The Analogy of Religion, Natural and Revealed, to the Constitution and Course of Nature* (London: John Chidley, 1838), 121.

99. Butler, *The Analogy of Religion*, 121.

100. Butler, *The Analogy of Religion*, 121, 126, 123.

101. Butler, *The Analogy of Religion*, 123.

not obey or speak truthfully for their own sake, but for some other reason (say, gain), the habit of obedience or veracity will not be strengthened (but rather the habit of avarice).

Beginning in the summer of 1825, Newman increasingly applied Butler's logic of habit formation to the process of sanctification. In a sermon on October 30, 1825, of which only the abstract is preserved, he insisted that a habit is "*acquired* not natural," and that it "depends on *principle*."[102] For the believer, this principle derives from faith. Newman certainly did not think human beings have the natural capacity to form holy habits. He insisted that "natural virtue" is "not Christian," and that "even the capacity" to acquire "habits of obedience . . . we owe to grace."[103] Nevertheless, he used the idea of habit to explain the dispositions of a person under grace. A habit, he argued, "cannot be inactive"; it issues in practice. It can neither be "inconstant nor partial"; thus, it issues in *consistent* practice. Habits, moreover, are *formed by* practice, so that they cannot be "acquired without effort." Actions, in fact, are "valuable only as they tend to habits." Finally, the process of habit formation is inescapable: "we are always confirming in habits good or bad." Hence, the importance of engaging in *right* actions.[104] A week later, Newman elaborated this idea in a sermon originally entitled, *The events of life, the means of acquiring habits*.[105] Since he retitled and extensively rewrote it for later preachings, only the sermon abstract is a reliable witness to his thought in the autumn of 1825.[106] It describes how temporal relations, afflictions, and temptations are means of forming "holy habits," so that this world becomes "on the whole a *school of virtue*."[107] Newman, in sum, began to conceptualize the sanctification of the baptized as a process of habit formation.

The idea of sanctification as habit formation increased Newman's emphasis on holiness as a requirement for ultimate salvation. In a Good Friday sermon March 24, 1826, he insisted that there are no shortcuts to holiness. If becoming holy means forming habits, it must be "the business of a life."[108] The sermon was on Luke's account of the crucified robber, who asked Jesus to remember him and was granted mercy.[109] Many evangelicals applied the case of the robber to that of ordinary Christians and held that salvation is simply there for the asking.

---

102. JHN, No. 113, "Habits of obedience to the law," October 30, 1825, *Serm.* 5, 343.

103. JHN, No. 113, "Habits of obedience," *Serm.* 5, 343.

104. JHN, No. 113, "Habits of obedience," *Serm.* 5, 343.

105. JHN, No. 114, "The events of life, the means of acquiring habits," November 6, 1825, *Serm.* 5, 355.

106. JHN, No. 114, "The world a discipline of moral character," *Serm.* 5, 344–54. The sermon was repreached (with different scripture texts) in 1826, 1827 (thrice), 1828 (thrice), 1830, 1835, 1838, and 1840.

107. JHN, No. 114, "The events of life," *Serm.* 5, 355.

108. JHN, No. 146, "On the penitent thief," March 24, 1826, *Serm.* 5, 397.

109. Luke 23:42–43.

Thomas Scott, for instance, had argued that "if a man should die, immediately after the first exercise of true faith, (as the thief on the cross did), . . . he would certainly enter heaven as a justified person."[110] Newman feared that such logic would serve to excuse the indefinite postponement of holy living on the supposition that "though men live on till the end of life in neglect of religion, yet then they will be able to turn to Christ [and] on their prayer for forgiveness will at once be freely pardoned."[111] To counter this conclusion (which Scott, of course, did not advocate), Newman drew on Whately. In a sermon at Halesworth, Whately had enlarged on the unique situation of the robber, who, in the face of the utter defeat of Jesus' chances of temporal success, was the only person to believe that his kingdom was not of this world. Such an exceptional act of faith cannot be matched by any contemporary Christian.[112] Newman adopted both Whately's arguments and his conclusion. The thief displayed "perhaps the most extraordinary instance of faith related in Scripture."[113] He was "as far as we are told the first, the only correct believer then in the world . . . the only one who could discern his Redeemer in His low estate, and see beauty in Him, and place his eternal interests into His hands."[114] Hence, the circumstances of his case are "quite singular." No English Christian will ever be in the like position: "his is no parallel case to any one among ourselves."[115]

Newman wanted to dispel the idea that a mere confession of faith in Christ is enough to fit us for heaven. "There is no[t] a more common practical error than . . . supposing everything done for us by Christ independently of ourselves," he argued.[116] People forget that Christ has two offices. He is not only "reconciling God to us" (justification) but also "reconciling us to God" (sanctification). In the former, human beings have no part. But the latter "is a *process*" requiring "time and labour." Of course, Christ remains "the sole author of all blessing and salvation." In baptism, he gives us "a principle which without Him we should never have had, to teach us what sin is, and what faith is, and what the love of God." But this principle must be actively developed. Accordingly, "the birth and growth of holiness in our souls . . . is a work of great effort and long time."[117] Hence, "a

110. Scott, *Essays on the Most Important Subjects in Religion*, 194.

111. JHN, No. 146, "On the penitent thief," *Serm.* 5, 393.

112. A country pastor [Richard Whately], *A View of the Scripture Revelations concerning a Future State* (London: B. Fellowes, 1829), 264–69.

113. JHN, No. 146, "On the penitent thief," *Serm.* 5, 393. Newman's later note of "Whateleyan" on the manuscript concerns this dependence. As Whately's sermons were only published a few years later, Newman must have either borrowed the manuscript or learned of Whately's take on this narrative in conversation (see p. 170 in this book).

114. JHN, No. 146, "On the penitent thief," *Serm.* 5, 394.

115. JHN, No. 146, "On the penitent thief," *Serm.* 5, 395.

116. JHN, No. 146, "On the penitent thief," *Serm.* 5, 395.

117. JHN, No. 146, "On the penitent thief," *Serm.* 5, 396.

mere prayer, a mere saying 'Lord remember me' is not enough to secure us heaven."[118] Only by a gradual process of learning to love what God loves, can we come to enjoy being with him. Without it, there can be no such enjoyment. To send "a worldly and unrenewed person . . . *to heaven*," Newman insisted, would be "a severe punishment."[119] He "would be miserable *in heaven*," because his desires would be at variance with those of God.[120] As Newman put it in a sermon of August 1826, heaven "is not a place of happiness, *except* to the holy."[121]

Election: Scripture and System

When discussing how Newman's religious crisis was brought to a head by the dilemma Sumner presented between Calvinism and baptismal regeneration, I noted that the doctrine of baptismal regeneration challenges the evangelical system in its entirety, not only its conception of conversion. It does so because it directly undermines the idea of efficacious grace (the idea, that is, that grace necessarily leads to salvation). If baptism conveys grace to all who receive it, and not every baptized person is saved, grace is not irresistible. In this way, the infallible sequence of predestination, election, conversion, and final perseverance comes undone. Soon after January 1825, Newman began to perceive these implications. A month later, in his annual birthday reflection, he noted, "I have taken many doctrines almost on trust from Scott &c and on serious examination hardly find them confirmed by Scripture."[122] "I have come to no decision of the doctrines of election &c," he added in explanation, "but the predestination of individuals seems to me hardly a scriptural doctrine."[123] Newman, then, began to realize that some of the Calvinistic convictions he had held as manifestly scriptural, rested, instead, on the authority of the evangelical authors he had read after his adolescent conversion. Sumner, once again, was at the root of this realization.

In his *Apostolical Preaching*, Sumner argued that the Calvinist take on predestination, election, and efficacious grace did not conform to the teaching of St Paul, because St Paul's use of the concepts of predestination and election is

118. JHN, No. 146, "On the penitent thief," *Serm.* 5, 397.
119. JHN, No. 146, "On the penitent thief," *Serm.* 5, 396.
120. JHN, No. 146, "On the penitent thief," *Serm.* 5, 397.
121. JHN, No. 153, "Holiness Necessary for Future Blessedness," August 6, 1826, *PaS* 1, 7.
122. JHN, "February 21, 1825," *AW*, 204.
123. JHN, "February 21, 1825," *AW*, 204. It is unclear how Newman distinguished predestination from election. But if we take Sumner's usage as a lead, what Newman seems to reject here is the idea that God has from all eternity decreed which individuals are to be saved, the position, that is, that makes election depend not on God's foreknowledge but on his "absolute decrees," as Sumner put it (*Apostolical Preaching*, 40). Election itself, and the efficacious grace that comes with it—which Sumner also rejected, as leading "to the same result" (*Apostolical Preaching*, 77)—Newman did not yet dare to jeopardize. But perhaps we should not make too much of the distinction.

communal rather than individual. What St Paul means, Sumner maintained, is that the Gentiles are now "admitted to privileges which had been confined to the Jews": "St. Paul speaks of election to the grace of the Gospel, and not of such personal election as Calvinists teach: election which leads infallibly to holiness as a mean of the salvation which has been determined from the foundation of the world."[124]

This description of the Calvinist position matches that of Newman in his 1821 *Collection*, and Sumner countered it not by theory but by scripture. When St Paul addresses the Corinthians, who "had admitted gross errors into their practice," or the Galatians, who "had swerved widely from sound doctrine," he does not, for that reason, treat them as unregenerate.[125] Instead, he reminds the Corinthians that "your body is the *temple of the Holy Ghost, which is in you*," and the Galatians that they "*have put on Christ*."[126] They are still regenerate, still elect, even though they abuse the grace given to them. By November 1825, Newman had come to agree with Sumner and began to use his arguments in preaching. Like Sumner, Newman maintained that "the Apostle in his letters to the churches addresses *all* who are called Christians[,] all who make up the visible body of the church as the children of God, as all elected in Christ and all heirs of grace," irrespective of their present behavior.[127] He substantiated his point by elaborating on Sumner's examples of the Galatians, with their "grievous heresy," and the Corinthians, with their "many sins," all of whom, "the weak, the inconsistent, the partially ignorant, and even the proud, the Apostle acknowledges as under grace."[128] To all of them, and, by extension, to "the whole body of the church is the Spirit given . . . and all have . . . more or less been partakers of His grace."[129] Every baptized person, in other words, is to be regarded as elect. Still, Newman's former belief in individual election was not quite rooted out.

In his birthday reflection for 1826, Newman seemed more certain than he had been a year before: "I am almost convinced against predestination and election in the Calvinistic sense, that is, I see no proof of them in Scripture."[130] The qualifier is important. Apparently, lack of scriptural proof was not enough to settle the question. Still, it sufficed for practical purposes. So much is clear from the farewell sermon Newman preached two months later, when he left St Clement's to become a tutor of Oriel. It discussed the widely held Calvinist notion that "there are certain individuals whom God hath chosen to salvation, and that all of these and none

<hr>

124. Sumner, *Apostolical Preaching*, 82, 90–91.

125. Sumner, *Apostolical Preaching*, 157.

126. Sumner, *Apostolical Preaching*, 158, 165; 1 Corinthians 6:16; Galatians 3:26.

127. JHN, No. 118, "Our admittance into the church," *Serm.* 5, 362.

128. JHN, No. 118, "Our admittance into the church," *Serm.* 5, 363–64.

129. JHN, No. 118, "Our admittance into the church," *Serm.* 5, 362.

130. JHN, "February 21, 1826," *AW*, 208.

but these can be saved."[131] Against this idea, Newman noted, "I cannot get myself to say a word . . . because *it may be true.*" But he added immediately, "*I cannot see it in the Bible,* and if it is not in the Bible, it *may be false.*"[132] For Sumner, as for many critics of Calvinism, the absence of scriptural evidence was compounded by what Sumner described as the manifest injustice of the idea that God "pardons whom he will . . . without any consideration than that of his own good pleasure," that is, without considering his foreknowledge of people's conduct.[133] Newman dared not make such a judgment. "I should talk neither reverently nor wisely if I attempted to show that election was an unjust thing," he observed, "because I think it would be no injustice in God if He had left us all to perish."[134]

At the same time, Newman also would not argue *for* individual election, since "Scripture assures us that God wishes *all men* to be saved . . . and declares those who have had grace given *may* fall away unto perdition."[135] God's universal salvific will, in other words, is at odds with the idea of individual election, while the scriptural assertion that grace can be lost is incompatible with the Calvinistic notions of efficacious grace and final perseverance. These are forceful observations, and they represent the thrust of Newman's argument. Despite his initial caveats, he drew on Sumner to argue that St Paul's usage of the term always has reference to the election of a *community*—first that of the Jewish people, and now that of the Gentiles, too—and not to the election of individuals. He clearly perceived the consequences of this take on election and drew them out for his congregation. "If this be all" that election means, he maintained, there is no "infallible and irreversible election unto life . . . the Jews we know *fell away* from their election, Christians then may in like manner from theirs."[136] The slight hesitation indicated by the "if this be all" either witnesses to a lingering apprehension on Newman's part that individual election "may be true," indeed, or to a sensitivity for evangelical leanings in his congregation. Whatever the case may be, he did not wish to depart from the parish of St Clement's while leaving the Calvinistic idea of efficacious grace uncontested.

The development of Newman's view on election is not just important in itself but also for the shift in theological method to which it testifies. Before, his take on election had been largely determined by the logical exigencies of the evangelical system. The idea of efficacious grace required that the elect will be both converted and ultimately saved. Newman's evangelical course of enquiry, then,

<hr>

131. JHN, No. 150, "General observations on the whole subject—conclusion," April 23, 1826, *Serm.* 5, 403.

132. JHN, No. 150, "General observations," *Serm.* 5, 403.

133. Sumner, *Apostolical Preaching*, 53; see 53–58.

134. JHN, No. 150, "General observations," *Serm.* 5, 403.

135. JHN, No. 150, "General observations," *Serm.* 5, 403.

136. JHN, No. 150, "General observations," *Serm.* 5, 404.

was from system to scripture. He admitted as much in July 1826, when he noted that he had written the 1821 *Collection "juxta praescriptum"*—according to precept.[137] By February 1825, he realized that his reliance on evangelical authors like Scott had been uncritical to a fault. Now, he insisted that, "I am persuaded that very many of my most positive and dogmatical notions were taken *from books*."[138] The evangelical system, in other words, had determined his interpretation of scripture. In 1825 and 1826, he began to invert this course of enquiry. When scripture indicated that God wishes *all* to be saved and that people *can* fall away, or when St Paul addressed even gross sinners or outright heretics as under grace, Newman could no longer gloss over such statements simply because the evangelical doctrine of election did not allow for them. We will return to this shift in theological method—from the *system* to the *data* of religion—below, after considering a final change entailed by Newman's adoption of the doctrine of baptismal regeneration.

The Turn to the Visible Church

A key consequence of accepting the doctrine of baptismal regeneration is an increased bestowal of meaning and value on the visible church. As Sumner intimated, belonging to the visible church had little salvific import on the Calvinistic model. The young Newman had regarded the individual as the focal point of God's salvific will. God had elected certain individuals to salvation, and they would consequently experience a conversion and ultimately be saved. This emphasis on individual election entailed a rigid distinction between the visible and the invisible church, that is, between membership—through baptism—of the social institution called the Church of England, and membership—through conversion—of the invisible community of the elect. Membership in the one did not entail membership in the other. By gradually accepting baptismal regeneration, Newman was forced to reconsider this distinction. At the same time, he began to rethink the role of the visible church in mediating religious truth. These developments are related because of the intrinsic connection between grace and truth. If grace is mediated through the social institution of the church, it stands to reason that the church fosters the necessary means to continue in that baptismal grace. The most important of these is a right faith, which depends on correct instruction in religious truth. It is no coincidence, then, that when Newman began to emphasize the communal character of the mediation of grace, he also stressed the communal character of the mediation of truth.

In a sermon on December 4, 1825, *On the use of the visible church*, Newman still rigidly distinguished the visible from the invisible church, much as any evan-

<hr>

137. JHN, "July 26, 1826," *AW*, 172.
138. JHN, "July 26, 1826," *AW*, 172.

gelical would. The one consists of "those who profess faith," the other "of all who have it."[139] Membership in the visible church comes by baptism, "an ordinance we see," but "the baptism of the Spirit," which makes one a member of the invisible church, "is in secret and without our knowing when and where it descends."[140] This rigid distinction is remarkable in view of Newman's argument two weeks earlier that all Christians are elect and that baptism entitles them to the Holy Spirit, but it does not directly contradict it. It merely shows that he thought many baptized Christians neglected the privilege they had acquired in baptism. "These two, the unseen and the actually seen Church, ought to be one and the same," he argued, but "this is far from being the case — too many are in the one who do not belong to the other — too many profess and call themselves Christians who were never led into her way of truth nor hold the faith in unity of spirit and in righteousness of life."[141] Perhaps this rather pessimistic assessment of the disparity between the visible and the invisible church shows how far the idea of baptism as entitlement to the Spirit still is from a full acceptance of baptismal regeneration. Yet, although Newman downplayed the role of the visible church in mediating grace to such a degree that, at least in tone, it jarred with his sermon of November 20, he magnified the role of the visible church in mediating truth. And this was, after all, the immediate topic of his sermon, which aimed at expounding St Paul's declaration that the visible church is "the pillar and ground of the truth" (1 Tm 3:15).

Newman's exposition was predicated on a simple premise: God did not intend scripture to be the only means of teaching religious knowledge. "In that case every Christian would have stood by himself unconnected with others," he argued, so that "he would have been bound to make out the Bible for himself, study it for himself alone, and look no further than his own personal salvation."[142] But this is not what God envisioned. By baptism, by the Lord's Supper, by communal prayer, and by appointing "an order of ministers, to watch over and rear His family," God "has bound the Church together in our visible union and fellowship."[143] As the sermon title indicates, it is the uses, or functions, of this visible church on which Newman focuses. His treatment is remarkable for the degree to which it relies on other people's thought, which indicates, at once, the relative novelty of the insights and his eagerness to present them to his congregation—perhaps even before properly digesting them.

From Butler's *Analogy*, which he had only just finished, Newman derived the idea that the visible church was instituted to preserve the faith; to keep it "from

<hr>

139. JHN, No. 121, "On the use of the visible church," December 4, 1825, *Serm.* 4, 28.
140. JHN, No. 121, "On the use of the visible church," *Serm.* 4, 28.
141. JHN, No. 121, "On the use of the visible church," *Serm.* 4, 28.
142. JHN, No. 121, "On the use of the visible church," *Serm.* 4, 29.
143. JHN, No. 121, "On the use of the visible church," *Serm.* 4, 29.

being lost and given up."[144] Butler's idea really must have struck a chord. It occupies only a page or two in the *Analogy*, but forty years later, in the *Apologia*, Newman still mentioned it as a central feature of Butler's argument. In the sermon, he slightly amended a citation from the *Analogy*, to enlarge on the church's call,

> to be, like a city on a hill, a standing memorial to the world, of the duty which we owe our Maker and Redeemer — to call men continually, both by example and instruction, to attend to it, and by the form of religion ever before their eyes, remind them of the reality — to take care of the Holy Scripture — to be a rallying point in times of irreligion and, to hold up and extend the knowledge of redemption till the whole earth should be turned unto God. [145]

The church, then, in Butler's robust conception of it, both preserves the faith and calls people to attend to it. To ensure that this function can be fulfilled in unimpaired continuity, Newman argued, "an order of ministers was instituted," who are "the descendants of the Apostles by the imposition of hands."[146]

From Edward Hawkins, Newman derived the idea that, beyond preserving religious truth in history, the visible church is our primary "*teacher* in the truth."[147] Newman's point was quite simple. In general, people learn about religion before they ever open a Bible, "from the ministers of God, from the public prayers and services, from the creeds and still earlier our parents, from our friends, guardians, masters and governors."[148] All these people or institutions are part of the visible church. Of course, such elementary teaching is "*from* the Bible, but not at first *by* the Bible." The church, in short, "is to *explain* and *teach* the truth, and the inspired word is to *prove* it."[149] This insight derived not only from actual religious practice; it also corresponded to the conduct of the Apostles. It was even suggested by the disparate "structure itself of the inspired books."[150]

This had been Hawkins' primary point in a University sermon of 1818, published the year after as *A Dissertation upon the Use and Importance of Unauthoritative Tradition, as an Introduction to the Christian Doctrines*. Hawkins' argument was as

<hr>

144. JHN, No. 121, "On the use of the visible church," *Serm.* 4, 29.

145. JHN, No. 121, "On the use of the visible church," *Serm.* 4, 28; Butler, *Analogy*, 200–1; and *Apo.*, 67. Newman substituted "to take care of the Holy Scripture" for Butler's "to be the repository of the oracles of God"—a role that Newman, at this time of lingering evangelicalism, presumably only ascribed to scripture.

146. JHN, No. 121, "On the use of the visible church," *Serm.* 4, 29, 30.

147. JHN, No. 121, "On the use of the visible church," *Serm.* 4, 30. See *Apo.*, 65–66; *AW*, 78–79.

148. JHN, No. 121, "On the use of the visible church," *Serm.* 4, 30.

149. JHN, No. 121, "On the use of the visible church," *Serm.* 4, 30.

150. JHN, No. 121, "On the use of the visible church," *Serm.* 4, 31.

straightforward as the title of his sermon suggests. It is a matter of plain observation that many doctrines that are considered central to the Christian faith are
very *"indirectly taught* in the Scriptures," even though the Bible could have easily
included "more *direct and systematic* statements of the main points of faith."[151]
While scripture "affords indeed the very strongest *proofs*" of such key doctrines
as the Trinity, "it is often the least adapted to the purpose of *teaching*" them.[152]
We can only explain this remarkable fact, Hawkins argued, if we consider *"tradition"* as a divinely intended "aid and guide" to teach doctrine. "The Church," in
short, "should *teach*, and the Scriptures *prove*, the doctrines of Christianity."[153]
Newman had always been aware that doctrines are not on the surface of scripture.
He used to consider their hiddenness a foil for the "proud & careless." They "<u>are</u>
explicitly & expressly contained in Scripture, but not to be seen without Divine
aid."[154] Hawkins taught him to expect such aid not directly, but mediately, through
the church. As Newman concluded in his sermon, scripture is "designed always
to have the assistance of the church in explaining it."[155]

Above, I suggested that Newman could retain a rigid distinction between the
visible and invisible church in this sermon, because he regarded baptism as conveying a title to, rather than reception of, the Holy Spirit. This interpretation is confirmed by his treatment of the church a year later, when he had come to accept
that the Spirit is received in baptism. Instead of beginning with a distinction between
the visible and invisible church, he now took the Nicene Creed's profession of
belief in "the One Catholic and Apostolic Church" as his point of departure.[156] He
asserted, without any qualifiers, that by "the *Church* in the Creeds is meant that
visible Christian body and society instituted by Christ and His Apostles professing
the one faith of the gospel, governed by certain officers, and associated by certain
laws."[157] Instead of focusing on the functions of the visible church, he now emphasized its corporate reality, whence these functions derive. The church, he argued,
"is not a mere collection of individuals, who have little or no connexion one with
another . . . but it is a society, a body corporate (so to say) a system composed of
many parts differing from one another yet all united." Human beings are, after all,
inherently social: "God has made us depend upon each other for every thing."[158]

151. Edward Hawkins, *A Dissertation upon the Use and Importance of Unauthoritative Tradition, as
an Introduction to the Christian Doctrines* (Oxford: J. Parker, 1819), 1, 2.
152. Hawkins, *A Dissertation*, 11.
153. Hawkins, *A Dissertation*, 22.
154. JHN, *Trinitas or Humanitas*, 1817, BOA A.9.1.b.
155. JHN, No. 121, "On the use of the visible church," *Serm.* 4, 32.
156. JHN, No. 157, "On the One Catholic and Apostolic Church," November 19, 1826, *Serm.*
4, 42. The *Book of Common Prayer* rendered the Niceno-Constantinopolitan Creed without the "holy"
as a mark of the church.
157. JHN, No. 157, "On the One Catholic and Apostolic Church," *Serm.* 4, 43.
158. JHN, No. 157, "On the One Catholic and Apostolic Church," *Serm.* 4, 43.

Thus, when St Paul speaks of the church as "*one* body," he means "a *visible* body," not just "a communion of spirits," because people "could not at all help or profit each other" if they were to be "united only in some unseen unknown manner" (e.g., by merely believing or feeling the same things).[159]

From the time of the Apostles, this one society was governed by ordained ministers, who had "spiritual power over the body of the people."[160] It was regulated, moreover, "by *certain laws* the due execution of which was in the hands of the ordained clergy."[161]

This "systematic form of church government," which has existed since the time of the Apostles, serves four ends. Three of these ends aim at preservation, namely, of "the Christian religion itself," of "*purity of doctrine*," and of "Christian piety, and holiness."[162] The church keeps Christianity in existence, maintains "sound doctrine," and ensures that its members grow in holy living.[163] In addition, the church promotes "*order*" by means of a set of fixed "rites, ceremonies, [and] ordinances."[164] Through an unbroken apostolic succession, this visible church has continued through the ages in different "branches" in various countries—"all members and descendants of that primitive church for which the Apostles laid down their lives."[165]

This view of the church entailed a rejection of religious dissent. "I see schism on all sides," Newman lamented, "Men see many sects called Christian, and think they have a right to choose their own — but God has given them no such right."[166] In England, the situation was simple: the "one Apostolic Church," to which every English Christian should belong, is "the Church of Bishops Priests and Deacons"—the Established Church.[167] This visible church is both geographically and historically unified: it is the one church of all England, and it is one with the church instituted by Christ through apostolic succession.

In a much later note on the manuscript, Newman wrote that this sermon was "one of the first, if not the first, declaration I made of High Church principles" (although he recognized that his sermon a year before had already tended in that direction).[168] Peter Nockles has broadly defined the theology of High Churchmen—or "Orthodox," as most preferred to call themselves—as emphas-

159. JHN, No. 157, "On the One Catholic and Apostolic Church," *Serm.* 4, 44.
160. JHN, No. 157, "On the One Catholic and Apostolic Church," *Serm.* 4, 47.
161. JHN, No. 157, "On the One Catholic and Apostolic Church," *Serm.* 4, 47.
162. JHN, No. 157, "On the One Catholic and Apostolic Church," *Serm.* 4, 48.
163. JHN, No. 157, "On the One Catholic and Apostolic Church," *Serm.* 4, 49.
164. JHN, No. 157, "On the One Catholic and Apostolic Church," *Serm.* 4, 49.
165. JHN, No. 157, "On the One Catholic and Apostolic Church," *Serm.* 4, 52.
166. JHN, No. 157, "On the One Catholic and Apostolic Church," *Serm.* 4, 52.
167. JHN, No. 157, "On the One Catholic and Apostolic Church," *Serm.* 4, 54.
168. JHN, No. 157, "On the One Catholic and Apostolic Church," *Serm.* 4, 42n2. The note was written on December 10, 1857.

izing, to varying degrees, "the doctrine of apostolical succession"; the "supremacy of Scripture," with due reference to "authorised standards such as the Creeds, the Prayer Book, and the Catechism"; the value of a consent of the "early Fathers . . . as witnesses and expositors of scriptural truth"; "the primacy of dogma"; "sacramental grace"; and "a practical spirituality based on good works rather than on any subjective conversion experience."[169] It is clear from what we have seen so far that Newman's theology began to fit these descriptors by the end of 1826. And yet, care is needed in their application, for Newman's shift entailed neither a break with his Oriel environment nor a turn to the High Church party.

Until fairly recently, it was common to pitch High Church theology against the school of Oriel thought developed by Copleston and Whately. This is accurate enough from the early 1830s onward, when Whately was at the helm of Oriel theology, but not for most of the 1820s.[170] In 1826, Newman asserted little more than what senior Oriel fellows like Hawkins, Whately, and Copleston would and did assert at the time. For instance, two Bosworth Lectures for Oriel undergraduates, written by Copleston for Whately, offer much the same argument as Newman's 1826 sermon, laying great stress on the church as the "*visible* society" of the baptized, of which "every single branch" is "regulated by certain officers" in a "continuous succession" from the Apostles for the sake of "the preservation and dissemination of . . . doctrines in their original purity" and "the maintenance of peace and good order among believers."[171] Newman, moreover, neither had nor sought to cultivate social connections with the High Church party in the Church of England, which was quite a closely-knit bunch due to "patronage and family networks."[172] Nor did he try to adopt its ideology (insofar as it had a homogeneous ideology).[173] Newman's claim to 'High Church principles' signifies his turn to the visible church—that of England, and by extension, that of the Apostles—not to party *in* that church.

This interpretation is borne out by a telling letter Newman wrote to Samuel Rickards on November 26, 1826, a week after his sermon *On the One, Catholic, and Apostolic Church*. The letter outlined a theological project for Rickards, who knew the Anglican theological tradition well, to undertake. "I begin by assuming," Newman wrote, "that the old worthies of our Church are neither orthodox nor evangelical, but untractable [*sic*] persons, suspicious characters, neither one thing nor the other."[174] Rickards should "give a kind of summary of their opinions,"

---

169. Peter B. Nockles, *The Oxford Movement in Context: Anglican High Churchmanship, 1760–1857* (Cambridge: Cambridge University Press, 1994), 25–26. See Turner, *John Henry Newman*, 12.

170. Pietro Corsi, *Science and Religion: Baden Powell and the Anglican Debate, 1800–1860* (Cambridge: Cambridge University Press, 1988), 73–79.

171. Copleston, *Remains*, 295, 299, 297, 296, 294; see also 300–3, 309–10.

172. Nockles, *The Oxford Movement in Context*, 15.

173. Nockles, *The Oxford Movement in Context*, 15.

174. JHN to Samuel Rickards, November 26, 1826, *LD* 1, 310.

taking them as "*the* English Church," and "distinctly marking out the grand bold scriptural features of that doctrine in which they all agree." In this way, the old divines would be "a band of witnesses for the truth, not opposed to each other (as they now are)," by High Churchmen and evangelicals. The proper subject for the enquiry was that which was bringing about his own theological transformation:

> that of regeneration — for it is at the very root of the whole system and branches out in different ways (according to the different views taken of it) into church of Englandism, or into *Calvinism, antipaedobaptism, the rejection of church government and discipline,* and *the mere moral system.* It is connected with the doctrines of freewill [*sic*], original sin, justification, holiness, goodworks [*sic*], election, education, the visible church, etc.[175]

Although nothing seems to have come of this rather ambitious project, the letter offering its prospectus is revealing in two respects. First, it shows that Newman's turn to the visible church was not the exchange of one theological system for another. He assumed, instead, that Church of England theology was neither that of High Churchmen nor of evangelicals. Its precise character was still to be determined. Second, the letter demonstrates that, by the end of 1826, Newman was aware of the theological implications of the course he had been taking. He realized that one's take on regeneration had many and varied ramifications for one's entire theology, just as it had had in his own case.

Another Family Controversy

Soon, Newman's new doctrinal stance led to tensions in his family. While he was gradually shedding his evangelicalism, his brother Francis's evangelical views were becoming increasingly radical, so that conflict was just a matter of time.[176] The issue that sparked controversy was at once unsurprising and highly instructive: infant baptism. In *Phases of Faith*, his 1850 religious autobiography, Frank described how the problem of infant baptism began to trouble him during his undergraduate days at Oxford. Like every student, he had to sign the Thirty-Nine Articles upon matriculation, and, once again, upon taking his BA degree. When he matriculated at Worcester in 1822, he had signed them gleefully. Like John, he had considered evangelicalism perfectly compatible with Church of England theology, but he, too, began to perceive incongruities, and his solution was the opposite of John's. When he was about to take his BA degree in 1826, he stumbled over the stipulation in the 27th Article that "the baptism of young children is in

---

175. JHN to Samuel Rickards, November 26, 1826, *LD* 1, 310.

176. See Timothy C. F. Stunt, *From Awakening to Secession: Radical Evangelicals in Switzerland and Britain 1815–1835* (Edinburgh: T&T Clark, 2000), 200–205.

any wise to be retained in the Church as most agreeable with the institution of
Christ," which he believed to be at odds with the whole bent of the New Testament. In the event, he signed, but his doubts remained.[177] By that time, he felt he
could no longer talk openly with John. Before, they had seen eye to eye on
religion. Both had gone to Ealing, and both were converted under the influence
of Walter Mayers. Years later, Frank recollected how heartily he had agreed with
a manuscript John gave him when they lodged together in Oxford in 1821 that
contained John's "controversy with a fellow-student *against* Baptismal Regeneration" (the *Dialogue—Merton—Spenser*).[178] But John had changed (and not he, as
Frank never tired of pointing out). After John accepted baptismal regeneration
and began to emphasize the importance of the visible church, Frank claims to
have "left off the attempt at intimate religious intercourse with him."[179] At home
though, Frank spoke his mind so that his sisters soon became uneasy about the
issue of baptism. In response, John began a long paper for them on February 13,
1827, entitled *Remarks on Infant Baptism*.[180]

Frank Turner, who seems not to have read much of the paper, has interpreted
Newman's move as a dogged effort "to assert religious dominance over the rest of
his family."[181] But this is a groundless attribution of motives. John insisted repeatedly
that he had been "called" to the controversy, one for which he had very little time
and which interfered with "studies which I was pursuing with advantage and for
which I was husbanding up my little leisure from Collegiate duties."[182] From the
paper, it seems that Frank was criticizing both the institution of infant baptism and
John's practice of it to such an extent that his sisters demanded that John explain
himself. John did so without enthusiasm, but with his usual sense of urgency and
duty, "as a minister of Christ."[183] This reading of the situation is confirmed by
John's argumentative strategy, which is defensive throughout. "I am only bound to
repel an <u>attack</u>, not to display my own forces," he insisted time and again.[184]

177. FWN, *Phases of Faith; or, Passages from the History of my Creed* (London: John Chapman,
1850), 3, 9–15.

178. FWN, *Contributions*, 11.

179. FWN, *Phases of Faith*, 12.

180. JHN, *Remarks on Infant Baptism*, 1827, BOA A.9.1.k. The editors of the *Letters and Diaries*
mistakenly consider February 13 as the finishing date of this paper (of sixty-six quarto pages) rather
than the date on which it was begun (*LD* 2, xix). They do so on the basis of Newman's letter to his
sisters, dated February 13, that opens the *Remarks*. This letter, however, clearly speaks of the essay
as yet to be begun (see *LD* 2, 4). Moreover, as Newman pointed out in a later note on the manuscript,
many of the sources in the *Remarks* are borrowed from William Wall's *The History of Infant-Baptism*
(1705), which he only borrowed from Oriel College library on February 11 (Parker). Sheridan
(*Newman on Justification*, 127–33) provides a useful summary of the text.

181. Turner, *John Henry Newman*, 124.

182. JHN, *Remarks on Infant Baptism*, BOA A.9.1.k, 45, 44; see also 54, 55.

183. JHN, *Remarks on Infant Baptism*, BOA A.9.1.k, 44.

184. JHN, *Remarks on Infant Baptism*, BOA A.9.1.k, 55; 44, 47, 54, 66.

Although it is clear that the *Remarks on Infant Baptism* is defensive in character, there has been some confusion about what it sought to defend. Sheridan has argued that defending "the institution of infant baptism" was *not* John's primary concern but only served as a foil to refute Frank's "denial of baptismal regeneration."[185] But this is a misreading, and it ultimately misses the point of the paper. If anything, the conflict between John and Frank was a clash of methods, much as John's argument with Charles had been (a parallel John recognized).[186] Recall that John countered Charles's objections to the content of revelation by arguing that he should consider revelation first as a fact. We should not judge of the doctrine of eternal damnation by considering whether it suits our sense of justice but by considering whether it has, in fact, been revealed. John countered Frank's objections in a similar way. The issue of infant baptism should not be decided on the basis of theological considerations about the *nature* of baptism but on the basis of historical arguments for the *fact* of its being practiced since the time of the Apostles. "We at present are inquiring into a <u>fact</u>," the opening line of Newman's paper read, "which must be proved, (as all facts are proved,) by <u>testimony</u>."[187]

John and Frank both recognized that this inquiry is complicated by the silence of the New Testament on baptizing infants; it neither commands nor prohibits the practice. For Frank, this silence alone almost settled the matter. When compounded with theological objections derived from the nature of baptism, it certainly justified the rejection of infant baptism. For John, the absence of scriptural evidence did not warrant a change of method in the inquiry, which remained one of fact rather than doctrine. Already in the summer of 1825, in controversy with Charles, John had distinguished the New Testament, as "the *record* of Christianity," from Christianity itself.[188] Like any other historical reality, Christianity does not fully coincide with what its records display. It is not because the Apostles did not *write* about infant baptism that they did not *practice* it. And there is only one way to find out whether they did: consulting ecclesiastical history. Thus, John turned to the fathers of the church, the first time he ever did so to solve a theological problem, albeit one of fact, not of doctrine. He was clear about this distinction: "While we accept the testimony of the Fathers as to the <u>fact</u>, we reject their authority in point of <u>doctrine</u>."[189] The fathers might have misunderstood the *nature* of baptism, but they believed the *practice* had been handed down from the Apostles, and since they were in a position to know, John regarded their testimony as conclusive. "I am asked why I baptize children," John concluded; "I answer

---

185. Sheridan, *Newman on Justification*, 134.
186. JHN, *Remarks on Infant Baptism*, BOA A.9.1.k, 45–46.
187. JHN, *Remarks on Infant Baptism*, BOA A.9.1.k, 1.
188. JHN to CRN, August 25, 1825, *LD* 1, 254. See p. 71 in this book.
189. JHN, *Remarks on Infant Baptism*, BOA A.9.1.k, 42; see 40–42.

because the universal church does & always has — because Hooker, Austin, and Cyprian did and thought it an act of duty to God so to do."[190]

This appeal to tradition did not imply that the New Testament had no bearing upon the question, only that its role was negative. "Infant baptism is a duty obligatory upon us," John argued, "unless it be proved from Scripture either directly or indirectly to be forbidden to us."[191] The "*onus probandi*" is on those who, like Frank, "deny its propriety."[192] Frank did offer scriptural arguments against infant baptism, and John addressed them in the second part of his paper. Frank's objections were premised on the idea that baptism "confers spiritual benefits," a presupposition that John shared, but from which Frank concluded that conversion must precede baptism.[193] Since baptism is "a ratification of the Christian covenant," Frank argued, it should be administered only to those who have shown, by faith and repentance, that they belong to it.[194] John replied that baptism *is* a ratification, but only in so far as it confirms an infant's election, which consists simply in being "born within the sound of the Gospel," that is, "in a Christian country."[195] To the objection that baptism always follows faith and repentance in the Acts of the Apostles, John responded that these particular instances from the period of "the creation of the Christian Church" should not be generalized.[196] They are subordinate to Christ's categorical declaration that "except one be born of water and the Spirit, he cannot enter into the Kingdom of God," which mentions no prior conditions whatever.[197] To Frank's argument that spiritual benefits only accrue to those who belong to the invisible church (the converted), John opposed Sumner's examples of the Corinthians and the Galatians. Even "when the one were in gross moral sin, the other in gross doctrinal error, the Apostle, while reproaching them, states boldly and fearlessly their then state of privileges."[198] Finally, like John before, Frank argued that "the actual conduct of the bulk of Christians proves they have not been benefitted by baptism."[199] John, by now, denied that human beings can make such judgments. "How presumptuous," he pointed out, "how shockingly presumptuous to attempt to decide whether baptism has or has not done good."[200] God alone

190. JHN, *Remarks on Infant Baptism*, BOA A.9.1.k, 47. Austin was a common (contracted) spelling for Augustine (of Hippo, in this case).

191. JHN, *Remarks on Infant Baptism*, BOA A.9.1.k, 20.

192. JHN, *Remarks on Infant Baptism*, BOA A.9.1.k, 20.

193. JHN, *Remarks on Infant Baptism*, BOA A.9.1.k, 46.

194. JHN, *Remarks on Infant Baptism*, BOA A.9.1.k, 48.

195. JHN, *Remarks on Infant Baptism*, BOA A.9.1.k, 50.

196. JHN, *Remarks on Infant Baptism*, BOA A.9.1.k, 50.

197. JHN, *Remarks on Infant Baptism*, BOA A.9.1.k, 52; John 3:5.

198. JHN, *Remarks on Infant Baptism*, BOA A.9.1.k, 59–60.

199. JHN, *Remarks on Infant Baptism*, BOA A.9.1.k, 60.

200. JHN, *Remarks on Infant Baptism*, BOA A.9.1.k, 60.

"knows the '<u>secrets</u>' of men's hearts." No one else "can discern the struggle between grace & sin which goes on many a year in a baptized Christian who appears outwardly to walk with the world, but who may still be a dear, but weak & erring, son of God."[201] This had been the lesson not only of his pastoral experience and of St Paul but also of his own spiritual life. "Indeed when I look upon the professing Christian world I grieve," he conceded to Frank, "but so I do when I look into my own heart — and with my perpetual & changing sins, my coldness and deadness, can I dare to think others certainly without grace, when in spite of my sins I think I am not myself?"[202]

Even though John went out of his way to counter Frank's arguments, his real qualms were with Frank's mode of arguing, which he considered as misguided as Charles's had been. John lamented the "minuteness, unmanly subtilty, and rashness" of Frank's arguments, which were based on "refinements & theorizings . . . indirect and circuitous reasonings . . . unsafe & uncertain surmises about the probable use or nature of baptism."[203]

In the end, John attributed Frank's inability or unwillingness to accept the ancient and prevailing practice of infant baptism to stubborn theological prejudice. On the evangelical system, the doctrinal case for baptizing infants was weak. Given the requirement of an experience of conversion, it would make more sense, as Frank argued, to reserve baptism for those who have had this experience. John, however, no longer viewed the issue as one of systematic theology but as one of historical fact. The question is not whether infant baptism fits a theological system (evangelical or otherwise), but whether it comes from the Apostles. This is a major shift in theological method, which is best described, as I suggested above, as a turn from the *system* to the *data* of religion.[204] A year before, John had recognized that, in the case of election, certain scripture texts militate against the Calvinistic ideas of irresistible grace and final perseverance, and he had chosen to rely on those data rather than the exigencies of the system. In the case of infant baptism, scripture was silent, so the clash of authorities was not between scripture and system but between system and tradition, and he opted for the datum of tradition.

Frank's mode of reasoning, by contrast, resembled that of Charles. Frank preferred to speculate about the doctrinal content of infant baptism, instead of considering the fact of its apostolicity. Accordingly, John argued that Frank's arguments betrayed "a <u>habit of mind</u>" dangerously like Charles's, which, "if this

---

201. JHN, *Remarks on Infant Baptism*, BOA A.9.1.k, 60.

202. JHN, *Remarks on Infant Baptism*, BOA A.9.1.k, 62.

203. JHN, *Remarks on Infant Baptism*, BOA A.9.1.k, 45, 65.

204. Newman's first university sermon defined respect for "data," rather than "excessive attachment to system," as the mark of a true scientist (No. 151, "The temper of mind injoined by Christianity, that which is indispensable in conducting scientific inquiries," July 2, 1826, BOA A.9.4, 11 [*OUS*, 9]).

particular evil is cured, may yet break out in other parts where the distemper may be more difficult of a remedy . . . [and] may as easily furnish arguments against revelation itself as against any of its peculiar doctrines."[205] John meant that if one is willing to trump the evidence for a doctrine's apostolicity because of the exigencies of a particular theological system, one might jeopardize any doctrine, ultimately revelation itself, if the requirements of the system change. In the event John's prediction came true. Frank did become a freethinker (albeit one with religious inclinations) who objected strenuously to traditional Christian doctrines. Years later, on May 12, 1874, Newman came across his own prescient words while sorting his early theological papers. He sadly commented on the facing page of the manuscript: "The denial of Infant Baptism was the <u>first</u> point on which Frank swerved from orthodox Christianity, as anticipated in the page opposite, it was, alas! <u>only</u> the first."[206]

Conclusion

This chapter has traced in detail what Newman called the "great change" in his religious views during his time at St Clement's.[207] It began with a single problem that struck him anew when he was about to be ordained. But when, after an intense struggle, he began to accept this one doctrine of baptismal regeneration, his entire theology was transformed. The inexorable logic of the evangelical system began to crumble. The obduracy of scripture and of pastoral experience undermined its rigid binaries and straightforward identifications. As a system, it became less and less satisfactory, as more and more religious data began to slip from its explanatory reach. In view of his acceptance of baptismal regeneration, Sheridan has concluded that Newman "can no longer be called an Evangelical" by March 1826.[208] It is certainly tempting to draw a line around this time. In July, Newman opened his theological journal for the first time since the summer of 1824 and noted how "greatly changed" his views were.[209] He observed how much of his earlier theology he had taken on trust from the evangelical authors of his youth, and he reinterpreted his own conversion along the lines of his new view of regeneration. His evangelicalism was in irreversible decline, and he knew it. Accepting baptismal regeneration had taken the life out of it, but it did not dis-

<hr>

205. JHN, *Remarks on Infant Baptism*, BOA A.9.1.k, 46. *Pace* Stunt (*From Awakening*, 202), who argues that the difference between John and Frank in these years was more political than doctrinal, and that John and Frank "were well aware that they were on the same side, in contrast to their wayward brother Charles."

206. JHN, *Remarks on Infant Baptism*, BOA A.9.1.k, 45v.

207. JHN, "Autobiographical Memoir," *AW*, 73. See p. 79 in this book.

208. Sheridan, *Newman on Justification*, 121.

209. JHN, "July 26, 1826," *AW*, 172.

appear overnight. Newman himself later admitted that "for a long while certain shreds and tatters of that doctrine [evangelicalism] hung about his preaching," and this is an understatement.[210] His take on regeneration had changed drastically, but for some years, he retained the key evangelical conviction that sanctification was premised on faith in the atonement and continued to structure much of his theology according to the evangelical pattern. These were not just "shreds and tatters," and, for all its impact on his theology, baptismal regeneration was not enough to undo them. He very much remained an evangelical adrift.

210. JHN, "Autobiographical Memoir," *AW*, 78.

CHAPTER 5

Questions of Conscience

The tensions in Newman's evangelical theology were compounded by a development that proved at least as disruptive as his acceptance of baptismal regeneration: his changing understanding of conscience. The precise signification of that term in Newman's vocabulary is harder to pin down than that of other theological notions he employs, not only because he seldom defined conscience, but also because the word itself is "a simmering pot of meanings," as C. S. Lewis put it, in which different senses influence, or "flavour" one another.[1] Its meanings include reflexive awareness in general (close in meaning to consciousness), the inner witness to one's deeds ("I have done this or that"), the inner judge of one's deeds ("This or that was bad"), the inner lawgiver ("It is bad to do this or that"), and an inner apprehension of punishment ("If I do this or that, I will be punished"), or even fear of hell (as in Hamlet's famous soliloquy).[2] For the evangelical Newman, the first three senses were incontrovertible. Even the most uncompromising Calvinist can see that human beings consciously register their actions and judge them either right or wrong, but any further step brings difficulties. They center on the existence, character, and extent of human beings' natural knowledge of the good, and, by implication, of God.

When conscience takes on the meaning of inner lawgiver (or moral sense), it becomes hard to square with the Calvinistic emphasis on human depravity and divine sovereignty. If everyone has a conscience and its judgments are not vacuous, a space for moral discernment and action is created that is not wholly dependent on divine intervention for its relation to the good. People can do good, even without express knowledge of revelation. When the meaning of conscience takes on personal overtones, as when punishment is feared, it contains an implied reference to the divine, as an invisible but omnipresent judge of actions. The idea of natural religion entailed by such a view, however, was contentious among evangelicals and other English Christians. With the Enlightenment tradition, nearly everyone held that God's existence and attributes could be proved by natural reason from the phenomena of the external world. This was natural religion in its uncontroverted sense, what is now called natural theology. Yet, many (and most evangelicals among them), were

---

1. C. S. Lewis, *Studies in Words* (Cambridge: Cambridge University Press, 1961), 202.
2. Lewis, *Studies in Words*, 205–8.

skeptical that such knowledge was ever actually acquired by natural means. In this second sense, as the actual religious beliefs and practices of the heathen, natural religion was a rather bleak affair. A lot is at stake, then, in how one conceives of conscience, and Newman's changing views had wide ramifications for his theology. Yet, this change has received little attention because it was long assumed that nothing changed.

From Louis Bouyer in the 1950s to Fabio Attard and Edward Tyler in the past decade, scholars have argued that Newman's understanding of conscience was essentially homogeneous from the time of his first conversion to his dying days. They disagree, at most, about its level of explicitness.[3] All agree that Newman's 1816 conversion issued in an understanding of conscience, which contained, at least by implication, his later idea that it is a means of relating to and acquiring knowledge of God. Such arguments by implication are always tricky, especially if the sources are as scarce, ambiguous, and purposively redacted as those concerning Newman's first conversion. I argue, by contrast, that if one leaves assumptions of continuity aside, there is no documentary evidence for a correspondence between Newman's early and late views of conscience in more respects than just one: his admission of its existence, as a judge of good and bad acts. Beyond this simple acknowledgement, just about every aspect of his view of conscience changed between the late 1810s and the early 1830s.

A Calvinist Conscience

Newman's conversion as an adolescent entailed an inversion of his prior understanding of the relation between morals and religion. At age fourteen, he used to contrast virtue and religion and prefer the former: "I should like to be virtuous but not religious." At school, he defended Alexander Pope's notion that, "Virtue alone is happiness below."[4] Such virtue was shaped by conscience more than religion. As Pope had it in his *Universal Prayer*:

3. Louis Bouyer, *Newman: sa vie, sa spiritualité* (Paris: Cerf, 1952); *Newman: His Life and Spirituality* (London: Burns and Oates, 1958); Fabio Attard, *Conscience in the* Parochial and Plain Sermons *of John Henry Newman* (Valetta: Midsea Books, 2008); and Edward Joseph Tyler, "The Historical Development of J. H. Newman's Idea of the Conscience, Viewed in the Context of his Defence of Religious Belief" (PhD diss., University of Sidney, 2016). For a summary of the development of Newman's idea of conscience treated in this chapter, and parts of chapters 7 and 8, see Geertjan Zuijdwegt and Terrence Merrigan, "Conscience," in *The Oxford Handbook of John Henry Newman*, ed. Frederick D. Aquino and Benjamin J. King (Oxford: Oxford University Press, 2018), 434–42, some of which is reproduced with permission. DOI: 10.1093/oxfordhb/9780198718284.013.22.

4. JHN, "January 19, 1823," *AW*, 169. The reference to Pope is a paraphrase. The line—the penultimate one of *An Essay on Man*—reads, in fact, "That virtue only makes our bliss below." See p. 19 in this book.

> What conscience dictates to be done,
> Or warns me not to do,
> This teach me more than hell to shun,
> That more than heaven pursue.[5]

These lines contrast a universalist morality based on conscience with the particularism of religious ethics. Virtue means cultivating adherence to conscience for its own sake rather than following religious dictates for fear of hell or desire of heavenly reward. After his conversion—which he experienced, quite literally, as a "turning around"—Newman inverted Pope's prioritizing of conscience over religion. Newman still believed in the existence of a natural conscience but made its proper functioning depend entirely on grace and revelation. Although this was to be expected in view of his early Calvinism, it is routinely overlooked. Take the following instance. In January 1817, Newman wrote to Walter Mayers, "I sincerely trust that my conscience, enlightened by the Bible, through the influence of the Holy Spirit, may prove a faithful and vigilant guardian of the principles of religion."[6] Edward Tyler makes much of the mention of conscience here but ignores Newman's stress on scripture and the Holy Spirit. To function properly, conscience depends for its content on revelation and for its operation on grace. Newman's conception of conscience here—as judge, but not as lawgiver—owed something to Beveridge's *Private Thoughts*, a gift from Mayers that Newman was reading at the time. Beveridge extolled conscience as a guide of actions. He called it "GOD's Vicegerent in my Soul," but he also insisted that it depends on external sources for the law by which it judges, primarily on "the Word of GOD."[7] Although conscience is key to the life of the converted, Newman's early theological papers (which Tyler did not consult) leave no doubt that it has no part in conversion itself.

This might come as a surprise. Given that conscience tells us what we do wrong, it would seem natural to assume that it can help people to acknowledge their sinfulness, which is the obvious precondition for accepting Christ's offer of redemption. But the young Newman did not think it could. In his 1821 *Comment on Phil 2,12 & 13*, he contrasted the irresistible "will & . . . longing after holiness," imparted by the Holy Spirit upon conversion, with the "transient, irregular, & inefficacious" pangs of "innate conscience." Conscience, he noted, is a mere "natural instinct of the mind, quite as much as the horse who snorts for the battle, the bird that watches over her young, the dog that flies at the thief."[8] It is alright

---

5. Alexander Pope, *The Universal Prayer* (London: R. Dodsley, 1738), 4. For Newman's familiarity with Pope's poem, see JHN, No. 20, "Parable of the Good Samaritan," September 12, 1824, *Serm. 5*, 102.

6. JHN to Walter Mayers, January 1817, *LD* 1, 30. See Tyler, *The Historical Development*, 66–68.

7. Beveridge, *Private Thoughts upon Religion*, 241–42.

8. JHN, *Comment*, BOA A.9.1.e, 1–2.

as far it goes, but it cannot contribute to the radical redirection of the affections from sin to God in which conversion consists. This is the sole work of the Holy Spirit. In fact, being aware of sin and desiring redemption do not precede conversion. They are its first stage. When "in the free mercy of our Lord" the time comes that the sinner is "to be translated into the Kingdom of God's dear Son," Newman argued in the *Collection*, the Spirit makes "an impression on his mind," and he enters "the first stage of his conversion, when he is 'convinced of sin.'"[9] In Newman's paper on holiness, we find a similar portrayal of the Holy Spirit as the sole "agent" in the process of conversion, which begins with a "sense of God's holiness & our own vileness" and a consequent "sorrow for sin."[10] The concept of conscience was not even mentioned in these latter accounts, nor did it need to be, but when Newman was confronted with an audience of parishioners who did not share his presuppositions, he felt the topic had to be addressed.

Newman's first sermons at St Clement's emphasized the impotence of conscience as a means of self-knowledge, not because it is a fickle instinct but because of human corruption. If someone "examines the recesses of his heart and deals truly with his conscience," he would know that he is "fallen, sinful . . . miserably polluted — without natural strength or spiritual health."[11] But "man naturally and of himself *never will* examine himself as he ought; — he either will not do it at all — or does it lightly and superficially — and thus he never arrives at an adequate knowledge of his own sinful and lost state."[12] Even though conscience is a means to arrive at the knowledge of one's sinful state, it is powerless because people will not use it. A person, therefore, must "be enlightened from above to discern his exceeding sinfulness."[13] Only when the Holy Spirit changes someone's will, or desires, can he adequately assess his corrupt state. The Spirit "descends to *change his heart* — to humble him, to make him see his own odiousness and criminality . . . and now sinful man, at length perceiving his guilt . . . comes for pardon to the cross."[14]

Although conscience cannot positively contribute to conversion, it is still important to adhere to it even for the unregenerate. It might not make them apprehend their sinfulness, but it does show their sincerity. Charles had once been a case in point. In August 1823, John told him that any person in his situation, sincerely trying to make up their mind about Christianity, should "read the Bible constantly and attentively . . . pray for grace to understand it incessantly, and . . . strive to live up to the dictates of conscience and what the mind acknowledges

<hr>

9. JHN, *Collection*, BOA A.9.1.c.4, 11.

10. JHN, *Nature of Holiness*, BOA A.9.1.g, 2, 6.

11. JHN, No. 1, "The work of man," June 27, 1824, *Serm.* 5, 19–20.

12. JHN, No. 1, "The work of man," *Serm.* 5, 20.

13. JHN, No. 4, "The wounded spirit," July 25, 1824, *Serm.* 5, 39.

14. JHN, No. 12, "[Religion alone sufficient for man]," *Serm.* 2, 269. Newman removed the passage cited when he repreached this sermon on July 26, 1843 (*Serm.* 2, 265).

to be right."[15] John reiterated these three markers of religious earnestness in one of his first sermons:

> If sincere, we shall study God's word *continually*. . . . We shall be in earnest in praying for the promised aid of God's Spirit, to lighten our darkness and renew our hearts. . . . We shall act up to our light — and keep God's commandments as far as we know them.[16]

If we abide by these precepts, we are in prime position to be converted, that is, to receive "the gift of knowledge, and spiritual light," which, in turn, issues in "sanctification and peace of mind."[17] Although conversion is a gift of God, it is a gift to those who seek. Faithfully adhering to conscience is one way to show that we are seeking in earnest.

Conscience in Transition

Up to mid-1824, the moral and religious import Newman could attribute to conscience was constricted by his evangelical understanding of conversion as a process by which some individuals (and not others) are transplanted from the realm of nature into the realm of grace. Since this process depends entirely on the supernatural intervention of the Holy Spirit, natural conscience cannot bridge the gap between those two realms, not even to the extent of perceiving human corruption. When this Calvinistic paradigm began to give way under the force of Hawkins's critiques, his reading of Sumner, and his parochial experience, Newman's understanding of conscience began to change as well. Sumner, for one, did not attribute the knowledge of our natural corruption to the work of the Holy Spirit but considered "the fact" of our "degeneracy" to be "familiar to all; it meets our eyes abroad, and is felt by our souls at home; it requires only to be stated, to produce practical conviction."[18] Soon after reading Sumner, Newman seems to have given up the idea—so prominent in his earliest sermons—that human beings are without natural knowledge of their sinful state. The idea, at least, no longer features in his sermons from September and thereafter.

On the 19th of that month, Newman preached a sermon titled *The corruption of human nature*, which treats of "the *extent* of our disobedience to the will of God."[19] Before turning to scripture, Newman investigated what "*conscience*" suggests about our disobedience, and he concluded that it shows that "our very nature is in

15. JHN, "August 9, 1823," *AW*, 193. See p. 59 in this book.
16. JHN, No. 2, "Waiting on God," June 23, 1824, *Serm.* 5, 9.
17. JHN, No. 2, "Waiting on God," *Serm.* 5, 10.
18. Sumner, *Apostolical Preaching*, 115. See Tyler, *The Historical Development*, 82–83.
19. JHN, No. 19, "The corruption of human nature," September 19, 1824, *Serm.* 1, 309.

fault" but that "how much of it is in fault is something beyond our powers of ascertaining."[20] Tyler has argued that because Newman acknowledges that conscience is a natural means to know our sinfulness, he also holds that it perceives, "implicitly, the Being and presence of an offended God."[21] Accordingly, Tyler traces Newman's idea of conscience as a faculty that offers "a natural knowledge of God" to mid-1824, and even suggests that he held it as early as 1817.[22] These claims are mistaken for two reasons. First, much of Tyler's argument rests, unwittingly, on a later introduction to the sermon on natural corruption (which Newman revised on subsequent preachings). More importantly, Tyler assumes that because conscience can perceive bad acts as disobedience to God, the idea of God must arise from conscience.[23] But this is an additional argumentative step. The fact that conscience, when coupled to the idea of God, suggests that we are disobedient, does not mean that conscience originates the idea of God. Newman did not yet make this latter claim. Thus, when Newman argued, in a later sermon, that "superstitions" result from "a guilty and a timorous conscience — which trembles at the idea of any intercourse with its Maker, and shrinks from the prospect of appearing before Him who is a holy and righteous and almighty Judge," he was not speaking about heathenism, as Tyler maintains, but about the misguided religiosity of some people in "Christian countries" who already know God through revelation.[24]

The interpretation I suggest here, that conscience has certain effects when linked to knowledge of God, but that this knowledge itself comes from elsewhere, is borne out by a sermon of June 1825 in which Newman made his first effort to define the concept of conscience.[25] "Conscience," he argued, "arises from the comparison of what we *do* with what *we believe to be our duty* — and is attended with a feeling of pleasure when our actions coincide with our belief — with a feeling of pain when they fall short of it."[26] On this definition, the faculty of conscience has two functions: it registers the consistency between our beliefs and our actions, and it administers correspondent pleasant or unpleasant stimuli. It is a judge, but not a lawgiver. As a result, conscience is both fallible, because our beliefs about right and wrong can be mistaken, and powerful, because it administers "pain and pleasure," by which "our whole life is governed."[27]

<hr>

20. JHN, No. 19, "The corruption of human nature," *Serm.* 1, 304, 311.

21. Tyler, *The Historical Development*, 90.

22. Tyler, *The Historical Development*, 88.

23. Tyler, *The Historical Development*, 83–85; *Serm.* 1, 303n3.

24. JHN, No. 29, "The effects on the mind of the doctrine of the Cross," October 31, 1824, *Serm.* 1, 271; Tyler, *The Historical Development*, 87.

25. Parts of this sermon, especially those relating to various malfunctions of conscience, were taken from the sermon outline "A good and evil conscience" in the evangelical Charles Simeon's *Helps to Composition*, which is reproduced in *Serm.* 5, 436–40.

26. JHN, No. 85, "Conscience its use etc," June 19, 1825, *Serm.* 5, 237.

27. JHN, No. 85, "Conscience," *Serm.* 5, 237.

Newman probably owed his formulation of this idea—that the judgments of conscience "depend, *not* upon the things we do being right or wrong, but upon their agreeing with what *we think* right or wrong"—to Sumner.[28] In his *Apostolical Preaching*, Sumner insisted that,

> Conscience, and reason, or that modification of it which is termed the moral sense, are not to be used by us as if they themselves furnished laws which we should obey, but for the purpose of pointing out when we agree with, and when we deviate from that rule of action, which has been previously established as our guide; whether that rule be the law of the land, or the precepts of a particular philosophy, or the customs of society, or the commands of God.[29]

Sumner's argument explicitly excludes the idea of conscience as a lawgiver, a position that confirmed Newman's earlier inclinations. In this way, Sumner evades the disruptive potential of the idea of conscience. He can retain the evangelical conviction that our knowledge of the good and of God depend on revelation as well as its corollary, that all good works spring from faith. If conscience is entirely dependent for its content on some external source, it has no intrinsic relation to a moral standard that must ultimately derive from God. Similarly, if obedience to conscience entails nothing more than modeling one's actions on one's beliefs, faith fully retains its priority over praxis.

Although formally adopting Sumner's definition of conscience, Newman did not wholly abide by it. Unlike Sumner, he would not admit that human beings completely lack a natural sense of right and wrong, even though this conclusion was entailed by his definition. Conscience might be "an imperfect guide," but it is a guide still, and although our "natural ideas of duty are slight, incorrect and feeble," we have them nonetheless.[30] In consequence, people, are under a double obligation. On the one hand, they must "enlighten" their conscience "by reading the word and prayer."[31] On the other hand, they must act up to its requirements: "since it is a powerful monitor, we must *obey* it."[32] Conscience, Newman concluded, is "the voice of God to the soul," not because it "could of itself inform us of God's will" but because—when supplied with the right moral and religious content, and rigidly attended to—it guards our progress in holiness.[33] Contrary to what Tyler suggests, Newman does not argue that conscience conveys an "impression of God."[34] He is not concerned with the situation of unbelievers but rather with

---

28. JHN, No. 85, "Conscience," *Serm.* 5, 237.
29. Sumner, *Apostolical Preaching*, 118.
30. JHN, No. 85, "Conscience," *Serm.* 5, 240.
31. JHN, No. 85, "Conscience," *Serm.* 5, 241.
32. JHN, No. 85, "Conscience," *Serm.* 5, 241.
33. JHN, No. 85, "Conscience," *Serm.* 5, 241, 240.
34. Tyler, *The Historical Development*, 100.

that of his parishioners, who are presumed to know God already. The believer acknowledges that conscience is the "voice of God," not because conscience itself tells her so but because, as a believer, she has learnt to identify it as such.

Still, there is tension in Newman's account. On the one hand, he argues that conscience has, as such, no content; it does not relate to the good but only to what *we think* is good. On the other hand, he maintains that the "more we strive to act up to our conscience, the more will conscience be enlightened to understand what is right and wrong."[35] This means that there is some connection between conscientious action and knowledge of the good, even if, as before, it were only conceived extrinsically, as a species of divine reward. But Newman opts for formulations that hint at a more intrinsic relationship: "A good man is always aiming to do what is holy and virtuous, and the more he strives, the more his conscience is enlarged — thus as his conduct rises nearer and nearer to heaven, his sense of duty and his conscience mount higher and higher with it."[36] What is described here is a dynamic relationship between the intimations of conscience and consequent actions that fuels moral insight. The active phrasing suggests that this dynamic is premised on an intrinsic relationship of conscience to the good.

This dynamic, moreover, takes on a religious hue, at least implicitly. Newman argued that conscience "is not likely to be very wrong in the grand principles of duty" and that someone who acts up to it is "doing God's will as far as he knows and in good time shall fully know it."[37] To be sure, this description applies to people already familiar with the basic truths of revelation, not to the religious situation of the heathen. Still, it shows that Newman would not dismiss the idea of conscience as a lawgiver as easily as Sumner. Moreover, when Newman did address the religious situation of the heathen a few months later, the tension with the evangelical account of nature and revelation exhibited by his view of conscience re-emerged in full force.

The Religion of the Heathen

Before the summer of 1825, Newman seems to have taken little interest in the subject of natural religion. As an evangelical, he was more interested in the distinction between real and nominal Christians than in that between Christians and pagans. His general outlook was that of Scott, who took the typical evangelical line: *"without revelation, there never was any true religion on the earth."*[38] Although

---

35. JHN, No. 85, "Conscience," *Serm.* 5, 238.

36. JHN, No. 85, "Conscience," *Serm.* 5, 238.

37. JHN, No. 85, "Conscience," *Serm.* 5, 241.

38. Thomas Scott, *The Holy Bible containing the Old and New Testaments, according to the Authorized Version; with Explanatory Notes, Practical Observations, and Copious Marginal References,* 5th ed., vol. 1 (London: L. B. Seeley, 1822), 2. See Turner, *John Henry Newman,* 37.

Scott believed that every human being has religious proclivities by nature, he denied that—barring one or two exceptions—anyone without revelation ever held the basic truths included under the Enlightenment concept of natural religion: "no such natural religion ever was discovered, and delineated, by men of any nation, who had never seen any part of the Bible, or any thing deduced from that source."[39] Newman, too, believed that it was a "fundamental doctrine" of Christianity that "the mind cannot arrive at religious truth . . . without a revelation."[40] As he put it in a sermon of September 1824,

> Who on looking around at the works of nature, will hesitate to own there is a God? or on observing their harmony and connexion to own there is but one God? Yet for these two truths which are so familiar to our minds, we are almost entirely, if not altogether, indebted to revelation.[41]

Reason could not discover those truths. Even among "the most learned and able philosophers of former times . . . scarcely two or three believed in a God at all, and not even those two or three believed there was but one God."[42] Conscience, too, is of no avail. "We have an innate consciousness of guilt," Newman noted in October 1824, so that "the idea of God is connected in our minds with feelings of dread and apprehension."[43] Historic "natural religion" institutionalized such fears with dramatic consequences. Because it was "slavish and grovelling," it made "the educated among the ancient heathen . . . disbelieve in the existence of superior intelligences altogether."[44] Without further revelations, conscience issues either in superstition or in atheism when coupled to the idea of God.

Natural religion is treated only cursorily in these early sermons. It is primarily introduced to throw Christianity into relief. The "twilight of philosophical conjecture" accentuates the clarity of revelation, while heathen religiosity contrasts with faith in Christ, which makes the "phantoms of the sinburdened [*sic*] conscience entirely disappear."[45] Only after the summer of 1825 did Newman begin to reflect on natural religion in its own right, and he did so because the topic had been forced upon his notice. Recall that at the tail end of their correspondence, in August 1825, Charles had challenged some of John's (implicit) assumptions about the relation between natural and revealed religion.[46] John did not address Charles's criticisms in his letters, but he did treat some of them in a course of

---

39. Scott, *The Holy Bible*, 2.
40. JHN to CRN, April 14, 1825, *LD* 1, 228.
41. JHN, No. 17, "Character of God and His holy law," September 12, 1824, *Serm.* 5, 94.
42. JHN, No. 17, "Character of God," *Serm.* 5, 94.
43. JHN, No. 29, "The effects," *Serm.* 1, 270.
44. JHN, No. 29, "The effects," *Serm.* 1, 271.
45. JHN, No. 29, "The effects," *Serm.* 1, 271.
46. See pp. 75–77.

sermons he began soon afterwards, on September 11, and concluded on December 18.[47] The course had the history of God's successive revelations to mankind for its main subject and treated the respective religious situations of heathens, Jews, and Christians. Frank McGrath has described the course as presenting "a crystal-clear system of haves versus have-nots, of light versus darkness," the haves being Jews and Christians, the have-nots, the heathen.[48] There is much truth in McGrath's assessment, but he overstates his case. It is not because Newman presents the religious situation of the heathen as dire that he thought they were without religion altogether.

The tenor of Newman's treatment of paganism was set in the first sermon of the course. Obliquely answering the Deist objection, voiced by Charles and Paine, that revelation ought to be universally accessible, Newman sought to account for the limited extension of Christianity over the world. God intended this to be the case, Newman argued, for the sake of contrast, that is, to display "the *weakness and helplessness of unaided man*" (man without revelation).[49] His discussion of pre-Christian heathenism in the second sermon of the course brought out the same point. The religiosity of ancient Greeks and Romans shows "the need *man* has of a revelation from God."[50] A year before, he had already argued that the ancient heathen "were truly without God in the world . . . for the most part with no hope or desire of a future life, no love of their Maker, no adequate sense of their own sinfulness and spiritual misery."[51] He now reiterated this judgment. Even the most learned heathen denied the "being of a God," their accountability in his sight, and "a future state of any kind."[52] Their ethical code, moreover, was "very defective," especially regarding humility and purity, and they did not "acknowledge themselves to be sinners."[53] Aristotle's "man of great mind" (μεγαλόψυχος) illustrates the arrogance of the heathen moral ideal.[54] Even the best of the heathen, in short, were in "spiritual darkness." "They knew not what they were, why they existed, to whom they belonged, and whither they were going."[55]

47. JHN, No. 85, "Conscience," *Serm.* 5, 449.

48. McGrath, *John Henry Newman*, 31.

49. JHN, No. 104, "Probable reasons for the partial extension of Christianity," September 11, 1825, *Serm.* 2, 348. This sermon constituted a response to Charles's argument (derived from Paine) that revelation entails universal accessibility.

50. JHN, No. 106, "State of the heathen world an evidence of the need of a revelation," September 18, 1825, *Serm.* 5, 306.

51. JHN, No. 19, "The corruption of human nature," *Serm.* 1, 309. This section was excised from later preachings of the sermon.

52. JHN, No. 106, "State of the heathen world," *Serm.* 5, 307.

53. JHN, No. 106, "State of the heathen world," *Serm.* 5, 308.

54. JHN, No. 106, "State of the heathen world," *Serm.* 5, 308; Aristotle, *Nicomachean Ethics*, IV.3 (not IV.2, as McGrath [*Serm.* 5, 308n9] has it).

55. JHN, No. 106, "State of the heathen world," *Serm.* 5, 310, 309.

In the next sermon of the course, Newman argued that all religious knowledge derives from revelation. A week before, he had claimed at a Church Missionary Society meeting that "Every part of our religious creed that relates to morality as well as to doctrine is from Christ."[56] Now, he explained that revelation alone teaches us "the existence of one and only one God," "His providence," "His moral governance, i.e. His approbation of virtue and hatred of sin" and his "attributes" ("infinite wisdom, knowledge, love, truth, and holiness").[57] These four fundamental doctrines characterize belief in revelation from patriarchal times to our own, and "never *were* found out and systematized by man for himself."[58] This is not to say that they *could* not have been discovered. "Whether the affairs and events of life were not enough to lead the mind to them, were it quite unprejudiced is a different question," Newman explained, "but in fact *they never did*."[59] Although the doctrines of God's existence, providence, moral governance, and attributes are no part of natural religion in its historic sense, they are, once revealed, derivable from nature by way of rational argument. They are "written, as it were in nature and might have been known even without direct revelation — but . . . man did not in fact deduce them from nature — he did not make use of the means put in his power, of arriving at knowledge."[60]

If the doctrines of natural religion can be known in principle but are never discovered in practice, the obvious question is: why not? The brief and unsurprising answer is sin. The heathen "did not follow conscience and seek the Lord in humility and prayer, and therefore did not find him," Newman argued; "Thus their mistakes arose ultimately from their dislike of the truth."[61] Both the content and phraseology of this argument echo Newman's 1821 article for the *Christian Observer* as well as his letters to Charles. Because unbelievers dislike the spiritual and moral demands of religion, they do not consider its evidences impartially.[62] In the case of Christianity, these evidences are miraculous. In the case of natural religion, they are derivable from the affairs and events of life. In both cases, however, prejudice stops people from considering them aright. In principle, faithfulness to conscience can overcome this impediment and facilitate an impartial consideration of nature as a source of knowledge of God, but in practice, human corruption bars such faithfulness from being achieved, so that we still owe all our knowledge of God to revelation.

56. JHN, "CMS speech," September 19, 1825, *LD* 1, 315.

57. JHN, No. 108, "On the *principles* common to all revelation," September 25, 1825, *Serm.* 5, 315, 318. See also No. 110, "On the *feelings* produced in common by all revelation," October 16, 1825, *Serm.* 5, 326.

58. JHN, No. 108, "On the *principles*," *Serm.* 5, 318.

59. JHN, No. 108, "On the *principles*," *Serm.* 5, 318; see also 315.

60. JHN, No. 110, "On the *feelings*," *Serm.* 5, 326.

61. JHN, No. 106, "State of the heathen world," *Serm.* 5, 310.

62. See pp. 25 and 62–63.

So far, the sermons seem to bear out McGrath's contention that Newman viewed the heathen as simply without knowledge of God, but it is not quite that simple. In August, for instance, Newman had written to Charles that all human-kind is at one in acknowledging a "feeling of *dependence* on a superior being."[63] In a sermon a month later, he summed up the state of the heathen by appealing to Socrates, "the wisest and most religious of them," who described the religious situation of his times as one of need: "we must wait till we learn from an heavenly instructor who careth for us and hath a wonderful concern for our interests, in what measure we are to conduct ourselves with regard to God and man."[64] The provenance of this remarkable citation is discussed below, but note how it wit-nesses to a deeply felt desire for religious knowledge, not merely to an absence. And Newman interpreted it as such. He identified a "longing after a revelation" among the heathen, which was not just Socrates's but that existed as "a general feeling among all classes of man."[65] Now it is hard to conceive how one can desire to know more of God, without already knowing something. Such knowledge, however, can be derived only from revelation, to which the heathen, on McGrath's reading, have no access. Newman had a solution to this conundrum, although not one that proved satisfactory.

McGrath assumes that by making revelation the only source of religious knowledge, Newman confined its possession to Jews and Christians, but this is not quite what Newman meant. His aim was not so much to restrict religious knowledge to the Judeo-Christian pale as to argue that whenever such knowledge is found beyond it, it does not derive from nature but from the Judeo-Christian revelation. Thus, in an 1824 review of a North-American travel book, the first review he ever wrote, Newman approvingly cited the author's contention that the religion of the indigenous Lenape, who "recognize the Unity of God, and believe him to be a Spirit . . . not to be represented by any visible symbol," originated in "obscured traditions received from patriarchal times."[66] He reiterated this idea in one of the sermons in his course, pointing to "constant traditions flying through the nations concerning the existence of one supreme maker and governor of the world, of His greatness and wisdom and knowledge and benevolence to man." Although Newman considered these traditions "*but* rumours"—and thus, "*as articles of faith* . . . peculiar to revelation"—they could conceivably originate the longing for revelation that is inexplicable on McGrath's reading.[67] Even so,

---

63. JHN to CRN, August 25, 1825, *LD* 1, 253. See p. 75 in this book.

64. JHN, No. 106, "State of the heathen world," *Serm.* 5, 309–10.

65. JHN, No. 106, "State of the heathen world," *Serm.* 5, 310.

66. JHN, "Duncan's Travels in North America," *British Review, and London Critical Journal* 22, no. 44 (May 1824): 147; John M. Duncan, *Travels through Part of the United States and Canada in 1818 and 1819*, vol. 2 (Glasgow: 1823), 99.

67. JHN, No. 110, "On the *feelings*," *Serm.* 5, 326–27.

Newman continued to verge on paradox. Although historic traces of the Judeo-Christian revelation might explain the heathens' desire for revelation, Newman's account of their religious situation remains contradictory. The heathen supposedly desire a religious truth that they at the same dislike (dislike being the cause of their ignorance). Somehow, they are supposed to long for what they hate. Just as he could not rid conscience of its intrinsic relation to the good, Newman could not conceive of the heathen as lacking all knowledge of God. If anything, the resulting tension shows how hard Newman struggled not to trespass evangelical boundaries concerning nature and revelation, even at the cost of rendering natural religion unintelligible. It was an uphill battle, though, and he soon realized as much. Before two months were over, he had found the beginning of a solution in a novel conception of conscience.

Conscience and Natural Religion

On December 4, 1825, Newman preached *On natural religion*, the ninth sermon of the course. He set out to discuss natural religion in its other sense, as a set of arguments, not of existing or historical forms of religiosity. Accordingly, he tried to demonstrate how "the being and attributes of God, His providence, and moral government may be seen in the system and scheme of things which is daily before our eyes."[68] To prove God's existence, attributes, and providence, Newman drew on Paley's *Natural Theology* (1802), a classic of Enlightenment apologetics. Just as we "never should fancy a watch or other piece of mechanism came into being without a contriver," so the existence and design of creation point to a Creator.[69] The uniformity of the laws of nature, moreover, points to God's unity, while their universal extension demonstrates God's "almighty power, and His infinite wisdom."[70] Finally, the beneficial ordering of the natural world, which is structured as if God had "studied, as it were, our comfort," witnesses to his good providence.[71] So far, Newman's argument is compatible with an emphasis on human corruption. "The heavens declared God's glory," he observed, "but they who shut their eyes could not expect to see."[72] It is easy to conceive how sin—a natural dislike of religion—would cause the heathen to dismiss the clear signs in nature of God's existence, attributes, and providence, so that they remained without religious

68. JHN, No. 119, "On natural religion," December 4, 1825, *Serm.* 2, 374.

69. JHN, No. 119, "On natural religion," *Serm.* 2. For the extensive elaboration of the watch-analogy, see William Paley, *Natural Theology: or, Evidences of the Existence and Attributes of the Deity, Collected from the Appearances of Nature* (London: R. Faulder, 1802), chaps. 1–6.

70. JHN, No. 119, "On natural religion," *Serm.* 2, 375; Paley, *Natural Theology*, chaps. 24, 25.

71. JHN, No. 119, "On natural religion," *Serm.* 2, 375–6. Newman follows Paley less closely here than in the three earlier arguments (compare to Paley, *Natural Theology*, chap. 26).

72. JHN, No. 119, "On natural religion," *Serm.* 2, 374.

knowledge, even though it could be acquired. But a very different picture emerges from Newman's argument for God's moral governance.

Newman derived his argument from Butler, whose *Analogy of Religion* he had just finished, but he made it very much his own. The apologetic target of the *Analogy* was Deism. As we have seen, Deists rejected certain religious tenets because they found them incompatible with belief in the God known through natural reason (recall Paine's remark that a believer in God cannot believe in Christ).[73] Butler turned this reasoning on its head. He assumed, as a lowest common denominator between Christians and Deists, a shared belief that God exists, has created the world, and continues to govern it. Given this shared premise, Butler argued, the Deists have no reasonable grounds for their rejection of additional tenets of natural and revealed religion. Controverted tenets, such as the belief that God punishes people for evil acts, or the idea of a mediator between God and man, are perfectly analogous to what we observe in the world around us every day. People routinely suffer the bad consequences of vicious behavior (think of hangovers after excessive drinking), and Deists agree that this is the natural course of things, willed and directed by God. Similarly, people depend, from infancy, on the mediation of others to acquire valuable goods (think of nutrition, education, careers), and this, too, is how Deists agree God has ordained it. Deists, therefore, are unreasonable when they reject divine punishment or Christ's mediation as incompatible with their supposed God of natural reason.

The *Analogy* begins with a discussion of controverted aspects of natural religion. After arguing for a future life, Butler defends the general idea that God governs human affairs by means of rewards and punishments. He then specifies this mode of government by arguing that it is not one of arbitrary rewards and punishments but consists of "rewarding the righteous and punishing the wicked."[74] God's governance, in short, is moral. Butler's case for God's moral governance consists of two lines of argument. One (the most important) is derived from human nature, the other (the most extensively developed) from the actual course of the world. Butler develops the first line in a brief dissertation subjoined to the *Analogy* entitled *Of the nature of virtue*. All of us, Butler argued, have, by nature,

> a capacity of reflecting upon actions and characters, and making them an object to our thought: and on our doing this, we naturally and unavoidably approve some actions, under the peculiar view of their being virtuous and of good desert; and disapprove others, as vicious and of ill desert.[75]

73. See p. 75.
74. Butler, *The Analogy of Religion*, 77.
75. Butler, *The Analogy of Religion*, 388; see also 160–61.

Butler cared little about what this "moral faculty" was called, be it "conscience, moral reason, moral sense, or divine reason," as long as its existence was admitted.[76] The most important characteristic of this faculty—and the one that does all the work in Butler's argument—is its conception of actions as not just good or bad but as deserving reward or punishment. Since "God has given us" this moral nature (which the Deists also affirmed), it is God himself who has "annexed to some actions an inseparable sense of good desert, and to others of ill," which entails that God will see to the just distribution of these deserts.[77] Conscience, in this argument, is not only judge and lawgiver, it also directly reflects God's justice.

Butler combined this argument from human nature with an argument from the actual course of the world, in which a desert-based order can already be discerned. Virtue already tends to happiness, while vice tends to misery, both because society rewards the one and punishes the other and because of the natural effects of virtuous and vicious actions.[78] Even though the current distribution of happiness and misery is not perfectly according to desert, there is a "natural" or "essential" tendency of virtue toward happiness, and of vice toward misery.[79] The current impediments to this "*natural* tendency" are "only *accidental*," so that it is reasonable to suppose that "the moral scheme of government established in nature shall be carried on much farther towards perfection hereafter."[80] This "presumption" (that the system of distribution of rewards and punishments will be perfected in a future life) is converted into a "practical proof" by taking into account the argument from "the moral nature which God has given us," which functions "as a presentiment of what is to be hereafter," namely, that "in the upshot and issue of things, happiness and misery shall, in fact and event be made to follow virtue and vice respectively."[81] Butler, then, presents a two-pronged argument for God's moral governance. We encounter God as both judge and lawgiver in our conscience, whose intimations confirm a tendency we can already observe in the world around us, namely, that vice will be punished and virtue rewarded.

Newman had begun the *Analogy* in July 1825 but did not finish it quickly. He was still reading it in October.[82] But once he had finished it, he eagerly adopted Butler's argument for God's moral governance (much as he had done with Butler's arguments about habit formation and a visible church). The "most striking evidence" of God's moral governance, Newman argued in his sermon on natural religion,

76. Butler, *The Analogy of Religion*, 388.
77. Butler, *The Analogy of Religion*, 79, 161.
78. Butler, *The Analogy of Religion*, 83–88.
79. Butler, *The Analogy of Religion*, 107.
80. Butler, *The Analogy of Religion*, 107; see also 189–90.
81. Butler, *The Analogy of Religion*, 107, 162.
82. *LD* 1, 239, 262.

is one lodged within us, the voice of conscience. This, as far as it goes, is truly said to be the voice of an observant and Holy Judge. It declares to us in plain language the general character of our duty — it condemns vice and impiety and sin — it applauds <approves> obedience and virtuous principle.[83]

Perhaps the most remarkable feature of this "inward voice" is that it is nearly impossible to silence:

> Men reason, argue, discuss, attempt to prove virtue vice and vice virtue . . . yet in vain — the moral sense within them, even natural conscience, reclaims — it does not deign to confute their reasonings, it brings forward no counter arguments, but it simply and plainly and boldly and as the messenger of God, declares that sin is sin — and thus by the unsupported energy, the weight of its own authority forces its way through every specious pretence and is a witness in every sinner's breast against himself and for that God before whom he will one day appears [*sic*] in judgment.[84]

In this way, as a "silent but stern monitor," conscience "evidences the being of an unseen but accurate Judge of actions."[85] When it came to the evidence for a moral governor in "the course of human affairs," Newman was less sanguine than Butler.[86] Like Butler, he argued that "even as it is we can observe the *tendency* of sin to be towards misery, of obedience towards peace and life," but he presented the common run of things as a prima facie contrast to, rather than a confirmation of, the idea of a moral governor derived from conscience. "It cannot be denied," he noted, that "there is a large infusion of evil in the system, an extensive irregularity." Still, although "natural reason . . . cannot pretend to account for the existence of prosperous wickedness," it "makes no objection against that doctrine of a Moral Governor, which both the voice of conscience and the general laws of human affairs firmly establish."[87]

Newman's portrayal of conscience in this sermon differs in crucial respects from his earlier account and, despite major convergences, from Butler's view. Following Butler, Newman exchanged the notion that conscience depends for its content upon some external moral law for the idea that it contains, by itself, a roughly accurate standard of right and wrong, what Butler expressively called "the moral rule of action interwoven in [our] nature."[88] Accordingly, conscience

<hr>

83. JHN, No. 119, "On natural religion," *Serm.* 2, 377.
84. JHN, No. 119, "On natural religion," *Serm.* 2, 377.
85. JHN, No. 119, "On natural religion," *Serm.* 2, 377.
86. JHN, No. 119, "On natural religion," *Serm.* 2, 377.
87. JHN, No. 119, "On natural religion," *Serm.* 2, 378. Note that the basic structure of Newman's argument in this sermon (conscience—God—world) would remain the same in his later writings (e.g., *Apo.*, 323, 376–79).
88. Butler, *The Analogy of Religion*, 392.

no longer merely registers discrepancies (between our beliefs and actions) but directly declares that something is wrong. Conscience is both judge and lawgiver. Newman also took up Butler's idea of a link between conscience and God, but he construed it in a different way. Unlike Butler, he did not emphasize the notion of desert. Instead, all the work in his argument is done by an analysis of the phenomenal qualities of the experience of conscience. What makes the operation of conscience unique is that it is experienced as a being spoken to. We somehow perceive it as having its referent outside our selves. The experience, moreover, is one of being spoken to in a certain way, namely, a being judged. In consequence, the operation of conscience is both distinct from reasoning (since it declares, rather than argues) and superior to it (since reason cannot easily silence it). Conscience, in short, is experienced as the voice of an authoritative judge, external and superior to the subject, which suggests, as the best available explanation, that there is, in fact, such a person—the "unseen but accurate Judge of actions"— who is doing the speaking by proxy.[89]

That Newman had not yet conceived of conscience in this way at the beginning of his course is evident from his treatment of the doctrine of God's moral governance in its earlier sermons. On September 25, he had argued emphatically that "the *moral governance of God* . . . is peculiar to revelation":

> Revelation alone makes God the witness of all our actions and thoughts, the approver of holiness and virtue, the rewarder of them that diligently seek him, the righteous Avenger of ungodliness. — Through revelation alone have we disclosed to us a moral system, a code of laws sanctioned by rewards and punishments, and founded on the authority of an Almighty Lawgiver. . . . Unaided reason . . . could but conjecture about virtue and religious worship — and where it has been correct in its opinions, it has been so apparently by chance.[90]

On this account, natural religious knowledge, insofar as it exists, should be attributed to "conjecture" and "chance." Two months later, Newman held the opposite view. If conscience witnesses to an implicit relationship between the subject and God, as he argued in the sermon on natural religion, such natural religious knowledge should not be attributed to mere chance or conjecture but to a recognition of this relationship. On his new account, moreover, conscience contains, at least implicitly, precisely that knowledge which is attributed solely to revelation in the earlier account: a standard of right and wrong (including a notion of good and ill desert) and the idea of an authoritative witness and judge of thoughts and actions. Both tenets establish significant continuity, rather than sheer

89. JHN, No. 119, "On natural religion," *Serm.* 2, 377.
90. JHN, No. 108, "On the *principles*," *Serm.* 5, 315.

discontinuity, between nature and revelation. This continuity is rooted in the specific character of Newman's argument from conscience.

Unlike Butler, Newman appears to have regarded the experience of conscience not only as an argument for God's moral governance but also for his existence. For Butler, the argument that our sense of good and ill desert entails God's moral government is premised on a prior conviction that we derive our nature (which contains this sense) from God. For Newman, it seems to be the experience of conscience itself—its peculiar quality as a phenomenon—that points to a something higher on behalf of which it speaks. Conscience suggests not so much that the God we know from other sources has a certain character (that of "an observant and Holy Judge") but that there is such a being in the first place. By identifying conscience as a point of contact between the self and God, Newman straddled the ontological divide between the natural and supernatural. In addition, he straddled the conceptual divide between natural religion understood as a historical reality and as a set of arguments. His understanding of the specific way in which conscience functions makes his argument distinct from his other arguments for God's existence and attributes. Given that Paley's arguments are all based on evidence external to the subject, it is easy to see how prejudice would cause people to ignore such evidence, or not perceive its significance (for the value of evidence depends on the questions with which it is approached). The voice of conscience, however, is well-nigh impossible to ignore: this is one of its main characteristics. It speaks, and it speaks in such a way that it inwardly conveys the impression of an omniscient judge. As a result, the experience of conscience is not just an evidence for God's existence or moral governance— like, say, the complexity of the human eye is an evidence for design—but is itself a religious phenomenon. Newman clearly realized as much, for the sermon on natural religion presents a significantly revised account of heathen religiosity.

At first sight, little seems to have changed. Newman still maintained that even the wisest heathens were "ignorant in the first principles of religion" and that "*sin* was the cause of their ignorance."[91] But he no longer thought human corruption utterly excludes the acquisition of religious belief and practice. "Suppose," he argued, "the case of a spiritually enlightened mind in the midst of heathen darkness." Now,

> conceive the misery with which he would discern the connection between sin and punishment which the world on the whole displays — *religion cannot exist without some degree of hope* — and though the goodness of Providence to sinners, the sun rising even upon the evil and the rain descending upon the unjust . . . would be some ground of hope, and render religious feelings not altogether incompatible with his darkness, yet the principle would be weak

91. JHN, No. 119, "On natural religion," *Serm.* 2, 379.

and sickly. . . . That there was a God and that obedience to that God was his duty, his conscience, the law written on his heart (as the Apostle says) would inform him — but sin would weigh him down and prevent him from a consistent and full acknowledgement of the truth.[92]

This depiction represents a major shift in Newman's understanding of the religious situation of the heathen. Before, he regarded their religiosity as, at best, the formulating of a question, to which revelation was the answer. Now, he conceived of it as itself a rudimentary form of religion. It consists of much ignorance and fear, but also of some hope, which makes authentic religiosity possible. Sin, moreover, cannot entirely efface the knowledge of God's existence and of a moral duty to him derived from conscience. The resulting religiosity is inconsistent and partial, to be sure, but it is there nonetheless.

Part of Newman's change of view was due to his continued reflection on the lines from Socrates cited in the sermon of September 19, which expressed a desire for divine instruction.[93] This remarkable citation was, in fact, a paraphrase that Newman pulled from one of the books he was reading in preparation for his *Essay on Miracles*. It appears verbatim in John Douglas's *The Criterion* (1754), where it is introduced for much the same reason as Newman's: to show the desperate need of a revelation among the heathen.[94] Douglas's paraphrase offers the gist of the conclusion to *Second Alcibiades*, a Socratic dialogue traditionally ascribed to Plato but now considered apocryphal.[95] The citation seems to have intrigued Newman, presumably because of the tension it brought to his account of heathen religious knowledge. On November 24, ten days before he preached the sermon on natural religion, he borrowed from Oriel College library a set of bound issues of *The Spectator*, the famous daily published by Joseph Addison and Richard Steele in 1711 and 1712. The issue for October 27, 1711, contained a paper by Addison that discussed *Second Alcibiades* in order to ascertain "the Notions of the most refined Heathens" about devotion.[96] Given that the dialogue contains Socrates's teaching on how to pray, Addison could not have selected his material better. Socrates explains to Alcibiades that we are never quite sure whether what we ask

92. JHN, No. 119, "On natural religion," *Serm.* 2, 379.

93. See p. 158.

94. John Douglas, *The Criterion; or Rules by which the True Miracles Recorded in the New Testament Are Distinguished from the Spurious Miracles of Pagans and Papists* (London: T. Cadell and W. Davies, 1807), 36–37: "*Socrates*, the most distinguished philosopher of heathen antiquity . . . expressly tells us *that we must wait till we learn from an instructor who careth for us and has a wonderful concern for our interests, in what manner we are to conduct ourselves with regard to God and our fellow creatures.*" Newman began reading Douglas (in the edition cited here) on August 29 and finished on September 1 (*LD* 1, 255).

95. D. S. Hutchinson, "Introduction to *Second Alcibiades*," in Plato, *Complete Works*, ed. John M. Cooper (Indianapolis, Ind.: Hackett, 1997), 596–97.

96. Joseph Addison, *The Spectator*, no. 207, October 27, 1711 (Parker).

is good for us. For that reason, he proposes the following short prayer to Alcibiades, which runs, in Addison's rendering,

> O Jupiter, *give us those things which are good for us, whether they are such things as we pray for, or such things as we do not pray for; and remove from us those things which are hurtful, though they are such things as we pray for.*[97]

Besides teaching him this prayer, Socrates advises Alcibiades "to apply himself to the Study of true Wisdom, and to the Knowledge of that which is his chief Good," so as to know better what to pray for.[98] Finally, Socrates points out that Alcibiades's prayer will be acceptable only when he practices "his Duty towards the Gods, and towards Men," because the gods prefer virtue to sacrifices.[99] Like Douglas, Addison noted Socrates's hope for an instructor to teach us "how we ought to behave ourselves towards the Gods, and towards Men," but frankly admitted that the Greek is obscure. He argued, nonetheless, that Socrates "saw, by the Light of Reason, that it was suitable to the Goodness of the Divine Nature, to send a Person into the World who should Instruct Mankind in the Duties of Religion, and in particular, Teach them how to Pray."[100] Christ, Addison concluded, fulfilled this expectation and confirmed and perfected Socrates's instructions about prayer.

Despite hoping for further instruction, the religious insight Socrates displays in *Second Alcibiades* clearly goes beyond the mere expression of a need. Addison saw this, while Douglas did not. Socrates does not just require further instruction on religion; he already knows its basics: that it is about the will of the gods, not of men, that it concerns our chief good, and that it requires virtue more than rites. Newman was struck by Addison's paper. Not only did he change his assessment of heathen religiosity in the sermon on natural religion, he also went to borrow *Second Alcibiades* from his college library ten days later, perhaps to make sure Addison's rendering was reliable.[101] Although Newman was not as sanguine as Addison, he became significantly more optimistic about the potential for heathen religious knowledge. This is shown by a section Newman added to the first sermon of his course when he preached it again in June 1826. The passage describes the many ways in which God makes himself known—in history, creation, and conscience—to render the heathen without excuse. Unlike before, Newman not only allowed for disparate traces of historic revelation but also affirmed the existence of "universal revelations":

<hr>

97. Addison, *Spectator*, no. 207, 1.

98. Addison, *Spectator*, no. 207, 1.

99. Addison, *Spectator*, no. 207, 1.

100. Addison, *Spectator*, no. 207, 2.

101. Jean De Serres, ed., *Platonis, augustiss. philosophi, omnium quae extant operum*, vol. 2 (Paris: Henri Estienne, 1578), 138–51 (Parker).

There was one to all the earth through Adam — another through Noah —
There is a revelation of God in the wonders of creation — there is a revelation in the moral law written on the heart — in conscience, God speaks to
all men in many ways — but if *they* neglect these many voices . . . can they
expect a fresh and clearer voice from heaven to reclaim them?[102]

All these voices, Newman calls revelation. This is a loose manner of speaking, to
be sure, but it shows how greatly enlarged his conception was of the potential
for religious knowledge among the heathen, even though such knowledge was
actualized only partially and in but a few instances.[103]

Conscience, Conversion, and the Atonement

Although Newman recognized that a genuine form of religion could be sustained among the heathen, he made the contrast with Christianity as stark as his
new framework allowed. Heathen religious knowledge could engender only the
mere rudiments of a religious life, if that. The experience of conscience might
usher in knowledge of God, but this knowledge is too limited to serve as a means
of genuine moral and religious growth. This contrast makes sense in view of
Newman's understanding of conversion. Drawing on Erskine, Newman had conceptualized conversion as a person's affective response to the cognitive content
of revelation, especially the doctrine of the atonement. Even though Newman
now believed that baptism ensures the participation of all Christians in this process, he still regarded apprehension of the gospel message as the precondition
for moral and religious progress. Neither his increased awareness that right actions
drive sanctification nor his discovery of the religious import of conscience made
him alter this narrative yet. In fact, the penultimate sermon of his sermon course
on revelation, preached on December 11, 1825, upheld the centrality of the atonement for conversion.

On the internal evidence of the evangelical doctrine was a companion sermon to
the one on natural religion, preached the week before. Whereas the latter had
provided reasoned arguments for the truths of natural religion, the present
sermon aimed to show how "the doctrines of the gospel," although "not dis-
coverable by human reason," still "contain much which recommends itself to
our reason."[104] Unsurprisingly, Newman practically limited those doctrines to
one: that of Christ's atoning sacrifice. He drew on Butler's *Analogy* to make a
negative point: since the mechanisms of mediation and vicarious suffering

102. JHN, No. 104, "Probable reasons," *Serm.* 2, 345; see 345n7.
103. JHN, No. 104, "Probable reasons," *Serm.* 2, 349n11.
104. JHN, No. 123, "On the internal evidence of the evangelical doctrine," December 11,
1825, *Serm.* 2, 381.

instantiated in the doctrine of the atonement have their counterparts in the ordinary course of human affairs, there is no reasonable ground to reject them. More importantly, he drew on Erskine to make a positive argument for the reasonableness of the atonement based on its efficacy in converting human beings. God's goal, Newman argued, is "to regenerate and sanctify our hearts, — to convert us from sin and make us love Him."[105] To achieve this end, "a display of His character was necessary — and a display of Himself in action — and a display not only of His holiness justice and truth, but also of His love — in order, through His grace, to warm our hearts."[106] All of these requirements are met by the "doctrine of the cross of Christ," which is a "manifestation of the character of God" in action, in which all "the various and distinct perfections of that character are . . . strikingly revealed," especially His "love."[107] The doctrine of the atonement, in short, is reasonable because it works, and it works because it wins over our affections.

Even as Newman discarded other aspects of evangelicalism, he remained wedded to the centrality of affect in the process of conversion. In August 1826, he preached a sermon with a High Church subject, the Creed, but defended its importance along Erskinian lines. Given that believing is "of no use" if it "does *not* make us better men," Newman aimed to show, "how *belief* in God and Christ (i.e. in the articles of the Creed) makes us holy."[108] His answer reads like a synopsis of the 1825 course on "the scheme of Christian doctrine," discussed in chapter 4.[109] We "are naturally *un*holy," Newman insisted, so that it is "a very difficult matter to make us holy."[110] God, in fact, tried various ways—all quite unsuccessful—until "He adopted a difficult and most wonderful mode for softening the heart of man" by sending "His son to die for man, to bear the punishment that man deserved to suffer for his sins."[111] The revelation of the atonement is intended to change our affections:

> Who does not feel his heart melt within him when he hears how much Christ suffered for us? Belief in the cross of Christ and in all that our Saviour underwent for us has a natural tendency to rouse our minds, to excite us to gratitude, and make us return in sorrow and selfabasement [*sic*] to Him who has loved us sinners who loved not Him.[112]

---

105. JHN, No. 123, "On the internal evidence," *Serm.* 2, 386.
106. JHN, No. 123, "On the internal evidence," *Serm.* 2, 386.
107. JHN, No. 123, "On the internal evidence," *Serm.* 2, 383, 384, 385, 386.
108. JHN, No. 155, "On the Creed," August 27, 1826, *Serm.* 3, 297, 298.
109. JHN, No. 103, "Holiness the end of the Gospel," September 4, 1825, *Serm.* 5, 292.
110. JHN, No. 155, "On the Creed," *Serm.* 3, 298.
111. JHN, No. 155, "On the Creed," *Serm.* 3, 298.
112. JHN, No. 155, "On the Creed," *Serm.* 3, 298.

Such faith in the atonement is not just one among several means to effect the emotional change that is part and parcel of becoming holy. It is "the *only* way in which the soul can be roused to spiritual feelings."[113]

The crucial corollary to this claim is that those without knowledge of Christ lack the means to achieve such affective (and the corresponding behavioral) change. The heathen, Newman concluded in June 1826, "had no *motives* to action," and lacked "habitual virtue, even were [*sic*] there was knowledge," because their knowledge was not of the right kind.[114] In a companion sermon to the one on the Creed, *On the Ten Commandments*, Newman even applied this reasoning to Judaism, although in a milder form. The Jews, he argued, needed a large body of precepts, because they "could not enter into [the] general principle of holiness as Christians may."[115] So "blind and hard is the human heart," Newman noted, "that no ordinary doctrines will move it to holiness or make it love God." In fact, it is only "the doctrine of Christ crucified which under grace has power to conquer and subdue the heart . . . and to plant the love of holiness and the principle of universal obedience in the soul."[116] This knowledge of their redemption the heathen lacked, and the Jews only dimly foresaw.[117]

Although Newman's evangelical emphasis on the necessity and efficacy of the doctrine of the atonement for conversion owed much to Erskine, his contrast between the religious condition of Christians and non-Christians also owed something to Whately, who was suspicious of natural religion, both as a historical phenomenon and as a set of arguments. His *Essays on Some of the Peculiarities of the Christian Religion* (1825) was devoted in its entirety to establishing the distinctiveness of (Protestant) Christianity as a religion, compared to heathenism, Judaism, Islam, and even Roman Catholicism.

One of those distinctive traits, Whately argued, was the New Testament appeal to the affections. Christianity does not so much teach people what to do as persuade them to do it. For Whately, such persuasion to act virtuously is achieved by engaging the affections. The Christian revelation's "continual appeal to the affections" constitutes one "of its most striking peculiarities," distinguishing it from paganism, Islam, and Judaism.[118] In the New Testament, "almost all the exhortations of the sacred writers are grounded on the infinite mercies of our great Instructor and Redeemer towards us, and on the gratitude, love, and reverence, which we ought to feel towards Him in return."[119]

113. JHN, No. 155, "On the Creed," *Serm.* 3, 298.

114. JHN, No. 104, "Probable reasons," *Serm.* 2, 349n11.

115. JHN, No. 154, "On the ten commandments," August 13, 1826, *Serm.* 1, 43.

116. JHN, No. 154, "On the ten commandments," *Serm.* 1, 43.

117. But compare JHN, No. 111, "On the compatibility of spiritual feelings with scanty knowledge in the ancient believers," October 23, 1825, *Serm.* 5, 335–42, which is decidedly more optimistic about the capacity for "really spiritual feelings . . . in the holy men of old" (336).

118. Whately, *Peculiarities of the Christian Religion*, 156.

119. Whately, *Peculiarities of the Christian Religion*, 156.

In his *Essays on Some of the Difficulties in the Writings of St. Paul* (1828), Whately used this insight to distinguish the spiritual nature of Christian obedience from the Jews' literal compliance with the Mosaic Law. It was "no part of the scheme of the gospel-revelation," Whately maintained, "to lay down any thing approaching to a complete system of moral precepts," meant to be obeyed to the letter.[120] This is evident from the structure of New Testament ethics. Jesus' moral injunctions often appear to contradict each other, regularly concern an "*insignificant* and *unimportant* . . . point of duty*," or are such that "literal compliance" is "*impossible*, or at least *extravagant* and *irrational*."[121] For instance, Jesus commands his disciples "to pray and give alms in secret," but also to "let their light shine before men." He likewise tells them to "hate father and mother," contradicting his own "exhortations to universal benevolence" as well as "common sense." Finally, some precepts, like turning the other cheek or going an extra mile with someone, are trivial when applied only literally.[122] Whately, therefore, concluded that the distinctive goal of Christianity was not to substitute some "*other* set of precise rules" for the Mosaic law but to implant "new and higher motives" to action, and to inculcate "sublime principles" by which a Christian is to freely regulate herself.[123]

Newman developed the same line of argument in a sermon on September 2, 1827, *On the Christian law of liberty*. He later dubbed it "a Whateleyan Sermon," and so it was.[124] It testifies to how much of Whately's influence was exercised through conversation rather than writing, as it drew on ideas that were published only a year later. Like Whately, Newman contrasted the distinctive "*liberty*" of the Christian's obedience with the "law of *bondage*" to which the Jews were subject.[125] He argued that "the rules for obedience which Christ has given us are . . . *not* full, precise, minute, systematic, but general only — exactly such as would be given if it were intended we should be guided by the spirit of the command."[126] In evidence, he summed up the same Gospel passages that Whately used and concluded, in the same vein, that the New Testament provides "high motives for obedience" and "broad principles of duty" rather than "specific precepts" to be complied with to the letter.[127] Like Whately, he believed that this provision of motives, or appeals to the affection, was a distinctive trait of Christianity. What "has been revealed" in Christianity, he argued, is "not so much a *knowledge* of our

<hr>

120. Richard Whately, *Essays on Some of the Difficulties in the Writings of St. Paul, and in Other Parts of the New Testament* (London: B. Fellowes, 1828), 232.

121. Whately, *Difficulties in the Writings of St. Paul*, 238.

122. Whately, *Difficulties in the Writings of St. Paul*, 239–46.

123. Whately, *Difficulties in the Writings of St. Paul*, 233, 234.

124. JHN, No. 161, "On the Christian law of liberty," September 2, 1827, *Serm.* 3, 301n2.

125. JHN, No. 161, "On the Christian law of liberty," *Serm.* 3, 304. The outline of this argument can already be found in the sermon *On the Ten Commandments* (*Serm.* 1, 41–43).

126. JHN, No. 161, "On the Christian law of liberty," *Serm.* 3, 306.

127. JHN, No. 161, "On the Christian law of liberty," *Serm.* 3, 306.

duty, as *motives to* perform it."[128] By now, he readily acknowledged that anyone could know his duty by means of conscience:

> We cannot put a limit to the power of natural conscience (if duly used) even independent of revelation in bringing us acquainted with our duty — and we know as a fact that not a single precept perhaps of the New Testament [exists] but has been somewhere or other laid down by heathen moralists who never saw the Scriptures.[129]

Such knowledge, however, is insufficient for practice because it does not engage the affections. What we need "is an excitement, something to stir us up and urge us on."[130] Without the gospel, conscience tends to issue in despair and moral impotence, not just with heathens, "but in good measure even with the Jews themselves."[131] The "doctrine of the sacrifice of Christ's . . . death instead of us" solves these problems. It liberates us both from the specter of guilt and the fetters of the law because it supplies us with "a means of *acceptance* with God" and "high motives" to live well.[132] Since heathens and Jews lack this "strong and constraining motive to holy action," their religiosity remains either inefficacious or bogged down by literal adherence to a code of law.[133] Religious knowledge, then, comes in degrees, and as long as it does not include knowledge of the atonement, it can sustain only a rudimentary moral and spiritual life.

An Essay on Miracles

As noted above, the shift in Newman's thought on conscience and natural religion was the outcome of a reflective process that originated in unresolved bits of the dispute with his apostate brother Charles. Now, John's new take on conscience and natural religion helped him to answer some of Charles's objections. John did so in the long entry on miracles that he wrote for the *Encyclopaedia Metropolitana* between August 1825 and April 1826.[134] The piece addressed three objections Charles had raised against miracles. First, contending religions all advance miraculous claims, which greatly reduces the evidential value of the biblical miracles. Second, our experience of the regular course of nature renders miracles, as

128. JHN, No. 161, "On the Christian law of liberty," *Serm.* 3, 307.
129. JHN, No. 161, "On the Christian law of liberty," *Serm.* 3, 307.
130. JHN, No. 161, "On the Christian law of liberty," *Serm.* 3, 307.
131. JHN, No. 161, "On the Christian law of liberty," *Serm.* 3, 308.
132. JHN, No. 161, "On the Christian law of liberty," *Serm.* 3, 303, 304.
133. JHN, No. 161, "On the Christian law of liberty," *Serm.* 3, 308.
134. The *Metropolitana* was a thematically arranged encyclopaedia, initiated by Samuel Taylor Coleridge. See Alan Rauch, *Useful Knowledge: The Victorians, Morality, and the March of Intellect* (Durham: Duke University Press, 2001), 35–37.

such, highly improbable.[135] And third, the probabilistic status of testimony to
miracles can never justify assent to implausible doctrines. In August 1825, John
had left these objections largely unanswered, but by April 1826, he had developed
a coherent account of the way Christian miracles are distinct from non-Christian
miracles, cohere with the God of nature's ordinary government of the world, and
function as (probabilistic) evidence for the Christian revelation.[136] These were
important achievements, to be sure, but it was the essay's novel conception of
the relation between nature and revelation that was to prove key in Newman's
theological development.

The *Essay on Miracles* was the apogee of Newman's constructive engagement
with Enlightenment apologetics. He began research for the article on July 15 by
studying the most famous eighteenth-century argument against miracles, David
Hume's chapter "Of Miracles" in the *Enquiry*, and he read several dozen other
works on miracles in the following months.[137] Newman defined a miracle as "an
event inconsistent with the constitution of nature."[138] Miracles, however, were
not to be regarded "as mere exceptions to physical order" because they are part
of God's providential governance and serve "a moral end," that is, the establishment of a revelation.[139] A miracle, then, is premised on our natural knowledge
of the existence and attributes of the God of nature; it is "the signature of God
to a message delivered by human instruments; and therefore supposes that signature in some degree already known, from his ordinary works."[140] On the
Enlightenment apologetic model, miracles could be proven only by testimony—
"the same *kind* of evidence as that by which we determine the truth of Historical
accounts in general."[141]

The Deists, however, with Hume in their wake, had questioned whether mere
testimony could ever prove miracles. For Hume, "violations of truth in the testimony of men" were infinitely more probable than "the violation of the laws of

135. CRN, *No 3*, BOA A.4.2.3, 16.
136. G. R. Evans's ("Newman's Letters," 97) suggestion that John's preoccupation with the
miraculous evidence for Christianity in his correspondence with Charles stemmed from his preparatory work on the *Essay on Miracles* is unlikely for three reasons: (i) John was steeped in the Enlightenment apologetic tradition long before the controversy with Charles commenced; (ii) John only began
to read up on the subject of miracles in July 1825, when his apologetic approach to Charles was
already well in place; and (iii) the *Essay on Miracles* develops themes that arose only in discussion with
Charles.
137. *LD* 1, 242ff; Jaki, "Newman and Miracles," 212–13.
138. JHN, "Apollonius Tyanaeus—Miracles," *Encyclopaedia Metropolitana*, vol. 10, *History and
Biography*, vol. 2, 626. The section on miracles runs from 626–44. The article was reprinted as the
essay "On the Miracles of Scripture," *Mir.*, 3–94.
139. JHN, "Miracles," 626 (*Mir.*, 5).
140. JHN, "Miracles," 627 (*Mir.*, 10). "A Miracle," John wrote, "is no argument to one who is
deliberately, and on principle, an atheist."
141. JHN, "Miracles," 628 (*Mir.*, 13).

nature by miracles."[142] On the basis of this a priori criterion, he rejected all known miracle accounts. Newman accorded little weight to Hume's argument; it had been satisfactorily answered by other authors, who had shown that it was based on "the *assumption*, that a Miracle is strictly a *causeless phenomenon*, a *self-originating violation of nature*" and could be met "by referring the event to *divine agency*."[143] The power that created the world could surely work miracles; hence, their intrinsic improbability was overcome. Yet, Hume and the Deists—echoed by Charles—had leveled a more popular objection against miracles drawn from the occurrence of miracles across incompatible religious traditions. "The alleged *similarity* of *all* Miraculous narratives," as Newman put it, provided such critics with "a reason for a common rejection of all."[144] This objection raised the pressing question: "*What* Miracles are in their nature and circumstances referable to divine agency," a question issuing naturally from a biographical study of the first-century miracle worker Apollonius of Tyana (the first part of Newman's essay), who was the favorite Deist parallel to Jesus.[145]

To answer this question, Newman, in a bold rhetorical move, adopted Hume's own principle that because God "discovers himself to us by his works, we have no rational grounds for ascribing to him attributes or actions dissimilar to those which his works convey."[146] Hume limited the application of this principle to God's "productions, in the usual course of nature" and argued that since we consistently experience nature as regular, testimony to miracles is infinitely unlikely to be true.[147] Newman, by contrast, argued that the works of the God knowable by natural reason are not limited to the laws of nature but include his moral law as well, an insight he derived from Butler's *Analogy*.[148] Besides the natural, there is "a *Moral* system; a system, which though but partially understood, and but general in its appointments as acting upon free agents, is as intelligible in its laws and provisions as the material world."[149] As in the sermon *On natural religion*, Newman argued that God's moral governance is evidenced inwardly and outwardly. In

---

142. Hume, *Enquiry*, 93 (129).

143. JHN, "Miracles," 628 (*Mir.*, 15). The argument was Paley's (*A View of the Evidences of Christianity*, 10–11).

144. JHN, "Miracles," 628 (*Mir.*, 15); Hume, *Enquiry*, 87–88 (121–22).

145. JHN, "Miracles," 628 (*Mir.*, 15); Burns, *The Great Debate on Miracles*, 72; and Jaś Elsner, "Beyond Compare: Pagan Saint and Christian God in Late Antiquity," in *Saints: Faith Without Borders*, ed. Françoise Meltzer and Jaś Elsner (Chicago: University of Chicago Press, 2011), 367–77. Although helpful, Elsner's presentation of Newman's article on Apollonius is skewed due to its ignoring the independent role of natural theology in the Enlightenment apologetic tradition.

146. JHN, "Miracles," 628 (*Mir.*, 15).

147. Hume, *Enquiry*, 93 (129). In addition to Hume, Newman ("Miracles," 629 [*Mir.*, 21]) also instanced Voltaire and Jeremy Bentham as limiting our natural knowledge of God's works to the laws of nature.

148. JHN, "Miracles," 628 (*Mir.*, 17). *Pace* Evans ("Newman's Letters," 95), reading the *Analogy* had no perceptible influence on John's response to Charles.

149. JHN, "Miracles," 628 (*Mir.*, 16). See Butler, *The Analogy of Religion*, pt. I, chap. 3.

terms of the subject, "we find certain instincts of mind; such as conscience, a sense of responsibility, and an approbation of virtue."[150] If we look at the external world, we see that, "in fact, Virtue is on the whole rewarded and Vice punished."[151] The order of nature, moreover, is subordinate to this moral system. On this premise, miracles make sense. They interrupt the laws of nature only to further a more important moral end: revelation. A miracle, then, "is a deviation from the subordinate for the sake of the superior system, and is very far indeed from improbable, when a great Moral end cannot be effected except at the expense of Physical regularity."[152] Although the idea that miracles should always serve a significant purpose was typical of Enlightenment apologetics, Newman's proximate source was the mathematician and astronomer Samuel Vince, who had emphatically argued that Hume's case against miracles failed because he "entirely neglected" God's moral purposes.[153] Newman's argument is a significant step forward from the controversy with Charles, where Newman had left the relationship between the God of nature and the God of revelation unspecified. Now, he located the continuity between natural and revealed religion, including the latter's miraculous evidence, squarely on the level of God's overarching moral ends.

It was precisely "Hume's canon"—"that *no work can be reasonably ascribed to the agency of God, which is altogether different from those ordinary works from which our knowledge of him is originally obtained*"—that provided Newman with a criterion to distinguish the Old and New Testament miracles from other allegedly miraculous events.[154] As the professed evidences for a divine revelation, the biblical miracles had a clear object, consonant with our natural knowledge of God's moral governance, "completing the Moral system, connecting Man with his Maker, and introducing him to the means of securing his happiness in another and eternal state of being."[155] This lofty object rendered the scriptural miracles antecedently probable, while it distinguished them from the miracles of non-Christian religions, as well as from apocryphal, patristic, and Roman Catholic miracles, which were either not referred to divine agency, were unworthy of the God of nature, lacked an object, or had an unimportant, questionable, or inconsistent object.[156] The conformity of mir-

---

150. JHN, "Miracles," 628 (*Mir.*, 17).

151. JHN, "Miracles," 628 (*Mir.*, 17).

152. JHN, "Miracles," 628 (*Mir.*, 18).

153. Samuel Vince, *The Credibility of the Scripture Miracles Vindicated in Answer to Mr. Hume*, 2nd ed. (Cambridge: J. Deighton and J. Nicholson, 1809), 6. See Butler, *The Analogy of Religion*, 224, and pp. 73–74 in this book.

154. JHN, "Miracles," 630 (*Mir.*, 26).

155. JHN, "Miracles," 629 (*Mir.*, 22).

156. JHN, "Miracles," 630–34 (*Mir.*, 27–45). Newman treated Paine's idea of "writing the Gospel on the skies" as the only "adequate attestation to a revelation" under the last heading, arguing that it required a perpetual, and therefore unnecessary miracle, given that "the recorded fact of their [the Biblical miracles's] once occurring [is] sufficient for a rational conviction" ("Miracles," 633 [*Mir.*, 40]).

acles to God's moral governance, then, provided Newman with a first criterion to distinguish biblical from nonbiblical miracles. Having demonstrated "that the Scripture Miracles *may* be ascribed to the Supreme Being," Newman set out to show that they could be attributed neither to "the power of invisible Beings, short of God," such as demons, nor to "the possible existence of causes in nature, to us unknown."[157]

With regard to the first, Newman rejected the opposite solutions of Locke, who argued that divine miracles could be distinguished from nondivine ones by their greater number and power, and Hugh Farmer, who simply denied the power of nondivine spirits to work miracles.[158] Newman also rejected the attempt to prove the divine origin of the miracle on the basis of the divine character of the doctrine it accompanied, arguing that such reasoning was circular and, more importantly, involved judging revelation by its contents.[159] Instead, he appealed to divine benevolence. Since "God has adopted Miracles as the seal of a divine message, we believe he will never suffer them to be so counterfeited as to deceive the humble inquirer."[160] With regard to the appeal to unknown natural causes, Newman admitted, with Locke, that the recognition of miracles was partly subjective, because it depended on the knowledge of nature on the part of those who witnessed the miracle.[161] Accordingly, some events might appear miraculous in one age but not in another. Newman, however, turned this problem into a second argument for the distinctive character of the scripture miracles. Whereas pagan, patristic, and Jansenist miracles could often easily be explained by natural causes, the biblical miracles were mostly impervious to such an explanation.[162]

Newman did not think *all* biblical miracles met his criteria. He candidly acknowledged that some biblical miracles appear either unworthy of God or explicable in natural terms. Yet, because they are part of one revelatory system, they are received on the basis of the vast majority of unobjectionable miracles as "exceptions (and as we suppose, but *apparent* exceptions) to the general rule."[163] Newman realized full well, moreover, that both the antecedent conformity of an alleged miracle to divine agency and the impossibility to explain it by other means did not *prove* the occurrence of the miracle: "the quality of the

157. JHN, "Miracles," 635, 636 (*Mir.*, 49, 50).

158. JHN, "Miracles," 635 (*Mir.*, 51–52); Locke, "A Discourse of Miracles," 223; and Hugh Farmer, *A Dissertation on Miracles* (London: T. Cadell, 1771).

159. JHN, "Miracles," 635 (*Mir.*, 51–52).

160. JHN, "Miracles," 635 (*Mir.*, 52).

161. JHN, "Miracles," 626 (*Mir.*, 5–6); Locke, "A Discourse of Miracles," 217–18.

162. JHN, "Miracles," 636–38 (*Mir.*, 53–67). For the many miracles reported at Port-Royal and at the tomb of François de Pâris, used to bolster the religious legitimacy of Jansenism, see B. Robert Kreiser, *Miracles, Convulsions and Ecclesiastical Politics in Early Eighteenth-Century Paris* (Princeton, N.J.: Princeton University Press, 1978), esp. chaps. 2–4.

163. JHN, "Miracles," 631 (*Mir.*, 30).

testimony on which the accounts rest can alone determine our *belief* in them."[164] Again, Newman's thinking had progressed since the controversy with his brother, who objected to the merely probabilistic nature of arguments from testimony. Appealing once more to Butler's *Analogy*, Newman argued that "in a practical question, as the divinity of a professed Revelation must be considered, even the weakest reasons are decisive when not counteracted by any opposite arguments."[165] Like Locke and most of the Enlightenment apologetic tradition, Newman believed the amount of evidence required was determined by what Robert Burns has called the 'principle of context': "those attendant circumstances, of which we have already spoken, the object of the Miracle, the occasion, manner, and human agent employed."[166] Since such antecedent considerations spoke in favor of the biblical miracles, even scanty evidence sufficed to prove their occurrence. Nevertheless, Newman was convinced that the biblical miracle accounts, in contrast to all other miracle stories, had a solid evidential basis and were written by honest and competent witnesses who had little to gain, and much to lose, by their testimony.[167]

All in all, the *Essay on Miracles* offered a coherent defense of the evidential import and unique status of biblical miracles and was a significant improvement on the *ad hoc* arguments developed in discussion with Charles. More importantly, however, it initiated two trajectories—both indebted to Butler—that would shape Newman's later thought. First, in line with his new understanding of conscience, Newman began to locate the continuity between natural and revealed religion on the moral plane. This was a decided move away from an alternative tendency, equally present in Enlightenment apologetics, to locate this continuity on the physical plane. Instead of merely resorting to the *power* required for performing miracles (which could only be that of the Creator of the universe), Newman bolstered the evidential import of miracles by showing their consonance with the God of nature's *moral* governance of the world.

Second, Newman began to appropriate Butler's emphasis on antecedent probability as a determining factor in evaluating miracles. This, too, implied taking one particular option within the tradition of Enlightenment apologetics. Rather than emphasize a miracle's intrinsic value as evidence for revelation—simply as an interruption of the course of nature—Newman stressed the contextual factors required for a miracle to qualify as evidence. Miracles never stand alone; they should be evaluated as part of a wider (moral) system from which they derive their

---

164. JHN, "Miracles," 639 (*Mir.*, 70).

165. JHN, "Miracles," 639 (*Mir.*, 70). Besides Butler's *The Analogy of Religion*, see Davison, *Discourses on Prophecy*, 5; James Pereiro, Ethos *and the Oxford Movement: At the Heart of Tractarianism* (Oxford: Oxford University Press, 2008), 90–91.

166. JHN, "Miracles," 639 (*Mir.*, 73); Burns, *The Great Debate on Miracles*, 49–51, 65–67.

167. JHN, "Miracles," 640–43 (*Mir.*, 75–91).

meaning. They are relative, rather than absolute, evidences of a revelation.[168] Since they are embedded within an antecedent set of expectations about God, moreover, the amount of historical testimony required to prove their occurrence, which would be insurmountable if they were "absolute" facts, can be relatively small.

Conclusion

For the development of Newman's fundamental theology and theological anthropology, conscience and natural religion were what baptismal regeneration had been for his doctrinal theology. After the summer of 1824, Newman began to invest conscience with increasing moral and religious significance. He gradually traded the notion that conscience has no content for the idea that it contains a roughly accurate sense of right and wrong: a moral sense. But conscience not only yields moral knowledge: it is also a means of acquiring knowledge of God's existence and moral governance. Although heavily impeded by sin and requiring the aid of other "universal revelations," the knowledge acquired through conscience can facilitate the rudiments of genuine religious praxis among the heathen. Where Butler's idea of conscience allowed Newman to establish a link between God and human nature, Butler's idea of God's moral governance helped Newman to conceptualize the relationship between God and the universe. The realms of nature and grace are unified by the overarching moral purposes of God's governance, expressed in ordinary providence as well as revelation. Still, Newman's evangelical take on conversion proved resilient. The cognitive and affective apprehension of Christ's atoning sacrifice still does most of the work. The religious knowledge acquired through conscience, or even through the Old Testament revelation, pales in comparison. Yet, the seeds of more radical developments had been sown.

---

168. Samuel Clarke's *Boyle Lectures* of 1705 are a good specimen of the opposite option within Enlightenment apologetics, which stressed the almost absolute probative value of miracles at the cost of contextual considerations such as the nature of the doctrine propounded and the character of the miracle worker (Burns, *The Great Debate on Miracles*, 99–105).

CHAPTER 6

Endings and Beginnings

The evangelical scene at Oxford in the mid-1820s was one of much soul-searching. The first generation of evangelical torchbearers in the Church of England was disappearing; John Newton and the Venn brothers had been dead for over a decade, Thomas Scott passed away in 1821, and Charles Simeon and William Wilberforce were becoming elderly men. They had no obvious successors, and the "second-hand legacy" that younger evangelicals inherited had lost much of its original sense of urgency and awakening.[1] A new generation, therefore, was beginning to reinterpret—or even reconsider—evangelicalism and its place in the Church of England. Newman was one of many. From 1824 onward, the theology he had drawn from evangelicalism's founding fathers—Newton, Milner, Scott, and Simeon—became subject to novel influences. The thought of an advanced evangelical like Erskine appealed to him and helped him to structure his theology of conversion. Oriel College also changed him. Whately left his mark, a mark that coincided, at times, with Erskine's but that also steered Newman toward a new appreciation of the visible church. Pusey, Hawkins, and Sumner furthered the crisis of Newman's evangelicalism by pressing the issue of baptismal regeneration. Newman read Butler in the autumn of 1825 and began to reconsider the theological import of conscience and the significance of heathen religiosity. By the summer of 1827, he had renounced many of his earlier evangelical beliefs, although some fundamental evangelical commitments continued to shape his theology. Amid these various developments, few people knew what to make of him.

The autobiography of the later Tractarian Isaac Williams is a testimony to the conflicting impressions people had of Newman. Williams recollects a visit to Llandrindod in 1827, where he met the evangelical curate of Deddington, John Hughes. Hughes frowned upon Oriel but still recommended for Williams's acquaintance "a most promising and excellent person there, Mr. Newman."[2] Hughes, Williams comments, evidently "considered Newman to be of his own

---

1. David Newsome, *The Parting of Friends: The Wilberforces and Henry Manning* (Grand Rapids, Mich.: William B. Eerdmans, 1993), 9; Grayson Carter, *Anglican Evangelicals: Protestant Secessions from the* Via Media, *c. 1800–1850* (Oxford: Oxford University Press, 2001), 254–55; and Stunt, *From Awakening to Secession*, 193.

2. Isaac Williams, *The Autobiography of Isaac Williams*, ed. George Prevost (London: Longmans, Green & Co., 1892), 43.

Calvinistic party."[3] In the same period, however, Williams received a letter from Thomas Keble (brother to John) explaining that Richard Hurrell Froude intended to take Newman to the Keble home to cure him of "his liberal principles."[4] As for Newman himself, he believed he was becoming rather High Church, albeit furtively so. "I was eagerly, but not very logically High Church," he wrote many years later, recollecting the Long Vacation of 1827.[5] When his former divinity professor, the High Churchman Charles Lloyd, became bishop of Oxford earlier in the year, Newman noted in his diary: "he says that our theological systems do not agree. They agree more than when I was in class with him, but I do not tell him so."[6] Evangelicalism, however, could accommodate Newman's tenets. It was quite a flexible creed in the mid-1820s, both at Oxford and elsewhere, and retained a good deal of common ground with High Church theology. Attitudes, as Timothy Stunt notes, only "polarised in the thirties."[7]

Newman's new convictions, therefore, did not estrange him from the evangelical world all at once. In July 1825, when he had made up his mind on baptismal regeneration, he still participated in the establishment of a local association of the Church Missionary Society, a plan spearheaded by the evangelical coterie of John Hill, vice-principal of St Edmund Hall and the key evangelical figure at the university.[8] Newman's first-ever public speech was delivered at the initial meeting of the society, at Deddington, where he already knew the evangelical vicar, Richard Greaves, whose curate Williams met at Llandrindod.[9] Newman also continued to subscribe to the Oxfordshire branch of the nondenominational Bible Society, despite his conviction that only the Church of England was that of the Apostles. In 1828, he could still give one of his parishioners *The Rise and Progress of Religion in the Soul*, a work by the dissenting evangelical Philip Doddridge.[10] And during the summer and Christmas holidays, he preached for the evangelical vicar Henry Venn Elliott at St Mary's, Brighton (where the Newman family had moved), a mark of distinction Newman shared with influential evangelicals like Charles Simeon and Josiah Pratt.[11] These events and associations, however, were the last

3. Williams, *The Autobiography of Isaac Williams*, 43.

4. Williams, *The Autobiography of Isaac Williams*, 43. On September 7, 1828, Froude could still write to Robert Wilberforce: "I would give a few odd pence if he [Newman] were not a heretic" (*Remains of the Late Reverend Richard Hurrell Froude*, vol. 1, ed. John Keble and John Henry Newman [London: J. G. & F. Rivington, 1838], 233).

5. JHN to J. G. Cazenove, January 16, 1867, *LD* 23, 38.

6. JHN, "February 21, 1827," *AW*, 210.

7. Stunt, *From Awakening to Secession*, 184, 188; Carter, *Anglican Evangelicals*, 256.

8. *LD* 1, 246.

9. *LD* 1, 178, 257, 315–16. See Stunt, *From Awakening to Secession*, 189, and p. 157 in this book.

10. *LD* 2, 100.

11. *LD* 2, 84, 114; Josiah Bateman, *The Life of the Rev. Henry Venn Elliott* (London: Macmillan, 1868), 119–20. Elliott was a nephew of John and Henry Venn.

convulsions of his life within evangelicalism. Developments in 1828 and early 1829 all but erased what had been distinctly evangelical about his theology. In part, this was only a continuation of his earlier trajectory, in which the influence of Butler, especially, became ever more prominent. But it was aided by personal and family drama and shaped by a new group of friends.

The Trower Paper and Oxford High Calvinism

In the second half of the 1820s, it became clear that High Church theology was not the only alternative tenet Oxford evangelicalism could accommodate. More radically Calvinist figures and ideas began to enter John Hill's circle. In 1826, Henry Bellenden Bulteel became curate of the Oxford parish of St Ebbe's, where, to cite an evangelical contemporary, he "created a most powerful sensation . . . by preaching ultra-Calvinism."[12] To the alarm of the university authorities, undergraduates trouped to his sermons. In May 1828, the vice-chancellor undertook a half-hearted attempt to stop university members from attending Bulteel's services. It failed, but Oxford was astir about high Calvinism.[13] Frank Newman, too, was part of Hill's circle, and he also was becoming more radical.[14] His qualms about infant baptism had jeopardized his allegiance to the Established Church, and these doubts were intensified when he went to Ireland, in September 1827, as tutor in an evangelical family. Frank met and was deeply impressed by John Nelson Darby, one of the future founders of the Plymouth Brethren, and became ardent about premillennialism.[15] While Frank and other Oxford evangelicals were drifting away from the Church of England, John's ecclesial ties were strengthening. In early 1828, he succeeded Hawkins as vicar of St Mary's, the University Church of Oxford, and returned to regular preaching. Soon, he began to formulate definite criticisms of evangelical theology and its developments at Oxford.

The impetus for Newman's critique of evangelical theology was the election of Walter John Trower as fellow of Oriel College in April 1828. Trower was a friend of Frank Newman and Benjamin Wills Newton, another radicalizing member of John Hill's circle of Oxford evangelicals.[16] According to Newton, Trower had been "a truly fixed evangelical" prior to his election, which means, presumably, that he was inclined toward high Calvinism.[17] But at Oriel he came

12. Thomas Byrth in 1827, cited in Stunt, *From Awakening to Secession*, 197.
13. Carter, *Anglican Evangelicals*, 260–61.
14. Stunt, *From Awakening to Secession*, 188.
15. Stunt, *From Awakening to Secession*, 205–9; *LD* 2, 56.
16. With Darby and George Wigram, Newton became one of the founders of the Brethren movement in the early 1830s.
17. Benjamin Wills Newton, cited in Stunt, *From Awakening to Secession*, 204.

under John Newman's influence.[18] Given his own experience, Newman had every reason to take an active interest in a young Calvinist trying to adapt to the Oriel environment. Their talk quickly turned theological. Debate must have been intense, for, in August, he presented Trower with a lengthy paper in criticism of evangelical doctrine, entitled *Remarks on the Covenant of Grace, in connexion with the doctrines of Election, Baptism, & the Church*.[19] He later noted that it "was written when I was <u>systematizing</u> my views against what is called Evangelical Religion."[20] This comment bears on the state of Newman's mind more than on the paper he wrote, which, he admitted, was "obviously unmethodical."[21] Not all of its content was new. From the summer of 1825 onward, Newman had begun to question, with growing openness, evangelical ideas about election, regeneration, and sanctification, but his criticisms were scattered throughout his sermons, often proposed hesitantly, and never extensive. They usually comprised only a few lines and seldom more than a paragraph.[22] The *Remarks* gathered these critiques into a more comprehensive argument against evangelical doctrinal theology, especially the high Calvinist variant that was making headway at Oxford.

It seems that the paper had some impact, for soon afterwards, Trower tried to convince Newton that baptism was necessary for salvation.[23] Trower was unsuccessful, but his focus on baptismal regeneration is telling. Newman's own turn away from evangelicalism had been precipitated by reconsidering the doctrine, and it was evidently on his mind in the early summer of 1828.[24]

The *Remarks* can be read as a discussion of the implications of baptismal regeneration for the evangelical understanding of election, the church, conversion, assurance, and perseverance. Recall that part of the appeal of Calvinistic evangelicalism was its simplicity, both regarding its internal consistency and its straightforward application to the religious life of individuals. Its belief in God's sovereignty was expressed in the core doctrine of efficacious grace, which connected the doctrines of predestination, election, assurance, and final perseverance. The experience of conversion was the point at which individuals began to participate in this doctrinal sequence; it actualized their elect status and led them on to ultimate salvation. The operation of grace is marked by a perfect identity between God's will and its effects:

18. *LD* 2, 63, 67, 71, 73, 75, 83–85.

19. JHN, *Remarks on the Covenant of Grace, in connexion with the doctrines of Election, Baptism, & the Church*, August 1828, BOA A.9.1. See *LD* 2, 65, 87. For a useful point by point summary, see Sheridan, *Newman on Justification*, 161–72.

20. JHN, *Remarks on the Covenant of Grace*, BOA A.9.1, title page. The comment is dated "May 12/74"; Newman wrote it on the same day that he was looking through his *Remarks on Infant Baptism* (see p. 144 in this book).

21. JHN, *Remarks on the Covenant of Grace*, BOA A.9.1, 6.

22. Newman's sermon on the penitent thief is one of few exceptions (see pp. 128–30 in this book).

23. Stunt, *From Awakening to Secession*, 204.

24. In June, Newman preached three consecutive sermons on infant baptism at St Mary's.

whomever he chooses, he saves. The doctrine of baptismal regeneration challenges this simple identification. If all the baptized receive grace, but not all are saved, there can be no perfect identity between God's will and its effects. At the end of his ministry at St Clement's, Newman had already questioned the scriptural support for an "infallible and irreversible election unto life" but would not dismiss the idea altogether.[25] In 1828, he did. "The question," he pointed out to Trower, "is not whether any can come without grace"—no one can—"but whether all who receive grace will come."[26] Here, he parted ways with Calvinism: not all will come.

After accepting baptismal regeneration, Newman increasingly emphasized the agentic dimension in the process of sanctification. From Butler, he learned that holy dispositions are acquired not only indirectly, by partaking of the means of grace, but also by trying to do good directly.[27] In June 1828, he formulated the theological principle implied by this shift: "man is so constituted that he cannot actually be saved (of course he cannot) without his own concurrence and cooperation."[28] Such a commitment to the freedom of human agency is a logical, though perhaps not a necessary, corollary to believing in baptismal regeneration, and it solves a practical problem introduced by that doctrine. Although baptismal regeneration accounts for the presence of goodness in otherwise not overly holy parishioners, it does not explain why some are holier than others. The most obvious solution to this problem—and the one that Newman gradually adopted—is to attribute the difference to the way people choose to respond to the grace given them in baptism. By the summer of 1828, this solution had become constitutive of his idea of regeneration.

"Regeneration," he explained to Trower, can be "viewed externally & internally — in the former point of view it is also called <u>justification</u> or <u>acceptance</u> . . . in the latter <u>conversion</u>."[29] These perspectives depend on whether one views regeneration as the product of divine or of human agency.

> The act of regeneration, as far as God's work is concerned, may be con
> sidered immediate & complete — we are at once transferred into a state of
> blessedness — part of it however (our sanctification) needing our own active
> cooperation, must, it stands to reason, be a <u>process</u>, the work of time, nay
> of our whole lives.[30]

25. JHN, No. 150, "General observations on the whole subject—conclusion," April 23, 1826, *Serm.* 5, 404. See pp. 131–32 in this book.

26. JHN, *Remarks on the Covenant of Grace*, BOA A.9.1, 14.

27. See pp. 127–28.

28. JHN, No. 169, "On Infant Baptism—part ii (as connected with the Christian scheme of salvation) i.e. baptism the seal of election," June 22, 1828, *Serm.* 1, 169.

29. JHN, *Remarks on the Covenant of Grace*, BOA A.9.1, 9. See also No. 169, "On Infant Baptism—part ii," *Serm.* 1, 165n3.

30. JHN, *Remarks on the Covenant of Grace*, BOA A.9.1, 9.

Newman had already emphasized this distinction in a June sermon on infant baptism. A person "is perfectly and irrevocably saved" upon baptism as "far as God's work is concerned," but only as far as that.[31] As far as we are concerned, "the whole of our earthly life is necessary for availing ourselves of privileges which were given promptly and in their fulness by Almighty God — for *we* are slow and imperfect in our acts, while God blesses at once."[32] Newman's use of the term conversion to denote this lifelong process of sanctification cemented the break with his own former evangelicalism as well as with that of John Hill's circle.

"Conversion," Newman wrote to Trower, "is the process, not the commencement of a religious course — the gradual changing, not an initial change."[33] He was adamant about this. There simply is no such a thing as an evangelical conversion: "a finished change introductory to a religious life . . . does not exist. No one is changed here."[34] This was at least a partial contradiction of his former views. As a young evangelical, Newman had understood conversion as the radical redirection of one's affection from sin to God. This primary and pivotal change in one's religious condition he termed regeneration, which, in turn, issues in sanctification: the secondary, but equally necessary, process of having one's praxis changed. Thus, although conversion is not a "finished change" (since it requires additional change), Newman did conceive of it as distinct from and introductory to sanctification.

When Newman accepted the idea that regeneration takes place in baptism, his former idea of conversion became redundant. All the baptized, by virtue of being baptized, are engaged in the process of sanctification. Increasingly, he came to think of this process as one of habit formation. But if sanctification—the only religious change required beyond baptism—consists in a change of habits (which, by definition, take time to form), there can be no such thing as a sudden change initiating a devout life. Accordingly, he denounced as pointless the evangelical quest for some point in time when a person "is first influenced by religious feelings."[35] Apart from baptism, there is no "first injection," as he had once called it, of religious feeling.[36] "Baptism is God's first time," he asserted categorically, and "no other can be definitely named."[37] Accordingly, "every baptized person is under a process of divine influence and sanctification — a process often interrupted, often given over — then resumed, irregularly carried on, heartily entered into, finally completed, as the case may be."[38]

---

31. JHN, No. 169, "On Infant Baptism—part ii," *Serm.* 1, 169.
32. JHN, No. 169, "On Infant Baptism—part ii," *Serm.* 1, 169.
33. JHN, *Remarks on the Covenant of Grace*, BOA A.9.1, 9.
34. JHN, *Remarks on the Covenant of Grace*, BOA A.9.1, 9.
35. JHN, *Remarks on the Covenant of Grace*, BOA A.9.1, 10.
36. JHN, *Nature of Holiness*, BOA A.9.1.g, 3.
37. JHN, *Remarks on the Covenant of Grace*, BOA A.9.1, 10.
38. JHN, *Remarks on the Covenant of Grace*, BOA A.9.1, 10.

Some of the more radical Calvinists in Hill's circle went further than the young Newman had gone. They not only identified the experience of conversion with regeneration but also rejected the necessity of progressive sanctification. They believed that the regeneration acquired upon conversion is *all* the change we need. Newman traced this "common & (as I think) hurtful error" to the misunderstanding of a metaphor. Evangelicals usually described the operation of grace "as issuing in a change of nature, of heart, of soul." As metaphor, this usage is "unexceptionable," but some strained the image "into a physical sense, as if something new actually took the place of something old."[39]

This reifying usage has two implications: first, because "a <u>nature</u> is always one & the same," it cannot be changed further (by a process of sanctification), and, second, because it literally replaces another nature, it cannot be lost.[40] Accordingly, high Calvinists argued that converted Christians must persevere: "Can a soul be <u>unborn</u>? Once regenerate, always regenerate."[41] Newman countered this logic by portraying the operation of grace as the infusion of a "new principle" rather than a new nature. This principle, received at baptism, contends with the "corrupt & sinful principle" that naturally governs us, and "like leaven is to spread & overcome the other."[42] Unlike a nature, such "a <u>principle</u> may increase or decrease without limit."[43] Its growth depends on the responsivity of the believer. As Newman put in his June sermon on infant baptism, "not a step can be advanced towards that complete regeneration without [one's] own active cooperation."[44] Because regeneration depends on human effort, there are no guarantees that all the baptized will achieve ultimate salvation. If "man has a share in a work," there must "from the nature of man be imperfection & uncertainty of final accomplishment."[45] Thus, even though all the baptized "are chosen in order to salvation, not all are ultimately saved."[46]

As a result of this view, Newman now denied the possibility of being assured of one's salvation. Already in March 1825, he had been wary of overly facile claims to assurance. "Many," he argued, "seem to have considered this inward assurance of God's favor as resulting immediately from faith."[47] But this is not the case. We should not judge of our saved status by our feelings—"an overflowing joy and fullness of spiritual comfort"—but by the actions that result from

<hr>

39. JHN, *Remarks on the Covenant of Grace*, BOA A.9.1, 9, 10.
40. JHN, *Remarks on the Covenant of Grace*, BOA A.9.1, 11.
41. JHN, *Remarks on the Covenant of Grace*, BOA A.9.1, 10.
42. JHN, *Remarks on the Covenant of Grace*, BOA A.9.1, 10.
43. JHN, *Remarks on the Covenant of Grace*, BOA A.9.1, 10–11.
44. JHN, No. 169, "On Infant Baptism—part ii," *Serm.* 1, 170.
45. JHN, *Remarks on the Covenant of Grace*, BOA A.9.1, 13.
46. JHN, No. 169, "On Infant Baptism—part ii," *Serm.* 1, 169.
47. JHN, No. 67, "Faith connected with, and confirmed by the inward witness," March 27, 1825, *Serm.* 5, 203.

our faith. Assurance "springs from faith, but not *at once* and immediately from faith, but from faith *through holiness* — it follows the *fruits* of faith."[48] This is what Newman meant in the *Apologia* when he traced back to Scott his conviction that "holiness" comes before "peace."[49] Still, he considered assurance a possible, perhaps even the normal, state of true believers. In 1828, he rejected the idea altogether because it was incompatible with human freedom. He did not think "a grace so absolutely over-ruling" that it precludes "the contingency of defection" was compatible "with the notion of our acting at all."[50] But even if it were, he argued, there is an epistemic problem with the idea of assurance: "how can I be certain" that I have the required "evidences" to make this judgment on my own state? How I do know that "I am not deceiving myself?"[51] Barring "a special revelation made to me personally," I have no means to be certain about my ultimate salvation.[52] All we have, therefore, is a "reasonable hope increasing with our increasing sanctification, that we shall persevere," and this is quite enough.[53]

Newman's definitive rejection of efficacious grace (with its implications for regeneration, sanctification, perseverance, and assurance) entailed that he could no longer construe the relationship between God's will and its effects as one of absolute identity. But if there is a disparity between what God wants and what he achieves, the difference must be accounted for. To do so, Newman introduced a rule for interpreting theological propositions that differentiated between what he called "the abstract doctrine" and the "actual state of the case."[54] This distinction was premised on a very un-Calvinistic theological conviction. Newman maintained that, by the act of creation, God imposed certain constraints on the exercise of his sovereignty. God's omnipotence is now bound by certain features of the created order. Accordingly, doctrinal statements about God's will in the abstract (without taking the created order into account) do not necessarily correspond to how God operates within the concrete bounds of creation. The import of this distinction is shown in Newman's discussion of the extent of the atonement: the question whether Christ died for all, or for the elect only.

Many Calvinists maintained that Christ died only for the elect and thus (because of efficacious grace) only for the ultimately saved. Newman rejected this idea of limited atonement, because he now fully affirmed God's universal

---

48. JHN, No. 67, "Faith connected with, and confirmed by the inward witness," *Serm.* 5, 203. See No 2, "Waiting on God," June 23, 1824, *Serm.* 5, 10–11.

49. *Apo.*, 61. See also JHN, No. 67, "Faith connected with, and confirmed by the inward witness," *Serm.* 5, 203n17.

50. JHN, *Remarks on the Covenant of Grace*, BOA A.9.1, 13.

51. JHN, *Remarks on the Covenant of Grace*, BOA A.9.1, 13.

52. JHN, *Remarks on the Covenant of Grace*, BOA A.9.1, 13.

53. JHN, *Remarks on the Covenant of Grace*, BOA A.9.1, 14.

54. JHN, *Remarks on the Covenant of Grace*, BOA A.9.1, 3.

salvific will. Strict Calvinism aside, he argued that determining the extent of the atonement was perhaps only a "verbal" difficulty.[55] He believed that "in <u>the divine intention</u>," everyone is "included within the pale of the Church," that is, among the elect.[56] In this "general, abstract" sense, "Church & human race are synonymous," and Christ died for all. In the concrete, however, not everyone is positioned such that she can join the church, because, "<u>in fact</u> the gospel is <u>gradually</u> communicated to the world."[57] Not everyone is born "within the sound of the Gospel" (which is what being elect means).[58] In this sense, Christ died "for the elect only," because they alone benefit from the atonement.[59] God's salvific will, which encompasses everyone, is constrained by the conditions of the created order, in this case, by its temporality, "time being in the system of Providence a condition of the actual communication of the knowledge of the gospel to the world."[60]

The distinction between God's abstract will and concrete creation also informed Newman's understanding of the church. By "church," he now meant the visible community of the baptized. He no longer thought that the term could be used to meaningfully signify some invisible reality. He drew Trower's attention to the "vast deal of confusion" that results from the "unscriptural distinctions between the visible & invisible Church" common among evangelicals.[61] "It is plain," he argued, that, "since we cannot know the hearts, we can only know the visible — the dearest & most exemplary friend we have, is known to us only through our senses, i.e. is but <u>visibly</u> a Christian."[62] Since we can never determine whether someone belongs to the invisible church, the distinction has no practical significance. And yet, "people talk, as if those, whose actions & outward character seemed to evidence their real religious principle, were actually <u>known to them</u> as members of the invisible Church."[63] Such reasoning, of course, is self-defeating. Once we assign people to an invisible church based on their conduct, we only create another visible church, one just as visible as the community of the baptized but with more restrictive membership criteria.

In principle, then, "the visible baptized Church is the external development of that spiritual body which God alone sees."[64] God provides this visible church with grace and, as far as this "divine grant of favor" is concerned, "the distinction

---

55. JHN, *Remarks on the Covenant of Grace*, BOA A.9.1, 2, 3.
56. JHN, *Remarks on the Covenant of Grace*, BOA A.9.1, 2.
57. JHN, *Remarks on the Covenant of Grace*, BOA A.9.1, 3.
58. JHN, *Remarks on Infant Baptism*, BOA A.9.1, 50. See p. 142 in this book.
59. JHN, *Remarks on the Covenant of Grace*, BOA A.9.1, 3.
60. JHN, *Remarks on the Covenant of Grace*, BOA A.9.1, 2.
61. JHN, *Remarks on the Covenant of Grace*, BOA A.9.1, 4.
62. JHN, *Remarks on the Covenant of Grace*, BOA A.9.1, 4.
63. JHN, *Remarks on the Covenant of Grace*, BOA A.9.1, 5.
64. JHN, *Remarks on the Covenant of Grace*, BOA A.9.1, 5.

between visible & invisible, apparent & real, is irrelevant & only perplexes."[65] Grace is given to the visible church, not to any other entity. This grace, moreover, is given to the visible church "as a whole or body or society." The New Testament addresses the church "as a body or society, not merely as individuals. . . . As a whole it is called, sanctified, & will persevere, triumph, be glorified."[66] Part of the evangelical mistake is to appropriate these "privileges . . . & promises" to individuals rather than to the church, so that they misrepresent the direction of grace, which is not from individuals to the community but from the community to individuals. Christ, Newman argued, "has lodged the promises to each individual in the body."[67] This is evident from the nature of the sacraments, which, as "the sole pledges of grace, the sole appointed instruments of participating in the benefits of redemption, are public and social, derived to individuals from the body."[68] If this primacy of the church as a means of grace is grasped, Newman pointed out to Trower, "the puritanical, calvinistic, & schismatical spirit . . . at present prevalent among us" is immediately overthrown.[69] Once people realize they are saved as members of a visible church on which they depend for grace, they will neither separate from that church nor put much stock in the idea of an invisible church.

But Newman still had to explain the relationship between the community of the baptized and the group of people that is ultimately saved. To do so, he distinguished once again between the abstract doctrine and the concrete situation. From God's point of view, the means of grace offered to the church "naturally & legitimately" issue "in final salvation." And thus, "as far as God is concerned, every elect person is saved."[70] Just as God intends the atonement to extend to everyone, so God both wishes and provides the means for all the elect to be saved. But here, too, a limiting condition in the created order institutes a disparity between God's will and its effects: the freedom of human agency. Since God's "purposes may be partially frustrated by man it is possible for individuals elected into the Church to fail of ultimate salvation."[71] As Newman put it in his June sermon on infant baptism,

> Although privileges are given us, which tend naturally and legitimately towards our complete <full> salvation from sin and misery, yet in many particular cases that tendency is not developed <realized> and the promise

<hr>

65. JHN, *Remarks on the Covenant of Grace*, BOA A.9.1, 5.
66. JHN, *Remarks on the Covenant of Grace*, BOA A.9.1, 5–6.
67. JHN, *Remarks on the Covenant of Grace*, BOA A.9.1, 6.
68. JHN, *Remarks on the Covenant of Grace*, BOA A.9.1, 6. See No. 162, "On general education as connected with the Church and religion (for National School)," August 19, 1827, *Serm.* 5, 424.
69. JHN, *Remarks on the Covenant of Grace*, BOA A.9.1, 6.
70. JHN, *Remarks on the Covenant of Grace*, BOA A.9.1, 1.
71. JHN, *Remarks on the Covenant of Grace*, BOA A.9.1, 1.

is in the event unaccomplished — not however from deficiency in His grace, but from human sinfulness.[72]

In the abstract, then, the visible church is ultimately saved, even though, in the concrete, some people are lost.

Accordingly, Newman described the two categories of the elect and the saved as broadly coextensive rather than absolutely identical. Despite "the quenching of divine grace by corrupt wills and hearts,"

> still, looking at Christians through all ages as one vast body, we may consider the first chosen and the finally saved in one sense the same. Who in a victory dwells upon the numbers that fell in the fight, and does not rather account the whole body conquerors who engaged? and so the Church militant and the Church triumphant may be counted one and the same.[73]

This was a creative solution to the thorny problem that the doctrine of final perseverance presented to many Anglicans. The seventeenth of the Thirty-Nine Articles dealt with predestination and described, in one continuous movement, how the elect are called by God, obey the call through grace, are justified, sanctified, and finally "attain to everlasting felicity." On the face of it, final perseverance was taught here, and many evangelicals appealed to the article in support of the doctrine. In 1891, Frank Newman still regarded this interpretation of the article as obvious. In an attempt to clear Walter Mayers from the charge of being a "high Calvinist," leveled by some readers of the *Apologia*, Frank argued that, "Like most other Evangelicals of my youth, his Calvinism consisted in this, that he did not *explain away* the 17th Article."[74] But John did not think he was explaining away the article.

When the seventeenth article "carries on the elect to salvation, Newman argued, it does not teach that every elect person will be saved, only that they usually are.[75] Again, he applied the distinction between abstract and concrete. Because the article is "<u>doctrinal & abstract,</u>" it does not add the qualification that in concrete cases people can and do fall away. No texts aimed at general truth specify every concrete eventuality. The same, he argued, is "constantly done in our sermons," where "no one after drawing the picture of a good man, would finish it with an account of his apostasy."[76] To draw such a picture would be "what Aristotle would call <u>contrary to general</u> truth, tho' <u>historically</u> and in <u>particular instances</u> possible."[77] Newman drew upon the *Poetics* here, where Aristotle argues

---

72. JHN, No. 169, "On Infant Baptism—part ii," *Serm.* 1, 169.
73. JHN, No. 169, "On Infant Baptism—part ii," *Serm.* 1, 169.
74. FWN, *Contributions*, 15.
75. JHN, *Remarks on the Covenant of Grace*, BOA A.9.1, 12.
76. JHN, *Remarks on the Covenant of Grace*, BOA A.9.1, 12.
77. JHN, *Remarks on the Covenant of Grace*, BOA A.9.1, 12.

that the poet (in contrast to the historian) does not deal with singulars but with "universal" phenomena. Instead of describing what this or that person has done, the poet deals with "what such or such a kind of man will probably or necessarily say or do."[78] The poet aims, in other words, to offer a generalizable and compelling portrait of the good or the bad person by means of her *typical* words and actions, not by what any individual specimen *has* said or done. In the same way, the 17th article portrays the *typical* course of the elect as one that issues in final salvation. In doing so, it simply follows the example of scripture, which should be interpreted according to the same rule. Take Philippians 1:6, a common proof-text for the final perseverance of individuals. When St Paul states that "he which hath begun a good work in you will perform it until the day of Jesus Christ," he presupposes, but leaves unstated, a qualifier like, "if we are true to ourselves."[79] To add this qualifier, Newman argued, would have been beside St Paul's purpose, because he was focusing on God's faithfulness, not on "the contingency of falling" due to our faithlessness.[80] Only a person already committed to the idea of efficacious grace would strain St Paul's assertion into a proof for the final perseverance of individuals.

Again, the idea is that God's abstract will and its concrete effects are broadly coextensive rather than absolutely identical. Besides using Aristotle's linguistic argument, Newman defended this idea by means of Butler's theory of the analogy between the realms of nature and revelation. Recall that Butler defended religious tenets such as God's punishment of vice, or the idea of a mediator between God and man, by showing their analogy to deeply ingrained features of the ordinary course of the world. The same, Newman argued, goes for the relation between God's will and its effects:

> The partial failure of what we call the divine <u>will</u> & intention as regards the condition of man hereafter, is but analogous to what we see in the natural world, where <u>general</u> rules only can be discovered; — ends are attained <u>on the whole</u>, after delay, loss, partial disappointment &c. vid the waste of seeds, flowers &c- the death of children &c &c (Butler's Analogy).[81]

We know from the natural world that the preservation of life by means of procreation is achieved generally, but not absolutely. Not every seed germinates, not

---

78. Aristotle, *Poetics*, 1451b8–9, trans. Ingram Bywater. For Newman's appropriation of Aristotle's conception of poetry, see "Greek Tragedy—Poetry," *London Review* 1, no. 1 (January 1829): esp. 160, 163–64. A slightly revised version of the piece was included as "Poetry, with reference to Aristotle's *Poetics*," in *Essays: Critical and Historical*, vol. 1 (London: Basil Montagu Pickering, 1871, 1–26 (esp. 9–10, 14–16), hereafter *Ess*.

79. JHN, *Remarks on the Covenant of Grace*, BOA A.9.1, 13.

80. JHN, *Remarks on the Covenant of Grace*, BOA A.9.1, 12.

81. JHN, *Remarks on the Covenant of Grace*, BOA A.9.1, 14; Butler, *The Analogy of Religion*, 171.

every child survives. If we accept that God governs the preservation of natural life by such general rules, we cannot object to the fact that he acts similarly in the supernatural realm, where eternal life is concerned.

The *Remarks* is a testimony to how pervasive Butler's influence on Newman's theology had become by 1828. It comes through in his understanding of the visible church, but even more so in his account of sanctification and his take on the relation between the natural and supernatural realms. In the second half of 1825, he had begun to apply Butler's theory of habit formation to the process of sanctification. Gradually, he became convinced that holiness is not just the result of interior disciplines (such as prayer and self-examination) or of external means (attending church and receiving communion) but also of outward acts done on principle. These acts are not meritorious, but they are indispensable because they help to create the stable inward disposition—"no mere transient feeling, but a state of heart"—in which holiness consists.[82]

In the same period, Newman began to rethink the relation between nature and revelation. As a young evangelical, he had conceived of the natural and supernatural realms as rigidly distinct; the one all corruption and ignorance, the other all grace and revelation. Under Butler's influence, he gradually perceived these two realms as continuous, or better, analogous. Both are governed by the same God whose revelatory and salvific activity parallels his providential operations. Newman first applied this idea to apologetics, in the *Essay on Miracles*, but in 1828, he felt confident enough to use it in theology. His increased confidence in Butler's theories owed much to a shift in friends.

The Keble Factor

In 1828, Newman's theological affinities shifted from one of Oriel's great luminaries—Whately—to another: John Keble. In a line made famous by James Pereiro's work on the Oxford Movement, Isaac Williams spoke of "the Keble school, which in opposition to the Oriel or Whatelian, set ἦθος [*ethos*] above intellect."[83] Newman, in the *Apologia*, characterized his drift toward liberalism in much the same terms: "I was beginning to prefer intellectual excellence to moral."[84] Although real theological differences existed within Oriel, they were problematized only during the Tractarian period, so that both comments are tinged with hindsight and can only be clarified by and by. For now, it is enough to note the

---

82. JHN, No. 162, "On general education," *Serm.* 5, 422.

83. Williams, *The Autobiography of Isaac Williams*, 46. See Pereiro, Ethos *and the Oxford Movement*, 1; "John Keble and the Ethos of the Oxford Movement," in *John Keble in Context*, ed. Kirstie Blair (London: Anthem Press, 2004), 59; and Peter Nockles, "Oriel and Religion, 1800–1833," in *Oriel College: A History*, ed. Jeremy Catto (Oxford: Oxford University Press, 2013), 313–14.

84. *Apo.*, 72.

parameters of Newman's shift—from intellect to moral character—and its connection to the thought of Keble. It was a shift that ended Newman's approximations to liberalism.

In the *Apologia*, he situated the termination of his liberal "dream at the end of 1827" and attributed it to "two great blows—illness and bereavement."[85] These blows followed in quick succession. In the last weekend of November 1827, Newman started to feel unwell, and on Monday, the 26th, he was too ill to continue as examiner in the Schools.[86] His doctor, George Babington, diagnosed his condition as "a determination of blood to the head arising from over exertion of the brain, with a disordered stomach." Newman took months to convalesce.[87] Five weeks later, on January 5, 1828, his nineteen-year-old sister Mary unexpectedly died. He loved her dearly and deeply suffered from the loss.[88] Newman never explained how these dramatic events impeded his liberal tendencies. He merely stated it, and that but once. Both events, however, drew him closer to Keble and his circle.

Newman's breakdown had been some time in the making. Weeks of hard preparatory work coupled with the stress of conducting public examinations had worn him out. He had other worries, too. His aunt Elizabeth was in serious financial trouble and had only the Newman family to turn to for aid. But it was the news that Copleston would vacate the Provostship of Oriel to become Bishop of Llandaff, which reached Newman on Friday, the 23rd, that was the straw that broke the camel's back. By Monday, he could no longer function and had "to leave the Schools in the middle of the day."[89]

Soon, the college was all in a flutter about the upcoming election. There were only two viable candidates: Hawkins and Keble. Newman supported Hawkins, whom, unlike Keble, he knew long and well, and thought was business-like enough to make a good provost—again, unlike Keble, whom he considered too otherworldly for the job. Besides, as he explained to Keble, Hawkins' "general views . . . practical notions, religious opinions, and habits of thinking" coincided with his own, as did his views on college government and university reform.[90] Hawkins was elected, and some believed Newman's advocacy had tipped the balance.[91]

Given the conflict that soon ensued between Newman and Hawkins about the content and organization of the Oriel tutorship, Newman had cause to regret his choice. Soon after Hawkins's election, he discovered that their views were not

---

85. *Apo.*, 72. See JHN, "June 25, 1869," *AW*, 268; Culler, *The Imperial Intellect*, 58–62.
86. *LD* 2, 37.
87. JHN, "February 21, 1828," *AW*, 212–13.
88. See, for example, JHN to Robert Isaac Wilberforce, January 14, 1828, *LD* 2, 48–50.
89. JHN, "February 21, 1828," *AW*, 212.
90. JHN to John Keble, December 19, 1827, *LD* 2, 44; Culler, *The Imperial Intellect*, 63–65.
91. See, for example, Williams, *The Autobiography of Isaac Williams*, 48.

as similar as they used to be. The irony, he later realized, was that his affinities had unwittingly shifted to the other camp. Years later, he commented: "strangely enough, Mr Newman, at the very moment of his friend Dr Hawkins entering upon the Provostship, became conscious for the first time of his own congeniality of mind with Keble."[92] This awareness did not come at once, nor, at first, because of Keble himself. It was mediated by two of Keble's disciples: Newman's fellow tutors Richard Hurrell Froude and Robert Isaac Wilberforce (the son of the leading evangelical, William Wilberforce). At Oriel, Froude and Wilberforce had come under Keble's sway rather than Whately's. After a brilliant undergraduate career at Corpus Christi College, Keble had taken double first-class honors in Latin and mathematics, won the English and Latin prize essays, and became first a fellow and then a tutor of Oriel. But in 1823, when his mother died, he left Oxford for the countryside. He accepted a curacy at Southrop to be near his father and sisters at Fairford. He seldom returned to Oxford, but organized reading-parties for Oriel students at Southrop in the Long Vacations.[93] Froude and Wilberforce were ardent members of his circle.[94] To Froude especially, Newman attributed the end of Whately's sway over his theology. In his *Autobiographical Memoir*, Newman noted that he was "under the influence of Dr Whately for four years, from 1822 to 1826, when, coincidently with his leaving Alban Hall, he began to know Mr Hurrell Froude."[95] Froude had been elected fellow of Oriel on March 31, 1826, and impressed Newman right away. "Froude is one of the acutest and clearest and deepest men in the memory of man," he wrote glowingly when briefing his mother about the election.[96] Their friendship grew slowly, however, and it was only when they were thrown together in the tutorship in the Michaelmas term of 1827 that he began to adopt some of the ideas Froude had derived from Keble.

Keble influenced many of the same areas of Newman's thought (church, sanctification, the relation between nature and revelation) that Butler had already begun to change. This was no coincidence, for Keble, too, had been deeply influenced by Butler's *Analogy*.[97] Hence, the "congeniality of mind" that Newman discovered in 1828. By that time, he had adopted many of the same Butlerian notions that had been shaping Keble's thought for years (and to which neither Erskine nor Whately was particularly receptive).[98] One of the ideas Keble derived

92. JHN, "Autobiographical Memoir," *AW*, 91.

93. Perry Butler, "Keble, John," *ODNB*.

94. Newsome, *The Parting of Friends*, 71–95.

95. JHN, "Autobiographical Memoir," *AW*, 69. See Piers Brendon, *Hurrell Froude and the Oxford Movement* (London: Paul Elek, 1974), 87–100.

96. JHN to Mrs Newman, March 31, 1826, *LD* 1, 282.

97. Pereiro, "John Keble," 60–66; Pereiro, Ethos *and the Oxford Movement*, 92–98.

98. *Pace* Pereiro (Ethos *and the Oxford Movement*, 102), Butler's influence did not come by way "of Keble's mind" but predated him, as Newman points out in the pages of the *Apologia* to which Pereiro appeals (see *Apo.*, 77).

from Butler was a specific view of the relation between cognition and moral praxis.[99] Recall that Erskine, and to a lesser extent Whately, construed the relation between knowledge and praxis as unidirectional. Knowledge of the gospel message (in Erskine's case) or of revelation generally (in Whately's case) resulted in behavioral change, by way of the affections.

Keble, by contrast, attributed to people a capacity to grasp and enact moral truth that is not dependent on the cognitive content of revelation. He distinguished this capacity from intellectual acuity, which only few have, and likened it to "the φρόνησις [*phronesis*] of the Grecian moralists: 'the practical understanding of our true interest,'" which everyone can acquire.[100] For both Butler and Keble, religion fell under the jurisdiction of such Aristotelian practical wisdom because it concerns our "chief good," that is, "the universal pursuit of happiness, and the universal art of living well."[101] Accordingly, it became a refrain in Keble's work that "we must look to the best man, not to the accomplished or most able, for the soundest views on moral and religious subjects."[102] Emphatically, this was not a commitment to some magical epistemic capacity that would allow, say, a chaste person to correctly interpret the finer points of Trinitarian doctrine. Keble, in fact, excluded from consideration "the great verities of the Christian faith, recognised by consent of all Churches, and registered in their Creeds." These doctrines "are like the first truths of natural religion; implicitly to be received at all risks, not to be judged of, but to be made a measure for judging of others."[103] Aristotle's theory of practical wisdom, moreover, held that someone is a judge only in those domains in which he has ample experience (as Keble's university audience would have known). Thus, a chaste person will be a good judge of whether certain moral or religious ideas promote or detract from chastity, but he is no expert in other domains. Finally, Keble did not emphasize just any virtue as necessary for the success of moral and religious inquiry but rather highlighted "the moral qualities of candour and attention, perseverance and self-control," qualities that are required for any earnest intellectual pursuit to succeed.[104]

Newman would have learned the outline of Keble's view from Froude, who, like Keble, held that a person's convictions depend to a large extent on her moral character. It is probable, he argued in an 1827 entry in a private notebook, "that

99. Pereiro, "John Keble," 62–65; Pereiro, Ethos *and the Oxford Movement*, 94–95.

100. John Keble, "Favour Shewn to Implicit Faith" (1822), in *Sermons, Academical and Occasional* (Oxford: John Henry Parker, 1847), 15.

101. Keble, "Favour Shewn to Implicit Faith," 10, 11; Butler, *The Analogy of Religion*, 26. Pereiro ("John Keble," 61–62) seems to underestimate the extent to which Butler and Keble understood religion as a practical matter, and thus makes their take on *phronesis* more distinct from Aristotle's than it is.

102. Keble, "Implicit Faith Recognised by Reason" (1822 or 1823), in *Sermons*, 25.

103. Keble, "Implicit Faith Reconciled with Free Enquiry" (1823), in *Sermons*, 62.

104. Keble, "Favour Shewn to Implicit Faith," in *Sermons*, 6.

a man who is *morally good*, will have a *right faith*," because "many of our *opinions* are the result of our *character*."[105] Froude's main concern in adopting this position was soteriological. Given that our salvation depends on what we believe *and* on what we do, he considered it "inconceivable" that these "two causes" should be "essentially independent; that is, of such a nature that the presence of one should in no way imply that of the other."[106] Rather than unilaterally prioritize faith over praxis, however, he suggested that although right faith implies right praxis, right praxis equally implies right faith. Thus, "particular opinions are essentially homogeneous with particular characters."[107] Froude's line of thought, undeveloped though it be, challenged the fundamental structure of the evangelical take on conversion. It opened a perspective in which moral character was not just the outcome of a set of beliefs but an independent reality that could shape as well as be shaped by those beliefs. Newman proved receptive to Froude's ideas, for by March 1828, he was expanding on them in a letter to another recent addition to the Oriel Common Room, Joseph Blanco White (1775–1841).

Blanco White had once been a Roman Catholic priest in Spain. After sundry religious and political wanderings, he ended up in England and joined the Established Church in 1812.[108] He took up residence at Oriel in October 1826, and Newman soon grew to like him.[109] At the end of February 1828, Blanco White proposed to set up an informal exchange of letters among "three or four friends . . . writing to each other upon subjects, moral and religious, requiring more thought than research."[110] The idea was to let someone broach a subject, have the letter go around, and let anyone so inclined compose an answer. The intended participants were Newman, his fellow tutors Froude and Wilberforce, and, of course, Blanco White himself. In his invitation, Blanco White insisted on the confidentiality of the correspondence. He noticed a general lack of "intellectual toleration, in religious matters," which he attributed to most people's—especially theologians'—inability to appreciate "the infinite variety of intellect which exists in mankind."[111] "Divines . . . are not satisfied with conformity, or Orthodoxy in results," he pointed out; "they demand for the most part conformity and Orthodoxy of arguments."[112] The aim of his project was to go beyond these constraints and have an open exchange among peers; not to question orthodox belief, or "to

105. Froude, "Occasional Thoughts," July 16, 1827, in *Remains*, 114, 116. See Pereiro, *Ethos and the Oxford Movement*, 99–100; Thomas, *Newman and Heresy*, 26–27.

106. Froude, "Occasional Thoughts," 114.

107. Froude, "Occasional Thoughts," 114.

108. G. Martin Murphy, "White, Joseph Blanco," *ODNB*.

109. JHN, "February 21, 1827," *AW*, 210.

110. Joseph Blanco White to JHN, February 24, 1828, BL, MS. Wilberforce c. 67, 151r. See Newsome, *The Parting of Friends*, 86–90.

111. Joseph Blanco White to JHN, February 24, 1828, BL, MS. Wilberforce c. 67, 152v.

112. Joseph Blanco White to JHN, February 24, 1828, BL, MS. Wilberforce c. 67, 152v.

pull it to pieces in the spirit of German rationalism," but to facilitate faithful and yet creative theological thinking.[113]

Newman was enthusiastic about the plan. Responding on March 1, he took for his subject Blanco White's assessment of "the incommensurability (so to speak) of the human mind." Newman fully agreed with Blanco White's view.[114] "We cannot gauge and measure by any common rule the varieties of thought and opinion," he argued. "Necessary as it is, that we should all hold the same truths (as we would be saved) still each of us holds them in his own way."[115] As the reason for this variance, he adduced the priority of moral character (or *ethos*) over intellect: "Words are not feelings — nor is intellect ἦθος [*sic*] — Intellect seems to be but the attendant and servant of right moral feeling in this own [*sic*: our] weak and dark state of being — defending it when attacked, accounting for it, and explaining it in a poor way to others."[116]

Unaware, perhaps, that this insight derived from Keble, Newman attributed it to Froude. "I have Froude's authority for lowering the intellectual powers into handmaids of our moral nature," he noted, "But I doubt whether he or Wilberforce will think it safe to proceed to the lengths to which I expatiate."[117] "For instance," Newman added, "it never occurs to me to measure the degree of a Socinian's error by the deficiency of his creed under the accuracy of the Athanasian — yet this is a common practice."[118] Accordingly, he challenged Wilberforce or Froude to offer "some account of the connexion (how far) of speculative error with bad ἦθος [*sic*] — e.g. *in what is a consistent Socinian a worse man than an orthodox believer.*" "*I* think him to be worse," Newman explained, "but I wish my mind clear on the subject, which it is not at present."[119]

As far as we know, Blanco White's plan came to nothing, as neither Froude nor Wilberforce responded. But Newman's letter is important in its own right, because it shows that he was reconsidering the relation between faith and moral praxis. On his earlier view, a Socinian, who neither believed in Christ's divinity nor in the propitiatory value of the atonement, was worse than an orthodox Christian because she lacked the decisive motive to live a holy life. Practice, after all, depends on faith. Now, Newman suggested that this relation should be inverted. Opinions are secondary to moral character: they only express, in a limited way, what is, in essence, an inexpressible moral reality. "Each mind pursues

---

113. Joseph Blanco White to JHN, February 24, 1828, BL, MS. Wilberforce c. 67, 153r.
114. JHN to Joseph Blanco White, March 1, 1828, *LD* 2, 60.
115. JHN to Joseph Blanco White, March 1, 1828, *LD* 2, 60.
116. JHN to Joseph Blanco White, March 1, 1828, *LD* 2, 60.
117. JHN to Joseph Blanco White, March 1, 1828, *LD* 2, 60. See Brendon, *Hurrell Froude and the Oxford Movement*, 93.
118. JHN to Joseph Blanco White, March 1, 1828, *LD* 2, 60.
119. JHN to Joseph Blanco White, March 1, 1828, *LD* 2, 60.

its own course," he wrote to Blanco White, "and is actuated in that course by ten-thousand [*sic*] indescribable incommunicable feelings and imaginings."[120]

Accordingly, it is a mistake to judge someone by her expressed opinions only. Yet, as we still hold some opinions to be erroneous, an account of how such errors arise is required. Although Newman suggested the vague outlines of such an account—that the error is somehow due to a moral flaw—his letter leaves more questions than it answers. None of its key concepts, such as intellect and moral feeling, are defined, and there is no indication of the way *ethos* is formed, or of the role of (the content of) revelation in the process. But this is what makes the letter significant. Rather than providing answers, it raises questions, and, in so doing, shows Newman in the act of rethinking the fundamental categories of his theology. In the year that followed, Newman continued to develop the idea that having a certain character shapes one's perspective on reality. His response to the death of his sister Mary shaped this development. Mourning her made Newman conceive of faith as a way of "seeing" the invisible God, shaped by one's moral character.

As noted, Newman adored Mary and was deeply affected by losing her. A week after her death, he described her to Robert Wilberforce as an angelic figure who "lived in an ideal world of happiness."[121] "All that happened to her she could change into something bright and smiling like herself," he noted, "and thus, having lived in this world as if it were heaven, before she discovered (as she must in time) that it was not so, she has been translated into the real and substantial heaven of God." Her unearthly loveliness had even worried him at times. "I have for years been so affected with her unclouded cheerfulness and extreme guilelessness of heart," he confessed to Wilberforce, "that I have be[en] impressed with the conviction that she would not live long, and have almost anticipated her death."[122] And, indeed, in October 1825 (not 1826, as he later thought), he wrote in his diary of his mother and sisters, "So much I love them, that I cannot help thinking. Thou wilt either take them hence, or take me from them, because I am too set on them."[123] After her death, Newman's sense of Mary's saintliness had transformed this somewhat crude sentiment—"I love her too much, so God will teach me a lesson"—into the subtler feeling that something so lovely cannot last on this corrupt earth.

Still, John took her death as a chastening of his affections and regarded it as "the heaviest affliction with which the good hand of God has ever visited me."[124]

---

120. JHN to Joseph Blanco White, March 1, 1828, *LD* 2, 60.

121. JHN to Robert Isaac Wilberforce, January 14, 1828, *LD* 2, 50.

122. JHN to Robert Isaac Wilberforce, January 14, 1828, *LD* 2, 50.

123. JHN, "October 30, 1825," *AW*, 207; see also "February 21, 1828," *AW*, 213.

124. JHN, "February 21, 1828," *AW*, 213. The entry was begun on his birthday, but Newman wrote his account of the loss of Mary only on Good Friday, April 4, 1828.

It served as a painful reminder that what is truly good belongs with God, so that all our affections should be directed heavenward. The death of Mary instilled in John a deep sense of the contrast between the present world—visible but perishable—and the unseen, eternal realm of God. Before, he had construed the contrast between the natural and the supernatural only incidentally in this way.[125] He usually subsumed it under the dichotomy between corruption and redemption. Now, the contrast between seen and unseen, temporal and eternal, became a recurrent theme in his letters whenever he brought up his significant dead. Only six weeks after Mary, Walter Mayers died an equally sudden and unexpected death. "This world is but a shadow and dream," John commented after the event, "we think we see things and we see them not — they do not exist, they die on all sides, things dearest and pleasantest and most beloved. But in heaven we shall all meet and it will be *no* dream."[126] Here, John's overwhelming sense of loss (first Mary, then Mayers) issues in a relegation of the visible world to unreality—as transient as a dream—along with the almost obstinate declaration that invisible heaven is "*no* dream," because it lasts.

When the first shock had subsided, John began to regard the visible world more positively: not as unreal altogether, but as real in a limited way, that is, as pointing beyond itself, to the unseen world. In a poem of April 13, he described the room in which Mary had died as a "sacred spot," hallowed by the departure of a saint. Just as Jacob found a heavenly ladder at Bethel (the story that inspired the poem) the holy space of Mary's room furnished a link between earth and heaven:

> Meanwhile, where last on earth she trod,
> This grace to faith is given,
> There to discern the house of God
> There find the gate of heaven.[127]

This referentiality of the material to the immaterial world was not limited to Mary's room. On Good Friday, Newman noted in his diary how everything in Oxford reminded him of her: "She was with us at Oxford, and I took a delight in showing her the place — and every building, every tree, seems to speak of her. I cannot realize that I shall never see her again."[128] Here, the world of matter both carries the memory of Mary and, by its almost disturbing visibility, reminds John of her invisibility. This referential quality gradually expanded to include all of nature. In May, he described to Jemima his regular morning rides in the countryside:

125. See, for example, JHN, No. 89, "against worldliness," July 10, 1825, *Serm.* 5, esp. 244–48.
126. JHN to Richard Greaves, February 27, 1828, *LD* 2, 58.
127. *LD* 2, 70.
128. JHN, "February 21, 1828 [written: April 4, 1828]," *AW*, 213.

The country too is beautiful — the fresh leaves, the scents, the varied land-scape. Yet I never felt so intensely the transitory nature of this world as when most delighted with these country scenes. . . . Dear Mary seems embodied in every tree and hid behind every hill. What a veil and curtain this world of sense is! beautiful but still a veil.[129]

The sentiment here is different: a sense of a beauty that cannot last. Nature is a veil that hides the real world—the unseen world that Mary now inhabits—and whose visible beauty speaks, at best, of the unseen.

A contrast between time and eternity is what many Christians would experience on the loss of a loved one, especially one so young as Mary, but the way Newman interpreted this experience owed much to Keble. In 1827, Keble had published *The Christian Year*, a volume of devotional poetry in the Romantic tradition, which quickly became very popular. In the *Apologia*, Newman maintained that it taught him "what may be called, in a large sense of the word, the Sacramental system; that is, that material phenomena are both the types and the instruments of real things unseen."[130] He had already begun to discover this idea by way of Butler, who argued that the realms of nature and religion are analogous, because they are governed by the one God. Keble, on the same premise, turned Butler's rational analogies into poetic types. At first, Newman spent little time on *The Christian Year*. He took his copy home and lent it to his mother and sisters. Mary liked it and learned some of the verses by heart.[131] On her deathbed, these poems were one of her chief consolations. This made John appreciate them anew.[132] On his May morning rides, he was struck by Keble's lines on spring nature, which, "Chanting with a solemn voice / Minds us of our better choice."[133] "I could hardly believe the lines were not my own," he wrote to Jemima, "and Keble had not taken them from me."[134] Nature conveyed the same message in its darker moods. When merry May had become dreary November, John wrote to his sister Harriett about these same rides: "I have learned to like dying trees and black meadows — swamps have their grace, and fogs their sweetness. A solemn voice seems to chant from every thing. I know whose voice it is — it is her dear voice."[135] All of nature has become referential here. It speaks of eternity both in beauty and decay, and it does so in

129. JHN to Jemima Newman, May 10, 1828, *LD* 2, 69.

130. *Apo.*, 77.

131. JHN to Jane Mozley, January 8, 1880, *LD* 29, 227–8; April 21, 1880, *LD* 29, 263.

132. JHN to Robert Isaac Wilberforce, January 14, 1828, *LD* 2, 49; JHN to John Keble, February 1, 1828, *LD* 2, 55.

133. John Keble, "First Sunday After Epiphany," in *The Christian Year: Thoughts in Verse for the Sundays and Holydays throughout the Year*, 6th ed. (Oxford: J. Parker, 1829), 52.

134. JHN to Jemima Newman, May 10, 1828, *LD* 2, 69.

135. JHN to Harriett Newman, November 23, 1828, *LD* 2, 108.

Mary's voice. Paradoxically, as time wore on and Mary's absence sank in more, John began to consider her ever closer. By November, it was no longer the trees that spoke of her, but she who spoke in the trees. Increasingly, Mary came to symbolize the unseen world.[136]

The poetic habit of perceiving the seen as a type of the unseen is an exercise of imagination, but not of just any imagination. Years before, in a review of Copleston's theory of poetry, Keble had pointed out that true poetic imagination has a moral or religious character. Keble agreed with Copleston that the object of poetry is to please, and thus, that "he who gives most pleasure, supposing the source of that pleasure poetical, is the best poet."[137] But Keble qualified Copleston's view by specifying that only particular kinds of pleasure are truly poetical. "It is to the awakening of some moral or religious feeling", he argued, "that we would refer all poetical pleasure."[138] Newman agreed with Keble's view and developed one of its implications in an article on poetry for the newly founded *London Review*—a short-lived but high-quality Oriel initiative.[139] Drawing on Aristotle, Newman argued that poetry is "a representation of the ideal."[140] "It delineates that perfection which the imagination suggests, and to which as a limit the present system of Divine providence actually tends."[141] Poetry represents the unseen bearings of the visible course of the world. Accordingly, "the poetical mind is one full of the eternal forms of beauty and perfection; these are its material of thought, its instrument and medium of observation—these colour each object to which it directs its view."[142] But to imagine the "*perfection* of the actual," which is the principle of poetry, the poet needs to accurately discern the fundamental tendencies of God's moral governance.[143] To do so requires a moral character that is formed according to this divine ordering, that is, a virtuous character. Thus, Newman argued that a "right moral state of heart is the formal and scientific condition of a poetical mind," or, put more simply: "poetry is ultimately founded on correct moral perception."[144]

---

136. For the further development of this tendency, compare poems 8, 9, 10, 12 and 16 in *Verses on Various Occasions* (London: Burns, Oates & Co., 1868), hereafter *VV*.

137. John Keble, "Copleston *Prælectiones Academicæ*," *The British Critic* 1 (June 1814), 578. The review was republished in Keble's *Occasional Papers and Reviews* (Oxford and London: James Parker, 1877), 148–62. Copleston was the Oxford Professor of Poetry from 1802 to 1812.

138. Keble, "Copleston *Prælectiones Academicæ*," 580.

139. "The London Review, 1829," in *The Wellesley Index to Victorian Periodicals, 1824–1900*, vol. 2, ed. Walter E. Houghton (Toronto: University of Toronto Press, 1972), 522–26. Newman's article was published in January 1829, but he had finished it three months before. The original is cited, but references below to the version in *Ess.* are included in parentheses.

140. JHN, "Greek Tragedy—Poetry," *London Review* 1, no. 1 (January 1829): 160 (*Ess.* 1, 9).

141. JHN, "Greek Tragedy—Poetry," 160 (*Ess.* 1, 9).

142. JHN, "Greek Tragedy—Poetry," 160 (*Ess.* 1, 10).

143. JHN, "Greek Tragedy—Poetry," 163 (*Ess.* 1, 14).

144. JHN, "Greek Tragedy—Poetry," 168 (*Ess.* 1, 21).

This habit of seeing all things, characters, and events through the lens of moral perfection had a directly religious application. "With Christians," Newman argued, "a poetical view of things is a duty":

> we are bid to colour all things with hues of faith, to see a divine meaning in every event, and a super-human tendency. Even our friends around are invested with unearthly brightness—no longer imperfect men, but beings taken into divine favour, stamped with his seal, and in training for future happiness.[145]

Faith, then, requires the poetic habit of seeing the eternal and invisible in the temporal and visible. Blanco White, the editor of the *London Review*, picked up on the irony of Newman's exposition of Aristotle's idea of poetry as a Platonic exchange of shadows in a cave for eternal forms.[146] "Adieu, my Oxford Plato," he signed off the letter acknowledging his receipt of the essay.[147] But Newman's point was moral rather than metaphysical: the right way of seeing depends on the right way of being.

Moral Character, Sanctification, and Natural Religion

In view of the developmental arc of his ideas about sanctification, it is no surprise that Newman was enthusiastic about all that the idea of moral character implied. The conviction that people need to become holy had always been the driving force of his theology. At first, he believed that sanctification is preceded by a radical change of the affections. As he accepted baptismal regeneration, he gave up the idea of such a radical prior change but retained the structure of his earlier model. The locus of change was still the affections, and what changed them was still the apprehension of the object of faith: God's holiness and mercy, manifested in Christ's atoning sacrifice. Only changed affections could yield a new and holy praxis.

Tensions emerged, however, when Newman began to conceive of sanctification as a process of habit formation. Under Butler's influence, he gradually realized that trying to do good contributes to making us good. Doing good helps to create the "state of mind" in which being holy consists.[148] The category of moral character, denoting the entire complex of a person's moral and religious habits, gave substance and stability to this idea. He began to use the term in this sense in July 1826 (drawing, no doubt, on Aristotle's *Nicomachean Ethics*, which he

---

145. JHN, "Greek Tragedy—Poetry," 169 (*Ess.* 1, 23).
146. See Plato, *Republic*, 514a-520a, in *Complete Works*, 1132–1137.
147. Joseph Blanco White to JHN, November 8, 1828, *LD* 2, 105; *Apo.*, 69.
148. JHN, No. 162, "On general education," *Serm.* 5, 423.

had just begun to teach as tutor of Oriel).[149] Under the influence of Froude and Keble, the idea became increasingly central to his theology. The Trower paper, for instance, described sanctification as "the formation of a new & holy character of soul."[150] And when Newman rewrote one of his 1825 sermons on habit formation for a later preaching, he retitled it: *The world a discipline of moral character.*[151] By early 1829, Newman's new conception of sanctification resulted in his first explicit critique of the evangelical idea that religious change is proportionate to the affective import of faith in the atonement.

In the first half of 1829, Newman preached a course of sermons on St Paul's Letter to the Romans that reinterpreted the role of the affections in the process of sanctification.[152] The third sermon of the course—the first of which a substantial portion is preserved—discussed how justifying faith establishes "an actual communion between the soul and God."[153] It is a mistake, Newman argued, to suppose that such "faith is a mere feeling."[154] "All feelings of self-abasement[,] anxiety[,] joy and comfort," he explained, "are but a delusion if they end in themselves, if they do not carry on the mind to progressive sanctification of itself from all evil." This was nothing new. He had said as much in March 1825. What was new was his account of how the feelings to which faith gives rise issue in sanctification. "It is a common, but a great error," he argued, "to think that faith will as an *immediate* consequence alter a man's character."[155] "Faith," he explained, "does not operate *at once* upon the character, but by the *means of self-discipline.*"[156] The will, and not the affections, is what turns believing into becoming holy. This is the logical outcome of his conviction that human beings must actively cooperate with grace. The feelings to which faith gives rise are, by themselves, powerless to effect lasting change. Newman's argument is so succinct as to approach syllogistic form: "Faith gives the motive — the motive is an impulse — all impulses are from their nature momentary — no impulse changes character."[157] The unstated premise in this enthymeme is that no lasting change (like a change

149. JHN, No. 151, "The temper of mind injoined by Christianity, that which is indispensable in conducting scientific inquiries," July 2, 1826, BOA A.9.4, 7, 12 (*OUS*, 7, 10); Culler, *The Imperial Intellect*, 75–76.

150. JHN, *Remarks on the Covenant of Grace*, BOA A.9.1, 9, 14.

151. *Serm.* 5, 344n8, 345. See p. 128 in this book.

152. *Serm.* 5, 453–54; *Serm.* 2, 133n1. The course, which is only partially preserved, was preached between January and June 1829 and consisted of fourteen sermons treating the first eleven chapters of the Letter to the Romans.

153. JHN, No. 184, "Rom iii, 27–v, 2," February 15, 1829, *Serm.* 2, 136. Of the introductory sermon of the course (No. 182), only the conclusion survives, while the second sermon (No. 183) is lost in its entirety (*Serm.* 2, 133n1, 135n1).

154. JHN, No. 184, "Rom iii, 27–v, 2," *Serm.* 2, 136.

155. JHN, No. 184, "Rom iii, 27–v, 2," *Serm.* 2, 136.

156. JHN, No. 184, "Rom iii, 27–v, 2," *Serm.* 2, 136–37.

157. JHN, No. 184, "Rom iii, 27–v, 2," *Serm.* 2, 137.

of character) can be produced by momentary causes. Newman was adamant about this point: "Impulses lose their force — they excite less and less as they are more and more applied."[158] The repeated application of emotional stimuli will numb people rather than change their lives.

Newman derived this insight from Butler, who argued in the *Analogy* that, due to "our very faculty of habits, passive impressions, by being repeated, grow weaker."[159] What Butler meant is that we become habituated to certain impressions the more we are exposed to them: "being accustomed to danger . . . lessens fear." In the course of a healthy moral development, the force of passive impressions will be inversely proportionate to the growth of active habits. Active habits will be "gradually forming and strengthening, by a course of acting upon such and such motives and excitements, whilst these motives and excitements themselves are, by proportionable degrees, growing less sensible, i.e. are continually less and less sensibly felt, even as the active habits strengthen."[160] Motives and excitements are necessary to begin to act. Pity for the poor can motivate us to help them. But the more we are exposed to poverty, the "less and less sensibly affected" we will be.[161] Hence, the original passive impression must be converted into an active habit, by acting on it. In this way, "benevolence, considered not as a passion, but as a practical principle of action, will strengthen." Although we will be less distressed by seeing the poor, we will "acquire a greater aptitude to assist and befriend them."[162]

In his sermon, Newman applied Butler's general theory of habit formation to the process of sanctification. "Faith," Newman summed up his new position, "does *not change* the heart." It is only "the motive leading to those separate efforts after holiness which in their turn act upon the heart and change it."[163] Moral change still depends on the motive provided by faith, but the motive itself does not do the changing: "the strongest emotions so far from changing the heart, will at length fail of being practically useful even for particular or transient purposes." Change only occurs because the motive leads "us to *acts* of virtue." Only such "separate and minute acts of obedience . . . have a gradual, indeed a sure and sensible effect upon our moral character." People change, in short, not because of what they *know* or *feel* but because of how they *act*: "By *doing* what is meek or humble, we become meek or humble."[164] Newman had been drawn to Butler's reasoning since the summer of 1825, but it took the influence of Keble (and Froude) to make him

<hr>

158. JHN, No. 184, "Rom iii, 27–v, 2," *Serm.* 2, 137.
159. Butler, *The Analogy of Religion*, 124.
160. Butler, *The Analogy of Religion*, 124.
161. Butler, *The Analogy of Religion*, 125.
162. Butler, *The Analogy of Religion*, 125.
163. JHN, No. 184, "Rom iii, 27–v, 2," *Serm.* 2, 137.
164. JHN, No. 184, "Rom iii, 27–v, 2," *Serm.* 2, 137.

assert its logical conclusion: that the affections are not the locus of religious change. Gradually, he had ceased to structure conversion according to the evangelical pattern of "faith—change of heart—change of practice," but he had lacked the conviction to formulate an alternative. Now he did, by structuring conversion as "faith—change of practice—change of heart." This new sequence no longer implied that a right faith necessarily issues in right practice (as the old one did). If we do not live holy lives, this might be because we lack the proper motives, but we might just as well be failing to act up to the motives we have; this is the crucial element of contingency introduced by free will.

Newman reiterated his new account of sanctification in *Holiness Necessary for Future Blessedness*, published as the first of his *Parochial Sermons* (1834). At first sight, this seems odd, for the sermon was originally written in August 1826, immediately before the sermons on the Ten Commandments and the Creed, which emphatically argued that faith in Christ's sacrifice is what changes the heart.[165] Newman reused the sermon, however, as the eighth one of his Romans course, on May 3, 1829, and seems to have revised it to fit his new emphases.[166] As in his February sermon, he argued that, "separate acts of obedience to the will of God . . . are of primary service to us, as the means of making our hearts good."[167] Holiness is not simply "the doing a certain number of good actions, but is an inward character which follows, under God's grace, from doing them." People, therefore, must learn "to practise good works, as the means of changing their heart, which is the end."[168] This is the only way holiness can be acquired: by "many patient, repeated efforts after obedience, gradually working on us, and first modifying and then changing our hearts."[169]

Newman's emphasis on good works as the means toward holiness and his corresponding suspicion of appeals to the affections increased his antagonism toward high Calvinist understandings of conversion. In a sermon of January 1826, he had averred, on a side note, that those who "think that growth in grace is a thing impossible and not promised to us" have nothing left of faith but "warm feelings."[170] In one of his Romans sermons, he expanded on this suggestion. He attributed the high Calvinist mistakes about conversion to their conception of total depravity. Although Newman certainly did not downplay human corruption, he mistrusted people "who declaim against human nature as *totally* sinful, utterly destitute of all kind of good."[171] He thought such people's "habit of uttering

---

165. See pp. 168–69.

166. *LD* 2, 140.

167. JHN, "Holiness Necessary for Future Blessedness," August 6, 1826, *PaS* 1, 9.

168. JHN, "Holiness Necessary for Future Blessedness," *PaS* 1,10.

169. JHN, "Holiness Necessary for Future Blessedness," *PaS* 1,11.

170. JHN, No. 130, "On the differences of religious opinions in the world," January 15, 1826, *Serm.* 3, 292.

171. JHN, No. 192, "The flesh," March 29, 1829, *Serm.* 2, 209.

indiscriminate revilings <railing> against [their] nature" was unreal. It betrays the fact that they believe in human corruption merely as "a *doctrine of Scripture*"; not as "a fact *ascertainable . . . by our experience.*"[172] If a person properly attends to his own concrete sins, "he will speak from *what he* knows" and be wary of indulging in "a vague indolent-railing against human nature in general."[173] When pursued "to its full extent," the outcome of belief in total depravity is antinomianism. If "*all* is to be changed in human nature," Newman argued, "*nothing* can really be changed." We are left with a "human corruption . . . so entire that amendment and sanctification are *impossible.*"[174] But to declare holiness unachievable is to give license to sin. Newman had never taken this route, but some high Calvinists, like Bulteel, had. They held "that there is a mass of evil in us which must remain the same in weight and measure till our death," and "that God has promised in Scripture to save those whom He loves, not *from* sin but *in spite* of sin."[175] As a result, emotions become the only test of one's religious state. The work of the Holy Spirit is regarded not as "one of *sanctification* but of mere *comforting,* not of *holiness* but of mere *joy and transport,* not as operating on *practice* but merely on the *affections.*"[176] The upshot of such a conviction is that "our feeling an inward assurance that we are saved" will be the measure of our religiosity.[177]

By conceiving of sanctification primarily in terms of good works, Newman was expunging the last traces of evangelicalism from his theology. And yet, he retained one very general but foundational evangelical conviction: that faith in the atonement is the indispensable motive to doing good. Even though he argued that the heart and its desires are changed not by means of an affective response to the content of revelation but by means of a sustained praxis of obedience, he continued to regard faith and obedience as essentially distinct habits of mind and adhere to the priority of faith in the process of sanctification. If obedience changes the heart, it does so only for the believer, that is, she who has faith first. Newman's account of natural religion in the sermon course on the Letter to the Romans bears this out. Recall Newman's argument in 1825 and 1826 that sin prevented the heathen from fully acknowledging and acting on the religious truths acquired through conscience. Their continual failure to obey conscience led to a religious despair that was only minimally tempered by hope, and which undermined their belief in God's existence and the demands of his law. Newman's 1829 account retained the outlines of his earlier position but construed the relation between obedience and belief in a new way.

172. JHN, No. 192, "The flesh," *Serm.* 2, 208.
173. JHN, No. 192, "The flesh," *Serm.* 2, 209
174. JHN, No. 192, "The flesh," *Serm.* 2, 209.
175. JHN, No. 192, "The flesh," *Serm.* 2, 209–10.
176. JHN, No. 192, "The flesh," *Serm.* 2, 210.
177. JHN, No. 192, "The flesh," *Serm.* 2, 210.

As before, Newman elaborated on the situation of well-meaning heathens. A "religious but unenlightened heathen," he argued, would reflect as follows:

> My conscience tells me at once that there is a Providence above me, and that I owe him obedience. I feel there is such a thing as sin — right and wrong are not mere names — I see an essential difference between them. I feel distressed when I do what I think wrong, even though I persist in doing it. I have a fear, a religious fear, a dread carrying my mind forward into the possibility of some unknown future evil, which Providence may connect with it. . . . But, alas!, I cannot do as I would — I continually offend the law of God written on my heart — Clearly if God deals with me as I deserve, I cannot escape punishment — What must I do then — I should *despair* unless I saw marks of the divine goodness around me. As it is I have some *hope*. Goodness in God seems to point to the possibility of *mercy*. — Yet what can I do?[178]

This crucial question barely arose on Newman's earlier account. He had assumed that the hope available to a religious heathen was simply not sufficient to result in such an existential dilemma. The heathen remained too bogged down by sin. Now, he perceived a way forward. "It stands to reason I ought to endeavour to obey in all things," the heathen would tell himself, "yet it equally stands to reason that after all I must throw myself unreservedly upon His [God's] pity and loving kindness."[179] And the latter is what a well-disposed heathen would do: "to confess himself wrong and to cast himself on the mercy of God."[180] At the heart of heathen religiosity, Newman discerned the possibility of passing dialectically from obedience to faith. Hope tempers the failure to obey to such a degree that, instead of merely undermining belief, it results in a proper act of justifying faith. In the failure of obedience, room is made for faith.

Despite its increased optimism about the religious situation of the heathen, this model was still premised on the evangelical dichotomy between faith and obedience. The relation between obedience and faith is not continuous but dialectical. The salvific import of a heathen's effort to obey his conscience is limited to the dialectical process by which it leads to faith. Obedience does not lead to salvation by making the heathen better but by making him realize that he is an utter failure. A heathen, Newman argued in another sermon of the course, "cannot approach God in that way which conscience and reason direct," that is, by "obedience to God's will."[181] Accordingly, since "adequate obedience he cannot

---

178. JHN, No. 185, "Faith the one condition of acceptance under every dispensation since the fall," February 8, 1829, *Serm.* 2, 141.

179. JHN, No. 185, "Faith the one condition," *Serm.* 2, 141.

180. JHN, No. 185, "Faith the one condition," *Serm.* 2, 142.

181. JHN, No. 188, "On Justification by faith only," January 18, 1829, *Serm.* 2, 167.

offer . . . his only offering is the confession that *he can offer nothing aright.*[182] Beyond issuing in this confession, which amounts to justifying faith, Newman envisaged no role for obedience in the religious progress of the heathen. The heathen's obedience, qua obedience, does not contribute to a change of heart, as it does in the believer, because both its role and its character are different from Christian obedience. "Before a man knows that Christ has died as a pledge of God's goodness to him and as a seal to that covenant which promises acceptance to faith," Newman argued, "his obedience will be slavish, because it will be an obedience of fear."[183] He will be in continual doubt "whether God really will pardon him" and thus never get beyond the dialectical progress toward justification.

The Christian, by contrast, enjoys "a comfortable happy free and unconstrained obedience," because he knows his justification is guaranteed by Christ's atoning sacrifice. The Christian's obedience, in consequence, is directed at sanctification; "he comes to God, not to gain *mercy* which he knows is secured to the Church for ever, but to gain *aid* in order to fit himself for an inheritance already purchased."[184] For Christians, obedience is rooted in knowledge of their acceptance by Christ and ends in sanctification. For non-Christians, it is rooted in anxiety and leads, at best, to an act of justifying faith. Christian obedience, in short, begins where heathen obedience ends: with faith.

Conclusion

By early 1829, Newman's commitment to the priority of faith over obedience was all that remained of his evangelical theology. Given that he expressed this commitment in a sermon written for Henry Venn Elliott's evangelical parish at Brighton, some might wonder whether he held it sincerely. But there is no reason to think that he was inclined to spare the prejudices of his hearers. On July 27, 1828, he had preached *Religion a Weariness to the Natural Man* to the same congregation. The sermon was on a verse from Isaiah 53: "He hath no form nor comeliness; and when we shall see Him, there is no beauty that we should desire Him."[185] It elaborated on the natural distaste everyone feels for religion, Christians included. We are simply not inclined to it. The sermon closed off all evangelical shortcuts to a holy life. "Truly it is a weariness to the natural man," Newman argued,

> to serve GOD humbly and in obscurity; it is very wearisome, and very monotonous, to go on day after day watching all we do and think, detecting our

182. JHN, No. 188, "On Justification by faith only," *Serm.* 2, 167.
183. JHN, No. 188, "On Justification by faith only," *Serm.* 2, 171.
184. JHN, No. 188, "On Justification by faith only," *Serm.* 2, 171.
185. JHN, No. 173, "Religion a Weariness to the Natural Man," July 27, 1828, *PlS*, 9; Isaiah 53:2.

> secret failings, denying ourselves, creating within us, under GOD's grace, those parts of the Christian character in which we are deficient.[186]

Nevertheless, this is the only way, even for "the confirmed servants of CHRIST."[187] The gospel message is not a spell that takes the toil away from sanctification: "there is no beauty that we should desire Him." Although not doctrinally incompatible with Elliott's brand of evangelicalism (the moderate variant of the likes of Simeon), the sermon made Elliott uneasy. Newman later noted that "Mr Elliott 'sat on thorns'" during the sermon.[188] Elliott was probably not the only one in the congregation who felt that Newman was drifting somewhat too far from the gospel preaching they were used to, but Newman's correspondence shows that he acted with deliberation.

The day after his sermon, Newman received a letter from Robert Wilberforce, who had just been ordained and was also asked to preach at Elliott's church. Wilberforce had felt up to it, but became confused after Newman had critiqued evangelical preaching:

> According to my old notions, I could have got on tolerably well — and, tho'
> I should have been dissatisfied with the execution, I should have believed
> myself on the right road. Now, you have convinced me I am altogether off
> the road, and every step I take, I only get deeper in the mire.[189]

Newman's reply was diffident and sympathetic, but unrelenting. He commiserated with Wilberforce's struggle to find an alternative for the evangelical mode of preaching with which he had been familiar all his life. He had been in the same situation when he began at St Clement's: "I have before now felt in my own mind the distress you speak of about the right mode of preaching — at one time . . . so sorely that I thought I must have given up my curacy, nay have left the Church."[190] But he did not counsel Wilberforce to quench his doubts. Newman's own doubts had centered on how to shape his preaching so as to help his parishioners become holy, whether by focusing on conversion and the atonement, or by some other means. As he accepted baptismal regeneration and appropriated Butler, he increasingly identified conversion with sanctification and highlighted the necessity of human agency in the process. By the summer of 1828, this had become a staple of his preaching, to be introduced even at Elliott's evangelical parish. Before long, even the rigid distinction between Christian and non-Christian obedience, the last vestige of his evangelicalism, was to disappear.

---

186. JHN, No. 173, "Religion a Weariness," *PlS*, 14–15.
187 JHN, No. 173, "Religion a Weariness," *PlS*, 15.
188. Note in a letter from Harriett and Jemima Newman, April 26, 1830, *LD* 2, 206.
189. Robert Isaac Wilberforce to JHN, July 28, 1828, *LD* 2, 85.
190. JHN to Robert Isaac Wilberforce, July 29, 1828, *LD* 2, 84.

CHAPTER 7

A New Vision

The year from early 1829 to early 1830 was a tipping point in the development of Newman's theology. In the preceding years, Newman had accepted baptismal regeneration and revised his understanding of sanctification, election, and the church. Conscience had become a way to God rather than an impotent instinct. Sanctification was no longer proportionate to the affective impact of the gospel message but rather to the moral effort to which faith gives rise. Still, obedience remained essentially distinct from, and conditional on, faith. By early 1829, his theology had lost all its evangelical features except for this structural reliance on the priority of faith over obedience: the idea that moral growth is dependent on an insight gleaned from revelation. In February 1829, this insight was what it had always been: knowledge of Christ's atoning sacrifice. Although it no longer brought about conversion by itself, it still had affective import. It functioned as a guarantee of our acceptance with God, which enabled a free and happy obedience that ushered in progressive sanctification.

By February 1830, Newman had discarded this model. By itself, this was a small step, long in the making, but its results were momentous. It was like reaching a mountain pass after a long climb. With each step—be it his gradual acceptance of baptismal regeneration or the gradual admission of conscience into his theology—he had left part of his evangelical heritage behind. When he dismissed the priority of faith over obedience, it was just another step; but it was also a final step, one that opened new vistas. New landscapes unfold upon reaching a mountain pass, and new paths are to be chosen. Similarly, by 1830, Newman was settling on a new vision of both the religious subject and the object of religious belief.

Faith, Obedience, and the Religious Character

Newman increasingly equated being religious with acquiring a specific moral character. He began to toy with this idea in his 1828 correspondence with Blanco White and developed it more thoroughly in his sermon course on the Letter to the Romans. One of its later sermons portrayed the religiosity of Christians as a "whole <one> character and complexion of mind, [a] general habit of thinking feeling and acting."[1] As in the earlier sermons, Newman contrasted this "Christian

---

1. JHN, No. 198, "The Christian's spiritual obedience; — the Holy Spirit author of it," June 7, 1829, *Serm.* 2, 188.

frame of mind" with the religiosity of the heathens, the patriarchs, and the Jews, who, in varying degrees, remained in their "*natural state* of guilt, gloom, and helplessness."[2] They exercised "an irregular, inconsistent, sorrowful obedience . . . laden with the consciousness of guilt and forebodings of punishments."[3] "Christian obedience," by contrast, is "free, enlightened, joyful, spiritual — for, instead of painfully conjecturing the truth and timorously sighing for pardon, it is our privilege to know, by the pledge given us by God in Christ's death, that acceptance *has* been gained for us."[4] At the same time—and this is new—Newman downplayed the importance of the contrast by qualifying it as "general and abstract"— terms that carry the same Butlerian meaning as they did in the 1828 *Remarks*. The contrast between Christians and non-Christians holds in theory, but concretely, it applies "more or less to this or that person, as the case may be."[5] Accordingly, "men who have *less* light often are *better* men and holier than those who have much light — Many an ungifted heathen, Rahab or Naaman or Cornelius, will at the last day shame us Christians — such have made much of their *one* talent."[6] In the 1828 *Remarks*, Newman had noted that ambiguous biblical figures like Samson, or the pagan prostitute Rahab, were "in Hebrews xi reckoned in the number of those who 'lived by faith.'"[7] A year later, he instanced Rahab not only for her faith but also as an example of sanctification through obedience. In theory, non-Christian obedience is aimed at justification, but in practice, sanctification can be, and is, attained.

In July 1829, Newman preached a sermon on Abraham that drew the logical conclusion from this insight. He labelled it *Character of Abraham,* a title showing his preoccupation with the idea of moral character. In fact, the moral and religious character of biblical figures became Newman's favorite sermon topic in the following year. Before the end of 1830, he had preached on the characters of Abraham, Lot, Isaac, Esau, Jacob, Moses, Saul, David, Solomon, Hezekiah, Josiah, Jeremiah, Mark, Matthew, Luke, John the Baptist, Peter, Bartholomew, Mary Magdalen, Barnabas, and James. In previous years, he had not even preached a handful of such sermons. The first of this genre, the sermon on Abraham, identified Abraham's particular virtue as "*faith,*" but immediately added that faith does not denote one specific disposition, distinct from others (such as obedience). Instead, it signifies a comprehensive habit of being religious: "a *religious temper* and *faith* mean in substance the very same thing."[8] Thus, Abraham's "faith was a character

---

2. JHN, No. 198, "The Christian's spiritual obedience," *Serm.* 2, 188.

3. JHN, No. 198, "The Christian's spiritual obedience," *Serm.* 2, 187–88.

4. JHN, No. 198, "The Christian's spiritual obedience," *Serm.* 2, 188.

5. JHN, No. 198, "The Christian's spiritual obedience," *Serm.* 2, 189. See pp. 186–91 in this book.

6. JHN, No. 198, "The Christian's spiritual obedience," *Serm.* 2, 189.

7. JHN, *Remarks on the Covenant of Grace,* BOA A.9.1, 11.

8. JHN, No. 202, "Character of Abraham," July 12, 1829, *Serm.* 2, 15.

imprinted on his mind, and influenced his conduct as a rooted principle."[9] To describe this habitual religiosity, Newman used the terms faith and obedience nearly interchangeably. Abraham gave up his life in Ur "simply *because God told him so to do* . . . for he felt God at all events was to be obeyed," and this "self-denying and unhesitating obedience was an act of strong faith."[10] Faith, then, denotes a specific moral and religious character. If we understand it as such, it matters little what we call it. Abraham, Newman argued,

> *preferred* God to all things and acted on his preference — and this is faith, or religious feeling <principle>, or a spiritual mind, or by whatever other name it is called; — for they all come to the same thing — denoting that one frame <state> of mind <heart>, that one character which renders us accepted in the sight of God.[11]

Here, the process of becoming acceptable to God is no longer divided into distinct and sequential theological steps (corruption—justification—sanctification) or distinct and sequential religious acts (repenting—believing—obeying). Instead, Abraham is rendered acceptable because of his comprehensive moral and religious character, which exhibits itself in various ways and is essentially the same as that of Christians.

In a sermon of December 13, Newman expanded this idea to cover all genuinely religious persons, not just Christians or paragons of salvation history like Abraham. The sermon, *Inward Prayer*, elaborated on St Paul's injunction to "Pray without ceasing," but explained this duty first as "taught us by natural reason and religious feeling."[12] Natural religion, Newman argued, teaches us "that we are creatures of the Great GOD, the Maker of heaven and earth; and that, as His creatures, we are bound to serve HIM and give HIM our hearts; in a word, to be religious beings."[13] Nature, then, obliges us to be religious, but the real question is what such religiosity looks like: "What is religion but a habit?" Newman answered,

> and what is a habit but a state of mind which is always upon us, a sort of ordinary dress or inseparable garment of the soul? . . . A man who is religious, is religious morning, noon, and, night; his religion is a certain character, a mould in which his thoughts, words, and actions are cast, all forming parts of one and the same whole.[14]

---

9. JHN, No. 202, "Character of Abraham," *Serm.* 2, 17.

10. JHN, No. 202, "Character of Abraham," *Serm.* 2, 16, 17.

11. JHN, No. 202, "Character of Abraham," *Serm.* 2, 17.

12. JHN, No. 220, "Inward Prayer," December 13, 1829, *PlS*, 131, 132. This sermon was retitled "Mental Prayer" in the collected *Parochial and Plain Sermons* (vol. 7, 205). See 1 Thessalonians 5:17.

13. JHN, No. 220, "Inward Prayer," *PlS*, 132.

14. JHN, No. 220, "Inward Prayer," *PlS*, 132.

This one character is marked by a single orientation: an orientation toward God. The religious person "sees GOD in all things; every course of action he directs towards those spiritual objects which GOD has placed before his heart; every occurrence of the day, every event, every person met with, all news which he hears, he measures by the standard of GOD's will."[15] Being religious, then, is a consistent habit of turning to God. It is a habit of seeing and doing, wholeheartedly oriented toward him. Within a few months, Newman came to realize that this unified conception of religious subjectivity was incompatible with the evangelical primacy of faith over obedience.

On his twenty-ninth birthday, February 21, 1830, Newman preached a sermon in a course on the liturgy, published as *Faith and Obedience* in 1836.[16] In all probability, the sermon was revised on its second preaching (on May 24, 1835), as the published version bases its argument on scripture rather than the liturgy.[17] Its central contention, however, was present in the original composition, because Newman reiterated it in a note drafted the day after first preaching the sermon. He knew he had adopted a controversial theological position, anticipating "certain objections which may be made to the doctrine of this Sermon."[18] The note succinctly defines that doctrine as follows: "our acceptance depends on our imperfect *obedience*."[19] A year before, Newman had maintained the opposite: "humble faith, not a profession of acceptable obedience . . . is the means of admission into God's favor."[20] Now, he argued that obedience could fulfil the same role as faith on the earlier account, even though it be imperfect. After all, "faith is imperfect," too, "in the very same sense that obedience is."[21] This shift in perspective went to the heart of Newman's theology of conversion.

In the opening sections of the sermon, Newman put the central question of his entire theology to his audience: "How are we sinners to be accepted by Almighty God?"[22] His answer was threefold. On the "meritorious cause of our justification," he had not budged since his early evangelical days. It remained "the sacrifice of Christ on the cross," the common confession of orthodox Christians the world over. As to the mediation of this grace, his views had developed considerably since 1824. Now, as in 1828, he unambiguously declared: "His Church is the ordained instrument of conveying it to us." His present concern, however, was neither with the cause, nor with the instrument of grace, but with "our own

---

15. JHN, No. 220, "Inward Prayer," *PlS*, 132.
16. JHN, No. 227, "Faith and Obedience," February 21, 1830, *PaS* 3, 83–95.
17. See *Serm.* 1, 80n2.
18. JHN, "N.B.," February 22, 1830, *Serm.* 1, 80.
19. JHN, "N.B.," February 22, 1830, *Serm.* 1, 80.
20. JHN, No. 188, "On Justification by faith only," January 18, 1829, *Serm.* 2, 169.
21. JHN, "N.B.," February 22, 1830, *Serm.* 1, 80.
22. JHN, No. 227, "Faith and Obedience," *PaS* 3, 85.

part in appropriating it," that is, with what *we* must do to be saved. On this subject, "Scripture makes two answers, saying sometimes 'Believe, and you shall be saved,' and sometimes 'Keep the commandments, and you shall be saved.'"[23] Up to early 1829, Newman had adopted, in some form or other, the evangelical solution to this conflict. He interpreted the former injunction in an unconditional sense and the latter in a conditional sense, as depending on the former: we must believe to be able to obey. Now, he chose a very different approach.

If we attentively consider faith and obedience as "two states of mind," Newman argued, we will find them to be "altogether one and the same," for: "To believe is to look beyond this world to God; and to obey is to look beyond this world to God; to believe is of the heart, and to obey is of the heart; to believe is not a solitary act, but a consistent habit of trust; and to obey is not a solitary act, but a consistent habit of doing our duty in all things."[24] Despite this identificatory language, Newman's point was not to bring about a conceptual synthesis between faith and obedience. As concepts, faith and obedience remain distinct. They "stand for separate ideas in our minds," but "they are not divided one from the other in fact. They are but one thing viewed differently."[25] In the concrete religious subject, faith and obedience manifest a single underlying reality: they are "exhibitions of one and the same spiritual character of mind."[26] Together, they make up the one "general character" or "temper of mind which has, in every age, been acceptable to Almighty God."[27] In consequence, "it is quite indifferent whether we say a man seeks God in faith, or say he seeks Him by obedience; and whereas Almighty God has graciously declared He will receive and bless all that seek Him, it is quite indifferent whether we say, He accepts those who *believe*, or those who *obey*."[28]

Part of the evangelical mistake was to treat the conceptual distinction between faith and obedience as an ontological one: representing, in the religious subject, two divergent realities, whereby the latter is subordinated to the former. For Newman, they are, instead, equal manifestations of a character that is habitually oriented toward God in thought and action: that *seeks* him. And by cultivating this habitual orientation, imperfect though it be, the subject appropriates God's grace.

This simple idea, that being religious means having a certain character, cut right through the logical and temporal sequences of the evangelical understanding of conversion. Recall that evangelicals structured the set of experiences, dispositions, and behaviors that characterize the religious subject according to their doctrinal system. The objective, doctrinal sequence of Fall, redemption by Christ,

---

23. JHN, No. 227, "Faith and Obedience," *PaS* 3, 85.
24. JHN, No. 227, "Faith and Obedience," *PaS* 3, 87.
25. JHN, No. 227, "Faith and Obedience," *PaS* 3, 87.
26. JHN, No. 227, "Faith and Obedience," *PaS* 3, 91.
27. JHN, No. 227, "Faith and Obedience," *PaS* 3, 88, 92.
28. JHN, No. 227, "Faith and Obedience," *PaS* 3, 86–87.

and gift of the Holy Spirit is transposed into the subjective sequence of deep misery, faith in Christ's atonement, and good works out of gratitude. Just as the Fall precedes the atonement, and the atonement precedes the giving of the Spirit, so repentance precedes faith, and faith precedes good works.

By early 1830, however, Newman had abandoned this model. His new account of the religious subject unified the distinct and sequentially ordered elements of evangelical subjectivity into a holistic (to use a trite term) orientation of the entire person, which underlies those elements and gives them substance. "Obedience, repentance, and faith," he argued, are all mentioned in scripture "as the means of obtaining God's favour because they are all names for one and the same substantial character, only viewed on different sides of it, that one character of mind which is pleasing and acceptable to Almighty God."[29]

Because they are expressive of one reality, obedience always entails faith: "habitually to obey God is to be constant in looking on to God,—and to look on to Almighty God, is to have faith."[30] Hence, obedience is not just doing good, but doing good for the right reasons; "on principle," as Newman had it before.[31] It has a certain directionality: there is something or someone that is obeyed. Accordingly, if someone "does right, *not* for religion's sake, but the world's sake, though he happens to be doing right . . . this is in no sense *obedience*, which is of the *heart*."[32] Given this understanding of obedience, Newman no longer needed the usual evangelical caveats when arguing that sanctification entails human effort. In a partially preserved sermon of July 1830, he maintained that the way of life is narrow, "because *obtaining the prize depends ultimately on ourselves.*"[33] True, he admitted, eternal life is a "gift," but "the taking it" is up to us.[34] Conversion, therefore, is the "process of converting *ourselves*, or changing our moral nature."[35] And we do so by "strict (unflinching) <resolute> habitual obedience, the *keeping the commandments* of God."[36]

The piling up of adjectives to characterize obedience underscores the dogged effort it takes to be religious. None of his former reluctance to present conversion as a work remained. His rejection of efficacious grace was complete: "if God does all and nothing is left to us, *then* there is no such thing as *our working out our own salvation.*"[37] There was nothing figurative about St Paul's injunction any

---

29. JHN, No. 227, "Faith and Obedience," *PaS* 3, 90.

30. JHN, No. 227, "Faith and Obedience," *PaS* 3, 87–88.

31. See p. 128.

32. JHN, No. 227, "Faith and Obedience," *PaS* 3, 87.

33. JHN, No. 249, "The life of St James the Greater — his request to Christ and its answer as teaching us the narrowness of the way of life," July 25, 1830, *Serm.* 3, 45.

34. JHN, No. 249, "The life of St James the Greater," *Serm.* 3, 45.

35. JHN, No. 249, "The life of St James the Greater," *Serm.* 3, 48, emphasis added.

36. JHN, No. 249, "The life of St James the Greater," *Serm.* 3, 49. See Galatians 5:6; No. 228, "The Liturgy teaching doctrine — concerning means of grace," February 28, 1830, *Serm.* 1, 86.

37. JHN, No. 249, "The life of St James the Greater," *Serm.* 3, 46.

longer.[38] Its emphasis on human agency was simply incompatible with the Calvinist scheme. Newman had said as much in 1828, but he used stronger terms now. "If our will could be changed without our own acting in the change," he argued, "we should [have] ceased to be men, we should no longer have souls."[39] Some of this vehemence was reactive. At twenty, he had professed this idea himself. Conversion was God's sovereign creation of "a soul with all its affections devoted to His service."[40] Nine years later, this notion had become reprehensible. "Matter only, the stone e.g. or the metal is passive under the workman's hands," Newman argued, "brute animals alone obey at the will of another."[41] But we are humans, and therefore, we are agents responsible for our salvation. We simply cannot be saved "without our accountableness or control."[42]

Still, Newman knew from experience that many people tended to skirt this responsibility. They desired an easier route to salvation, a shortcut that bypasses obedience, or replaces it with something else, a "charm . . . so as at once to convert us."[43] In the opening sermon of his liturgy course, preached on January 31, he had attacked the very "common and natural error" of thinking that people can "be saved without their own personal trouble."[44] Thus, some evangelicals reduced Christianity to the maxim "*believe* and you are safe." They forgot that faith "does not purify and convert us fully and at once, it does not change our nature *as a charm.*"[45] Similarly, a High Churchman might think that "the Sacraments . . . will *work* his *sanctification,* as a charm, without his trouble." But there is nothing magical about faith. The only way to be saved is "through our own painful selfdiscipline [*sic*]."[46] In a March sermon of the same course, he reiterated that holiness is conditional on ascesis. The way to purify ourselves from "the thoughts of this world's joys, honors or emoluments" is by "*selfdenial* [*sic*]."[47] To learn to love God, we must "unlearn the love of this world," which comes naturally to us. This means "thwarting our natural wishes and tastes," refraining not merely from the "*sinful* pleasures" to which we naturally incline but also "from *innocent* comforts of this world."[48] The latter, "*self-*

---

38. See p. 33.
39. JHN, No. 249, "The life of St James the Greater," *Serm.* 3, 50.
40. JHN, *Comment*, BOA A.9.1.e, 2.
41. JHN, No. 249, "The life of St James the Greater," *Serm.* 3, 50.
42. JHN, No. 249, "The life of St James the Greater," *Serm.* 3, 50.
43. JHN, No. 249, "The life of St James the Greater," *Serm.* 3, 50.
44. JHN, No. 224, "The Liturgy the service of the Christian Priest," January 31, 1830, *Serm.* 1, 64.
45. JHN, No. 224, "The Liturgy the service of the Christian Priest," *Serm.* 1, 65.
46. JHN, No. 224, "The Liturgy the service of the Christian Priest," *Serm.* 1, 65.
47. JHN, No. 232, "The Liturgy forming the character — viz to self denial — the Commination and Lent Services," March 28, 1830, *Serm.* 1, 97. Parts of this sermon survive in manuscript, other parts were published as "The Duty of Self-Denial," in *PlS*, 57–66.
48. JHN, No. 232, "The Duty of Self-Denial," *PlS*, 57; JHN, No. 232, "The Liturgy forming the character," *Serm.* 1, 99.

denial in things lawful," is "real selfdenial"; it is the "peculiar virtue of a Christian."[49] Only by practicing it can the Christian train herself to look beyond the world to God, who is her eternal good. People who have just begun to take religion seriously are especially prone to forget this. In their initial enthusiasm, Newman argued on November 14, they tend to think that it is an "easy task," or that "though hard in itself, it will be easy to them, for God's grace will take all the toil of it from them."[50] Such people "must be reminded . . . of the greatness of the work which they have undertaken, viz. the sanctification of their souls."[51] If they do not realize this, conversion becomes impossible, for "we cannot do it rightly without a deep settled conviction of the exceeding difficulty of the work."[52] Without this conviction, people easily fall into the high Calvinist trap of thinking that it is not just difficult but "*impossible* to overcome our evil selves," so that "all we have to do, is to believe in Christ who is to save us, and to dwell on the thought of his perfect work for us."[53] But this attitude betrays a misconception of the work of Christ.

"Christ," Newman had pointed out on January 31, "has not lived *instead* of you, nor was holy *instead* of you;" living and becoming holy are up to us.[54] The typical evangelical conversion experience suggested the contrary. Take Newman's own description in the 1821 *Collection*: we try and try, until we realize we can do nothing of our own and must simply rely on Christ's atoning sacrifice.[55] It is easy to conclude from such an experience that Christ has done all and we need to do nothing, but this is a mistake. "Christ has not *lived* instead *of you*, but He *died instead* of you," Newman explained, "He saved you from the wrath to come, He purchased for you the gifts of grace, and thus is ultimately the sole author of your salvation."[56] People, Newman argued in October, assume that "strict obedience is not necessary under the Gospel, and that something else will be taken, for Christ's sake, in the stead of it," be it faith, repentance, or ritual observances.[57] They assume, in other words, that "Christ came to gain for us easier terms of admittance into heaven than we had before." But "instead of making obedience less strict, He has enabled us to obey God more strictly; and instead of gaining *easier* terms of *admittance*, He has gained us *altogether* our admittance into heaven."[58]

---

49. JHN, No. 232, "The Liturgy forming the character," *Serm.* 1, 99.

50. JHN, No. 268, "Obedience is the remedy for perplexities," November 14, 1830, published as "Obedience the Remedy for Religious Perplexity," in *PaS* 1, 270.

51. JHN, No. 268, "Obedience the Remedy," *PaS* 1, 269.

52. JHN, No. 268, "Obedience the Remedy," *PaS* 1, 270.

53. JHN, No. 268, "Obedience the Remedy," *PaS* 1, 269–70.

54. JHN, No 224, "The Liturgy the service of the Christian Priest," *Serm.* 1, 65.

55. See pp. 29–30.

56. JHN, No 224, "The Liturgy the service of the Christian Priest," *Serm.* 1, 65–66.

57. JHN, No. 265, "Obedience to God the Way to Faith in Christ," October 31, 1830, *PlS*, 298.

58. JHN, No. 265, "Obedience to God," *PlS*, 299.

In consequence, the "Gospel leaves us just where it found us, as regards the necessity of our obedience to GOD."[59]

It is important that people realize obedience is still demanded. If they do not, they will measure their religious progress by the wrong test: "not by their power of obeying God in practice . . . but by the warmth and energy of their religious feelings."[60] They will *talk* religiously, but forget

> that a Christian spirit is the growth of time; and that we cannot force it upon our minds, however desirable and necessary it may be to possess it; that by giving utterance to religious sentiments we do not become religious, rather the reverse; whereas, if we strove to obey God's will in all things, we actually should be gradually training our hearts into the fullness of a Christian spirit.[61]

Still, it is not because devout feelings and pious phrases are no measure of one's religious state that emotion has no function whatsoever in the formation of a Christian character. It has, but it should be handled with care. Newman warned his parishioners especially "against impetuous feelings in religion."[62] The perfect Christian temper is one of "calm, full, reverent, contemplative, obedient" love, so that we should neither encourage nor "*think highly* of violent emotion."[63] Of course, strong emotions sometimes overcome us. For religious beginners, it is natural to "feel bitter sorrow and keen repentance" at their sins.[64] But such emotions are "not the essence of true faith;" they might be "sometimes natural, sometimes suitable; but they are not religion itself."[65] Being religious, after all, is having a stable moral character, while emotions are transient. Feeling, Newman argued in a later sermon, "comes & goes & having no root in our nature, speaks with no divine authority," whereas "the moral perception, though varying in the mass of men, is fixed in each individual, and is an original part of us."[66] Still, emotions can serve a religious purpose. The excitements people experience when they first take up religion can help them to overcome "the first distastefulness and pain of doing their duty."[67] Obedience is hard, and fervent emotion makes it a little easier at first. The only proper response to feeling remorse, anxiety, or joy is the one

---

59. JHN, No. 265, "Obedience to God," *PlS*, 300.

60. JHN, No. 268, "Obedience the Remedy," *PaS* 1, 269.

61. JHN, No. 268, "Obedience the Remedy," *PaS* 1, 268. See also No. 197, "Spiritual freedom, which the Jews had not," May 31, 1829, *Serm.* 2, 185.

62. JHN, No. 292, "Religious Emotion," March 27, 1831, *PaS* 1, 208.

63. JHN, No. 292, "Religious Emotion," *PaS* 1, 208, 209.

64. JHN, No. 292, "Religious Emotion," *PaS* 1, 209, 210.

65. JHN, No. 292, "Religious Emotion," *PaS* 1, 210, 213.

66. JHN, No. 321, "On the so-called 'march of intellect' at the present day," December 11, 1831, BOA A.9.4, 8v; published as "The Usurpations of Reason," *OUS*, 44–45.

67. JHN, No. 305, "The Religious Use of Excited Feelings," July 3, 1831, *PaS* 1, 134.

Butler had recommended: action. As Newman advised his parishioners, "hasten to commit yourself to certain definite *acts* of obedience."[68] Emotions are there to *use*, to turn "into principles by acting upon them," and not, as some evangelicals did, to indulge in "for their own sake."[69]

Conscience in Quest of God

Without the priority of faith over obedience, Newman's latest solution to the problem of heathen religion—the idea of obedience to conscience as issuing dialectically in justifying faith—made little sense. If God graciously accepts imperfect obedience as well as faith, the salvific import of obedience does not depend on the faith it results in, but on itself. This conviction fit the Butlerian idea that the relation between natural and revealed religion is continuous rather than dialectical. "Christianity," Butler claimed in the *Analogy*, contains "a republication of natural religion"; it is natural religion and something besides.[70] As Keble had it, "the true view of human happiness, revealed to us fully by the Gospel of Christ, differs from former views, philosophical and religious, not so much in contradicting them, as in going beyond them."[71] Already in January 1829, Newman echoed these views to argue that revelation neither originates nor undoes the Christian's obligation to obey God:

> For God has given him a conscience, writing on his heart the difference between good and evil — God does by nature speak to his heart, bidding him avoid sin. And God never contradicts Himself — what He has said once as a moral and eternal truth, He will never unsay by a subsequent revelation — The gospel does not destroy the religion of nature — it does but add to it.[72]

And yet, Newman still contrasted Christian and non-Christian obedience in terms of their character and goal. In June, Newman abandoned this contrast when reflecting on Abraham's religious character, and by August, he extended his new logic to natural religion. In a manuscript note, he argued:

> When even a heathen as Aristotle says "I will follow moral excellence without reference to the pleasure which may or may not attend it, because it is good and my best instincts prompt me to follow it," he is but acting the part of Abraham who took God as his portion without definite promise. In both is

68. JHN, No. 305, "The Religious Use of Excited Feelings," *PaS* 1, 135.
69. JHN, No. 305, "The Religious Use of Excited Feelings," *PaS* 1, 137, 136.
70. Butler, *The Analogy of Religion*, 197.
71. Keble, "Implicit Faith Recognised by Reason," *Sermons*, 25.
72. JHN, No. 188, "On Justification by faith only," January 18, 1829, *Serm.* 2, 170.

the same self neglect and self denial, and resolute and noble disinterestedness
in trusting to the voice of God without reference to present enjoyment.[73]

Heathen obedience to conscience, then, is the same in kind as Abraham's, or,
indeed, a Christian's obedience to God's express commands.

In a university sermon on April 13, 1830, Newman explicated his new understanding of the relation between natural and revealed religion. He identified conscience as "the essential principle & sanction of religion in the mind."[74] As such,
it has a double role. On the one hand, its inward operations generate an impression of the religious object. "Conscience implies a relation between the soul and
a something exterior to itself — and moreover something superior to itself, a
relation to an excellence which it does not possess and to a tribunal over which
it has no power."[75] This had been Newman's belief since December 1825. The
experience of conscience suggests that the self has reference to something
beyond it, something better and more authoritative, under whose jurisdiction it
falls. On the other hand, conscience sanctions the phenomenon of religion as it
exists in the world. Newman had never believed that natural religion is generated
solely by conscience.[76] Natural religion is not, in fact, quite natural. When "religion
of some sort is said to be natural," he now argued, "it is not here meant that any
religious system has been actually traced out by unaided reason," for the simple
reason that "we know of no time or country in which human reason was
unaided."[77] Revelations, he explained, "were granted to the first fathers of our
race, concerning the nature of God and man's duty to Him." Besides being
anchored in the subject, natural religion has a historic source. It retains, in various
forms and degrees, the memory of an original divine communication. "No people
has been denied a revelation from God — tho' but a portion of the world has
enjoyed a written revelation."[78] Therefore, nearly all peoples have a traditional
belief in unseen powers and their interference with nature as well as humankind.
It is the function of conscience to sift the primordially revealed truth from these
corrupted traditions.

73. JHN, Note of August 1829 (BOA A.7.1) cited in JHN, *Fifteen Sermons Preached before the
University of Oxford*, ed. James David Earnest and Gerard Tracey (Oxford: Oxford University Press,
2006), 278, and in McGrath, *John Henry Newman*, 42.

74. JHN, No. 234, "Natural and revealed religion contrasted in point of practical effect," April
13, 1830, BOA A.9.4, 5, published as, "The Influence of Natural and Revealed Religion Respectively,"
OUS, 19.

75. JHN, No. 234, "Natural and revealed religion," BOA A.9.4, 5 (*OUS*, 19–20).

76. See pp. 166–67.

77. JHN, No. 234, "Natural and revealed religion," BOA A.9.4, 4 (*OUS*, 19). See also No. 231,
"Steadfastness in the Old Paths," March 21, 1830, *PIS*, 159.

78. JHN, No. 234, "Natural and revealed religion," BOA A.9.4, 4 (*OUS*, 19). This was also
Butler's opinion (*The Analogy of Religion*, 222).

Conscience and Natural Religion

Although Newman retained the basic structure of his earlier argument, he premised his new account of conscience as a way to God on the perfective dimension of conscience: the fact that the functioning of conscience is improved if it is obeyed. Up to early 1829, he was reluctant to grant that obedience to conscience yields substantial moral progress in natural religion. He tended to portray conscience as a series of distinct pangs, which, when analysed, yield the idea of God as moral governor. By April 1830, it was *obedience* to conscience, rather than its singular pangs, which yields such knowledge. The "more closely this innate monitor [conscience] is respected & followed," he argued, "the clearer, the more exalted, and the more varied its dictates become, and the standard of excellence seems ever to fly before, while it guides, our obedience."[79] When conscience is obeyed, it improves; but while it improves, its demands also increase. The moral standard it upholds always escapes our reach. As a result, "a moral conviction is . . . at length obtained of the unapproachable nature as well as the supreme authority of that, whatever it is, which is the object of the mind's contemplation."[80] Knowledge of God is the outcome of a course of consistent obedience to conscience. It is the result of sedulously trying to be good, realizing all the while that, although we improve, we could still be better. In this way, conscience eventually suggests an absolute good and an absolute judge as its referent. Thus, faithfulness to conscience provides us with "the elements of a religious system," that is, the "system of relations existing between us and a Supreme Power, claiming our habitual obedience."[81]

These two beliefs, that there is a God and that we owe him obedience, make up the essence of natural, and indeed of all, religion. But conscience has additional religious implications. First, it issues in "the presentiment of a future life, and of a judgment to be past [*sic*] upon present conduct, with rewards & punishments annexed."[82] The idea of a future life was an important corollary to Butler's argument in the *Analogy*. Seeing that our God-given moral nature demands just deserts for virtue and vice, and that such justice is not fully established in the present world, a future life is suggested in which all accounts will be settled. Newman assumed all this, but foregrounded, once again, his perfective understanding of conscience. He parsed the idea of conscience into three constituent components: it "implies a difference in the nature of actions, the power of acting in this way or that as we please, and an obligation of acting in one particular way in preference to all others."[83] Conscience says that actions are either good or bad,

---

79. JHN, No. 234, "Natural and revealed religion," BOA A.9.4, 5 (*OUS*, 20).
80. JHN, No. 234, "Natural and revealed religion," BOA A.9.4, 5 (*OUS*, 20).
81. JHN, No. 234, "Natural and revealed religion," BOA A.9.4, 5–6 (*OUS*, 20).
82. JHN, No. 234, "Natural and revealed religion," BOA A.9.4, 6 (*OUS*, 20).
83. JHN, No. 234, "Natural and revealed religion," BOA A.9.4, 6 (*OUS*, 20).

that we are free agents, and that we, therefore, should do good rather than evil. If we do so, we improve. But "the more our moral nature is improved, the stronger innate power of improvement it seems to possess." In this way, conscience impresses on us a sense of responsibility, not just for what we do, but for what we ultimately become. It unfolds a view of "the capabilities & prospects of man, and the awful importance of that work which the law of his being lays upon him."[84] Conscience impresses on us the ultimate bearings of our task. It suggests that death is not some great leveller but rather opens onto a state in which each will be held accountable for what she has become.

Secondly, habitual obedience to conscience implies habitual faith. Conscience, Newman argued, "brings with it no proof of its truth, & commands attention to it on its own authority."[85] In consequence, "all obedience to it is of the nature of <u>faith</u>."[86] Again, echoes of Butler resound. In his *Sermons at the Rolls Chapel* (1726), Butler had noted that conscience, "without being consulted, without being advised with, magisterially exerts itself"; it simply "carries its own authority with it."[87] Newman read Butler's *Sermons* for the first time in 1827, nearly two years after studying the *Analogy*, and returned to the book in the autumn of 1829.[88] As with the *Analogy*, he did not slavishly reproduce Butler's work but integrated it creatively into his own thinking. Butler's main point in the early *Sermons* is that conscience is superior among our mental faculties. Because it magisterially judges the self and its actions, it is "in kind and in nature supreme over all others" and "bears its own authority of being so."[89] Being a judge, in other words, entails authority, and judging all that pertains to the self entails supreme authority. Again, Newman assumed all this, but he asked the further question how the supremacy of conscience is established in practice. His answer was: by a kind of faith. "Habitual obedience" to conscience, he argued,

> implies the <u>direct exercise</u> of a clear & vigorous faith in the truth of its suggestions, triumphing over opposition both from without & within the mind — quieting the murmurs of reason perplexed with the disorders of the

84. JHN, No. 234, "Natural and revealed religion," BOA A.9.4, 6 (*OUS*, 20).

85. JHN, No. 234, "Natural and revealed religion," BOA A.9.4, 7 (*OUS*, 21).

86. JHN, No. 234, "Natural and revealed religion," BOA A.9.4, 7 (*OUS*, 21).

87. Joseph Butler, "Upon Human Nature," in *The Works of the Right Reverend Father in God Joseph Butler*, vol. 2, ed. Samuel Halifax (Oxford: Clarendon Press, 1820), 32, 44. This was the edition Newman read. The book was originally published as *Fifteen Sermons Preached at the Rolls Chapel* (London: James and John Knapton, 1726).

88. Newman borrowed Butler's *Sermons* from the Oriel College library on April 4, 1827, and again on September 14, 1829 (Parker). Although the idea of conscience as bearing its own authority is already present in the sermon on natural religion of December 1825, this is not enough—in the absence of corroborating evidence—to conclude to an earlier reading of Butler's *Sermons*.

89. Butler, "Upon Human Nature," in *Works*, vol. 2, 32–33.

present scheme of things, and subduing the appetites, clamorous for goods which promise an immediate and keen gratification.[90]

The supremacy of conscience, then, is not a simple given. It must be established in the subject. In proportion as it is obeyed, conscience gains power over other faculties, such as reason and sense, quelling doubt and directing desire from transient goods to the good itself. To use Butler's terms: it has supreme *authority*, but supreme *power* it must acquire.[91] And to accord it the power suiting its authority, one must believe that it tells truly. Again, faith and obedience are mutually constitutive.

So far, Newman's argument concerns only the religious bearings of conscience, not its moral function. This is no coincidence. One of the most remarkable features of his take on conscience is that its moral quality does not fully determine its religious significance. Conscience "is, as such, essentially religious; but moral it is not necessarily, only in proportion as it happens to be refined & strengthened in each particular mind."[92] Newman did not mean to say that conscience has no intrinsic reference to morality. Since it has actions for its immediate object, it is concerned with morality even before religion. His point is merely that even though conscience might be mistaken about the good (and thus sanction immoral acts, and be, strictly speaking, immoral), it always retains its religious significance. There is some "uncertainty" in "the innate <u>moral</u> law," but this uncertainty does not at all interfere with "the certainty of that general <u>religious</u> sense, which is implied in the remorse and vague apprehension of evil which the transgression of conscience occasions."[93] Even an erroneous conscience has its religious function unimpaired, because transgressing it will still produce feelings of unease regarding both the past and the future, which leaves it intact as a witness to a supreme power that claims our obedience.

Despite allowing for a "discordancy of human opinions on the excellence or demerit of <u>particular</u> actions," Newman insisted that sedulous obedience to conscience will issue in "a continually growing expertness in the science of <u>morals</u>."[94] In fact, there is no limit to the moral and religious knowledge that can be acquired by obeying conscience. A "mind, habitually conforming itself to its own sense of duty," he argued, "will at length enjoin or forbid with an authority second only to an inspired oracle."[95] In "a heathen country," moreover, "it will have power to discriminate with precision between the right and wrong in tradi-

90. JHN, No. 234, "Natural and revealed religion," BOA A.9.4, 7 (*OUS*, 21).
91. Butler, "Upon Human Nature," in *Works*, vol. 2, 36–37.
92. JHN, No. 234, "Natural and revealed religion," BOA A.9.4, 7 (*OUS*, 21).
93. JHN, No. 234, "Natural and revealed religion," BOA A.9.4, 8 (*OUS*, 21).
94. JHN, No. 234, "Natural and revealed religion," BOA A.9.4, 8 (*OUS*, 21).
95. JHN, No. 234, "Natural and revealed religion," BOA A.9.4, 8 (*OUS*, 21–22).

tionary superstitions, and will thus gain confirmation to its faith even from corruptions of the truth."[96]

In all likelihood, Newman was again thinking of Socrates. In 1825, he had been struck by Socrates's religious insight for the first time. By 1830, Socrates had become the paragon of a good heathen for Newman and his friends. In September 1829, Newman wrote to Froude that he, like Pusey, believed in "the inspiration of . . . all good men (e.g. Socrates)."[97] This private comment went beyond the view he expressed publicly in the university sermon, and it was later echoed by Froude, who noted that, "as to Socrates, I can scarcely belief [*sic*] that he was not inspired."[98] Given Newman's understanding of conscience, his appreciation for Socrates can hardly surprise. His view of the faculty as a magisterial voice uncannily resembles Socrates's famous "divine or spiritual sign:" his *daimonion*. In Plato's *Apology*, which contains its fullest description, Socrates calls it "a voice," which "turns me away from something I am about to do" and recounts how this "spiritual manifestation [*daimonion*] frequently opposed me, even in small matters, when I was about to do something wrong."[99] Just as in Newman, we encounter in Plato an inward voice, a magisterial dictate, and the suggestion of a relationship to the divine. Socrates's resolute obedience to conscience—his *daimonion*— explained his moral authority and his capacity to accurately sift the truth out of the Greek religious traditions.

If we recall Newman's earliest accounts of heathen religious knowledge, the contrast with his present views could hardly be more striking. Then, as now, he based himself on "the extant works of heathen writers," but what he now drew from those works was directly opposite to what he had previously concluded.[100] All the doctrines he now regarded as attainable, and at times attained, by the heathen—the being and attributes of God, our duty to obey him, and a future state and judgment—he had reserved to Jews and Christians prior to December 1825. By April 1830, he declared, by contrast, that it "may be even questioned whether there be any essential character of Scripture doctrine which is without its place in this moral revelation" (that is, natural religion):

> For here is the belief in a Principle exterior to the mind to which it is instinctively drawn, infinitely exalted, perfect, incomprehensible; the hopes & the fears of a judgment to come; the knowledge of unbounded benevolence, wisdom, & power, as traced in the visible creation — and of moral laws unlimited in their operation — further there is something of hope respecting

96. JHN, No. 234, "Natural and revealed religion," BOA A.9.4, 8–9 (*OUS*, 22).
97. JHN to Richard Hurrell Froude, September 11, 1829, *LD* 2, 163.
98. Richard Hurrell Froude to JHN, August 11, 1831, *LD* 2, 349.
99. Plato, "Apology," 31c-d, 40a, in *Complete Works*, 29, 35.
100. JHN, No. 234, "Natural and revealed religion," BOA A.9.4, 9 (*OUS*, 22).

the availableness of repentance, so far (i.e.) as suffices for religious support; lastly, there is expertness in the rule of duty, increasing with the earnestness with which obedience to it is cultivated.[101]

In part, this description of the religious condition of the heathen repeats views developed between late 1825 and early 1829, but the final clause reveals the shift in vision. Instead of presenting natural religiosity as hopeless and forlorn (1825), or as resulting, at best, in a confession of moral impotence (1829), Newman allowed for both moral growth and the acquisition of substantial religious knowledge in proportion not so much to faith, let alone to the felt apprehension of Christ's atoning sacrifice, but to how earnestly conscience is obeyed.

Conscience and Revealed Religion

Newman held that natural religion not only issued from conscience but also depended on historic traces of revelation. He elaborated on the interplay between the two in a memorandum of August 1830 originally intended for (but never sent to) his brother Charles. "I believe in an *universal* revelation," Newman stated there, "the doctrines of which are preserved by tradition in the world at large, in Scripture, in the Christian Church. The only difference in this respect between us and the heathen nations, is, that *we* have a written, *they* an unwritten memorial of it."[102] And even this difference should not be absolutized. The world of religion is not "simply divisible into classes," not of converted and unconverted, and not of those with and without revelation.[103] Echoing Butler's *Analogy*, he explained: "Revelation is a gift, like all gifts, diffused with indefinite inequality over the earth." Just as the gifts of Providence in the natural realm, things like health, wealth, and weather, are distributed unequally, so God's gift of revelation "varies indefinitely in its degree." Thus, "Islamism in its different forms, and Polytheism besides in its numberless varieties, contain revelations from God. I do not say they *are* revelations, but they *embody* revealed truths with more or less clearness and fullness. And this has ever been the case since Noah's time."[104] Newman found patristic confirmation for the idea of universal revelation when he studied Clement of Alexandria († c. 215) in 1831, in preparation of the volume that would become *The Arians of the Fourth Century*.

---

101. JHN, No. 234, "Natural and revealed religion," BOA A.9.4, 9–10 (*OUS*, 22–23).

102. JHN, "Memorandum on Revelation," *LD* 2, 281. There is no evidence for Francis McGrath's contention (*John Henry Newman*, 41) that Newman's views on the universal extent of revelation derived from Justin Martyr, since Newman had already hit on the idea in early 1826, two years before he read Justin Martyr.

103. JHN, "Memorandum on Revelation," *LD* 2, 281.

104. JHN, "Memorandum on Revelation," *LD* 2, 281.

The "Alexandrian school" to which Clement belonged upheld a distinct doctrinal tenet that Newman termed *"the divinity of Traditionary Religion."*[105] Newman's description of this idea in the *Arians* echoed the memorandum for Charles. It held that revelation is "an universal, not a partial gift," so that "there is something true and divinely revealed, in every religion all over the earth," even if "the Church of God ever has had, and the rest of mankind never have had, *authoritative documents* of truth."[106] Citing Clement's conviction that the Greeks had received philosophy as their "covenant" in preparation of Christ, he considered the truths contained in heathen religion a distinct *"dispensation of Paganism."*[107] He even believed that God remained active among the heathen: "the traditions, thus originally delivered to mankind at large, have been secretly re-animated and enforced by new communications from the unseen world."[108] Scripture offered numerous instances of this fact. Just think of "the dreams of Pharaoh and Abimelech," or of "Nebuchadnezzar," Or take the story of Job, who "was a Pagan in the same sense in which the Eastern nations are Pagans in the present day," but who "heard the voice of God out of the whirlwind."[109] These examples suggest that "there may have been heathen poets and sages, or sibyls again, in a certain extent divinely illuminated, and organs through whom religious and moral truth was conveyed to their countrymen."[110] Socrates, again, would have been among the number.

Given that such illumination was rare, limited, and unsupported by miraculous evidence, obedience to conscience remains the key to become good and acquire religious truth. In his memorandum for Charles, Newman argued that "to all men,"

> light enough is given for practical religious purposes — enough to lead them to heaven, and to condemn them if they do not employ themselves in disciplining and changing their moral nature. For all have a natural conscience, which at once exhorts them to virtue and by an instinctive vigor extracts from even the worst religious systems those better parts and real truths which relate to the being, providence, and moral governance of God.[111]

---

105. *The Arians of the Fourth Century, their Doctrine, Temper, and Conduct, Chiefly as Exhibited in the Councils of the Church, between A.D. 325, and A.D. 381* (London: J. G. & F. Rivington, 1833), 88, hereafter *Ari*.

106. *Ari.*, 88–89.

107. *Ari.*, 89; Clement, *Stromata*, bk. 6, chap. 8. The phrase also occurs in the printed edition of Newman's 1830 university sermon, but its position in the manuscript (as an insertion on the facing page) as well as the handwriting, suggest that he added the clause later, after he had become familiar with the *Stromata* in the course of 1831. See *OUS*, 22; No. 234, "Natural and revealed religion," BOA A.9.4, 8v, 9.

108. *Ari.*, 89.

109. *Ari.*, 90.

110. *Ari.*, 91.

111. JHN "Memorandum on Revelation," *LD* 2, 282.

God enables every human being to know him and improve her moral character, that is, to become engaged in the process of conversion. Heathens, just like Christians, are responsible for how well they turn out. The difference is one of degree only. The "whole world," Newman argued, is "under religious training" but "with varying light." The successful outcome of such a course of religious training depends on earnest obedience to conscience. Such obedience not only enables the acquisition of truth and goodness within a specific religion but also secures the passage between one tradition and another: "every good man under a worse religious system will (as a general rule) joyfully accept the news of a more perfect system, and after examination pass on into it." The obverse is also true: "the fact of a person being an unbeliever under the light of the Gospel truth, is to my mind a general evidence of a defect in his moral character or ἦθος."[112] Had John sent the memorandum, Charles would have been stung by the remark, which unambiguously attributed his rejection of Christianity to a moral flaw. Some things had not changed.

In a sermon of September 1830, Newman illustrated the positive relation between virtue and religious progress from the history of the Jewish king Josiah.[113] Writing before historical criticism deconstructed the Old Testament narrative, Newman took the story of Josiah's finding of the Book of the Law in the Temple at face value. Nevertheless (or for that reason), the sermon is a fine character study, one of his best, written with great literary sensitivity to its Old Testament sources. Josiah was ignorant of Moses's Law when he succeeded to the throne at the tender age of eight, brought up as he was "among very wicked men—in a corrupt court— after an apostasy of more than half a century; far from GOD'S Prophets, and in the midst of idols."[114] Yet, when he was sixteen, "he began to seek after the GOD of David his father."[115] Given his context, hardly anyone, whether Christian or heathen, could be "in more disadvantageous circumstances than Josiah" for such a quest. And yet he succeeded, because he "had that, which all men have, heathen as well as Christians, till they pervert or blunt it—a natural sense of right and wrong; and he did not blunt it . . . he acknowledged a constraining force in the Divine voice within him—he heard and obeyed."[116] Josiah listened to his conscience and found God: "amid all the various worships offered to his acceptance, this same inward sense of his, strengthened by practice, unhesitatingly chose out the true one, the worship of the GOD of Israel. It chose between the better and the worse, thought it could not have discovered the better of itself."[117]

112. JHN, "Memorandum on Revelation," *LD* 2, 282.
113. Compare Attard, *Conscience*, 84–86.
114. JHN, No. 257, "Josiah, A Pattern for the Ignorant," September 5, 1830, *PlS*, 229.
115. JHN, No. 257, "Josiah," *PlS*, 230; 2 Chronicles 34:3.
116. JHN, No. 257, "Josiah," *PlS*, 230.
117. JHN, No. 257, "Josiah," *PlS*, 231. Note, once again, the dialectic between conscience as a way toward God and historic revelations which provide the material, so to speak, for religious belief.

And thus, at twenty, and still without the law, Josiah began a reform. He took "such measures as natural conscience suggested," that is, he "put away idolatry generally," for conscience speaks of one God only.[118] He did so, Newman insisted, without "accurate knowledge."[119] Josiah "set out, not knowing wither he went. But this is the rule of GOD's providence, that those who act up to their light, shall be rewarded with clearer light. To him that hath, more shall be given."[120] And thus, Josiah found "the Book of the Law," not before but "in the *course* of his reformations."[121]

Josiah, then, progressed from natural to revealed religion, because he earnestly sought God by attending to conscience. Again, Newman was not particular about terms. The "strict virtue" Josiah displayed "is called *faith*, he argued. But he immediately added:

> It is no matter whether we call it faith or conscientiousness, they are in substance one and the same: where there is faith, there is conscientiousness—where there is conscientiousness, there is faith; they may be distinguished from each other in words, but they are not divided in fact. They belong to one, and but one habit of mind—dutifulness; they show themselves in obedience, in the careful anxious observance of GOD's will, however we learn it.[122]

The point is almost word for word that of *Faith and Obedience*. There, he stressed the dimension of obedience in the one character that is acceptable to God. Here, he stresses the dimension of faith, understood as a turn from the seen to the unseen. It "is called *faith*," he explained, "because it implies reliance on the mere word of the unseen God overpowering the temptations of sight." Whether we "read and accept his word in Scripture . . . or His word in our conscience . . . in either case, it is by following it, in spite of the seductions of the world around us, that we please GOD."[123]

Newman explained the passage from natural to revealed religion more systematically in a sermon of October 31, tellingly titled *Obedience to conscience leads to the knowledge of Christ*.[124] Early in the sermon, he concisely summed up its main argument: "obedience to conscience leads to obedience to the Gospel, which, instead of being something different altogether, is but the completion and perfection of that religion which natural conscience teaches."[125] The obedience of

118. JHN, No. 257, "Josiah," *PlS*, 231.
119. JHN, No. 257, "Josiah," *PlS*, 231.
120. JHN, No. 257, "Josiah," *PlS*, 231–32.
121. JHN, No. 257, "Josiah," *PlS*, 232.
122. JHN, No. 257, "Josiah," *PlS*, 237.
123. JHN, No. 257, "Josiah," *PlS*, 237.
124. JHN, No. 265, "Obedience to conscience leads to the knowledge of Christ," October 31, 1830, *Serm.* 5, 497, published as, "Obedience to God the Way to Faith in Christ," *PlS*, 297–306.
125. JHN, No. 265, "Obedience to God," *PlS*, 297.

natural religion, moreover, is not just of the same character as Christian obedience; it is also its precondition. Scripture tells us "again and again, that obedience
to God leads on to faith in Christ; that it is the only recognized way to Christ,
and, that therefore, to believe in Him, ordinarily implies that we are living in obedience to God."[126] Religion is a quest: we progress from worse to better depending
on how earnestly we *seek*. This applies not only to someone like Josiah, who
passed from natural religion onto Judaism, but also to Jews who embrace Christ.
The New Testament clearly instances this. The "early Christian Church," Newman
observed, "was principally composed of those who had long been in the habit
of obeying their consciences carefully, and so preparing themselves for CHRIST'S
religion."[127] Zacharias, Elisabeth, Mary's husband Joseph, Simeon, Nathanael,
Joseph of Arimathea, the heathen centurion Cornelius—all are qualified as righteous, just, or good *before* they come to know of Christ. Even St Paul is no exception to this rule, for though he sinned in persecuting the church, he "was not
transgressing, but obeying his conscience" when he was converted on the way to
Damascus. His "conscience was ill-informed," and he should have known better,
but still "he obeyed it such as it was."[128] St Paul was doing what he strongly
believed was right: "not sinning *against light*, but *in* darkness."[129]

People, therefore, should not take comfort from St Paul's case by hoping for
a sudden conversion. It is, at most, a ground of hope "to furious, intolerant bigots,
and bloodthirsty persecutors" who act up to "their own notions of duty." It offers
none whatsoever "to the slothful and negligent and lukewarm."[130] Obviously, this
is not to say that sinners cannot come to Christ. "Of course all who come to HIM
will be received," Newman argued, but the question is "whether they are likely to
come."[131] And here, he answered in the negative:

> When sinners truly repent, then, indeed, they are altogether brothers in
> CHRIST'S kingdom with those who have not in the same sense "need of
> repentance;" but that they should repent at all is (alas!) so far from being
> likely, that when the unexpected event takes place it causes such joy in heaven
> (from the marvelousness of it) as is not even excited by the ninety and nine
> just persons who need no such change of mind.[132]

This is a striking reading of the parable of the lost sheep. It illustrates Newman's
deep-seated conviction that obedience alone is a proper preparation for the recep-

---

126. JHN, No. 265, "Obedience to God," *PlS*, 297.
127. JHN, No. 265, "Obedience to God," *PlS*, 301. See also *Ari.*, 52.
128. JHN, No. 265, "Obedience to God," *PlS*, 304.
129. JHN, No. 265, "Obedience to God," *PlS*, 303.
130. JHN, No. 265, "Obedience to God," *PlS*, 304.
131. JHN, No. 265, "Obedience to God," *PlS*, 302.
132. JHN, No. 265, "Obedience to God," *PlS*, 302. See Luke 15:1–7.

tion of Christ. Sinners, therefore, are always at a disadvantage, even if they do repent. A "sinner, who has formed his character upon unbelief," he had argued the week before, "can overcome himself and new make his heart . . . in only one way, in *the way of His commandments*."[133] There are no shortcuts, only "a slow, tedious, toilsome self-discipline; slow, tedious, and toilsome, that is, to one who has been long hardening himself in a dislike of it."[134] As he put it a few weeks later, giving another remarkable twist to a familiar gospel trope: "Christ's 'yoke is easy,' true, to those who are accustomed to it, not to the unbroken neck."[135] There is simply no way around obedience as the principle of religious progress.

Revelation and the Incarnate God

Newman's conviction that obedience to conscience and obedience to Christ are on a continuum was mirrored in his understanding of the relation between the object of natural and of revealed religion. Before, he had conceived of the atonement as the distinctive trait of Christianity. Now, his account of the unicity of revealed religion centered on the doctrine of the incarnation. Natural religion, he argued in his university sermon, taught "the infinite power & majesty, the wisdom & goodness, the moral governance, the intelligence, & in one sense the unity of the Deity."[136] But "it gave little or no information respecting what may be called His <u>Personality</u>."[137] Forty years later, when annotating his university sermons for a third edition, he questioned this judgment. He considered it "too strongly said" and "inconsistent" with an 1832 sermon in the same volume.[138] Even at the time, it did not quite reflect his considered view. In both earlier and contemporaneous texts, he always assumed that conscience witnesses to an agent, rather than a mere principle.[139]

So why this downplaying of natural religion? A note prefixed to the manuscript of the sermon suggests that it had more to do with his understanding of Christianity than with his take on natural religion. The note is addressed to an unknown correspondent (probably an Oriel colleague) and transcribes, in Greek, part of the opening verse of St John's first Epistle, which, Newman wrote, "seems to me to express very vividly the feeling you were speaking of relative to a

133. JHN, No. 264, "Pride trusts reason more than conscience," October 24, 1830, published as "The Self-wise Inquirer," *PaS* 1, 259.

134. JHN, No. 264, "The Self-wise Inquirer," *PaS* 1, 259–60.

135. JHN, No. 268, "Obedience the Remedy," *PaS*, 271; Matthew 11:30.

136. JHN, No. 234, "Natural and revealed religion," BOA A.9.4, 11 (*OUS*, 23).

137. JHN, No. 234, "Natural and revealed religion," BOA A.9.4, 11 (*OUS*, 23).

138. JHN, *Fifteen Sermons Preached before the University of Oxford, between A.D. 1826 and 1843* (London: Rivingtons, 1872), 22n1.

139. Think of his 1825 and 1829 accounts of natural religion, his sermons on prayer and on Josiah, and his letter to Charles on revelation.

personal God."[140] It was this text about which he preached his university sermon: "That which was from the beginning, which we have heard, which we have seen with our eyes, which we have looked upon, and our hands have handled."[141] Brief as it is, the note crucially links the idea of the incarnation with the idea of a personal God. God's personhood is manifested in his coming in the flesh. It is this unique notion, vividly expressed by St John, that struck Newman so deeply that he thought natural religion paled in comparison. And yet, he presented the relation between the natural and revealed religious object as fundamentally continuous.

Belief in the incarnation, Newman argued in his sermon, allows for the keeping together of two aspects of religious truth separated in Greco-Roman thought. The God of heathen philosophy embodied intellectual and moral perfection but remained abstract and unrelatable. The pagan philosopher's "conviction of the <u>Infinitude</u> & <u>Eternity</u> of the Divine nature" could not "lead to any just idea of [God's] <u>Personality</u>, since there can be no circumscribing lineaments of the Immeasurable, no external condition, or fortune to that Being who is all in all."[142] The idea of personality is incommensurable with the idea of the absolute. Polytheistic religion did not remedy this shortcoming. For all its concreteness, it could not credibly introduce the personal into the abstract philosophical conception of God, because it degraded "His Invisible majesty by unworthy, multiplied and inconsistent images of Him."[143] At best, it underscored the religious need for concrete figures, but it did not supply a satisfying image of the divine. Newman concluded:

> The God of philosophy was infinitely great, but unreal — the God of paganism was intelligible, but degraded by human conceptions — reason and nature could produce no joint work — it was left for an express revelation to propose the object in which they would both be reconciled & to satisfy the desires of both in a real & manifested incarnation of the Deity.[144]

Human beings' natural striving toward God tends to devolve either into an exercise of abstract reason, which ignores God's personal character, or into a projection of the imagination, which yields concrete but all too human mythologies, irreconcilable with what reason represents as the good and the true. The Christian revelation, by contrast, satisfies the yearnings of both the intellect and the religious imagination in the incarnation of the Son.

140. JHN, No. 234, "Natural and revealed religion," BOA A.9.4, prefixed note.

141. JHN, No. 234, "Natural and revealed religion," BOA A.9.4, prefixed note: "ὃ ἦν ἀπ᾽ ἀρχῆς, ὃ ἀκηκόαμεν, ὃ ἑωράκαμεν τοῖς ὀφθαλμοῖς ἡμῶν, ὃ ἐθεασαμεθα [sic], καὶ αἱ χεῖρες ἡμῶν ἐψηλάφησαν" (1 John 1:1).

142. JHN, No. 234, "Natural and revealed religion," BOA A.9.4, 12 (OUS, 24).

143. JHN, No. 234, "Natural and revealed religion," BOA A.9.4, 14–15, 14v (OUS, 25).

144. JHN, No. 234, "Natural and revealed religion," BOA A.9.4, 15 (OUS, 25–26).

In Christ, the one God, without compromising his divinity, becomes a tangible, concrete human being. "In <u>His</u> life," Newman explained, "we discern the real nature of the Invisible God, drawn out into action in accommodation to our weakness."[145] In the New Testament, the moral perfection ascribed by philosophers to the Absolute is predicated of a concrete human being. Christ has "all those abstract titles of moral excellence bestowed upon Him which philosophers have invented — He is the Λόγος, the light, the life, the truth, wisdom, the divine glory."[146] As St John had it in the text Newman preached on: "the Life was manifested & we <u>have seen</u> it."[147] St Paul employed the same logic when he engaged the Epicurean and Stoic philosophers of his day on the Areopagus. Having noticed an "altar dedicated to the Unknown God," he made known to them "Him 'whom they ignorantly worshiped.'"[148] He began "to condemn their polytheistic and anthropomorphic errors, and to disengage the notion of a Deity from the base earthly attributes in which Heathen religion had encompassed it."[149] He appealed to Greek poetry and philosophy (Aratus and Epimenides) to do so, and thus acknowledged "the abstract correctness of the philosophical system" of the heathen.[150]

Next, however, "he preaches unto them Jesus and the Resurrection — i.e. he embodies the moral character of the Deity in those historical notices of it which have been made the medium of the Christian manifestation of His attributes."[151] St Paul, in other words, presents Christ as the summation of all that is good in natural religion. Christ's life "brings together and condenses truths concerning the chief good & the laws of our being, which are seen straggling over the surface of the moral world."[152]

Christ is the epitome of God's personhood, but a preference for personality over abstraction marks all of revelation. The Bible constantly aims "to relate some course of action, some conduct, a life (to speak in human terms) of the One Supreme God," emphasizing "those marks of character . . . which imply the most extreme opposition to an eternal fated system."[153] Throughout scripture, God is represented as having "inherent free will, power of change . . . long-suffering, placability, repentance, delight in the praises & thanksgivings of His

145. JHN, No. 234, "Natural and revealed religion," BOA A.9.4, 18 (*OUS*, 27).
146. JHN, No. 234, "Natural and revealed religion," BOA A.9.4, 20 (*OUS*, 29).
147. JHN, No. 234, "Natural and revealed religion," BOA A.9.4, 20 (*OUS*, 29); 1 John 1:1.
148. JHN, No. 234, "Natural and revealed religion," BOA A.9.4, 15 (*OUS*, 26); Acts 17:22–34.
149. JHN, No. 234, "Natural and revealed religion," BOA A.9.4, 15–16 (*OUS*, 26).
150. JHN, No. 234, "Natural and revealed religion," BOA A.9.4, 16 (*OUS*, 26).
151. JHN, No. 234, "Natural and revealed religion," BOA A.9.4, 16 (*OUS*, 26).
152. JHN, No. 234, "Natural and revealed religion," BOA A.9.4, 19–20 (*OUS*, 29). See also No. 228, "The Liturgy teaching doctrine — concerning means of grace," February 28, 1830, *Serm.* 1, 82–83; JHN, No. 337, "Revelation of God in the New Testament," May 1, 1832, *Serm.* 3, 334–36.
153. JHN, No. 234, "Natural and revealed religion," BOA A.9.4, 16, 17 (*OUS*, 26, 27).

creatures, failure of purpose, & the prerogative of doing what He will with His own."[154] God, in other words, is presented as a being that can genuinely act and be affected. In the New Testament, this idea of divine personhood is stretched to the point of paradox:

> the Divine character is exhibited to us not merely as love, or mercy, or holiness (attributes which have a vagueness in our conceptions of them from their immensity), but these & others as seen in an <u>act of self-denial</u> — a mysterious principle when ascribed to Him who is all things in Himself, but especially calculated (from the mere meaning of the term) to impress upon our minds the personal character of the Object of our worship. 'God so loved the world,' that He <u>gave up</u> His only Son; and the Son of God "pleased not Himself."[155]

In these passages, the Absolute is described not just as an agent but as an agent capable of denying or limiting its own capacity for agency for the sake of something else. Thus, the Father denies himself by giving up his Son for humanity, and the Son denies himself to please the Father. The latter idea even inscribes an act of self-denial into the immanent Godhead, which is thus not only in relationship with creation but, as Trinity, relational in itself. The distinguishing mark of revealed religion, then, is its emphasis on God's personhood, and, in Christianity, on its definitive manifestation in the incarnate Son.[156]

None of this detracts from natural religion, whose importance is, in fact, enhanced. The idea of God incarnate as the embodiment of natural religion means that the "revealed system is rooted deep in the natural course of things, of which it is merely the result and completion."[157] Thus, revelation is "evidenced & interpreted by those awful far-reaching analogies of mediation & vicarious suffering, which we discern in the visible course of the world."[158] This was another of Newman's creative reworkings of Butler, facilitated, perhaps, by Keble and

---

154. JHN, No. 234, "Natural and revealed religion," BOA A.9.4, 17 (*OUS*, 27).

155. JHN, No. 234, "Natural and revealed religion," BOA A.9.4, 17–18 (*OUS*, 27); John 3:16; Romans 15:3. See No. 232, "The Duty of Self-Denial," *PlS*, 60–61.

156. The centrality of the personal in Christianity extends beyond its conceptualization of God or the incarnation. There is a "method of personation (so to call it) . . . carried throughout the revealed system." Scripture consistently witnesses to a personal reality rather than an abstract system. Thus, "the principle of good, when implanted & progressively realized in our hearts, is still continually personified" (as the Holy Spirit). Likewise, "the doctrine of original sin is centered in the person of Adam," while the "evil principle is revealed to us in the person of its author, Satan." And even when actual persons are not concerned, the same method is applied, so that the church becomes "invested with a metaphorical personality" (No. 234, "Natural and revealed religion," BOA A.9.4, 23–24 [*OUS*, 31–32]). See Poston, *The Antagonist Principle*, esp. 50–52.

157. JHN, No. 234, "Natural and revealed religion," BOA A.9.4, 26 (*OUS*, 33).

158. JHN, No. 234, "Natural and revealed religion," BOA A.9.4, 25 (*OUS*, 33).

Froude.[159] In the *Analogy*, Butler had countered Deist objections to Christ's mediation and atonement by pointing to analogous processes of mediation and vicarious suffering in the natural and social world. This was a negative argument, aimed
at showing the Deists' inconsistency, which Newman turned into a positive one.
Natural religion, on his view, points to and prepares for Christianity by deeply
familiarizing people with the realities of mediation and vicarious suffering. At the
same time, these natural analogies remain diffuse until they can be seen to converge on Christ, who "has interpreted . . . the difficult language of the natural
system."[160] In this way, Newman even turned the "very deficiency of nature"—
its lack of divine personhood—into a strength. He made it the lock to Christianity's key. While the biblical "doctrines of atonement & mediation are paralleled
by phenomena in the visible course of things," revelation provides a religious
breakthrough in the "one solitary doctrine, which from its nature has no parallel
in this world, an incarnation of the Divine Essence."[161] Christ, then, as God incarnate, comes to comprehend into a single personal center the entire history of
divine providence.

Newman's new emphasis on the incarnation increased his aversion to religious systems that denied Christ's divinity (and, by extension, the Trinity). By doing
so, Newman argued, "Anti-trinitarians," such as Deists and Socinians, "go far to
destroy the very advantages which the revealed system possesses over the natural;
& throw back the science of morals & of man's supreme good into that state of
vagueness and inefficiency from which Christianity has extricated it."[162] It is only
because Christ is God that his life can be regarded as embodying the divine
attributes. If it can no longer function in this way, religious knowledge lacks its
focal point and risks relapsing into the disarray of natural religion. This danger is
aggravated by the form anti-Trinitarian objections to Christ's divinity usually take.
As early as 1821, Newman had identified the imposing of a criterion of rational
perspicuity on religious truth as the core problem of Deism and Socinianism.
Both positions are rooted in the principle that "a true religion can have no mysteries" and thence infer, respectively, "either that Christianity is not a true religion
because it contains mysteries—or that it contains no mysteries, because it is a true
religion."[163] But Newman now realized that a consistent application of this principle endangers the notion of a personal God altogether.

Socinians object to "a plurality of Persons in the Godhead" but forget that
it is just as "inconceivable how personality can in any way be an attribute of the

<hr>

159. On the creative uses of Butler in Keble's circle, see Pereiro, Ethos *and the Oxford Movement*, 93.

160. JHN, No. 234, "Natural and revealed religion," BOA A.9.4, 26 (*OUS*, 33).

161. JHN, No. 234, "Natural and revealed religion," BOA A.9.4, 27 (*OUS*, 33–34).

162. JHN, No. 234, "Natural and revealed religion," BOA A.9.4, 27 (*OUS*, 34).

163. [JHN], "On the Study of the Mathematics," 295; *LD* 1, 104. See p. 25 in this book.

Infinite Incommunicable essence of the Deity, or in what particular sense it is ascribed to Him."[164] This notion of divine ineffability is key to Newman's argument. The natural religious conception of God did not fall short because heathens lacked the conceptual tools that Christians have. No one, either before or after revelation, can rationally establish *how* the ineffable God is personal. The best that human beings *can* come up with, is what the Greeks *did* come up with, namely, two divergent visions of the divine, as either an abstract absolute, or a society of all too human deities. Revelation, then, does not *explain* God's personhood, it merely *declares* it. In consequence, as Newman noted in a crossed-out sentence in the manuscript, it is "equally an act of simple faith (unsuspiciously accepting the word revealed,) to adopt the notion of a God in unity of person or in trinity."[165] For that reason, the Socinian objection to Trinitarian doctrine proves too much. To "be consistent," Socinians "should find a difficulty in the doctrine of an Unity of Person, as well as in that of a Trinity, and, having ceased to be Athanasians, should not stop till they become Pantheists," that is, until they revert to the impotent heathen philosophy that Christ came to surpass.[166]

Evangelicalism and the Person of Christ

Newman's conception of revelation as centering on the person of God incarnate not only jarred with Socinianism but was also at odds with the crucicentrism of evangelical theology. Evangelicals, Newman noted in his university sermon, pride themselves on "<u>preaching Christ,</u>" by which they mean, as he used to put it himself, "the doctrine of Christ crucified."[167] He now resolutely opposed such an unwarranted reduction of Christ's person and life to the atonement. Preaching Christ, he argued, does not mean "putting natural religion out of sight, nor the separating one doctrine of the gospel from the rest as having an exclusive claim to the name of gospel."[168] Instead, it means "the displaying <u>all</u> that nature & Scripture teach concerning Divine Providence (for they teach the same truths) whether of His majesty, or love, or mercy, or holiness, or His fearful anger at sin, thro' the medium of the life of His Son Jesus Christ."[169] The object of religious belief, then, is the same in natural and revealed religion. "It is not that <u>natural</u> teaching gives merely the law, & <u>Christian</u> teaching gives the tidings of pardon," Newman

---

164. JHN, No. 234, "Natural and revealed religion," BOA A.9.4, 28 (*OUS*, 34).

165. JHN, No. 234, "Natural and revealed religion," BOA A.9.4, 28.

166. JHN, No. 234, "Natural and revealed religion," BOA A.9.4, 27v (*OUS*, 34).

167. JHN, No. 234, "Natural and revealed religion," BOA A.9.4, 30 (*OUS*, 36); JHN to Mrs Newman, July 28, 1824, *LD* 1, 181.

168. JHN, No. 234, "Natural and revealed religion," BOA A.9.4, 30 (*OUS*, 36).

169. JHN, No. 234, "Natural and revealed religion," BOA A.9.4, 30 (*OUS*, 36).

argued, "for nature speaks of God's goodness as well as of His severity, & Christ surely of His severity as well as of His goodness."[170]

Instead, the crucial difference is the clarity and comprehensiveness with which the religious object is represented: "in the Christian scheme we find <u>all</u> the divine attributes (not mercy only tho' mercy pre-eminently) brought out & urged upon us, which were but latent in the visible course of things."[171] The divine attributes are revealed in the whole of Christ's life and person, not just in the atonement, and we know that they are such because Christ is the Son of God incarnate. And thus, it is "the Divinity of Christ, rather than any doctrine drawn from a partial view of Scripture" that constitutes the fundamental and distinctive Christian truth.[172]

These two elements—the continuity of natural and revealed religion and the centrality of Christ's personhood—are paralleled in Newman's account of the relation between the natural and the Christian moral character. Just as Christ is the personal center who focuses and exalts the disparate truths of natural religion, so the Christian saint comprehends and elevates the various natural virtues. In a university sermon in March 1831, Newman qualified the difference between the "extraordinary Christian πνεῦμα, and the virtue and faith of human nature," in precisely such terms:

> while they are the <u>same in kind</u>, the one is indefinitely higher in degree than the other, more rooted in the mind, more consistent, more vigorous, of more intense purity, of more sovereign authority, more lasting — the choicest elements of our moral nature being collected, fostered, matured into a determinate character by the gracious influences of the Holy Ghost.[173]

This saintly character, in turn, mirrors Christ, who is not only its model but actively indwells the subject in whom this character is formed. We should, therefore, always "urge & illustrate virtue in the name & by the example of our blessed Lord."[174] Accordingly, "the gospels are the great instruments of fixing and instructing our minds in a religious course — the epistles being rather comments on them than intended to supersede them, as is sometimes inconsiderately

170. JHN, No. 234, "Natural and revealed religion," BOA A.9.4, 30–31 (*OUS*, 36).

171. JHN, No. 234, "Natural and revealed religion," BOA A.9.4, 31 (*OUS*, 36).

172. JHN, No. 234, "Natural and revealed religion," BOA A.9.4, 30v (*OUS*, 37).

173. JHN, No. 288, "Spiritual excellence, which the gospel promises us, is the completion of natural virtue," March 6, 1831, BOA A.9.4, 10; "Evangelical Sanctity the Completion of Natural Virtue," *Fifteen Sermons*, 43. The sermon was published only in the third, 1871 edition of the university sermons. See also No. 233, "The Liturgy forming the character — viz. to charity. — The Litany," April 4, 1830, *Serm.* 1, 106–7.

174. JHN, No. 234, "Natural and revealed religion," BOA A.9.4, 30 (*OUS*, 36).

maintained."[175] For the same reason, "the primitive creeds insist almost exclusively upon the facts, not the doctrines, of Christianity — it being thro' our Lord's <u>history embodying</u> the revelation that doctrine is to be taught." This is what it means to "preach Christ."[176]

Newman's understanding of Christ as embodying natural and revealed religion explains his growing aversion to the evangelical use of the atonement as an emotional stimulant to action or a sedative for guilt and despair. In a sermon of November 1830, Newman considered the case of people who "from ill health or other cause . . . fall into religious despondency" and worry about their salvation. Unsurprisingly, he considered "obedience to God's will" the only way to "soothe and calm the mind" of such people.[177] Many evangelicals, however, applied a different remedy to episodes of religious gloom. They try "to console themselves by those elevated Christian doctrines which St. Paul enlarges on; and others encourage them in it."[178] This is a grave mistake. "St. Paul's doctrine," the whole theology of Christ's atoning sacrifice, "is not intended for weak and unstable minds" but for mature Christians. Revelation not only integrates natural religion but also presumes it. Accordingly, there is an order to be observed in religious instruction, moving from the simple truths of natural religion to more arcane doctrines like the atonement. The proper reception of the latter is premised on a thorough knowledge and praxis of the former. It is only in "proportion as we gain strength" that "we shall be able to understand and profit by the full promises of the Christian covenant."[179]

Newman was thinking of a concrete pastoral case here: that of Mary Birmingham. His parish of St Mary the Virgin included the village of Littlemore, which he began to visit regularly soon after his induction in March 1828.[180] After a while, his brother Frank started to assist him with parish visits. One of their regular stops was the Birmingham family, whose daughter Mary was sickly when John first met her.[181] Both John and Frank called upon her regularly in the following years, as she was given to fits of religious anxiety. Frank once described

---

175. JHN, No. 234, "Natural and revealed religion," BOA A.9.4, 31 (*OUS*, 37). In *Faith and Obedience*, Newman wryly noted that the latter mistake caused many evangelicals to explain away Jesus' words about the necessity of keeping the commandments by means of St Paul's teaching of justification by faith (*PaS* 3, 84). See also No. 337, "Revelation of God in the New Testament," May 1, 1832, *Serm.* 3, 336: "If we study His [Christ's] life, as given us in the Gospels, we gain all the knowledge of God we can have here, all we *want* for our need, as His creatures whose duty it is to serve Him."

176. No. 234, "Natural and revealed religion," BOA A.9.4, 31–32 (*OUS*, 37).
177. JHN, No. 268, "Obedience the Remedy," *PaS* 1, 276, 277.
178. JHN, No. 268, "Obedience the Remedy," *PaS* 1, 277.
179. JHN, No. 268, "Obedience the Remedy," *PaS* 1, 277.
180. *LD* 2, 76–77.
181. "May 12, 1828," *LD* 2, 70; "June 19, 1828," *LD* 2, 76.

her to John as "deeply convinced of sin." She said she had "seven devils" and feared that "she was too bad to be saved."[182] Here was despondency indeed, and it was aggravated by an incident in the late spring of 1830, which involved her letting an unmarried man into the house, causing serious suspicions of impropriety (though little happened). Apparently, the man was an Oxford student, for Mary was afraid that the case would be brought before the proctors, the university officers responsible for discipline. For that reason, she asked John to offer a testimonial for her character, as he had been appointed proproctor on April 21.[183] Frank visited Mary after the incident and put her through the evangelical works, first stressing her sin and how she had "caused Christ to be blasphemed," and then elaborating on "the sympathy of Christ."[184] He had no doubt, however, that "God's grace" had made her "stop short in sin" and wrote to John: "she is really a child of God, and shall deeply repent, though thro' much suffering; and be restored for his mercy's sake."[185] From Frank's evangelical viewpoint, Mary was still on the side of the saved.

Unsurprisingly, John took issue with Frank's approach. "I give no credit to *words*," he summed up his position to Frank, "tho' a man spoke like an angel."[186] He did not believe that "the habit of religious conversation, the expression of opinions, fears, hopes, desires etc" said much about people's hearts. "My ground of sure hope as to another's spiritual state," he argued, "is the sight of a consistent *life*," and it was Mary's life that was in question.[187] John's comments entailed a fundamental critique of Frank's evangelical take on conversion. In 1827, he had pointed out to Frank that it is a mistake to think that baptized people have *no grace* because they lead inconsistent lives.[188] Now, he added that it is just as much of a mistake to think that because someone has religious feelings, or talks religiously, there is *grace only*. Of course, "she has wishes and views which could come only from God," but this does not mean that she is converted in any special sense, that is, more than any other baptized person. "Words," after all, "are no evidence by themselves — but works." And, considering the incident, John pointed out that he had "no evidence" that "she is much better than the world in general, or in any sense "a child of God," in which others around her are not."[189] Her error, he explained,

---

182. FWN to JHN, undated but before January 1830, BOA, Personal Collection, Francis William Newman, 2.

183. FWN to JHN, undated, BOA, Personal Collection, Francis William Newman; *LD* 2, 205. The four proproctors were deputies to the two proctors.

184. FWN to JHN, undated, BOA, Personal Collection, Francis William Newman, 3.

185. FWN to JHN, undated, BOA, Personal Collection, Francis William Newman, 3.

186. JHN to FWN, undated 1830, *LD* 2, 183.

187. JHN to FWN, undated 1830, *LD* 2, 183.

188. See pp. 142–43.

189. JHN to FWN, undated 1830, *LD* 2, 183.

is that of multitudes in the so-called religious world . . . who think they know
things because they can say them, and understand because they have heard
them — or, account themselves Christians because they use Scripture
phrases — or, to believe in Christ with the heart and to be changed in their
moral nature because they assent fully to certain doctrines (not hard to admit
as intellectual truths without any moral preparation) that we can do nothing
of ourselves, have no merit, or are saved by faith; — or (again) imagine they
have habits or a character when they have only feelings.[190]

Her error, in other words, was to have evangelical views of conversion; "or
rather," he added, this was "the error of some others in judging of her." This
was a clear jibe at Frank, for John did not think Mary herself had ever pretended
to "special holiness."[191] It was Frank who had entered her as converted on the
evangelical register.

Given their contrasting diagnoses of the case, John could only lament Frank's
"method of treatment . . . as irrelevant, if not mischievous."[192] To "address her
as a child of God except so far as she has the general privileges of a Christian,
and to apply high Christian doctrines as medicines, John argued, is "but to inflame
the disease — the disease, namely, of mistaking words for things."[193] Habitual
obedience is the only proper preparation for receiving truths such as the atonement; they "require a faith . . . grounded on deep self-knowledge and a long course
of self discipline [*sic*]."[194] One must be ready for certain teachings, and whether
one is ready depends on one's habit of obedience, not on one's emotional state.
Frank had spoken either to no effect or with the bad effect of convincing Mary
that the use of evangelical formulae made her a true Christian. He had made the
evangelical mistake of resorting to theory to solve a practical problem, that is, to
talk of the doctrine of the atonement to make a sinner amend. But the atonement
is not the answer to religious despondency. That answer is Christ, who embodies,
at once, nature and grace, law and gospel, obedience and faith. To believe, emulate,
and obey Christ, step by step, is the only path to sanctification

Newman found confirmation for these views in the Alexandrian church
fathers. Their catechetical schools embodied the pedagogical model he had discerned in St Paul and suggested to Frank: the practice of dispensing Christian
truth according to the level of people's religious proficiency. What catechumens
were taught, he observed in the *Arians*, "varied with the time of their discipleship,
advancing from the most simple principles of natural religion to the peculiar

190. JHN to FWN, undated 1830, *LD* 2, 183.
191. JHN to FWN, undated 1830, *LD* 2, 183.
192. JHN to FWN, undated 1830, *LD* 2, 183. Note that "mischievous" does not bear the sense
of "naughtiness" or "petty annoyance" here, but that of "inflicting real harm."
193. JHN to FWN, undated 1830, *LD* 2, 184.
194. JHN to FWN, undated 1830, *LD* 2, 184.

doctrines of the Gospel, from moral truths to the Christian mysteries."[195] Until after their baptism, "they were granted nothing beyond a formal and general account of the articles of the Christian faith; the exact and fully developed doctrines of the Trinity and the Incarnation, and still more, the doctrine of the Atonement . . . being the exclusive possession of the serious and practised Christians."[196]

The ancient catechumenate supplied Newman with an additional argument against the evangelical conviction of his own day that "the evangelical doctrines are the appointed instruments of conversion" because they transform the affections.[197] He now resolutely rejected this idea. Neither scripture nor the early church, he argued, offer any sanction, "whether of precept or of example, in behalf of the practice of stimulating the affections, (e.g., gratitude or remorse,) by means of the doctrine of the atonement, in order to the conversion of the hearers."[198] Instead, the "uniform method" of Apostles, evangelists, and church fathers is "to connect the gospel with natural religion, and to mark out obedience to the moral law as the ordinary means of attaining to a Christian faith, the higher evangelical truths . . . being received as the reward and confirmation of habitual piety."[199] These lines occur in the *Arians*, but they might have been written in 1830. Even though Newman learned of the catechumenal model from the Alexandrian fathers, it confirmed a set of theological principles he had discovered and formulated in his sermons over a year before.

A Private Reckoning

Newman summed up the implications of his new religious vision for evangelicalism in a lengthy manuscript paper entitled *Critical Remarks on Dr Chalmers' Theology*. Years later, he had trouble dating the manuscript correctly. On its top left corner, he scribbled "1830 or 1831?" but later crossed it out and put "1834?"[200] His last surmise was right, but the wavering is telling. Given its theme and content, the paper would have fit 1830 or 1831 just as well as 1834, but a reference to one of his *Parochial Sermons* ruled out such an early date, as he must have realized on closer inspection. In fact, the manuscript was written on March 17, 1834, for John Frederic Christie, a younger Oriel colleague with whom Newman had walked and dined two days earlier.[201] There must have been some

195. *Ari.*, 49.
196. *Ari.*, 49–50.
197. *Ari.*, 50.
198. *Ari.*, 50.
199. *Ari.*, 51.
200. JHN, *Critical Remarks on Dr Chalmers' Theology*, March 17, 1834, BOA A.9.1, 1.
201. *LD* 4, 206.

serious discussion, for Newman was prompted to pen a systematic demolition of evangelical theology and expound his alternative vision in 28 quarto pages. He focused, "by way of specimens," on the sermons of Thomas Chalmers (1780–1847), a hugely influential evangelical leader in the Church of Scotland and professor of theology in Edinburgh, but he left no doubt that his attack concerned all of evangelicalism.[202] The paper, in fact, was a reckoning: a settling of accounts, not least with his former self.

In the opening paragraph of the *Critical Remarks*, Newman set out to oppose "a religious system exerting considerable influence among us," which, he argued, could be characterized from a variety of viewpoints:

> It may be said to be the system, which supersedes the efficacy of baptism is [*sic*: as] the means of regeneration, and makes this change in our privileges, hope, condition &c. take place at a certain period independent altogether of this, & called the time of conversion. Or it may be described as the system which considers obedience upon conscience as different in kind from obedience on Christian faith; or which considers the love of God to be unknown to the human heart independent of [the] reception of the gospel revelation; — or again, which considers that the revelation of gospel mercy is the especial instrument of conversion, & that, by exciting the principle of gratitude; or again that human nature is totally corrupt — or again that there is a broad line between perfect Christian believers and men without faith, without any intermediate state — or that Christ satisfied the justice of God & that therefore the gospel is "a free & full salvation."[203]

Together, these propositions sum up evangelicalism, with a specific focus on its theory of conversion. To each of these propositions Newman had formerly subscribed, and all of them he now rejected.

Unlike his 1828 *Remarks on the Covenant of Grace*, which criticized distinct doctrinal elements of (Calvinistic) evangelicalism, Newman's 1834 paper attacked the fundamental structure of evangelical theology: the idea that faith in the atonement brings about conversion by changing the affections. Like his own early theology, Chalmers's account of conversion was premised on a Calvinistic commitment to total depravity, the idea that "till a man receives the gospel he cannot love God."[204] Accordingly, it is "the message of pardon . . . which makes him love God." More specifically, "the doctrine exciting this gratitude &c" is the "Atonement," which therefore becomes "the characteristic & sole instrument" of conversion, operating as "an appeal to the

---

202. Newman was thoroughly familiar with Chalmers's sermons, of which he had long owned a copy: Thomas Chalmers, *Sermons, Preached in the Tron Church, Glasgow*, 2nd ed. (Glasgow: Chalmers and Collins, 1821).

203. JHN, *Critical Remarks on Dr Chalmers' Theology*, BOA A.9.1, 1.

204. JHN, *Critical Remarks on Dr Chalmers' Theology*, BOA A.9.1, 12.

affections."[205] As a result, one's relation to the atonement becomes the touchstone of one's religious state: "the difference between a . . . truly religious man & a carnal, is his clearly appropriating the doctrine of the Atonement."[206]

In response to Chalmers, Newman boldly asserted the opposite view: "I . . . altogether deny that the gospel message is the instrument of conversion."[207] First, he dismissed the idea of total depravity. Human beings are "by nature in a certain religious state."[208] Despite human corruption, people are naturally oriented toward God: "in unregenerate man there is a principle (in its poor degree certainly, but still there) of love towards God . . . grounded on the existence of the rudiments of truth & holiness in man's natural heart."[209] Secondly, he rejected the idea that conversion is rooted in an "excited affection," as Chalmers suggested.[210] He agreed that "we must base faith upon some natural principle or other," but chose to follow the example of Christ, who "bases it on conscientious obedience."[211] The natural religiosity that issues from such obedience has both an affective and an intellectual component. When someone "obeys the light of nature," his religion "will consist in hope and fear, and more in fear than in hope, and its object will be the Divine Attributes."[212] Natural religion, then, is based on conscientious obedience, engenders the affective states of hope and fear, and has the divine attributes for its object.

Revelation does not fundamentally change this natural religiosity: "the essence of religion is the same with or without the gospel."[213] Like Butler, who also described natural religion as "essential religion," Newman believed that natural religion remained a basic constituent of Christianity.[214] Imagine a heathen like Cornelius, or even an Englishman raised as a Christian but with no "definite knowledge of the gospel doctrines." How would "his state of mind change" if he were to "believe in Christ as his satisfaction," Newman wondered. "Not at all," he answered, "in the kind of its religion, tho' very much in the degree and excellence of it."[215] He still fears, but less so. He still hopes, but more so. And his "view of the Divine attributes is far clearer & truer & fuller than before — yet not substantially different."[216] Faith in the doctrine of the atonement, then, does

205. JHN, *Critical Remarks on Dr Chalmers' Theology*, BOA A.9.1, 12.

206. JHN, *Critical Remarks on Dr Chalmers' Theology*, BOA A.9.1, 13.

207. JHN, *Critical Remarks on Dr Chalmers' Theology*, BOA A.9.1, 19.

208. JHN, *Critical Remarks on Dr Chalmers' Theology*, BOA A.9.1, 2.

209. JHN, *Critical Remarks on Dr Chalmers' Theology*, BOA A.9.1, 11–12.

210. JHN, *Critical Remarks on Dr Chalmers' Theology*, BOA A.9.1, 25.

211. JHN, *Critical Remarks on Dr Chalmers' Theology*, BOA A.9.1, 25.

212. JHN, *Critical Remarks on Dr Chalmers' Theology*, BOA A.9.1, 25, 2–3.

213. JHN, *Critical Remarks on Dr Chalmers' Theology*, BOA A.9.1, 8.

214. Butler, *The Analogy of Religion*, 197.

215. JHN, *Critical Remarks on Dr Chalmers' Theology*, BOA A.9.1, 3–4.

216. JHN, *Critical Remarks on Dr Chalmers' Theology*, BOA A.9.1, 4.

not fundamentally change the character of one's religiosity, and thus, it cannot be the operative principle of conversion. In "no case," Newman argued,

> do I make the gospel doctrine <u>as such</u> the instrument of a change from disobedience to obedience — the one set of men are obedient (in their degree) already — the others are converted but not by any particular doctrine of the gospel, but by a faithful manifestation of the Attributes of God.[217]

Whether a person accepts revealed religion depends on his former habit of obedience, as well as on "his previous view of God in all His varied Attributes fearful & amiable."[218] Revealed religion "does but fulfil the desires which his former view created" so that the change from natural religion to Christianity does not come about "by a <u>revolution</u> of sentiment, but a <u>completion</u>."[219] There is, in short, "nothing peculiar in the evangelical doctrines to <u>convert the heart</u> . . . a man who does not obey God under natural religion, will not under the Law, nor under the gospel."[220] The only revolution is the "revolution in changing from disobedience to obedience," and this is effected not by preaching the atonement to the disobedient but by proclaiming "the <u>whole</u> counsel of God — i.e. <u>all</u> the attributes of God in <u>harmony</u>."[221]

The idea, once again, is that belief in God is belief in a person, not in one specific doctrine, however touching it might be. Accordingly, all aspects of God's personality should be presented in a balanced way. Just as our knowledge of another human being depends on our being acquainted with all her character traits, and giving them their due respective weight, so our knowledge of God depends on apprehending his character as a whole. This is precisely why we preach Christ: he is "more tangible and visible — God is unseen — Christ is seen — the Attributes of God are scattered in nature, are collected in Christ."[222] As in his university sermon (to which he referred Christie), Newman appealed to St Paul's preaching in Athens, where "<u>natural religion</u> is taught, but in clearer, more definite form — with authority — and with (so to say) visibleness & personality — i.e. as shown in Christ."[223] The gospel, moreover, must be exhibited gradually. Just as in the *Arians*, Newman pointed out that "the disclosure of the Sacred Doctrines <u>varies with</u> the Christian proficiency of the hearer," so that the doctrine of the atonement is introduced not at the beginning but toward the end of a course of

---

217. JHN, *Critical Remarks on Dr Chalmers' Theology*, BOA A.9.1, 6.
218. JHN, *Critical Remarks on Dr Chalmers' Theology*, BOA A.9.1, 4.
219. JHN, *Critical Remarks on Dr Chalmers' Theology*, BOA A.9.1, 4.
220. JHN, *Critical Remarks on Dr Chalmers' Theology*, BOA A.9.1, 8.
221. JHN, *Critical Remarks on Dr Chalmers' Theology*, BOA A.9.1, 8, 5–6.
222. JHN, *Critical Remarks on Dr Chalmers' Theology*, BOA A.9.1, 9.
223. JHN, *Critical Remarks on Dr Chalmers' Theology*, BOA A.9.1, 10.

religious instruction, "as a <u>reward</u>, as a <u>remedy</u>, as a <u>completion</u>, not as an especial & peculiar quickener and enlightener of the dead."[224]

Conclusion

Although Newman's gradual development away from evangelicalism had taken at least five years, its theological outcome was so dramatically different from what he had held before, that even those who knew him well marveled at the change. By late 1834, Frank Newman had read his brother's first volume of *Parochial Sermons*, which contained the gist of John's new vision. He was shocked. Writing to John from Bristol, he wistfully recalled the time "when you were curate at St. Clement's, how you seemed to be preaching the blessed gospel of the Lord Jesus."[225] Now, Frank had to conclude that John "had utterly abandoned all that, which when first ordained as a minister of Jesus Christ . . . you believed to be the truth of the gospel." He could only express his "deep affliction at <u>your</u> changes, concerning . . . the marrow of all religion."[226] He did not so much mind that John was "too little of a Calvinist"—although he minded that too—but he "was anxious for the vital truth in which the peace & spirituality of the soul is concerned, & without which it has no fellowship with the Father & with the Son."[227] And thus, he appended a twenty-one-page critique of John's sermons to his letter. It was premised on some of the same convictions he and John had shared a decade earlier: God's absolute sovereignty, the radical priority of faith over works, and faith in the atonement as the only means of salvation.

It was John's emphasis on obedience as the way to holiness that troubled Frank the most. This was "human salvation affected by human effort" rather than "faith which <u>looks out of itself</u> to the power of Christ."[228] He could only read John's injunction to obey as a pseudo-Jewish return to the "works of the law" denounced by St Paul. John, he concluded, "plainly sets <u>works</u> (under the name of <u>obedience</u>) in the place of <u>faith</u>."[229] The idea of faith and obedience as mutually constitutive was incomprehensible to him. To say, as John did, "that faith <u>means</u> a life of persevering obedience, is . . . as gratuitous as to say that black means white." John's theology, Frank argued, completely obscured the fact "that

224. JHN, *Critical Remarks on Dr Chalmers' Theology*, BOA A.9.1, 7, 8–9.

225. FWN to JHN, 1834, BOA, Personal Collection, Francis William Newman, 1. Except for the year, the letter is undated, but Frank moved to Bristol (from which the letter was sent) only at the end of 1834. See *LD* 4, 338, 370; William Robbins, *The Newman Brothers: An Essay in Comparative Intellectual Biography* (Cambridge, Mass.: Harvard University Press, 1966), 58–59.

226. FWN to JHN, 1834, BOA, Personal Collection, Francis William Newman, 1.

227. FWN to JHN, 1834, BOA, Personal Collection, Francis William Newman, 2.

228. FWN, *Extracts from Newman's Parochial Sermons, &c.*, 1834, BOA, Personal Collection, Francis William Newman, 18, 7.

229. FWN, *Extracts*, BOA, Personal Collection, Francis William Newman, 13.

the <u>gospel</u> is <u>glad tidings</u>"; it is "not uncertainty & disquietude, fear & bondage, but power & love & much assurance."[230] John never responded to Frank's criticisms. His new theological outlook was the result of an extended and conscious struggle with precisely those views Frank raised as objections, views that had lost so much of their appeal that John could hardly experience them as criticisms. By now, moreover, their fundamental theological convictions and principles were so far apart that it would have taken a volume to explain his position in terms that Frank would understand. Besides, he had other fish to fry: liberal fish.

230. FWN, *Extracts*, BOA, Personal Collection, Francis William Newman, 13.

CHAPTER 8

The Usurping Intellect

By early 1830, Newman's evangelicalism had come undone and was being replaced by a novel theological vision. Newman no longer thought that belief in the atonement brings about religious change by redirecting the affections. Instead, he held that conversion consists in the cultivation of a specific moral character, acquired by obedience to the God who speaks in conscience as well as revelation. The object of faith is God as revealed in Christ, not just in the atonement, but in Christ's entire life and work. Accordingly, the difference between natural and revealed religion is not that the one preaches condemnation and the other redemption but that Christianity authoritatively reveals what natural religion only faintly suggests: that God is person, rather than principle. That is why Christ's divinity is the central Christian doctrine. Before, Newman measured the value of doctrines like the atonement or the Trinity by the subjective effects of believing them. Now, he held that doctrine derives its importance from revealing to us the person we already love and obey in conscience. Revelation is not about us; it is about God. These new commitments jarred with the religious culture of the late 1820s. Society at large downplayed the importance of doctrine and sought truth in the wrong way, valuing independent inquiry over tradition and cultivating the intellect rather than moral character. Society, in short, was turning liberal. Or so, at least, Newman thought.

Whether Newman's verdict was correct is matter for debate, but that he gave it is not. And yet, this is precisely what Frank Turner disputes. Turner, we will recall, claims that Newman's invective in the early 1830s concerned evangelicalism, not liberalism, the latter being an invention of the *Apologia*. Although this is a mistake, it is, perhaps, an understandable one in view of Note A, which defined liberalism in the 1865 edition of the *Apologia*; not because Note A is a ruse, as Turner has it, but because it focuses exclusively on Oxford University. Given the amount of energy Newman spent in combating Oxford liberals during the Tractarian period, this focus is understandable, and if one were to take this as all he meant by liberalism, Turner's mistake becomes understandable, too. After all, Newman did attack evangelicalism some years before the Tractarian Movement began, which makes it easier to interpret as a gloss Newman's assertion that his "battle was with liberalism."[1] What Turner overlooks, however, is what Newman

1. *Apo.*, 120.

does not mention in Note A: that Newman did not develop his concept of liberalism with an eye to Oxford theology but in response to broad societal shifts during the tumultuous late 1820s and early 1830s.

As early as 1821, Newman had begun to discern the key features of an emergent liberal worldview, but it was Catholic emancipation in 1829 and its Oxford aftermath that convinced him that a novel social and religious culture was becoming entrenched in English society, spearheaded by parts of its political and intellectual elite. Within a year or two, liberalism had become his favorite denominator for this ideology, which he denounced using the same terms and for the same reasons he later listed in the *Apologia*. It is the burden of the following two chapters to prove this claim. The present chapter describes how Newman's concept of liberalism emerged historically as a critique of culture, in response to a series of sociopolitical events that set England on a new course. It also analyses what Newman considered the driving force of liberalism on both the individual and societal levels: an undue reliance on the intellect to acquire and assess religious truth. The next chapter argues that Newman conceived of liberalism as not only undermining traditional religion but supplanting it with a pseudoreligious worldview of its own. It also shows how Newman used the ideas of the mystery of revealed truth and the doctrinal authority of the early church to counter this worldview. I end by picking up the historical thread that opens the present chapter, and that leads straight into the beginning of the Tractarian Movement.

Reconfiguring Culture: Peel and Catholic Emancipation

The British historian Jonathan Clark has argued that the passage of the Reform Act in 1832, along with the events leading up to it, signified the end of the *ancien régime* in England. Between the repeal of the Test and Corporation Acts in May 1828 and the reform of the electoral system in 1832, "a whole social and political order had been destroyed", or so, at least, thought the defenders of the status quo.[2] Newman, for one, experienced the period as one of dramatic upheaval and change. He saw the old order rapidly fading and something new, and altogether unpromising, taking its place. The shift in his understanding of culture was prompted by a series of national and local political events in early 1829.[3] Soon after the repeal of the Test and Corporation Acts had removed the hindrances barring Protestant dissenters from public office, the Roman Catholic

2. J. C. D. Clark, *English Society, 1688–1832: Ideology, Social Structure and Political Practice during the Ancien Regime* (Cambridge: Cambridge University Press, 1985), 409.

3. This section incorporates material from Geertjan Zuijdwegt, "Richard Whately," in *The Oxford Handbook of John Henry Newman*, ed. Frederick D. Aquino and Benjamin J. King (Oxford: Oxford University Press, 2018), 196–216, reproduced with permission. DOI: 10.1093/oxfordhb/9780198718284.013.10.

Relief Act was brought to the vote. It would abolish further tests (such as taking the Oath of Supremacy and abjuring transubstantiation) to allow Catholics to sit in Parliament. Characteristically, Newman became involved in the event only once it affected Oxford, but when he did, it was a political awakening.

On February 4, 1829, Sir Robert Peel, home secretary in the Duke of Wellington's cabinet and Member of Parliament for Oxford University, resigned his seat because he had come out in support of Catholic emancipation, a measure he had opposed for years, and which was unpopular at Oxford because it encroached on the privileges of the Established Church.[4] Newman took an informed view of the event. About the passing of the Catholic Relief Act, he felt "indifferent." He did not consider it "a religious question" but one of political expediency, which it was.[5] In July 1828, the popular Irish lawyer and political activist Daniel O'Connell had surprisingly won the by-election at County Clare. Because he was a Catholic, he could not take his seat at Westminster, and disturbances in Ireland were feared. Wellington and Peel believed that Catholic emancipation was the only way to conciliate the Irish, and, after some hesitation, pushed the measure through.[6] Newman was well-aware that Irish grievances were more political than religious. "The clamours of the Catholics," he wrote to Samuel Rickards, "are but the accidental development of the jealousy Ireland must feel towards a country which has stolen her Parliament and independence."[7] Still, as he commented to his sister Harriett, he found it "most deplorable" that "the Government should have been bullied by Mr O'Connell into concession."[8] Newman was enough of a political realist to want Peel to bear the consequences of his volte-face. Oxford annually petitioned against the Catholic claims, and Newman found it impossible to swallow that "because a Minister chooses *deliberately* to change his opinion . . . Oxford must *suddenly* in a few days change too."[9] "It is not pro dignitate nostrâ to have a Rat our member [for Parliament]," he wrote to Rickards.[10] To show its constancy and independence, the university had to oust Peel.

Although Newman feared Peel would be reelected, "for want of a better man," all seemed headed in the right direction, at least for a few days.[11] Then, opposition arose from an unexpected quarter. On February 9, Hawkins returned

4. Robert Peel, *Memoirs by the Right Honourable Sir Robert Peel* (London: John Murray, 1856), 312–15; W. R. Ward, *Victorian Oxford* (London: Frank Cass, 1965), 71–75.

5. JHN to Samuel Rickards, February 6, 1829, *LD* 2, 118. See also JHN to Harriett Newman, March 19, 1827, *LD* 2, 7.

6. Boyd Hilton, *A Mad, Bad, and Dangerous People? England 1783–1846* (Oxford: Oxford University Press, 2006), 379–91, esp. 387–89.

7. JHN to Samuel Rickards, February 6, 1829, *LD* 2, 118.

8. JHN to Harriett Newman, March 16, 1829, *LD* 2, 132.

9. JHN to Jemima Newman, March 4, 1829, *LD* 2, 127.

10. JHN to Samuel Rickards, February 6, 1829, *LD* 2, 118.

11. JHN to Samuel Rickards, February 6, 1829, *LD* 2, 118.

from London, where he had joined the pro-Peel party, and began to canvas for Peel's reelection without consulting the members of his college.[12] A protracted struggle ensued, which divided Oxford at large as well as Oriel. Newman was vexed with his "meddling Provost" and took sides with his new friends. He joined Keble, Froude, and Robert Wilberforce to campaign for Sir Robert Inglis, a staunch Conservative, while Whately, Hawkins, Blanco White, and others of their coterie supported Peel. On February 28, Inglis was elected with a large majority, and Newman basked in the "glorious Victory."[13] "It is the first public event I have been concerned in," he wrote to his mother, "and I thank God from my heart both for my cause and its success. We have proved the independence of the Church and of Oxford."[14] He had also proved his independence from former mentor Whately. Even though in hindsight the affair forebodes the future rift at Oriel, at the time, no one made much of it.[15] Still, Whately was sore about Newman's stance, although relations remained cordial. Assuming that his opposition to the Peel campaign meant that he was making common cause with the old High Church party, Whately took a humorous revenge by inviting Newman to dinner, seating him between two unintellectual, port-loving, "high and dry" principals, and asking him if he was "proud" of his "friends."[16]

Yet, as Peter Nockles points out, Newman's "stand was only incidentally at one" with that of the High Church party.[17] Just as in 1826, when he first turned to the visible church, Nemwan was carving out a position of his own. In the *Apologia*, he portrayed his opposition to Peel as a mere university affair; it had rested "on a simple academical, not at all an ecclesiastical or a political ground."[18] Although his primary concern was indeed the university, this assessment is misleading, and Newman corrected it in his *Autobiographical Memoir*. Besides being "a question of politics," he noted there, Peel's reelection "was a moral, an academical,

---

12. *LD* 2, 121; JHN to Harriett Newman, February 17, 1829, *LD* 2, 122; and "Autobiographical Memoir," *AW*, 98. Ward (*Victorian Oxford*, 72) points to Whately as the instigator of the pro-Peel campaign but provides no evidence for the claim.

13. JHN to Mrs Newman, March 1, 1829, *LD* 2, 125.

14. JHN to Mrs Newman, March 1, 1829, *LD* 2, 125.

15. See Richard Whately to JHN, August 3, 1830, *LD* 2, 262. The emergent divide at Oriel was deepened by a conflict over tutorial arrangements that pitted three of the four tutors—Newman, Froude, and Wilberforce—against their provost. It centered on different conceptions of the tutorship, which Newman, along with Froude and Wilberforce, considered above all a pastoral office that demanded more attention to private instruction of the tutor's own pupils than to public lectures, and it ended with Hawkins deciding to stop their supply of pupils in June 1830. See "Memorandum. The Oriel Tuition," *LD* 2, 246–50; *AW*, 86–107; Culler, *The Imperial Intellect*, 48–53, 65–74; Peter Nockles, "Oriel and the Making of John Henry Newman—His Mission as a College Tutor," *Recusant History* 29, no. 3 (2009): 411–21; and Nockles, "Oriel and Religion," 316–25.

16. *Apo.*, 73. See *LD* 2, 131.

17. Nockles, "Oriel and Religion," 324.

18. *Apo.*, 72.

an ecclesiastical, nay a religious question; at least it grew to be such."[19] This more accurately describes his state of mind at the time. The Peel affair spurred the development of his thought unlike any previous public event. He was simply brimming with intellectual excitement. "My mind is so full of ideas," he wrote to his mother, "and my views have so much enlarged and expanded that in justice to myself I ought to write a volume."[20]Although Peel's reelection was a university matter and the passing of the Roman Catholic Relief Act a political question, the societal agitation in its favor was grounds for ecclesiastical and religious alarm. "Emancipation," Newman observed to Rickards, "is the *symptom* of a systematic hatred to our Church borne by Romanists, Sectarians, Liberals, and Infidels."[21]

This vision of a burgeoning cultural coalition of anti-Church of England forces suffused his letters home in the next month.[22] "I think there is a grand attack on the Church in progress from the Utilitarians and Schismatics," he wrote to Jemima on March 4.[23] A week later, he warned his mother that the "stream of opinion is setting against the Church" and detailed its "enemies."[24] Danger came from "schismatics, in and out of the Church" of a mostly evangelical cast, whose publicity channels were the nondenominational *Eclectic Review* and the evangelical *Christian Guardian and Church of England Magazine*. He considered "Baptists" a danger, too, "whose system is consistent Calvinism." Given Calvin's commitment to paedobaptism, this comment might seem confused, but it is not. Newman's long struggle with the doctrine of baptismal regeneration and his controversy with Frank (which their mother had witnessed) had convinced him that believer's baptism was the logical outcome of Calvin's system. Accordingly, he considered the moderate Calvinism of many Anglican evangelicals an amalgam of irreconcilable tenets: "as far as I can see, Thomas Scott etc are inconsistent, and such inconsistent men would in times of commotion split, and go over to this side or that."[25] When seriously challenged, moderate Calvinists would either choose Church of England theology—as he had done—or the more robust Calvinism of one of the dissenting bodies—as Frank was doing. There was no middle way.

Besides Calvinist evangelicals, Newman identified Radicals and Whigs as the primary enemies of the Established Church. He feared the "uneducated or partially educated mass in towns," who were "almost professedly deistical or worse"

<hr>

19. JHN, "Autobiographical Memoir," *AW*, 97.

20. JHN to Mrs Newman, March 13, 1829, *LD* 2, 130.

21. JHN to Samuel Rickards, February 6, 1829, *LD* 2, 119.

22. Roman Catholics are absent from his later inventories, presumably because they were a negligible quantity at home (unlike in Ireland). In England, dissenters and liberals were his chief worry.

23. JHN to Jemima Newman, March 4, 1829, *LD* 2, 128.

24. JHN to Mrs Newman, March 13, 1829, *LD* 2, 130.

25. JHN to Mrs Newman, March 13, 1829, *LD* 2, 130.

and had their views shaped by "Carlisle's [*sic*] publications."[26] It was the poor laboring class as well as Radicals like his brother Charles that Newman had in mind here. One step up the ideological ladder, he listed the "Utilitarians, political economists, useful knowledge people — their organs the Westminster Review, the London University, etc."[27] This catalogue pinpoints the shared ideological (but not political) agenda of the Philosophic Radicals around Jeremy Bentham, the founder of modern utilitarianism, and Whigs of the professional classes, like Henry Brougham. Together with his main populariser James Mill, Bentham had launched the *Westminster Review* in 1823 to serve as a party platform for the Philosophic Radicals. London University was also inspired by Bentham's utilitarian principles. It was founded as a nondenominational alternative to Oxbridge in 1826, with Mill and Brougham as its driving forces. In the same year, Brougham initiated the Society for the Diffusion of Useful Knowledge (SDUK), aimed at educating the masses by means of cheap popular scientific publications. Finally, Newman registered the aristocratic branch of Whiggism—"the high circles in London"—as enemies of the Established Church.[28]

Amid the different ideologies of these groups, Newman discerned the common features of an emergent worldview that threatened to erode convictions he held sacred. He had been wary of this trend since 1821.[29] In 1826, apropos of the founding of London University and the SDUK, he had warned an academic audience against "the present philanthropic advocates of improvements in the condition of society, and encouragers of universal science," who "appear confidently to expect that the progress of discovery and general diffusion of knowledge must terminate in the fall of Christianity."[30] But only after Catholic emancipation and the Peel affair did he realize how imminent the danger was. "We live in a novel era," he wrote to his mother, "one in which there is an advance to universal education. Man have hitherto depended on others, and especially on the Clergy, for religious truth, now each man attempts to judge for himself."[31] He did not think Christianity was, in principle, "opposed to free inquiry," but he still considered it "*in fact* at the present time opposed to the particular form which that liberty of thought has now assumed."[32] Newman's stress on the "novel," the "now," and the "present" in these

---

26. JHN to Mrs Newman, March 13, 1829, *LD* 2, 130. The London publisher Richard Carlile, a fierce advocate of free speech, was tried (and imprisoned) for publishing Paine's *Age of Reason* in 1818 (Philip W. Martin, "Carlile, Richard," *ODNB*).

27. JHN to Mrs Newman, March 13, 1829, *LD* 2, 130.

28. JHN to Mrs Newman, March 13, 1829, *LD* 2, 130. See William Thomas, *The Philosophic Radicals: Nine Studies in Theory and Practice, 1817–1841* (Oxford: Clarendon Press, 1979), 46–94.

29. See pp. 38–39.

30. JHN, No. 151, "The temper of mind injoined by Christianity, that which is indispensable in conducting scientific inquiries," July 2, 1826, BOA A.9.4, 3 (*OUS*, 3).

31. JHN to Mrs Newman, March 13, 1829, *LD* 2, 129.

32. JHN to Mrs Newman, March 13, 1829, *LD* 2, 129.

lines indicates that he felt he was getting at the very "spirit of the age," much as the young John Stuart Mill did in his 1831 essay of that title. Mill, too, defined the age as one of "transition," whose main feature was that people "will not be led by their old maxims, nor by their old guides."[33] Although John Stuart was not as self-congratulatory as his father, James Mill, he, too, lauded the change. Newman, by contrast, derided the spirit of the age as "one of latitudinarianism, indifferentism, republicanism, and schism, a spirit which tends to overthrow doctrine, as if the fruit of bigotry, and discipline as if the instrument of priestcraft."[34]

Despite his use of staunchly conservative pejoratives to denounce his age and his selection of enemies from dissenting, Whig, and Radical ranks, Newman's reaction was no mere Toryism (although it was that, too).[35] From the outset, Newman's diagnosis of culture was based on a cogent view of tradition as the process of transmitting profound moral and religious truths, truths that are hard to prove—and thus easily dismissed—but crucial to hold. He expounded this idea to his mother:

> As each individual has certain instincts of right and wrong, antecedently to reasoning, on which he acts and rightly so . . . so, I think, has the world of men collectively. God gave them truths in His miraculous revelations, and other truths, in the unsophisticated infancy of notions, scarcely less necessary and divine. These are transmitted as "the wisdom of our ancestors," through men, many of whom cannot enter into them, or receive them themselves, still on, on, from age to age, not the less truths, because many of the generations, through which they are transmitted, are unable to prove them, but hold them either from pious and honest feeling (it may be) or from bigotry or prejudice.[36]

Conscience and (universal) revelation have provided humankind with a set of fundamental moral and religious truths, whose transmission is a vitally important but fragile process. This process is endangered if the right to always judge for oneself becomes a supreme cultural value. Many people will realize that they hold traditional beliefs they cannot justify and relinquish them accordingly. For Mill, this was only proper. People had simply "outgrown old institutions and old doctrines."[37] Although Newman disagreed, he admitted that much of the populace would find it "most difficult to prove" such traditional beliefs: "great men alone

---

33. John Stuart Mill, "The Spirit of the Age," January 1831, in *Collected Works of John Stuart Mill*, vol. 22, ed. Ann P. Robson and John M. Robson (Toronto: University of Toronto Press, 1986), 230, 231.

34. JHN to Mrs Newman, March 13, 1829, *LD* 2, 129.

35. See Peter B. Nockles, "'Church and King': Tractarian Politics Reappraised," in *From Oxford to the People: Reconsidering Newman & the Oxford Movement*, ed. Paul Vaiss (Leominster: Gracewing, 1996), 93–123.

36. JHN to Mrs Newman, March 13, 1829, *LD* 2, 130–31.

37. Mill, "The Spirit of the Age," in *Collected Works*, vol. 22, 230.

can prove great ideas or grasp them."[38] "Such a mind," he added, "was Hooker's, such Butler's; and, as moral evil triumphs over good on a small field of action, so in the argument of an hour, or the compass of a volume, would men like Brougham, or again Wesley show to far greater advantage than Hooker or Butler."[39] This unlikely linkage of Brougham and Wesley—the one the patron of utilitarian learning, the other of the evangelical revival—reinforced the image of an unholy alliance against the Established Church, with liberals and dissenters as strange bedfellows. Conflicting ecclesiologies were at stake here.

Liberals, Evangelicals, and the Established Church

In Newman's view, liberals and (dissenting) evangelicals both disregarded the visible church as the indispensable means of grace and truth. God, Newman argued in an 1827 sermon, "has founded a Church, with whom He has lodged both grace and teaching."[40] By the fact "that the means of grace and instruction belong to the Church, it is meant that God has not promised his grace in the sacraments or his blessing on teaching to private individuals standing by themselves separating from and independent of other Christians." Rather, "He has willed His followers to be *one body*."[41] Newman had defended this idea of the church since 1826, and it explains why he responded so vehemently to liberal and dissenting efforts to minimize or actively undermine the religious role of the Established Church. Scripture expressly enjoins "union in a visible body" on all Christians, he reiterated in a sermon of November 1829.[42] The New Testament witnesses to "the existence of a strict Church government:" a hierarchical system under the authority of the Apostles, who ordained other ministers, instituted rules of communion, and censured dissent.[43] The objects of this system are the "preservation of the faith, purity of doctrine, the quiet growth of piety in private Christians, and precision and clearness in the general <public> operations of the Church." The "only known means to *attain* these objects," Newman added, are "fixed rules."[44] Since this ordered ecclesial system has continued, in different branches, "in regular and unbroken succession from the Apostles," its "rule of order" is to be obeyed now as it was then.[45]

---

38. JHN to Mrs Newman, March 13, 1829, *LD* 2, 131.

39. JHN to Mrs Newman, March 13, 1829, *LD* 2, 130–31.

40. JHN, No. 162, "On general education as connected with the Church and religion," August 19, 1827, *Serm.* 5, 424.

41. JHN, No. 162, "On general education," *Serm.* 5, 424.

42. JHN, No. 216, "On Church-union, and the sin of schism," November 15, 1829, *Serm.* 4, 56.

43. JHN, No. 216, "On Church-union," *Serm.* 4, 59.

44. JHN, No. 216, "On Church-union," *Serm.* 4, 61.

45. JHN, No. 216, "On Church-union," *Serm.* 4, 62–63.

The Peel affair had made Newman realize that people questioned the entire idea of the church as an ordered society. He considered this a new state of affairs. Until the Reformation, he argued in his sermon, the formal organization of the church was hardly ever questioned, and even after it, nearly all Protestants "considered sober continuance *in some form or other* a solemn duty."[46] Only of late, "multitudes both in and out of the Church have set up as a great discovery and glory in the principle that forms are *nothing*, and make it a boast that they belong to *no party*." Instead, they maintain that, "provided men agree in the <some> principal doctrines of the gospel, it matters little whether they agree in anything else."[47] Liberals and dissenters acted as if Christianity's spiritual kernel could be extracted from its institutional husk. For Newman, this was "the very spirit of unbelief," an explicit disavowal of a clear divine injunction.[48] Every organized ecclesial act—baptism, the Lord's Supper, even public worship as such—is a form. We use those forms not because we like or comprehend them but because scripture tells us to: "they are *commanded*."[49]

Yet, even though we use forms because we are told to, we can still perceive their value. Newman, by now, was deeply attached to the forms of the Church of England, and he did not think he was alone. "I am sometimes tempted to think associations connected with the Liturgy and affection for it is the great hold of the Church in the minds of the multitude," he wrote to Edward Rudd in January 1830.[50] For that reason, he began a sermon course on "the English Church and Liturgy" at the end of the month.[51] The course defined the liturgy as "the *form* of prayer" by which the priest offers up "the sacrifice of prayer and praise of the whole congregation."[52] Although a liturgical form is always necessary for the sake of order and reverence, Newman wanted to highlight "the particular excellencies of *our own* forms of prayer (the Liturgy contained in our *Prayer book*)."[53] The course identified three such qualities. First, "it contains in it a record of the *doctrines* of the gospel;" through its forms of worshipping God, the various collects, prayers, lessons, services, and creeds, it teaches "the substance of revealed truth."[54] Secondly, the liturgical forms "impress upon our hearts the true *image of the Christian character*."[55] By selecting judiciously from scripture and drawing on

46. JHN, No. 216, "On Church-union," *Serm.* 4, 63.
47. JHN, No. 216, "On Church-union," *Serm.* 4, 63.
48. JHN, No. 216, "On Church-union," *Serm.* 4, 64.
49. JHN, No. 216, "On Church-union," *Serm.* 4, 64.
50. JHN to Edward Rudd, January 21, 1830, *LD* 2, 191.
51. JHN to Jemima Newman, November 29, 1829, *LD* 2, 175–76.
52. JHN, No. 224, "The Liturgy the service of the Christian Priest," January 31, 1830, *Serm.* 1, 61.
53. JHN, No. 225, "The Liturgy public — its three peculiar uses," February 7, 1830, *Serm.* 1, 70.
54. JHN, No. 225, "The Liturgy public," *Serm.* 1, 71.
55. JHN, No. 225, "The Liturgy public," *Serm.* 1, 71.

ages of Christian wisdom, the liturgy teaches what it means to be holy. Finally, the liturgy forges union among believers by engendering "mutual love."[56] It moves "our hearts from our long intimacy with it — its words are bound up with our recollections from childhood, it has been heard in grief often and soothed us, and it has hallowed our joy."[57] Birth, marriage, death: all are worked into the liturgical life of the church, so that it becomes "a permanent bond of union" among its members.[58] The liturgy, in short, transforms the head, the will, and the heart. It is "calculated to convert your souls from sin to a complete holiness."[59]

As an evangelical, Newman had used nearly the same words to describe the preaching of the atonement. But by the end of 1829, the liturgy had supplanted preaching as the main Christian ordinance. Unlike missionaries, parish priests are sent "not to preach the gospel but to baptize principally and to teach His disciples and to minister the other ordinances of His holy religion."[60] "We have not the duty of *preaching the gospel* committed to us," he asserted categorically.[61] Accordingly, as he argued in another sermon, it is a mistake to act "as if hearing so called preaching was *the* great ordinance of the Christian religion," which actually is "joint prayer and praise"—public worship.[62] Given that "God's grace is promised, not through preaching, but through the Sacraments," preaching is only a secondary affair.[63] The liturgy of the Church of England, then, is what mediates grace and truth. No other institution can fulfil this role, because the true church is defined neither by its order nor its teaching, but by its history. The church "is not a mere *form of discipline,* nor (again) a voluntary association founded on a profession of certain *doctrines.*"[64] It is, instead, "as a matter of history, an existing divine ordinance" whose identity is determined by episcopal succession from the time of the Apostles. Accordingly, "the Apostolic ministry" is "the essence and the bond of the Church of Christ." In consequence, there cannot be any other church than the church: "you *cannot* make a Church by copying the existing body." Even if you "make the form and discipline those of the Church you have discarded, and secure the orthodoxy of its doctrines; still you have made no advance towards

56. JHN, No. 225, "The Liturgy public," *Serm.* 1, 73.
57. JHN, No. 225, "The Liturgy public," *Serm.* 1, 73.
58. JHN, No. 225, "The Liturgy public," *Serm.* 1, 74.
59. JHN, No. 225, "The Liturgy public," *Serm.* 1, 74.
60. JHN, No. 214, "On preaching," November 1, 1829, *Serm.* 1, 20.
61. JHN, No. 214, "On preaching," *Serm.* 1, 20.
62. JHN, No. 290, "On the objects and effects of preaching — (on the anniversary of my entering on my living)," March 20, 1831, *Serm.* 1, 25.
63. JHN, No. 290, "On the objects and effects of preaching," *Serm.* 1, 26. See also No. 246, "St Peter's authority — and thence on Church authority etc.," June 29, 1830, *Serm.* 3, 31; No. 225, "The Liturgy public," *Serm.* 1, 69; No. 323, "On the Ministerial Order, as an existing divine institution. Ordination Sermon," December 18, 1831, *Serm.* 4, 82.
64. JHN, No. 323, "On the Ministerial Order," *Serm.* 4, 82.

your object — you have but the shadow of a Church."[65] All of this, liberals and dissenters seemed to forget.

For that reason, Newman began to distrust the great panevangelical institutions of his day. On June 8, 1830, he resigned from the British and Foreign Bible Society, but this was not his first clash with organized evangelicalism. He had just been ousted as secretary of the local branch of the Church Missionary Society after a head-on collision with the Oxford evangelical set. He had affronted John Hill by an outright attack on Bulteel in December 1829 and created another row two months later with an anonymous pamphlet calling clergyman to join the CMS and bring it under stricter ecclesial control. His brother Frank exposed his authorship and incited Benjamin Wills Newton to propose his removal as secretary. At the annual meeting in March, with "Bulteel and his satellites, and half Edmund Hall, being in attendance," the proposal was carried, and Newman was replaced by Joseph Philpot, a high Calvinist like Bulteel.[66] Although the CMS admitted dissenters, it was officially an organ of the Established Church, so that Newman could continue his subscription for several years, and even preach in its behalf. The Bible Society was a different case. It was explicitly nondenominational and included Anglicans and dissenters on a basis of equality, even though at Oxford it was run by nearly the same people as the CMS.[67] But after the debacle in March, that made leaving only easier.

In August, Newman explained his decision to quit the Bible Society to Simeon Lloyd Pope in terms of resisting liberalism. "The tendency of the age," he wrote to Pope, "is towards *liberalism* — i.e. a thinking established notions worth nothing — in this system of opinions a disregard of religion is included."[68] By mid-1830, the term liberalism had replaced the profusion of earlier adjectives to capture what was wrong with the age. "No religion," Newman argued, "can stand if deprived of its forms."[69] It might be true, but its truths are, as a rule, unpalatable: "*moral* truth is not acceptable to man's heart." And thus, religion "must be enforced by authority of some kind."[70] In Christianity, this authority is the church. It was "*actually established* by the Apostles, and is thus the *legitimate* enforcement of Christian truth." "The liberals," Newman argued, "know this — and are in every possible manner trying to break it up." The Bible Society, because it downplayed

---

65. JHN, No. 323, "On the Ministerial Order," *Serm.* 4, 82.

66. Thomas Mozley to Anne Mozley, March 14, 1830, *LD* 2, 199. See *LD* 2, 129, 178–79, 198–99; [JHN], "Suggestions Respectfully Offered to Certain Resident Clergyman [*sic*] of the University, in behalf of the Church Missionary Society," February 1, 1830, *Serm.* 4, 339–44; Timothy Stunt, "John Henry Newman and the Evangelicals," *Journal of Ecclesiastical History* 21.1 (1970): 65–74.

67. Stunt, "John Henry Newman and the Evangelicals," 66.

68. JHN to Simeon Lloyd Pope, August 15, 1830, *LD* 2, 264.

69. JHN to Simeon Lloyd Pope, August 15, 1830, *LD* 2, 264.

70. JHN to Simeon Lloyd Pope, August 15, 1830, *LD* 2, 265.

confessional identity, "(unconsciously) is a means of aiding their object." Hence, prominent liberals, such as the Whig Lord George Nugent, would join it for a time. They realized that it professed "no *Church principles*" to which Anglicans could rally, so that dissent was implicitly acquiesced in. Anglicans, "by coming *on common ground* with Dissenters . . . seem to come on *middle* ground . . . and to allow that they ought to concede *as well* as Dissenters."[71] When Newman joined the Bible Society in 1824, he had been unimpressed by this argument. He believed that the society's mixed composition promoted "charity" among Anglicans and dissenters, who, as long as they were "spiritual," agreed "in substance."[72] Now, he maintained the contrary: "IT MAKES CHURCHMEN LIBERALS — it makes them undervalue the guilt of schism — it makes them feel a wish to conciliate Dissenters at the expence [*sic*] of truth."[73]

If the Bible Society fostered the relativizing of religious truth because of its institutional structure, the incessant evangelical brandishing of the atonement equally contributed to religious indifference. "The Children of evangelical parents," Newman pointed out to Charles Portales Golightly in January 1831, "if they see the world, will generally turn liberals."[74] They are so constantly exposed to the Gospel message that it loses all its appeal. For instance, the prominent evangelical Daniel Wilson, a former authority for Newman, had "roused and spiritualized" the people at his Oxfordshire parish of Worton "till they were fairly knocked up, defatigati — worn out."[75] They simply cared no longer. Newman reminded Golightly that,

> Bishop Butler tells us that, if we say things over without feeling them, we become worse not better. Children, who are taught, since they were weaned, to rely on the Christian atonement, and in whose ears have been dinned the motives of gratitude to it etc before their hearts are trained to understand them, are deadened to them by the time they are 21.[76]

People become impervious to the gospel if they are told incessantly to feel its emotional pull. Its doctrines will mean little more to them than they did to the likes of Brougham. But liberal indifference was rife beyond the evangelical pale, as well. Two months later, Newman asked John Bowden whether "the persons you meet generally are (I do not say, consistently religious, we can never expect that in this world) but believe in Christianity in any true meaning of the word?"

71. JHN to Simeon Lloyd Pope, August 15, 1830, *LD* 2, 265. See also JHN to Simeon Lloyd Pope, April 9, 1832, *LD* 3, 42–43.

72. JHN, *Marsh's Pamphlet*, BOA A.9.1.e, 2, 8. See pp. 41–42 in this book.

73. JHN to Simeon Lloyd Pope, August 15, 1830, *LD* 2, 265.

74. JHN to Charles Portales Golightly, January 3, 1831, *LD* 2, 308.

75. JHN to Charles Portales Golightly, January 3, 1831, *LD* 2, 308.

76. JHN to Charles Portales Golightly, January 3, 1831, *LD* 2, 308.

He provided the answer himself: "No, they are liberals, and in saying this, I conceive I am saying almost as bad of them as can be said of any man."[77]

Newman's apprehensions about the spread of liberalism were increased by the volatile political situation of the early 1830s. In November 1830, the Whigs acceded to power for the first time in his conscious memory. He viewed the event as a political confirmation of the cultural shift he had been observing since 1829. With Brougham as Lord Chancellor in Earl Grey's new government, this assessment can hardly surprise. Under such a government, the future of the Church of England looked troubled, indeed. Already in March 1829, Newman had predicted that Catholic emancipation was not the ending but the beginning of difficulties, only to be "settled with the downfall of the Established Church."[78] This was a bleak prospect, but not a daunting one. It strengthened his resolve to forego marriage and devote himself completely to the church. He realized "the importance of staying in Oxford many years," because there needed to be "men in the Church, like the R[oman] Catholic friars, free from all obstacles to their devoting themselves to its defence."[79] This was not the romantic reverie of a cloistered academic, but it was a practical solution to a real problem. The Peel campaign had used the patronage system to exert pressure on prospective Inglis voters, whose families depended on the income generated by their benefices. Unmarried clergy, especially those at the university, were free from such constraints and could act independently. As he put it to Pope a few years later: "The Church wants *expeditos milites* [unencumbered soldiers] — not a whole camp of women at its heels, forbye brats."[80]

Newman still worried about what the Whigs would do to the church, especially in terms of episcopal appointments, but he cared more for its purity than for its political fortunes. "I would rather have the Church severed from its temporalities and scattered to the four winds than such a desecration of holy things," he wrote to Bowden in March 1831, "I dread above all things the pollution of such men as Lord Brougham affecting to lay a friendly hand upon it. This vile Ministry, I cannot speak of them with patience."[81] Newman and his friends did not court disestablishment, but they also did not fear it. The liberal threat was an opportunity for the church to rally and hold its own. "Depend upon it," he assured Henry Wilberforce in May, "we shall prove a tough mouthful, when the nation fastens upon us."[82] With the Reform Bill in Parliament since March, amid

---

77. JHN to John William Bowden, March 13, 1831, *LD* 2, 317.

78. JHN to Harriett Newman, March 16, 1829, *LD* 2, 132.

79. JHN to Jemima Newman, March 17, 1829, *LD* 2, 133.

80. JHN to Simeon Lloyd Pope, April 9, 1832, *LD* 3, 43. The citation is from Livy (*Ab urbe condita*, bk. 35, chap. 27).

81. JHN to John Bowden, March 13, 1831, *LD* 2, 317. For an overview of various Whig religious outlooks at the time, see Brent, *Liberal Anglican Politics*, 106–18.

82. JHN to Henry Wilberforce, May 13, 1831, *LD* 2, 331.

much popular frenzy, this was no mere brag. "If it was not for a personal hatred of the Whiggs [*sic*]," Froude summed up the mood on October 4, "I should care comparatively little for the reform bill. For the Church can never right itself without a blow up."[83] He nearly got the blow up he wanted three days later, when the bill was thrown out of the House of Lords on its second reading, with nearly all the bishops voting against it. Reform, by now, garnered massive popular support, and the bishops' intransigence resulted in an upsurge of anticlerical agitation, mob violence, and, in some places, outright insurrection. Clergymen and bishops were no longer safe. Similar scenes ensued next May, when Grey resigned after a Tory amendment of the bill was carried in the Lords, again with substantial episcopal support. Because Wellington could not form a government, Grey returned on the king's promise to create the peers necessary to get the bill through the Lords, and it received the royal assent on June 7.[84]

Despite his invective, Newman was not in principle against political reform. He mainly challenged its current premise. People, he explained to Samuel Wood, "imagine they can put things right by applying their scientific knowledge to the improvement of the existing system."[85] This assumption entailed a misconception of the nature both of systems of governance and of human beings. First, the most important facets of governance "depend on personal and private virtue," so that "the difference between this and that system is *as nothing* compared with the effects of the human will upon them." Accordingly, "till the will be changed from evil to good, the difference of the results between two given systems will be imperceptible."[86] Second, Newman rejected the popular idea that societal progress inevitably demands change in individual behavior and sociopolitical structures. Behind the narrative "that the march of opinion, of events, of civilization *forces* on us certain changes" lurked a denial of human responsibility. "It is the fashion of the day to consider the human mind as a machine and to think that education will do any thing for it; — in fact that *it is not responsible*."[87] A few years earlier, only a radical Owenite like his brother Charles would hold such views.[88] Now, they began to suffuse culture as a whole.

There was no easy remedy. As long as the English retained their supreme confidence in the inevitable progress of their own culture, Newman saw only one corrective to their mistaken premises: "nothing but the reality of severe suffering will bring us to a right estimate of what we are — and rouse us from this indolent

---

83. Richard Hurrell Froude to JHN, October 4, 1831, *LD* 2, 365.

84. Clark, *English Society*, 403–7; Owen Chadwick, *The Victorian Church*, vol. 1, (London: A. and C. Black, 1971), 25–32.

85. JHN to Samuel Francis Wood, September 4, 1832, *LD* 3, 90.

86. JHN to Samuel Francis Wood, September 4, 1832, *LD* 3, 90–91.

87. JHN to Samuel Francis Wood, September 4, 1832, *LD* 3, 91.

88. See p. 60.

contemplation of our advances in the useful arts and the experimental sciences, to the thought and practice of our duties as immortal beings."[89] The Whigs in power typified the cultural complacency that needed to be dismantled. To his aunt, Newman complained that the Whigs were "deeply infected with the cold-hearted indifferent spirit of liberalism; mere Gallios."[90] Like the Roman proconsul in Acts, they considered religious questions far beneath them. Hence, Newman's reservations about removing from the Athanasian Creed the clauses proclaiming damnation for unbelief—a proposal that was rapidly gaining in popularity. Edward Berens, among others, had suggested it in his influential *Church-Reform* (1828).[91] Although Newman was sympathetic to the book, he pointed out to a correspondent that removing the damnatory clauses from the Athanasian Creed entailed the "extreme danger of countenancing the false liberality of the age, which would fain have it believed that differences of *opinion* are of slight consequence."[92] Newman responded to such liberal indifference from the pulpit by analysing and countering its structure and origins both in the individual and in society at large.

Intellect and the Quest for God

Newman believed that liberalism had its roots in a misconception of the quest for religious truth. Liberals interpreted religious plurality as an argument for relativism and regarded the intellect as the only proper judge of religious truth claims. Reading Thomas Scott's religious biography as a teenager had taught Newman that confessional diversity does not relativize religious truth claims but rather spurs one to earnestly seek for the correct ones. This is what he had told Charles in August 1823, and he reiterated it in his sermons at St Clement's. "If all men were to seek in earnest," he noted in a January 1826 sermon, "there would be *no* difference of opinion."[93]

But he also knew that this was only one response to religious plurality. In December 1823, he had cautioned Charles that it may also lead people "hastily to conclude that opinions diametrically opposite to each other may be held without danger."[94] Such people, he explained in the 1826 sermon, infer either that one form of religion "is as good as another or even supposing there be one better than the rest at least that it is impossible for us to discover which it is."[95] By 1830,

<hr>

89. JHN to Samuel Francis Wood, September 4, 1832, *LD* 3, 90.

90. JHN to Elizabeth Newman, August 24, 1832, *LD* 3, 81. See Acts 18:12–17.

91. JHN to E. M. Rudd, January 21, 1830, *LD* 2, 191; Edward Berens, *Church-Reform* (London: John Murray, 1828), 123–29.

92. JHN to E. M. Rudd, January 21, 1830, *LD* 2, 191.

93. JHN, No. 130, "On the differences of religious opinions in the world," January 15, 1826, *Serm.* 3, 290.

94. JHN to CRN, December 12, 1823, *LD* 1, 169–70.

95. JHN, No. 130, "On the differences of religious opinions," *Serm.* 3, 288.

he believed that this proclivity to make light of religious truth was on the ascendant. In a sermon October 17, the first of a course entitled *Seeking and Finding*, he observed that "our religious creeds and professions at this day are many."[96] Some conclude from this plurality that "religious truth is not worth seeking at all, or that it is not given us."[97] "The present confused and perplexed state of things" they see as "a proof that religious truth cannot be obtained; that there is no such thing as religious truth; that there is no right or wrong in religion; that, provided we *think* ourselves right, one set of opinions is as good as another." Scripture teaches the opposite. It tells us "that religious truth is *one* — and therefore that all views of religion *but* one are wrong."[98] Accordingly, every Christian is bound to "seek the truth with all his heart and strength."[99]

Newman, by now, identified obedience to conscience as the means to acquire sound religious views. Intellectual enquiry plays only a very minor role. "Seek truth in the way of *obedience*," he admonished his parishioners, "try to act up to your conscience, and let your opinions be the result, not of mere chance reasoning or fancy, but of an improved heart."[100] Correct religious views are acquired over time by habitually obeying conscience. This is the central principle of religious progress, for Christians as much as for heathens and Jews. On the basis of this conviction, Newman, like Keble, challenged the liberal myth that intellectual proficiency or scientific learning issue in moral and religious progress. We have no reason, Newman argued, to be startled when "men of learning and ability . . . more or less reject the Gospel."[101] Although such surprise is the natural response of an age that prizes talent and education as the high road to truth, it is misguided. The "Christian revelation addresses itself to our hearts, to our love of truth and goodness, our fear of sinning, and our desire to gain GOD's favour," none of which are acquired by intellectual endeavour.[102] Accordingly, whether we accept revelation depends on our "religious principles and feelings," not on "what is commonly called reason."[103] Where religion is concerned, intellectual ability is on a par with other natural gifts, such as wealth or strength: "belief in Christianity has hardly more connexion with what is called talent, than it has with riches, station, power, or bodily strength."[104] If being a millionaire, an MP, or a bodybuilder does not make one a Christian, neither does being a genius or a professor.

96. JHN, No. 263, "Indolence and heartlessness do not seek the truth," October 17, 1830, published as "Truth Hidden when not Sought after," *PlS*, 287. See *Serm.* 4, 67n2; *Serm.* 5, 456–57.

97. JHN, No. 263. "Truth Hidden," *PlS*, 292.

98. JHN, No. 263. "Truth Hidden," *PlS*, 287.

99. JHN, No. 263. "Truth Hidden," *PlS*, 293.

100. JHN, No. 263. "Truth Hidden," *PlS*, 295.

101. JHN, No. 263. "Truth Hidden," *PlS*, 288, 289.

102. JHN, No. 263. "Truth Hidden," *PlS*, 289.

103. JHN, No. 263. "Truth Hidden," *PlS*, 290.

104. JHN, No. 263. "Truth Hidden," *PlS*, 291.

In the next sermon of the course, Newman drew on St Paul to explain why reliance on reason alone to acquire religious truth is "foolishness."[105] Our "reasoning powers," he argued, "are very weak in all inquiries into moral and religious truth."[106] When morality and religion are concerned, the intellect is out of its proper element. "Clear-sighted as reason is on other subjects, and trust-worthy as a guide, still in questions connected with our duty to God and man, it is very unskilful and equivocating," because it cannot provide the proper starting points for religious inquiry.[107] Newman was aware that "we must trust our notions in one shape or other," or we could not think at all. Thought requires some basis. Such accurate starting points for thought "come to us by way of our conscience, for such come from God."[108] Conscience provides everyone with the elements of morality and of religion: "that there is a right and wrong, that some things ought to be done, and other things not done; that we have duties, the neglect of which brings remorse; and further, that God is good, wise, powerful, and right-eous, and that we should try to obey Him."[109] Only these notions provide safe principles for a person to think by, for "they will, if obeyed, of a certainty lead him to a firm belief in Scripture."[110] Accordingly, the maxim Newman had used to capture Josiah's religious progress applied to his parishioners as well: "Act up to your light, though in the midst of difficulties, and you will be carried on, you do not know how far. . . . To him that hath, more shall be given."[111]

Keble had been defending a similar position for years. The proper response to doubts about religion is "taking, practically, the side of virtue and self-denial, where-ever the evidence seems doubtful." Such an exercise of "implicit Faith," Keble maintained, is "sure to bring even a plain man safe through all material difficulties in religion."[112] Newman explicitly related such a mode of action to conscience. In another sermon of his course, he argued that conscience will always assure us that "there is a God above us, and that it is our duty to obey His voice in our hearts in all things."[113] "We may have darkness on the right hand and the left," he explained, "but we have none straight on before us — in that quarter there is a guiding light, inviting us forward amid the gloom."[114] Here, the metaphor

105. JHN, No. 264, "Pride trusts reason more than conscience," October 24, 1830, published as "The Self-wise Inquirer," *PaS* 1, 247. See 1 Cor 3:19.

106. JHN, No. 264, "The Self-wise Inquirer," *PaS* 1, 251.

107. JHN, No. 264, "The Self-wise Inquirer," *PaS* 1, 251.

108. JHN, No. 264, "The Self-wise Inquirer," *PaS* 1, 248.

109. JHN, No. 264, "The Self-wise Inquirer," *PaS* 1, 248–49.

110. JHN, No. 264, "The Self-wise Inquirer," *PaS* 1, 249.

111. JHN, No. 263, "Truth Hidden," *PlS*, 293, 294. See pp. 226–27 in this book.

112. Keble, "Implicit Faith Recognised by Reason," *Sermons*, 32.

113. JHN, No. 269, "Doubts in religion do not interfere with practical obedience," November 21, 1830, *Serm.* 4, 171.

114. JHN, No. 269, "Doubts in religion," *Serm.* 4, 171. The imagery might have come from Butler. See "Upon the Ignorance of Man," in *Works*, vol. 2, 270–71.

of light points beyond conscience itself to the person speaking through it. An echo of this usage—God in conscience—resounds three years later in the most famous of Newman's poems, *The Pillar of the Cloud.*[115] Acting up to conscience is not just the execution of an impersonal dictate but a means of relating to God, who will, if obeyed, lead us to religious truth. As Newman had declared quite categorically the week before: "To all those who are perplexed in any way soever, who wish for light but cannot find it, one precept must be given—OBEY."[116]

Culture, however, with its emphasis on the intellect, was taking the opposite route. "In the world," Newman noted in his sermon of October 24, "reason is set against conscience, and usurps its power."[117] He chose the image of usurpation deliberately; it is not just rhetorical flourish but carries a precise meaning. It denotes the encroachment of the intellect on the territory of conscience, both individually and culturally. These two levels tended to coincide. It was particularly tempting for highly intelligent people, "whose gift of reason is something especial—clear, brilliant, or powerful," to join the liberal "march of intellect," as it was commonly (and, by 1830, often satirically) called.[118] "The first sin of men of superior understanding," Newman explained, "is to *value* themselves upon it, and look down upon others."[119]

He was speaking from experience. For years, he had struggled with the pride he took in his own unquestionable acuity, "the devilish imaginations of my superiority of intellect," as he put it in 1824.[120] "I have been very vain this year," he reiterated on his birthday in 1826, "inordinately vain of my acuteness, clearness of mind &c despising others."[121] In 1827, still feeling "conceited and vain," he even admitted to "becoming somewhat worldly; thoughts about livings, the Provostship, promotions &c come before my mind."[122] This self-conceit was shattered at the turn of the year, when he could not bear up to the stress of having to elect a provost (let alone be one), and the death of Mary impressed upon him the transitory character of the world. These blows had cured him, but he formu-

---

115. JHN, "The Pillar of the Cloud," *VV*, 133. Its first stanza reads:

> Lead, Kindly Light, amid the encircling gloom,
> > Lead thou me on!
> The night is dark, and I am far from home —
> > Lead thou me on!
> Keep thou my feet; I do not ask to see
> The distant scene, — one step enough for me.

116. JHN, No. 268, "Obedience the Remedy for Religious Perplexity," November 14, 1830, *PaS* 1, 266.

117. JHN, No. 264, "The Self-wise Inquirer," *PaS* 1, 252.

118. JHN, No. 264, "The Self-wise Inquirer," *PaS* 1, 257.

119. JHN, No. 264, "The Self-wise Inquirer," *PaS* 1, 257.

120. JHN, "February 21, 1824," *AW*, 196. See Culler, *The Imperial Intellect*, 3–4.

121. JHN, "February 21, 1826," *AW*, 208. See also "February 21, 1825," *AW*, 205.

122. JHN, "February 21, 1827," *AW*, 210.

lated an account of the disease only in hindsight. He did so in the sermon of October 24, using the exact terms he would later use to qualify his drift toward the liberalism of the day in the *Apologia*. It is the tendency to "make intellect the measure of praise and blame," that is, to "cast down moral excellence from its true station, and set up the usurped empire of mere reason."[123]

While Newman's usurping intellect might have been halted, it was running rampant in many of the great minds of the day. Without naming names, Newman left his parishioners in little doubt that he was talking of liberals like Bentham, Mill, and Brougham. Such people, he argued, dream of replacing the church, as the communion of believers, by "some other fellowship of civilization, refinement, literature, science, or general illumination."[124] They value "all truths exactly in proportion to the possibility of proving them by . . . mere reason." As a result, "moral and religious truths are thought little of . . . because they fall under the province of *conscience* far more than of the intellect."[125] Since moral character rather than reason differentiates between religious truth claims, liberals tend "to think all religions alike." Utilitarian theory was an application of the same logic to "the code of morals," which it acknowledged only "so far as its dicta can be proved by reasoning, by an appeal to sight, and to expedience."[126] Finally, liberals projected their own mania for "intellectual advancement" onto society at large. Because they think that if "men grow in knowledge, they will grow in virtue," they are "bent on improving the world by making *all men* intellectual," a clear jibe at Brougham's SDUK.[127]

Newman provided an extensive critical analysis of this individual and cultural propensity toward liberalism in a university sermon of December 1831. Upon publication, it was aptly titled *The Usurpations of Reason*. This is a more captivating title than the original one, *On the so-called 'march of intellect' at the present day*, but the latter has the advantage of showing that its aim was a critique of contemporary culture.[128] The sermon explicated the axiom that had undergirded Newman's previous sermons, that "there is no connexion between the intellectual and moral principles of our nature."[129] On "religious subjects," Newman explained, "we may prove any thing or overthrow any thing, and can arrive at truth but accidentally, if we investigate by the mere reason, which is here but the instrument at best in

<hr>

123. JHN, No. 264, "The Self-wise Inquirer," *PaS* 1, 257.

124. JHN, No. 264, "The Self-wise Inquirer," *PaS* 1, 257.

125. JHN, No. 264, "The Self-wise Inquirer," *PaS* 1, 257.

126. JHN, No. 264, "The Self-wise Inquirer," *PaS* 1, 258.

127. JHN, No. 264, "The Self-wise Inquirer," *PaS* 1, 258. See also No. 224, "The Liturgy the service of the Christian Priest," January 31, 1830, *Serm.* 1, 65.

128. JHN, No. 321, "On the so-called 'march of intellect' at the present day," December 11, 1831, BOA A.9.4, title page. The original title explains why the manuscript uses "intellect" in many places where the published version has "reason."

129. JHN, No. 321, "On the so-called 'march of intellect,'" BOA A.9.4, 2 (*OUS*, 40).

the hands of the legitimate Judge, expertness in right conduct."[130] In the published version of the sermon, reason is hardly defined, but this was not for lack of trying. In the manuscript, Newman crossed out one lengthy definition, composed another just as long, and then gave up the attempt.[131] Still, these abortive definitions are informative. First, they clarify the sense in which he was not using the term. Reason did not bear the traditional signification of "all in which man differs from the brutes."[132] It denoted neither the rational soul of Aristotle and the medieval scholastics nor the "Λόγος" used "in Scripture & in the writings of the primitive Christians."[133] In this traditional sense, reason includes "the power of discriminating between right and wrong, & of guiding the actions," but this is precisely the sense Newman wanted to exclude.[134]

Instead, he defined intellect as "the mere speculative faculty."[135] He viewed it as a compound, made up of those "powers of mind" that "are naturally & adequately exhibited in speaking & writing," and which, "without influencing conduct themselves, can collectively describe & pass judgment on conduct — such as the reasoning faculty, imagination, generalization, memory & the like."[136] Much remains unclear in these attempts at definition, but they contain two basic ideas. First, the intellect is the faculty of cogent verbal expression. It is the faculty not of conceiving or having ideas but of explaining and defending them; not of holding something, but of arguing for it. Secondly, intellect signifies all those mental powers which operate without providing an impetus to action; all but conscience and the will. Memory, imagination, generalization, and reasoning all contribute to assessing praxis but do not originate it, because they lack a conception of right and wrong and thus, of a good for which to act. Hence, Newman's contrastive definition of the "moral powers." They "depend on <u>character</u>, which itself depends in turn on the cultivation of our natural sense of right & wrong," that is, on a deliberate course of action aimed at the good.[137]

In 1828, Newman had tentatively suggested this view of the relation between intellect and moral character to Blanco White. By 1830, it was a fact he took for granted. He used it not only for theorizing and preaching but also to account for his own choices. When Simeon Lloyd Pope asked him to write "just *two* lines" explaining his withdrawal from the Bible Society, Newman was "amused."[138] He did not think the grounds for such a decision could be put into syllogisms or for-

---

130. JHN, No. 321, "On the so-called 'march of intellect,'" BOA A.9.4, 2 (*OUS*, 40).
131. JHN, No. 321, "On the so-called 'march of intellect,'" BOA A.9.4, 6v, 7, 7v (*OUS*, 43).
132. JHN, No. 321, "On the so-called 'march of intellect,'" BOA A.9.4, 7v (*OUS*, 43).
133. JHN, No. 321, "On the so-called 'march of intellect,'" BOA A.9.4, 8.
134. JHN, No. 321, "On the so-called 'march of intellect,'" BOA A.9.4, 7v (*OUS*, 43).
135. JHN, No. 321, "On the so-called 'march of intellect,'" BOA A.9.4, 7v.
136. JHN, No. 321, "On the so-called 'march of intellect,'" BOA A.9.4, 6v-7v.
137. JHN, No. 321, "On the so-called 'march of intellect,'" BOA A.9.4, 7, 7v.
138. Simeon Lloyd Pope to JHN, August 13, 1830, *LD* 2, 264n2.

mulas. "Practical matters cannot be defended by argument, or explained on paper," he argued, "they are determined by the ἦθος of the agent — who (whether he be correct or not) still adopts his measures, not on a process of reasoning which words will do justice to, but on feeling, on the dictates of an internal unproduceable sense."[139]

The sermon formalized this contrast between the inward (and preverbal) moral springs to action and their reflexive verbal expression and argumentative evaluation. Thus, it described "theorists on religious subjects" as "those who have speculated without acting on their sense of right, or (again) who have rested their cause on mere argument, instead of a direct contemplation of its subject matter."[140] Such mere intellectuals err, first, because their thinking is not rooted in the moral and religious premises derived from conscientious action, and secondly, because their views result from a mere linkage of propositions, rather than a perception of the unseen object of faith. Newman's belief in the priority of moral character over intellect in the pursuit of religious truth altered his understanding of the relation between faith and reason.

Faith, Reason, and Apologetics

Recall that in 1825, Newman had defined faith as attaining to conviction "from reliance on something else which gives the information."[141] He had paralleled it with belief in the correctness of our "senses," our "memory," and our "reasoning powers," all of which we trust to tell truly.[142] He reiterated this line of argument in a sermon in May 1829 but admitted that the analogy was not quite perfect. After all, "to trust our senses and reason is in fact nothing more than to trust ourselves," which is different from "trusting another person." And the latter is faith in the "Scripture sense of the word."[143] Accordingly, he defined faith as *"reliance on the words of another."*[144] Religious belief, in this sense, is still analogous to ordinary exercises of belief in matters of fact. His parishioners knew they "are in an island." But none "has *seen* the land all around, and has proved for himself that the fact is so." They simply believe it on "the *report of others*."[145] Likewise, we all know that we will die, and arrange our affairs accordingly. But "*what proof* has

---

139. JHN to Simeon Lloyd Pope, August 15, 1830, *LD* 2, 264.

140. JHN, No. 321, "On the so-called 'march of intellect,'" BOA A.9.4, 15 (*OUS*, 49). See also No. 264, "The Self-wise Inquirer," *PaS* 1, 256.

141. JHN, No. 57, "Nature and object of faith," February 20, 1825, *Serm.* 5, 166. See p. 89 in this book.

142. JHN, No. 57, "Nature and object of faith," *Serm.* 5, 166.

143. JHN, No. 196, "Religious Faith Rational," May 24, 1829, *PaS* 1, 222.

144. JHN, No. 196, "Religious Faith Rational," *PaS* 1, 222.

145. JHN, No. 196, "Religious Faith Rational," *PaS* 1, 223.

any of us that he shall die?" Deaths around us are usually few and far between. Again, we believe it because "it is *a received fact*."[146]

Religion, however, is not about ordinary events within the range of our experience but about "a future life."[147] People, therefore, might rejoin that since God is the only reliable source of information about supernatural facts, they have a right to be "*certain*" that God has spoken, and that they are not because "it is not *His voice* we hear, but *man's* speaking in His name," an objection Charles had raised.[148] Newman admitted this was "a very large and weighty question," but did not consider it "a very practical one," since most people who wonder about "our reasons for believing the Bible came from God" "dislike" religion to begin with.[149] This had been his diagnosis of Charles's condition some years before, but he now countered it by appealing to conscience rather than to the evidences: "It is a mistake to suppose that our obedience to God's will is merely founded on our belief in the word of such persons as tell us Scripture came from God. We obey God primarily because we actually feel His presence in our consciences bidding us obey Him."[150] If we attend to conscience, belief in revelation will come naturally: "let us obey God's voice in our hearts, and I will venture to say we shall have no doubts practically formidable about the truth of Scripture."[151] This does not mean that Newman deemed the evidences unsound, only that he downplayed their import. A new altercation with his brother Charles made this clear.

In May 1830, Charles tried to revive his earlier controversy with John. He thought John had argued unfairly five years earlier and sent a new batch of papers expounding his skeptical views. John sent them back unread but responded in August with the longest letter he ever wrote.[152] Most of it was an exasperated attempt to set the record straight by minutely reconstructing their earlier discussion. But even though he defended his earlier course of argument, his vision of the relation between faith and reason had changed. Recall that Charles had understood John's appeal to external evidences as the ground of belief in revelation to mean that he considered them beyond doubt. When Charles realized that they were merely probabilistic, he was so elated that he thought John had become, in the latter's words, "a brother-sceptic, if not a brother-infidel."[153]

Because Charles had considered the discussion closed, John had never responded to the charge, but now he did. He attributed Charles's objection to a

146. JHN, No. 196, "Religious Faith Rational," *PaS* 1, 224.
147. JHN, No. 196, "Religious Faith Rational," *PaS* 1, 224.
148. JHN, No. 196, "Religious Faith Rational," *PaS* 1, 226.
149. JHN, No. 196, "Religious Faith Rational," *PaS* 1, 226, 229.
150. JHN, No. 196, "Religious Faith Rational," *PaS* 1, 229.
151. JHN, No. 196, "Religious Faith Rational," *PaS* 1, 231.
152. JHN to CRN, August 19, 1830, *LD* 2, 266–81.
153. JHN to CRN, August 19, 1830, *LD* 2, 276. See p. 77 in this book.

misunderstanding of the idea of certainty. "You seem to think," John argued, "that no evidence for an alleged fact is certain, which admits of the chance of it being otherwise — i.e. you would hold that demonstration alone is certain proof."[154] But this is an unwarranted extension of the standards of rational justification in one domain of knowledge to all. "No facts are known, no practical matters conducted on demonstrative proof," John maintained, "which is found in pure mathematics alone and subjects of a similar nature."[155]

Like Butler, Newman held that where contingent rather than necessary truth is concerned, we judge and act on the basis of probabilistic evidence: "every thing we do, is done on probabilities."[156] In consequence, "there is always *a* chance of error, or even if we have overwhelming evidence, things *could* be otherwise than they seem.[157] But such contingency does not justify confining certainty to the realm of necessary truth. In many concrete cases, we think and act without doubt. We are, in fact, certain, even though contingent facts, like our eventual death, admit of "theoretical doubt."[158] This had been Butler's argument in the *Analogy*, when he argued that "probability is the very guide of life."[159] Even scant evidence "in matters of practice will lay us under an absolute and formal obligation, in point of prudence and interest, to act upon that presumption, or low probability."[160] "*Certainty* in the business of life," Newman likewise concluded, "means a *conviction sufficient for practice.*"[161] Apologists had offered more than enough evidences to warrant such a conviction. As Newman put it in his university sermon of December 1831, the "alternation of arguments, for & against, results indeed in an indefinitely vast balance on the side of Christianity."[162] But even so, it still "does not get beyond the first suggestions of plain religiously trained reason."[163] Obedience to conscience remains the primary means of acquiring religious knowledge.

John tried to explain this idea to Charles, but eventually omitted the explanation from the letter "for want of time and space," happily so, he thought a few months later, "for it would not profit him now, and may at some future day."[164] Half of these reflections I discussed in Chapter 7. They dealt with the universality of revelation and its relation to conscience. The other half of the memorandum concerned the relation between evidence and religious belief. Newman admitted

154. JHN to CRN, August 19, 1830, *LD* 2, 280.
155. JHN to CRN, August 19, 1830, *LD* 2, 280.
156. JHN to CRN, August 19, 1830, *LD* 2, 280.
157. JHN to CRN, August 19, 1830, *LD* 2, 280.
158. JHN to CRN, August 19, 1830, *LD* 2, 280.
159. Butler, *The Analogy of Religion*, 25.
160. Butler, *The Analogy of Religion*, 25.
161. JHN to CRN, August 19, 1830, *LD* 2, 280.
162. JHN, No. 321, "On the so-called 'march of intellect,'" BOA A.9.4, 18v (*OUS*, 51).
163. JHN, No. 321, "On the so-called 'march of intellect,'" BOA A.9.4, 18v (*OUS*, 51).
164. JHN, January 2, 1831, *LD* 2, 281.

that although "the evidence for the Christian Revelation is more than sufficient for the proof of the fact, still it is not so great as it might have been."[165] In part, this is due to the nature of the case. Because "there *is no limit* to the accumulation of evidence for *any fact*," probabilistic evidence can always increase. "We should have more abundant proof that there has been a revolution in France," he observed, "had we read 10 distinct Newspapers instead of 9." As in the case of the July Revolution, we have sufficient evidence to believe in revelation, and yet, the evidence "might have been indefinitely greater." This might seem a drawback, but Newman did not think it was. He regarded the fact that the evidence for Christianity could have been greater as a constitutive aspect of the economy of salvation, an idea he also gleaned from Butler. The "formation of a virtuous char-acter depends on trial," Newman argued, and one such trial is the difficulty of believing in revelation: "this world is a world of temptation — and among these, the temptation to unbelief is one." Revelation, therefore, "was never intended to force truth upon any one, but to give to those who *seek*." Accordingly, the evidence for the divinity of Christianity is "very strong but not overpowering, that men might not *be forced* to accept it as if they were mere machines, but in order to try what each man was made of."[166] The quest for God is driven by conscientious obedience and thus premised on human responsibility. It is a test of character. Had Charles reiterated Paine's objection that the gospel ought to have been written on the sun, John would now have responded in the words of Butler. The idea of life as "a state of discipline and improvement, necessarily excludes such sensible evidence and conviction of religion."[167]

Because Newman thought that too much emphasis on the evidences obscures the role of moral character in the acquisition of religious truth, he became increasingly critical of the apologetic tradition of the English Enlighten-ment. He did not question its cogency but doubted its efficacy and pertinence. In his December 1831 university sermon, Newman highlighted its limitations, appealing, almost flippantly, to one of its greatest detractors:

> Hume, in his Essay on Miracles, has well propounded a doctrine which at the same time he misapplies. He speaks of "those dangerous friends or dis-guised enemies to the Christian religion, who have undertaken to defend it by the principles of human reason." "Our most holy religion (he proceeds) is founded on <u>Faith,</u> not on reason"; this is said in irony, but it is true as far as every important question in revelation is concerned.[168]

<hr>

165. JHN, "Memorandum on Revelation," *LD* 2, 282.

166. JHN, "Memorandum on Revelation," *LD* 2, 282.

167. Butler, "Upon the Ignorance of Man," in *Works*, vol. 2, 267; see also 268; Butler, *The Analogy of Religion*, 203.

168. JHN, No. 321, "On the so-called 'march of intellect,'" BOA A.9.4, 9–10 (*OUS*, 45); Hume, *Enquiry*, 94 (130).

Hume rightly held that faith is not founded on reason but did not see what its real foundation was. Reason, Newman argued, "incroaches [*sic*] on the province of religion" when it attempts "to judge of those truths which are subjected to another part of our nature, the moral sense."[169] This does not mean that arguments for Christianity are logically unsound but that relying on them is misguided: "it is as absurd to argue men, as to torture them, into believing."[170] If faith does not originate in the intellect but in moral character, treating it as if it was the conclusion of an argumentative process is to misrepresent it fundamentally.

Newman, therefore, regarded the evidences more like "splendid philosophical investigations than practical arguments."[171] "In matter of fact," he asked rhetorically, "<u>how</u> many men do we suppose in a century out of the whole body of Christians have been primarily brought to belief or retained in it by an intimate & lively perception of the force of what are technically called the evidences?"[172] The reason there are "so few" is that religious conviction is not rooted in argument:

> to the mind already familiar with the truths of natural religion, enough of evidence is at once afforded by the mere fact of the present existence of Christianity, which, viewed in its connexion with its principles & upholders & effects, bears on the face of it the signs of a divine ordinance in the very same way in which the visible world attests to us its own divine origin.[173]

The conscientious person who believes in God and obeys him will recognize, at once, that Christianity embodies the perfection of those moral and religious convictions she already holds: "so alert is the instinctive power of a sedulously improved conscience that by some secret faculty & without any refined reasoning process it seems to detect moral truth wherever it lies hid . . . and this especially in the case of revealed religion, which is one comprehensive moral fact."[174]

This idea should not be confused with the practice of judging individual doctrines by their content, as Charles had done. The person who already believes the truths of natural religion on the authority of conscience accepts revealed religion as a whole, difficult doctrines included, on the authority of scripture and the church, because she recognizes that the same God who speaks through conscience also speaks through scripture and the church. Such a mode of judging is more like perceiving that two different paintings are from the same artist, although from different periods or in different styles, than like giving a verdict based on the weighing of forensic evidence.

169. JHN, No. 321, "On the so-called 'march of intellect,'" BOA A.9.4, 9 (*OUS*, 44).
170. JHN, No. 321, "On the so-called 'march of intellect,'" BOA A.9.4, 14 (*OUS*, 48).
171. JHN, No. 321, "On the so-called 'march of intellect,'" BOA A.9.4, 18 (*OUS*, 50).
172. JHN, No. 321, "On the so-called 'march of intellect,'" BOA A.9.4, 18 (*OUS*, 50–51).
173. JHN, No. 321, "On the so-called 'march of intellect,'" BOA A.9.4, 19 (*OUS*, 51).
174. JHN, No. 321, "On the so-called 'march of intellect,'" BOA A.9.4, 19 (*OUS*, 51).

Besides being ineffective, an undue emphasis on the evidences obscures the structure of faith as belief upon authority. Along with the other "usurpations of the intellect," Newman traced evidential apologetics back to "the Reformation," when, "together with the tyranny, the legitimate authority of the Church was more or less overthrown; [and] in some places its ultimate basis also, the moral sense."[175] Recall that in March 1829, Newman had argued for an ancient tradition of moral and religious insight, "the wisdom of our ancestors," which is transmitted in history by prejudice more than argument.[176] Because the vast majority of people cannot prove these religious and moral insights, they have to accept them on authority, and whether they do so depends on their moral character. This transmissive process broke down at the Reformation:

> The Lutherans resisted the <u>Christian</u> ordinance; — the Calvinists went farther & rejected the supreme authority of the law of conscience. Accordingly, revealed religion was in a great measure stripped of its proof; — for the existence of the Church had been its external evidence, and its internal had been supplied by the moral sense.[177]

People, in other words, used to accept Christianity based on a convergence of two realities: the objective reality of the one, authoritative body proclaiming it and the subjective reality of their cultivated conscience. By breaking up the one church into several competing bodies, the Lutheran Reformation undermined the authority of the church. By introducing the idea of total depravity, Calvinism denied people the subjective proof of religion: the innate sense of right and wrong. Both developments originated from a rejection of ecclesial authority and the attempt to judge for oneself, that is, from the usurping intellect.

But reason did not stop there. It tried to fill the vacuum it had created. "The intellect undertook to repair the demolition it had made, and to render the proof of Christianity independent both of the Church & of the law of nature."[178] This is how Enlightenment apologetics came about. Since the "proof of the authority of Scripture" was no longer "the testimony borne to it by the actually existing Church," post-Reformation thinkers evidenced the truth of revelation by means of the historicity of certain supernatural events recorded in the Bible (miracles and prophecy).[179] In this way, a plain argument accessible to all became "subtle and complicated in its form" and fully perspicuous only to "the oligarchy of learning."[180] At the same time, natural theologians began to limit themselves almost

175. JHN, No. 321, "On the so-called 'march of intellect,'" BOA A.9.4, 23 (*OUS*, 54).
176. JHN to Mrs Newman, March 13, 1829, *LD* 2, 130.
177. JHN, No. 321, "On the so-called 'march of intellect,'" BOA A.9.4, 23–24 (*OUS*, 54).
178. JHN, No. 321, "On the so-called 'march of intellect,'" BOA A.9.4, 24 (*OUS*, 54).
179. JHN, No. 321, "On the so-called 'march of intellect,'" BOA A.9.4, 24 (*OUS*, 54–55).
180. JHN, No. 321, "On the so-called 'march of intellect,'" BOA A.9.4, 24 (*OUS*, 55).

exclusively to arguments from "the marks of design in the creation, which are beautiful and interesting to the believer in a God" but fail to convince those who "have not already recognized God's voice within them," a flaw that is aggravated by a possible "unsoundness in the intellectual basis of the argument."[181] Reason, in short, first undermined the authority of church and conscience, and then sought to remedy the loss by grounding religious belief on itself. And it went further still. By severing the connection between religion and ethics, utilitarian theory constituted a "still bolder encroachment . . . by the intellect."[182] It tried "to deprive the moral law of its intrinsic authority, & to rest it upon a theory of present expediency." In this way, it "constituted itself the court of ultimate appeal in religious disputes, under pretence of affording a clearer & more scientifically arranged code than is to be collected from . . . conscience."[183] The upshot of these historical processes of usurpation was the growing prevalence of liberalism in the culture of Newman's day.

Conclusion

Like his rejection of evangelicalism, Newman's critique of liberalism stemmed from his conviction that religious belief is grounded in moral character. Human beings are responsible agents first and foremost: responsible to their conscience, to the God who speaks through it, and to Christ, who is that God incarnate. People's intellectual functioning and the knowledge it yields are only subsidiary to the more basic awareness of God and his demands, which they acquire through conscience. We relate to God before we ever think of proving anything about his existence or attributes. If we are aware of this relationship and cultivate it, we will accept his self-revelation in Christ when we encounter it, and reasonably so. If we do not acknowledge this primordial relationship, no amount of evidence will ever convince us that Christianity is true. This conviction remained key to Newman's religious epistemology. Although he was keener to highlight the rational aspects of faith in later life than now, when he was newly sensitized to the dangerous spread of unfettered intellectual inquiry, he continued to insist that faithfulness to conscience determines belief more than explicit argumentations. In the early 1830s, however, Newman's main concern was to resist the usurping intellect, which corroded the dictates of conscience and traditional understandings of religious belief. Still, this was only one aspect of Newman's response to liberalism.

181. JHN, No. 321, "On the so-called 'march of intellect,'" BOA A.9.4, 25 (*OUS*, 55).
182. JHN, No. 321, "On the so-called 'march of intellect,'" BOA A.9.4, 26 (*OUS*, 55).
183. JHN, No. 321, "On the so-called 'march of intellect,'" BOA A.9.4, 26 (*OUS*, 55).

CHAPTER 9

The Religion of Liberalism

Liberalism was a multifaceted construct in Newman's thought. Ideologically, it stressed scientific knowledge and free enquiry, was suspicious of tradition and belief based on authority, and relativized religious truth claims. Its *ethos*, to use Newman's term, was one of casual indifference about religious truth, without dismissing it entirely. Liberalism was socially embedded in utilitarian institutions of Whig and Radical inspiration, such as London University and the Society for the Diffusion of Useful Knowledge (SDUK). Politically, it was embodied by a succession of Whig governments from late 1830 onward. Both individually and culturally, liberalism was driven by a misguided reliance on reason to acquire moral and religious truth, but it was not only a mistaken mode of religious enquiry.

Liberalism was also a substantive pseudoreligious worldview that called for deconstruction. It was closely allied with the ideology of progress that lauded the changes that had turned Merrie Olde Englande into a scientific, technological, and industrial powerhouse and an empire on which the sun never set. Theologically, liberalism had close affinities with Socinianism. It was characterized by a shallow optimism about human beings that ignored sin and evil. Morals and religion had no independent claim on people's allegiance but were reduced to mere markers of being civilized. Nor did mystery and tradition have any place in the liberal worldview. They were bugbears from a bygone era of intellectual darkness. It was the encroachment of the Whig torchbearers of this worldly ideology on the Established Church that set the Tractarian machine in motion. But I will not get ahead of my story.

Liberal Religion, Socinian Theology, and the Civilizing Process

If experience had drilled one conviction into Newman's mind, it was this: being religious means turning from the world to God, not just from sin to holiness but also from time to eternity. He explained why this was so in a March 1829 sermon published as *The World our Enemy*. Scripture, Newman observed, describes the world in some cases as "positively sinful" but in others as simply "the present visible system of things, without taking into consideration whether it is good or bad."[1] In the latter sense, it means the "course of things which we see carried on

---

1. JHN, No. 189, "The World our Enemy," March 8, 1829, *PlS*, 18, 21. The sermon was preached in the same period as, but not as part of, the Romans course. Newman preached it again on December 17, 1837, so that revisions cannot be ruled out (see *LD* 6, 178).

273

by means of human agency, with all its duties and pursuits"—the realm of society and culture. In principle, nothing is wrong with this realm. It "is framed . . . by GOD Himself, and therefore cannot be otherwise than good."[2] This is not to say that specific social structures are of divine origin but that the characteristically human endeavour to seek social and cultural organization is willed by God. Yet, even in this sense—whatever its concrete form of organization—the world "is not to be trusted, because it cannot last."[3] Only what is eternal merits our trust. And yet, we tend to invest too much in our perishable world nonetheless. The "state of things which we see, fair and excellent in itself, is very likely (for the very reason that it is seen, and because the spiritual and future world is not seen) to seduce our wayward hearts from our true and eternal good."[4] This is not because the world is bad, but because we are. The world "is an enemy of our souls . . . because the love of it is dangerous to beings circumstanced as we are; things in themselves good being not good to us sinners."[5] Natural corruption makes us short-sighted. We focus on what is around us and find it difficult to look beyond the here and now: "sight has more power over us than belief, and the present than the future," and thus we are tempted to stake too much on this world, which is "divine," but "temporal."[6]

Newman had learned this truth the hard way, through his father's professional failure, his own defeats, illnesses, financial worries, family conflicts, and, most of all, his sister Mary's untimely death. But liberalism denied it. That is why Newman's list of liberal enemies of the church included political economists. Political economy—what we now call economics—was a relatively new science in Newman's day (at Oxford, the chair was founded in 1825). He distrusted it because it focused exclusively on "the well-being of men in this life." "The sciences," he argued, "of good government, of acquiring wealth, of preventing and relieving want, and the like, are for this reason especially dangerous." By "fixing, as they do, our exertions on this world as an end, they go far to persuade us that they have no other end; they accustom us to think too much of success in life and temporal prosperity."[7] Political economy can even tempt us to think that religion, with its otherworldly focus, acts as a brake on socioeconomic progress. It can make us "jealous of religion and its institutions, as if these stood in our way, preventing us from doing so much for the worldly interests of mankind as we might wish."[8] For that reason, Newman considered political economy the

2. JHN, No. 189, "The World our Enemy," *PlS*, 19.
3. JHN, No. 189, "The World our Enemy," *PlS*, 19.
4. JHN, No. 189, "The World our Enemy," *PlS*, 20.
5. JHN, No. 189, "The World our Enemy," *PlS*, 19–20.
6. JHN, No. 189, "The World our Enemy," *PlS*, 20.
7. JHN, No. 189, "The World our Enemy," *PlS*, 20.
8. JHN, No. 189, "The World our Enemy," *PlS*, 20.

characteristic science of the emergent liberal worldview, which basked in a self-satisfied sense of security and optimism based on imperial power, prosperity, and intellectual and technological advancement.

In a sermon of December 1830, Newman indicted the whole of English culture along these lines. "Do not we constantly hear mention made of our glorious farspreading empire on which the sun never sets," he observed, and "do we not think ourselves wise, sagacious, enlightened, dexterous, beyond all former ages?"[9] Are "we not quite intoxicated," he added, "with that new knowledge of the wonders of nature which scientific discoveries have given us, or with the power over nature and the ingenious contrivances thence resulting?"[10] And how about "the love of money"—"the root of all evil, now sovereign among us?"[11] Money, Newman argued, has become "the measure of every thing — and things are called good things or bad things according as they are lucrative or no."[12] Imperial power, scientific knowledge, technological innovation, uninhibited capitalism; these were the key tenets of England's cultural consensus, and they all contributed to a false sense of security: a security of self, without God. This "self-trust" explained why culture was permeated by religious indifference and relativism, expressed in

> a contempt for the Church, and an undervaluing of ancient notions on the ground that they ARE ancient — and a consequent avowed neglect and ignorance of the system of Christian truth — [and] an opinion, certainly increasing in quarters of most influence in civil matters, that one belief is as good as and no better than another.[13]

These corrosive tenets sum up what liberalism did to religion, but it was not all there was to it. From liberalism's secure sense of self emerged an optimistic religion of civilization, meant to replace traditional Christianity.

In a university sermon of April 8, 1832, Newman applied to liberalism the words Jeremiah had used to denounce the teachings of Israel's false prophets: "They have healed the hurt of the daughter of My people slightly, saying: Peace, peace — when there is no peace."[14] These false prophets were deceitful, "not in promising a _cure_ for the wounded soul, but in healing the hurt of the daughter of God's people _slightly_, saying, Peace, peace, before either the evil or the remedy

---

9. JHN, No. 273, "Christ will come in a wicked age — with a reference to these times," December 12, 1830, _Serm._ 3, 172–73.

10. JHN, No. 273, "Christ will come in a wicked age," _Serm._ 3, 173.

11. JHN, No. 273, "Christ will come in a wicked age," _Serm._ 3, 175.

12. JHN, No. 273, "Christ will come in a wicked age," _Serm._ 3, 175.

13. JHN, No. 273, "Christ will come in a wicked age," _Serm._ 3, 174, 176.

14. Jeremiah 8:11; JHN, No. 334, "On the principle of Justice as one of intrinsic & external authority, and not merely subservient to the ends of Benevolence," April 8, 1832, BOA A.9.4, published as "On Justice, as a Principle of Divine Governance," _OUS_, 86–107. See also No. 273, "Christ will come in a wicked age," _Serm._ 3, 170.

for the hurt had been rightly ascertained by them."[15] The worldly optimism of the liberal was premised on the same misconception of human nature. When preparing the sermon, Newman explained to Froude that liberalism's "cheerful hopeful view of human nature" is deceptive, because it "is *nominally* like the Christian's cheerfulness, but *superficial*."[16] Christian hope is the outcome of an inward discipline of conscientious obedience, in which evil is not ignored but acknowledged and gradually overcome. Liberal optimism, by contrast, overlooks inward evil. It reflects only outward circumstances. It is the product of "times of political peace & safety . . . when the laws of a country are upheld & obeyed, and property [is] secure."[17] It issues from empire, science, technology, and prosperity, not from a persistent effort to amend our corrupt selves by obeying God.

Nevertheless, liberals sought to reconcile their optimism with religion. The resulting worldview coincided with a theology Newman had long rejected. The liberal worldview, Newman argued, "when assuming a definite doctrinal basis, will be found to centre in Socinianism or Theophilanthropism, a different name being given to the system as it admits or rejects the authority of Scripture."[18] Theophilanthropy was a species of Deism that flourished briefly at the end of the French revolutionary period. It was founded by Thomas Paine (among others), did indeed reject the Bible, and valued religious belief only as a constituent of individual and social well-being. Socinianism has a more complex history, but most of it can be safely ignored. Newman was not primarily concerned with the precise beliefs of Fausto Sozzini and the Polish Brethren who published his Racovian Catechism, nor even with the beliefs of the recently organized denomination of English Unitarians.[19] Rather, Newman was concerned with "the <u>spirit</u> of this system," which had a long history in England and was, he thought, infecting "great numbers of men, who are unconscious of the origin & tendency of their opinions."[20]

Recall that Socinians were committed to God's absolute unity, denied Christ's divinity, and rejected the atonement. Often, Newman focused on the former tenets (as in his April 1830 university sermon).[21] Now he critiqued the latter, because of the optimistic understanding of God and human nature upon which it was premised. Socinians, Newman argued, hold,

15. JHN, No. 334, "On the principle of Justice," BOA A.9.4, 5 (*OUS*, 88).
16. JHN to Richard Hurrell Froude, April 5, 1832, *LD* 3, 35.
17. JHN, No. 334, "On the principle of Justice," BOA A.9.4, 7 (*OUS*, 90).
18. JHN, No. 334, "On the principle of Justice," BOA A.9.4, 9 (*OUS*, 91). See also JHN to Richard Hurrell Froude, April 5, 1832, *LD* 3, 35.
19. H. L. Short, "Presbyterians under a New Name," in *The English Presbyterians: From Elizabethan Puritanism to Modern Unitarianism*, ed. C. Gordon Bolam et al. (London: George Allen & Unwin, 1968), 240.
20. JHN, No. 334, "On the principle of Justice," BOA A.9.4, 9 (*OUS*, 91).
21. See pp. 233–34.

that the rule of Divine Government is one of benevolence, & nothing but benevolence, that evil is but remedial & temporary, that sin is of a venial nature; that repentance is a sufficient atonement for it; [and] that the moral sense is substantially but an instinct of benevolence.[22]

Newman had long held that the Socinian denial of the atonement downplayed the depth of sin and evil.[23] The discovery that Socinians subordinated the divine attribute of justice to that of benevolence was more recent. He found it in Joseph Priestley (one of the English founders of Unitarianism), whom he had read while doing research for *The Arians of the Fourth Century*. In the context of an attack on the atonement, Priestley insisted that, in "the deity, *justice* can be nothing more than a modification of *goodness*, or *benevolence*, which is his sole governing principle."[24] Newman encountered the same view among the liberal intellectuals of his day.

The instance Newman used in his sermon was that of the MP James Mackintosh, a renowned Scottish intellectual who had just published an acclaimed treatise on the development of moral philosophy in the past two centuries as part of the latest edition of the *Encyclopaedia Britannica*.[25] As a prominent philosophic Whig, Mackintosh tried to distance himself from the utilitarianism of Bentham and the Philosophic Radicals, although he shared many of their values. Against utilitarianism, he argued that people have an innate "moral sense . . . which immediately approves what is right and condemns what is wrong."[26] People are "so constituted as instantaneously to approve certain actions without any reference to their consequences." And yet, Mackintosh agreed with the utilitarians that, upon analysis, we invariably find "that a tendency to produce general happiness is the essential characteristic of such actions."[27] Utilitarianism, in short, is mistaken about moral motivations but correct about what is right in actions. As a result, Mackintosh's definition of God's moral governance was one that could ruffle few utilitarians. "A perfectly good Being," he argued, "cannot indeed be conceived by us to have any other end in view than general wellbeing."[28] Just as our moral sense is geared

22. JHN, No. 334, "On the principle of Justice," BOA A.9.4, 9–10 (*OUS*, 91).

23. JHN, "May 16, 1821," *AW*, 166.

24. Joseph Priestley, *An History of the Corruptions of Christianity*, vol. 1 (Birmingham: J. Johnson, 1782), 158, see also 277. Newman borrowed this edition of the work from Oriel College Library on June 17, 1831, and kept it nearly four months (Parker). The book was dedicated to Theophilus Lindsey, who founded the first openly Unitarian congregation in England (see Short, "Presbyterians under a New Name," 229–32).

25. See JHN to Richard Hurrell Froude, April 5, 1832, *LD* 3, 35; James Mackintosh, "Dissertation Second; Exhibiting a General View of the Progress of Ethical Philosophy, Chiefly during the Seventeenth and Eighteenth Centuries," in *Encyclopaedia Britannica*, 7th ed., vol. 1 (Edinburgh: Adam and Charles Black, 1842), 293–429. All installments were dated 1842, but the first were published in 1830.

26. Mackintosh, "Progress of Ethical Philosophy," 298.

27. Mackintosh, "Progress of Ethical Philosophy," 298.

28. Mackintosh, "Progress of Ethical Philosophy," 402.

toward "general happiness," so is God's governance.[29] Accordingly, Mackintosh attributed God's "whole government to benevolence" as its "sole principle."[30]

Newman vigorously challenged this idea. On Mackintosh's conception, he argued, justice disappears "as an original absolute principle of the moral law"; it becomes subservient to the "ultimate end" of general happiness.[31] But there is no reason to think that benevolence is more basic than justice, either in human motivation or in divine providence. "If it be natural to pity & wish well to men in general, without reference to their character or our personal knowledge of them," Newman argued, "it is also natural to feel indignation when vice triumphs, & to be dissatisfied and uneasy till the inequality is removed."[32] Our moral nature is not just benevolent, it also clamors for the punishment of vice and the reward of virtue. This demand for retributive justice is not just a part of our moral subjectivity. As Butler had emphasized, retribution is built into the moral constitution of the world. Like Butler, Newman pointed to the sometimes disastrous consequences of "<u>single</u> sins, as furnishing some foreboding of the full & final judgment of God upon us."[33] Often, such consequences "neither effect, nor evince a tendency towards effecting, the moral benefit of the individuals thus punished," and thus they cannot be understood as subservient to people's happiness.[34] As he wrote to Froude, they "are *retributive* essentially, not *remedial*."[35] This view, that of natural religion, is not superseded by revealed religion, only complemented by it. Mercy, Newman told Froude, is "supplemental not substitutive for justice"; it tempers the *fear* of retribution, but it does not efface the *principle* of retribution.[36]

Newman did not mean to expose liberals like Mackintosh as covert Socinians. He merely tried to show that the ideas they promoted coincided—possibly unbeknownst to them—with Socinian theology. The resultant worldview, therefore, was not Socinianism but something distinct, a novel, liberal religiosity, exemplified by the Whigs in power. Newman considered it too complacent and shallow to have much life in it. "The present reign of Whiggery cannot last," he wrote to Simeon Lloyd Pope a day after his sermon, "the notion is an absurdity."

When good and evil fight together, Tories and Radicals come into the field —
but Whigs are neither fish, flesh, nor fowl — and have no resting place — their

29. Mackintosh, "Progress of Ethical Philosophy," 402; JHN, No. 334, "On the principle of Justice," BOA A.9.4, 11 (*OUS*, 92).

30. Mackintosh, "Progress of Ethical Philosophy," 402; JHN, No. 334, "On the principle of Justice," BOA A.9.4, 12 (*OUS*, 92–93).

31. JHN, No. 334, "On the principle of Justice," BOA A.9.4, 14 (*OUS*, 93–94).

32. JHN, No. 334, "On the principle of Justice," BOA A.9.4, 12 (*OUS*, 92–93).

33. JHN, No. 334, "On the principle of Justice," BOA A.9.4, 21 (*OUS*, 99).

34. JHN, No. 334, "On the principle of Justice," BOA A.9.4, 22 (*OUS*, 100).

35. JHN to Richard Hurrell Froude, April 5, 1832, *LD* 3, 36.

36. JHN to Richard Hurrell Froude, April 5, 1832, *LD* 3, 36.

whole view is a supercilious theory — their policy is liberalism, and their basis Socinianism — they have no root in the heart Superstition may last for ages, and true religion, and Manicheeism, and fanaticism — any thing that has depth and reality in it — but as to that cold and scoffing theory, which says there is no great evil in the world, affects non-chalance [*sic*], and says all religions are about the same, nothing can come of it — it is a shortlived dream.[37]

The dream was not quite as short-lived as Newman expected. When he wrote the *Apologia* in 1864, he realized that the situation had only worsened. Liberalism was no longer the badge of a single party but a "deep, plausible scepticism" saturating the entire "educated lay world."[38] But even in 1832, he felt it was a worldview that needed to be actively resisted.

Newman did so most emphatically in one of his best-known sermons, *The Religion of the Day*, preached on August 26, 1832. In "every age of Christianity," Newman argued, "there has been what may be called a *religion of the world*, which so far imitates the one true religion, as to deceive the unstable and unwary."[39] In "rude and fierce" medieval times, "the darker side of the Gospel" issued in a religion "of *fear*," which abounded in cruelty and superstition.[40] The "civilized" nineteenth century saw the contrasting evil. "It has taken the brighter side of the Gospel," he argued, "its tidings of comfort, its precepts of love; all darker, deeper views of man's condition and prospects being comparatively forgotten."[41] Such a religion suits an age of political, economic, and scientific success, of growing prosperity and wide education, but it originates in something akin to what Norbert Elias has called the civilizing process, more than in Christianity:[42] "As the reason is cultivated, the taste formed, the affections and sentiments refined," Newman observed, "a general decency and grace will of course spread over the face of society, quite independently of the influence of revelation."[43] As part of this broad civilizing process, religion and morality become subsumed under the mores of polite society:

Our manners are courteous; we avoid giving pain or offence; our words become correct; our relative duties are carefully performed. Our sense of propriety shows itself even in our domestic arrangements, in the embellishments of our houses, in our amusements, and so also in our religious profession.[44]

37. JHN to Simeon Lloyd Pope, April 9, 1832, *LD* 3, 42.
38. *Apo.*, 402.
39. JHN, No. 341, "The Religion of the Day," August 26, 1832, *PaS* 1, 355.
40. JHN, No. 341, "The Religion of the Day," *PaS* 1, 357.
41. JHN, No. 341, "The Religion of the Day," *PaS* 1, 357–58.
42. See Norbert Elias, *The Civilizing Process*, trans. Edmund Jephcott (Oxford: Blackwell, 1994).
43. JHN, No. 341, "The Religion of the Day," *PaS* 1, 358. For an earlier intimation of this idea, see No. 228, "The Liturgy teaching doctrine — concerning means of grace," February 28, 1830, *Serm.* 1, 85.
44. JHN, No. 341, "The Religion of the Day," *PaS* 1, 358.

Vice is avoided because it is "unseemly," while "elegance" becomes "the test and standard of virtue."[45] Morality is mere decency, and religion becomes a cult of good manners.

Newman considered such civilized religion another encroachment of the intellect on the domain of conscience. "Conscience," Newman argued, "is no longer recognized as an independent arbiter of actions, its authority is explained away." It is superseded by good taste, or "the rule of expediency."[46] But excising conscience cuts Christianity off from its roots in natural religion, "the dark side of religion," as Newman called it.[47] Conscience "is a stern gloomy principle," he explained, "it tells us of guilt and prospective punishment."[48] To believe in Christ in the right way requires a thoroughgoing awareness of our guilt and God's justice. "The gospel," he argued in his April university sermon, "is in its very name a message of peace, but it must never be separated from the _bad_ tidings of our fallen nature which it reverses."[49] He did not mean this in the evangelical sense of an experiential passage from guilt, via redemption, to assurance and gratitude; quite the contrary. Conscience and the sense of moral shortcoming that comes with it remain constitutive of Christianity. They spur us on to do what Christ has enabled us to do: obey God better.

Newman's insights into the constitutive role of the dark side of religion led him to revise his earlier assessment of the frantic search for redemption in the religious behavior of the heathen. Such behavior was no longer a mere illustration of human weakness without God but constituted, under the circumstances, a fitting posture toward the divine. Always and everywhere, Newman argued, people have felt the need to propitiate the divine by sacrifice and "self-tormenting" mortifications.[50] Compared to "true religion," these natural religious behaviors surely qualify as "superstition."[51] But it is "man's truest & best religion, _before_ the gospel shines on him."[52] If we are indeed fallen people, then "to be in gloom, to view ourselves with horror" and to grasp at every straw for relief —in a word, to be superstitious"—is the right thing to do "in the presence of an Holy and offended God."[53] It bespeaks a proper estimate of our natural spiritual condition before Christian faith. Only such a correct estimate of who we are makes us actively religious, and only active religiosity—the effort to pray, to do good, etc.—makes

<hr>

45. JHN, No. 341, "The Religion of the Day," _PaS_ 1, 358.
46. JHN, No. 341, "The Religion of the Day," _PaS_ 1, 358–59.
47. JHN, No. 341, "The Religion of the Day," _PaS_ 1, 368.
48. JHN, No. 341, "The Religion of the Day," _PaS_ 1, 359.
49. JHN, No. 334, "On the principle of Justice," BOA A.9.4, 5 (_OUS_, 88).
50. JHN, No. 334, "On the principle of Justice," BOA A.9.4, 30–31 (_OUS_, 105).
51. JHN, No. 334, "On the principle of Justice," BOA A.9.4, 31 (_OUS_, 105).
52. JHN, No. 334, "On the principle of Justice," BOA A.9.4, 32 (_OUS_, 106).
53. JHN, No. 334, "On the principle of Justice," BOA A.9.4, 32 (_OUS_, 106).

us receptive to revelation. Newman, therefore, concluded that people "who are not superstitious without the gospel, will not be religious with it."[54]

The fault of liberalism is to forget this. It bypasses the "gloomy religion" of nature but still pretends to a hope that it calls Christian.[55] And this pretence of Christian hope is what makes it so deceptive. The person "who speaks of the state of the world in a sanguine way, may indeed be an advanced Christian, but he may also be much less even than a proselyte of the gate."[56] True faith is not so much to have no superstition as to have overcome it. If a person's "security & peace of mind be merely the calm of ignorance, surely the men whom he looks down upon as narrow-minded & superstitious, whose religion consists in fear not in love, shall go into the kingdom of heaven before him."[57] Given that such worldly optimism was the condition of many Englishmen, Newman expressed his "firm conviction," in *The Religion of the Day*, "that it would be a gain to this country, were it vastly more superstitious, more bigoted, more gloomy, more fierce in its religion, than at present it shows itself to be"; to profess anything, that is, but "that shallowness of religion, which is the result of a blinded conscience."[58]

Doctrine and Mystery

In a sermon preached a week before *The Religion of the Day*, Newman had critiqued liberal religion from the angle of the authority of revelation. He qualified upper-class respectability as a form of religiosity "based upon self and the world, a mere civilization of the mind."[59] Since Christianity happens to be the "religion of the land," the upper classes accept it, but it does not change them. Instead, "they add it to what they *are*, they ingraft it upon the selfish and worldly habits of an unrenewed heart." For such people, revelation has no independent authority. "They in no sense obey *because* it commands. They do right where they *would* have done right had it not commanded."[60] Many liberals of the SDUK variety, who want to promote "the happiness of their fellow-creatures, and have formed a system of morality and religion of their own" evince the same laissez faire attitude: "a moral and decent conduct, (on *whatever* principles,) seems to them to be enough."[61] The fact that the "spread of knowledge" issues in "a selfish temperance, a selfish peaceableness, a selfish benevolence, the morality of expedience,

---

54. JHN, No. 334, "On the principle of Justice," BOA A.9.4, 32–33 (*OUS*, 106).

55. JHN, No. 334, "On the principle of Justice," BOA A.9.4, 28 (*OUS*, 104).

56. JHN, No. 334, "On the principle of Justice," BOA A.9.4, 5 (*OUS*, 88–89).

57. JHN, No. 334, "On the principle of Justice," BOA A.9.4, 5 (*OUS*, 89).

58. JHN, No. 341, "The Religion of the Day," *PaS* 1, 368, 370.

59. JHN, No. 340, "Knowledge of God's Will without Obedience," August 19, 1832, *PaS* 1, 34.

60. JHN, No. 340, "Knowledge of God's Will," *PaS* 1, 34.

61. JHN, No. 340, "Knowledge of God's Will," *PaS* 1, 36.

this satisfies them"; as long as people behave decently, it does not matter why they do so. And thus, they applaud religion only when it suits them: "They care for none of the truths of Scripture, *on the ground* of their being in Scripture," nor do they "obey *because* they are told to obey, on faith; and the need of this divine principle of conduct they do not comprehend."[62] They forget that the essence of being religious is to obey because God commands, through conscience or revelation, and to believe what God says, because he says it.

It had always been obvious to Newman that doctrines ought to be believed because they are revealed, not because of what they say. And yet, his theology in the mid-1820s had tended to value doctrines for their effects and intelligibility. Christianity's central doctrine, the one that changed lives, did so precisely because it was perspicuous. Newman had still accepted that certain doctrines, such as that of the Trinity, contained incomprehensible elements, but these could be safely ignored. His reading of Butler had begun to undermine this assumption. The *Analogy* insisted that revelation is a "mysterious economy" and thus "quite beyond our comprehension."[63] Accordingly, theology can never be a perspicuous system. It must remain a collection of truths that cannot be made to cohere fully, a point stressed in Butler's sermons.[64]

In his altercations with Frank, Newman had applied this logic to the case of infant baptism. Even if its theological sense remains unclear, infant baptism should be accepted because it was practiced by the Apostles. In the wake of the Peel affair, Newman began to view the desire for perspicuous doctrine as one of the liberal usurpations of the intellect. In response, he began to emphasize the value of the limited intelligibility of doctrine.

In his Trinity Sunday sermon for 1829, Newman still maintained that the end of revelation is moral and religious change. It "is given, not that we may know more, but that we may do better."[65] Yet, Newman no longer premised this change on doctrinal intelligibility. The "illumination" of Pentecost, celebrated the week before, does not concern "the mere light of the reason, the gifts of the intellect; inasmuch as the Gospel has its mysteries, its difficulties, and secret things, which the Holy Spirit does not remove."[66] Throughout history, Newman pointed out, people have denied this and considered "mysteries inconsistent with the light of the Gospel."[67] In Enlightenment England, many thought "Christianity to be, what

---

62. JHN, No. 340, "Knowledge of God's Will," *PaS* 1, 36–37.

63. Butler, *The Analogy of Religion*, 247, 246.

64. Butler, "Upon the Ignorance of Man," in *Works*, vol. 2, 261–78.

65. JHN, No. 199, "The Christian Mysteries," June 14, 1829, *PaS* 1, 233. The sermon was probably revised on its June 1832 preaching and/or its publication in 1834, but there is no reason to doubt that its substance dates from the time of its composition.

66. JHN, No. 199, "The Christian Mysteries," *PaS* 1, 233.

67. JHN, No. 199, "The Christian Mysteries," *PaS* 1, 235.

they term, a 'rational religion.'"[68] Socinians argued "that no doctrine which was *mysterious*, i.e. too deep for human reason, or inconsistent with their self-devised notions, could be contained in Scripture."[69] This was still the line of the newly organized Unitarian body, but such a mode of arguing is antithetical to genuine religious belief. "Faith receives with reverence and love whatever God gives, when convinced it is His gift."[70] And mysteries happen to be part and parcel of this gift.

To begin with, the Christian revelation does not solve the mysteries inherent in prior dispensations. Thus, the difficulties of natural religion "remain as great as before Christ came."[71] The origin of pain and suffering, for instance, is as incomprehensible after revelation as it was before. Likewise, the intellectual difficulties of Judaism remain what they were. Just as Jews did not know how animal sacrifices pleased God, or why they were God's elect people, so Christians are ignorant of how Christ's sacrifice atones, or why some people are born of Christian parents and others are not.[72] What is more, Christianity even *"increases our difficulties"*: "The very revelation that brings us *practical and useful knowledge* about our souls, in the very *act of doing* so, nay (as it would seem), in *consequence of* doing so, brings us mysteries."[73] The New Testament tells us of eternal life, but "we learn in connexion with this joyful truth, that there is a *state of endless misery* too"—a doctrine impossible to comprehend.[74] Similarly, we have the "inexpressible comfort" to know that we are saved by the sufferings and death of Christ, but we also learn that this suffering and dying man is "the Very Son of God, Begotten of God and One with God from everlasting, God incarnate"—another baffling truth.[75] The doctrine of the Trinity, too, is "religious light and comfort." We learn that "both Son and Spirit are separately God" so that we "cannot love Them too much." At the same time, "if Christ be by Himself God, and the Spirit be by Himself God, and yet there be but one God, here is plainly something altogether beyond our comprehension."[76]

Newman summed up this mystifying trait of revelation in a bold principle: *"religious light is intellectual darkness."*[77] This phrase is the key to his understanding of religious mystery. "We gain spiritual light," he explained, "at the price of intellectual perplexity."[78] The contrast with his former views is striking. Before,

<hr>

68. JHN, No. 199, "The Christian Mysteries," *PaS* 1, 235.
69. JHN, No. 199, "The Christian Mysteries," *PaS* 1, 235.
70. JHN, No. 199, "The Christian Mysteries," *PaS* 1, 243.
71. JHN, No. 199, "The Christian Mysteries," *PaS* 1, 236.
72. JHN, No. 199, "The Christian Mysteries," *PaS* 1, 236–39.
73. JHN, No. 199, "The Christian Mysteries," *PaS* 1, 239.
74. JHN, No. 199, "The Christian Mysteries," *PaS* 1, 239–40.
75. JHN, No. 199, "The Christian Mysteries," *PaS* 1, 240.
76. JHN, No. 199, "The Christian Mysteries," *PaS* 1, 241.
77. JHN, No. 199, "The Christian Mysteries," *PaS* 1, 242.
78. JHN, No. 199, "The Christian Mysteries," *PaS* 1, 239.

Newman could attribute little meaning to mystery, because revelation achieves its goal—conversion—by being intelligible. Now, he believed that mystery was constitutive of revelation itself. Since God is ineffable, he can never be fully revealed to cognitively limited creatures. And because we can learn only something of God, not everything, we end up with mystery. Mysteries, Newman explained,

> are as shadows brought out by the Sun of Truth. When you knew nothing of revealed light, you knew not revealed darkness. Religious truth requires you should be told *something* . . . and to know *something*, and *not all – partial knowledge* – must of course perplex; doctrines imperfectly revealed must be mysterious.[79]

Revelation, then, is a trade-off. With increased religious knowledge comes increased intellectual perplexity. This is why scholarship or learning are of limited benefit to the believer. The *"learned study* of Scripture," Newman noted in an 1830 sermon, can only solve "small difficulties." But even when it does, it *"gives rise to more* difficulties than it *removes."*[80] The earnest seeker "conquers one set of difficulties only to encounter another — the light, by which he detected the former to be unreal, is only just strong enough to show him others — *as* formidable in appearance, the emptiness of which he *cannot* detect."[81] There is no getting around perplexity as a thinking Christian. "The grant of mercy," Newman pithily concluded, "is conveyed by *means* of incomprehensible doctrines."[82] Of course, the most incomprehensible doctrine of all was that of the Trinity.

In the mid-1820s, Newman had been sympathetic to Whately's exclusively practical take on the doctrine, but he had never gone on to deny that the scriptural distinction between Father, Son, and Spirit says something about the immanent Godhead. When he attempted to explicate this distinction in April 1827, Whately's critique had put him off, but he did not waver on the issue itself. In his Trinity Sunday sermon of 1828, Newman affirmed the distinction between Father, Son, and Spirit with new vigor. Because scripture so often speaks of "the Spirit being *sent* by the Son, and the Spirit and Son by the Father," the "Son and Spirit must . . . in some very strong and true sense be distinct from the Father and from one another."[83] Newman believed that this distinction was properly expressed in the ecclesial doctrine of the Trinity: "first that there is only one God — second that this God is sometimes spoken of as the Father, sometimes as the Son, sometimes as the Holy Spirit — Thirdly that yet the Father is not the Son, nor the Son the

79. JHN, No. 199, "The Christian Mysteries," *PaS* 1, 242.
80. JHN, No. 269, "Doubts in religion," *Serm.* 4, 168.
81. JHN, No. 269, "Doubts in religion," *Serm.* 4, 168–69.
82. JHN, No. 269, "Doubts in religion," *Serm.* 4, 169.
83. JHN, No. 166, "On the Doctrine of the Trinity," June 1, 1828, *Serm.* 3, 318.

Spirit — nor the Spirit the Father."[84] At the same time, he drew the attention of his parishioners away from this mystery by emphasizing that "God is revealed, not as He is in Himself, but as *He is to us*" and that "the doctrine of the Trinity is revealed . . . practically as concerns ourselves."[85] In his Trinity Sunday sermon a year later, the one on mystery, Newman was expunging the last traces of this Whatelyan take on revelation. By Trinity Sunday 1831, they were gone.

Newman's sermon for that day based its argument on the Matthean command to baptize "in the Name of the Father, and of the Son, and of the Holy Spirit."[86] For Newman, this revelation of the divine name made sense only on the supposition that the orthodox doctrine of the Trinity was true. If it had run, "in the Name of God, Jesus Christ, and the Comforter," a non-Trinitarian interpretation, along the lines of "an Author of grace and His instruments," might have been possible.[87] As it stands, however, the injunction clearly conveys the idea "that the Three Sacred Names introduced have a meaning relatively to each other, and not to any temporal dispensation."[88] The terms Father, Son, and Spirit, deliberately used together in such a formal setting, signify distinctions in the immanent and not just in the economic Trinity. Newman readily admitted that this doctrine was a mystery, not because it was couched in obscure terms, as some contemporary critics of the Athanasian Creed had it but because it dealt with an incomprehensible reality. What people really mean when they discard "the Creed of St. Athanasius as being unintelligible," he wittily observed, "is that it is too plain."[89] Taken one by one, its constituent propositions are very simple and precise. Problems arise "not in any one singly, but in their combination."[90] This only shows, however, that the difficulty "is in the nature of things, in the adorable mystery spoken of, which no wording can remove or explain."[91]

A Christian firmly believes that God is one and that God is three, "not as if that Trinity were a name only, or stood for three manifestations, or qualities, or attributes, or relations," but that he is truly three, and truly one:

> The Eternal Three are worshipped by the Catholic Church as distinct, yet One—the Most High God being wholly the Father, and wholly the Son, and wholly the Holy Ghost; yet the Three Persons being distinct from each other, not merely in name, or by human abstraction, but in very truth.[92]

---

84. JHN, No. 166, "On the Doctrine of the Trinity," *Serm.* 3, 317.
85. JHN, No. 166, "On the Doctrine of the Trinity," *Serm.* 3, 323.
86. Matthew 28:19.
87. JHN, No. 300, "The Mystery of the Holy Trinity," May 29, 1831, *PaS* 6, 374.
88. JHN, No. 300, "The Mystery of the Holy Trinity," *PaS* 6, 374.
89. JHN, No. 300, "The Mystery of the Holy Trinity," *PaS* 6, 376.
90. JHN, No. 300, "The Mystery of the Holy Trinity," *PaS* 6, 376.
91. JHN, No. 300, "The Mystery of the Holy Trinity," *PaS* 6, 377.
92. JHN, No. 300, "The Mystery of the Holy Trinity," *PaS* 6, 382.

To believe in the Trinity is to believe, quite literally, an incomprehensible thing. This mysterious quality, moreover, adheres to everything we predicate of God, although other doctrines strike us as less incomprehensible. The unity of God's attributes, for instance, is almost as puzzling as the unity of persons. These attributes "are many in one mode of speaking, yet all One in God."[93] Thus, when "we speak of God as Wisdom, or as Love, we mean to say that He is Wisdom, and that He is Love; that He is each separately and wholly, yet not that Wisdom is the same as Love, though He is both at once." Here, too, we are confronted with our creaturely condition: the "simple accuracy of statement which would harmonize all of them is beyond us, because the power of contemplating the Eternal, as He is, is beyond us."[94]

Despite Newman's repeated affirmations that God's essence is unknowable, his understanding of divine ineffability differed from that of Whately, for whom it was premised on a specific theory of analogical predication. Since such predication concerns the resemblance of two relations, rather than the resemblance of two realities, we never predicate anything directly of Godself, who therefore remains unknown.[95] Newman, by contrast, understood analogy in Butler's sense, as a likeness or similarity between substances or attributes.[96] Since we "are endowed by nature and through grace with a portion of certain excellences which belong in perfection to the Most High—as benevolence, wisdom, justice, truth, and holiness," we discern "a sort of parallel" between such "qualities, properties, powers, and habits of our own minds" and God's attributes.[97] These analogies are real, but partial. Divine ineffability, then, does not mean that we can predicate nothing of the immanent Godhead but that such predication yields only limited knowledge:

> We understand things unknown, by the pattern of things seen and experienced; we are able to contemplate Almighty God so far as earthly things are partial reflexions of Him; when they fail us, we are lost. And as of course nothing earthly or created is His exact and perfect image, we have at best but dim glimpses of His infinite glory.[98]

Accordingly, when scripture speaks of God's wisdom, or his strong arm, the analogy of our own wisdom or agency allows for a faint understanding of what is signified. But in the case of the Trinity, we lack such analogies, so that "we feel the weight of that mystery, which exists also when mention is made of the Divine

---

93. JHN, No. 300, "The Mystery of the Holy Trinity," *PaS* 6, 379.
94. JHN, No. 300, "The Mystery of the Holy Trinity," *PaS* 6, 379–80.
95. See pp. 99–101.
96. Butler, *The Analogy of Religion*, 23–35.
97. JHN, No. 300, "The Mystery of the Holy Trinity," *PaS* 6, 384.
98. JHN, No. 300, "The Mystery of the Holy Trinity," *PaS* 6, 386.

Wisdom, or the Divine Arm, though we feel it not."[99] Everything that is predicated of God, in short, is mysterious, in the sense that we know something, but not all, and that our partial knowledge yields incomprehension.

Doctrine and the Fathers

Newman's vigorous defense of the Athanasian Creed in 1831 shows the extent to which he had overcome his antipathy toward terms and ideas he used to consider overly speculative and technical. It also witnesses to his growing conviction that the church's doctrinal formulations are the authoritative key to the interpretation of scripture, an idea he had gleaned from Hawkins.[100] In his 1828 Trinity Sunday sermon, Newman admitted that scripture does not state the ecclesial doctrine of the Trinity systematically, although it affirms its constituent propositions "separately."[101] There was good reason for the "omission" of such a systematic exposition. "Since this great and fundamental truth does not appear on the surface of Scripture, it is plain we must *search* if we wish to be sure that it is contained in Scripture."[102] This is a crucial inference. It is not because scripture is less clear about the Trinity than about other doctrines that its ecclesial exposition loses value. The obscurity of scripture is a spur to seek more earnestly, not to dismiss the quest, and the direction of this quest is from church teaching to the Bible, not the other way around.

In the liberal climate of the day, the authority of the Established Church as the legitimate expositor of revealed truth was increasingly disputed. Accordingly, when an opportunity came to rally to its defense in writing, Newman eagerly took it. The result was *The Arians of the Fourth Century*, which drew on Patristic theology to explain the genealogy, authority, and meaning of the doctrinal definitions of the early church. That Newman would turn to the fathers was far from obvious. As a young evangelical, he had become enamoured of them, especially of Ambrose and Augustine, through reading Joseph Milner's *History of the Church of Christ*.[103] But some of this early enthusiasm dissipated under the influence of Whately, who spoke of the fathers disparagingly as "certain old divines."[104] By the time Newman wrote his *Essay on Miracles*, he dismissively classed patristic miracle reports with those of pagans and medieval Roman Catholics—a flippancy he later attributed

99. JHN, No. 300, "The Mystery of the Holy Trinity," *PaS* 6, 387.

100. See pp. 135–36.

101. JHN, No. 166, "On the Doctrine of the Trinity," *Serm.* 3, 317.

102. JHN, No. 166, "On the Doctrine of the Trinity," *Serm.* 3, 322.

103. JHN to Henry Wilberforce, September 24, 1846, *LD* 11, 252–53; *Lectures on Certain Difficulties Felt by Anglicans in Submitting to the Catholic Church* (London: Burns & Lambert, 1850), 301, hereafter *Diff.*; *Apo.*, 62; and "Autobiographical Memoir," *AW*, 83.

104. JHN, "Autobiographical Memoir," *AW*, 70.

to his incipient liberalism.[105] He also believed that doctrinal error was rife in the patristic period. His first serious resolve to read the church fathers, in early 1826, was part of an ambitious plan "to trace the sources from which the corruptions of the Church, principally the Romish, have been derived."[106] A year later, this plan was still on his mind, even though he now accepted the trustworthiness of the fathers as historical witnesses to the practice of infant baptism.[107]

At the end of 1827, Newman acquired a large set of patristic works, which Pusey had bought for him in Germany, and in July 1828, he began to read them chronologically, beginning with the Apostolic Fathers.[108] Although he had now abandoned his original plan of mining the fathers for error, their impact on his theology was slight. In 1842, he wrote to Thomas Allies that he had "measured and systematized them by the Protestant doctrines and views, and by this sort of cross division . . . managed to spend a good deal of time on them and got nothing from them."[109] He reiterated the point after he had become a Catholic: "I had read them simply on Protestant ideas, analyzed and catalogued them on Protestant principles of division, and hunted for Protestant doctrines and usages in them. My headings ran, 'Justification by faith only,' 'Sanctification,' and the like."[110] Later, he thought there had been more to his course of reading. In the *Apologia*, he interpreted it as a renewal—on moving "out of the shadow of liberalism"—of the interest he had taken in the fathers as a youth.[111] In his *Autobiographical Memoir*, he even reversed the causal sequence and argued that "the ancient Fathers" had prevented his adopting the "cold Arminian doctrine" of "Tillotson and Barrow, Jortin and Paley" when his Calvinism came undone.[112] The latter claim, that the fathers saved him from latitudinarianism, was wistful exaggeration.

In fact, Newman seriously engaged Patristic theology only in 1831, in view of his contribution to a projected Theological Library edited by the High Churchmen Hugh James Rose and William Rowe Lyall. Even then, a study of the fathers was not his first thought. He wanted to write a book on the Thirty-Nine Articles, but Rose suggested that he compose an introductory volume first, on the history of church councils up to Trent.[113] Soon, Newman realized such a project was

---

105. JHN, "Miracles," 630–34 (*Mir.*, 27–45); *Apo.*, 72. See p. 174 in this book.

106. JHN to Jemima Newman, May 1, 1826, *LD* 1, 285.

107. JHN, "February 21, 1827," *AW*, 210. See p. 141 in this book.

108. *LD* 2, 30; JHN to Joseph Blanco White, July 4, 1828, *LD* 2, 80.

109. JHN to T. W. Allies, September 30, 1842, *LD* 9, 119.

110. *Diff.*, 302. The "headings" refer to Newman's theological commonplace book (BOA D.18.1), which he had begun in 1826, and the first part of which concerned the Apostolic Fathers. See McGrath, *John Henry Newman*, 39, 44n29.

111. *Apo.*, 87.

112. JHN, "Autobiographical Memoir," *AW*, 83.

113. See the correspondence between Rose and Newman in March and April 1831 (*LD* 2, 321–25).

beyond the scope of a single volume. He proposed, at first, to limit himself to the first seven ecumenical councils, but ultimately settled on a history of "the Councils concerning the Trinity," that is, up to the First Council of Constantinople (in 381).[114] Eventually, the book did not even become that. It turned, in Lyall's words, into "a History of *Arianism*," and a very curious one at that.[115] But writing it had momentous effects. By delving into Christian antiquity with the help of earlier High Church scholarship, Newman came to regard it as "the true exponent of the doctrines of Christianity and the basis of the Church of England," as he put it in the *Apologia*.[116] This was not a foregone conclusion: it was formed along the way.

Despite its historiographical character, the *Arians* was written with an eye to the times. The spectacle of defining orthodox doctrine in the early church, with all its heresies, provided neat parallels with contemporary (religious) culture. "I am resisting the innovations of the day," Newman wrote to Simeon Lloyd Pope in April 1832, "and attempting to defend the work of men indefinitely above me (the Primitive Fathers) which is now assailed."[117] In the church of Alexandria, especially, he encountered ideas and ways of thinking that dovetailed with the theological vision he had been crafting for several years. Like himself, the Alexandrian fathers discerned a fundamental continuity between natural and revealed religion, on which they based their religious instruction. In the catechumenal model, profound Christian mysteries, such as the Trinity and the atonement, were held back until the learner had reached proficiency in more basic beliefs and was baptized. Newman used this model to criticize the common evangelical practice of preaching the atonement as a means of conversion.[118] But this idea of the "*disciplina arcani*," a doctrinal tradition transmitted only to the initiate, informed his entire account of the genealogy of creedal orthodoxy. The outline of his argument is that the councils of Nicea and Constantinople were forced to explicate the oral tradition derived from the Apostles in creeds because of the rationalizing attacks on revealed truth by heretics like Arius. The essence of ancient heresy turned out to be the same as that of the liberalism of Newman's own day: the encroachment of the intellect on the territory of religion.[119]

114. JHN to Samuel Rickards, June 5, 1832, *LD* 3, 54. See also JHN to Hugh James Rose, August 24, 1831, *LD* 2, 352–53.

115. William Rowe Lyall to Hugh James Rose, October 19, 1832, *LD* 3, 105. For detailed analyses of the sources, genesis, and argument of the *Arians*, see Rowan Williams, "Newman's *Arians* and the Question of Method in Doctrinal History," in *Newman after a Hundred Years*, ed. Ian Ker and Alan G. Hill (Oxford: Clarendon Press, 1990), 263–85, and Benjamin John King, *Newman and the Alexandrian Fathers: Shaping Doctrine in Nineteenth-Century England* (Oxford: Oxford University Press, 2009), 70–126.

116. *Apo.*, 88.

117. JHN to Simeon Lloyd Pope, April 9, 1832, *LD* 3, 42.

118. See pp. 238–39.

119. Stephen Thomas identifies Joseph Milner as a model for this aspect of the *Arians*' historiography (*Newman and Heresy*, 46–49).

In antiquity, the nearest parallel to contemporary liberalism was the Neoplatonist "rationalism" of the Eclectic School of Ammonius Saccas, but all heresy embodied liberalism to some extent.[120] Neoplatonist philosophy, Newman argued, was bred in the Alexandrian church but crucially denied "the peculiar divinity of the Scripture revelations" and rejected the evidential value of the miracles by which it was introduced.[121] By treating all philosophies as on a level, Neoplatonism threw the inquirer "upon the examination of the doctrines for the evidence of the divinity of Christianity; there being no place left for a claim on his allegiance to it as a whole, and for what is strictly termed faith, he admitted or rejected, as he chose."[122] Christ, in consequence, was on a par with human sages, so that the "claims of religion" were "no longer combined, defined, and embodied in a personal Mediator between God and man." As a result,

> its various precepts were dissipated back again and confused in the mass of human knowledge, as before Christ came; and in its stead a mere intellectual literature arose in the Eclectic School, and usurped the theological chair as an interpreter of sacred duties, and the instructor of the inquiring mind.[123]

This judgment echoed Newman's earlier condemnation of Socinian and utilitarian thought, and he did not leave his readers to discern the parallel for themselves. Everyone, he argued, could "recognize in this old philosophy the chief features of that school of liberalism and false illumination, political and moral, which is now Satan's instrument in deluding the nations," but whose "cold scoffing spirit" is even worse.[124] Although he was careful to distinguish Arians from Neoplatonists, Newman insisted that both agreed in "rejecting from their theology all *mystery*, in the ecclesiastical notion of the word."[125] Besides, he enlarged on the "disputatious character" of Arianism, which was in its origin "a sceptical rather than a dogmatic teaching" and used the argumentative methods of the sophist to critique "the received creed."[126] Just as in nineteenth-century England, the tenets that undermined religion in antiquity were a combined reliance on reason and opposition to traditional truth. This was no surprise, for the "heretical spirit is ever one and the same in its various forms."[127]

---

120. *Ari.*, 115. This conflation of Neoplatonism with eclecticism was the accepted theory in Newman's day. See Myrto Hatzimichali, *Potamo of Alexandria and the Emergence of Eclecticism in Late Hellenistic Philosophy* (Cambridge: Cambridge University Press, 2011), 9–13.

121. *Ari.*, 115–16.

122. *Ari.*, 116.

123. *Ari.*, 117.

124. *Ari.*, 117. See pp. 278–79 in this book.

125. *Ari.*, 124; see also 238–9.

126. *Ari.*, 29–30.

127. *Ari.*, 153.

If Newman recognized an early manifestation of the usurping intellect in the history of heresy, he regarded the church's response as based on the primacy of moral character. He summed up his position in a statement at once complete and concise:

> The systematic doctrine of the Trinity may be considered as the shadow, projected for the contemplation of the intellect, of the Object of scripturally-informed piety; a representation, economical; necessarily imperfect, as being exhibited in a foreign medium, and therefore involving apparent inconsistencies or mysteries; given to the Church by tradition contemporaneously with those apostolic writings, which are addressed more directly to the heart; kept in the background in the infancy of Christianity, when faith and obedience were vigorous, and brought forward at a time when, reason being disproportionately developed, and aiming at sovereignty in the province of religion, its presence became necessary to expel an usurping idol from the house of God.[128]

It would not be too much to say that the *Arians* is the historical and theological unpacking of this single statement. It was premised on Newman's earlier distinction between the intellect and moral character, the true addressee of revelation. Revelation, Newman argued, does not address "itself to the intellect, except so far as it is necessary for conveying and fixing its truths on the heart."[129] Since scripture has an intelligible content, the intellect is required to perceive its meaning, but the message itself is addressed to one's moral character. Revelation does not aim at satisfying the intellect. It is not a perspicuous system but rather a set of distinct truths which cannot be made to fully cohere with one another.

"Before the mind has been roused to reflection," Newman explained, "it acquiesces, if religiously trained, in that practical devotion to the Blessed Trinity, and implicit acknowledgment of the divinity of Son and Spirit, which holy Scripture at once teaches and exemplifies."[130] Such devotion is based on what we read in scripture, but our resultant conception of the Trinity can be preverbal, and perhaps even precognitive. "Moral feelings," Newman pointed out, "do not directly contemplate and realize to themselves the objects which excite them." Thus, a child loves and reveres her parents, without knowing how or why, and the "heathen in obeying his conscience, implicitly worships Him of whom he has never distinctly heard."[131] To explicate the religious object is the natural impulse of our cognitive faculties. When our intellect is cultivated, it begins "to analyze the vision which influences the heart, and the Object in which that vision centres"

---

128. *Ari.*, 159–60.
129. *Ari.*, 239.
130. *Ari.*, 158.
131. *Ari.*, 158.

and does not "stop till it has, in some sort, succeeded in expressing in words, what has all along been a principle both of the affections and of practical obedience."[132] In consequence, "a system of doctrine becomes unavoidable; being framed . . . not with a view of explaining, but of arranging the inspired notices concerning the Supreme Being, of providing, not a consistent, but a connected statement."[133] As soon as this is achieved, enquiry ought to end. The "inquisitiveness of a pious mind" stops "when it has pursued the subject into the mystery which is its limit."[134]

To respect this boundary of enquiry is what distinguishes orthodoxy from heresy. Ancient heretics, like modern Deists and Socinians, "assumed as an axiom that there could be no mystery in the Scripture doctrines respecting the nature of God."[135] The idea that all heresy derives from a denial of mystery was by no means new to Newman. Years ago, he had read in Scott's *Force of Truth* that,

> when reflecting men, in order to avoid those *mysterious*, and as they imagine, *unreasonable* conclusions, which, according to the true meaning of words, the Scriptures contain, have become *Arians*, it is wonderful they do not, for the same cause, embrace the *Socinian* system. This is the natural progress of unhumbled reason; from *Arianism* to *Socinianism*; from *Socinianism* to *Deism*; and thence to *Atheism*.[136]

Once we admit the demand for perspicuous doctrine into our theology, Scott suggests, there is no end to the intellectual objections we can level at religious truth. The same logic that questions the Son's eternal generation, will proceed to baulk at his divinity, at the idea of revelation, and, ultimately, even at God's existence. Scott's point was that scripture requires submission, a conviction Newman had always shared, but now, Newman added that such mysteries are constitutive of revelation. Heresy, he explained, fails to recognize that "a mystery in doctrine" is only "a difficulty or inconsistency in the intellectual expression" of a truth that transcends human comprehension.[137]

As before, he insisted in the *Arians* that doctrine is necessarily mysterious because it represents in human terms an ineffable reality. This is the reason a doctrine like that of the Trinity appears self-contradictory when we think it through, not because it is misconceived and should be worded more logically but because its object is such that it cannot become perspicuous to human beings. By now, Newman held that the encounter with mystery pervades our cognitive relation to

132. *Ari.*, 159.
133. *Ari.*, 161.
134. *Ari.*, 161.
135. *Ari.*, 238.
136. Scott, *The Force of Truth*, 31. See Thomas, *Newman and Heresy*, 10.
137. *Ari.*, 239.

all of reality, beginning with God, but ultimately encompassing the world as well. He pointed out that "everlasting and unchangeable quiescence is the simplest and truest notion we can obtain of the Deity."[138] Strictly speaking, the idea of God in action, that is, of "any Divine procedure, greater or less, which consists of means and an end," is a representation of God in human terms: an *economy*.[139] He concluded with the Alexandrian fathers that,

> all those so-called Economies or dispensations, which display His character in action, are but condescensions to the infirmity and peculiarity of our minds, shadowy representations of realities which are incomprehensible to creatures such as ourselves, who estimate every thing by the rule of association and arrangement, by the notion of a purpose and plan, object and means, parts and whole.[140]

The same logic applies to the "general moral laws" that govern human affairs. Already in 1828, he had emphasized that Providence governs the course of human affairs not by absolute but by general rules: laws that apply for the most part. Now, he explained their failure—"their infringement, their tedious victory, the endurance of the wicked"—as witnessing to their being "an οἰκονομία of greater truths untold, the best practical communication of them which our minds in their present state will admit."[141] What we perceive of God's moral governance is an economical representation of truths that are beyond us but which suffices for practical purposes.

Newman even suggested that the same holds for material creation. "What are the phenomena of the external world," he wondered,

> but a divine mode of conveying to the mind the realities of existence, individuality, and the influence of being on being, the best possible, though beguiling the imagination with a harmless but unfounded belief in matter as distinct from the impressions on their senses?[142]

In the *Apologia*, Newman traced these insights back to Keble, and thence to Butler. They had taught him the rudiments of "the Sacramental system; that is, the doctrine that material phenomena are both the types and instruments of real things unseen."[143] Although Butler and Keble provided the theory, only the death of his sister Mary had brought its reality home to him. Reflecting on her

---

138. *Ari.*, 82.
139. *Ari.*, 82.
140. *Ari.*, 83. See JHN to Hugh James Rose, August 16, 1832, *LD* 3, 78.
141. *Ari.*, 83.
142. *Ari.*, 83. See Butler, "Upon the Ignorance of Man," in *Works*, vol. 2, 263.
143. *Apo.*, 77.

death is what taught him to see the unseen bearings of the visible world.[144] When he encountered these same ideas in the "broad philosophy of Clement and Origen," he was deeply responsive: their teaching "came like music to my inward ear."[145] The Alexandrian fathers shaped his conviction that "the exterior world, physical and historical, was but the outward manifestation of realities greater than itself."[146]

Newman was aware that this idea of the world as an economy (and thus an intellectual mystery) might disorient people. As he noted in the *Arians*, "on the mind's first mastering this general principle, it seems to itself at the moment to have cut all the ties which bind it to the universe, and to be floated off upon the ocean of interminable scepticism."[147] If nothing in the external world is what it seems, all certainties seem to evaporate. But Newman did think there was an indubitable ground to our convictions: the primordial relation of the moral self to God. This explains his take on the design argument for God's existence (whose cogency he had questioned two years earlier) as an economy, teaching people "in the simplest way the active presence of Him, who after all dwells intelligibly, prior to argument, in their heart and conscience."[148] This interior encounter of a responsible self with a personal God is the ultimate reality, by which everything else that goes for reality pales in comparison. Losing our cognitive bearings upon becoming aware of the economical character of the external world will throw us back upon this primordial relationship with God, which is more constitutive of the self than our relationship with the world. Because of "a sure confidence in the love of Him who cannot deceive, and who has impressed the image and thought of Himself and of His Will upon our original nature," we realize that the mind "must be intended to rely on something, and therefore that the information given, though philosophically inaccurate, must be practically certain."[149] And this is true for revelation as much as for nature: "whatever is told us from heaven, is true in so full and substantial a sense, that no possible mistake can arise practically from following it."[150] Our greatest danger, by contrast, is to attempt "to be wiser than God has made us, and to outstep in the least degree the circle which is prescribed as the limit of our range."[151] This is the attitude that defines both ancient and contemporary heresy.

---

144. See pp. 198–200.

145. *Apo.*, 88–89.

146. *Apo.*, 89. For the resonance of Newman's ideas with earlier British Christian Platonism and the possible influence of Ralph Cudworth (1617–1688) in the early 1830s, see Mark Allen McIntosh, "Newman and Christian Platonism in Britain," *The Journal of Religion* 91, no. 3 (2011): 344–64.

147. *Ari.*, 84.

148. *Ari.*, 84. See pp. 270–71 in this book.

149. *Ari.*, 84.

150. *Ari.*, 84.

151. *Ari.*, 84.

In antiquity, the intellectual speculations of heretics forced the church to define its creed and combat reason with reason. But this was settling for second best: "freedom from symbols and articles is abstractedly the highest state of Christian communion and the peculiar privilege of the primitive Church."[152] In his university sermon of December 1831, Newman had already intimated as much.

> What an extreme exercise of intellect is shown in the composition of our Creeds! — yet how was it necessary? from the previous errors of heretical reasonings in subjects addressed to the moral perception. For while the religious principle was engaged in that exact & well instructed devotion to Christ which no words can suitably describe, the forward reason stepped in upon the yet uninclosed [sic] ground of doctrine and attempted to describe there an image of the Invisible. Henceforth, the Church was obliged in self-defence to employ the gifts of the intellect in the cause of God, to trace out (as near as might be) the true shadow of those truths, which unlearned faith admits & acts upon without the medium of intellectual representation.[153]

Heresy forced the church to explicate its implicit dogmas. This is not to say that it merely reasoned out its doctrines. As Newman noted in the *Arians*, "the Creeds imposed have been compiled either from Apostolical traditions, or from primitive writings."[154]

Given that "the Apostles conversed, and their friends had memories, like other men," it was obvious to Newman that such a tradition existed.[155] Its content, moreover, would have been more systematic than scripture, since the Apostles would have been concerned to safeguard the correct interpretation of their writings. By the end of the third century, however, "the line of tradition, drawn out as it was, to the distance of two centuries from the Apostles, had at length become of too frail a texture, to resist the touch of subtle and ill-directed reason."[156] As a result, the church, unwillingly, had "recourse to the novel, though necessary measure, of imposing an authoritative creed" on its ministers.[157] Although the creeds of Nicea and Constantinople drew on apostolical tradition, Newman did not think they replicated it verbally. Besides being "derived from direct Apostolical Tradition," ante-Nicene Trinitarian theology "was the result of intuitive spiritual perception in scripturally-informed and deeply religious minds."[158] He held, moreover, that even though it appears technical, its terminology is either "found or

---

152. *Ari.*, 41.
153. JHN, No. 321, "On the so-called 'march of intellect,'" BOA A.9.4, 16 (*OUS*, 49–50).
154. *Ari.*, 165.
155. *Ari.*, 60.
156. *Ari.*, 40.
157. *Ari.*, 41.
158. *Ari.*, 95.

strictly implied in the New Testament itself."[159] With the formulation of the creeds, the gist of the tradition derived from the Apostles was made public, and ceased to exist as an independent source of religious knowledge.

Despite its elaborate defense of the early church and its creeds, the *Arians* was not what Rose and Lyall had expected or hoped for their Theological Library. Not only was it not what it had set out to be, a history of councils, but it also contained views that Lyall, at least, found objectionable. He tried to understate his criticisms, but Newman was right when he thought his work had been "*plucked.*"[160] Lyall challenged the central thesis of the *Arians* by insisting that its idea of tradition—the *disciplina arcani*—was "directly adverse to that which Protestant writers of our own church have contended for."[161] He also critiqued the dispensation of paganism, and questioned the fathers' reserve about preaching "our Lord's atonement."[162] These ideas belonged to the core of Newman's theology, and he was not inclined to give them up. But even had he done so, the *Arians* would have been unsuited to the Theological Library. With some regret, especially on Rose's part, the book was published as a standalone title.[163] Although writing the *Arians* opened a new world for Newman and initiated crucial developments beyond the scope of the present study, much of its vision was rooted in what he had discovered before: the primacy of moral character over intellect, the continuity between natural and revealed religion, and the ineluctable mysteriousness of doctrine.

Choosing Sides

If we compare the core features of liberalism as Newman understood it in the early 1830s with the eighteen propositions that defined it in the *Apologia*, there can be no doubt that he was thinking of the same thing. The theological theses of Note A, which Turner dismisses as modeled on the papal condemnations of Pius IX, capture what Newman had long rejected about liberalism.[164] They instance the usurpations of the intellect, stating that a person should only believe what reason shows to be important (no. 1), what is "brought home to him by actual proof" (no. 4), or what coheres with "scientific conclusions" (no. 6).[165] They reject incomprehensible doctrine, holding that "there are no mysteries in

159. *Ari.*, 95.

160. *LD* 3, 84.

161. William Rowe Lyall to Hugh James Rose, October 19, 1832, *LD* 3, 105.

162. William Rowe Lyall to JHN, November 9, 1832, *LD* 3, 113. See Williams, "Newman's *Arians*," 272–73; Introduction, in JHN, *The Arians of the Fourth Century* (Leominster: Gracewing, 2001), xix–xlvii.

163. Hugh James Rose to JHN, November 21, 1832, *LD* 3, 120n1.

164. The list also includes politically oriented theses, with which the present study is not directly concerned.

165. *Hist.*, 294, 205.

true religion" (no. 2). They proclaim religious indifference, stating that "theological doctrine" is nothing more "than an opinion which happens to be held by bodies of men," so that "no creed, as such, is necessary for salvation" (no. 3). They profess that a person may judge doctrine by its content and believe only that which "he can spontaneously receive as being congenial to his moral and mental nature." Thus, he "is not bound to believe in eternal punishment" (no. 5) (an instance showing that even in 1865, Charles was on his mind).[166] The theses also claim that Christianity has to change with the times (no. 7) and that no institution has a right to impose doctrinal tests (no. 9).[167] They uphold "utility and expedience" (no. 13) and argue, finally, that "virtue is the child of knowledge and vice of ignorance" (no. 18).[168]

The evidence reviewed in the last two chapters shows that Newman indeed "earnestly denounced and abjured" these tenets, not just during the Tractarian period but even several years earlier.[169] From 1829 onward, he took a definite stance in a time of social, political, and cultural transition, in which, as John Stuart Mill put it,

> The wisdom of ancestors, and the march of intellect, are bandied from mouth to mouth; each phrase originally an expression of respect and homage, each ultimately usurped by the partisans of the opposite catchword, and in the bitterness of their spirit, turned into the sarcastic jibe of hatred and insult.[170]

Newman sided with the wisdom of ancestors, but his attack on the march of mind was no mere bigotry. He believed that liberalism entailed a misconception of just about everything: human nature, God, religion, morals, doctrine, truth. And he did not just jibe but presented arguments to substantiate his case. It was the massive danger Newman perceived in the onset of liberalism that made him launch the Tractarian campaign to reassert the authority, apostolicity, and purity of the Church of England and its theology. The vision and determination needed to engage in such unremitting public agitation had grown out of the experience— well expressed by Jonathan Clark—"of the shattering of the old order by [Catholic] Emancipation."[171] "Two years back the State deserted [the church]," Newman wrote to Bowden in 1831.[172] Since then, it had had to fend for itself, and Newman welcomed the challenge.

---

166. *Hist.*, 294.
167. *Hist.*, 295.
168. *Hist.*, 296.
169. *Hist.*, 294.
170. Mill, "The Spirit of the Age," in *Collected Works*, vol. 22, 228.
171. Clark, *English Society*, 409.
172. JHN to John William Bowden, March 13, 1831, *LD* 2, 317.

None of this sense of urgency abated when Newman left England for seven months, in December 1832, to tour the Mediterranean with Froude and his father. To Hugh James Rose, Newman pointed out that they were not "running away as truants for mere pleasure."[173] Their trip was not a desertion of the cause of the embattled English church. "I have been for years suffering from duties too many for me," Newman explained, "and take the opportunity of recruiting myself for further service."[174] As an earnest of such service, he proposed to "systematize a poetry department" for the *British Magazine* (which Rose edited). Its title would be *Lyra Apostolica*, and it was to "bring out certain truths and facts, moral, ecclesiastical, and religious, simply and forcibly, with greater freedom, and clearness than in the Christian Year."[175] The contemporary situation required a more outspoken presentation of Christian truth than Keble's a few years earlier. The *Lyra* was to be "an effective quasi-political engine" in "stirring times."[176] By mid-January, Newman had composed nearly fifty verses, and by the end of April, his tally was over a hundred.[177] Meanwhile, the prospects of the Established Church had worsened.

In February, at Naples, Newman received news that the Whigs, who had won a landslide victory in the first election after the passing of the Reform Act, had turned their reforming zeal to the Church of Ireland and proposed a bill that included the suppression and merging of dioceses and a revised collection and distribution of taxes at considerable expense to the church.[178] "We have just heard the Irish Church Reform Bill," Newman fiercely wrote to his mother, "well done, my blind Premier, confiscate and rob, till, like Samson, you pull down the political structure on your own head, tho' without his deliberate purpose and his good cause!"[179] It was another sign of the times, "as if the whole world (Western) were tending towards some dreadful crisis."[180] As before, he was at once aghast at "the accursed Whig spoliation bill" and welcomed the prospect of open battle. To George Ryder, he confided that he was "perhaps not sorry, in a bad matter, to see things proceed so quickly to a crisis — since it is very annoying and disheartening to linger on in an ague, and to feel every one around you neither hot nor cold. The time is coming when every one must choose his side."[181] By April, he

173. JHN to Hugh James Rose, November 26, 1832, *LD* 3, 119.

174. JHN to Hugh James Rose, November 26, 1832, *LD* 3, 119.

175. JHN to Hugh James Rose, November 26, 1832, *LD* 3, 120. The series eventually included contributions from Newman, Keble, Froude, Robert Wilberforce, Isaac Williams, and John Bowden.

176. JHN to Frederic Rogers, December 1, 1832, *LD* 3, 121.

177. JHN to Isaac Williams, January 16, 1833, *LD* 3, 195; JHN to Harriett Newman, April 25, 1833, *LD* 3, 304.

178. Chadwick, *The Victorian Church*, vol. 1, 56–57.

179. JHN to Mrs Newman, February 28, 1833, *LD* 3, 224.

180. JHN to Mrs Newman, February 28, 1833, *LD* 3, 224.

181. JHN to George Ryder, March 14, 1833, *LD* 3, 249.

was preparing his side's resistance, tentatively suggesting "clubs and societies under the title of Apostolical" to advocate "a return to the primitive state of the Church, when it was not a mere instrument of civil government."[182]

Initially, there had been a good deal of Tory concern for the Establishment in Newman's response to the politics of the day. Around 1830, much of his writing had teemed "with the spirit of high Establishmentism."[183] And even in 1832, he could still portray Whig ideology as an insubstantial hovering between the real alternatives of "good and evil" represented by "Tories and Radicals."[184] By the spring of 1833, his commitment to Toryism was evaporating. "By this time I am become neither Whig nor Tory," he wrote to Walter John Trower in April. "In proportion as a Government disconnects itself with the Church, so does it cease to be the duty of a Churchman to be a Politician, and both the Tories and the pious Whigs are disconnected since the Reform Bill, and other political measures have been past."[185] From now on, he would be politically "neuter, with a tendency, which may grow, towards agitating for a more effectual Church discipline, for the independence of Bishops of the Crown which has now become but a Creature of an Infidel Parliament, and for the restoration of the practice of excommunication."[186] It was time for the church to assert itself. This principled vision of an independent, apostolic Church of England explains Newman's vociferousness about Irish church reform. He knew well enough that the Roman Catholic peasantry suffered from the tithes levied for the Church of Ireland, but it was not a social justice issue. "Perhaps it is not *unjust* to take away property from the Church," he conceded to Trower, but it was decidedly irreligious. "The Church thus deprived was founded by St Patrick. It has continued by regular succession of clergy ever since." And thus, "it is one of the oldest ecclesiastical bodies in the world."[187] The "demolition of this Church (not the mere alienation of property but the extinction of one half of the sees)" was sacrilegious indeed.[188]

Nothing better illustrates Newman's combative mindset on the eve of the Tractarian Movement than the motto of the *Lyra*, whose first installments were sent to Rose in March. Froude and Newman borrowed a Homer at Rome, and Froude selected for a motto part of Achilles' speech on rejoining the battle against

<hr>

182. JHN to Henry Arthur Woodgate, April 17, 1833, *LD* 3, 300.

183. JHN to Hugh James Rose, May 23, 1836, *LD* 5, 304.

184. JHN to Simeon Lloyd Pope, April 9, 1832, *LD* 3, 42. See pp. 278–79 in this book.

185. JHN to Walter John Trower, April 16, 1833, *LD* 3, 293. "Pious" is a sarcasm.

186. JHN to Walter John Trower, April 16, 1833, *LD* 3, 293. See also No. 347, "[Separating Oneself from the World]," April 14, 1833, *Serm.* 3, 219–28.

187. JHN to Walter John Trower, April 16, 1833, *LD* 3, 292. Newman regarded the "Romish Priests" in Ireland as "mere intruders, and a creation from Rome of these last centuries," a view he derived from William Palmer's *Origines Liturgicae* (JHN to Richard Hurrell Froude, January 8, 1832, *LD* 3, 4).

188. JHN to Walter John Trower, April 16, 1833, *LD* 3, 292–93.

Troy: "Γνοῖεν δ᾽, ὡς δὴ δηρὸν ἐγὼ πολέμοιο πέπαυμαι."[189] "Long time have I been absent from the field / And they shall know it," it ran in William Cowper's famous translation; or, as Newman paraphrased it in the *Apologia*: "You shall know the difference, now that I am back again."[190] Although the motto was never intended to apply to his person, Newman's return to England in July made a difference indeed. After the summer of 1833, his hidden years were over. He had been known at Oxford as tutor of Oriel and vicar of St Mary's, but he was not in the public eye. Even his publications had been anonymous so far. All this changed when he launched the *Tracts for the Times* in September and became one of the leading figures in a movement that shook up the nation and its church. The *Arians* was published in November, followed by his first volume of parochial sermons in March 1834. Both appeared under his own name. A year into the movement, he summed up his new public status: "my name, which was not known out of Oxford circles before I went abroad, is now known pretty generally."[191] Achilles had joined the fray, and people knew it.

Conclusion

Newman began the Tractarian effort as a defense of the Church of England against the encroachments on its rights and authority by a hostile Whig government and its liberal ideology, but he soon realized that he was not fighting only forces external to the church. The enemy was also within. A subtle redaction of one of his verses for the *Lyra* illustrates this well. *The Zeal of Jehu*, written at Palermo in June 1833, attacked the civilized religiosity of liberalism in terms by now familiar. It was the attempt "to halve the gospel of God's grace" by ignoring its "dread depths":

> And so ye halve the Truth; for ye in heart,
> At best, are doubters whether it be true,
> The theme discarding, as unmeet for you; —
> Yet seeming Christian. O new-compassed art
> Of the ancient Foe! — but what, if it extends
> O'er our own camp, and guiles our patron-friends?[192]

Liberalism stressed the cheering and comfortable aspects of Christianity, but rejected its more austere features—its "zeal and quick-eyed sanctity"—because

---

189. Homer, *Iliad*, bk. 18.125; "Lyra Apostolica," no. 1, *British Magazine* 3 (June 1833): 656; and JHN to Hugh James Rose, March 16, 1833, *LD* 3, 251.

190. William Cowper, *The Iliad and Odyssey of Homer*, vol. 1 (London: J. Johnson, 1791), 488; *Apo.*, 98.

191. JHN, "My illness in Sicily," August 31, 1834, *AW*, 123.

192. JHN, "The Zeal of Jehu," *British Magazine* 5 (April 1834): 431. He sent the first version to his mother on June 9, 1833 (*LD* 3, 319).

it was, at bottom, indifferent to religious truth.[193] With the Irish Church Temporalities Act still to be passed, the last lines conjure an image of the (Tory) patrons of the Established Church misled by liberalism in its benevolent guise. When the *Lyra* was published in book form three years later, a shift had taken place. Its title was changed to *Liberalism*, and the final lines now read: "but what if it extends / O'er our own camp, and rules amid our friends."[194] This small emendation makes a world of difference. Instead of a mere beguiling, Newman conjures the spectre of a reigning liberalism, while "patron" is not dropped just for the metre but to suggest the sway of liberalism over the whole church.

This shift in view was not just a polemical response to those Anglicans who opposed Tractarianism. It reflected a new way of framing the contest with liberalism, rooted in the theological history of the Church of England. Before the Oxford Movement began, Newman had lamented the fact that the church's prospective defenders knew so little of its past. "I am much afraid we shall not know our own principles, if we are not allowed a little time to get them up," he wrote to Ryder in March 1833; "you must get up the history of Church changes at the time of the Reformation, and set others to do the same."[195] Following his own advice, Newman, too, began to immerse himself in Church of England divinity, especially that of the seventeenth century. He saw his own reverence for the early church reflected in the theologians of the reign of the two Charleses (the Caroline divines) and the nonjurors, who refused to swear allegiance to William and Mary after the Glorious Revolution of 1688, and he came to despise the latitudinarian thinkers of the same century and after. Now as then, he thought, the conflict was between catholicity and "pure Protestantism or latitudinarianism," which accepted only the Bible as a source of religious truth, questioned the authority of the church's doctrinal tradition, downplayed mystery, ritual, and the importance of a visible church, and tended toward Socinianism.[196]

Newman's course of reading issued in an increasingly agonistic understanding of Church of England theology. Already in 1829, he had argued that Anglican evangelicals were theologically inconsistent and would under pressure of conflict become either genuine churchmen or dissenters.[197] Six years later, he used the same logic to construe the entire Protestant element in the Church of England as an incoherent amalgam of rationalist and Catholic attitudes and beliefs.

<hr>

193. JHN, "The Zeal of Jehu," 431.

194. JHN, "Liberalism," in *Lyra Apostolica* (Derby: Henry Mozley, 1836), 131–32.

195. JHN to George Ryder, March 14, 1833, *LD* 3, 249.

196. JHN, untitled manuscript beginning: "The Revolution in 1688," 1834, BOA D.5.13, 8, 21. See Andrew Starkie, "The Legacy of the 'Caroline Divines', Restoration, and the Emergence of the High Church Tradition," in *The Oxford Handbook of the Oxford Movement*, ed. Stewart J. Brown, Peter B. Nockles, and James Pereiro (Oxford: Oxford University Press, 2017), esp. 11–13, 16–17.

197. See p. 249.

"Protestants," he wrote to Maria Giberne in September 1835, should "make up their minds to be more consistent one way or other, to become rationalists or true Catholics."[198] In language that echoed his earlier description of Whigs in comparison to Tories and Radicals, he argued:

> A rationalist is intelligible though very offensive — so is a Roman Catholic — so is a Catholic — but the piebald system, which at present is thought so delightful and promising, is 'neither fish, flesh, nor good red herring,' and cannot stand the sifting of controversy.[199]

Establishment Protestantism was a violent forging of irreconcilable elements by state power. "Nothing but the State, i.e. the secular interests of men, expediency acting through force, keeps it up," Newman argued, "it is based upon no homogeneous principle in the heart, no perspicuous doctrine of the reason."[200] Thankfully, there was a viable alternative: the Tractarian resuscitation of "the system which nourished our great divines of the 17th Century, Taylor and the rest!"[201]

In the spring of 1836, Newman reiterated this line of argument in a revealing correspondence with Rose, who had begun to challenge Tractarian pessimism about the Church of England.[202] Newman frankly admitted: "I cannot love the 'Church of England' commonly so designated."[203] He objected to the theological unity Rose invested it with: "Surely it is matter of fact, the 'Church of England' has never been one reality, except *as* an Establishment."[204] "Viewed *internally*," he explained, "it is the battle field of two opposite principles; Socinianism and Catholicism — Socinianism fighting for the most part by Puritanism its unconscious ally."[205] The history of the Established Church showed that Socinianism was not just an ideological force outside of the church but a principle eroding it from within, aided unwittingly by (Calvinistic) evangelicalism and its precursors—an idea that derived support from Socinian trends in continental Protestantism.[206] Still, there was more to the church than what it became at the Reformation, and there were bright spots ever after:

198. JHN to Maria Giberne, September 4, 1835, *LD* 5, 134.
199. JHN to Maria Giberne, September 4, 1835, *LD* 5, 135. See pp. 278–79 in this book.
200. JHN to Maria Giberne, September 4, 1835, *LD* 5, 135.
201. Jeremy Taylor (1613–1667) was a famous Caroline divine.
202. Hugh James Rose to JHN, May 13, 1836, in John William Burgon, *Lives of Twelve Good Men*, vol. 1 (London: John Murray, 1888), 214–21. See JHN to Hugh James Rose, May 1, 1836, *LD* 5, 291–92; Hugh James Rose to JHN, May 9, 1836, in Burgon, *Lives*, 209–13; and JHN to Hugh James Rose, May 11, 1836, *LD* 5, 294–95.
203. JHN to Hugh James Rose, May 23, 1836, *LD* 5, 301.
204. JHN to Hugh James Rose, May 23, 1836, *LD* 5, 302.
205. JHN to Hugh James Rose, May 23, 1836, *LD* 5, 302.
206. See, for example, JHN to Mrs Newman, February 28, 1833, *LD* 3, 224.

The Anglican Church, the old Church of 1200 or 1600 years, the Church of the builders of our Cathedrals, the Church again of Andrews, Laud, Hammond, Ken, and Butler (so far forth as they agree together, and are lights shining in a dark place) the Church discriminated by imposition of hands, not a tyrant's jurisdiction, I love indeed, and the later not a whit less fervently than the earlier.[207]

Newman believed the Tractarian mission was to revive in the church of his own day the Catholic principle instanced throughout English history. Quickly, the battle *of* the church (against antagonistic cultural and political forces) had become a battle *for* the church: a struggle to define and uphold its catholic identity over against contending theological visions, which soon turned out to be those of former allies and inspirations.

207. JHN to Hugh James Rose, May 23, 1836, *LD* 5, 301.

CHAPTER 10

Tractarian Reckonings

The first targets of Newman's critique of evangelical religion had been high Calvinists like his brother Frank or Bulteel. When he turned to face liberalism a year or two later, Newman singled out prototypical progressives like Bentham and Brougham. Newman's attacks on both evangelicalism and liberalism began at the extreme ends of the spectrum, but his invective moved closer to the center as time went by. What is more, these two targets gradually began to overlap. To be sure, antiliberalism is what kicked off the Tractarian Movement; on this point, Frank Turner was wrong. But he was right to identify the resemblance between Newman's denunciation of liberalism in the 1860s and 1870s and his attack on "evangelical Protestant religion" in the 1830s.[1] Turner's mistake is not one of perception but of causation. Newman did not model his later antiliberalism on his earlier antievangelicalism, as Turner claims. Instead, Newman's Tractarian polemic against evangelicalism (and Protestantism more generally) was premised on his rejection of liberalism. To be precise, Newman attacked (evangelical) Protestantism *because* he believed it issued in liberalism or Socinianism. This identification of a liberal tendency in much of the Protestant theology of the day was rooted in his own intellectual history.

Recall that part of Newman's theological development in the mid-1820s consisted in a drift toward liberalism, as he later called it. The influence of Whately and Erskine caused him to explicate a tendency—only implicit in his earlier theology— toward valuing doctrine according to its affective import and practical effect. In consequence, Newman's theology centered on the atonement as the primary means of conversion and downplayed doctrines less obviously conducive to a holy life, such as the Athanasian Creed's formulation of Trinitarian theology. There is no evidence that Newman identified this tendency as liberal prior to the Tractarian period, and even during the Tractarian years, he never stated unequivocally that his own theology had tended toward liberalism. But the content of his polemics as well as his selection of targets warrant the conclusion that he was very much aware of it.

In 1834 and 1835, Newman fell out with Whately and blamed the Oriel theology that derived from his thought for fostering liberalism and Socinianism. He identified similar tendencies in evangelical theology at large and selected Erskine as instancing its rationalistic bearing. Even if Newman could not or would not

1. Turner, "Editor's Introduction," 59.

305

openly admit to their sway over his earlier theology, his dissection of their respective views was based on long familiarity with their thought and personal experience of its perilous attractions. I use this final chapter to show how this very private bit of personal history shaped Newman's public polemic during the early years of the Tractarian Movement. Obviously, I do not aim at comprehension. My only purpose is to show both that Newman attacked evangelicalism as well as Oriel theology because they tended toward liberalism and that he could discern this tendency because they had once made *him* drift toward liberalism.

Trouble at Oriel

Amid his anger over the Whigs' "wicked Spoliation Bill," Newman looked to Keble as "a second St Ambrose" leading the defense of the church.[2] But even though Keble had been his guide for a while now, Newman was still anxious to know what Whately thought of "the atrocious Irish sacrilege bill" (assuming, all the while, that his former Oriel mentor opposed it).[3] It was a pertinent question because Whately was at the heart of the trouble. In September 1831, he had become Archbishop of Dublin upon Earl Grey's recommendation. Froude was glad, at the time, that the hated "Whiggs [*sic*] should by a strange accident have blundered upon an honourable and kind hearted man."[4] Newman even expected an invitation to accompany his old mentor to Ireland— a dreaded prospect, for he believed his place was at Oxford.[5] But the invitation was never extended. Whately, Newman later realized, "knew me better than I knew myself."[6] Newman had not only misjudged himself. He also misjudged Whately, who did, in fact, agree with Whig policy on many counts.[7] For instance, Whately wholeheartedly supported the Whig effort to set up a national school system in Ireland that disregarded confessional fault lines.[8] Such a stance was

---

2. JHN to Jemima Newman, March 20, 1833, *LD* 3, 264. The reference is to Ambrose's excommunication of emperor Theodosius I after the massacre at Thessalonica in AD 390. This section and the following incorporate material from Geertjan Zuijdwegt, "Richard Whately," in *The Oxford Handbook of John Henry Newman*, ed. Frederick D. Aquino and Benjamin J. King (Oxford: Oxford University Press, 2018), 196–216, reproduced with permission. DOI: 10.1093/oxfordhb/9780198718284.013.10.

3. JHN to Thomas Mozley, March 9, 1833, *LD* 3, 242. See JHN to Richard Whately, November 11, 1834, *LD* 4, 359.

4. Richard Hurrell Froude to JHN, October 4, 1831, *LD* 2, 365–66.

5. JHN to Harriett Newman, October 16, 1831, *LD* 2, 367.

6. JHN to Harriett Newman, October 16, 1831, *LD* 2, 367n3.

7. David de Giustino, "Finding an Archbishop: The Whigs and Richard Whately in 1831," *Church History* 64, no. 2 (1995): 218–36, esp. 228–29.

8. E. Jane Whately, *Life and Correspondence of Richard Whately, D.D.*, vol. 1 (London: Longmans, Green, and Co., 1866), 137–39. See John Coolahan, "The Daring First Decade of the Board of National Education, 1831–1841," *The Irish Journal of Education* 17 (1983): 35–54.

beyond Newman's imagination. He regarded the "Irish Education Commission" as a "precious specimen" of liberal indifferentism. His hearty wish that "the good Whately," whom he thought "neither a Whig nor a Liberal," "had nothing to do with such dirt" illustrates Newman's naiveté about his former mentor.[9] Whately, who was tasked with the Irish church's actual administration, could not comprehend Newman's principled opposition to state interference with its governance. Whately scornfully recalled the opponents of Irish church reform, Newman included: "they only contributed fine speeches and tracts . . . but as for coming down with the *money*, nobody thought of that. It was cheaper to declaim against the horrible enormity of suppressing bishoprics and taxing benefices."[10]

Newman learned Whately's real position because of a painful incident that happened upon his arrival in England from the Mediterranean. On June 6, Bishop Phillpotts of Exeter had vigorously argued in the House of Lords that the proposed Church Temporalities Act violated the king's solemn oath at his coronation to "maintain and preserve inviolably the settlement of the United Church of England and Ireland [and] all such rights and privileges" as lawfully appertained to its churches and clergy.[11] Earl Grey offered the standard Whig response that the Coronation Oath "applied to the Sovereign, not in his legislative, but in his executive capacity," but desisted from arguing the point.[12] Whately, however, agreed with Grey and somehow felt the need to come out in his support a month later. The Coronation Oath, Whately argued in the Lords, "could not prevent the King from assenting to any Bill that might have been passed by both Houses of Parliament," because it was only "intended to prevent the King from encroaching upon the laws, or from acting against them"; that is, it only "affected his Majesty in his executive, and not in his legislative capacity."[13] Although Phillpotts's appeal to the Coronation Oath was bound to come to nothing—the strategy had failed in 1828 and 1829 and was sure to fail again— Newman still regarded Whately's "evasions about the Coronation Oath" as a betrayal of the church.[14] In an aborted manuscript pamphlet, he countered the "detestable sophistry" of Whately's Whig argument that "the King is bound to uphold the Church, not in his legislative, but merely in his executive capacity" by suggesting that the same logic would justify church members in considering

9. JHN to Simeon Lloyd Pope, April 9, 1832, *LD* 3, 42.

10. E. J. Whately, *Life*, vol. 1, 241.

11. HL Deb, June 6, 1833, *Hansard* 3.18, 382. See Henry Phillpotts, *A Letter to an English Layman on the Coronation Oath* (London: John Murray, 1828).

12. HL Deb, June 6, 1833, *Hansard* 3.18, 385. See Clark, *English Society*, 355–56.

13. HL Deb, July 9, 1833, *Hansard* 3.19, 305. See Nockles, "Church and King," 103.

14. JHN to Henry Arthur Woodgate, August 7, 1833, *LD* 4, 27. See Chadwick, *Victorian Church*, vol. 1, 14–16; Hilton, *A Mad, Bad, and Dangerous People*, 389–90.

themselves "bound to obey the King, only so far forth as he was a Churchman, & not when his Ministers were her [the church's] enemies."[15] And then there were the circumstances of the case. Whately had gratuitously shielded a Whig prime minister from the attack of a brother bishop concerning a measure encroaching on ecclesial rights. He had sided with the Whigs against the church. "Poor Whately is lost," Newman wrote to Christie; "I am much distressed at it — but there is no help for it, and one ought to cease to think of him. He has almost severed himself from Catholic Communion."[16]

Whately learned what Newman thought of him only a year later, and that by accident. In October 1834, Whately wrote Newman apropos of a persistent rumor that, on his last visit to Oriel, Newman stayed away from College Chapel "to avoid receiving the Communion along with me." Although Whately had been refuting the allegation, he still wanted "to be able to contradict the report from your own authority."[17] Newman responded that the accusation was untrue, he had simply taken communion at St Mary's that Sunday, but took the opportunity to vent his grievances. He lamented "the secular and unbelieving policy" to which the Irish church had submitted: "the Union of her members with men of heterodox views [in the Board of National Education], and the extinction (without ecclesiastical sanction) of half her candlesticks."[18] He attributed Whately's sanctioning these "perilous measures" to

> principles, difficult to describe in few words, with which your reputation is especially associated; principles, which bear upon the fundamentals of all argument and investigation, and affect almost every doctrine and every maxim on which our faith or our conduct depend.[19]

This charge was as vague as it was strong, and it deeply offended Whately. He thought that because Newman appealed to his "reputation," he had formed his judgment on calumnious hearsay. In response, he cited Newman's warm professions of friendship of eight years before and charged him with injustice—given the frankness of their earlier relationship—for not bringing up his qualms before.[20]

Like most people, Newman tended to overestimate the continuity between his former and his current views. He claimed he had never agreed with Whately's "line of opinions," even though he admitted he had said things that might have

---

15. JHN, untitled manuscript beginning: "It is not the intention of this pamphlet," 1833, BOA D.6.3, 2.

16. JHN to John Frederic Christie, August 6, 1833, *LD* 4, 26.

17. Richard Whately to JHN, October 25, 1834, *LD* 4, 348.

18. JHN to Richard Whately, October 28, 1834, *LD* 4, 349.

19. JHN to Richard Whately, October 28, 1834, *LD* 4, 349.

20. Richard Whately to JHN, November 3, 1834, *LD* 4, 356–57. See JHN to Richard Whately, November 14, 1826, *LD* 1, 306–7.

suggested the contrary.[21] He now qualified these opinions as "Liberal," including "the undervaluing of antiquity, and resting on one's own reasonings, judgments, definitions etc rather than authority and precedent." "I think I gave very little into this," he added. "Of course every one changes in opinion between 20 and 30," he noted, "doubtless I have changed; yet I am not conscious that I have so much *changed* as made up my mind on points on which I had no opinion."[22] If Newman intended this statement as a description of his theological development as a whole, it is simply false. But even if he was thinking only of the specific areas in which he now disagreed with Whately, which is probable, given the context, it downplays the depth and extent of his change in views. Even his letter suggests as much. In explanation of his new opinion of Whately's views—an undeniable change—he argued: "it is natural, that, when two persons pursue different lines from the same point, they should not discover their divergence for a long while; especially if there be any kind feeling in the one towards the other."[23] This is much nearer the truth. Even while he shared Whately's practical views on revelation and purely economic understanding of Trinitarian doctrine, Newman retained (in part latently) his earlier commitment to dogma, evinced by his continued insistence on the reality of the personal distinctions in the Godhead. This conviction broke through in his 1827 sermon *On the Mediatorial Kingdom of Christ.* It was the first sign of divergence from what had seemed a common starting point, even though, at the time, he tried to conform to Whately's critiques. From 1827 onward, Newman's theology so rapidly evolved away from that of Whately that only his continued affection explains that he did not problematize their differences any earlier. It was precisely the love he had expressed in 1826 (which Whately took to imply culpable lack of candor now) that had blinded Newman for so long. Thus, at Naples, Newman had still "indignantly rejected the notion" that Whately acquiesced in "the project of destroying the Irish sees." It was only upon returning to England that he realized "all was over."[24] And even when he gave up Whately, it was with regret. "He has so many good qualities, that it is impossible also not to feel for him," Newman confided to Bowden at the time.[25]

Two weeks after his parting letter to Whately, Newman clashed with another member of the Oriel Common Room: Renn Dickson Hampden (1793–1868). Again, the occasion was politico-religious. In March 1834, the Earl of Radnor had initiated a public debate about the statute requiring Oxford undergraduates

21. JHN to Richard Whately, November 11, 1834, *LD* 4, 358.
22. JHN to Richard Whately, November 11, 1834, *LD* 4, 358.
23. JHN to Richard Whately, November 11, 1834, *LD* 4, 358–59.
24. JHN to Richard Whately, November 11, 1834, *LD* 4, 359.
25. JHN to John William Bowden, August 31, 1833, *LD* 4, 34. In 1860, after years of bearing Whately's acrimonious attacks in print, Newman still wrote: "There is scarcely any one, whom in memory I love more than Whately even now" (note dated November 10, 1860, *LD* 1, 307).

to subscribe to the Thirty-Nine Articles upon matriculation. Dissenters, backed by Earl Grey in Parliament, clamoured for its abrogation, and the university administrators (the Board of Heads of Houses) began to give way to the political pressure by the end of 1834.[26] Hampden, as principal of St Mary's Hall, not only advocated abrogation in the board but also was the first to support reform in print. His *Observations on Religious Dissent* made the theological point that dissent does not touch the substance of Christianity but expresses only a difference of opinion. At first, Newman chose to ignore the pamphlet, but when Hampden presented him with a copy of its second edition, he could no longer contain himself. Emboldened, perhaps, by his distancing himself from Whately, he wrote to Hampden on November 28 to express his "very sincere and deep regret" that the pamphlet had been published: "I dare not trust myself to put on paper my feelings about the principles contained in it, tending as they do in my opinion altogether to make shipwreck of Christian faith."[27] Just as in his letters to Whately, Newman's concern was with principles that, if consistently applied, cut at the root of Christian belief and praxis. In an earlier draft of his letter to Hampden, he had specified these principles as "legitimately leading to formal Socinianism."[28] As in the case of Whately, Newman explicitly aligned Hampden's theology with the liberalism he had been challenging for several years now.

Despite his private ire at Hampden, it took two further events to provoke Newman to public action. On March 20, 1835, he learned that Blanco White had converted to Unitarianism. Blanco White had joined Whately in Dublin in 1832 but left for Liverpool in early 1835 when his Unitarian convictions would have compromised the archbishop.[29] A few days earlier, on March 16, Edward Hawkins had published an anonymous pamphlet in favor of abolishing subscription. It dismissed as imaginary the fear that the proposal implied "some insidious attempt against the great doctrines of Christianity."[30] People mistakenly "think of Arians and Socinians," Hawkins argued, "and imagine a connexion between the present proposal for a change in the Subscription of Undergraduates, and the assault upon Subscription to Articles in all cases whatever in 1772."[31] In view of the

---

26. Ward, *Victorian Oxford*, 89–99; Chadwick, *The Victorian Church*, vol. 1, 89–95.

27. JHN to Renn Dickson Hampden, November 28, 1834, *LD* 4, 371.

28. JHN to Renn Dickson Hampden, November 28, 1834, *LD* 4, 371n4; BOA, Various Collections, Hampden and H. Wilberforce, 1835.

29. John Hamilton Thom, ed., *The Life of the Rev. Joseph Blanco White*, vol. 2 (London: John Chapman, 1845), 71–72.

30. [Edward Hawkins], *A Letter to the Earl of Radnor upon the Oaths, Dispensations, and Subscription to the XXXIX Articles at the University of Oxford* (Oxford: J. H. Parker, 1835), 18.

31. [Edward Hawkins], *A Letter to the Earl of Radnor*, 18. In 1771, the latitudinarian Feathers Tavern petitioners requested the abolishment of subscription to the articles because it interfered with "their undoubted right as Protestants of interpreting Scripture for themselves" (*The History, Debates, and Proceedings of Both Houses of Parliament of Great Britain, from the Year 1743 to the Year 1774,*

explicitly theological nature of Hampden's recent pamphlet, this was a bit rich. Compounded by the "defection of poor Blanco White," it was too much.[32] Newman responded swiftly. On March 23, he asked Henry Wilberforce to attack the Oriel theology that had taken its lead from Whately in a pamphlet to be entitled "Socinianism in Oxford."[33] It should show that subscription reform originated with a "school" of doubtful orthodoxy, now known as the Oriel Noetics, whose theology tended toward Socinianism.[34] Although the Noetics had no formal organization, they did share a common intellectual outlook largely derived from Whately. As Pietro Corsi argues, the Noetics became "Whately's school" after Copleston left for Llandaff in 1828.[35] By and large, the members Newman listed are those identified with the school in modern scholarship: Whately, Hampden, Blanco White, Thomas Arnold, Samuel Hinds, and Nassau William Senior.[36] In Newman's conception, Wilberforce's pamphlet was to demonstrate that Noetic advocacy for reform at Oxford "was but the *advanced guard* of a black host."[37] Their many doctrinal errors, and especially "Hampden's century of heresies," all tended toward Socinianism.[38] This charge had two layers. On a doctrinal level, it meant that the Noetics expounded views on subjects like the Trinity or the atonement that resembled or led to the Socinian position. These errors of doctrine, in turn, were rooted, on a fundamental theological level, in a mistaken conception of the source and nature of revealed truth.

---

vol. 6 [London: J. Debrett, 1792], 169). Shortly after the proposal was defeated in the Commons in 1772, one of its main advocates, Theophilus Lindsey, left the Established Church and opened his Unitarian congregation. See John Gascoigne, "Anglican Latitudinarianism and Political Radicalism in the Late Eighteenth Century," *History* 71 (1986): 22–38; G. M. Ditchfield, "Feathers tavern petitioners (*act.* 1771–1774)," ODNB; and Young, *Religion and Enlightenment*, 45–80.

32. JHN to Henry Wilberforce, March 23, 1835, *LD* 5, 51.

33. JHN to Henry Wilberforce, March 23, 1835, *LD* 5, 50.

34. JHN to Henry Wilberforce, March 23, 1835, *LD* 5, 51. Although the precise meaning of the designation Noetic and its currency in the 1830s remains unclear, the term was widely and enthusiastically adopted by commentators and historians after Thomas Mozley first used it in print in 1882. See Mozley, *Reminiscences*, 18–26; Richard Brent, "The Oriel Noetics," in *The History of the University of Oxford*, vol. 6, *Nineteenth-Century Oxford*, ed. M. G. Brock and M. C. Curthoys (Oxford: Clarendon Press, 1997), 72–76.

35. Corsi, *Science and Religion*, 74. See Nicholson, "Eveleigh," 279. Whately was Arnold's and Hampden's senior at Oriel, and he strongly influenced Blanco White. Hinds, Nassau Senior, and Baden Powell had all been his pupils. Recall Isaac Williams's juxtaposition of the "Oriel or Whateleian" school with that of Keble (Williams, *Autobiography*, 46). See p. 191 in this book.

36. In his response, Henry Wilberforce suggested also having "a slap at Baden Powell," the missing Noetic in Newman's original list (Henry Wilberforce to JHN, March 25, 1835, *LD* 5, 52).

37. JHN to Henry Wilberforce, March 23, 1835, *LD* 5, 51.

38. JHN to Henry Wilberforce, March 23, 1835, *LD* 5, 51.

Noetic Heresies

In his letter to Wilberforce, Newman argued that Whately approached Socinianism via "Sabellianism" and "Nestorianism."[39] The idea of an intrinsic connection between these three heresies had been gestating for several years in Newman's thought, but he formulated it with increasing clarity after his final exchange with Whately in November 1834. Newman must have been reminded of the critiques Whately had penned on the manuscript of his 1827 sermon on Christ's mediatorial kingdom. Perhaps he even consulted them. Reviewing Whately's remarks on the Trinity in light of the patristic framework he had developed in the *Arians* would have given Newman abundant cause for censure. Although Whately studiously tried to remain agnostic about distinctions in the immanent Godhead, his way of treating the divine persons suggested that he viewed them only as aspects or modes of the one God's activity toward creation. In the etymological sense Whately adopted in the *Logic*, "person" only meant "(assumed) character." It did not denote God's *being* but rather his *relating to us* as Father, Son, and Spirit.[40] The 1829 edition was even more explicit. It cited the seventeenth-century mathematician John Wallis to argue that God's unity requires that "person" be understood as signifying a mere difference in "*state, quality*, or *condition*," just as when we say that "the same man may at once sustain the Person of *a King* and a *Father*, if he be invested both with *regal* and *paternal* authority."[41] Perhaps subconsciously recalling these passages from the *Logic*, Newman had resolutely rejected such a reading in the *Arians*, arguing that to take "person" in "its etymological sense of persona or πρόσωπον, i.e. *character*" amounts to "what is popularly called Unitarianism."[42] The premise for this radical conclusion was the work's earlier sketch of Sabellianism.

In the *Arians*, Newman defined Sabellianism as "the denial of the distinction of Persons in the Divine Nature" and identified two variants, distinguished by their respective Christologies.[43] Sabellians rejected the idea that in Christ one of three distinct divine persons has become incarnate, but that idea left them with a

---

39. JHN to Henry Wilberforce, March 23, 1835, *LD* 5, 51. For a detailed discussion of developments in Newman's Christology between 1834 and 1836, see King, *Newman*, 127–61.

40. Thomas Mozley, who had to deliver Whately's Bosworth lectures in 1835 (the ones Newman used approvingly in his 1825 sermon on the Trinity) had a similar impression. He later recalled that they seemed to present divine personality as a mere "Office," whereby "the Second Person in the Trinity was a representation of the Father's mercy, and the Third of His sanctifying power" (*Reminiscences*, 21; see p. 102 in this book).

41. Whately, *Elements of Logic*, 3rd ed. (London: B. Fellowes, 1829), 311; John Wallis, *A Fifth Letter Concerning the Sacred Trinity* (London: Tho. Parkhurst, 1691), 16. Newman read Wallis's *Letters* in 1842 and judged them "Sabellian" (JHN to Thomas Mozley, March 14, 1842, *LD* 8, 485).

42. *Ari.*, 390.

43. *Ari.*, 129.

puzzle. They still had to explain "in what sense they believed God to be united to the human nature of Christ."[44] Two different accounts emerged, the one engendering the other. The first argued "that God was literally one with Christ, and therefore . . . in no sense distinct from Him." Since this position entailed that the Father suffered and died on the cross, it was labelled patripassianism. It had the advantage of retaining "the doctrine of the hypostatic union," which Newman considered "the only safeguard against a gradual declension into the Ebionite, or modern Socinian heresy." But its problem was that it was nearly impossible to reconcile with scripture, which clearly suggests that "there is *some* real sense in which the Father is not the Son."[45] It is almost impossible to interpret the relational dynamic between Christ and the Father—portrayed in the New Testament as serving and being served, being sent and sending, descending from and ascending to—as reflecting a merely verbal distinction. The only way for a Sabellian to solve this problem and maintain the absolute divine unity was to construe the relation between God and Christ as one of mere "*presence*," "*emanation*," or "inspiration," rather than substantial union, and thus to land in a form of Socinianism. Sabellianism, in short, gradually and inevitably tends toward Socinianism.[46] Newman thought that Whately's modalism was of the second variety. Although Whately affirmed Christ's divinity, he refused to distinguish Father and Son, so that he had to interpret all New Testament passages about Christ's relationship to the Father as expressing the relationship between Christ's human nature alone and the one God.[47] As a result, Whately invited Newman's second charge, that of Nestorianism: the abandonment of the idea of a personal union of divine and human natures in Christ. Whately, however, was not the only one with Nestorian leanings; far from it.

"At present you hear Nestorianism preached in every other pulpit," Newman wrote to Froude in January 1835.[48] For five years now, Newman had considered the doctrine of the incarnation as the distinctive and central tenet of Christian theology, but all around him, he saw Christians who hardly realized what it meant to affirm that in Christ, God became man, such that a single person at once was truly God and truly man. To most people, he argued in a sermon of March 8, the words "Son of God" meant little more than that Christ "came from God, that

44. *Ari.*, 133.

45. *Ari.*, 133.

46. *Ari.*, 136. Newman's interpretation of Sabellianism was indebted to that of Edward Gibbon (who claimed that "the Sabellian ends where the Ebionite had begun") but reversed its genealogy. For Gibbon, it was the startled realization of some Sabellians that they had to give up Christ's divinity that turned them into patripassians (Edward Gibbon, *The History of the Decline and Fall of the Roman Empire*, vol. 3 [Dublin: William Halhead, 1781], 321). Frank Newman also followed Gibbon in identifying Sabellianism as a "concealed" form of Unitarianism (*Phases of Faith*, 87).

47. *Serm.* 1, 336n21. See pp. 105–6 in this book.

48. JHN to Richard Hurrell Froude, January 18, 1835, *LD* 5, 10.

He was the well beloved of God, and that He is much more than a mere man."[49] "This is all that the words convey to many men at the most," Newman argued, "while many more refer them merely to His human nature," as Whately did.[50] Newman's point was not that people explicitly denied the hypostatic union but that they did not realize its implications. What it means is the following. The Son of God, eternally one with and yet distinct from the Father,

> took into His own Infinite Essence man's nature itself in all its original fulness, creating a soul and body, and, at the moment of creating, making them His own, so that they never were other than His, never existed by themselves or except as in Him. . . . And, while thus adding a new nature to Himself, He did not in any respect cease to be what He was before.[51]

Accordingly, Christ is fully and at once God and man: "whatever our Lord said and did upon earth was strictly and literally speaking the word and deed of God Himself."[52] But most believers cannot hold together the divine and human nature in the one person of the Son. "We speak of Him in a vague way as God . . . [but] when we proceed to consider His humiliation, we are unable to carry on the notion of His personality from heaven to earth."[53] We first speak of the Son of God "as God, without mention of the Father from whom He is," and then "as if a creature."[54] But "these distinct notions of Him" do not "hold together in our minds."[55] The result of speaking in this way—"first of God, then of man"—is that "we seem to change the Nature without preserving the Person." We end up with a being who was one thing first, and then quite another, with no unifying link whatsoever. People, in sum, speak of Christ's "human nature and His Divine nature so separately as not to feel or understand that God is man and man is God."[56] Newman warned his congregation that such people "begin by being Sabellians, that they go on to be Nestorians, and that they tend to be Ebionites and to deny Christ's Divinity altogether."[57] This was the precise accusation Newman had leveled at Whately.

Conceptually, the trajectory Newman sketches can be summed up as follows. If the Son is in no way distinct from the Father (Sabellianism), the incarnation must be thought of either as an absolute identification of the one God with human nature (and thus we arrive at patripassianism) or as a mere relationship

---

49. JHN, No. 380, "The Humiliation of the Eternal Son," March 8, 1835, *PaS* 3, 176.
50. JHN, No. 380, "The Humiliation of the Eternal Son," *PaS* 3, 176.
51. JHN, No. 380, "The Humiliation of the Eternal Son," *PaS* 3, 179.
52. JHN, No. 380, "The Humiliation of the Eternal Son," *PaS* 3, 180.
53. JHN, No. 380, "The Humiliation of the Eternal Son," *PaS* 3, 185.
54. JHN, No. 380, "The Humiliation of the Eternal Son," *PaS* 3, 185.
55. JHN, No. 380, "The Humiliation of the Eternal Son," *PaS* 3, 186.
56. JHN, No. 380, "The Humiliation of the Eternal Son," *PaS* 3, 186.
57. JHN, No. 380, "The Humiliation of the Eternal Son," *PaS* 3, 186.

of two distinct entities (Nestorianism). But once we conceive of the incarnation in terms of God "relating to" rather than "becoming" man, we will tend to construe this relationship in ever looser (because more intelligible) ways. And thus, the door is opened to forms of adoptionism (such as that of the Ebionites) or an understanding of Christ as a merely inspired human being: the Socinian view. The progression from Sabellianism via Nestorianism to Socinianism resulted from a mistaken concept of divine personhood, precisely where all had gone wrong with Whately. Accordingly, it could only be halted by insisting "upon the Personality of the Word as distinct from the Father," as Newman put it in the *Arians*.[58] The "Divine Sonship," Newman claimed in his sermon, "is that portion of the sacred doctrine on which the mind is providentially intended to rest throughout, and so to preserve for itself His [the Son's] identity unbroken."[59] Those who lose sight of this, lose sight of the Son "as a really existing being, external to our minds" and reduce him, instead, to "a mere name on which titles and properties may be affixed without congruity and meaning."[60]

The logic of Newman's position has not always been clear. Reading some of the literature, one might think that Newman was imagining heresies everywhere (Stephen Thomas) or merely using their names as empty catchwords (Turner), but his Trinitarian theology and patristic knowledge were quite sophisticated, more so than those of his opponents or of many later commentators. Given his long familiarity with Whately's thought, the surprise is not that he denounced it as Sabellian but that it took him until 1835 to do so. Besides, it was hard not to see Blanco White's defection as the practical validation of Newman's theoretical model of the progression from Sabellianism to Socinianism. And if more evidence were needed, Blanco White provided it himself. In the summer of 1835, he published a defense of his new convictions: *Observations on Heresy and Orthodoxy.* In the preface, he explained how he had taken "refuge in a modification of the Sabellian theory"—praying to God via Christ as his image—to be able to remain in the Church of England. But the "*devout* contrivance" could not satisfy his reason, and he realized that "Sabellianism is only Unitarianism disguised in words."[61] For Newman, these lines were an unexpected confirmation of "the tendency of certain opinions" he had long suspected, and he made the most of them in controversy.[62] At the same time, he did not think Trinitarian doctrine was the only problem of Noetic theology, nor, perhaps, even its most fundamental.

<hr>

58. *Ari.*, 138.

59. *Ari.*, 138.

60. *Ari.*, 184, 185.

61. Joseph Blanco White, *Observations on Heresy and Orthodoxy* (London: J. Mardon, 1835), viii.

62. JHN to Richard Hurrell Froude, August 9, 1835, *LD* 5, 119. See also JHN to John William Bowden, August 3, 1835, *LD* 5, 114; JHN to Hugh James Rose, August 6, 1835, *LD* 5, 116; and JHN to Elizabeth Newman, August 9, 1835, *LD* 5, 121.

The conflict of views between Newman and Whately on Christ and the Trinity issued from their respective understandings of the sources and nature of doctrine. For Newman, all doctrine derived its meaning from the incarnation.[63] We can grasp what it means—that Christ was born, lived, died, harrowed hell, rose, and ascended to heaven—only when we understand that he was the Son of God in the flesh: truly man, truly God, one person. Newman was convinced that this was how the Apostles and their early followers understood Christ. Their writings witness to this revelation of God in Christ, albeit unsystematically. The Apostles and their successors instructed the initiate in its doctrinal sense, until the continual attacks of heretics forced the church to formulate this oral tradition in its creeds.[64] Although the doctrines they contain, especially those of the Trinity and the incarnation, are only partially comprehensible, they are the nearest approximation that human language can provide to the ineffable truth about Godself. Accordingly, they are binding on later generations of Christians as the authoritative key to the doctrinal sense of scripture.

Whately's theology militated against such an understanding of doctrine. Like Newman, Whately agreed with Hawkins's insight that scripture does not "furnish us with any thing of the nature of a systematic Creed."[65] Instead of interpreting this fact as an argument for a doctrinal tradition of greater (Newman) or lesser (Hawkins) authority, however, Whately used it to argue for the limited importance of doctrine. Given the human penchant for theorizing, the fact that the Apostles never wrote down a systematic creed is inexplicable. It can only be explained if we assume that God "*supernaturally* withheld" the Apostles from doing so, so as to leave "Christians at large in respect of those points in which variation might be desirable."[66] Accordingly, no creeds are binding. Given that "*uninspired* writers" composed them in response to specific circumstances, "we need not scruple to *alter* them from time to time, as occasions may require."[67] Each community of believers is "to steer its own course by the Chart and Compass which [God's] holy Word supplies."[68] Whately's theory of the nature of revelation further diminished the value of traditional creeds. Scripture records only what God does and says, not who he is. It does not reveal "the *intrinsic* nature of the Deity."[69] We only

63. See JHN to James Stephen, March 16, 1835, *LD* 5, 45.

64. See JHN to Thomas Falconer, about January 26, 1834, *LD* 4, 179–80.

65. Whately, "On the Omission of a System of Articles of Faith, Liturgies, and Ecclesiastical Canons," in *Essays on Some of the Peculiarities of the Christian Religion*, 3rd ed. (London, B. Fellowes, 1831), 312. Newman owned a copy of the original pamphlet version (Earnest and Tracey, *John Henry Newman*, 20.201).

66. Whately, *Peculiarities of the Christian Religion*, 3rd ed., 330, 332–33.

67. Whately, *Peculiarities of the Christian Religion*, 3rd ed., 345.

68. Whately, *Peculiarities of the Christian Religion*, 3rd ed., 337.

69. Richard Whately, *The Errors of Romanism Traced to their Origins in Human Nature* (London: B. Fellowes, 1830), 82.

know God as he appears to us, not as he is in himself; hence Whately's principled stance against affirming distinctions in the immanent Godhead. As a result, Whately had no patience for the doctrinal debates of the early church. They were mere exercises in "human folly and learned ignorance": the "miserable disputes of pretended Christians."[70]

Hampden radicalized Whately's suspicions of doctrine. His *Observations on Religious Dissent* used the subscription debate to challenge the theological grounds of denominational division as such. On November 12, Newman had complained of the pamphlet to Froude as proving "all articles and creeds (but the Apostles) human composition, theological statements and pious opinions."[71] Although imprecise in its wording, the gist of the comment is correct. Hampden instituted a rigid distinction between the data of scripture and "the intellectual, or speculative, or theological conclusions" drawn from them.[72] The former are revealed and must be believed. They make up "religion": the collection of "truths which are simply contained in divine revelation, with the affections, dispositions, and actions suggested by them." The latter constitute the field of "theological opinion," on which we are free to disagree.[73] This distinction was premised on a specific theory of revelation. Like Whately, Hampden believed that scripture reveals only "the doings and actions of God."[74] It wholly "consists of matter of fact."[75] Unlike natural facts, these revealed facts are beyond our ordinary field of experience, so that we cannot use them as premises for theorizing. Where scripture is concerned, "texts, *as texts*, prove nothing"; they cannot be used to infer the truth of doctrines, because their only referents are "real facts in the history of Divine providence."[76] And thus, Hampden insisted that "no conclusions of human reasoning, however correctly deduced, however logically sound, are properly religious truths."[77] This idea radically opposes scripture to tradition, which Hampden believed to be "nothing more than expositions of the text of Scripture, reasoned out by the Church and embodied in a code of doctrine."[78] No creed, therefore, should ever be treated as religious truth. This was true especially for traditional creeds like the Nicene and Athanasian, which have the additional defect of being premised on the obsolete conceptual framework of ancient philosophy, whose central distinctions (form-matter, substance-accident) were conclusively

70. Richard Whately, *Elements of Logic*, 4th ed. (London: B. Fellowes, 1831), 335, citing James Douglas, *Errors Regarding Religion* (Edinburgh: Adam Black, 1830), 54.

71. JHN to Richard Hurrell Froude, November 12, 1834, *LD* 4, 360.

72. Renn Dickson Hampden, *Observations on Religious Dissent* (Oxford: J. H. Parker, 1834), 13.

73. Hampden, *Observations*, 20.

74. Hampden, *Observations*, 15.

75. Hampden, *Observations*, 14.

76. Hampden, *Observations*, 15; see also 17–19.

77. Hampden, *Observations*, 8; see also 17.

78. Hampden, *Observations*, 4.

debunked by Francis Bacon.[79] Obviously, all of this greatly relativizes the significance of dissent. Doctrinal divergence is only a difference of opinion, whereas in "religion, properly so called, few Christians, if any, really differ."[80] Accordingly, Hampden argued that even "Unitarians deserve "the name of Christians," because they accept the Bible.[81]

Although Hampden's theology jarred with Newman's deepest convictions, Newman hoped to avoid having to respond in person. That is why he asked Henry Wilberforce to do so. But Wilberforce hesitated: despite having been Newman's private pupil at Oriel, he was not quite as familiar with the Noetics and their work. He had neither seen nor heard of Hampden's pamphlet and knew little of the theology of Blanco White, Hinds, or Senior.[82] To get him going, Newman drew up "a sketch of what might be," which included lengthy citations from the works of Hampden, Arnold, Hinds, and Blanco White.[83] Wilberforce turned it into a pamphlet proper but would not put his name to it—"the pamphlet being really yours."[84] Newman probably agreed, for it appeared anonymously in May under a title Wilberforce had suggested: *The Foundation of the Faith Assailed in Oxford*.[85] It presented the proposed change in the university statutes as part of a more sweeping reform program, aimed at modifying "our system by a series of liberal changes, tending to make knowledge, rather than moral discipline the object of our studies," so that Oxford would no longer inculcate "high and chivalrous loyalty" to the Church of England but instead yield only scientific and commercial prodigies who hardly believe "that in religious and moral subjects there is anything decidedly and intrinsically true."[86]

Hampden and some of his Oriel cronies were cited as providing the theological rationale for this program. They constituted "a party" at Oxford that almost merited "the awful name of Socinian."[87] Wilberforce had to admit that Hampden did not directly assert Socinian views, but by objecting "to all statements of doctrine of whatever kind, if they claim to be regarded as expressing any thing of intrinsic truth; and, by representing the points of difference as trifling, he certainly paves the way for others to formal Socinianism, however he may himself escape it."[88]

---

79. Renn Dickson Hampden, *The Scholastic Philosophy Considered in its Relation to Christian Theology* (Oxford: J. H. Parker, 1833), 378–79.

80. Hampden, *Observations*, 20.

81. Hampden, *Observations*, 21.

82. Henry Wilberforce to JHN, March 25, 1835, *LD* 5, 52.

83. JHN to Henry Wilberforce, April 3, 1835, *LD* 5, 55.

84. Henry Wilberforce to JHN, April 26, 1835, *LD* 5, 65.

85. A clerical member of Convocation [Henry Wilberforce], *The Foundation of the Faith Assailed in Oxford: A Letter to His Grace the Archbishop of Canterbury* (London: J. G. & F. Rivington, 1835).

86. [Wilberforce], *Foundation*, 8–9.

87. [Wilberforce], *Foundation*, 34.

88. [Wilberforce], *Foundation*, 15.

Hampden bore the brunt of the pamphlet's attack, but Whately was never mentioned. As Wilberforce pointed out in a letter, Newman had omitted Whately from his collection of citations, perhaps because of personal affection, perhaps because he thought it inappropriate or inopportune to attack an archbishop.[89] Still, Whately's theology was dealt with vicariously, through Hinds, his closest associate and domestic chaplain in Dublin. Like Whately, Hinds argued that all we learn from scripture is that "God has assumed a threefold *character* . . . and that distinct views of the Divine nature attach to Him accordingly." As to "further distinctions *unrevealed*," these "can only be derived, *by inference*, from God's apparent design in creating a threefold impression of Himself."[90] The fate of such inferences, like the distinction of persons in the Trinity, Hampden had made clear.

The pamphlet had a tempestuous aftermath. Hampden was furious when he discovered that it came from a mere upstart like Wilberforce and more than suspected that Newman had egged him on.[91] Matters got worse when Newman, as editor, included the *Foundation* in a collection of pamphlets in defense of subscription. The preface of the collection reiterated another of the *Foundation*'s charges, that Hampden's understanding of the atonement was "Socinian," by citing instances from his 1832 *Bampton Lectures* that denied "that Christ's atonement, considered as a truth of Scripture, included in it the idea of having propitiated the Father."[92] Hampden protested vehemently against the collection and its preface, and before a single copy had been sold, it was reissued without Wilberforce's pamphlet and the offending matter in the preface.[93] The *Foundation* was by no means a great text. Wilberforce did not know enough about the subject to argumentatively tighten up Newman's loose outline, and some of his claims were exaggerated beyond what is tolerable even in the alarmist genre—due in part, no doubt, to his characteristic impudence.[94] Still, Newman liked the *Foundation* "very much" and reiterated many of its charges when Hampden was appointed Regius Professor of Divinity in

89. Henry Wilberforce to JHN, April 26, 1835, *LD* 5, 65. Senior was also omitted, probably because Newman could not procure his relevant publications on short notice (most of the citations in the pamphlet are from works in Newman's private library).

90. [Wilberforce], *Foundation*, 32, (probably) Newman's emphases; Samuel Hinds, *The Three Temples of the One True God Contrasted* (London: B. Fellowes, 1830), 130–31.

91. See the correspondence between Wilberforce, Hampden, and Newman at *LD* 5, 73–74.

92. JHN, Preface, in *Pamphlets in Defence of the Oxford Usage of Subscription to the XXXIX Articles at Matriculation*, 1st ed. (Oxford: J. H. Parker, 1835), 11, 12. See Wilberforce, *Foundation*, 32–33. Newman distinguished this idea "from that of satisfaction or compensation, which goes on to assign the *mode* in which He effected the propitiation." See p. 335 in this book.

93. The omission was mainly due to the fact that William Sewell threatened to withdraw his pamphlet if the collection contained personal attacks on Hampden. See the correspondence between Hampden, Newman, and Sewell at *LD* 5, 83–86, and JHN to Richard Hurrell Froude, June 27, 1835, *LD* 5, 89–90.

94. Froude once called him "the most impertinent fellow that ever existed" (Richard Hurrell Froude to George Ryder, November 26, 1832, *LD* 3, 117n1). See Newsome, *Parting of Friends*, 108–17.

February 1836, an event that incited one of the bitterest of Newman's Tractarian campaigns, but which is beyond the scope of the present study.[95]

The Stakes: Apostolical Tradition

Amid the ferocious flurry of Oxford's pamphlet wars, it is easy to lose sight of the fact that a serious theological issue was at stake, an issue Newman could and did address quite soberly when he wanted to. One way to interpret the theological conflict at Oriel is to view it as the result of opposing responses to Hawkins's insistence that the Bible contains no systematic exposition of doctrine. Whately took scripture as the model of divine pedagogy and concluded to the relative unimportance of doctrinal propositions. Hampden went a step further and argued that scripture contains no doctrine whatsoever. When he considered St Paul's injunction to Timothy to "Hold fast the form of sound words," Hampden dismissed the idea that St Paul was "alluding to some formal exposition of doctrines." St Paul simply meant "faith in Christ," that is, "the collection of facts involved in that general expression, 'Christ crucified,' which is the sum and substance of his writings."[96] Newman had drawn the opposite conclusion from Hawkins's argument. Because scripture is unsystematic, Newman thought, the church is the legitimate teacher of doctrine. Accordingly, Newman's interpretation of St Paul's injunction to Timothy was the polar opposite of Hampden's. In a sermon of August 28, 1834, Newman argued:

> The Christian doctrine committed to Timothy was contained in a definite form of sound words, not a mere general message left for this or that man to interpret or deliver as he would, but a certain fixed creed which every Christian Minister was bound to preach and to transmit entire as he had received it.[97]

More than in the *Arians*, Newman insisted that the fact that scripture is unsystematic does not make it undogmatic. The New Testament shows, both in the text from St Paul and elsewhere, that the Apostles taught definite doctrinal formulae, and scattered passages confirm that their content corresponds to the traditional creeds.[98]

---

95. JHN to Henry Wilberforce, May 3, 1835, *LD* 5, 63. See JHN, *Elucidations of Dr. Hampden's Theological Statements* (Oxford: J. H. Parker, 1836); Zuijdwegt, "Richard Whately," 211.

96. Hampden, *Observations*, 16; 2 Timothy 1:13.

97. JHN, No. 354, "The Form of sound words, a trust committed to the Christian Minister," August 28, 1834, *Serm.* 3, 341. See also 346: "ὑγιαινόντων λόγων is clearly an outline of *doctrine* and *precept*, of the *objects*, the *articles* of Christian faith and obedience."

98. JHN, No. 354, "The Form of sound words," *Serm.* 3, 346–48.

After reading Hampden's *Observations*, Newman realized how pertinent his sermon was, and he rewrote it for inclusion in his second volume of *Parochial Sermons*.[99] Countering Hampden, he argued that the "Faith of Christ" is not "vague, indeterminate, a matter of opinion or deduction" but rather "a definite deposit, a treasure, common to all, one and the same in every age, conceived in set words, and such as admits of being received, preserved, transmitted."[100] Upon baptism, a believer receives it in the form of the Apostles' Creed, which "will then unfold, first, into the Nicene Creed (as it is called), then into the Athanasian."[101] "All these unfoldings of the Gospel Doctrine," Newman argued, "are in fact nothing more or less than the one true explanation of them delivered down to us from the first ages, together with the original Baptismal or Apostles' Creed itself."[102] In 1825, Newman had eagerly adopted Hawkins's idea that the church teaches and explains, while scripture proves doctrine. His patristic research several years later convinced him that this was especially true of the early church, not so much because it had exceptional expository qualities but because it possessed the doctrinal teaching of the Apostles. As Newman put in August 1834,

> What was generally received in the early times must have been sanctioned by the Apostles; and what the Apostles ordained and taught in every Church is the best comment on what they said in Scripture, the fullest and truest development of those principles of faith which they have put into writing, much truer than any private judgment and private interpretation.[103]

Newman simply did not see a way around Christian antiquity to arrive at religious truth. "As to Scripture being practically sufficient for making the Christian," he had written to Pusey in December 1832, "it seems to me a mere dream — nor do I find it anywhere said so in Scripture."[104] What belief in the sufficiency of scripture led to was instanced by Blanco White. He had chosen to rely on scripture alone and, using the same argument as Hampden, justified his defection from the Church of England on the grounds that "the whole *Patristical* theology, which makes up the greatest part of the Thirty-Nine Articles, consists of groundless speculations which could never have obtained currency among Christians without the aid of a false philosophy."[105] Socinianism was the natural outcome of such a line of reasoning.

99. *LD* 5, 381.

100. JHN, No. 367, "The Gospel, A Trust Committed to Us," December 1834, *PaS* 2, 283; see also 285.

101. JHN, No. 367, "The Gospel, A Trust," *PaS* 2, 283–84.

102. JHN, No. 367, "The Gospel, A Trust," *PaS* 2, 284.

103. JHN, No. 354, "The Form of sound words," *Serm.* 3, 354.

104. JHN to Edward Bouverie Pusey, December 5, 1832, *LD* 3, 127.

105. Blanco White, *Observations*, v.

Newman applied his argument beyond Noetic theology to all *sola scriptura* Protestantism. Again, this was the result of personal experience. For some years, his brother Frank (now a dissenting evangelical) had been championing reliance on scripture alone, along with questioning the religious value of definite doctrinal beliefs.[106] John had distanced himself from Frank soon after both returned from abroad (John from the Mediterranean, Frank from a missionary journey to Persia) because Frank was preaching to dissenting congregations.[107] On November 8, 1835, John received a letter from Frank that worried him. "I do fear his verging towards liberalism," he wrote to Froude on November 17.[108] A few days later, he heard from Samuel Wilberforce that Frank's qualms about the Trinity had issued in a denial of "the personality of the Holy Spirit and the duty of praying to Christ."[109] John now interpreted Frank's avowed aversion to dogmatism as a cover for the fact that he simply retained few definite beliefs. "So it is then," John wrote to Frank on November 23, "latitudinarianism *is* a secret Socinianizing, as is often said. One does not like to believe these things till one sees them."[110] But he considered Frank's attitude to scripture the real cause of his mistakes.

"That wretched Protestant principle about Scripture," Newman had told Froude the week before, "when taken in by an independent and clear mind, is almost certain to lead to errors I do not like to name."[111] He now told his brother the same:

> That wretched, nay (I may say) cursed Protestant principle, (not a principle in which our Church has any share, but the low arrogant cruel ultra-Protestant principle) — your last letter showed me you had so imbibed it as to be in great peril — but I had no notion you had gone so far.[112]

The principle in question, that every individual is equipped to interpret scripture for himself and will arrive at truth without the aid of church or tradition, John wrote to Frank, "is the πρῶτον φεῦδος [faulty premise] of your notions." Instead, Frank should accept that "the unanimous witness of the whole Church (as being a witness to an *historical fact,* viz that the Apostles so taught), where attainable, is as much the voice of God (I do not say as sacredly and immediately so, but as

---

106. FWN, *Phases of Faith*, esp. 26–105.

107. JHN to Richard Hurrell Froude, November 17, 1835, *LD* 5, 164; *Apo.*, 118; and FWN, *Phases of Faith*, 55.

108. JHN to Richard Hurrell Froude, November 17, 1835, *LD* 5, 164. Frank's letter is not preserved.

109. JHN to FWN, November 23, 1835, *LD* 5, 166. See also JHN to Samuel Wilberforce, December 4, 1835, *LD* 5, 171; FWN, *Phases of Faith*, 52.

110. JHN to FWN, November 23, 1835, *LD* 5, 166.

111. JHN to Richard Hurrell Froude, November 17, 1835, *LD* 5, 164.

112. JHN to FWN, November 23, 1835, *LD* 5, 166.

really) as Scripture itself."[113] If an acute thinker like Frank would continue without this conviction, John had little hope for him. The history of Charles immediately came to mind. Frank, too, would "unravel the web of selfsufficient inquiry" and end up with very few beliefs left.[114] Some of John's fears were alleviated when Frank denied that he rejected the tenets John had instanced. "He does not deny the two points you mentioned to me," John wrote to Wilberforce, "but he holds them in such a way that I fear they may slip through his fingers any day," as they did soon afterwards.[115] Still, the episode left a mark.

Between late 1835 and early 1836, Newman wrote a lengthy article for the *British Critic* that expanded on the views he had expressed to Frank. It was a review of a recently published correspondence between an Anglican minister and his Unitarian brother-in-law, aptly—and ironically, in view of Frank—entitled *The Brother's Controversy*. Newman's discussion of the book occupied only six pages. He devoted the rest of the article to a demonstration of the existence and importance of "a known Apostolical Tradition on the subject of the Trinity, and therefore an unerring interpreter of Scripture so far," in opposition to the latitudinarian tradition represented by Chillingworth and Locke, the Unitarianism of Blanco White, and the views proposed by Hampden.[116] Newman used the book under review to set up his argument. Its two protagonists labored under the same misconception. Both assumed "that truth of doctrine is to be gained from Scripture by each person for himself."[117] As in Frank's case, he termed this "the πρῶτον ψεῦδος of the controversy."[118] He reminded his readers that this had been the "latitudinarian argument" as well, which he summed up as follows: "Scripture is the sole informant of religious truth; there is no infallible interpreter of Scripture, therefore every man has a right to interpret it for himself, and no one may impose his own interpretation on another."[119] He cited Locke as a case in point. Locke advocated toleration of doctrinal differences because no one is bound to accept another's deductions from the Bible: "however clearly we may think this or the other Doctrine to de deduced from Scripture, we ought not therefore to impose it upon others, as a necessary Article of Faith."[120]

---

113. JHN to FWN, November 23, 1835, *LD* 5, 166. Read ψεῦδος for φεῦδος—a not uncommon (mis)spelling at the time.

114. JHN to FWN, November 23, 1835, *LD* 5, 166.

115. JHN to Samuel Wilberforce, December 4, 1835, *LD* 5, 171.

116. JHN, "The Brothers' Controversy/Apostolical Tradition," *British Critic* 20 (July 1836): 172. The article was included in the first volume of Newman's *Essays: Critical and Historical* from the fifth edition onward (London: Pickering and Co., 1881). It was so drastically revised that corresponding pagination cannot be provided.

117. JHN, "The Brothers' Controversy/Apostolical Tradition," 166.

118. JHN, "The Brothers' Controversy/Apostolical Tradition," 166.

119. JHN, "The Brothers' Controversy/Apostolical Tradition," 174.

120. John Locke, *A Letter concerning Toleration* (London: Awnsham Churchill, 1689), 60; JHN, "The Brothers' Controversy/Apostolical Tradition," 173. See Young, *Religion and Enlightenment*, 24–28.

For Newman, the fundamental problem with this argument was not that it rejected the revealed status of deductions from the Bible but that it interpreted the traditional creeds as such deductions. "The doctrinal statements of the creeds are not to be viewed as mere deductions from Scripture," he argued, "but as the appropriate expressions and embodying of apostolical teaching, known to be such, and handed down in the Church as such from age to age."[121] He had already emphasized this point to Frank:

> Observe I am not urging the testimony of the Church, as if the *opinion* of a number of persons of the meaning of Scripture, but as an independent source of truth, viz an historical testimony to *a fact* viz the Apostles' having taught such and such doctrines.[122]

In contrast to Roman Catholicism, the Church of England believed that this doctrinal tradition was subordinate to scripture. Although it is an independent *source*, it is not an independent *authority*: "Scripture is the sole verification of the creeds, as of all professed Apostolical traditions whatever."[123] But insofar as they neither contradict scripture, nor speak where scripture is silent (such as the Tridentine decree on indulgences), "the creeds are the legitimate exposition of Scripture doctrine."[124] And this, neither Locke nor Hampden understood.

Newman argued that it is clear from the early fathers that "there was a certain body of doctrine in the Church Catholic called the dogma fidei or depositum transmitted from bishop to bishop, and taught to every member of it." Its outline was summed up in baptismal creeds, whose "articles varied somewhat in the different branches of the Church" but expressed the same body of doctrine.[125] When forced to decide a contentious issue, as at Nicea, the bishops in council determined what the doctrine was. They did not reason it out but formulated it by comparing the tradition each had received. Newman was enough of a historian to realize "that the very articles of the Creed are not Apostolic in such a sense that we can pronounce them to be literally spoken by the Apostles."[126] Still, they "convey that view which is Apostolic"; they represent its sense. Thus, "certain words, as ὁμοούσιος, θεοτόκος and the like," were used at various times "as the criterion of certain doctrines which required the seal of public authority;" they function as "representations, more or less arbitrary, as the case might be, of the Apostolic tradition on

121. JHN, "The Brothers' Controversy/Apostolical Tradition," 181.

122. JHN to FWN, November 23, 1835, *LD* 5, 167. For a slightly more careful formulation of this view, see "The Brothers' Controversy/Apostolical Tradition," 168–69.

123. JHN, "The Brothers' Controversy/Apostolical Tradition," 170.

124. JHN, "The Brothers' Controversy/Apostolical Tradition," 170.

125. JHN, "The Brothers' Controversy/Apostolical Tradition," 187.

126. JHN, "The Brothers' Controversy/Apostolical Tradition," 188.

the subject."[127] Nevertheless, these terms represent "the one doctrine . . . preached and confessed all over Christendom."[128] In this way, "Catholic tradition . . . attests the proper divinity of Christ, and anathematizes Socinianism and all other heresy on the subject." It does so, in sum, "not by arguing and deducing from Scripture, as Dr. Hampden would say, but as being a separate apostolic information, parallel with Scripture, verified by, but not subsisting in it."[129]

Liberalism, Evangelicalism, and the Contemplation of Self

Newman's lumping together of Locke, Hampden, Blanco White, and his evangelical brother Frank shows that by the end of 1835, his critiques of latitudinarianism, Noetic theology, and evangelicalism began to converge. This development was not entirely new, but initially, Newman had emphasized other routes by which evangelical theology approached to Socinianism. In his March 1834 *Critical Remarks on Dr Chalmers' Theology*, Newman pointed out that "a very great deal might be said on the approximation made by this system to liberalistic views."[130] First, he discerned a parallel between liberal and evangelical understandings of divine justice. The "essence" of the evangelical system, Newman argued, is "that God <u>was</u> a God of justice — but that now justice is satisfied & its claims destroyed — & God solely a God of love."[131] Thus, Chalmers "certainly enlarges on the moral attributes of God, yet in some places . . . he almost narrows them to benevolence — thus remarkably agreeing with the liberals, e.g. Sir James Macintosh [*sic*] in his Treatise."[132]

On the evangelical model, the converted Christian relates to God's justice only as something of the past, overcome by Christ's atoning sacrifice. But without a lively perception of God's justice, rooted in conscience, belief in the darker and deeper aspects of Christianity will gradually give way to the shallow and comfortable religion of polite society. Paradoxically, the theology of the great defenders of the atonement—the evangelicals—implied the same reduction of God's attributes to benevolence as that of its great detractors, the Socinians.

Secondly, Newman argued that the "<u>tendency</u> of Dr Chalmers's theory is to make the reception of the great doctrines of the gospel chiefly important as <u>leading to practice</u> — & therefore to undervalue any doctrine or part of a doctrine which does not visibly lead to practice."[133] Doctrines, in other words, "are tried by a cer-

---

127. JHN, "The Brothers' Controversy/Apostolical Tradition," 188–89.
128. JHN, "The Brothers' Controversy/Apostolical Tradition," 194.
129. JHN, "The Brothers' Controversy/Apostolical Tradition," 194.
130. JHN, *Critical Remarks on Dr Chalmers' Theology*, BOA A.9.1, 27.
131. JHN, *Critical Remarks on Dr Chalmers' Theology*, BOA A.9.1, 27.
132. JHN, *Critical Remarks on Dr Chalmers' Theology*, BOA A.9.1, 28.
133. JHN, *Critical Remarks on Dr Chalmers' Theology*, BOA A.9.1, 27.

tain rule of expedience — & their importance is determined, not by Scripture, but by their practical influence."[134] If the relative value of a doctrine depends on its usefulness, however, those doctrines that do not obviously change practice can be safely ignored. Hence, "so many persons at this day would give up the Trinity & Incarnation as necessary to salvation, & rest instead upon the Atonement & Sanctification." This is bad enough as it is, but the same logic endangers faith in doctrine altogether. If expedience is the sole criterion, one can do without doctrine if other measures yield the same result. Accordingly, some people "go on even to give up creeds altogether, & talk of an union of <u>hearts</u> as the one thing needful."[135] In this way, evangelicalism tends to engender an indifference to doctrinal truth comparable to that of liberalism, not just because it leads to emotional exhaustion (his argument in 1831) but because of the fundamental structure of its theology.[136]

Both critiques of evangelical theology implied an indictment of Newman's own earlier views, especially the latter. Although his earliest theology was predicated on a stark contrast between divine justice and mercy (in which the latter effaces the former), Newman's growing emphasis on sanctification made God's holiness (which entails justice) constitutive of the Christian life. The tendency to judge the value of doctrine based on its effects was more deeply ingrained in Newman's early theology. The idea that faith in the atonement drives the process of sanctification (and therefore is the central Christian doctrine) continued to shape his thought in one form or other until the late 1820s. In the early 1830s, it was replaced with the conviction that sanctification depends on habitual obedience to conscience. Along with it, Newman stressed the importance of faith in doctrine irrespective of its practical effect, as revealing, albeit mysteriously, the God in whom we believe. His first volume of *Parochial Sermons* was largely made up of sermons that expressed these new convictions. Unsurprisingly, they rubbed many evangelicals the wrong way, not only those of the radical kind, such as his brother Frank, but also those of moderate views and more congenial minds.

One of them was Samuel Wilberforce, who, unlike his brothers Robert and Henry, had never been close to Newman at Oxford.[137] In a letter of January 23, 1835, Wilberforce critiqued Newman's "apparently studious effort to supress the doctrine of spiritual influences," that is, the belief that the Holy Spirit freely and at once changes human hearts.[138] He also enclosed a critical comment on the sermons by his evangelical friend James Stephen, who appreciated Newman's devout-

---

134. JHN, *Critical Remarks on Dr Chalmers' Theology*, BOA A.9.1, 28.

135. JHN, *Critical Remarks on Dr Chalmers' Theology*, BOA A.9.1, 28.

136. See p. 256.

137. See David Newsome, "Justification and Sanctification: Newman and the Evangelicals," *Journal of Theological Studies* 15, no. 1 (1964): 32–53.

138. Samuel Wilberforce to JHN, January 23, 1835, *LD* 5, 14n1; Newsome, "Justification and Sanctification," 38–39.

ness, depth, and acuity but lamented his effort to distance himself from "the poor Evangelicals whom he despises."[139] A correspondence ensued with both in which Newman emphasized the dangerous tendencies of evangelical thought. "Rightly or wrongly," he wrote to Wilberforce, "*I think they* [evangelicals] *tend as a body to Socinianism*."[140] But he did not despise them. Although "a very heterogenous party," he looked "most hopefully towards numbers of them," since the evangelicals had "some of the highest and noblest elements of the Christian character among them."[141] Still, as he pointed out to Stephen, he had to speak out strongly against "the *spirit* of their school," which "tends to liberalism and Socinianism."[142] Evangelicalism, he argued, is "a system of doctrine which eats out the heart of godliness, where truer and holier instincts do not exclude it from producing its legitimate results."[143] He explained this charge in two sermons written for his second volume of *Parochial Sermons* at the time of his correspondence with Stephen and Wilberforce. Together with the letters, this pair of sermons constituted his most penetrating critique of evangelical religiosity to date.

The gist of Newman's criticisms was that the evangelical emphasis on affective change turned the believer's focus away from the objects and fruits of faith toward her own state of mind. It was a religiosity that ultimately revolved around the self rather than around love of God and neighbor. Much of evangelical religiosity, he argued, consists in examining "the heart, with a view of ascertaining whether it is in a spiritual state or no."[144] Such a state consists in perceiving our complete sinfulness, utterly depending on Christ's atoning sacrifice, and living gratefully in prayer and obedience.[145] The linchpin of this spirituality is "the necessity of renouncing our own righteousness for the righteousness provided by our Lord and Saviour."[146] Such complete trust in the atonement is tortuous to come by, and to have acquired it—that is, to be converted—is "the especial and critical event which marks a man, as issuing from darkness, and sealed unto the privileges of the sons of God."[147] Thus, "the doctrine of Justification by Faith,

---

139. James Stephen to Samuel Wilberforce, *LD* 5, 21n1; Newsome, "Justification and Sanctification," 40. James Stephen was a high-ranking civil servant at the Colonial Office, whose father (also named James) was a close friend and brother-in-law of William Wilberforce. James partly grew up at Clapham, where many prominent evangelicals (such as the Wilberforces and Venns) resided, and married John Venn's daughter Jane. See Patrick C. Lipscomb III, "Stephen, James (1758–1832)"; A. G. L. Shaw, "Stephen, Sir James (1789–1859)," *ODNB*.

140. JHN to Samuel Wilberforce, March 10, 1835, *LD* 5, 40.

141. JHN to Samuel Wilberforce, February 4, 1835, *LD* 5, 21. See also JHN to Jemima Newman, October 2, 1834, *LD* 4, 337–38.

142. JHN to James Stephen, February 27, 1835, *LD* 5, 32.

143. JHN to James Stephen, February 27, 1835, *LD* 5, 32.

144. JHN, No. 373, "Self-contemplation," January/February 1835, *PaS* 2, 181.

145. JHN, No. 373, "Self-contemplation," *PaS* 2, 181–82.

146. JHN, No. 373, "Self-contemplation," *PaS* 2, 182.

147. JHN, No. 373, "Self-contemplation," *PaS* 2, 182–83.

is accounted to be the one cardinal point of the Gospel."[148] But what matters to the evangelical is not so much *that* we hold it, but *how* we hold it. It is not enough "to admit it readily as a clear Scripture truth (which it is,) and to attempt to go on unto perfection." It must be paramount in the religious life: "the very wish to pass forward is interpreted into a wish to pass over it, and the test of believing it at all, is in fact to insist upon no doctrine but it."[149] Accordingly, to be religious means believing the doctrine of the atonement in the right way, that is, in a way that yields perceptible affective change. As a result—and this was Newman's primary objection—evangelicals become preoccupied with their own (and others') state of mind. Their religion is self-oriented.

Newman believed that the misguided orientation of evangelical religiosity issued from its understanding of conversion, more specifically, as Wilberforce had rightly seen, from its conception of the work of the Holy Spirit. For a decade now, Newman had been distancing himself from the evangelical idea that a changed heart "is formed by the Holy Spirit immediately acting upon our minds."[150] Instead, the heart is changed gradually, "by our own particular acts, (whether of faith or obedience,) prompted, guided, and prospered by Him."[151] The Holy Spirit, he pointed out to Wilberforce, acts through the natural means of our mind: "our reason, affections, conscience, passions, natural-affections, tastes, associations etc," and it requires our cooperation.[152] Salvation, in other words, "depends on ourselves, on our own willing or not, i.e. prompted, enlightened, aided, carried on, perfected by the influences of grace," but not over-ruled by them.[153] Because the Holy Spirit uses natural means and sanctification requires effort, Newman rejected as chimerical the evangelical attempt "to secure directly and primarily that 'mind of the Spirit,' which may savingly receive the truths, and fulfil the obedience of the Gospel." To this "modern system" he opposed the "ancient and universal teaching of the Church," which focuses, instead, "on the Objects and fruits of faith" and considers "the spiritual character of that faith itself sufficiently secured, if these are as they should be."[154] He had explained before that "the whole duty and work of a Christian is made up of . . . Faith and Obedience; 'looking unto Jesus,' the Divine Object as well as Author of our faith, and acting according to His will."[155] The "essence of Faith is to look out of ourselves," he argued.[156] Being religious is not about contemplating our

148. JHN, No. 373, "Self-contemplation," *PaS* 2, 183.
149. JHN, No. 373, "Self-contemplation," *PaS* 2, 183.
150. JHN, No. 373, "Self-contemplation," *PaS* 2, 184.
151. JHN, No. 373, "Self-contemplation," *PaS* 2, 184.
152. JHN to Samuel Wilberforce, January 29, 1835, *LD* 5, 14.
153. JHN to Samuel Wilberforce, January 29, 1835, *LD* 5, 15–16.
154. JHN, No. 373, "Self-contemplation," *PaS* 2, 184.
155. JHN, No. 372, "Saving Knowledge," January/February 1835, *PaS* 2, 170–71.
156. JHN, No. 372, "Saving Knowledge," *PaS* 2, 180.

own mental states. It is about believing and obeying someone external to us: God, as revealed in Christ. The requisite spiritual state is "sure to follow, if our hearts do but grow into these two chief contemplations, the view of God in Christ, and the diligent endeavour to obey Him in our conduct."[157]

The evangelical misconceptions of obedience as well as doctrine arose from not acknowledging this. If people think that they are saved because they experience deep trust in Christ's atonement, obedience can have very little place in their religious life: "men *do* think that a saving state is one, where the mind merely looks to Christ — a virtual antinomianism."[158] Such people do not view "works as the concomitant developement [*sic*] and evidence, and instrumental cause of faith" but instead consider faith as something that "must first be secured, and that, by some means in which works have no share." Accordingly, they "lay all the stress upon the direct creation, in their minds, of faith and spiritual-mindedness, which they consider to consist in certain emotions and desires."[159] The commonness of this mistaken view of obedience was the reason Newman selected the sermons he did for the *Parochial Sermons*. We require "*the Law* not the Gospel in this age," he explained to Wilberforce, "we want rousing — we want the claims of duty and the details of obedience set before us strongly."[160] Christians are bid to obey: "*how* they do it, is another matter — we know it is through the Spirit nevertheless, as a fact, *they do it* — and this age forgets they do it."[161] And thus there was little of comfort or encouragement in his sermons. Evangelicalism and the religion of polite society had enough of that. As Newman strikingly put it to Wilberforce: "We need a continual Ash-wednesday."[162]

The evangelical preoccupation with the believer's state of mind came not only at the cost of obedience but also of belief in doctrine as expressive of a divine reality. If the mind recognizes its converted status by its affective states, and these states are responses to the gospel message, the value of doctrine comes to depend on its affective import. Evangelicals, Newman argued, "lay it down as self-evident, that the main purpose of revealed doctrine is to affect the heart, that that which does not seem to affect it, does not affect it, — that what does not affect it is unnecessary."[163] In all cases, this principle results in "disproportionate attention to the doctrines connected with the work of Christ, in comparison with

157. JHN, No. 372, "Saving Knowledge," *PaS* 2, 171.
158. JHN to Samuel Wilberforce, February 4, 1835, *LD* 5, 22.
159. JHN, No. 373, "Self-contemplation," *PaS* 2, 187. Newman believed this attitude either fostered "self-confidence and spiritual pride" (since those "who make self instead of their Maker the great object of their contemplation, will naturally exalt themselves") or, if people are not aware of having the right affections, "a feverish anxiety about their religious state" (191–92).
160. JHN to Samuel Wilberforce, February 4, 1835, *LD* 5, 22.
161. JHN to Samuel Wilberforce, February 4, 1835, *LD* 5, 22.
162. JHN to Samuel Wilberforce, March 10, 1835, *LD* 5, 40.
163. JHN, No. 373, "Self-contemplation," *PaS* 2, 185.

those which relate to His Person, from their more immediately interesting and exciting character."[164] People of a reflective cast of mind will go further and conclude that "the Atonement and Sanctification" are "the essence of the Gospel."[165] The principle can even issue in a denial that "in matters of doctrine there is any one sense of Scripture such, that it is true and all others false." As long as a doctrine works for a given individual, it is true for him. Thus, "one man may say that Christ is God, another deny His pre-existence, yet each have received the Truth according to the peculiar constitution of his own mind, the Scripture doctrine having no real independent substantive meaning."[166] On this view, doctrine no longer delineates a definite Being, so that "the system under consideration tends legitimately to obliterate the great Objects brought to light in the Gospel." Just like Unitarianism, it throws "us back into the vagueness of Heathenism, when men only felt after the Divine Presence" and thus frustrates "the design of Christ's incarnation so far as it is a manifestation of the Unseen Creator."[167]

Rationalism and Mystery

Newman believed that the evangelical approach to doctrine was based on a fundamentally flawed premise: that we know *why* God has revealed Himself.[168] Evangelicals "have rested the whole Gospel upon the doctrines of the Atonement and Sanctification," because they believe its end is "the salvation of the world, or the conversion of sinners" and value "all the Scripture doctrines by their respective sensible tendency to effect this end."[169] But this was not just an evangelical problem. Alluding to the Noetics, Newman pointed out that others hold "that the object of the Gospel Revelation is merely practical, and therefore, that theological doctrines are altogether unnecessary, mere speculations."[170] The content of revelation is remodelled to fit such assumptions:

> instead of accepting reverently the doctrinal Truths which have come down to us, an attempt is made on the part of these reasoners to compare them together, weigh and measure them, analyze, simplify, refashion them; to reduce them to system, to arrange them into primary and secondary, to harmonize them into an intelligible dependence upon each other.[171]

---

164. JHN, No. 373, "Self-contemplation," *PaS* 2, 185–86.
165. JHN, No. 373, "Self-contemplation," *PaS* 2, 186.
166. JHN, No. 373, "Self-contemplation," *PaS* 2, 186.
167. JHN, No. 373, "Self-contemplation," *PaS* 2, 186. See pp. 233–34 in this book.
168. JHN, No. 367, "The Gospel, A Trust," *PaS* 2, 287; No. 354, "The Form of sound words," *Serm.* 3, 342–44.
169. JHN, No. 367, "The Gospel, A Trust," *PaS* 2, 289.
170. JHN, No. 367, "The Gospel, A Trust," *PaS* 2, 288, 287.
171. JHN, No. 367, "The Gospel, A Trust," *PaS* 2, 287.

Such a procedure is mistaken because it absolutizes one end of revelation, out of the many scripture mentions, by which to determine the relative importance of what is revealed. But the plain truth is that "we do not know, and cannot form a notion, what is the real final object of the Gospel Revelation."[172] God simply has not told us. Thus, our responsibility toward the revealed deposit is not to systematize it but "to commit it to our hearts, to preserve it inviolate, and to deliver it over to our posterity."[173]

This understanding of revelation was the outcome of the emphasis on mystery that had begun to suffuse Newman's theology in 1829. We cannot comprehend who God is, and yet, God has told us something of himself. To enhance the perspicuity of these doctrines is beyond us, since we lack both the required cognitive capacities and the necessary information. Accordingly, our duty is to safeguard what we have received. We must "jealously maintain . . . our Creed, lest, by dropping jot or tittle, we suffer the truths concealed therein to escape from us."[174] In September 1835, Newman began a long tract (No. 73) that used the idea of mystery to criticize the evangelical (and, covertly, the Noetic) understanding of revelation.[175] It aimed to expose a "peculiar and subtle form" of "Rationalism . . . in the popular religion of this day" and took Thomas Erskine as one of its expounders.[176] It was aimed against evangelicalism at large, identifying "a widely spread, though variously received School of doctrine among us, within and without the Church, which intends and professes peculiar piety, as directing its attention to the *heart itself*, not to any thing external to us, whether creed, actions, or ritual."[177] Newman's central argument was that "this doctrine is based upon error, that it is really a specious form of trusting man rather than God, that it is in its nature Rationalistic, and that it tends to Socinianism." The tract constituted, in short, Newman's definitive and public verdict on the theology that had inspired his preaching at St Clement's.[178]

Newman did not treat rationalism as a system or a philosophical position but as an attitude. "To Rationalize," he argued, "is to ask for *reasons* out of place; to

172. JHN, No. 367, "The Gospel, A Trust," *PaS* 2, 295.

173. JHN, No. 367, "The Gospel, A Trust," *PaS* 2, 284.

174. JHN, No. 365, "Mysteries in Religion," December 1834, *PaS* 2, 235–36.

175. *Ess.* 1, 101; JHN to Richard Hurrell Froude, September 10, 1835, *LD* 5, 40; and *On the Introduction of Rationalistic Principles into Religion*, Tracts for the Times 73 (London: J. G. & F. Rivington, 1836). The republished version (*Ess.* 1, 30–99) is so drastically revised that corresponding pagination cannot be provided.

176. JHN, *On the Introduction of Rationalistic Principles*, 1. The other was Jacob Abbott (1803–1879). Although Newman critiqued Abbott more severely than Erskine, only the section on Erskine is of real interest for our purposes, given the light it sheds on Newman's intellectual development.

177. JHN, *On the Introduction of Rationalistic Principles*, 53.

178. Placid Murray regards the tract "as a retraction or refutation, point by point" of Newman's October 1824 sermon "The effects on the mind of the doctrine of the cross" (*Serm.* 1, 268n1; see pp. 93–94 in this book). See also Strange, *Newman*, 98–102.

ask improperly how we are to *account* for certain things, to be unwilling to believe them unless they can be accounted for."[179] It is "to be unduly set upon *accounting* for what is offered for our acceptance."[180] The stress here is on "unduly," because, in principle, there is nothing wrong with trying to make sense of things. Rationalism only begins if we stipulate that things must make sense before we accept them: when we "set up our existing system of knowledge as a legitimate test of the credibility of testimony," or demand "to be told the mode of reconciling alleged truths to other truths already known, the *how* they are, and *why* they are."[181] The impulse to rationalize betrayed "forgetfulness of God's power, disbelief of the existence of a First Cause sufficient to account for any events or facts."[182] Instead of measuring a purported revelation by God's omnipotence, the rationalist insists that it conform to her existing intellectual and imaginative frameworks. Hume, who considered it "unphilosophical to suppose that Almighty God can do anything, but what we see He does," is prototypical here.[183] This rationalist procedure is self-centered in much the same way as the evangelical concern with the subjective effects of doctrine. "Instead of looking out of ourselves, and trying to catch glimpses of God's working," Newman explained, "we sit at home bringing everything to ourselves, enthroning ourselves as the centre of all things, and refusing to believe any thing that does not force itself upon our minds as true."[184] This captures the key distinction between rationalism and faith: the one shuts us up in ourselves, the other opens us up and propels us outward.

In a veiled critique of Blanco White, Newman distinguished between "Objective Truth"—reality as "existing in itself, external to this or that particular mind"—and "Subjective Truth:" "that which each mind receives in particular" and holds to be true.[185] Blanco White had used this distinction in an 1834 work to argue that religious convictions can only ever be subjective truth, that is, "truth for the person who has the conviction" because they cannot be verified experimentally—a view Newman had denounced via Wilberforce's *Foundation*.[186] Now, Newman redefined the terms for his own purposes, anticipating his much later distinction between assent and apprehension. "To believe in Objective Truth," he argued,

> is to throw ourselves forward upon that which we have but partially mastered or made Subjective, to embrace, maintain, and use general propositions

179. JHN, *On the Introduction of Rationalistic Principles*, 2.
180. JHN, *On the Introduction of Rationalistic Principles*, 2.
181. JHN, *On the Introduction of Rationalistic Principles*, 3.
182. JHN, *On the Introduction of Rationalistic Principles*, 3–4.
183. JHN, *On the Introduction of Rationalistic Principles*, 4.
184. JHN, *On the Introduction of Rationalistic Principles*, 4.
185. JHN, *On the Introduction of Rationalistic Principles*, 4.
186. Joseph Blanco White, *The Law of Anti-Religious Libel Reconsidered* (Dublin: Richard Milliken and Son, 1834), 34; [Wilberforce], *Foundation*, 24–25.

which are greater than our own capacity, as if we were contemplating what
is real and independent of human judgment.[187]

Such assent is not conditional upon apprehension; we believe truths whose bearing we cannot discern. On the rationalist model, by contrast, assent is conditional
upon apprehension. It consists in "the reception of doctrine, as, and so far as it
is met and apprehended by the mind, which will be differently in different persons."[188] The rationalist, in short, "professes to *believe* in that which he *opines*," so
that the challenge of being religious is not "the submission of the reason to external truths partially disclosed," but to form one's opinions responsibly, that is, by
means of persistent and candid intellectual inquiry.[189]

As noted, Newman attributed the rationalist demand for perspicuous doctrine to the "refusal to take for granted the existence of a First Cause, in religious
inquiries, which it prosecutes as if commencing in utter ignorance on the subject."[190] Religious truth claims are evaluated in the same way as, say, theories in
the natural sciences. And thus, the rationalist "receives only so much as may be
strictly drawn out to the satisfaction of the reason." With an insightful play on
the word "subject," Newman evoked a contrast between the submissiveness of
faith and the dominance of the rationalist intellect. Whereas faith submits to
truth, rationalism "limits Truth to our comprehension of it, or *subjects* it to the
mind, and admits it only so far it is subjected."[191] Accordingly, it "considers faith
to have reference to a *thing* or *system*, far more than to an *agent*, for an agent may
be supposed as acting in unknown ways, whereas a system cannot be supposed
to have existence beyond what is ascertained of it."[192] All of this would be reasonable enough, if the scientific method, and the (methodological) agnosticism
that goes with it, were the proper approach to religious inquiry. But it is not.
Newman was convinced that every meaningful quest for religious truth ought to
be driven by the knowledge of God's existence and attributes acquired through
conscience. This knowledge should be—and was for nearly everyone at the
time—a common starting point. But once "we *assume the existence of* an unseen
Object of Faith, then we already possess the main truth, and may well be content
even with half views as to His operations."[193] If we truly believe in God as an
independent being, we are ready to accept whatever it is that he has chosen to
reveal to us, even if we understand it only partially.

187. JHN, *On the Introduction of Rationalistic Principles*, 4.
188. JHN, *On the Introduction of Rationalistic Principles*, 4–5.
189. JHN, *On the Introduction of Rationalistic Principles*, 5.
190. JHN, *On the Introduction of Rationalistic Principles*, 7.
191. JHN, *On the Introduction of Rationalistic Principles*, 7; see also 18, 19.
192. JHN, *On the Introduction of Rationalistic Principles*, 7.
193. JHN, *On the Introduction of Rationalistic Principles*, 7.

Newman believed that the theology of Erskine instanced the rationalist equation of assent with apprehension and the concomitant reduction of the object of faith to a system. Recall that Erskine held that "I cannot believe any thing which I do not understand," so that we must comprehend the Gospel (which reveals "the system of God's dealings with men") before we can believe it.[194] For Newman, this suggested that Erskine held that "the main *object* of Christian faith is, not Almighty God, but a certain work or course of things which He has accomplished."[195] Erskine's frequent use of the term *"Manifestation"* epitomizes this view, "as if the system presented to us were such as we could trace and connect into one whole, complete and definite."[196] For that reason, Newman took the term "as a token of the [rationalist] philosophy under review" and contrasted it with "the word 'Mystery,'" as "the badge or emblem of orthodoxy."[197] He interpreted Erskine's work as a sophisticated exposition of "the popular theology of the day:" the broadly evangelical view that "the Atonement is the chief doctrine of the Gospel," whose centrality derives from "its experienced effects on our minds," that is, "the change it effects where it is believed."[198]

Erskine formalized these convictions in the idea that revelation, especially the atonement, is a manifestation of God's character intended to mould the human character into its likeness.[199] Ten years earlier, Newman had wholeheartedly concurred. Now, he vigorously challenged the idea "that the object of the Christian revelation is ascertainable by us."[200] To change human beings is *"an* object," that much we know from scripture, but we have no reason to think it is *"the* object" of revelation, or "the *leading idea* of Christianity."[201] The result of making it so is to undervalue all doctrine that has no perceptible effect on character, like the Trinity. And thus, Erskine's theory leads "pretty nearly to Socinianism."[202] If character change is the ultimate goal of revelation, its Aristotelian "τέλος τελειότατον," people might well wonder: "What is the *harm* of being, *e.g.,* a Sabellian?"[203] Newman had

---

194. Erskine, *An Essay on Faith,* 28–29; JHN, *On the Introduction of Rationalistic Principles,* 7–8; and p. 90 in this book.

195. JHN, *On the Introduction of Rationalistic Principles,* 7.

196. JHN, *On the Introduction of Rationalistic Principles,* 8.

197. JHN, *On the Introduction of Rationalistic Principles,* 8. Newman acknowledged that the idea of manifestation is part of the idea of revelation and had continued to use the word to characterize aspects of the incarnation (in line with St John's gospel—see p. 230 in this book). He only objected to it as denoting the reduction of revelation to an intelligible system, which can only be believed if it is understood.

198. HN, *On the Introduction of Rationalistic Principles,* 13.

199. Erskine, *An Essay on Faith,* 43; *Remarks on the Internal Evidence,* 12, 49; and JHN, *On the Introduction of Rationalistic Principles,* 16.

200. JHN, *On the Introduction of Rationalistic Principles,* 17.

201. JHN, *On the Introduction of Rationalistic Principles,* 17, 18.

202. JHN, *On the Introduction of Rationalistic Principles,* 20.

203. JHN, *On the Introduction of Rationalistic Principles,* 17, 20.

raised the same issue in December 1834 as one implication of the Noetic approach to revelation, and he reiterated it in a letter to his aunt Elizabeth the following August.[204] "The most religiously-minded men are ready to give up important doctrinal truths because they do not *understand their value*," he noted, "Sabellianism has been spreading of late years, chiefly because people have said 'What is the harm of Sabellianism?'"[205] By that time, he could point to Blanco White, who not only instanced its danger but was aware of it (although not as danger). In Tract 73, Newman cited the actual passage from Blanco White's *Observations*, not so much to show that Sabellianism "*leads* to Socinianism"—which it might also do—but that, as in Blanco White's case, it is a conviction "under which Socinianism may *lie hid*, even from a man's own consciousness."[206]

The same Socinian tendency was instanced in Erskine's take on the atonement as "a Manifestation, not only of GOD's love, but of His justice," a view Newman too had accepted into the 1820s.[207] Now, he denied outright that the atonement was a "*Manifestation* of His *justice*."[208] Henry Wilberforce was puzzled by this claim and questioned Newman about it. Newman explained that although scripture says that the atonement propitiates God's wrath, it not does not tell us "*how* His wrath is put away."[209] If scripture clearly stated that God's *justice* was satisfied by Christ's death—which Newman did not believe—Newman was ready to "receive it as a mystery (which Mr Erskine *would not* do)." But it was in no sense a *manifestation* of God's justice, "for how *God's justice* (according to any sense we attach to the word) could be satisfied by one suffering for another, is past my conception." If it were revealed, it would be "a mystery as great in its way as the Trinity," for "it seems in the abstract contradictory to the first notions of mere justice." The atonement might be taken to exemplify many things, but it is "no *instance* of justice — you may as well say that God's creating the stars is an instance of justice."[210] Some people had felt this difficulty, and they tried to solve it by subsuming "GOD's justice" under "the well-being of His creation, as *a final end*, as if it might in fact be considered a modification of his benevolence."[211] This was Mackintosh's theory, which Newman had denounced as Socinian in 1831, but his time, he instanced it by citing Thomas Scott. Liberal and evangelical morphed continually in Tract 73.

For Newman, the rationalist attitude, espoused alike by liberals, evangelicals, and Noetics, was premised on a fatal misunderstanding of the nature of revelation.

---

204. JHN, No. 367, "The Gospel, A Trust," *PaS* 2, 288.
205. JHN to Elizabeth Newman, August 9, 1835, *LD* 5, 120.
206. JHN, *On the Introduction of Rationalistic Principles*, 40.
207. JHN, *On the Introduction of Rationalistic Principles*, 29. See pp. 29 and 95–96 in this book.
208. JHN, *On the Introduction of Rationalistic Principles*, 29.
209. JHN to Henry Wilberforce, August 11, 1836, *LD* 5, 337.
210. JHN to Henry Wilberforce, August 11, 1836, *LD* 5, 337.
211. JHN, *On the Introduction of Rationalistic Principles*, 30.

Years ago, he had learned from Butler that we cannot comprehend revelation; it is a mystery. "No revelation," Newman now reiterated, "can be complete and systematic, from the weakness of the human intellect; *so far as* it is not such, it is mysterious."[212] He disagreed with theologians like Whately, who maintained that in the New Testament, mystery means "a *secret*," which is "always, when mentioned, associated with the notion of its being now revealed."[213] When St Paul uses the term, Whately had argued, it does not denote "something we cannot understand at all" but something that was "*formerly* unknown" and is now disclosed.[214] The New Testament describes certain truths as mysteries, "not *so far forth as* they are hidden and unintelligible, but so far forth as they are *revealed* and *explained*."[215] From 1829 onward, Newman had rejected this idea. Echoing his earlier sermons on the subject, he now argued that "Religious Truth is neither light nor darkness, but both together; it is like the dim view of a country seen in the twilight, with forms half extricated from the darkness, with broken lines, and isolated masses."[216] Revelation, then, "is not a revealed *system*, but consists of a number of detached and incomplete truths belonging to a vast system unrevealed."[217] We know *that* these truths cohere, but we cannot know *how* they do. Hence Newman's adamance about safeguarding the revealed deposit. Since we do not know why God has revealed certain truths, how these truths relate to each other, or even what they mean exactly, there is no way to get at the spirit of revelation apart from its letter. For that reason, "we should religiously adhere to the form of words and the ordinances under which it comes to us, through which it is revealed to us, and apart from which the revelation does not exist, there being nothing else given us by which to ascertain or enter into it."[218]

Conclusion

By the summer of 1835, Newman had come to believe that the two formative theologies of his youth, that of the evangelicals and that of the Noetics, converged toward Socinianism. His earlier critique of liberalism had broadened into

---

212. JHN, *On the Introduction of Rationalistic Principles*, 9.

213. JHN, *On the Introduction of Rationalistic Principles*, 9.

214. Richard Whately, *Essays on Some of the Difficulties in the Writings of St. Paul, and in Other Parts of the New Testament*, 2nd ed. (London: B. Fellowes, 1830), 229n; *The Errors of Romanism*, 78. Whately referenced John Parkhurst's *A Greek and English Lexicon to the New Testament*, 3rd ed. (London: G. G. and J. Robinson, 1808), 446–47. Characteristically, Newman instanced the view from the Scottish Enlightenment thinker George Campbell, not from Whately.

215. Whately, *Difficulties in the Writings of St. Paul*, 230n. See also *The Errors of Romanism*, 77–80.

216. JHN, *On the Introduction of Rationalistic Principles*, 9. See p. 284 in this book.

217. JHN, *On the Introduction of Rationalistic Principles*, 9; see also 12.

218. JHN, *On the Introduction of Rationalistic Principles*, 13.

a critique of most forms of Protestantism, which also instanced reliance on the intellect, doctrinal relativism, and rejection of tradition and mystery. Newman, too, had bordered on these views at one time, albeit unawares. Without this very particular set of personal experiences, he would never have been as sensitive as he was to the liberal tendencies of Noetic and evangelical theology. Despite the dangers to the church that he perceived all around, Newman remained hopeful about the outcome of Tractarianism and was supremely confident in his theological position. "No other doctrine but ours has substance and reality in it," he wrote to Arthur Philip Perceval in April 1836.[219] It did not take long before these hopes were shattered. In 1841, the fallout after Tract 90 proved one controversy too many. Newman left cushy Oriel College for a cottage at Littlemore and gathered a small band of celibate friends around him. In October 1845, three decades after his teenage conversion, he was received into the Roman Catholic Church. A few years later he moved to Birmingham, where he founded the first Oratory in England. With him came a little book by the Deist Thomas Paine. It was once his father's, and reading it had been the high point of Newman's teenage scepticism. I do not know why he kept it. Perhaps it was just a family heirloom, but maybe he held on to it to remind him of what he might have been had God not intervened in that fateful autumn of 1816. In the preceding pages, I have traced the transformation of Newman's religious thought in the two decades after his adolescent conversion. In some ways, I have barely gotten beyond the beginning. My tale finishes where most others start, but I hope to have shown that the prologue, as often happens, gives away much of the later story.

219. JHN to Arthur Philip Perceval, April 25, 1836, *LD* 5, 285.

Conclusion

It is tempting to complete the present study by recounting, however briefly, the many ways in which the ideas Newman developed before 1833 continued to shape his thought as a Tractarian and a Roman Catholic. Most readers familiar with Newman's main writings will have thought of one or another arc to which his pre-Tractarian development was tending: his *Lectures on the Prophetical Office of the Church* (1837), his *Lectures on Justification* (1838), *The Tamworth Reading Room* (1841), his later university sermons on faith and reason (1839–1843), his *Essay on Development* (1845), the theological bits of the *Apologia* (1864), and even *An Essay in Aid of a Grammar of Assent* (1870). Much could be said about each of these, but to do so here would be to flout the rule of careful and detailed analysis by which this study has abided. Newman's ideas continued to change, by intense reflection and under the influence of new friends, authors, and events. These developments merit as considered a study as the ones I have discussed above. To trace even their outlines here would be presumptuous. Still, it seems fair to say that Newman's theological vision in the early 1830s more nearly resembled that of the Newman of the *Apologia* or the *Grammar* than that of the evangelical Newman of the early 1820s. In this sense, the pre-Tractarian years were, indeed, the most formative of his intellectual life. A summary of the major lines of this development can suffice by way of conclusion, even though it must necessarily be partial and simplistic.

Upon his adolescent conversion, Newman attained a deep conviction of God's reality. From Scott and the tradition of English Enlightenment apologetics, he learned that to believe in God's self-revelation means to believe what God says, because he says it. To assess whether a purported revelation is, indeed, a revelation, we must evaluate the evidence that it comes from God, not the message it contains. Miracles are the most important of those evidences. If credibly reported, they invincibly establish that the person who worked them speaks divine truth, for only God can overrule the laws of nature. The miracles of scripture (and of scripture only) are historically reliable, so that we can reasonably hold that scripture contains God's self-revelation. This was the old Enlightenment argument by which Newman defended Christianity from his brother Charles's assaults, but he also stipulated that vicious prejudice can keep people from seeing the cogency of these evidences; they convince only if studied impartially. In his *Essay on Miracles*, Newman explained that miracles do not derive their evidential import just from being interruptions of natural laws but also from the fact that revelation conforms to moral ends we can discern in God's providential governance of the world (an idea he derived from Butler). As far as the human subject is concerned, this continuity between the natural and supernatural realms was rooted in conscience (another of Butler's ideas), which testifies to the existence of a just and good God. These ideas softened the stark contrast Newman used to draw between the natural realm, defined by corruption and ignorance, and the supernatural realm, defined by grace and revelation.

This development in Newman's apologetic coincided with his discarding of the more Calvinistic elements of his early evangelical theology. After his own religious awakening as a teenager, he believed that a postbaptismal experience of conversion is necessary to be saved—a change wrought sovereignly by God the Holy Spirit, who uses the message of Christ's atoning sacrifice to radically reorient our desires and affections, so as to live holily and assured of our salvation. Newman's struggle with the doctrine of baptismal regeneration at the time of his ordination initiated his gradual relinquishing of this model. Under the influence of Hawkins, Sumner, and Butler, he began to realize that the rigid binaries of the Calvinistic system did justice neither to the lives of his parishioners nor to scripture, whose data refused to fit the machinery of efficacious grace. Increasingly, appeals to fact—whether of experience, scripture, or ecclesiastical history—replaced the exigencies of system. Newman also began to emphasize that conversion is not just the work of the Holy Spirit but demands our active exertion to do good. Under the influence of Froude and Keble, this fledgling conviction grew into the firm belief that moral character is what defines being religious. This belief was premised on the idea that human beings are free and responsible for how they behave and what they become. Only such freedom and responsibility ensure that we relate to God as persons. Obedience to conscience is how this responsibility is exercised. The path to God does not lie in argument, but in praxis. Accordingly, the Enlightenment emphasis on evidence is not so much mistaken as misguided. Coming to believe the truth is not a test of intellectual acuity but a test of character; that is why God left the evidence as it is: sufficient, but not overwhelming.

As an evangelical, Newman had believed that obedience depends on faith, through whose appropriation of the gospel message our hearts are converted. Under the influence of Erskine and Whately, he concluded that God intended the gospel message to work this affective change. Since doctrines derive their relative value from how well they serve this overarching end of revelation, his theology centered on the atonement as the most touching display of God's attributes and ignored purportedly arid statements of doctrine, such as the Athanasian Creed's formulation of the Trinity. As Newman began to understand conversion as habit formation, this approach to doctrine gradually disappeared from his theology. Obedience is not the result of, but rather a disposition coequal with, faith, manifesting the one moral and religious character in quest of God. Thus, the responsible self is placed in a face-to-face relationship with God. It no longer relates to God via a series of prestructured dispositions but wholly and at once. It repents, believes, and obeys, not sequentially, or according to pattern, but habitually and progressively, gradually cultivating the Christian character. This account resists all mechanical explanations of the religious life. be it the (high) Calvinist conception of faith as a kind of charm, or the liberal conception of the mind as a kind of machine, which both yield predetermined outcomes depending on cognitive input, whether of the atonement or the felicific calculus. Instead, it relies on the free responsibility of the agent toward her own conscience.

The possibility of obeying conscience ensures that the naturally religious subject is no longer a self without God, waiting to learn of Christ's atoning sacrifice, but a self that enters a relationship with the one God, faintly known at first, but fully revealed in the person of Christ. Christ embodies and unifies the stray notices of God's existence and attributes in nature and universal revelation. Accordingly, the incarnation—the Son assuming human nature—becomes the central Christian doctrine. Only as God incarnate can Christ be the definitive manifestation of the divine, a manifestation not in the sense of a perspicuous system but in the sense of a tangible person. By denying Christ's divinity, Unitarianism robs faith of its personal object, while evangelicalism obscures it by focusing almost exclusively on the atonement. The revelation of God in Christ is necessarily mysterious. It consists of propositions we can grasp individually but cannot render coherent as a whole. Its doctrines are divine accommodations to our limited cognitive capacities, expressing, as well as language can express, a reality that is beyond linguistic expression. We believe and value them not because we understand them but because it is God who has given them. Nature, too, partakes of this mystery. After his sister Mary died, Newman increasingly conceived of faith as a seeing of the unseen: a seeing beyond the sight of sense experience. Again, continuity replaces dichotomy between the natural and the supernatural. Instead of a law-governed machine, the natural world becomes a symbol of God's personal providence.

Newman had always believed that the doctrines taught by the Church of England were to be found in scripture, although they did not lie on its surface. As a young evangelical, he thought the Holy Spirit would reveal them to every sincere Bible reader. Hawkins taught him not to expect such individual divine aid. The tradition of the church is what mediates divine truth, just as its sacraments mediate divine grace. Newman's study of the fathers increased the authority he accorded to the church's creeds as the definitive expositions of scripture's doctrinal sense. His qualms with latitudinarians like Chillingworth, Tillotson, and Locke, were not about why revelation ought to be believed but about what constitutes revelation. Revelation is not primarily a book. It is Christ: a divine person entering history. We have come to know this person through his followers. Inspired by Christ's Spirit, they wrote down some of what they had learned from him—about God, about his person, his life, his teachings, his work—and orally transmitted other truths, explaining their writings to their followers. The gist of these apostolic traditions was definitively formulated by the church in its battle with heresy and constitutes the only proper exposition of the apostolic writings.

Like the resistance to mystery, the reliance on scripture alone tends toward Socinianism. The intellect is equipped neither to fully understand doctrine, nor to deduce it from scripture. Faith, therefore, entails intellectual submission to both mystery and apostolic authority, submission, that is, not to a system or an ideology but to a person. As the Tractarian Movement progressed, Newman realized that the influences that had shaped much of his early thought—evangelicalism and Oriel theology—flouted this principle with potentially disastrous consequences.

Ultimately, what liberalism, rationalism, or Socinianism (depending on the angle) jeopardize is the relationship of responsible selves to a personal God. To understand this, consider what the liberal approach would mean for any of our intimate relationships—with parents, spouse, lover, friend. Imagine treating your partner as if you do not care who he is, feeling at liberty to construe whatever he says however you like, or even interpreting whatever he says or does from your perspective of what his ultimate intentions are. Obviously, these are recipes for relational disaster. Such behavior does not take the other person seriously at all. It suggests, in fact, that he is not even there. For Newman, this is what liberals did to God. They failed to take God seriously, as a being with his own integrity and freedom to speak and act, transcending, nonetheless, all he says or does. If God is the supremely real person, as Newman believed, to deny him this is to virtually deny his existence, and thus to undermine any genuine relationship between God and the self. This explains the *Apologia's* charge that religion without dogma is "a dream and a mockery."[1] It is like loving a picture instead of a real person; or, as Tract 73 put it, "Rationalism takes the words of Scripture as signs of Ideas; Faith, of Things or Realities."[2]

This study has described and analyzed Newman's convictions at various times, how he came to hold them, and how these transforming views related to one another. Something, too, has been said about how he experienced these intellectual transitions. For a time in the mid-1820s, his theology was in crisis. He hardly knew where he stood. As he relinquished his evangelicalism and moved from under Whately's wings toward the more mature friendship of Froude and Keble, his views acquired a clarity and coherence they did not have before. After the struggle of the mid-1820s, one can sense his elation at having found a cogent position in his sermons and letters from 1829 onward. He began to speak like a

1. *Apo.*, 120.
2. JHN, *On the Introduction of Rationalistic Principles*, 5.

man who knows where he stands and why. In the *Apologia*, he prefaced his treatment of the beginning of the Tractarian Movement by enlarging on his "supreme confidence" in his cause, to explain, among other things, the "fierceness" of some of his language and behavior: the martial spirit of the *Lyra*, his defence of gloom and superstition, breaking off relations with his brother Frank.[3] Other instances suggest themselves. Think of his treatment of Hampden, which contained, in addition, some of the "sport" and "wantonness" he also attributed to the "absolute confidence" in what he believed.[4] Nevertheless, his confidence was more ambivalent than appears at first sight.[5] He firmly believed that what he taught was true, but he could keenly question the way he had come by his convictions and the mode in which he held them. In December 1834, he wrote down the thoughts he had during the illness in Sicily that had brought him near to death in May 1833. "I seemed to see more & more my utter hollowness," he recounts, "I began to think of all my professed principles, & felt they were mere intellectual deductions from one or two admitted truths. I compared myself with Keble, and felt that I was merely developing his, not my convictions."[6]

Newman could have easily attributed such thoughts to the despondency that can come with being very ill, but he thought there was more to them. He still held these thoughts to be "in the main true ones" a year and a half later.

> Indeed this is how I look on myself; very much (as the illustration goes) as a pane of glass, which transmit[s] heat being cold itself. I have a vivid perception of the consequences of certain admitted principles, have a considerable intellectual capacity of drawing them out, have the refinement to admire them, & a rhetorical or histrionic power to represent them; and, having no great (i.e. no vivid) love of this world, whether riches, honors, or any thing else, and some firmness and natural dignity of character, take the profession of them upon me, as I might sing a tune which I liked — loving the Truth, but not possessing it — for I believe myself at heart to be nearly hollow — i.e. with little love, little self denial. I believe I have some faith, that is all.[7]

At first sight, these are strangely self-deprecating remarks for someone whose theology developed by a process of such intense and sustained reflection. Newman forgot, for instance, that what he learned from Keble had been fermenting in his mind before, through Hawkins, Sumner, and, most of all, Butler. But on closer inspection, his comments are understandable. It is precisely the fact

---

3. *Apo.*, 113, 116–18.

4. *Apo.*, 114, 116. See Klaver, "The Apologia," 469–70.

5. Poston makes much of the "alternating self-effacement and aggression" in Newman's personality (*The Antagonist Principle*, 6).

6. JHN, "My Illness in Sicily," *AW*, 125.

7. JHN, "My Illness in Sicily," *AW*, 125.

that his development was one of thought that troubled him. His comments witness to the psychological strain put on one who had long known that his "quickness of logic" was remarkable but who believed, at the same time, that moral character rather than intellectual acuity determines religious progress.[8] He saw the truth, loved it, desired it, but did not feel he had it, for the having is not in the intellect. And yet, by deprecating his own convictions, he shows how firmly he held them. This is no mere paradox. Newman thought he was "hollow" because he thought he had come by his convictions intellectually. But he could only think so because he absolutely believed that right convictions were rooted in moral character, which is precisely what he felt he lacked: love and self-denial. Surely, one test of the reality of our convictions is whether we can admit when we fall short of what they demand. And this, Newman could certainly do. He did, indeed, have "some faith" after all.

8. JHN, "about 1826," *AW*, 173.

Bibliography

Manuscript Works by John Henry Newman

Scott vs. Mant on Baptism. 1816. BOA A.9.1.b.

Trinitas or Humanitas. 1817. BOA A.9.1.b.

On the necessity of a thorough reception of the doctrines contained in the 9th article & first part of the 10th, to a belief in the rest. May 1821. BOA A.9.1.e.

A collection of Scripture passages setting forth in due order of succession the doctrines of Christianity. June 1821. BOA A.9.1.

Comment on Phil 2,12&13. June 1821. BOA A.9.1.e. Dialogue—Merton—Spenser. January 1822. BOA A.9.1.e.

The Nature of Holiness. 1822 or 1823. BOA A.9.1.g.

Remarks on Herbert Marsh's Pamphlet on the Bible Society. April 1823. BOA A.9.1.e.

Correspondence with Charles Robert Newman (letters and papers). 1825. BOA A.4.2.1–8.

Remarks on Infant Baptism. 1827. BOA A.9.1.k.

Remarks on the Covenant of Grace, in connexion with the doctrines of Election, Baptism, & the Church. August 1828. BOA A.9.1.

Untitled manuscript beginning: "It is not the intention of this pamphlet." 1833. BOA D.6.3.

Untitled manuscript beginning: "The Revolution in 1688." 1834. BOA D.5.13

Critical Remarks on Dr Chalmers' Theology. March 17, 1834. BOA A.9.1.

Primary Sources

Addison, Joseph. *The Spectator*. No. 207, October 27, 1711.

Bateman, Josiah. *The Life of the Rev. Henry Venn Elliott*. London: Macmillan, 1868.

Berens, Edward. *Church-Reform*. London: John Murray, 1828.

Beveridge, William. *Private Thoughts upon Religion*. London: Smith, 1709.

Blanco White, Joseph. *The Law of Anti-Religious Libel Reconsidered*. Dublin: Richard Milliken and Son, 1834.

Blanco White, Joseph. *Observations on Heresy and Orthodoxy*. London: J. Mardon, 1835.

The Book of Common Prayer. Cambridge: John Baskerville, 1762.

The Book of Common Prayer. Edited by Richard Mant. Oxford: J. Parker, 1820.

Boyle, Robert. *The Christian Virtuoso*. London: 1690.

Burgon, John William. *Lives of Twelve Good Men*. 2 vols. London: John Murray, 1888.

Butler, Joseph. *Fifteen Sermons Preached at the Rolls Chapel*. London: James and John Knapton, 1726.

————. *The Works of the Right Reverend Father in God Joseph Butler*. 2 vols. Edited by Samuel Halifax. Oxford: Clarendon Press, 1820.

————. *The Analogy of Religion, Natural and Revealed, to the Constitution and Course of Nature*. London: John Chidley, 1838.

Chalmers, Thomas. *The Evidence and Authority of the Christian Revelation*. 6th ed. Andover: Mark Newman, 1818.

————. *Sermons, Preached in the Tron Church, Glasgow*. 2nd ed. Glasgow: Chalmers and Collins, 1821.

Chillingworth, William. *The Religion of Protestants a Safe Way to Salvation*. Oxford: Leonard Lichfield, 1638.

Clarke, Samuel. *A Collection of the Promises of Scripture under their Proper Heads*. Philadelphia: J. H. Cunningham, 1820.

Conway, Moncure Daniel. *Autobiography: Memories and Experiences*. Vol. 1. London: Cassell and Company, 1904.

Copleston, Edward. *An Enquiry into the Doctrines of Necessity and Predestination*. London: John Murray, 1821.

————. *Remains of the Late Edward Copleston, D.D., Bishop of Llandaff*. Edited by Richard Whately. London: John W. Parker, 1854.

Cowper, William. *The Iliad and Odyssey of Homer*. Vol. 1. London: J. Johnson, 1791.

Davison, John. *Discourses on Prophecy*. London: John Murray, 1824.

Douglas, John. *The Criterion; or Rules by which the True Miracles Recorded in the New Testament Are Distinguished from the Spurious Miracles of Pagans and Papists*. London: T. Cadell and W. Davies, 1807.

Duncan, John M. *Travels through Part of the United States and Canada in 1818 and 1819*. 2 vols. Glasgow: 1823.

Erskine, Thomas. *Remarks on the Internal Evidence for the Truth of Revealed Religion*. 5th ed. Edinburgh: Waugh & Innes, 1821.

————. *An Essay on Faith*. 2nd ed. Edinburgh: Waugh & Innes, 1822.

Evanson, Edward. *The Dissonance of the Four Generally Received Evangelists, and the Evidence of their Respective Authenticity*. Ipswich: B. Law, 1792.

Farmer, Hugh. *A Dissertation on Miracles*. London: T. Cadell, 1771.

Froude, Richard Hurrell. *Remains of the Late Reverend Richard Hurrell Froude*. 2 vols. Edited by John Keble and John Henry Newman. London: J. G. & F. Rivington, 1838.

Gibbon, Edward. *The History of the Decline and Fall of the Roman Empire.* Vol. 3. Dublin: William Halhead, 1781.

Hampden, Renn Dickson. *The Scholastic Philosophy Considered in its Relation to Christian Theology.* Oxford: J. H. Parker, 1833.

————. *Observations on Religious Dissent.* Oxford: J. H. Parker, 1834.

Hawkins, Edward. *A Dissertation upon the Use and Importance of Unauthoritative Tradition, as an Introduction to the Christian Doctrines.* Oxford: J. Parker, 1819.

[Hawkins, Edward]. *A Letter to the Earl of Radnor upon the Oaths, Dispensations, and Subscription to the XXXIX Articles at the University of Oxford.* Oxford: J. H. Parker, 1835.

Hinds, Samuel. *The Three Temples of the One True God Contrasted.* London: B. Fellowes, 1830.

The History, Debates, and Proceedings of Both Houses of Parliament of Great Britain, from the year 1743 to the year 1774. 7 vols. London: J. Debrett, 1792.

Hopkins, Ezekiel. *The Works of the Right Reverent Father in God, Ezekiel Hopkins.* 4 vols. Edited by Josiah Pratt. London: L. B. Seeley, 1809.

Horne, Thomas Hartwell. *An Introduction to the Critical Study and Knowledge of the Holy Scriptures.* Vol. 2. London: T. Cadell and W. Davies, 1818.

Howell, Thomas Jones, ed. *A Complete Collection of State Trials and Proceedings for High Treason and other Crimes and Misdemeanors.* Vol. 31. London: 1823.

Hume, David. *An Enquiry concerning Human Understanding.* Edited by Peter Millican. Oxford: Oxford University Press, 2007.

Lardner, Nathaniel. *A Large Collection of Ancient Jewish and Heathen Testimonies.* In *The Works of Nathaniel Lardner, D.D. In Eleven Volumes,* edited by Andrew Kippis. Vols. 7–9. London: J. Johnson, 1788.

Law, William. "The Case of Reason, or Natural Religion, Fairly and Fully Stated." In *Works of the Reverend William Law,* vol. 2, 55–138. London: J. Richardson, 1762.

Leslie, Charles. *A Short and Easie Method with the Deists.* London: C. Brome, 1699.

Less, Gottfried. *The Authenticity, Uncorrupted Preservation, and Credibility of the New Testament.* Edited by Roger Kingdon. London: F. C. and J. Rivington, 1804.

Locke, John. *An Essay Concerning Human Understanding.* 2 vols. Edited by John W. Yolton. London: J. M. Dent, 1961.

————. *A Letter concerning Toleration.* London: Awnsham Churchill, 1689.

————. "Mr. Locke's Reply to the Bishop of Worcester's Answer to his Second Letter." In *The Works of John Locke,* vol. 3, 193–498. London, 1794.

————. "A Discourse of Miracles." In *Posthumous Works of Mr. John Locke,* 215–31. London: A. and J. Churchill, 1706.

"Lyra Apostolica," No. 1. *British Magazine* 3 (June 1833): 656–57.

Lyttelton, George. *Observations on the Conversion and Apostleship of St. Paul.* London: R. Dodsley, 1747.

Keble, John. "Copleston *Prælectiones Academicæ.*" *The British Critic* 1 (June 1814): 577–88.

———. *The Christian Year: Thoughts in Verse for the Sundays and Holydays throughout the Year.* 6th ed. Oxford: J. Parker, 1829.

———. *Sermons, Academical and Occasional.* Oxford: John Henry Parker, 1847.

———. *Occasional Papers and Reviews.* Oxford: James Parker, 1877.

Mackintosh, James. "Stewart's *Introduction to the Encyclopaedia.*" *Edinburgh Review* 36 (October 1821): 220–67.

———. "Dissertation Second; Exhibiting a General View of the Progress of Ethical Philosophy, Chiefly during the Seventeenth and Eighteenth Centuries." In *Encyclopaedia Britannica*, 7th ed., vol. 1, 293–429. Edinburgh: Adam and Charles Black, 1842.

Mant, Richard. *An Appeal to the Gospel.* Oxford: J. Parker, 1812.

Marsh, Herbert. *An Inquiry into the Consequences of Neglecting to Give the Prayer Book with the Bible.* 4th ed. London: Rivingtons, 1812.

Mayers, Walter. *Sermons, of the late Rev. Walter Mayers.* London: James Nisbet, 1831.

Michaelis, Johann David. *Introduction to the New Testament.* Vol. 1. Edited by Herbert Marsh. Cambridge: J. Archdeacon, 1793.

Mill, John Stuart. *Collected Works of John Stuart Mill.* Vol. 22. Edited by Ann P. Robson and John M. Robson. Toronto: University of Toronto Press, 1986.

Mozley, Anne. *Letters and Correspondence of John Henry Newman, During his Life in the English Church.* 2 vols. London: Longmans, Green, and Co., 1891.

Mozley, Thomas. *Reminiscences: Chiefly of Oriel College and the Oxford Movement.* 2 vols. London: Longmans, Green, and Co., 1882.

Newman, Charles Robert. *Essays in Rationalism.* Edited by George Jacob Holyoake and J. M. Wheeler. London: Progressive Publishing Company, 1891.

Newman, Francis William. *Phases of Faith; or, Passages from the History of my Creed.* London: John Chapman, 1850.

———. *Contributions Chiefly to the Early History of the Late Cardinal Newman.* London: Kegan Paul, Trench, Trübner & Co., 1891.

Newman, John Henry. "On the Study of the Mathematics." *Christian Observer* 20, no. 5 (May 1821): 293–95.

———. "Duncan's Travels in North America." *British Review, and London Critical Journal* 22, no. 44 (May 1824): 144–67.

———. "Apollonius Tyanaeus—Miracles." *Encyclopaedia Metropolitana*, vol. 10; *History and Biography*, vol. 2, 619–44.

————. "Greek Tragedy—Poetry." *London Review* 1, no. 1 (January 1829): 153–71.

————. "The Zeal of Jehu." *British Magazine* 5 (April 1834): 431.

————. Preface. In *Pamphlets in Defence of the Oxford Usage of Subscription to the XXXIX Articles at Matriculation*, 1st ed., 1–14. Oxford: J. H. Parker, 1835.

————. "Liberalism." In *Lyra Apostolica*, 131–32. Derby: Henry Mozley, 1836.

————. *Elucidations of Dr. Hampden's Theological Statements*. Oxford: J. H. Parker, 1836.

————. *On the Introduction of Rationalistic Principles into Religion*. Tracts for the Times 73. London: J. G. & F. Rivington, 1836.

————. "The Brothers' Controversy/Apostolical Tradition." *British Critic* 20 (July 1836): 166–99.

————. *Fifteen Sermons Preached before the University of Oxford, between A.D. 1826 and 1843*. 3rd ed. London: Rivingtons, 1872.

————. *Fifteen Sermons Preached before the University of Oxford*. Edited by James David Earnest and Gerard Tracey. Oxford: Oxford University Press, 2006.

[Newton, John, and William Cowper]. *Olney Hymns*. London: W. Oliver, 1779.

Owen, Robert. *A New View of Society: or, Essays on the Formation of the Human Character, Preparatory to the Development of a Plan for gradually ameliorating the Condition of Mankind*. 3rd ed. London, 1817.

Paine, Thomas. *The Age of Reason. Part the Third. Being an Examination of the Passages in the New Testament, Quoted from the Old and Called Prophecies concerning Jesus Christ*. London: Daniel Isaac Eaton, 1811.

Paley, William. *A View of the Evidences of Christianity*. 2nd ed. 2 vols. London: R. Faulder, 1794.

————. *Natural Theology: or, Evidences of the Existence and Attributes of the Deity, Collected from the Appearances of Nature*. London: R. Faulder, 1802.

Parkhurst, John. *A Greek and English Lexicon to the New Testament*. 3rd ed. London: G. G. and J. Robinson, 1808.

Peel, Robert. *Memoirs by the Right Honourable Sir Robert Peel*. London: John Murray, 1856.

Philalethes [Thomas Morgan]. "A Letter to Eusebius." In *The Moral Philosopher*, vol. 2. London: 1739.

Phillpotts, Henry. *A Letter to an English Layman on the Coronation Oath*. London: John Murray, 1828.

Plato. *Platonis, augustiss. philosophi, omnium quae extant operum*. 2 vols. Edited by Jean De Serres. Paris: Henri Estienne, 1578.

————. *Complete Works*. Edited by John M. Cooper. Indianapolis, Ind.: Hackett, 1997.

Pope, Alexander. *The Universal Prayer*. London: R. Dodsley, 1738.

Priestley, Joseph. *An History of the Corruptions of Christianity*. 2 vols. Birmingham: J. Johnson, 1782.

"Reviews of Pamphlets, &c., on the Peterborough Question," *Christian Observer* 20, no. 3 (March 1821): 160–90; 20, no. 4 (April 1821): 235–58; 20, no. 5 (May 1821): 295–316.

Romaine, William. *Discourses upon Solomon's Song, preached at St Dunstan's Church*. London: T. Chapman, 1789.

Scott, Thomas. *The Force of Truth: An Authentick Narrative*. 8th ed. London: L. B. Seeley, 1808.

———. *Essays on the Most Important Subjects in Religion*. 7th ed. London: L .B. Seeley, 1814.

———. *The Holy Bible containing the Old and New Testaments, according to the Authorized Version; with Explanatory Notes, Practical Observations, and Copious Marginal References*. 5th ed. Vol. 1. London: L. B. Seeley, 1822.

Stillingfleet, Edward. *Origines Sacrae, or a Rational Account of the Grounds of Christian Faith*. London: Henry Mortlock, 1675.

Sumner, John Bird. *Apostolical Preaching Considered, in an Examination of St. Paul's Epistles*. 6th ed. London: J. Hatchard and Son, 1826.

Thom, John Hamilton, ed. *The Life of the Rev. Joseph Blanco White*. 3 vols. London: John Chapman, 1845.

Thomson, James. "Scripture." In *Encyclopaedia Britannica*, 3rd ed., vol. 17, 106–74. Edinburgh: A. Bell and C. Macfarquhar, 1797.

Tillotson, John. *The Works of the Most Reverend Dr. John Tillotson*. 2 vols. London: 1722.

Van Mildert, William. *An Historical View of the Rise and Progress of Infidelity*. 4th ed. 2 vols. London: Rivington, 1831.

Vince, Samuel. *The Credibility of the Scripture Miracles Vindicated in Answer to Mr. Hume*. 2nd ed. Cambridge: J. Deighton and J. Nicholson, 1809.

Wallis, John. *A Fifth Letter Concerning the Sacred Trinity*. London: Tho. Parkhurst, 1691.

Whately, E. Jane. *Life and Correspondence of Richard Whately, D.D.* 2 vols. London: Longmans, Green, and Co., 1866.

Whately, Richard. *Historic Doubts relative to Napoleon Buonaparte*. London: J. Hatchard, 1819.

———. *The Right Method of Interpreting Scripture, in what Relates to the Nature of the Deity, and His Dealings with Mankind, illustrated in a Discourse on Predestination by Dr. King*. London: John Murray, 1821.

———. *The Use and Abuse of Party-Feeling in Matters of Religion*. Oxford: J. Parker, 1822.

———. *Essays on Some of the Peculiarities of the Christian Religion*. Oxford: John Murray, 1825.

————. *Elements of Logic.* 1st ed. London: J. Mawman, 1826.

————. *Essays on Some of the Difficulties in the Writings of St. Paul, and in Other Parts of the New Testament.* London: B. Fellowes, 1828.

————. *Elements of Logic.* 3rd ed. London: B. Fellowes, 1829.

————. *A View of the Scripture Revelations concerning a Future State.* London: B. Fellowes, 1829.

————. *The Errors of Romanism Traced to their Origins in Human Nature.* London: B. Fellowes, 1830.

————. *Essays on Some of the Difficulties in the Writings of St. Paul, and in Other Parts of the New Testament.* 2nd ed. London: B. Fellowes, 1830.

————. *Essays on Some of the Peculiarities of the Christian Religion.* 3rd ed. London, B. Fellowes, 1831.

————. *Elements of Logic.* 4th ed. London: B. Fellowes, 1831.

[Wilberforce, Henry]. *The Foundation of the Faith Assailed in Oxford: A Letter to His Grace the Archbishop of Canterbury.* 1st ed. London: J. G. & F. Rivington, 1835.

[Wilberforce, Henry]. *The Foundation of the Faith Assailed in Oxford: A Letter to His Grace the Archbishop of Canterbury.* 2nd ed. London: J. G. & F. Rivington, 1835.

Williams, Isaac. *The Autobiography of Isaac Williams.* Edited by George Prevost. London: Longmans, Green & Co., 1892.

Secondary Sources

Altholz, Josef L. "The Mind of Victorian Orthodoxy: Anglican Responses to *Essays and Reviews*, 1860–1864." *Church History* 51, no. 2 (1982): 186–97.

Atkins, Gareth. "'True churchmen'? Anglican Evangelicals and History, c. 1770–1850," *Theology* 115, no. 5 (2012): 339–49.

————. "Evangelical Writers." In *The Oxford Handbook of John Henry Newman*, edited by Frederick D. Aquino and Benjamin J. King, 173–95. Oxford: Oxford University Press, 2018.

Attard, Fabio. *Conscience in the* Parochial and Plain Sermons *of John Henry Newman.* Valetta: Midsea Books, 2008.

Baker, William J. *Beyond Port and Prejudice: Charles Lloyd of Oxford, 1784–1829.* Orono: University of Maine at Orono Press, 1981.

Barr, Colin, and Simon Skinner. "Political and Social Thought." In *The Oxford Handbook of John Henry Newman*, edited by Frederick D. Aquino and Benjamin J. King, 395–415. Oxford: Oxford University Press, 2018.

Bebbington, David W. *Evangelicalism in Modern Britain: A History from the 1730s to the 1980s.* London: Routledge, 1989.

Bouyer, Louis. *Newman: sa vie, sa spiritualité.* Paris: Cerf, 1952.

———. *Newman: His Life and Spirituality.* London: Burns and Oates, 1958.

Brendon, Piers. *Hurrell Froude and the Oxford Movement.* London: Paul Elek, 1974.

Brent, Richard. *Liberal Anglican Politics: Whiggery, Religion, and Reform, 1830–1841.* Oxford: Clarendon Press, 1987.

———. "The Oriel Noetics." In *Nineteenth-Century Oxford,* edited by M. G. Brock and M. C. Curthoys, 72–76. Vol. 6 of *The History of the University of Oxford.* Oxford: Clarendon Press, 1997.

Burns, Robert M. *The Great Debate on Miracles: From Joseph Glanvill to David Hume.* Lewisburg, Pa.: Bucknell University Press, 1981.

Carter, Grayson. *Anglican Evangelicals: Protestant Secessions from the* Via Media, *c. 1800–1850.* Oxford: Oxford University Press, 2001.

Chadwick, Owen. *The Victorian Church.* 3rd ed. Vol. 1. London: A. and C. Black, 1971.

Clark, J. C. D. *English Society, 1688–1832: Ideology, Social Structure and Political Practice during the Ancien Regime.* Cambridge: Cambridge University Press, 1985.

Conn, Walter E. *Conscience & Conversion in Newman: A Developmental Study of Self in John Henry Newman.* Milwaukee, Wisc.: Marquette University Press, 2010.

Coolahan, John. "The Daring First Decade of the Board of National Education, 1831–1841." *The Irish Journal of Education* 17, no. 1 (1983): 35–54.

Corsi, Pietro. *Science and Religion: Baden Powell and the Anglican Debate, 1800–1860.* Cambridge: Cambridge University Press, 1988.

Culler, Dwight. *The Imperial Intellect: A Study of Newman's Educational Ideal.* New Haven, Conn.: Yale University Press, 1955.

Daston, Lorraine. "Marvelous Facts and Miraculous Evidence in Early Modern Europe." *Critical Inquiry* 18, no. 1 (1991): 93–124.

Davis, Robert A. "Robert Owen and Religion." In *Robert Owen and His Legacy,* edited by Chris Williams and Noel Thompson, 91–111. Cardiff: University of Wales Press, 2011.

de Giustino, David. "Finding an Archbishop: The Whigs and Richard Whately in 1831." *Church History* 64, no. 2 (1995): 218–36.

Dessain, Stephen. "Newman's First Conversion." *Newman Studien* 3 (1957): 37–53.

———. *John Henry Newman.* London: Thomas Nelson, 1966.

Dulles, Avery. *A History of Apologetics.* San Francisco: Ignatius Press, 2005.

Egner, G. [P. J. FitzPatrick]. *Apologia pro Charles Kingsley.* London: Sheed and Ward, 1969.

Elias, Norbert. *The Civilizing Process.* Translated by Edmund Jephcott. Oxford: Blackwell, 1994.

Elsner, Jaś. "Beyond Compare: Pagan Saint and Christian God in Late Antiquity." In *Saints: Faith Without Borders*, edited by Françoise Meltzer and Jaś Elsner, 363–91. Chicago: University of Chicago Press, 2011.

Enright, Edward J. "The Letters to Charles Newman as Background to the *Grammar*." In *Personality and Belief: Interdisciplinary Essays on John Henry Newman*, edited by Gerard Magill, 161–72. Lanham, Md.: University Press of America, 1994.

Evans, Gillian R. "'An organon more delicate, versatile, and elastic': John Henry Newman and Whately's *Logic*." *Downside Review* 97 (1979): 175–91.

———. "Newman's Letters to Charles." *Downside Review* 100 (1982): 92–100.

Ffoulkes, E. S. *A History of the Church of S. Mary the Virgin, Oxford*. London: Longmans, Green, and Co., 1892.

Garnett, Jane. "Joseph Butler." In *The Oxford Handbook of John Henry Newman*, edited by Frederick D. Aquino and Benjamin J. King, 135–53. Oxford: Oxford University Press, 2018.

Gascoigne, John. "Anglican Latitudinarianism and Political Radicalism in the Late Eighteenth Century." *History* 71 (1986): 22–38.

Gilley, Sheridan. *Newman and His Age*. London: Darton, Longman and Todd, 1990.

Goslee, David. *Romanticism and the Anglican Newman*. Athens: Ohio University Press, 1996.

Grant, Edward. *Planets, Stars, and Orbs: The Medieval Cosmos, 1200–1687*. Cambridge: Cambridge University Press, 1994.

Griffin, Martin I. J. *Latitudinarianism in the Seventeenth-Century Church of England*. Edited by Richard H. Popkin and Lila Freedman. Leiden: E. J. Brill, 1992.

Harrison, Peter. "Miracles, Early Modern Science, and Rational Religion." *Church History* 75, no. 3 (2006): 493–510.

Hart, Trevor A. *The Teaching Father: An Introduction to the Theology of Thomas Erskine of Linlathen*. Edinburgh: Saint Andrew Press, 1993.

Hatzimichali, Myrto. *Potamo of Alexandria and the Emergence of Eclecticism in Late Hellenistic Philosophy*. Cambridge: Cambridge University Press, 2011.

Haykin, Michael A. G. "Evangelicalism and the Enlightenment: A Reassessment." In *The Emergence of Evangelicalism: Exploring Historical Continuities*, edited by Michael A. G. Haykin and Kenneth J. Stewart, 37–60. Nottingham: Inter-Varsity Press, 2008.

Hindmarsh, D. Bruce. *The Evangelical Conversion Narrative: Spiritual Autobiography in Early Modern England*. Oxford: Oxford University Press, 2005.

Herrick, James A. *The Radical Rhetoric of the English Deists: The Discourse of Scepticism, 1680–1750*. Columbia: University of South Carolina Press, 1997.

Hilton, Boyd. *A Mad, Bad, and Dangerous People? England 1783–1846*. Oxford: Oxford University Press, 2006.

Horrocks, Don. *Laws of the Spiritual Order: Innovation and Reconstruction in the Soteriology of Thomas Erskine of Linlathen*. Carlisle: Paternoster Press, 2004.

Houghton, Walter E., ed. *The Wellesley Index to Victorian Periodicals, 1824–1900*. 5 vols. Toronto: University of Toronto Press, 1972.

Hylson-Smith, Kenneth. *Evangelicals in the Church of England, 1734–1984*. Edinburgh: T. & T. Clark, 1989.

Jaki, Stanley L. "Newman and Miracles." *Downside Review* 400 (July 1997): 193–214.

James, William. *The Varieties of Religious Experience: A Study in Human Nature*. London: Longmans, Green, and Co., 1928.

Jolley, Nicholas. "Locke on Faith and Reason." In *The Cambridge Companion to Locke's "Essay Concerning Human Understanding,"* edited by Lex Newman, 436–55. Cambridge: Cambridge University Press, 2007.

Ker, Ian. *John Henry Newman: A Biography*. Oxford: Clarendon Press, 1988.

Ker, Neil, and Michael Perkin. *A Directory of the Parochial Libraries of the Church of England and the Church in Wales*. London: Bibliographical Society, 2004.

King, Benjamin John. *Newman and the Alexandrian Fathers: Shaping Doctrine in Nineteenth-Century England*. Oxford: Oxford University Press, 2009.

Klaver, J. M. I. "The Apologia." In *The Oxford Handbook of John Henry Newman*, edited by Frederick D. Aquino and Benjamin J. King, 454–74. Oxford: Oxford University Press, 2018.

Kreiser, B. Robert. *Miracles, Convulsions and Ecclesiastical Politics in Early Eighteenth-Century Paris*. Princeton, N.J.: Princeton University Press, 1978.

Kroll, Richard, Richard Ashcraft, and Perez Zagorin, eds. *Philosophy, Science, and Religion in England, 1640–1700*. Cambridge: Cambridge University Press, 1992.

Larsen, Timothy. "The Reception Given *Evangelicalism in Modern Britain* Since its Publication in 1989." In *The Emergence of Evangelicalism: Exploring Historical Continuities*, edited by Michael A. G. Haykin and Kenneth J. Stewart, 21–36. Nottingham: Inter-Varsity Press, 2008.

Ledger-Lomas, Michael. "Unitarians and Presbyterians." In *The Nineteenth Century*, edited by Timothy Larsen and Michael Ledger-Lomas, 99–123. Vol. 3 of *The Oxford History of Protestant Dissenting Traditions*. Oxford: Oxford University Press, 2017.

Lewis, C. S. *Studies in Words*. Cambridge: Cambridge University Press, 1961.

Linnan, John E. "The Evangelical Background of John Henry Newman, 1816–1826." 2 vols. PhD diss., Université Catholique de Louvain, 1965.

Lucci, Diego, and Jeffrey R. Wigelsworth. "'God does not act arbitrarily, or interpose unnecessarily:' Providential Deism and the Denial of Miracles in Wollaston, Tindal, Chubb, and Morgan." *Intellectual History Review* 25, no. 2 (2015): 167–89.

Lowe, E. J. *Locke on Human Understanding*. London: Routledge, 1995.

Marshall, P. J., and Donald Bryant, eds. *The Writings and Speeches of Edmund Burke*. Vol. 4. Oxford: Oxford University Press, 2015.

Martin, Roger H. *Evangelicals United: Ecumenical Stirrings in Pre-Victorian Britain, 1795–1830*. Studies in Evangelicalism 4. London: The Scarecrow Press, 1983.

McGrath, Francis. *John Henry Newman: Universal Revelation*. Macon, Ga.: Mercer University Press, 1997.

McIntosh, Mark Allen. "Newman and Christian Platonism in Britain." *The Journal of Religion* 91, no. 3 (2011): 344–64.

Meldrum, Patricia. *Conscience and Compromise: Forgotten Evangelicals of Nineteenth-century Scotland*. Carlisle: Paternoster, 2006.

Merrigan, Terrence. "*Numquam minus solus, quam cum solus*—Newman's First Conversion: Its Significance for his Life and Thought." *Downside Review* 103 (April 1985): 99–116.

Needham, Nicholas R. *Thomas Erskine of Linlathen: His Life and Theology*. Edinburgh: Rutherford House Books, 1990.

Newsome, David. "Justification and Sanctification: Newman and the Evangelicals." *Journal of Theological Studies* 15, no. 1 (1964): 32–53.

———. *The Parting of Friends: The Wilberforces and Henry Manning*. Grand Rapids, Mich.: William B. Eerdmans, 1993.

Nicholson, Ernest. "Eveleigh and Copleston: The Pre-Eminence of Oriel." In *Oriel College: A History*, edited by Jeremy Catto, 247–90. Oxford: Oxford University Press, 2013.

Nockles, Peter. "'Church and King': Tractarian Politics Reappraised." In *From Oxford to the People: Reconsidering Newman & the Oxford Movement*, edited by Paul Vaiss, 93–123. Leominster: Gracewing, 1988.

———. *The Oxford Movement in Context: Anglican High Churchmanship, 1760–1857*. Cambridge: Cambridge University Press, 1994.

———. "Oriel and the Making of John Henry Newman—His Mission as a College Tutor." *Recusant History* 29, no. 3 (2009): 411–21.

———. "Oriel and Religion, 1800–1833." In *Oriel College: A History*, edited by Jeremy Catto, 291–327. Oxford: Oxford University Press, 2013.

North, John. *Cosmos: An Illustrated History of Astronomy and Cosmology*. Chicago: University of Chicago Press, 2008.

O'Faolain, Sean. *Newman's Way*. London: Longmans, Green, and Co., 1952.

Parker, Kenneth, and C. Michael Shea. "Johann Adam Möhler's Influence on John Henry Newman's Theory of Doctrinal Development: The Case for a Reappraisal." *Ephemerides Theologicae Lovanienses* 89, no. 1 (2013): 73–95.

Pereiro, James. "John Keble and the Ethos of the Oxford Movement." In *John Keble in Context*, edited by Kirstie Blair, 59–72. London: Anthem Press, 2004.

———. Ethos *and the Oxford Movement: At the Heart of Tractarianism*. Oxford: Oxford University Press, 2008.

Poston, Lawrence. *The Antagonist Principle: John Henry Newman and the Paradox of Personality*. Charlottesville: University of Virginia Press, 2014.

Purnell, Thomas. "Charles Robert Newman." *Athenaeum*, March 29, 1884, 408.

Rauch, Alan. *Useful Knowledge: The Victorians, Morality, and the March of Intellect*. Durham, N.C.: Duke University Press, 2001.

Reedy, Gerard. *The Bible and Reason: Anglicans and Scripture in Late Seventeenth-Century England*. Philadelphia: University of Pennsylvania Press, 1985.

Robbins, William. *The Newman Brothers: An Essay in Comparative Intellectual Biography*. Cambridge, Mass.: Harvard University Press, 1966.

Shaw, Ian J. *High Calvinists in Action: Calvinism and the City—Manchester and London, c. 1810–1860*. Oxford: Oxford University Press, 2003.

Sheridan, Thomas. *Newman on Justification*. Staten Island, N.Y.: Alba House, 1967.

Short, Edward. *Newman and His Family*. London: Bloomsbury, 2013.

Short, H. L. "Presbyterians under a New Name." In *The English Presbyterians: From Elizabethan Puritanism to Modern Unitarianism*, edited by C. Gordon Bolam et al., 229–52. London: George Allen & Unwin, 1968.

Sidenvall, Erik. *After Anti-Catholicism? John Henry Newman and Protestant Britain, 1845–c.1890*. London: T&T Clark, 2005.

Skinner, Simon. "History *versus* Hagiography: The Reception of Turner's *Newman*." *Journal of Ecclesiastical History* 61, no. 4 (2010): 764–81.

Spurr, John. "'Latitudinarianism' and the Restoration Church." *The Historical Journal* 31, no. 1 (1988): 61–82.

Starkie, Andrew. "The Legacy of the 'Caroline Divines', Restoration, and the Emergence of the High Church Tradition." In *The Oxford Handbook of the Oxford Movement*, edited by Stewart J. Brown, Peter B. Nockles, and James Pereiro, 9–22. Oxford: Oxford University Press, 2017.

Stevenson, Mark R. *The Doctrines of Grace in an Unexpected Place: Calvinistic Soteriology in Nineteenth-Century Brethren Thought*. Eugene, Ore.: Pickwick Publications, 2017.

Stewart, M. A. "Arguments for the Existence of God: The British Debate." In *The Cambridge History of Eighteenth-Century Philosophy*, edited by Knud Haakonssen, 710–30. Cambridge: Cambridge University Press, 2006.

———. "Revealed Religion: The British Debate." In *The Cambridge History of Eighteenth-Century Philosophy*, edited by Knud Haakonssen, 683–709. Cambridge: Cambridge University Press, 2006.

Strange, Roderick. *Newman and the Gospel of Christ.* Oxford: Oxford University Press, 1981.

Stunt, Timothy C. F. "John Henry Newman and the Evangelicals." *Journal of Ecclesiastical History* 21, no. 1 (1970): 65–74.

———. *From Awakening to Secession: Radical Evangelicals in Switzerland and Britain 1815–1835.* Edinburgh: T&T Clark, 2000.

Sullivan, Robert E. *John Toland and the Deist Controversy: A Study in Adaptations.* Cambridge, Mass.: Harvard University Press, 1982.

Svaglic, Martin J. "Charles Newman and his Brothers." *PMLA* 71, no. 3 (1956): 370–85.

Thomas, Stephen. *Newman and Heresy: The Anglican Years.* Cambridge: Cambridge University Press, 1991.

Thomas, William. *The Philosophic Radicals: Nine Studies in Theory and Practice, 1817–1841.* Oxford: Clarendon Press, 1979.

Thompson, David M. *Cambridge Theology in the Nineteenth Century: Enquiry, Controversy and Truth.* Aldershot: Ashgate, 2008.

Trevor, Meriol. *Newman.* Vol. 1, *The Pillar of the Cloud.* Vol. 2, *Light in Winter.* London: Macmillan, 1962.

Turner, Frank M. *John Henry Newman: The Challenge to Evangelical Religion.* New Haven, Conn.: Yale University Press, 2002.

———. "Editor's Introduction: The Newman of the *Apologia* and the Newman of History." In John Henry Newman, *Apologia Pro Vita Sua and Six Sermons,* edited by Frank Turner, 1–115. New Haven, Conn.: Yale University Press, 2008.

Tyler, Edward Joseph. "The Historical Development of J. H. Newman's Idea of the Conscience, Viewed in the Context of His Defence of Religious Belief." PhD diss., University of Sidney, 2016.

Vaiss, Paul. *Newman. Sa vie, sa pensée et sa spiritualité.* Paris: L'Harmattan, 1991.

———. "Newman's State of Mind on the Eve of his Italian Tour." In *From Oxford to the People: Reconsidering Newman & the Oxford Movement,* edited by Paul Vaiss, 203–22. Leominster: Gracewing, 1996.

Vandrunen, David. "The Two Kingdoms Doctrine and the Relationship of Church and State in the Early Reformed Tradition." *Journal of Church and State* 49, no. 4 (2007): 743–63.

Ward, Maisie. *Young Mr. Newman.* London: Sheed & Ward, 1952.

Ward, W. R. *Victorian Oxford.* London: Frank Cass, 1965.

Ward, Wilfrid. *The Life of John Henry Cardinal Newman.* 2 vols. London: Longmans, Green, and Co., 1912.

Watts, Michael R. *The Dissenters: From the Reformation to the French Revolution.* Oxford: Clarendon Press, 1978.

Williams, Rowan. "Newman's *Arians* and the Question of Method in Doctrinal History." In *Newman after a Hundred Years*, edited by Ian Ker and Alan G. Hill, 263–85. Oxford: Clarendon Press, 1990.

———. Introduction. In John Henry Newman, *The Arians of the Fourth Century*, xix–xlvii. Leominster: Gracewing, 2001.

Wolterstorff, Nicholas. *John Locke and the Ethics of Belief.* Cambridge: Cambridge University Press, 1996.

Young, Brian. *Religion and Enlightenment in Eighteenth-Century England.* Oxford: Oxford University Press, 1998.

Zuijdwegt, Geertjan. "Newman's Disputed Honesty: A Case Study in Victorian Religious Controversy." *Louvain Studies* 34 (2010): 361–84.

———. "Scepticism and Credulity: Victorian Critiques of John Henry Newman's Religious Apologetic." *Journal for the History of Modern Theology* 20, no. 1 (2013): 1–24.

———. "Richard Whately's Influence on John Henry Newman's Oxford University Sermons on Faith and Reason." *Newman Studies Journal* 10, no. 1 (2013): 82–95.

———. "Richard Whately." In *The Oxford Handbook of John Henry Newman*, edited by Frederick D. Aquino and Benjamin J. King, 196–216. Oxford: Oxford University Press, 2018.

Zuijdwegt, Geertjan, and Terrence Merrigan, "Conscience." In *The Oxford Handbook of John Henry Newman*, edited by Frederick D. Aquino and Benjamin J. King, 434–53. Oxford: Oxford University Press, 2018.

Index